ADVANCED MODERN MACROECONOMICS

ANALYSIS AND APPLICATION

Max Gillman
Cardiff Business School, Cardiff University

Financial Times
Prentice Hall
is an imprint of

Harlow, England • London • New York • Boston • San Francisco • Toronto • Sydney • Singapore • Hong Kong
Tokyo • Seoul • Taipei • New Delhi • Cape Town • Madrid • Mexico City • Amsterdam • Munich • Paris • Milan

Pearson Education Limited
Edinburgh Gate
Harlow
Essex CM20 2JE
England

and Associated Companies throughout the world

Visit us on the World Wide Web at:
www.pearsoned.co.uk

First published 2011

© Pearson Education Limited 2011

ISBN: 978-0-273-72652-4

British Library Cataloguing-in-Publication Data

A catalogue record for this book is available from the British Library

Library of Congress Cataloging-in-Publication Data

Gillman, Max.
  Advanced modern macroeconomics : analysis and application / Max Gillman.
     p. cm.
  ISBN 978-0-273-72652-4 (pbk.)
1. Macroeconomics. I. Title.
  HB172.5.G55 2011
  339—dc22

                                                      2010037491

10 9 8 7 6 5 4 3 2 1
14 13 12 11 10

Typeset in Stone Serif 9/11.5 by 73
Printed and bound by Ashford Colour Press Ltd., Gosport

BRIEF CONTENTS

CONTENTS

Supporting resources
Visit **www.pearsoned.co.uk/gillman** to find valuable online resources:

For instructors

- Complete, downloadable Instructor's Manual
- PowerPoint slides that can be downloaded and used as OHTs

For more information please contact your local Pearson Education sales representative or visit **www.pearsoned.co.uk/gillman**

CUSTOM PUBLISHING

Pearson Education's custom publishing programme began in response to customers' desire to create textbooks and online resources that match the content of their course. Every university course is unique and custom publishing allows a bespoke product created by you for your students and your course.

As a result, content choices include:

- Chapters from one or more of our textbooks in the subject areas of your choice
- Your own authored content
- Case studies from any of our partners including Harvard Business School Publishing, Darden, Ivey and many more
- Third party content from other publishers
- Language glossaries to help students studying in a second language
- Online material tailored to your course needs

The Pearson Education custom text published for your course is professionally produced and bound – just as you would expect from a normal Pearson Education text. You can even choose your own cover design and add your university logo.

To find out more visit **www.pearsoncustom.co.uk** or contact your local representative at: **www.pearsoned.co.uk/replocator**

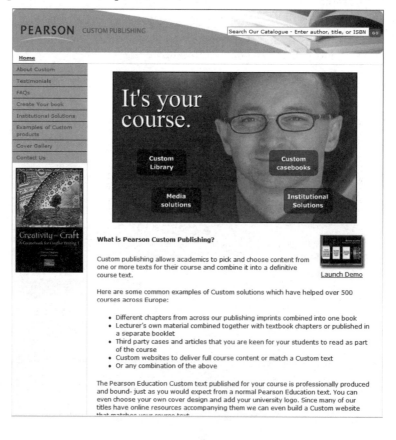

This book presents the elements of macroeconomics in terms consistent throughout with microeconomics. This gives the book the sense of a fully developed course of 'micro-founded' macroeconomics. It presents a methodologically consistent approach from beginning to end. It starts with the labour–leisure choice and the two-period intertemporal investment decision as a static analysis. And then it presents a fully worked out dynamic analysis.

Aggregate supply and demand for output (AS–AD) are presented both in static and dynamic chapters throughout the book. The book's derivation of AS–AD is novel for the dynamic analysis. Yet the book shows that by solving the capital stock, the aggregate supply and demand for output can be formulated and graphed. The labour market is also graphed throughout, using only exact functional forms derived in the book, as is done with the AS–AD analysis.

The general equilibrium is also graphed with both goods and labour markets implicit in the utility level curve and production function graphs. And in the dynamic analysis, the isoquant and isocost curves are also represented in the input markets, again using exact functional forms of the example economy being examined. Thus the equilibria are graphed both in the separate goods and labour markets along with the general equilibrium output and input dimensions, with the goods market known as the AS–AD graphs.

One theme of the book is to explain business cycles and important trends using just comparative static analysis. This approach revives the 'real business cycle' model approach of explaining expansions and contraction using changes in productivity. The goods sector productivity is changed in a comparative static fashion, as is the time endowment, with the result being an ability to explain rudimentary elements of business cycles.

The comparative static analysis is extended in the dynamic equilibrium analysis with endogenous growth so that a change in the productivity of the human capital sector replaces the change in time endowment. And a third productivity change is found in the chapter on banking, with a decrease in bank productivity able to reproduce a bank-led major recession.

The other main focus is on economic growth. This is presented with 'exogenous growth' and then with 'endogenous growth', using human capital. Trend changes in the human capital sector productivity also allow for explanations of rising growth, falling labour hours, and rising education levels. Thus the real business cycle and growth theory approach of changing productivities is extended to include changes in human capital productivity.

Another focus is how taxes affect the equilibrium, both in the static and dynamic analysis. The main taxes are the labour income tax, the capital income tax, the goods 'value added' tax, and the implicit inflation tax. And with endogenous growth, the effect of taxes on growth can also be discerned.

Who this book is for

The book is intended for those with a background only in microeconomics, and with basic mathematics skills in terms of taking derivatives and solving systems of equations. The book probably appeals most to those wanting to teach and learn macroeconomics in a way consistent with advanced methods that are found in graduate school and university research. It makes for a more seamless transition to higher level study, as compared to books that present aggregate analysis without derivation from microeconomic methods.

Inevitably there may be some greater appeal to teachers who have learned advanced research methods in their own graduate study, in that use of the book avoids the typical compromise of using models that are mostly obsolete at advanced levels. The book hopefully offers a respite from the chore of teaching what we may not think of as modern macroeconomics.

The book can be used in intermediate or advanced undergraduate courses, as well as in introductory graduate level courses.

ACKNOWLEDGEMENTS

I owe elements of Part 2 of the text to the undergraduate class notes of Professor Robert E. Lucas, Jr. These notes stimulated the idea of laying out the elements of modern macro-economics in a comprehensive fashion that is accessible to undergraduates. The book benefited from the support from my wife Anita, the guidance of my editors Ellen Morgan, Kate Brewin, Philippa Fiszzon, Linda Dhondy, my proofreader – Philip Tye, and the interaction with Cardiff University, Central European University and the University of New South Wales faculty and students. I am indebted to the price-theoretic heritage of Milton Friedman, Gary Becker and George Stigler, to manuscript revisions suggested by Joe Peng Zhou, Robert E. Lucas, Jr., Michal Kejak and Helmuts Azacis, to discussion with Glenn Otto, Viatcheslav Vinogradov, Mark N. Harris, Charles Nolan, Christoph Theonissen, Robert Kollmann, Toni Braun, Bob McNabb, Patrick Minford, Mike Wickens, Kent Matthews, Laurence Copeland, Anton Nakov, Szilard Benk, and Parantap Basu, and also to Lucy Moon, and to Narayana Kocherlakota for emphasising banking, and to research assistance from Joe Peng Zhou, Jing Dang, Hao Hong, and Szilard Benk. Also I am grateful for recurrent participation in conferences of the Society of Economic Dynamics, the Center for Dynamic Macroeconomic Analysis, the Euro Area Business Cycle Network, the Konstanz Seminar on Monetary Theory and Policy and the European Monetary Forum; and for association with the Institute of Economics of the Hungarian Academy of Sciences and with the Academy of Sciences of the Czech Republic, along with annual visits to CERGE-EI in Prague, and a research semester at the University of Melbourne. Responsibility for the contents of the text resides solely with me.

Publisher's acknowledgements

The publishers wish to thank the following reviewers for their valuable input:

Hector Valle, University of Bristol
Joe Byrne, University of Glasgow
Paul Scanlon, Trinity College Dublin
Wlodek Bursztyn, University of Gothenburg
Petra Geraats, University of Cambridge
Espen Henriksen, University of Oslo

We are grateful to the following for permission to reproduce copyright material:

Figure
Figure 17.1 from Robert J. Shiller, http://www.econ.yale.edu/~shiller/

In some instances we have been unable to trace the owners of copyright material, and we would appreciate any information that would enable us to do so.

PART 1

MICROFOUNDATIONS OF MACROECONOMICS

Thus the history of the individual firm cannot be made in the history of an industry any more than the history of an individual man can be made into the history of mankind. And yet the history of mankind is the outcome of the history of individuals and the aggregate production for a general market is the outcome of the motives which induce individual producers to expand or contract their production. It is just here that our device of a representative firm comes to aid. (Alfred Marshall, *Principles of Economics*, 8th edition, pp. 380–381). 'Thus the representative firm is in a sense an average firm' (Ibid., p. 265).

CHAPTER 1

Overview of the book

1.1 Introduction

This chapter provides an overview of the book within different dimensions. First it motivates how it is an extension of the microfoundation approach of using general equilibrium theory for macroeconomics. It highlights new elements of the text in terms of providing aggregate demand and supply analysis in the dynamic context, and in explaining business cycles with basic comparative statics of goods and time endowment changes.

The role of human capital in the text is explained and then the text is outlined in terms of fundamental margins of economic activity. Concepts of permanent income and wealth are traced across the chapters of the book, in a section providing a summary mathematical reference section. The single agent and heterogeneous agent approach are outlined. Finally, a brief summary of uses of the text in teaching are presented.

1.1.1 Learning objective

The aim of the chapter is to provide the intuition for the approach of using only microeconomics to derive all of macroeconomics. Then the specifics are presented so that a complete overview of the text can be glimpsed. This chapter is meant as a reference to pull together all of the separate chapters of the book. It provides a basis to which the student might return at later points so as to get additional intuition into the subsequent Chapters 2–20.

1.1.2 Who made it happen?

Paul A. Samuelson's PhD thesis, published as *Foundations of Economic Analysis* (1947), is often cited as the beginning of modern economic analysis. For example it formulated the modern mathematical analysis of changes in equilibrium, known as comparative statics. Samuelson (Nobel Laureate 1970) developed static macroeconomic analysis in multiple editions of his textbook, *Economics: An Introductory Analysis*, starting in 1948, and finishing with a 19th edition in 2009 co-authored with William Nordhaus. In this he developed the aggregate supply and demand analysis that became known as the Keynesian Cross, and which morphed into the *IS–LM* analysis that remains the dominant paradigm of introductory macroeconomic analysis.

Robert E. Lucas, Jr. writes in his 2001 'Professional Memoir': 'Samuelson was the Julia Child [American television kitchen Chef] of economics, somehow teaching you the basics and giving you the feeling of becoming an insider in a complex culture all at the same time. I loved the *Foundations*. Like so many others in my cohort, I internalized its view that if I couldn't formulate a problem in economic theory mathematically, I didn't know what I was doing. I came to the position that mathematical analysis is not one of many ways of doing economic theory: It is the only way. Economic theory is mathematical analysis. Everything else is just pictures and talk.'

R.D.G. Allen provided a summary of the state of mathematical macroeconomic analysis in his 1968 *Macro-Economic Theory,* but utility maximisation was not a part of this. Jump forward to the current statement of dynamic macroeconomic theory such as in Stokey and Lucas, with Prescott, in their 1989 *Recursive Methods in Economic Dynamics*. This expounded the two-period approach to capturing the full infinite horizon of the dynamic consumer problem. This text follows that approach in its simplest form, while attempting the contextual approach of aggregate supply and demand that Samuelson motivates. In certain ways it also formalises and extends the general equilibrium approach seen in Robert Barro's Macroeconomics textbook.

Note that subsections called 'Who made it happen?' give some of the background of how the ideas presented in the particular chapter evolved over time. Those economists named here are not an exclusive group but rather a partially representative group that inevitably omits others that are equally deserving in credit for the development of certain theories. The idea is to give historical flavour that presents the concepts as an evolving part of economics rather than a fixed law of a textbook that never will be amended. People make economics as a science develop and it can be thought-provoking to view it that way.

1.2 The microfoundations approach

Macroeconomics has had a history of divorcing itself from the need to derive its equilibrium conditions, which is the basis of microeconomics. Sets of equilibrium conditions have been presented and analysed, but not derived from the consumer and firm maximisation frameworks. Microeconomics is the study of how the consumer and firm do maximise subject to constraints, thereby giving the supply and demand of goods and the factor markets of labour and capital. Modern macroeconomic practice has returned to the microeconomic foundation of deriving the equilibrium conditions through optimisation problems using microeconomic principles. This has given name to the microfoundations approach to macroeconomics.

Deriving the equilibrium conditions from the agent's optimisation problem is the central part of the microfoundations to macroeconomics. This approach also has come to mean avoiding the addition of features into the model that are not arguably technological features of the aggregate economy or particular industries. The pure microfoundations approach avoids so-called 'ad hoc' elements, since this is the characteristic feature of macroeconomic models not derived from optimisation.

A microfoundations approach is extremely popular in modern macroeconomics, but many ad hoc elements are nonetheless found in most work. This evolution of macro shows that while the microfoundations approach is the goal, it is still subject to compromise in order to better explain certain aggregate events. But now the compromise more often takes place by adding in the ad hoc features into the optimisation problem itself. This way all of the equilibrium conditions are still derived. There are important exceptions though, with equilibrium conditions simply added onto the model after optimisation, and such instances are further from a pure microfoundations approach.

A text for modern macroeconomics at the intermediate undergraduate level can well justify presenting only the pure microfoundations approach to macroeconomics and so leave detailed ad hoc elements for higher graduate level study. And this is what this text does. Yet it is astonishing how much of the subject of macroeconomics can be covered in this way. Arguably all of the elements of macroeconomics are covered in this way, and this text lays out an extensive set of these elements. In its pure microfoundations approach, only the utility and production technology plus goods and time constraints account for all of the equilibrium conditions of the text. And only standard utility and technology forms are used.

1.2.1 Building macro from micro: new elements

The modern macroeconomics here implies equilibrium supply and demand conditions in all of its extensions such that a modern definition of aggregate supply and demand emerges and permeates the text. The text's basic novelty is that the equilibrium conditions and implied aggregate markets are derived strictly by using standard microeconomics. This makes the transition from microeconomics to macroeconomics a direct extension, rather than a new learning of the science.

Many previous books have integrated increasing amounts of microeconomically founded macroeconomics into more traditional macroeconomic approaches that are not strictly based on microeconomics. In a sense, this text departs from this model by starting with a clean slate and building the macroeconomics without any recourse to the usual approaches except those consistent with pure microeconomics. This is both the goal and the methodology of the text: to write what we think of as modern macroeconomics solely in terms of pure microeconomics. This gives a methodologically consistent structure from the beginning to the end, with each chapter building upon the last.

The full approach of the book is made accessible to the student in that every model solution is an explicit analytic solution. Simulations are not used, but rather only explicit functional forms that give the solutions of the variables. For the baseline dynamic model, all variables including the state variable are found with explicit analytic solutions, with all variables being solved as an exact function of the economy's exogenous parameters. In extensions including human capital, the solution involves an analytic equation in just one variable, with the equilibrium solution being the solution of a quadratic equation.

Every model in the book thus can be solved and graphed using the exact functional form. And the graphs are those we are familiar with: aggregate supply and demand. The aggregate supply and demand equations are also used to derive the analytic solution to the economy. And these graphs are even extended to show a complete graphical exposition of the general equilibrium solution that includes graphical derivation of the capital stock in the dynamic model.

1.2.2 Microeconomic foundations of macroeconomics

Deriving aggregate markets in general equilibrium follows directly from decentralising the representative agent general equilibrium problem into consumer and firm parts. Starting with the centralised economy, the consumer maximises utility subject to the technology of goods production, thereby acting as both consumer and firm simultaneously. Here prices are not explicit or necessary for the optimisation problem to be solved.

The decentralisation allows the prices and profit to become explicit, in contrast to the centralised general equilibrium. Decentralisation allows the consumer to only consume, while the firm does the production. However, the consumer still owns the firm and receives back any profit of the firm as part of the budget constraint. The consumer then maximises utility subject to the budget constraint. The firm maximises the same budget constraint, which now is in the form of the firm's profit, subject to the production technology. Thus the budget constraint becomes the means of separating the centralised economy without prices and profit into the decentralised economy with consumer and firm problems.

The equilibrium of the consumer and firm problems then implies the supply and demand for quantities of goods, labour and capital as functions of the relative prices.

The decentralisation into the consumer and firm problems, which are the mainstays of microeconomics, thereby allows for the markets of goods, labour and capital to be made explicit. The aggregate demand and supply of goods, labour and capital can all be derived in functional forms and this is done throughout the text.

1.3 Static versus dynamic general equilibrium

While the derivation of the static aggregate demand and supply is commonplace, the derivation of the dynamic aggregate supply and demand of goods, labour and capital markets is not so easy to find. And this difference is what makes fully microeconomic founded macroeconomics different from microeconomics. Microeconomics considers capital a fixed factor and does not solve the problem dynamically. Micro-founded macroeconomics solves the dynamic problem with the equilibrium capital as an integral part of the solution.

Apparently the exact derivation of the aggregate supply (*AS*) and demand (*AS*) of the dynamic 'neoclassical' model, instead of the *AS–AD* that we write down loosely in introductory textbooks, is a new approach of this textbook. The *AS–AD* is right there in the modern macroeconomics model, waiting to be made clear to students, but up until now it has remained buried. This focus of the book brings the modern dynamic method down to terms of *AS* and *AD*, with the advantage of greatly simplifying the results in terms of common graphs. Of course this is why we have always liked to use supply and demand in economics: to make intuitively obvious the nature of the results.

The text brings out the dynamic model exactly as it is, and really how it must be. There are many ways to derive the *AS–AD* model in non-microfounded macroeconomic approaches, with each textbook seeming to offer a different way to do such a derivation of our fundamental concept of supply and demand in the aggregate context. Here it could be said is just one more approach to *AS–AD*. But it may emerge over time that there is one standard way to derive *AS–AD* in a pure microfoundations approach within the standard dynamic neoclassical model and this approach is presented here.

Such *AS–AD* analysis is useful by making exact how changes to the equilibrium in aggregate markets occur. And these changes are the foundation of the dynamic growth and business cycle theory of modern macroeconomics. Showing how these changes can be formulated within *AS–AD* and applied is a central task of the text.

To make the modern macroeconomics of *AS–AD* as clear as possible, the first part of the text previews the two marginal rates of substitutions that are the bedrock of the *AS–AD* by deriving them in a static framework. The static warm-up takes these margins one dimension at a time. Then when they are derived in the equivalent form in the dynamic framework they are already old friends to whom students can compare stories of equilibrium. This makes the dynamic framework immediately approachable since the equilibrium conditions are nearly the same as those that have been derived statically.

Similarly by deriving the *AS–AD* in these static frameworks, the derivation of *AS–AD* in the dynamic framework likewise is a reasonable next step from what has already been learned. Students can then focus on seeing how this aggregate framework is used in all of its extensions.

Changes in the equilibrium known as comparative statics are also developed in a similar fashion, first in the static frameworks and then again in the dynamic framework with the static framework available for comparison. In particular the change in sectoral productivity is the main comparative static exercise that is found throughout the book, first in the static context and then dynamic. And this lays the foundation for understanding the neoclassical growth and business cycle models, as an extension of the same productivity shift studied from the very beginning of the text. Dynamic models can be described in terms of their essential comparative static exercise, even if this occurs over time.

1.3.1 Dynamic *AS–AD*

Some tricks are necessary to accomplish the expiation of the modern *AS–AD* and its standard extensions. It is analysed as a stationary equilibrium concept as its first presentation. There are no 'transitional dynamics' discussed in the text; rather only the movement from one stationary equilibrium state to another. The study of stationary equilibrium is the first step upon which transition dynamics can then be studied at advanced levels.

The use of stationary equilibrium also suggests how to present the analysis. Dynamic analysis requires that an output growth rate of the economy needs to be assumed, or derived endogenously. Therefore, along with the concept of an output growth rate must be the concept of a balanced growth path equilibrium. Then the dynamic *AS–AD* can be derived, which is done starting in Part 4.

To derive the dynamic *AS–AD* along the balanced growth path stationary equilibrium still requires thought about what makes the modern dynamic analysis in fact dynamic. The dynamic part is the accumulation of capital. This creates a fundamental 'state' variable that must be consistent with the *AS–AD* equilibrium; the *AS–AD* is written as a function of the state variable, and it must be the correct value of the state variable. Therefore the third trick, after assuming a growth rate and realising that the equilibrium must be along the balanced growth path, is that the state variable must be computed accurately for the equilibrium to be correct.

To see the complexity that arises with the need for computation of the equilibrium state variable, consider that for any comparative static change in the parameters of the model, the *AS–AD* functions that have been derived as a function of the state variable must be recomputed with the new equilibrium state variable substituted in. This is really the only hard part of the computation of the *AS–AD*: the computation of the state variable, and how it changes with comparative static exercises. Only then can the analysis show the change from one balanced growth path equilibrium to another balanced growth equilibrium.

The computation of the state variable is shown in the text and at the same time the importance of the state variable in the equilibrium also influences the modern approach of presenting the optimisation problem. The 'recursive' framework of writing down the optimisation problem as a function of the state variable provides a concise, helpful way of deriving the equilibrium conditions. It avoids the more cumbersome infinite horizon approach that speaks almost immediately to the graduate level but not below. It puts in place a simple structure of two time periods that once understood and accepted makes it possible for the student to accept the dynamic model and so derive its equilibrium conditions. And it helps that the text shows that using the recursive approach gives the same two, now familiar, margins already learned in the preceding static problems of Parts 2 and 3. The only difference is that now both are derived at the same time.

In summary, Parts 2 and 3 build the static elements of *AS–AD* analysis that are consistent with the dynamic development of *AS–AD*. Part 4 then presents the dynamic *AS–AD* analysis. And then this dynamic analysis is applied in the remaining parts of the book, with a set of fundamental extensions. A full graphical analysis of the dynamic general equilibrium *AS–AD* that includes the derivation of the capital stock is provided in Chapter 10.

1.3.2 General equilibrium output and input dimensions

A complementary feature to showing the supply and demand in goods and labour markets, with the goods market being called the *AS–AD* analysis, is to show the general equilibrium output in terms of both goods and leisure. In addition we have the general equilibrium inputs in terms of labour and capital, the input equilibrium.

In the output dimensions, this is done using what is typically called a production possibility curve and a utility level curve. Here this same graph is constructed for the equilibria throughout the book using the exact production functions and exact utility level curves. For the dynamic analysis that starts in Part 4 and continues to the end of the book, the input space is in terms of labour and capital. And these dimensions are also graphed for examples using the exact functional forms throughout Parts 4–7 of the text.

1.3.3 Consumption smoothing

A central theme of the economics of the text is that consumption is always guided by the natural desire by the consumer to 'smooth' consumption of goods across different dimensions of the economic problem. This smoothing is the result of optimisation of a normally shaped utility function subject to the resource constraints. For goods and leisure in Part 2, this means that the consumer chooses a balance of goods consumption versus leisure, in the 'intratemporal' decision that allocates resources during the current time period. For goods consumption across time in Part 3, this means that the consumer chooses a balance of consumption today versus consumption tomorrow, in the 'intertemporal' decision that allocates resources across time periods. For intratemporal and intertemporal consumption in Part 4, this means that the consumer chooses a balance of consumption simultaneously intratemporally and intertemporally.

The heart of Part 4 is the dynamic baseline model in which the consumer's consumption demand is derived (Chapter 8). And consumption is shown to depend upon permanent income. This is an important concept in macroeconomic theory that is expostulated here in terms of the elements from the labour–leisure intratemporal choice and the current–future consumption intertemporal choice. The consumption demand is shown to be a simple fraction of permanent income, just as in the permanent income hypothesis of consumption that was first specified as the modern dynamic baseline model was being developed.

By consuming a fraction of permanent income, the consumer smooths the consumption across time and during the period. To raise permanent income, the consumer needs to invest in capital. A steady amount of investment is necessary for sustained economic growth, a subject of Part 5 (Chapter 11). Permanent income is also affected by how much the consumer invests in other forms of capital. The investment into human capital raises the permanent income and consumption stream, while determining the output growth rate. Such endogenous growth is also the subject of Part 5 (Chapter 12). How the consumption stream is affected by variations in income around the permanent income level comprises the 'business cycle' study of the economy also in Part 5 (Chapter 13). Trade also affects consumption in the dynamic model with endogenous growth in the last part of Part 5 (Chapter 14).

Investment by the consumer in other forms by transferring capital across time and space, and the subsequent smoothing of consumption across time and space, is the subject of the next Part 6. This shows a general problem of smoothing consumption across uncertain states of nature, such as good and bad states that arise with certain probabilities. The analysis involves an extension of the so-called Arrow-Debreu theory of uncertain state consumption smoothing. Here costs are assumed to be involved in such consumption smoothing, giving rise to an extension of the theory, but in a very intuitive way. With costs introduced, consumption smoothing is not perfect, but instead is done as best as resources allow. Banks are also introduced in Part 6 as the means of making such transference of consumption across uncertain states, time and space (Chapter 15). And then the consumer's investment in banks as financial intermediaries to do this consumption smoothing is introduced (Chapter 16). Consumer investment directly in asset markets and asset pricing is also introduced, in the last part of Part 6 (Chapter 17).

Part 7 shows how government intervenes to try to implement better consumption smoothing by the representative consumer. The government does this using its budget constraint (Chapter 18), and the corresponding fiscal (Chapter 19) and monetary policy (Chapter 20). Taxes necessary to raise funds for such government efforts in themselves create distortions that decrease the ability of the consumer to smooth consumption, and this is a problem. But the government can try to balance this loss of consumption smoothing from taxation against a greater ability to smooth consumption through government programmes involving 'social insurance' as it appears in its many manifestations.

1.3.4 Taxes, regulations and inefficiencies

The text provides full descriptions and general equilibrium examples of how taxes on goods, labour and capital affect the economy, and how this decreases the consumption smoothing. So-called 'wedges' get driven between the consumer and producer so that there is less work and less consumption during the period, with goods and labour taxes, and/or less investment and consumption over time with capital taxes. Using human capital, goods, labour and capital taxes are all shown to decrease the growth rate of the economy. So all taxes cause less current and future consumption through their distortions on the consumer's incentives to work, save, and invest compared to when there are no taxes. Of course taxes are necessary if there is government spending. And it is possible that the effect of government spending is so positive as to more than offset such negative incentive effects.

Regulations likewise act like taxes. Government regulations are analysed in a similar way to government taxes (Chapter 2). And the analysis also allows for privately induced regulations to result in effect upon the economy, such as through unions or corruption. Analysing taxes and regulations in general equilibrium in the different dimensions of intratemporal work–leisure, and intertemporal savings–investment provides a introduction to the effect of such distortions on the economy.

Chapters 3 and 6 have labour, goods and capital taxes in a static environment. Chapter 9 shows the effect of a labour tax in the dynamic baseline model. Chapter 19 focuses within the dynamic model on the effect of labour, capital and goods taxes on both output levels and on the economy's growth rate. And Chapter 20 shows the distorting effect of the inflation tax to be similar to a labour tax.

1.4 Comparative statics and business cycles

Comparative statics are done by changing one exogenous parameter of the economy and finding the new equilibrium, and comparing it to the initial equilibrium before the parameter was changed. Such analysis is conducted throughout the book, being a comparison of new balanced growth path equilibria in the dynamic models of Parts 4–7. And these are used to show how a typical business cycle might be explained.

1.4.1 A focus on productivity changes

Productivity changes are key to studying modern research-based macroeconomics. Productivity increases in the aggregate goods production sector are the way that economic growth is formulated. And fluctuations in such productivity is how business cycles are explained. Therefore productivity changes are examined throughout the text.

Parts 2 and 3 introduce the comparative static experiment of increasing productivity and seeing how this affects equilibrium in the economy. Part 4 shows how such productivity changes affect the dynamic *AS–AD* framework, including the subsequent change in the capital stock. Part 5 shows that continuous productivity increases over time, within the dynamic model, provide a modern theory of economic growth; and changes to such productivity likewise can introduce the modern theory of business cycles. Productivity increases in the human capital sector allow for changes in the growth rate, in Part 5. And human capital productivity increases that occur along with the general aggregate goods sector productivity changes allow for resolution of certain puzzles of the baseline dynamic model.

Productivity increases also allow for increased ability to smooth consumption across uncertain states of nature in Part 6. Similarly, banking productivity changes can cause changes in capital. And unexpected productivity changes in the banking sector can introduce so-called aggregate risk into such uncertain state consumption smoothing, also in Part 6.

1.4.2 Basic puzzle of too much smoothing

The basic dynamic model of Part 4 can explain major parts of the economy. However productivity changes show that the model cannot explain changes in labour employment very well. And so in a sense the model can be said to yield employment that is too smooth relative to the evidence.

A productivity increase leads to no change in labour employed in the static model in Part 2, and also in the dynamic model in Part 4. Yet business cycles are formulated as being a result of changes in aggregate goods sector productivity. This presents a problem in that labour employment does not change when a productivity change occurs and the business cycle occurs. It is a problem because a rise and fall in the employment rate of labour are a key feature of business cycles and one that needs to be a part of a good business cycle explanation. Thus labour employment is too smooth in the baseline static and dynamic model.

One approach to the smoothing puzzles is to look at market distortions that keep markets from working properly. In effect what is assumed is that there is some 'ad hoc' reason for the market not to be working as the general equilibrium economy demands. The text presents the simplest case for this type of ad hoc approach. Labour, goods and capital markets are shown to be non-clearing by assuming that the input prices of labour and capital, these being the wage rate and the capital rental rate, are for some reason fixed at the current level. The inability to lower the wage rate and/or the interest rate when there is an aggregate productivity decrease causes 'unemployment' of labour and/or capital (Chapters 3 and 5).

The assumption of fixed relative prices is outside of a full general equilibrium analysis or, more accurately, in violation of the assumptions of general equilibrium. As part of the microeconomic foundations to macroeconomics is to use proper general equilibrium analysis, the text does not favour this approach as a full understanding of the resolution of the smoothing puzzles. It is a segmented, temporary solution that allows the model to have unemployed resources. But fixed relative prices violate the notion of equilibrium and so are hard to accept as a full solution of the problem.

Instead, the text shows a basic approach towards ameliorating the smoothing puzzle, under conditions of a complete general equilibrium analysis, without assumed violations to the equilibrium. It does this through the introduction of a second comparative static experiment: a change in the time allowed for goods and leisure. This is done by changing the time endowment in Parts 2–4. And then in Part 5, a change in the time for goods and leisure is made endogenous. This is done by allowing for changes in the productivity of human capital investment. And this leads to changes in the time devoted to human capital investment. The result is that the time devoted to goods and leisure is then endogenously changed as the productivity of the human capital investment sector is changed. And this human capital approach also solves a related major complication of the baseline model: it cannot explain endogenously the growth rate, but human capital accumulation does explain growth.

1.4.3 Human capital

The text extends the mainstream dynamic model by including the long tradition in human capital study. It does this for the fundamental reason of providing solutions to the problems of the baseline model. Sufficient changes in the labour employment rate during the business cycle are accomplished first by changing the time endowment exogenously. And then with human capital this is accomplished by having a second production sector, besides the aggregate goods sector. This second sector is the production of human capital investment.

With a change in human capital productivity, the text shows how the output of the goods sector expands as the human capital sector moves in the other direction. Labour flows from the 'non-market' human capital sector to the goods sector, and this gives the central result. The employment rate rises in the goods sector. And in reverse, employment shifts towards the human capital sector, and the employment rate falls in the goods sector, this being a key fact of a business cycle contraction.

The human capital sector allows the growth rate to be endogenous rather than being assumed as exogenous and so unexplained as in the baseline dynamic model. Goods sector productivity changes have no effect on the growth rate. But changes in the human capital sector productivity do affect the growth rate of output. This gives a fuller explanation of economic growth and, in particular, how tax distortions affect the output growth rate.

1.4.4 Banking in general equilibrium

Alongside the introduction of human capital is the introduction of banking in general equilibrium. Human capital allows the economic choice of the capitalisation rate of the consumer's time value, over time. The banking sector allows the economic choice of the transfer of goods, rather than time, over space, time and states of nature under certain conditions. These conditions are that it is no longer a 'frictionless' world in which such transfers can take place without any cost. When such transfers are costly, and involve entire large industries to manifest the transformation of goods across various dimensions, then it is desirable to analyse how this costly transformation is performed in an optimal way. And this is where banking is introduced, in order to model how the economy does this transformation of goods, or capital.

Banking is modelled as the way in which goods are transferred across uncertain states of nature, in the case when such transformation involves cost. This can be thought of generally as insurance being provided by the insurance industry, which itself can be considered more broadly as part of the financial intermediation, or banking, industry. Banking in this way can also be viewed as the conduit for providing pensions, and even health insurance. This approach of modelling financial intermediation in general equilibrium results in an extension of the Arrow-Debreu theory of how goods are transferred across uncertain states of nature under the assumption of no cost in manifesting the goods transfer. Banking is a way to model these costs. This provides a window into the view of how a drop in banking productivity can cause such disruption to the economy, and be a cause of so-called unexpected aggregate risk (Chapter 15).

Banking also allows the economy to intermediate the savings of the consumer into the investment of the firm, when such intermediation cannot be done by the consumer directly. Describing the production of this intermediation service is the way in which banking is brought into the general equilibrium. The banking extension then again focuses on productivity changes, this time to the productivity of producing the intermediation service in the banking industry. When for example there is a downwards drop in productivity, as in a banking crisis, then less savings are turned into investment, and consumption is not smoothed as well as otherwise (Chapter 16).

1.4.5 Private and public finance

The text tries to minimise the extensions to the baseline model while still covering the elements of modern macroeconomics, including private and public finance. Initially the consumer can directly invest in physical capital, which the consumer then rents to the firm. Then the consumer is assumed to no longer be able to invest directly in physical capital, and instead can either use financial intermediation through banks (Chapter 16), or invest in ownership shares of the firm, getting back profit in the form of dividends. And the firm itself then invests in capital directly, as occurs in actual economies (Chapter 17).

The private finance of firms by the consumer is then extended also to allow the public finance of the government by the consumer. Here the consumer is allowed to invest directly in government bonds, making another form of investment without directly investing in physical capital (Chapter 17).

When the consumer invests in government bonds, either directly or through the private bank, this is a way in which the consumer takes part in government finance (Chapter 18). The nature of government finance can affect the economy's growth rate (Chapter 19). The consumer's holding of money printed by the government's central bank is also a part of government finance and this also affects the economy's growth rate (Chapter 20).

1.5 Explaining business cycles and growth

The text shows how the neoclassical model succeeds in explaining business cycles in simple elemental terms of comparative static exercises. This is contrary to conventional wisdom of standard textbooks. Conventional wisdom says that a productivity change in the output sector is the basis of the business cycle model. Yet comparative statics show the sense in which the productivity change causes insufficient employment change. In other words, for the labour market, the worker has no external margin for labour, about whether to enter the labour force or not, but only an internal one on how many hours to work. And the internal margin does not change because income and substitution effects of the productivity change result in little or no employment change.

This problem is overcome by considering not only changes in the productivity of the output sector, but also changes in the endowment of time. The goods productivity increase, given the production technology, amounts to an increase in the endowment of goods in the economy. And this is just one major side of the economic equation of directing goods and time efficiently. The endowment of time also is the other major side of the balancing of resources. Sickness affects this; age affects this; and perhaps most important for basic analysis, education time affects the time endowment left over for everything else. Thus both the goods and time endowment can be affected by productivity changes, either in goods production, or in human capital production.

Allowing the endowment of time to increase or decrease in a comparative static fashion is intuitively similar to allowing changes in the labour force participation rate, or the external margin. This causes a shift out and back of the labour supply, with a rise and fall in the time endowment; and the result is a rise and fall of the equilibrium employment rate. But in Part 2 it also makes the wage rate go down when time endowment increases and up when time endowment decreases. Allowing the time endowment to go up in a business cycle expansion allows labour employment to rise, but counterfactually the wage rate falls. However, combining this with the goods productivity change solves the problem.

A comparative static explanation of business cycles that extends the standard approach is to allow both the goods productivity and the time endowment to rise in an expansion. In Chapter 3 this is done with an equal percentage rise in the expansion and decrease in a contraction. The result is that in an expansion, labour employment rises, as labour supply shifts out, but so also does the wage rate rise, as productivity rises and offsets the fall in the wage from the shift out in the labour supply. In a contraction, the employment and wage rate fall. This explains normal expansions and contractions.

A fixed wage rate is additionally allowed to show an occasional extreme decrease in employment, in both static and dynamic economies (Chapters 3 and 9). This is done by having the productivity decrease and the time decrease occur at the same time that the wage is fixed. Then employment drops severely as in a depression, in a way to illustrate Keynes's original ideas.

Such goods and time comparative statics mark an approach that allows for a more cohesive story to emerge. The same comparative statics that are performed in the model without dynamic capital accumulation in Part 2 are performed with the baseline dynamic model in Part 4. The same results occur, so that a business cycle is explained with the same combination of comparative static changes in goods and time endowment, even within the dynamic model. Further, in the dynamic model the fixed wage is added onto such productivity changes to again show a depression-like decrease in employment as in Part 2.

In Part 5, the model is extended with human capital and endogenous growth to again examine the business cycle. When the productivity of the human capital sector rises, more time is spent producing human capital. This causes a decrease in the time left for labour and leisure. This decrease in time left over is analogous to a decrease in the time endowment for labour and leisure that is performed in the exogenous growth standard dynamic model. Changing human capital productivity thereby endogenises the exogenous change in time endowment seen in earlier chapters of the text. And it does this in a way consistent with explaining the business cycle.

When human capital productivity shifts up, labour in the goods sector decreases as in a business cycle contraction, and time spent in the human capital sector increases as has been interpreted to occur when labour shifts from the market to the non-market sector in a contraction. When human capital productivity falls, labour shifts back to the goods production sector, as the time endowment for labour and leisure is endogenously increased by the fall in human capital productivity. This gives the movement of labour as seen in the business cycle.

Combining the fall in human capital productivity with a rise in goods sector productivity, the wage rate indeed rises in an expansion. In a contraction, a decrease in goods sector productivity combined with a rise in human capital sector productivity produces a decrease in the wage rate and in employment in the goods sector. Therefore human capital theory endogenises the previously exogenous change in the external margin, being the amount of time endowed for labour and leisure.

The occasional use of fixed real wages to generate a depression on top of a normal contraction is ad hoc. This feature is eliminated by making the occasional depression endogenous to the model, through banking. In Part 6, a banking sector is specified that intermediates savings into investment. Using the standard approach of changing productivity, a third productivity comparative static exercise is introduced. When the banking sector productivity is decreased sharply, as occurs occasionally such as in the 1930s and 2007–09, the model shows how a normal recession can become a depression, but now without fixed wages.

The story that results is that normal business cycles can be explained by changing productivity in the goods and human capital sector. And a further depression can be explained by decreasing productivity in the banking sector. It demonstrates a surprising vigour of the standard model to explain what is often our main focus: business cycles. And it does this without any ad hoc elements that are outside of the model other than model parameters. In particular only productivity parameters end up being changed.

The human capital feature that is crucial to this elemental business cycle explanation also explains important long term phenomena: the long secular fall in the labour workweek, the long secular increase in the time spent in education, and the long gradual increase in the worldwide growth rate. These are all a direct result within the model of the human capital sector productivity increasing very slightly but steadily over time.

Human capital therefore allows for long term growth puzzles to be explained, as well as business cycles, all within the *AS–AD* analysis, and using only comparative static changes in productivity parameters. Banking adds the further productivity event that plausibly adds to the model's repertoire the explanation of the Great Depression, again within *AS–AD* analysis of shifting aggregate supply and demand. This gives a slowly expanded baseline model, with each step consistent with earlier elements, but with added fundamentalism so that only comparative static changes in sectoral productivities are used in the end to explain a broad set of phenomena. The elemental expansion slowly builds from Chapter 2 and continues until the end of the text.

1.6 Content by margins

A theme of the book is that just two basic types of margins can explain the behaviour of the representative agent. Economic margins are simply the equilibrium conditions that describe the simultaneous balancing of the costs and benefits of alternatives during the period, across time, and across states of nature. The two primary margins are the marginal rate of substitution between goods and time (leisure) during the period and the marginal rate of substitution between goods, or time, over time or across states of nature.

The goods–leisure margin links goods to time during the period. The intertemporal–interstate margin links the transfer of goods or time across time or across states of nature to the investment set aside for such transfers during the current period. Such investment is reaped only in a future time or a different state of nature. While the investment of goods or time for transfer across states of nature might be thought of as a separate, additional, margin to the intertemporal transfer of goods or time across time, both are forms of investment of goods or time now for a return from the investment in another time or state-space. In this sense, no other margins are introduced in the book.

Part 2 first develops the goods–leisure margin for the single representative agent, 'closed economy' (Chapter 2). The marginal disincentive effect of a tax on goods or labour income is presented (Chapter 3). And the text presents the same margin but for two representative agents identical in utility but different in labour productivity. This creates comparative advantage between the two agents, one being better at goods production and the other being better at leisure consumption, and equilibrium requires trade between the agents (Chapter 4).

Within the goods–leisure margin, the real wage focuses the consumer's decision of whether to consume goods or instead to consume leisure. As the relative price of leisure versus goods, the real wage w plays both a substitution and an income role in this dimension of consumption theory. The substitution effect, as the wage rises, is that the consumer chooses less leisure, more work, and more goods consumption. The income effect causes, as the real wage rises, every hour of work to yield more real income, and this induces higher goods consumption. And from the firm side, this real wage is the marginal product of labour in producing goods.

Part 3 develops the intertemporal margin for the representative agent that explains how the consumer decides how much to save and invest today in order to get a certain amount of goods at a future point in time (Chapter 5). Business cycles and taxes are investigated on the basis of this margin (Chapter 6), and the analysis is extended to two representative agents again with identical utility but different productivity of capital (Chapter 7).

Physical capital theory focuses on investment of goods to create even more future period goods, thereby balancing the consumption of goods across time. The interest rate, like the real wage, is a relative price; it gives the price of goods consumed today or in the current period, relative to goods consumed tomorrow or in the next period. Consider that goods consumed today could be instead invested with a net rate of return equal to r so that tomorrow the abstaining consumer would have $1 + r$ multiplied by the goods invested today. Thus r, the net interest rate, or $1 + r$, the gross interest rate, is the 'cost' of the current relative to the future consumption. And from the supply or producer side in equilibrium the interest rate r equals the marginal product of capital.

The substitution effect of an increase in the interest rate is less current consumption in favour of more future consumption. The income effect of a change in the interest rate depends on whether the consumer is a borrower or lender (Chapter 7). On balance, the representative consumer has zero net borrowing since this represents the net borrowing of the whole closed economy, which must be zero. This zero net borrowing means the lack of any income effect on the representative consumer. But with two agents, one can borrow from the other (Chapter 7).

Part 4 develops the baseline model which simultaneously derives the two main margins of intratemporal consumption, being goods versus leisure, and of intertemporal consumption, about savings and investment (Chapters 8, 9, 10). Part 5 extends both margins. Growth in the baseline model depends on exogenous changes in labour and capital productivity (Chapter 11). Human capital requires time to accumulate and it enables higher wage earnings in the future, which makes it a form of savings/investment. Here time is in effect invested today in order to yield more time in the future. Thus the balance is again current versus future consumption, but of time rather than goods.

Time is increased in effect by increasing the human capital stock so that the effective time, which is the raw time multiplied by the human capital stock, is higher. And the higher the human capital, the higher is the effective wage for the human capital augmented time. Because time is the ultimately scarce resource that cannot be reproduced, the decision on how much human capital to accumulate thereby determines how fast the economy can grow (Chapter 12).

In Part 5, changing the productivity of production alters how the consumer decides across both intratemporal and intertemporal margins. And the consumer response to the changes then gives rise to an explanation of the business cycle (Chapter 13). Allowing the productivity of human capital production to be different across agents, and then allowing for trade between agents, allows for a simultaneous combination of the wage and interest rate bases of labour trade in Chapter 4 and capital trade in Chapter 7. With different wage rates and interest rates under autarky, the trade equilibrium establishes international factor price equalisation, and the trade flows between nations required to establish this, a key theorem of international trade (Chapter 14).

Part 6 allows for the intertemporal margin to be extended to allow for investment across uncertain states (Chapter 15), for investment across time through banking (Chapter 16), and for investment directly into asset markets as a conduit of the private finance of the firm's capital investment (Chapter 17). Part 7 considers the public finance dimensions intertemporally (Chapter 18). This introduces tax distortions to the goods–leisure intratemporal margin, and to the return on intertemporal capital investment (Chapter 19). And with money comes the inflation tax distortion to the goods–leisure margin that lowers the human capital investment return, and lowers the growth rate of output (Chapter 20).

1.7 Consumption, permanent income and wealth

Understanding the mathematical structure of the text's macroeconomics requires study of the consumer problem, from its simplest form to a continually extended form. A mathematical overview of consumption and output demand can be provided in order to outline some of the mathematical content. The presentation of certain equations thereby provides an overview that can be returned to as a reference while deriving these progressively throughout the text.

The mathematics is made as simple as is possible. The log-utility function is used throughout the text, on the consumer side. And the standard Cobb–Douglas production function is also used throughout, on the firm side. These standard functions are described in Chapter 2. The optimisation problems are reduced to the task of taking the partial derivative with respect to just one variable in many of the models. This requires use of the chain rule of derivation in order to get the 'first-order' equilibrium condition or conditions of the optimisation problem. And the other challenge is solving the full set of equilibrium conditions for the unknown variables of the model.

All of the following equations concerning consumption are derived and worked out at length in the text. The first mathematical current consumption function, derived in Part 2, is that consumption is a fixed fraction of permanent income from wages and profit from the firm that produces goods. Here c^d denotes the consumer's demand for consumption goods, w the real wage rate, l^s the fraction of time supplied as labour, Π the profit from firm production of goods that goes to the consumer, x the fraction of time spent as leisure, and α a positive parameter indicating degree of preference for leisure. The budget constraint is that consumption purchases are made with labour income wl^s and profit from goods production Π,

$$c^d = wl^s + \Pi.$$

The exogenous time allocation of T is assumed to be divided between work and leisure, so that $T = l^s + x$ and so consumption is also written as

$$c^d = w(T - x) + \Pi.$$

It will be shown in detail that the marginal rate of substitution between goods and leisure with log utility tells us that

$$x = \frac{\alpha c^d}{w}.$$

And substituting in for x, and solving for c^d, the result is that consumption is a constant fraction, $\frac{1}{1+\alpha}$, of the flow value of time, wT, plus the profit, that is $wT + \Pi$, or

$$c^d = \frac{1}{1+\alpha}(wT + \Pi). \tag{1.1}$$

Since consumption equals total output here, this is also the aggregate demand for output as a function of the real wage.

Alternatively, with permanent income defined as

$$y_P \equiv wT + \Pi,$$

then consumption is the fraction $\frac{1}{1+\alpha}$ of permanent income:

$$c^d = \frac{y_P}{1 + \alpha}.$$

(1.2)

Inversely, to get an aggregate demand, or AD, curve that can be easily graphed as a downward sloping function of the relative price, the relative price needs to be solved for as a function of the consumption, rather than solving for the consumption as a function of the relative price as in equation (1.1). Solving for the price of goods relative to leisure, which is the goods price of 1, divided by the leisure shadow price of w, then $\frac{1}{w}$ is the relative price and the AD function is also given by

$$\frac{1}{w} = \frac{T_t}{c^d (1 + \alpha) - \Pi}.$$

This gives a downsloping demand for goods as a function of the relative price $\frac{1}{w}$. Given the parameters T, α, and given Π (for now, although this is found to be a function of w that needs to be substituted in), then as c^d goes up, the price goes down: a downward sloping demand function.

In Part 3, the two-period model is very useful in establishing the idea of how intertemporal consumption relates to the interest rate and time preference. The static consumption demand of equation (1.1) is modified when the dynamic model is specified. Dynamics means that there is an accumulation of capital over time. As a step towards the dynamic aspect of capital accumulation, Part 3 develops at length how savings of capital and investment in capital are optimally chosen over just two periods. With log utility, this captures that main intertemporal margin mathematically. With c_0 and c_1 denoting consumption in time periods 0 and 1, the growth in consumption over the two periods depends on whether the interest rate $\hat{r}$ exceeds the consumer's rate of time discount, a positive parameter denoted by ρ:

$$\frac{c_1}{c_0} = \frac{1 + \hat{r}}{1 + \rho}.$$

(1.3)

Note that here in the two-period model, full depreciation of capital is assumed, so that $\frac{c_1}{c_0} = \frac{r}{1+\rho}$, using the standard definition of r. But with $1 + \hat{r} \equiv r$, the intuition can be developed that carries over to the full dynamic model (see Appendix A5).

In the dynamic model over the complete time horizon rather than just two periods, Part 4 shows how the consumption function of Part 2 is modified. This is done by using the additional intertemporal equilibrium concept of Part 3. Consumption depends on wages as before and now, instead of profit, on the interest income from the capital stock at time t, with this stock denoted by k_t. This means that the profit of Part 3, which is similar to capital income in a model in which capital is not yet explicitly introduced, is replaced by the explicit capital income in Part 4. This capital income forms part of the consumer's permanent income, as the interest flow on capital that adds to the wage flow from labour. Also depreciation of capital is introduced, with the depreciation rate denoted by δ_k.

Using time t subscripts, the Part 4 dynamic model is the simplest next step in developing the consumption function. The model is developed to show that the modified consumption demand is

$$c_t^d = \frac{1}{1 + \alpha}[w_t T_t + (r - \delta_k) k_t].$$

(1.4)

Optimal dynamic capital accumulation also implies that

$$\frac{c_t}{c_{t-1}} = \frac{1 + r_t - \delta_k}{1 + \rho},$$ (1.5)

which is similar to equation (1.3) except for the time subscripts and the depreciation rate.

The interest flow on capital is then found in the equilibrium with zero growth. Zero growth of the economy implies that $c_t = c_{t-1}$, and so that the interest rate net of depreciation is equal to the rate of time preference: $r_t - \delta_k = \rho$. The consumption demand becomes simply

$$c_t^d = \frac{1}{1 + \alpha}(w_t T_t + \rho k_t).$$ (1.6)

Again consumption is a simple fraction, $\frac{1}{1+\alpha}$, of permanent income, which in turn is the flow value of time $w_t T_t$ and the interest flow from capital, or $w_t T_t + \rho k_t$. The profit in the previous definition of permanent income is made more explicit in this extension with dynamic capital accumulation. Now the interest flow on capital ρk_t replaces profit Π in the permanent income of Part 3, and now this interest flow is added to the flow value of time $w_t T_t$.

The consumer wealth can also be specified. The concept of wealth is that it is the capital value of the permanent income. Given the consumer's permanent income of

$$y_{Pt} = w_t T_t + \rho k_t,$$

wealth W_t can be defined as the present value of the infinite income stream of $w_t T_t + \rho k_t$, discounted with the interest rate $r_t - \delta_k = \rho$. Then wealth is

$$W_t = \frac{w_t T_t + (r - \delta_k) k_t}{r - \delta_k} = \frac{w_t T_t}{\rho} + k_t.$$

This means that wealth is the sum of both the discounted flow value of time, or 'human capital', and the physical capital.

To get the aggregate demand AD for the output y_t, with capital accumulation and zero growth, Part 4 shows that the investment demand is added to the consumption demand of equation (1.6). With zero growth, investment need only cover the depreciated capital, and so it equals $\delta_k k_t$. The AD function adds this $\delta_k k_t$ investment to the consumer demand for goods, to get that

$$y_t^d = c_t^d + \delta_k k_t = \frac{1}{1 + \alpha}\left(w_t T_t + \left[\rho + \delta_k (1 + \alpha)\right] k_t\right).$$ (1.7)

Output is a fraction of permanent income, made up of the time value flow $w_t T_t$ and the capital income flow plus capital depreciation of $\left[\rho + \delta_k (1 + \alpha)\right] k_t$. This can be written inversely by solving for the relative price of goods, $\frac{1}{w}$, so as to graph the AD function in price-quantity dimensions, as

$$\frac{1}{w_t} = \frac{T_t}{y_t^d (1 + \alpha) - \left[\rho + \delta_k (1 + \alpha)\right] k_t}.$$

This gives a downward sloping aggregate demand function.

When there is a positive but exogenous growth rate of g in the equilibrium, the aggregate demand is modified accordingly. Part 5 develops the growth model and shows that greater growth changes the capital income to $k_t (r_t - \delta_k - g)$, instead of $k_t (r_t - \delta_k)$ when there is zero growth. With this change, and using equation (1.5) to define the growth rate as the consumption growth rate,

$$1 + g_t \equiv \frac{c_t}{c_{t-1}} = \frac{1 + r_t - \delta_k}{1 + \rho},$$

this implies that $r_t - \delta_k - g$ can be rewritten as $\rho\left(1+g\right)$. This makes the modified consumption function a simple fraction of permanent income, with this income now being $w_t + \rho\left(1+g\right)k_t$:

$$c_t^d = \frac{1}{1+\alpha}\left[w_t T_t + \rho\left(1+g\right)k_t\right]. \tag{1.8}$$

With a growth rate of g, the permanent income is

$$y_{Pt} = w_t T_t + \rho\left(1+g\right)k_t,$$

while wealth is again given by the discounted infinite stream of the permanent income. With the discount rate $r_t - \delta_k - g$,

$$W_t = \frac{w_t T_t + (r_t - \delta_k - g)k_t}{r_t - \delta_k - g} = \frac{w_t T_t}{\rho\left(1+g\right)} + k_t.$$

Moving back to the aggregate demand for goods, investment is higher than just the depreciated capital when there is positive growth. The investment is shown to become $\delta_k\left(1+g\right)k_t$, so that adding this to the consumer's goods demand gives an aggregate demand AD of

$$y_t^d = \frac{1}{1+\alpha}\left(w_t T_t + k_t\left[\rho\left(1+g\right) + (\delta_k + g)\left(1+\alpha\right)\right]\right). \tag{1.9}$$

Inversely in terms of the relative price $\frac{1}{w}$, this AD is

$$\frac{1}{w_t} = \frac{T_t}{y_t^d\left(1+\alpha\right) - k_t\left[\rho\left(1+g\right) + (\delta_k + g)\left(1+\alpha\right)\right]}.$$

Part 5 goes the next step by making the growth rate endogenous. To do this, time is invested in human capital, and the growth rate is higher the higher is this human capital investment. But investing time in this way reduces time available for work. This makes the current wage flow lower, yet it ultimately makes the human capital stock and wage flow higher.

Let the time invested in human capital at time t be denoted by l_{Ht}. Then Part 5 develops the consumption function and shows it is given by

$$c_t^d = \frac{1}{1+\alpha}\left[w_t\left(1 - l_{Ht}\right)h_t + \rho\left(1+g\right)k_t\right]. \tag{1.10}$$

The time in human capital is solved within the model and the result is that it depends on the productivity of human capital investment, denoted by A_H, and the depreciation rate of human capital, denoted by δ_h, along with the growth rate g. Using the actual solution that $l_{Ht} = \frac{g+\delta_h}{A_H}$, the consumption function becomes

$$c_t^d = \frac{1}{1+\alpha}\left[w_t\left(1 - \frac{g+\delta_h}{A_H}\right)h_t + \rho\left(1+g\right)k_t\right]. \tag{1.11}$$

The consumption demand can also be written by defining the sum of the labour and leisure time as T_t, as in Parts 2, 3 and 4. Then $1 - l_{Ht} = T_t$, and consumption is

$$c_t^d = \frac{1}{1+\alpha}\left[w_t T_t h_t + \rho\left(1+g\right)k_t\right], \tag{1.12}$$

as in Part 4, when $h_t = 1$.

The permanent income stream is

$$y_{Pt} = w_t T_t h_t + \rho\left(1+g\right)k_t,$$

and with $r_t - \delta_k - g = \rho\left(1+g\right)$, wealth is

$$W_t = \frac{w_t T_t h_t + (r_t - \delta_k - g)\, k_t}{r_t - \delta_k - g} = \frac{w_t T_t h_t}{\rho\left(1+g\right)} + k_t.$$

Using that $T_t = 1 - \frac{g+\delta_h}{A_H}$, aggregate output AD becomes

$$y_t^d = \frac{1}{1+\alpha}\left[w_t\left(1 - \frac{g+\delta_h}{A_H}\right)h_t + k_t\left[\rho\left(1+g\right) + (\delta_k + g)\left(1+\alpha\right)\right]\right],$$

or inversely,

$$\frac{1}{w_t} = \frac{\left(1 - \frac{g+\delta_h}{A_H}\right)h_t}{y_t^d\left(1+\alpha\right) - k_t\left[\rho\left(1+g\right) + (g+\delta_k)\left(1+\alpha\right)\right]}. \tag{1.13}$$

Normalising $h_t = 1$, and using $1 - \frac{g+\delta_h}{A_H} = T_t$, this AD function is the same as in Part 4:

$$\frac{1}{w_t} = \frac{T_t}{y_t^d\left(1+\alpha\right) - k_t\left[\rho\left(1+g\right) + (g+\delta_k)\left(1+\alpha\right)\right]}. \tag{1.14}$$

Endogenising the growth rate through human capital accumulation helps solve certain problems in the exogenous growth model and provides a better explanation of a variety of long term and even business cycle issues. This does complicate the model, and so it is focused upon primarily in Part 5. Endogenous growth appears again in Part 7 in order to show the effect of taxes on growth, which requires an endogenous growth model.

Part 6 of the text has the same consumption function as the baseline dynamic model of Part 4 with exogenous growth, but now the capital financing is done in a variety of ways. Capital savings from the consumer are intermediated through the banking sector to the firm for investment. With a banking crisis that lowers the productivity of the banking sector, the cost of capital rises and the capital stock falls. And this lowers the k_t that enters the standard AD function of equation (1.6).

Part 6 also shows how capital is raised by the firm through asset markets. And capital is raised by the government through taxation in Part 7. The basic AD is affected only if there are costs of raising the capital, either through asset markets or through the government. Taxes on labour, goods, capital and on money use all cause the basic AD function to be affected by changes in the after tax real wage and real interest rate.

1.8 A methodological outline

Starting with a representative agent framework, there is a certain methodology available to build the fundamentals first for the closed and then for the open economy. This is done by having a single agent for the closed economy and having multiple agents for the open economy who differ in some fashion. The difference in agents gives rise to the name of 'heterogeneous' agents, meaning that they are not homogeneous with all of the same features but rather differ in some way. The text assumes a simple case of the heterogeneous agent economy: only two different types of agents exist. These two agents then differ in only one way: different marginal productivities. In Chapter 4, the type A and B agents have different marginal productivities of labour. In Chapter 7, the type A and B agents have a different marginal productivity of capital. In Chapter 14, the two agents, 1 and 2, have different human capital productivities, which result in different equilibrium marginal products of both labour and capital when they exist in isolation without trade. Trade makes these marginal products the same in both countries.

1.8.1 Closed economy methodology

The closed economy is derived under two equivalent views of the representative agent. There are no externalities introduced in any part of the text. Therefore there is what can be called a 'centralised' version of the economy that is equivalent to what is called the 'decentralised' version of the economy. The difference is that prices and profit, and supply and demand functions within markets, are explicit only once the economy is decentralised. Then relative prices reflect all conditions that affect the equilibrium when there are no externalities and so the centralised and decentralised economies are equivalent.

If there are factors external to the markets, then the relative prices do not reflect all of these factors and so the centralised and decentralised economies would not be the same. With externalities, a set of relative prices cannot 'support' the same equilibrium found in the centralised economy. This complication gives rise to the concept of a 'central planner' that makes allocations in the centralised economy. But all of these complications are avoided in the text by not introducing any externalities, and there are no central planners that might internalise any externalities.

Instead the text allows the representative agent to act jointly as consumer/producer, in the centralised economy, or to be split into being each a separate consumer and a separate firm, in the decentralised economy, with the relative prices separating the consumer from the firm.

Centralised economy

The agent that acts jointly as consumer and firm simply maximises utility subject to production technology, like Robinson Crusoe living alone on an island. Relative prices are not needed to find the general equilibrium. The aggregate demand and supply are equal at the equilibrium point. The relative prices and profit are implicit and not explicitly solved. And this lack of explicit prices does not allow for supply and demand functions to be derived. But this provides a simple and valid characterisation of the equilibrium. It is analogous to a closed world economy with the agent as the average agent.

Decentralised economy

Alternatively the agent acts in separate problems each as consumer and as firm. This puts a market line, also called either a budget line or a budget constraint, into the problem. This enables the derivation of aggregate demand and supply functions, and for the solutions of the equilibrium relative prices and profits. The consumer maximises utility subject to a budget constraint, and the firm maximises profit subject to production technology. The trick here is that the consumer budget constraint is the same equation in equilibrium as the firm profit function.

Acting each as consumer and as firm/producer, the agent has separately identifiable supply and demand functions for outputs and for factor inputs. This is still a closed economy, with a particular known equilibrium set of quantities demanded and supplied. But now rather than just the quantities of supply and demand being known, the functions of supply and demand, which say how quantities depend on the relative prices, are known. This allows for examination of how the equilibrium changes when prices change. And this decentralisation is useful for tax analysis and for the open economy model.

Mathematically, the equilibrium price is determined from the market clearing condition. For example, for the consumption good as a function of the price, $c\left(\frac{1}{w}\right)$, setting the demand function for consumption, $c^d\left(\frac{1}{w}\right)$, equal to the supply function of consumption, $c^s\left(\frac{1}{w}\right)$, allows for determination of the equilibrium price $\frac{1}{w}$:

$$c^d\left(\frac{1}{w}\right) = c^s\left(\frac{1}{w}\right).$$

1.8.2 Open economy methodology

By adding just one more type of agent, the model can represent the open general equilibrium economy with trade. With two representative agents that differ only in productive capacity, each of the agents acts separately as both consumer and firm. Different supply and demand functions can then be derived for each agent, and trade patterns established as functions of relative prices. Now the consumption demand is the sum of both agents A and B, as is consumption supply:

$$c^d = c_A^d + c_B^d;$$
$$c^s = c_A^s + c_B^s.$$

And the equilibrium relative price is determined by setting the total supply equal to the total demand of both agents. This gives the expanded market clearing condition:

$$c^d = c_A^d + c_B^d = c_A^s + c_B^s = c^s.$$

Different productivities induce comparative advantage and open up gains from trade. Trade 'triangles' result when moving from autarky (which means no trade) to trade. This approach assimilates part of the microeconomic 'pure theory of international trade'. Different cultures with different technologies can trade with each other.

The representative agent approach to the open economy, with two types of agents, is easily extended to any number of agents. Say there are 1000 agents in all, 400 of A and 600 of B type. The first-order equilibrium conditions for each type of agent are completely unaffected by the number of each type of agent. Only when the market clearing condition is applied to find the equilibrium price does the number of agents affect the computation of the equilibrium solution. In particular, now to get total consumption goods demand equal to consumption goods supply, and so to find the equilibrium relative price, the market clearing condition is instead

$$c^d = 400c_A^d + 600c_B^d = 400c_A^s + 600c_B^s = c^s.$$

And with consumption a function of $\frac{1}{w}$, this altered market clearing condition determines the new equilibrium $\frac{1}{w}$.

A two-agent general equilibrium, with the agents differing only in productivity, is presented in Chapters 4, 7 and 14. These chapters cover the labour-only dimension, the capital-only dimension, and the fully dynamic model with both labour and capital. Factor price equalisation occurs in each chapter. The wage equalises in Chapter 4, the interest rate equalises in Chapter 7 and both equalise in Chapter 14. However Chapter 14 requires endogenous growth so that the interest rate is endogenous and both interest rates and wage rates can as a result be equalised. And while Chapters 4 and 7 assume the agents differ only in their goods productivities, in Chapter 14 the agents differ only in their human capital investment productivities.

1.9 Suggested ways to use the text

The book can be read by students focusing on the intuition of the margins, learning to derive the margins presented, and working through the examples that are presented. It allows conceptual thinking about how each margin is first formulated and then how a margin is being affected by each extension.

Familiarity of the margins of the baseline recursive model then allows for the extensions to be made as just one more step beyond well-known compounds. Parts 2, 3 and 4 are designed to be a one-semester course in modern macroeconomics. The elements of modern macroeconomics are derived along the two static margins in Parts 2 and 3 and then brought together simultaneously in the baseline dynamic model in Part 4.

The Part 5–7 extensions of the model beyond the baseline formulation make up what is designed to be the second semester course in undergraduate modern macroeconomics. These extensions are along four dimensions: Part 5, growth and business cycles; Part 6, risk, banking and asset prices; Part 7 fiscal and monetary policy.

1.9.1 Possible course usage of text

The text is intended to bring to undergraduates the main elements of macroeconomics used in research. This involves additional mathematical rigour. And yet, while the mathematics is involved, it uses only derivatives and solving systems of equations. The solution of a quadratic equation is also used at times, although this is not essential as the solution is also shown graphically. And the text allows a graphical representation to be emphasised over the mathematics if that is desired. All of the graphs show the exact mathematical form of the equations of the particular example, and so the graphs are exact representations of the economy.

Undergraduates can be taught the text as a single intermediate macroeconomics one-semester course, as a two-semester course in intermediate macroeconomics, or as an advanced macroeconomics one-semester course. For example, for a full two semesters in undergraduate macroeconomics, the book's 20 chapters can be split in half. Master's level courses are typically as in undergraduate intermediate courses or as in advanced undergraduate courses, and so a Master's level course could select across the entire book. More advanced graduate courses could use the book as an introduction.

1.9.2 A summary

1. Two-semester undergraduate intermediate Macroeconomics sequence:
   (a) Semester one, first 10 chapters, selectively.
   (b) Semester two, second 10 chapters, selectively.
2. One-semester undergraduate intermediate Macroeconomics course:
   (a) Emphasise the first half of the book, in Parts 1–4.
   (b) Select across the first half of the book, in Parts 1–4 and add in other sections such as growth theory and banking in Part 5, and fiscal and monetary policy in Part 6.
   (c) Emphasise only the static analysis of Parts 1–3, if you do not want to do the full dynamic analysis.
3. Undergraduate advanced Macroeconomics course: one semester, selected chapters across all seven Parts of the book.
4. Master's level Macroeconomics course: one semester, the entire book, selectively.

1.10 Questions

1. The microfoundations approach to macroeconomics stresses
   (a) the representative agent analysis;
   (b) relative price analysis;
   (c) *AD–AS* analysis;
   (d) more than one of the above.
2. From the general equilibrium economy, where there are two outputs, x and y, and a representative consumer/producer, we can derive
   (a) the amount of goods 'traded' (the difference between consumption and production, if any);
   (b) the quantity supplied of x;

(c) the demand schedule for y;

(d) all of the above.

3. If the representative agent consumes goods c, according to the consumption function $c = \left(\frac{1}{1+\alpha}\right) y_P$, where y_P is permanent income, and α a constant parameter, then

(a) an increase in permanent income raises consumption;

(b) an increase in the interest rate raises wealth;

(c) an increase in the real wage rate lowers consumption;

(d) all of the above.

4. Suppose the consumption function is

$$c = \left(\frac{1}{1+\alpha}\right) y_P$$

where y_P is permanent income and α a constant parameter. Focusing on substitution and income effects, indicate how to use this function to explain each of the following:

(a) business cycles;

(b) economic growth;

(c) old age pension insurance;

(d) the distribution of income.

5. What are the main margins of economic analysis that make up the microfoundations approach to macroeconomic analysis?

6. What role does the capital stock play in forming the aggregate demand and supply analysis in the dynamic model?

7. Define permanent income and explain how it affects the consumer's demand for goods.

8. Explain how the consumer's demand for goods, or consumption function, changes as the economy goes from a static one to a dynamic one.

9. Explain how aggregate demand is formed from the consumer's demand for goods, in terms of capital investment?

10. What role can comparative statics play in explaining business cycles and severe recessions?

11. What economic facts can be explained by the inclusion of human capital?

1.11 References

Allen, R.D.G. 1968, *Macro-Economic Theory*, Macmillan, London.

Barro, Robert J., 1984, *Macroeconomics*, John Wiley and Sons, Inc; and various subsequent editions.

Lucas, Robert E., Jr., 2001, 'Professional Memoir', manuscript, University of Chicago, http://home.uchicago.edu/~sogrodow/homepage/memoir.pdf.

Marshall, Alfred, 1920, *Principles of Economics*, 8th edition, Macmillan and Co. Limited, London.

Samuelson, Paul Anthony, 1947, *Foundations of Economic Analysis*, Harvard Economic Studies, vol. 80, Harvard University Press, Cambridge.

Samuelson, Paul Anthony, 1948, *Economics: An Introductory Analysis*, McGraw-Hill Publishing Company Ltd, New York.

Samuelson, Paul Anthony and William D. Nordhaus, 2009, *Economics: An Introductory Analysis*, 19th edition, McGraw-Hill Higher Education.

Stokey, Nancy L. and Robert E. Lucas, Jr., with Edward C. Prescott, 1989, *Recursive Methods in Economic Dynamics*, Harvard University Press, Cambridge.

PART ②

LABOUR AND GOODS MARKETS

CHAPTER ②

Labour, leisure and productivity

2.1 Introduction

The chapter analyses the general equilibrium demand and supply for goods and for labour. This involves deriving the labour–leisure trade-off, or margin, for the representative agent. First the general equilibrium is set out in which the agent maximises utility subject to a production of goods with a labour-only technology. Then the agent problem is split into two separate but related problems of the consumer and the firm. The consumer maximises the same utility but now subject to an income constraint rather than subject to the production function itself. The firm maximises profit, subject to the production function. This still gives the same equilibrium but now markets can be made explicit.

The marginal rate of substitution between goods and leisure is derived in a general equilibrium for the representative agent, and then again through the consumer and the firm sides of the problem. The latter allows the prices to be made explicit, through a 'market line', or budget constraint, and for profits to be also determined. This allows for the aggregate supply and demand for labour and goods markets to be made explicit and for the equilibrium wage to be found.

A change in labour productivity is postulated through an increase in the parameter that factors the production function. Doubling this causes the marginal product of labour to double. And this causes substitution and income effects that can be decomposed in general equilibrium. The substitution effect of higher productivity is to work more; the income effect is to work less. With standard utility and production functions, it is shown that the higher productivity leads to more consumption by both substitution and income effects, while working time remains stable as substitution and income effects go in opposite directions and offset each other. The effects on the aggregate demand and supply of goods and labour markets is shown, and the new equilibrium wage found.

2.1.1 Building on the last chapter

The last chapter discussed what it means to model macroeconomics using only microeconomics. Requiring only the assumption of a representative consumer, this methodology of the general equilibrium, and then separate consumer and firm problems is applied in full here to the labour problem. The last chapter discussed closed versus open economies; this chapter is a closed economy setting, with explicit utility and production function specifications. The last chapter focused also on how two central margins are specified and applied throughout the text, and here the intratemporal margin is developed, of the labour–leisure time trade-off during the current period.

2.1.2 Learning objective

You will develop one of the essential margins in economics: the marginal rate of substitution between goods and leisure. The aim is to see why this is equal to the real wage rate in equilibrium. And then the goal is to understand how this margin leads to the derivation of the aggregate supply and demand of both goods and labour. The general equilibrium centralised economy and the general equilibrium decentralisation into goods and labour markets are a primary learning objective. Understanding comparative statics within these equilibria is the final aim.

2.1.3 Who made it happen?

Giving shape to modern economics, Alfred Marshall wrote his eight editions of *Principles of Economics* from 1890 to 1920 while a debate raged on the 'natural laws' that determined wages. John Bates Clark is recognised for first postulating the marginal productivity theory of wages, in his 1899 book *The Distribution of Wealth: A theory of wages, interest and profits* and in his 1901 article 'Wages and Interest as Determined by Marginal Productivity', in the *Journal of Political Economy*. This was followed up by such notables as Henry Ludwell Moore who tested the theory in his 1911 *Laws of Wages*, and by Nobel Laureate (1972) J. R. Hicks who linked the marginal product theory back to Marshall's first edition of *Principles* and then expanded the theory in the context of unions, wage regulation and unemployment, in his 1932 *The Theory of Wages*.

Gary S. Becker (Nobel Laureate 1992) made prominent the theory that all of our time is valued 'at the margin' at the same value as our work time, as implied by marginal productivity theory. His 1965 article 'The Allocation of Time' in the *Economic Journal* allowed all uses of time to be analysed in terms of the factors determining how people spend their non-work time (reprinted in Becker 1976). This includes the so-called 'leisure' time in general, but more specifically time spent studying in school, or on-the-job training, or for fertility and child raising, as discussed in his books *Human Capital, The Economic Approach to Human Behaviour* and *A Treatise on the Family*.

Becker is well-known for showing how including time allows for analysis of such 'non-economic' issues such as drug addiction, marriage and discrimination, by understanding the constraints on the representative agent that help determine social behaviour. In the *American Economic Review* in 2005, he and his co-authors applied the shadow value of time to the worldwide distribution of income: by counting the shadow value of the world population's increasing health the worldwide distribution of income is getting more equal rather than less equal as some argue on the basis of income alone.

2.2 Representative agent goods–leisure choice

The building blocks of the representative agent model are to show how an average agent acts given a utility function, a time allocation endowment, a production function, and a goods allocation endowment. First consider how the model with an average agent works. The representative agent acts as someone, sometimes called Robinson Crusoe, after the fictional book of a mariner living alone on an island (Daniel Defoe, 1719, *Robinson Crusoe*), who both produces and consumes goods, with a time endowment and production technology. This is a paradigm for the average person in an economy, and one that goes back to early classical economics; even Karl Marx refers to Robinson Crusoe economies. And Alfred Marshall employed this device in his text that established neoclassical economics.

In economic terms, this translates here into a consumer that maximises utility with respect to goods and leisure, while facing constraints on production technology and on goods and time endowments. The model can be set up with prices being only implicit, in a centralised form, or prices can be made explicit by decentralising the problem into both consumer and firm problems. In the centralised form the firm problem is implicit in the single consumer optimisation.

The equilibrium is solved and graphed using normal-shaped, 'homothetic' utility and production functions. Utility is specified always as log utility, and production always in a Cobb–Douglas form. Utility, time allocation, technology and goods constraints are specified next.

2.2.1 Utility and production elements

Let utility u be a function of goods c and leisure x, given in general by

$$u = u(c, x).$$

It is assumed that both goods and leisure increase utility, so that $\frac{\partial u(c,x)}{\partial c} > 0$, and $\frac{\partial u(c,x)}{\partial x} > 0$. And it is assumed that such utility increases occur at a decreasing rate (diminishing marginal utility of increased consumption of goods or leisure) so that both second derivatives of utility are negative. With a utility function such as log utility, these conditions are satisfied.

Log utility

The equilibrium can be solved and graphed using normal-shaped utility and production functions. Consider the log form, with additive separability between the terms involving goods c and leisure x:

$$u(c, x) = \ln c + \alpha \ln x. \tag{2.1}$$

The parameter α tells of the degree to which the agent likes leisure. For example let $u(c, x) = \ln c + 0.5 \ln x$. Figure 2.1 graphs this function, showing how utility rises with each goods and leisure. Note that the numerical value of utility is negative, and it rises as does the quantity of goods and leisure, approaching 0 as the upper limit of utility. As the numerical value of utility indicates nothing in itself, it is fine to have a negative value.

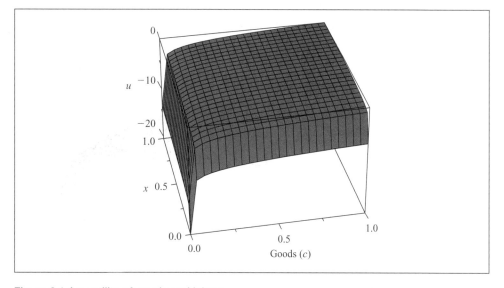

Figure 2.1 Log utility of goods and leisure

And as log utility is very standard in macroeconomics, and easy to work with, a log utility form, such as in equation (2.1), will be used through the text.

Cobb–Douglas production

For the production of output, denoted by y, a Cobb–Douglas production function is the standard one used in the modern macroeconomic theory. Consider that it is specified with two factors, labour and capital. Let capital be denoted by k, assume a productivity parameter $A_G > 0$, where the G subscript represents the $Goods$ output sector, and let there be a parameter γ between zero and one, so that $\gamma \in (0, 1)$. Then the production function is in general specified as

$$y = f(l, k) = A_G l^\gamma k^{1-\gamma}.$$

Figure 2.2 graphs the Cobb–Douglas output function with the assumptions on parameters that $A_G = 1$ and $\gamma = \frac{1}{3}$. Output rises as either factor, labour or capital, rises. With $A_G = 1$, then $y = 1$ in the case when labour and capital both are equal to 1.

As we are focusing on the labour–leisure trade-off in this chapter, let $k = 1$ so that

$$f(l) = A_G l^\gamma. \tag{2.2}$$

In Part 2, in contrast, the labour is kept at 1, and changes in k are focused on. And in Part 4 and throughout the rest of the book, the labour and capital are both allowed to be chosen optimally. Details about the Cobb–Douglas function are given in Appendix A2.10.4.

Log utility and Cobb–Douglas production are simple and form the bedrock of modern research. Empirical research supports these specifications, with some variation allowed. More general utility functions can be examined in advanced work, as can further extensions from Cobb–Douglas technology.

Further, log utility is almost the same functional form as the Cobb–Douglas production function. Consider that if we transform the utility function by taking the exponential of both sides of the equation, then

$$u(c, x) = \ln c + \alpha \ln x;$$
$$u(c, x) = \ln c + \ln x^\alpha = \ln(c x^\alpha); \tag{2.3}$$
$$e^u = c x^\alpha. \tag{2.4}$$

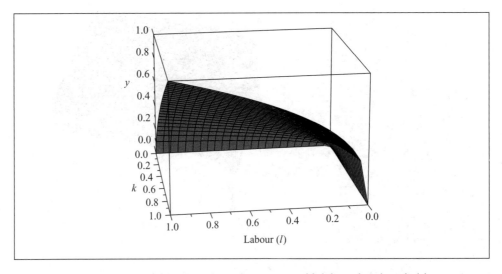

Figure 2.2 Cobb–Douglas production of goods output y with labour l and capital k

More generally the log utility function can be given with parameters α_1 and α_2, with

$$\alpha_1 + \alpha_2 = 1,$$

whereby

$$u(c, x) = \alpha_1 \ln c + \alpha_2 \ln x;$$
$$u(c, x) = \ln c^{\alpha_1} + \ln x^{\alpha_2} = \ln \left(c^{\alpha_1} x^{\alpha_2} \right);$$
$$e^u = c^{\alpha_1} x^{\alpha_2}. \tag{2.5}$$

Then the utility function e^u in equation (2.5) is also in the form of a Cobb–Douglas production function. We will use the simpler form of equation (2.1). But the point here is that log utility and Cobb–Douglas production are similar functions that have nice smooth utility level curves, and production isoquants. These functions are called 'homothetic' functions because of these smooth properties, but we will not use this terminology elsewhere in the text.

2.2.2 Time and goods constraints

There are two constraints, one on time and one on goods. Time and goods can be thought of as being exogenously endowed, and then distributed optimally between alternative uses. Or they can be produced and distributed between alternative uses. However the production of time is taken up only later in Chapter 12 on human capital.

Time allocation constraint

The representative agent maximises utility with respect to goods and to leisure, subject to a time constraint, a goods constraint and a production technology. The 'allocation of time' constraint assumed here is that the time available for labour l and leisure x in general sums up to the amount T, which is an assumed exogenous parameter. This makes the constraint:

$$l + x = T. \tag{2.6}$$

Certainly, there are other uses of time than work and leisure, such as education time which takes up a huge part of many young adult lives. For now such other uses of time are not included. But as education time plays an important role in a fuller analysis, this time is included explicitly in Parts 5 and 7.

One way to think of T is that labour and leisure time add up to 100% of the time, disregarding education time for now. Instead of 100, the number 1 can be used more simply, so that the allocation of time constraint can be specified as

$$l + x = 1. \tag{2.7}$$

Then labour and leisure are fractions of the total time endowment.

Alternatively, the exogenous time endowment can be thought of in terms of hours in a day, 24, and this specification is also used in this chapter, again ignoring education time for now. But even 24 could be replaced for example by 16 if 8 hours of sleep are not included in the consumer's time allocation for work and leisure. The most typical specification is $T = 1$, but others will be used to supply additional intuition.

Goods endowment constraint

The goods constraint indicates how much output can be divided into consumption and investment. The output is determined by the production technology, this being the Cobb–Douglas function. And if the output increases or decreases, this endows the consumer with more or fewer goods to divide between consumption and investment.

In this Part 2, the investment is zero since the capital stock is assumed fixed at $k = 1$. Therefore the goods endowment constraint is very simple: consumption equals output:

$$c = y = f(l, k) = A_G l^\gamma k^{1-\gamma} = A_G l^\gamma.$$

This last equality follows because as yet there is no investment, allowing all output to be consumed.

2.2.3 Equilibrium with capital fixed

A simple method of consumer optimisation of utility subject to the technology, time and goods constraints is to substitute the constraints directly into the utility function. This way there is only one variable left in the utility function for which the consumer takes the derivative. Then the equilibrium is given by one straightforward derivative. Appendix A2.10.1 at the end of the chapter alternatively includes the constraints as in the 'Lagrangian optimisation' method, which is almost absent in this text because it appears more complicated to most students.

Utility will be put into a form so that it depends only upon the time spent working, l. This is done by solving for x from equation (2.7) as $x = 1 - l$, using that $c = y$ from the goods constraint, and using that $y = f(l)$ from the production technology of equation (2.2). This puts both x and c in terms of l, with $c = y = f(l)$.

Substituting for x and c into the utility function turns the maximisation problem into one involving only the one unknown of labour time l (it is arbitrary as to which one variable is used, in this case l is the single variable):

$$\text{Max}_{l} \; L = u[f(l), 1 - l].$$

Taking the derivative with respect to l, by using the 'chain rule' of calculus, gives that

$$\frac{\partial u}{\partial c}\frac{\partial f(l)}{\partial l} + \frac{\partial u(c, x)}{\partial x}\frac{\partial(1 - l)}{\partial l} = 0.$$

Rearranging this gives the basic characterising equilibrium condition of the economy:

$$\frac{\partial f(l)}{\partial l} = \frac{\frac{\partial u(c,x)}{\partial x}}{\frac{\partial u(c,x)}{\partial c}}.$$

The marginal product of labour (MP_n) equals the marginal rate of substitution between goods and leisure $(MRS_{c,x})$, or

$$MP_l \equiv \frac{\partial f(l)}{\partial l} = \frac{\frac{\partial u(c,x)}{\partial x}}{\frac{\partial u(c,x)}{\partial c}} \equiv MRS_{c,x}. \tag{2.8}$$

The ratio of marginal utilities is called the 'marginal rate of substitution' between goods and leisure. Altogether this tells us that the incremental rate of productivity in output supply is set equal to the incremental rate at which goods are substituted for leisure in the equilibrium. It is the most basic 'intratemporal' (during the period) trade-off that the agent encounters. It links together production and consumption so that both are efficiently used. This margin will be developed in this chapter and used throughout the text. It is one of two key margins, when both labour and capital are simultaneously used, starting in Part 4.

The equilibrium solution when the agent maximises log utility subject to the Cobb–Douglas technology with $k = 1$ is the same as in equation (2.8), but now with the particular functional forms used in the derivatives. To see this, write down the representative agent problem as

$$\text{Max}_{l} \; u[f(l), 1 - l] = \ln\left(A_G l^\gamma\right) + \alpha \ln\left(1 - l\right). \tag{2.9}$$

And this implies the first-order equilibrium condition, from taking the derivative with respect to l, and setting it equal to zero, of

$$\frac{\partial u[f(l),1-l]}{\partial l} = \frac{\partial \left[\ln\left(A_G l^{\gamma}\right) + \alpha \ln\left(1-l\right)\right]}{\partial l} = 0; \tag{2.10}$$

$$0 = \frac{A_G \gamma \,(l)^{\gamma-1}}{A_G l^{\gamma}} - \alpha \left(\frac{1}{1-l}\right). \tag{2.11}$$

Note that this makes use of the mathematical rule for taking the derivative of the natural logarithm function: $\frac{\partial \ln z(n)}{\partial n} = \frac{\frac{\partial z(n)}{\partial n}}{z(n)}$.

The equilibrium condition can also be rewritten as in equation (2.8):

$$MP_l \equiv \frac{\partial f(l)}{\partial l} = A_G \gamma \,(l)^{\gamma-1} = \frac{\frac{\alpha}{1-l}}{\frac{1}{A_G l^{\gamma}}} = \frac{\frac{\alpha}{x}}{\frac{1}{c}} = \frac{\frac{\partial u(c,x)}{\partial x}}{\frac{\partial u(c,x)}{\partial c}} \equiv MRS_{c,x}. \tag{2.12}$$

The solution for the labour l can be found since this equilibrium condition is just one equation in the unknown l. Simplifying either equation (2.11) or (2.12), the solution for l follows:

$$\gamma\left(1-l\right) = \alpha l,$$
$$\gamma = (\alpha + \gamma)\,l,$$
$$l = \frac{\gamma}{\alpha + \gamma}. \tag{2.13}$$

This gives a solution for l in terms of given, known, parameters, γ and α. Note here that the productivity parameter A_G cancels out and does not affect this basic allocation result. The parameters γ and α are specified as part of utility and technology specifications. Here they have been given in general form without specific values, but that is done in Example 2.1. Note that once l is solved, the rest of the solution in terms of parameters follows immediately:

$$c = y = A_G l^{\gamma} = A_G \left(\frac{\gamma}{\alpha + \gamma}\right)^{\gamma}, \tag{2.14}$$

$$x = 1 - l = 1 - \frac{\gamma}{\alpha + \gamma}.$$

2.2.4 Example 2.1: Baseline model

Assume the log utility and Cobb–Douglas production functions as in equation (2.9). Now the equilibrium solution will be found for an example specification of the parameters of the economy. Such a parameter set specification is often called a calibration of the economy, with the idea that the parameter values result in an equilibrium that is consistent with particular empirically based notions about the economy.

Calibration

Now assume specific values for the utility and technology parameters, in particular that $A_G = 1$, $\gamma = \frac{1}{3}$ and $\alpha = 0.5$. Then it follows that $c = y = f(l) = l^{\frac{1}{3}}$. The equating of the marginal product of labour to the marginal rate of substitution between leisure and goods, in equation (2.12), now becomes:

$$\left(\frac{1}{3}\right)l^{\left(\frac{1}{3}-1\right)} = \frac{\frac{1.5}{x}}{\frac{1}{c}} = \frac{\frac{1.5}{1-l}}{\frac{1}{l^{\frac{1}{3}}}}.$$

This is solved as $l = \frac{\gamma}{\alpha+\gamma} = \frac{\frac{1}{3}}{0.5+\frac{1}{3}} = 0.4$. Then leisure is $x = 1-0.4 = 0.6$, and consumption is $c = l^{\frac{1}{3}} = 0.40^{\frac{1}{3}} = 0.737$. And utility is

$$\ln(c) + \alpha \ln(x) = \ln(0.737) + 0.5\ln(0.6) = -0.56058.$$

Utility can be a negative number without any problem, as in Figure 2.1; a less negative number means a higher utility level.

In equilibrium, 40% of time is spent working, 60% is spent in leisure, and goods consumed are equal to 0.737. This example specification of parameters, which in general is called the 'calibration' of the model, is similar to what is found in the full dynamic model that is researched and extended in economic journals.

Note that in this baseline example with $\gamma = \frac{1}{3}$, the amount of labour income relative to profit income will be $\frac{1}{3}$ for labour and $\frac{2}{3}$ for profit, when the economy is decentralised as in Section 2.4. This comes from the Cobb–Douglas properties of the production function (see Appendix A2). Some calibrations are instead chosen in reverse in that $\gamma = \frac{2}{3}$ so that labour income is two-thirds and profit (capital income) is one-third. The baseline specification here of choosing $\gamma = \frac{1}{3}$ is however consistent with models that view the capital as also containing human capital and not just physical capital (see Mankiw, Romer and Weil, 1992). The inclusion of human capital is indeed an important part of the latter parts of the text and so the choice of $\gamma = \frac{1}{3}$ is consistent with this approach.

Graphically
To graph the equilibrium requires the utility level curve at its equilibrium level and the production function. These will be illustrated in the c and x dimensions, of goods and leisure. As in equation (2.4), utility can be written as $e^u = cx^\alpha$. Solving for consumption gives the utility level curve to be graphed in $(c : x)$ dimensions:

$$c = \frac{e^u}{x^{0.5}} = \frac{e^{-0.56058}}{x^{0.5}}. \tag{2.15}$$

For the production function, let $c = f(l) = l^{\frac{1}{3}}$. Substituting $l = 1 - x$ into the production function gives a version of the production function that can also be graphed in $(c : x)$ space:

$$c = (1-x)^{\frac{1}{3}}. \tag{2.16}$$

Although there is an entire 'map' of such utility level curves, Figure 2.3 graphs only the equilibrium utility curve of equation (2.15) in black along with the production function of equation (2.16) in blue.

The graph shows the equilibrium tangency point at $c = 0.737$ and $x = 0.60$. This is the optimal amount of goods and leisure for the representative agent. The 'interior solution' occurs between the endpoints of the production and utility curves, indicating that indeed the agent achieves a balancing of goods versus leisure.

In general, the marginal rate of substitution between goods and leisure, denoted by $MRS_{c,x}$, equals the negative of the slope of the indifference curve at every point. The marginal product of labour, MP_l, is equal to the negative of the slope of the production function at every point. At the tangency point between the production function and the indifference curve, the $MRS_{c,x}$ equals the MP_l.

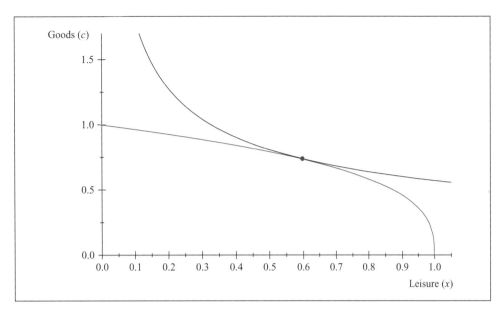

Figure 2.3 Consumption and leisure equilibrium at tangency point of Example 2.1

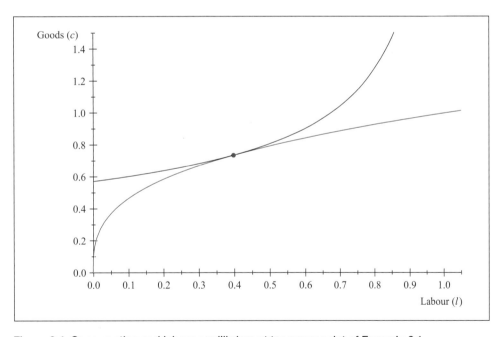

Figure 2.4 Consumption and labour equilibrium at tangency point of Example 2.1

Graphed in reverse, in terms of goods c and labour l, the equations are

$$c = \frac{e^u}{(1-l)^{0.5}} = \frac{e^{-0.56058}}{(1-l)^{0.5}}; \tag{2.17}$$

$$c = (l)^{\frac{1}{3}}. \tag{2.18}$$

And Figure 2.4 graphs the same equilibrium of Example 2.1 in $(c:l)$ space.

2.2.5 Smoothing consumption

The equilibrium in Figure 2.3 illustrates that the agent engages in a balance between leisure and goods consumption. This is a type of 'smoothing' of consumption through an optimal balancing of different opportunities, of consuming goods and taking leisure. If, instead, a different equilibrium resulted with only work and no leisure, then the equilibrium would occur at a 'corner' solution. In Figure 2.3, there would be zero leisure and so only work; the solution would be $l = 1$ and $c = 1$ at the point where the production function intersects the vertical axis. Such an equilibrium would not be very nice for the agent since it would be a very unbalanced life of only working. Consumption across different 'economic goods', these being the actual consumption good and also the leisure time, would not be 'smoothed' or balanced.

Whether a balance occurs or not depends on several factors, mainly being the shape of the production function and the shape of the utility function in $(c : x)$ space. If production functions are linear, as can be assumed, a convex shaped utility level curve in Figure 2.3 may still result in a balance between work and leisure; or there may be a corner solution. But production is typically concave as this represents the fundamental idea that the marginal product of labour is positive but diminishing, so that the slope of the production function is positive (negative however as graphed in Figure 2.3), and that the marginal product is rising but at a diminishing rate as labour increases (the second derivative of output is negative, $f''(l) < 0$). Production function concavity helps ensure the equilibrium is not a corner solution.

And utility typically has the convex shape as seen in Figure 2.3. This means simply that as the agent chooses to consume, say, less leisure, and to work more, then the marginal utility of leisure rises, while the marginal utility of goods consumed gets smaller. With less leisure, an hour of it becomes worth more. And with more goods, getting even more goods is not so beneficial. Thus the ratio of marginal utilities $\frac{\partial u(c,x)}{\partial x} / \frac{\partial u(c,x)}{\partial c}$ gets higher as the agent works more. The convex feature of utility level curves is natural and drives the actual equilibrium towards a balance between work and leisure.

This shows the concept of the 'smoothing' of items that enter the utility function, in particular goods and leisure. The equilibrium is not the most goods possible, nor the most leisure possible, but rather a balance of the two that represents equating the utility value of each activity, at the margin.

Another way to look at this margin is in terms of equalising the marginal utility of expenditure across the different types of utility-yielding events, which here are consuming goods and taking leisure. The value of the marginal utility per unit cost for goods is $\frac{\partial u(c,l)}{\partial c}$ divided by the cost of 1 per unit. And this the consumer sets equal in equilibrium to the value of the marginal utility of leisure $\frac{\partial u(c,l)}{\partial x}$ divided by its 'shadow' per unit cost, which is the marginal product of labour $\frac{\partial f(l)}{\partial l}$:

$$\frac{\frac{\partial u(c,l)}{\partial c}}{1} = \frac{\frac{\partial u(c,l)}{\partial x}}{\frac{\partial f(l)}{\partial l}}.$$

This other way to write the equilibrium condition shows the property of consumption 'smoothing' from the basic microeconomic paradigm of equating benefits per unit cost at the margin.

2.3 Goods productivity increase

Now suppose that the productivity changes. This happens when the exogenous parameter A_G changes. If A_G rises, then the production function $y = A_G l^\gamma$ shifts upwards.

2.3.1 Example 2.2

Let $\gamma = \frac{1}{3}$ and $\alpha = 0.5$, as in Example 2.1, but now let A_G double from 1 to 2. By equation (2.13), the equilibrium labour, and therefore leisure is unaffected by changes in A_G since A_G does not enter that equation. So $l = 0.60$ and $x = 0.40$. By equation (2.14), consumption rises to twice what it was, now to

$$c = 2l^{\frac{1}{3}} = 2\left(0.40\right)^{\frac{1}{3}} = 1.474. \tag{2.19}$$

And utility is

$$\ln(c) + \alpha \ln(x) = \ln\left(1.474\right) + 0.5\ln\left(0.6\right) = 0.13257;$$
$$c = \frac{e^u}{x^{0.5}} = \frac{e^{0.13257}}{x^{0.5}}. \tag{2.20}$$

Figure 2.5 graphs equations (2.19) and (2.20) of Example 2.2 in bolder blue and bolder black, in comparison to the Example 2.1 equilibrium in normal blue and normal black.

The productivity increase shifts up the production function and the utility level, while leaving leisure unchanged.

2.3.2 Substitution and income effects

Figure 2.5 shows that consumption rises but leisure remains the same. For consumption, both income and substitution effects go towards increasing consumption. For leisure, it remains the same because the substitution and income effects go in opposite directions and exactly offset each other. This offsetting feature is common to the aggregate labour specification because it results with normal (homothetic) production and utility functions, such as the Cobb–Douglas production and log utility used here. While common it is also acceptable because it implies realistically that as productivity rises, the working hours per week stay the same.

A change in productivity of Example 2.2 can be decomposed graphically into its substitution and income effects. A pure substitution effect occurs when the marginal product

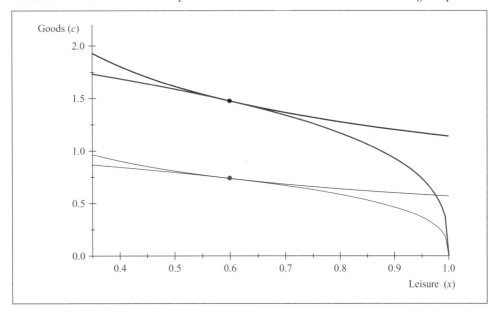

Figure 2.5 Productivity doubling of Example 2.2 (bolder blue and bolder black)

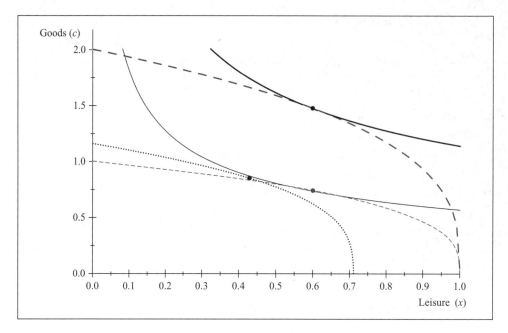

Figure 2.6 Substitution and income effects from a productivity doubling

of labour changes and the utility level remains the same as in the original equilibrium. Figure 2.6 adds into Figure 2.5 the dotted black curve that illustrates the substitution effect for Example 2.2.

This curve is tangent to the light black utility curve, at a lower level of leisure than 0.6, but with the same equilibrium marginal product of labour as when productivity doubles. The higher marginal product of labour than in the initial equilibrium induces more labour (and more goods) and less leisure while holding utility constant.

The income effect is a shift of the production function with the marginal product kept at its new higher value such as when productivity doubles in Example 2.2. The income effect in Figure 2.6 is the shift up in the utility level curve to its final equilibrium value, from the light black curve to the bold black curve, at the tangency between the higher dashed bold blue curve and the higher utility curve. The income effect causes more leisure (and more goods). Substitution and income effects on leisure are exactly offsetting, leaving $x = 0.60$.

2.3.3 Example 2.3: An eight-hour day

In an alternative model specification used in the text, the time endowment is 24, for '24 hours in a day', instead of 1 for '100% of time', in order to give intuitive results in terms of hours worked per day. Therefore assume that $T = 24$, and also that $\alpha = 1$, $A_G = 1$, and let $\gamma = 0.5$.

The log utility function is therefore

$$u = \ln c + \ln x.$$

The Cobb–Douglas production function is

$$c = \sqrt{l}.$$

The utility maximisation problem is

$$\text{Max}_{l} \; u = \ln\left(\sqrt{l}\right) + \ln\left(1 - l\right), \tag{2.21}$$

with the equilibrium condition rearranged to give the equality between the marginal product of labour and the marginal rate of substitution between goods and leisure:

$$MP_l \equiv \frac{\partial f}{\partial l} = 0.5l^{-0.5} = \frac{\frac{1}{x}}{\frac{1}{c}} = MRS_{x,c}.$$

Substituting in for $x = 24 - l$, and $c = l^{0.5}$, gives the one equation in one unknown, l:

$$0.5l^{-0.5} = \frac{\frac{1}{24-l}}{\frac{1}{l^{0.5}}} = \frac{l^{0.5}}{24 - l},$$

$$0.5\left(24 - l\right) = l,$$

$$12 = 1.5l,$$

$$l = 8.$$

The solution is $l = 8$, $x = 16$, and $c = \sqrt{8} = 2.83$. Utility is $u = \ln 2.83 + \ln 16 = 3.81$. So the agent works a normal eight-hour day. Increasing productivity by any factor leaves $l = 8$, just as in Example 2.2. For example, doubling goods productivity so that

$$c = y = 2\sqrt{l},$$

gives the solution equation that

$$l^{-0.5} = \frac{\frac{1}{24-l}}{\frac{1}{2l^{0.5}}} = \frac{2l^{0.5}}{24 - l},$$

$$24 - l = 2l,$$

$$24 = 3l,$$

$$l = 8.$$

Then $x = 16$, and consumption increases to $c = 2\sqrt{8} = 5.66$.

Therefore even in this differently calibrated economy, although still with log utility and Cobb–Douglas production, for leisure the income and substitution effects again exactly offset each other. The agent still works eight hours a day despite having a higher marginal productivity and consuming more goods.

2.3.4 Example 2.4: Linear indifference curves

As a final example here consider how a corner solution can result with a linear utility function. Let utility be given by

$$u = c + x,$$

and production again as in Example 2.3 equal to

$$c = \sqrt{l},$$

with the time endowment of $T = 1$, and so $1 = l + x$. The maximisation problem, in the simple one-step form, is

$$\text{Max}_{l} \; u = \left(1 - l\right) + \sqrt{l}.$$

This gives the first-order equilibrium condition:

$$\frac{\partial u}{\partial l} = -1 + 0.5l^{-0.5} = 0.$$

It implies the solution $l = 0.25$, which gives in turn that $x = 1 - 0.25 = 0.75$, $c = \sqrt{0.25} = 0.5$, and that $u = \sqrt{0.25} + 0.75 = 1.25$. This is an 'interior' solution in that the consumer has some of both work and leisure.

Now suppose that the labour productivity doubles so that instead the production function is given by

$$c = 2\sqrt{l}.$$

The new equilibrium comes from the maximisation problem:

$$\underset{l}{\text{Max }} u = \left(1 - l\right) + 2\sqrt{l},$$

and yields the equilibrium condition that

$$\frac{\partial u}{\partial l} = -1 + l^{-0.5} = 0.$$

The solution is $l = 1$, $x = 0$, $c = 2$, and $u = 2$. The consumer only works, with zero leisure, a 'corner' solution.

Graphically, the linear utility function gives linear indifference curves, or level curves. Using $u = c + x$, with the initial equilibrium utility of $u = 1.25$, the level curve in $\left(c : x\right)$ dimensions at the maximum is

$$c = 1.25 - x, \tag{2.22}$$

and at the more productive case, the utility level curve is

$$c = 2 - x. \tag{2.23}$$

The alternative production functions can be written as

$$c = \sqrt{1 - x}, \tag{2.24}$$
$$c = 2\sqrt{1 - x}. \tag{2.25}$$

Figure 2.7 graphs equations (2.22) and (2.24) as the light black line, and light blue production function, and equations (2.23) and (2.25) in bold black and blue.

The initial equilibrium is $x = 0.75$ and $c = 0.5$ before the productivity increase. With the productivity increase, the bold blue curve intersects the bold black utility level curve at a 'corner' equilibrium of $x = 0$ and $c = 2$. Income and substitution effects do not offset each other with respect to leisure, since there is no effect on leisure from the income effect. This leaves only the substitution effect towards more work and less leisure. This is the problem of linear utility functions.

The Example 2.4 productivity increase can be decomposed graphically. Figure 2.8 adds the dotted black curve into Figure 2.7; this curve intersects the light black utility level line at $x = 0$; this shows the substitution effect, from the initial equilibrium of $x = 0.75$ to $x = 0$. The jump up in the level curve to the upper dashed black line leaves the leisure at $x = 0$, as the income effect takes hold and has no effect on leisure.

Such a linear utility function is abnormal. With a zero income effect on leisure, leisure is a 'borderline normal' good. For a 'normal' good, leisure would rise with a positive income effect rather than staying constant. So this linear utility function leads to a corner solution when productivity rises and it is not a realistic function to use in modelling the macroeconomic economy. In contrast, with log utility, both leisure and consumption are 'normal' goods that rise with a positive income effect.

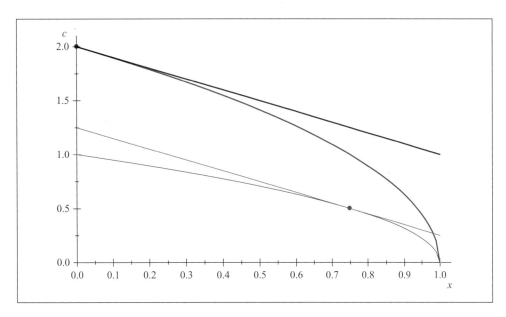

Figure 2.7 Linear utility with a doubling of goods productivity in Example 2.4

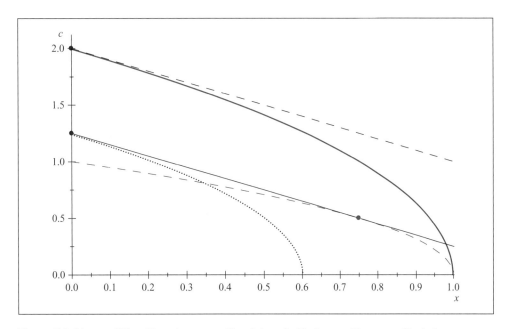

Figure 2.8 Linear utility with a decomposition into substitution and income effects in Example 2.4

2.4 Consumer and firm problems

The representative agent problem can be divided into consumer and firm problems. This is known as 'decentralising' the representative agent problem into separate consumer and firm problems, with the same equilibrium still resulting. The advantage of the decentralisation is that it makes the relative prices explicit, within a supply and demand framework for each market that is a part of the general equilibrium. In the case of this chapter, and throughout most of the text, these are the markets for goods and labour. The price of goods in terms of labour is the inverse of the real wage, and the price of labour versus goods is the real wage itself.

The decentralisation is important when explicit prices help with the analysis, and when supply and demand functions within each market offer additional intuition of the equilibrium. To make demand and supply functions explicit, where these functions depend on relative prices, the separate consumer and firm approach must be followed. Or when there are taxes, for example on wage income, then the approach again requires the separate consumer and firm problems.

The separate consumer problem is to maximise utility subject to the budget constraint. The separate firm problem is to maximise profit, which is exactly the same budget constraint of the consumer, subject to the production technology. The consumer problem here yields that the marginal rate of substitution between goods and leisure $MRS_{c,x}$ is equal to the real wage, denoted by w. The firm problem here yields that the marginal product of labour MP_l is equal to the real wage w. Instead of an equilibrium whereby $MRS_{c,x} = MP_l$, now the equilibrium gives that

$$MRS_{c,x} = w = MP_l. \tag{2.26}$$

The budget line of the consumer, and profit line function of the firm, are different names for the 'market line' that separates the utility and production functions. The budget/profit/market line goes through the tangency equilibrium point between utility and production. Put differently, the equilibrium occurs at the same tangency point as in the problem when the agent acts as both consumer and firm, and this is described by equivalence of the marginal rates of substitution and 'marginal technical rate of transformation' (the marginal product of labour). But now the market line also goes through the tangency point, with its slope being constant at the value of the real wage w. The market line is the budget constraint for the consumer, and it is exactly the same as the profit function for the firm. Solving the consumer and firm problems together gives each side of the famous marginal condition of equation (2.26).

2.4.1 Consumer: demand for goods, supply of labour

The consumer now works for the firm, supplying labour hours, and demands the consumption goods that the firm supplies. The consumer receives a real wage rate, denoted by w, for hours supplied for working at the firm, denoted by l^s. Here we will use s and d superscripts for supply and demand. In equilibrium, market clearing requires that $l^s = l^d$, and so in equilibrium the superscripts can be dropped.

The consumer's budget constraint is the new part of the separate consumer problem. It says that expenditure equals revenue. Expenditure is on consumption goods, c, and revenue is from working and earning wages, and from receiving profit from the firm, which the consumer implicitly owns.

Note that explicit ownership through equity share ownership is specified in Chapter 17 on financial markets. But for the representative agent, the consumer owns 100% of the equity shares anyway, making the implicit ownership equally valid as explicitly deriving share prices. The difference is that now the consumer receives the profit as a lump sum transfer, while as an owner of shares, the consumer receives the same profit as a dividend return on the shares.

And although the profit is comparable to the return on capital, as will be seen in later chapters, here capital is fixed and therefore profit is just like a given capital income that is the return on a fixed factor (capital). This means, as is important to realise in taking derivatives, that when the consumer solves the optimisation problem, the profit income is assumed to be fixed.

The total wages earned are wl^s. The consumer as owner of the firm receives the profit denoted by Π. The total income is $wl^s + \Pi$, and the total expenditure is simply c^d, the amount of goods demanded. This is because the price of the demanded goods is normalised to 1. The budget constraint is thereby

$$c^d = wl^s + \Pi.$$

The consumer problem is to maximise utility $u\left(c^d, x\right)$ subject to the budget constraint $c^d = wl^s + \Pi$, and subject to the allocation of time constraint. Again let $T = 24$. The time constraint is

$$x + l^s = 24.$$

Substituting the constraints directly into the utility function, the consumer problem is to maximise with respect to the supply of labour l^s

$$\operatorname*{Max}_{l^s} \; u\left(wl^s + \Pi, 24 - l^s\right). \tag{2.27}$$

The equilibrium condition using the 'chain rule of calculus' is

$$\frac{\partial u}{\partial c} \frac{\partial \left(wl^s + \Pi\right)}{\partial l^s} + \frac{\partial u}{\partial x} \frac{\partial \left(24 - l^s\right)}{\partial l^s} = 0.$$

This becomes

$$\frac{\partial u}{\partial c} w + \frac{\partial u}{\partial x} \left(-1\right) = 0,$$

or

$$w = \frac{\frac{\partial u(c, l^s)}{\partial x}}{\frac{\partial u(c, l^s)}{\partial c}} = MRS_{c,x}.$$

The real wage equals the marginal rate of substitution between leisure and goods. From this margin, the real wage w is sometimes called the 'shadow price' of leisure relative to goods, another name for the $MRS_{c,x}$.

2.4.2 Firm: supply of goods, demand for labour

The firm problem is actually the problem of the representative agent who now is acting as the goods producer. The firm chooses the amount of labour demanded, or l^d, to input into the production function so as to produce the supply of goods, or c^s, that maximises profit Π. Profit equals receipts of goods purchased by the consumer minus wage payments to the consumer:

$$\Pi = c^s - wl^d.$$

It is the same as the budget line of the consumer, except that now it involves the supply of goods and demand for labour, while for the consumer it is the demand for goods and the supply of labour.

It is assumed that the firm owns the fixed capital stock, $k = 1$, and so does not have to pay any capital rental costs as part of the cost of production. It simply returns the residual profit after production to the consumer. When the capital is made a variable input in Part 4, the consumer rents the capital to the firm, the firm incurs the capital rental cost as an explicit cost, and the firm's subsequent residual profits are zero, assuming a Cobb–Douglas production function. This is shown in this chapter's appendix, A2.10.4.

The firm maximises profit subject to the constraint that the output of goods is produced with the technology,

$$y = f\left(l\right).$$

And there is also the constraint that the supply of consumer goods equals the total output:

$$c^s = y.$$

By substituting directly into the profit line the production function for $c^s = y = f(l)$, the firm problem is to choose l^d so as to maximise profit:

$$\text{Max}_{l^d} \; \Pi = f\left(l^d\right) - wl^d. \tag{2.28}$$

The solution is that the marginal product of labour equals the real wage

$$MP_l = \frac{\partial f\left(l^d\right)}{\partial l^d} = w. \tag{2.29}$$

When the production function is explicitly specified, the equilibrium condition is used to solve for l^d, y, c^s, and the profit Π. See also Appendix 2.10.3.

2.5 Aggregate demand and supply

With specific utility and production functions the supply and demand functions can be derived as functions of the relative price of goods to leisure, which is $1/w$. Put differently, the relative price of leisure to goods is the wage rate w. And then the equilibrium w is found, so that all of the equilibrium quantities are then solved.

2.5.1 Example 2.5

As in Example 2.3, let $T = 24$, $\alpha = 1$, $\gamma = 0.5$, and $A_G = 1$. By equation (2.27), the consumer problem is

$$\text{Max}_{l^s} \; u = \ln\left(wl^s + \Pi\right) + \ln\left(24 - l^s\right). \tag{2.30}$$

The first-order equilibrium condition is

$$\frac{\partial L}{\partial l^s} = \frac{\partial u}{\partial c^d}(w) + \frac{\partial u}{\partial x}(-1)$$

$$= \frac{w}{wl^s + \Pi} - \frac{1}{24 - l^s} = 0.$$

Solving for l^s, we get the supply of labour as a function of the real wage and profits:

$$l^s = 12 - \frac{\Pi}{2w}. \tag{2.31}$$

As is clear, this is a standard form of a supply function: as the price of labour w rises, the supply of labour increases since $\frac{\partial l^s}{\partial w} = \frac{\Pi}{2w^2} > 0$ given that profit Π is positive. Solving this supply function in terms of w, the resulting function gives the rising marginal cost of labour supply as the quantity of labour is increased; and then that gives a standard upward sloping labour supply curve that is interpreted as the marginal cost of labour curve, as seen in the graph in Figure 2.9.

The solutions for c^d, and x, as a function of the real wage w, are readily obtained by substituting the labour supply into the budget constraint and into the time constraint:

$$c^d = wl^s + \Pi = w\left(12 - \frac{\Pi}{2w}\right) + \Pi = 12w + \frac{\Pi}{2},$$

$$x = 24 - l^s = 12 + \frac{\Pi}{2w}$$

$$l^s = 12 - \frac{\Pi}{2w}.$$

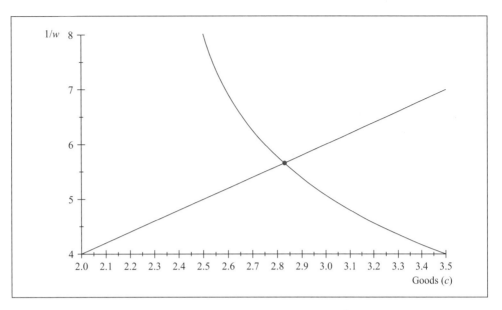

Figure 2.9 Aggregate goods demand and supply as a function of $\frac{1}{w}$ in Example 2.5

This gives the demand for goods and the supply of labour as functions of the real wage w, and profit Π. Before the graphs of these can be drawn, the profit needs to be solved in terms of the real wage w, from the solution to the firm problem. Note that this substitution for Π in terms of w can only be made now, after the consumer's equilibrium conditions have been derived.

The firm problem is to maximise profit Π, which equals receipts from supplying goods, denoted by c^s, minus the cost of the wage payments, subject to the production function. Let the production be given by

$$c^s = \sqrt{l^d}, \tag{2.32}$$

where the demand for labour is denoted by l^d. The wage payments are wl^d, and the maximisation problem then is

$$\underset{l^d, c^s}{\text{Max}} \ \Pi = c^s - wl^d + \lambda \left(\sqrt{l^d} - c^s \right). \tag{2.33}$$

In the simpler form, obtained by substituting in the production function for c^s, this is

$$\underset{l^d}{\text{Max}} \ \Pi = \sqrt{l^d} - wl^d. \tag{2.34}$$

The equilibrium condition is

$$0.5 \left(l^d \right)^{-0.5} - w = 0. \tag{2.35}$$

From this, the demand for labour can be derived directly by solving the equation for l^d.

$$l^d = \frac{1}{4w^2}. \tag{2.36}$$

As can be readily computed, the demand for labour is a downsloping function of the wage rate. As the wage goes up the demand for labour goes down; $\frac{\partial l^d}{\partial w} = -\frac{1}{2w^3} < 0$. Goods supply and profit can then be solved as functions of the wage rate:

$$c^s = \sqrt{l^d} = \frac{1}{2w},$$ (2.37)

$$\Pi = \sqrt{l^d} - wl^d = \frac{1}{2w} - \frac{w}{4w^2} = \frac{1}{4w}.$$ (2.38)

Note that the supply of goods c^s is a typically upward sloping function of the relative price of goods to leisure, or $\frac{1}{w}$; $\frac{\partial c^s}{\partial \left(\frac{1}{w}\right)} = \frac{1}{2} > 0$.

Given the firm's demand for labour, supply of goods, and profit, all as functions of w, the consumer demand for goods, and supply of labour, can now be completed by adding in that $\Pi = \frac{1}{4w}$:

$$c^d = 12w + \frac{\Pi}{2} = 12w + \frac{1}{8w}.$$ (2.39)

$$l^s = 12 - \frac{\Pi}{2w} = 12 - \frac{1}{8w^2}.$$ (2.40)

Now all four of the demand and supply functions have been derived: the consumer's supply of labour and demand for goods and the firm's demand for labour and supply of goods.

In this economy there is no capital investment. Therefore output equals consumption; $y = c$. Deriving the demand for consumption in equation (2.39) is the same as deriving the demand for output, or the aggregate output demand. Similarly, the supply of goods by the firm in equation (2.37) is the same as the supply of output, or aggregate output supply.

2.5.2 The goods markets: *AS* and *AD*

Demand and supply functions for both goods and labour can now be graphed as functions of the real wage. Since the consumption is equal to output in this economy, the supply and demand for consumption are also the supply and demand for aggregate output. Therefore this is a derivation of the 'static' aggregate demand *AD* and aggregate supply *AS* when capital is fixed.

To put the relative price of goods $\frac{1}{w}$ on the vertical axis and c on the horizontal, rewrite the supply and demand for goods by solving for $\frac{1}{w}$. For supply, from equation (2.37),

$$\frac{1}{w} = 2c^s,$$ (2.41)

which is a straight line from the origin with a slope of 2.

For demand there is a small problem in this simple economy in that to solve for $\frac{1}{w}$ from the *AD* equation (2.39) requires forming a quadratic equation in $\frac{1}{w}$. Multiplying through by 8, and dividing by w:

$$c^d = 12w + \frac{1}{8w},$$ (2.42)

$$\frac{8\left(c^d\right)}{w} = \frac{8\left(12w\right)}{w} + \frac{\frac{1}{w}}{w},$$

$$\left(\frac{1}{w}\right)^2 - 8c^d \frac{1}{w} + 96 = 0.$$ (2.43)

This quadratic of $A\left(\frac{1}{w}\right)^2 + B\frac{1}{w} + C = 0$, where $A = 1$, $B = -8c^d$, and $C = 96$, is solved by using the general solution formula for quadratics whereby $\frac{1}{w} = \frac{-B - \sqrt{B^2 - 4AC}}{2A}$. Using this, the solution for $\frac{1}{w}$ is given by

$$\frac{1}{w} = \frac{8c^d - \sqrt{64\left(c^d\right)^2 - 4\left(96\right)}}{2} = 4c^d - 4\sqrt{\left(c^d\right)^2 - 6}; \tag{2.44}$$

this gives a normal downward sloping demand curve in Figure 2.9.

Figure 2.9 (see page 45) graphs the *AS* and *AD* functions of equations (2.37) and (2.44), against the relative price of goods to labour, or $\frac{1}{w}$.

The downward sloping curve is the demand for goods, and the upwards sloping line from the origin is the supply of goods. The equilibrium inverse wage $\frac{1}{w} = 5.65$ is given at the intersection. The equilibrium consumption quantity can be found from the equilibrium wage, using the consumption demand equation (2.42), as

$$c^d = 12w + \frac{1}{8w} = \frac{12}{5.65} + \frac{1}{8}\left(5.65\right) = 2.83.$$

2.5.3 Aggregate labour market

The labour market supply and demand can also be graphed, now from equations (2.36) and (2.40), by inverting these functions so as to solve for w. This gives the downsloping labour demand and upward sloping labour supply equations:

$$w = \frac{1}{2}\sqrt{\frac{1}{l^d}}, \tag{2.45}$$

$$w = \sqrt{\frac{1}{8\left(12 - l^s\right)}}. \tag{2.46}$$

Figure 2.10 graphs equations (2.45) and (2.46).

The equilibrium wage is $w = 0.177$ and the employment is $l = 8$.

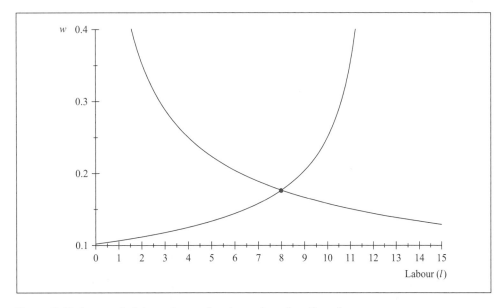

Figure 2.10 Aggregate labour demand and supply as function of *w*

2.5.4 Market equilibrium: the real wage rate

The equilibrium wage rate can be solved exactly by letting the supply of goods equal the demand for goods, and solving for $\frac{1}{w}$, or by letting the supply of labour equal the demand for labour and solving for w. Solving for w in either the goods or the labour market will give the same answer. This also provides a way to check that the markets are indeed both clearing at the equilibrium wage rate: solve for w in both markets and check that the answer is the same.

Setting goods supply equal to demand in equations (2.37) and (2.39) gives that

$$c^S = \frac{1}{2w} = 12w + \frac{1}{8w} = c^d,$$

which implies that

$$w = \sqrt{\frac{3}{96}} = 0.177.$$

Similarly, setting labour supply equal to demand in equations (2.40) and (2.36) gives that

$$12 - \frac{1}{8w^2} = \frac{1}{4w^2},$$

which implies the same answer that $w = \sqrt{\frac{3}{96}} = 0.177$, or $\frac{1}{w} = \frac{1}{0.177} = 5.65$. With this equilibrium wage rate, the labour supply and demand functions show that $l^s = l^d = 8$; eight hours are worked. And consumption and leisure are also the same as in Example 2.3 with $x = 16$, $c = 2.83$ and utility $u = \ln(2.83) + \ln(16) = 3.81$.

2.5.5 General equilibrium representation

A general equilibrium representation of decentralised goods and labour markets in Example 2.5 can be made in a way similar to Figure 2.2, except that now there is also the dashed blue budget line/profit line drawn in-between the black utility level curve and blue production function. The budget line is graphed as

$$c^d = wl^s + \Pi = w(24 - x) + \Pi$$
$$c^d = (0.177)(24 - x) + \frac{1}{4(0.177)} \tag{2.47}$$

with $w = 0.177$, and $\Pi = \frac{1}{4(0.177)}$; the utility level curve is graphed as

$$c = \frac{e^u}{x} = \frac{e^{3.81}}{x}, \tag{2.48}$$

with $u = 3.81$; and the production function is graphed as

$$c = \sqrt{l} = \sqrt{24 - x}. \tag{2.49}$$

Figure 2.11 graphs equations (2.47), (2.48) and (2.49).

The tangency to the dashed blue line with the black curve is the equilibrium for consumer problem, and the tangency between the dashed blue line and the blue curve is the equilibrium for the firm problem. The dashed blue line is both the budget constraint of the consumer and the profit function of the firm. Eliminating the dashed blue line does not

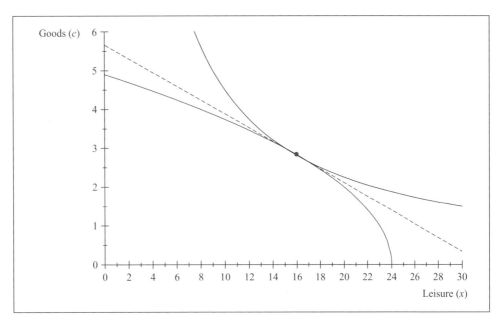

Figure 2.11 General equilibrium goods and labour market with budget/profit line in Example 2.5

change the equilibrium solution but only eliminates the explicit derivation of the price w and profit Π.

2.6 Labour productivity increase

Suppose the productivity of labour in Example 2.5 doubles, so that the production function for the firm problem is now $c = 2\sqrt{l}$ instead of $c = \sqrt{l}$. The consumer problem is not affected in its functional form of equation (2.39). However the profit will rise and the new profit must be substituted in, and this shifts the demand for goods. The firm problem is affected more directly, as the higher productivity directly shifts the firm's demand for labour and supply of output.

2.6.1 Example 2.6

Parameters are as in Examples 2.3 and 2.5, with $T = 24$, $\alpha = 1$, $\gamma = 0.5$, except that now $A_G = 2$ instead of $A_G = 1$. The consumer problem is unchanged. The firm problem is now

$$\underset{l^d}{\text{Max}} \ \Pi = 2\sqrt{l^d} - wl^d. \tag{2.50}$$

The equilibrium condition is

$$\left(l^d\right)^{-0.5} - w = 0; \tag{2.51}$$

the demand for labour is

$$l^d = \frac{1}{w^2}; \tag{2.52}$$

and the goods supply and profit is now

$$c^S = \frac{2}{w};$$ (2.53)

$$\Pi = \frac{2}{w} - \frac{w}{w^2} = \frac{1}{w}.$$ (2.54)

The new profit then is substituted into the consumer's demand for goods, and supply of labour from equations (2.39) and (2.40):

$$c^d = 12w + \frac{\Pi}{2} = 12w + \frac{1}{2w};$$ (2.55)

$$l^S = 12 - \frac{\Pi}{2w} = 12 - \frac{1}{2w^2}.$$ (2.56)

The new equilibrium wage can be found by setting supply equal to demand in either the labour or goods market. Using the labour market, in equations (2.52) and (2.56), this implies the one equation in the one unknown of w:

$$l^S = 12 - \frac{1}{2w^2} = \frac{1}{w^2} = l^d.$$ (2.57)

The real wage is found from $12 = \frac{3}{2w^2}$, or $w = \sqrt{\frac{1}{8}} = \frac{1}{4}\sqrt{2} = 0.354$, an increase from 0.177 when $c = \sqrt{l}$. The results imply that the wage rate doubles as labour productivity doubles.

Goods market

From equations (2.55) and (2.53), the supply and demand for goods can be written inversely so as to solve for $\frac{1}{w}$:

$$c^d = \frac{12}{\frac{1}{w}} + \frac{1}{2}\frac{1}{w},$$

$$0 = \frac{1}{2}\left(\frac{1}{w}\right)^2 - c^d\left(\frac{1}{w}\right) + 12.$$

This is a quadratic of $A\left(\frac{1}{w}\right)^2 + B\frac{1}{w} + C = 0$, where $A = \frac{1}{2}$, $B = -c^d$, and $C = 12$. Using the general solution formula for quadratics or $\frac{1}{w} = \frac{-B - \sqrt{B^2 - 4AC}}{2A}$,

$$\frac{1}{w} = \frac{c^d - \sqrt{\left(c^d\right)^2 - 4\left(\frac{1}{2}\right)(12)}}{2\left(\frac{1}{2}\right)}.$$ (2.58)

And for supply,

$$c^S = \frac{2}{w},$$

$$\frac{1}{w} = \frac{c^S}{2}.$$ (2.59)

Figure 2.12 graphs equations (2.58) and (2.59) in black along with the aggregate goods demand and aggregate goods supply from the Example 2.5 equilibrium, in blue.

It shows that the productivity increase shifts out both the aggregate goods demand and aggregate goods supply. Equilibrium goods output and the wage rate rise. Here the new equilibrium output is $c = \frac{2}{0.354} = 5.65$.

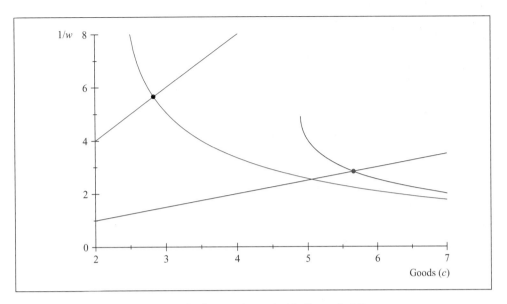

Figure 2.12 Productivity increase in the goods market in Example 2.6

Labour market

The labour market supply and demand can be solved for w from equations (2.52) and (2.56) so that the standard supply and demand can be graphed with the price w on the vertical axis:

$$l^s = 12 - \frac{1}{2w^2},$$

$$w = \sqrt{\frac{1}{2\left(12 - l^s\right)}}; \tag{2.60}$$

$$l^d = \frac{1}{w^2},$$

$$w = \frac{1}{\sqrt{l^d}}. \tag{2.61}$$

Figure 2.13 graphs equations (2.60) and (2.61) from Example 2.6 in black, along with the equilibrium of equations (2.45) and (2.46) in Example 2.5 in blue.

Labour demand shifts out because of higher productivity while labour supply shifts back because of the higher income from higher firm profit. Employment remains unchanged while the wage rate rises.

2.6.2 General equilibrium

Figure 2.14 shows in the general equilibrium how the dashed black budget line of Example 2.6 has a steeper (negative) slope in equilibrium than the dashed blue line of Example 2.5, due to the higher wage rate. This budget line is graphed as

$$c^d = wl^s + \Pi = w\left(1 - x\right)l^s + \Pi$$

$$c^d = \left(0.3535\right)\left(24 - x\right) + \frac{1}{0.3535},$$

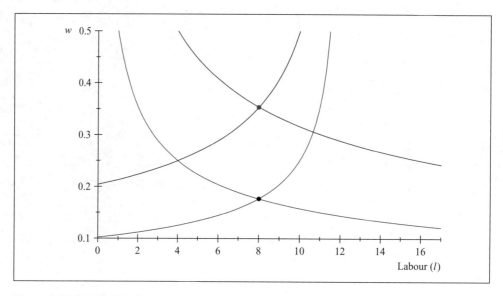

Figure 2.13 Productivity increase in the labour market of Example 2.6

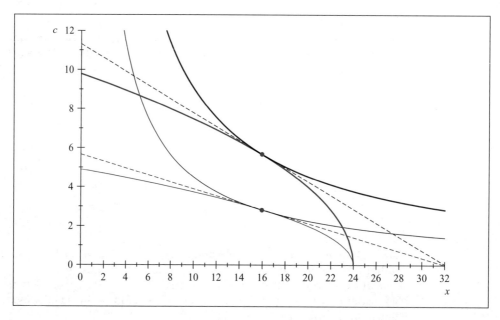

Figure 2.14 General equilibrium goods and labour market in Example 2.6 (black) and Example 2.5 (blue)

while the new bold black utility level curve with $u = \ln 16 + \ln 5.65 = 4.505$ is

$$c^d = \frac{e^u}{x} = \frac{e^{4.505}}{x} = \frac{90.5}{x},$$

and the bold blue production function is

$$c^S = 2\sqrt{24 - x}.$$

2.7 Application: productivity and growth

2.7.1 Growth policy

The basis of growth theory is already captured in our simple representative agent economy. It is the productivity increase. With a productivity increase, the output per hours worked increases. The labour hours remain the same. And this is exactly how economic theory has come to explain economic growth. The productivity of factor inputs rises gradually and steadily over time. There are fluctuations in how productivity changes, which give rise to business cycles. But the steady rise in productivity, despite any fluctuations, creates an upward trend that establishes what we view as economic growth: a rising per capita income with a stable amount of work per period by each agent.

Decades ago a policy of achieving high economic growth was not a common proclamation of governments. Rather it was to decrease unemployment, to decrease inflation and to attain the highest output possible. Since the apparent taming of inflation in the 1980s and 1990s, and the modernisation and growing acceptance in economics of growth theory, the policy emphasis has shifted. From a focus on levels of output, the focus has gone to the growth rate of output. In other words, policy regarding output has evolved from a level to the change in the level. Employment theory is discussed in Chapters 3 and 9, and growth theory is set out in Chapters 11 and 12.

2.7.2 US legislation

A policy focus on economic growth, instead of on 'stabilisation policy', dramatically changes the political and even economic landscape as to what becomes important to study and develop. For example, since just after WWII the US under President Truman enacted the Employment Act of 1946, and this is still in force today in amended form. This piece of legislation shows that the focus was squarely on the level of employment and output. Section 2 of the Act states that the objective is to 'promote the maximum employment, production and purchasing power'. It required Congress to provide the investment needed to create full employment; in the words of Section 2(c) of the Act, the federal government must 'provide such volume of Federal investment and expenditure as may be needed ...to assure continuing full employment'. It was to do this by creating deficits sufficient to provide such investment during times of unemployment, and likewise creating surpluses when output was above the level required for maximum employment. Full employment language was specifically excluded from the Act, with 'maximum' employment inserted instead after Congressional debate.

The wording of full employment entered the Act upon its amendment in 1978 under President Carter. And notably this is when a consideration of economic growth entered the legislation. The amended Act is entitled the Full Employment and Balanced Growth Act. It enhanced the employment goal to one of full employment, and added the goals of balanced economic growth, growth in productivity, and a balanced government budget (Title I,1). It also 'encourages the adoption of a fiscal policy that would reduce federal spending as a percent of GNP', a topic discussed in Chapter 19. And, amazingly, it also set inflation targets of 3% by 1983 and 0% by 1988, a topic we will discuss in Chapter 20.

2.7.3 Modern economic views on stabilisation vs growth

Robert E. Lucas, Jr. popularised amongst economists that it is possible that the cost of business cycles to the representative agent is much less than the gain from a small amount of increased economic growth. Lucas, in his 1987 book *Models of Business Cycles*, constructs an analysis of the representative agent who has uncertainty over the future consumption stream due to random fluctuations in consumption as occur during the business cycle. He shows that the amount of consumption that the consumer needs to be compensated with in order to not be worried about the consumption variation is much less than the amount of consumption increase that results from a small amount of economic growth. The implication was to focus on growth not 'stabilisation'.

Lucas's analysis was a startling use of economic theory to address the central policy issue of the time: whether to try to stabilise aggregate output or instead go for increasing the growth rate of output. Many have since written on this subject using Lucas's approach to show that the cost of business cycles can be higher than what Lucas derived, while others have argued that Lucas's analysis is quite reasonable. This leaves the concept in place that focusing on fostering productivity increases and so facilitating economic growth may be the most important policy a government might pursue.

2.8 Questions

1. If goods and leisure are 'normal' then
   (a) an increase in relative prices causes a decrease in the consumption of each;
   (b) the substitution effect dominates the income effect;
   (c) a positive income effect causes consumption of goods and leisure to increase;
   (d) all of the above.

2. In the equilibrium, an amount of goods c produced using labour in a production function $f(l) = l^{0.5}$, also involves
   (a) a negative marginal product of labour;
   (b) a diminishing marginal product of labour;
   (c) a positive marginal utility of work;
   (d) all of the above.

3. Maximisation subject to constraints (optimisation) by a representative agent, as producer of goods, demander of labour, supplier of labour, and consumer of goods and leisure, implies
   (a) that the marginal rate of substitution between leisure and goods equals the real wage;
   (b) the marginal product of labour equals the real wage;
   (c) that the marginal product of labour equals the marginal rate of substitution between leisure and goods;
   (d) all of the above.

4. The labour–leisure trade-off in general equilibrium
   (a) is determined in part by the marginal rate of substitution between goods and leisure;
   (b) is determined in part by the marginal product of labour;
   (c) is determined in part by the real wage;
   (d) all of the above.

5. For the representative consumer of only goods and leisure, a rise in the real wage, with the log utility level held constant, causes
   (a) the relative price of leisure to goods to stay the same;
   (b) an increase in leisure;
   (c) an increase in consumption;
   (d) all of the above.

6. For a representative agent who consumes only goods and leisure, and produces goods only with labour time, an increase in the marginal product of labour causes
   (a) a substitution effect towards less leisure;
   (b) an income effect towards more leisure;

(c) a 'pivoting up' of the production function;

(d) all of the above.

7. With only goods and leisure entering the representative consumer's utility function in general equilibrium, an increase in the marginal product of labour

    (a) creates a substitution effect towards more leisure;

    (b) creates an income effect towards more goods;

    (c) creates a substitution effect and an income effect towards more leisure;

    (d) all of the above.

8. Applications of the representative agent economy, with consumption of only goods and leisure, and production of goods with only labour time, are that

    (a) young people work more as their real wage rises, because the income effect dominates the substitution effect of the wage rise;

    (b) hours worked per week have fallen gradually over time as the real wage has risen, because the income effect has dominated the substitution effect of the wage rise;

    (c) labour force participation has risen because the real wage for women has fallen gradually since WW II;

    (d) all of the above.

9. Suppose that the utility is $u = \ln c + \ln \left(24 - l\right)$.

    (a) Graph the 'level curves': $\bar{u} = 3.81$; $\hat{u} = 4.0$; $\tilde{u} = 5.0$; with c being the vertical axis variable and l the horizontal axis variable. For each curve, assume that $l = 8$ and find the different values of c consistent with the utility level.

    (b) Graph the curve $c = \sqrt{l}$ separately and then together with the level curves in part a.

    (c) Graph $c = \sqrt{l}, c = 2\sqrt{l}, c = 3\sqrt{l}, c = 4\sqrt{l}$. Find the exact equilibrium c, l, and u, both when $c = 3\sqrt{l}$ and when $c = 4\sqrt{l}$, and then find the corresponding equilibrium utility level curves. Graph the four equilibria production and utility level curves. In what sense does economic growth correspond to your graph?

10. Suppose the representative consumer's utility depends on goods, c, and leisure, $24 - l$, where l is the quantity of hours worked: $u = \ln c + \ln \left(24 - l\right)$. And suppose the consumer's production function is $c = 6\sqrt{l}$.

    (a) Find the equilibrium c, l, and u.

    (b) Suppose the marginal product of labour rises for all l. Indicate the direction of the substitution and income effects both for l and for c.

    (c) What changes in the production function over time would be required to generate economic growth?

11. Over time, economic growth gradually raises the real wage in industrial societies.

    (a) Decompose a real wage rise, in goods–leisure space $(c : l)$, into substitution and income effects.

    (b) Explain the downward trend in weekly hours worked using the substitution and income effects of part a.

    (c) Explain the historic (or 'secular') rise in women's labour force participation rate in terms of substitution and income effects.

12. Assume

$$u\left(c, n\right) = \ln\left(c\right) + \ln\left(24 - l\right)$$
$$y = \sqrt{l}$$
$$c = y.$$

The equilibrium work l, consumption c, and output is $l = 8$, $c = 2\sqrt{2}$, $y = 2\sqrt{2}$.

    (a) Verify this equilibrium.

    (b) Suppose the production function shifts from $y = \sqrt{l}$ to $y = 2\sqrt{l}$. Find the new equilibrium n, c and y.

(c) Graphically decompose the change, from the equilibrium in part a to the equilibrium in part b, into income and substitution effects, for both c and l.

(d) Indicate which, if any, effect dominates the movement in each c and l.

(e) In parts a and b, determine whether the productivity of labour, defined as $\frac{y}{l}$, exceeds, equals or falls below the marginal product of labour.

13. Find the representative agent economy of

$$u(c, l) = \ln(c) + \ln\left(24 - l\right),$$
$$y = 7\sqrt{l},$$
$$y = c,$$

(a) find the equilibrium consumption of goods c, the labour supply l, the output y, the utility level u, and graph the equilibrium in $(c : l)$ space;

(b) with w the real wage, find the supply and demand for goods as a function of $\frac{1}{w}$, the supply and demand for labour as a function of w, and graph both the goods and the labour market;

(c) indicate graphically how the supply and demand for goods and labour are affected by an increase in labour productivity.

14. Modify Example 2.5 by instead assuming that $\gamma = \frac{2}{3}$. Derive the aggregate output supply as a function of $\frac{1}{w}$, and graph this in $\left(\frac{1}{w} : c\right)$ space. Is the new AS curve convex, concave or linear? Put differently, does the AS function rise at an increasing rate as $\frac{1}{w}$ increases, at a constant rate, or at a decreasing rate?

15. Show that in Figure 2.4 the vertical axis distance between the origin and the vertical axis intersection of the implicit budget line of the decentralised economy is exactly equal to profit Π.

16. What is the chain rule of calculus and how does this give us the standard set of first-order equilibrium conditions that the partial derivatives are equal to zero?

17. *Numerical substitution point.* In Example 2.4, when there is an increase in the productivity of labour with linear utility, the decomposition into income and substitution effects is shown graphically; this may be computed numerically as well. To do this analysis, we will set up three equations, which describe the 'substitution point', in three unknowns, c^s, l^s and z. Here c^s and l^s are the goods and labour at the substitution point where the original utility level curve is tangent to the slope of the production function that is given by the new equilibrium (with a doubled productivity). The third parameter, z, is the parallel shift in income, as measured from the c-axis, of moving from the substitution point up to the new equilibrium (with a doubled productivity). Thus the change in equilibrium is decomposed into moving from the original equilibrium point to (c^s, l^s), with the same utility level and a pure substitution effect, and then from (c^s, l^s) to the new equilibrium in a parallel shift upwards that is a pure income effect. Given that the original equilibrium solution is $(c, l) = \left(0.5, 0.25\right)$, the three equations are

(a) $u\left(0.5, 0.25\right) \equiv u(c^s, l^s)$, so that utility at (c^s, l^s) is the same as at the initial equilibrium before the productivity increase;

(b) $c^s = 2\sqrt{l^s} - z$, so that consumption of goods in the new equilibrium (after the productivity increase) is shifted down by z to the point (c^s, l^s); and

(c)
$$\frac{-\frac{\partial u}{\partial l^s}}{\frac{\partial u}{\partial c^s}} = \frac{\partial(f(l^s))}{\partial l^s} = \frac{\partial\left(2\sqrt{l^s}\right)}{\partial l^s},$$

so that the slope of the indifference curve at the substitution point equals the slope of the dotted black production function in Figure 2.8.

i. Using the functional forms for the linear utility function and the production function, verify that these translate into the following three equations:

$$u = c^s + 24 - l^s = 0.5 + 24 - 0.25;$$
$$c^s = 2\sqrt{l^s} - z;$$
$$1 = (l^s)^{-0.5}.$$

ii. Verify that the last of these equations implies that $l^s = 1$; substituting this into the first of these gives that $c^s = 1.25$. And substituting these into the second of these three equations gives that $z = 0.75$. So the substitution point is

$$(c^s, l^s) = \left(1.25, 1\right),$$

and the income shift up to the equilibrium equals 0.75 as measured by the vertical axis.

iii. Re-graph Figure 2.8 now including the point (c^s, l^s) in Figure 2.8.

2.9 References

Becker, Gary S., 1975, *Human Capital: A Theoretical and Empirical Analysis, with Special Reference to Education*, 2nd edition, The University of Chicago Press, Chicago.

Becker, Gary S., 1976, *The Economic Approach to Human Behavior*, The University of Chicago Press, Chicago.

Becker, Gary S., 1981, *A Treatise on the Family*, NBER Books, National Bureau of Economic Research, Inc., number beck81-1, March.

Becker, Gary S., Tomas J. Philipson and Rodrigo R. Soares, 2005, 'The Quantity and Quality of Life and the Evolution of World Inequality', *American Economic Review*, American Economic Association, vol. 95(1) (March): 277–291.

Clark, John Bates, 1899, *The Distribution of Wealth: A Theory of Wages, Interest and Profits*, The Macmillan Company, New York.

Clark, John Bates, 1901, 'Wages and Interest as Determined by Marginal Productivity', *Journal of Political Economy*, 10(1)(December): 105.

Hicks, J. R., 1932, *The Theory of Wages*, Macmillan, New York; 2nd edition 1937.

Lucas, Robert E. Jr., 1987, *Models of Business Cycles*, Basil Blackwell, Oxford, England.

Mankiw, N. Gregory, David Romer and David N. Weil, 1992, 'A Contribution to the Empirics of Economic Growth', *The Quarterly Journal of Economics*, MIT Press, vol. 107(2)(May): 407–437.

Marshall, Alfred, 1920, *Principles of Economics*, 8th edition, Macmillan and Co., London.

Moore, Henry Ludwell, 1911, *Laws of Wages*, The Macmillan Company, New York.

2.10 Appendix A2: Optimisation

The maximisation problem can be set up using the 'Lagrangian optimisation' technique. This allows us to maximise the objective function, utility u, while the agent is constrained in choice. The constraints define the agent's 'opportunity sets', and because of these there is a scarcity consideration that drives economic decisions. Constraints are added onto the maximisation problem using Lagrangian multipliers for each constraint.

Note that in adding the constraints we still add 'zero' to the utility in that each constraint is an equation that adds up to zero. For example, the time constraint is $1 = l + x$. We add this to utility by adding it in the form of $1 - l - x = 0$; we are still only adding zero. However the way we add these zero-value constraints is by factoring them by the Lagrangian multiplier. In this way the derivative of the objective, utility, with respect to the constrained quantity (like total time allocation) tells us the change in utility from a change in the value of the total time. Thus these multipliers in equilibrium can be solved to reveal one type of 'shadow value' of the constrained variables.

Should the multipliers have a zero value themselves, then this implies that the constraints are non-binding in equilibrium, and so do not apply. In that case, for example, time would be effectively unconstrained with a consequent shadow price of zero; and time would not affect the equilibrium. Generally, we will be assuming throughout the text for simplicity that these constraints are binding. Otherwise a slightly more formal analysis, with inequality constraints such as $l + x \leq 1$ is necessary. But we can confirm that the constraints are binding in examples by solving for the equilibrium value of the multipliers and finding them to be non-zero.

2.10.1 General representative agent problem

Denoting the Lagrangian multipliers by λ_1 and λ_2, for each the time and goods constraint, the maximisation problem can be stated as being the maximisation of constrained utility, and with respect to the decision variables, which in this economy are goods, leisure and work, or c, x and l, and the multipliers themselves, λ_1 and λ_2. Taking the partial derivatives with respect to λ_1 and λ_2 just gives back the constraints themselves, so that the constraints become part of the set of equilibrium conditions. The constrained maximisation problem is also called the optimisation problem and in this case it is given by

$$\underset{c,x,l,\lambda_1,\lambda_2}{\text{Max}} \quad L = u(c,x) + \lambda_1 \left(1 - l - x\right) + \lambda_2 \left[f(l) - c\right]. \tag{2.62}$$

This gives the five first-order equilibrium conditions, of the derivative of the maximisation problem, with respect to goods, leisure, labour and the two Lagrangian multipliers (which themselves give the shadow values of time and goods):

$$\frac{\partial L}{\partial c} = \frac{\partial u}{\partial c} - \lambda_2 = 0; \tag{2.63}$$

$$\frac{\partial L}{\partial x} = \frac{\partial u}{\partial x} + \lambda_1 = 0; \tag{2.64}$$

$$\frac{\partial L}{\partial l} = -\lambda_1 + \lambda_2 \left(\frac{\partial f}{\partial l}\right) = 0; \tag{2.65}$$

$$\frac{\partial L}{\partial \lambda_1} = 1 - l - x = 0; \tag{2.66}$$

$$\frac{\partial L}{\partial \lambda_2} = c - f(l) = 0. \tag{2.67}$$

To see that these partial derivatives are the equilibrium conditions, consider the more formal approach. Totally differentiate L and set the derivative equal to zero, so as to get a maximum. The result is that $dL(c, x, l, \lambda_1, \lambda_2) = \frac{\partial L}{\partial c}dc + \frac{\partial L}{\partial x}dx + \frac{\partial L}{\partial l}dl + \frac{\partial L}{\partial \lambda_1}d\lambda_1 + \frac{\partial L}{\partial \lambda_2}d\lambda_2 = 0$. Because dc_0, dx, dl, $d\lambda_1$ and $d\lambda_2$ each generally are not zero, it happens that the $dL = 0$ condition is met only by setting each of the partial derivatives equal to zero, $\frac{\partial L}{\partial c} = \frac{\partial L}{\partial x} = \frac{\partial L}{\partial l} = \frac{\partial L}{\partial \lambda_1} = \frac{\partial L}{\partial \lambda_2} = 0$. This is an application of the so-called 'chain rule' of calculus. And it gives the equilibrium conditions of equations (2.63) to (2.67).

The first two equilibrium conditions in equations (2.63) and (2.64) tell us that the multipliers are equal to the marginal utility of goods and leisure, respectively. These marginal utilities are the 'shadow prices' of goods and leisure; these are their values without using explicit prices. Combining the first three equations (2.63) to (2.65) implies the basic characterising equilibrium condition of the economy: that the marginal product of labour (MP_l) equals the marginal rate of substitution between goods and leisure ($MRS_{c,x}$), or

$$MP_l \equiv \frac{\partial f(l)}{\partial l} = \frac{\frac{\partial u(c,x)}{\partial x}}{\frac{\partial u(c,x)}{\partial c}} \equiv MRS_{c,x}. \tag{2.68}$$

2.10.2 Simpler one-step method of maximisation

A much simpler method of maximisation is to substitute the two constraints directly into the utility function. This is done by solving for x from equation (2.6) as $x = 1 - l$, and by using $c = y$ from the goods constraint and that $y = f(l)$ from the production technology, giving that $c = f(l)$. Substituting these for x and c into the utility function turns the maximisation problem into one involving only the one unknown of labour time l (it is arbitrary as to which one variable is used as the one unknown, in this case l):

$$\underset{l}{\text{Max}} \; L = u[f(l), 1 - l].$$

Taking the derivative with respect to l, by using the 'chain rule' of calculus, gives that

$$\frac{\partial u}{\partial c} \frac{\partial f(l)}{\partial l} + \frac{\partial u}{\partial x} \frac{\partial (1 - l)}{\partial l} = 0.$$

This yields the same equilibrium condition that

$$\frac{\partial f(l)}{\partial l} = \frac{\frac{\partial u(c,x)}{\partial x}}{\frac{\partial u(c,x)}{\partial c}}.$$

2.10.3 Separate decentralised problems

In Lagrangian form, the decentralised consumer problem is

$$\underset{c^d, x, l^s, \lambda_1, \lambda_2}{\text{Max}} \; L = u\left(c^d, x\right) + \lambda_1 \left(24 - l^s - x\right) + \lambda_2 \left(w l^s + \Pi - c^d\right), \tag{2.69}$$

with similar derivatives.

Similarly, the firm Lagrangian problem is to choose c^s and l^d so as to maximise profit constrained by the production function:

$$\underset{l^d, c^s, \lambda}{\text{Max}} \; \Pi = c^s - w l^d + \lambda \left[f\left(l^d\right) - c^s\right]. \tag{2.70}$$

2.10.4 Cobb–Douglas profit

One property of the general Cobb–Douglas production function,

$$y = A_G l^\gamma k^{1-\gamma}, \tag{2.71}$$

is that the share of labour costs in output equals the labour-related Cobb–Douglas parameter γ when markets are assumed to be competitive. This means that

$$\frac{wl}{y} = \gamma. \tag{2.72}$$

This can be proved simply by deriving the marginal product of labour from equation (2.71) and substituting it in for the real wage w in the above equation (2.72):

$$\frac{wl}{y} = \frac{\partial y}{\partial l} \frac{l}{y} = \frac{\left(\gamma A_G l^{\gamma-1} k^{1-\gamma}\right) l}{y} = \frac{\gamma y}{y} = \gamma. \tag{2.73}$$

And also the share of capital cost in output is the capital-related Cobb–Douglas parameter $1 - \gamma$. Denote by $\hat{r}$ the rental cost of capital; this property is

$$\frac{\hat{r}k}{y} = 1 - \gamma;$$

this is proved by substituting in the marginal product of capital for $\hat{r} = (1 - \gamma) A_G l^\gamma k^{-\gamma}$:

$$\frac{\hat{r}k}{y} = \frac{\partial y}{\partial k} \frac{k}{y} = \frac{\left[(1 - \gamma) A_G l^\gamma k^{-\gamma}\right] k}{y} = \frac{(1 - \gamma) y}{y} = 1 - \gamma.$$

Note that in Part 3, Chapters 5–7, the interest rate $\hat{r}$ is actually defined in terms of $1 + r$, in order to abstract from the depreciation rate that makes the two-period model difficult to solve. From Part 4 onwards, in the infinite horizon model, $\hat{r}$ is defined normally as r_t, the rate at time t.

With the firm profit in this chapter given by

$$\Pi = y - wl,$$

this expression is equivalent to

$$rk = y - wl,$$

where $\Pi = rk$, when capital is variable. And again this can be proved by substituting in for w and r the respective marginal products of labour and capital.

Or, profit can be divided by output y so that

$$\frac{\Pi}{y} = \frac{y}{y} - \frac{wl}{y} = 1 - \gamma.$$

Therefore profit is simply

$$\Pi = (1 - \gamma)\, y = (1 - \gamma)\, f\,(l).$$

This shortcut can be used, or not. To use it, the equilibrium labour supply l^s is substituted into $f\,(l)$. The solution for profit will be the same as the other, perhaps more direct, way to solve for profit by substituting in the equilibrium labour supply l^s into $\Pi = f\,(l) - wl$. The two ways are equivalent.

CHAPTER 3

Employment cycles and taxes

3.1 Introduction

The chapter adds a second comparative static change in given parameters onto the standard change in goods productivity. The time endowment for goods and leisure is also allowed to change. An expansion of the business cycle with employment rising and goods consumption increasing is explained in terms of an increase in both the goods and time endowment. A contraction with employment and goods falling is explained with these endowments falling. These are all equilibrium movements of labour and goods.

A second type of analysis is added onto the contractionary decrease in the goods and time endowments. The real wage is assumed to be fixed, although this is ad hoc. Then the employment level is found to drop by significantly more, as in a deep recession or depression.

Taxes on goods and labour are also introduced, with consequent effects on employment and output. The taxes have similar effects that are compared. The tax revenue is transferred back to the consumer as income, in a way similar to certain unemployment compensation policies. A tax on goods, with the income transfer back to the consumer, causes labour supply to shift back, and goods demand to shift back. The equilibrium wage rises, but it is shown that the wage rate 'net of taxes' falls.

The theory of economic regulation as implicit taxes and transfers is introduced along with applications of the chapter's analysis to unemployment policy, moral hazard and insurance. Taxes are discussed as a means of employment policy. And the theory of economic regulation is applied to a discussion of certain industries.

3.1.1 Building on the last chapters

The last chapter derived the equilibrium conditions of the general equilibrium closed economy with a labour-only Cobb–Douglas production function. It then derived the markets for goods and labour as functions of the real wage, also within the closed economy, and it showed the effect of increasing the productivity of labour. This chapter extends those results by adding onto the change in labour productivity a change in time endowment, so as to explain business cycles with employment rising and falling. This analysis uses the supply and demand developed in the last chapter.

The supply and demand schedules of the last chapter are also affected by the imposition of taxes in this chapter, with the equilibrium wage higher as a result. The incentive of the consumer to work and take leisure from the last chapter is now distorted on the margin by the taxes imposed in this chapter. The distortion is seen by the effect of the tax rate on the marginal rate of substitution between goods and leisure that is developed in the last chapter.

3.1.2 Learning objective

The aim is to provide an understanding of how an equilibrium business cycle might occur in terms of employment and output, using simple comparative static analysis of a baseline model. Then the challenge is to see how a non-equilibrium theory of unemployment is specified, with the result that there is surplus labour, or more specifically an excess supply of labour at the fixed wage rate. The effect of taxes on employment levels is the third main analysis for the student to learn. This allows for an understanding of how tax and transfer policies relate to unemployment policy.

3.1.3 Who made it happen?

Paul A. Samuelson (1951) provided analysis whereby during a recession unemployment could be formalised in terms of an equilibrium at less than full employment. Samuelson used equilibrium conditions suggested by Keynes (1936) and Hicks's (1937) interpretation of Keynes. These theories proposed the existence of surplus labour that resulted from rigid wages during the 1930s international depression.

Samuelson, who did his undergraduate education at the University of Chicago during the 1930s Depression and was a long-time professor at Massachusetts Institute of Technology, considered that during crisis economic periods the Keynesian idea of unemployment, in markets which were not clearing, was relevant and that government should do something actively to end such crises. Such analysis is now formalised in models that add rigid wages and prices to otherwise standard dynamic general equilibrium models. And this type of unemployment, along with lower employment using comparative statics, is shown in this chapter.

Samuelson (1947) included an analysis of how taxes affect the equilibrium, showing how they can cause a distortion of incentives that end up decreasing output and long term employment. Arnold Harberger (1974) showed further welfare consequences of taxation in terms for example of comparing labour and goods taxes. The similarity of the effect of goods versus labour taxes in raising wage rates and decreasing long term output and employment, an issue studied since Ricardo, is also studied in this chapter.

David Ricardo in his 1817 *Principles of Political Economy and Taxation* discusses nearly all of the major taxes and how for example goods and labour wage taxes generally cause a rise in the cost of goods and labour. He writes:

> Taxes on wages will raise wages, and therefore will diminish the rate of profits on stock. We have already seen that a tax on necessities will raise their prices, and will be followed by a rise of wages.

It is therefore an old idea that similar effects can result from financing government spending by levying income taxes that fall on wages earned, or by putting taxes on goods purchases such as a value added tax. And both of such taxes can cause distortions that end up lowering output and the supply of labour. The output distortions of taxation became well recognised. Henry George in his 1926 *Progress and Poverty* wrote (p. 408):

> The checking of production is in greater or less degree characteristic of most of the taxes by which the revenues of modern governments are raised. . . . All such taxes have a tendency to reduce the production of wealth, and should, therefore, never be resorted to when it is possible to raise money by taxes which do not check production.

George's solution was to find the least distortive tax and so proposed taxing the ownership of land, so that the government could extract the 'rents' of land without resorting to confiscating private property. Such land taxes have become a predominant part of modern government finance, where for example home property values are taxed to raise funds for financing local education in the United States, and where 'council taxes' on home property finance local government services in the United Kingdom.

Modern economics views taxation as generally falling on either labour, capital or goods, with land and housing property viewed as a form of capital. Rigid wages or prices can be analysed as regulations imposed upon markets, just as an implicit tax. Economists have shown how implicit taxes have similar effects to explicit taxes. Gary Becker argues in his 1957 book, *The Economics of Discrimination*, that people are willing to implicitly tax other people because of a desire to discriminate. For example, an employer who is less willing to hire a certain type of worker will typically pay a higher rate for a given level of productivity, while employing someone more desirable. The firm's marginal cost increases, and one worker is implicitly taxed with the proceeds of the implicit tax in effect getting transferred to the other worker.

The theory of economic regulation that Nobel Laureate (1982) George Stigler (1971) and Samuel Peltzman (1976) put forth argues that the rents get used up by those seeking to have the legislation that creates protection from open market competition. The rents can also be tangible, in the form of corrupt payments. And the concept of rent seeking behaviour has been applied to the making of laws such as in the economics and law literature that Judge Richard Posner fostered with his *Economics of Law* text of 1973, with a 7th edition in 2007.

3.2 Business cycles and employment

During an economic downturn, factor productivity falls. This is represented by a decrease in the parameter A_G in our economy. However in such a downturn, in our log utility and Cobb–Douglas production economy, the labour worked does not fall. This creates a dilemma in that the labour employed is too 'smooth' relative to what occurs in fact over the business cycle. In fact employment is perfectly smooth, and this is part of the too-smooth features of the standard modern model.

The comparative statics of an increase in labour productivity, as shown in Chapter 2, indicate that the substitution and income effects exactly offset each other with respect to the quantity of labour employed for log utility and Cobb–Douglas production technology; this also holds for a productivity decrease. Thus, despite a common description of the business cycle as being explained by a rise and then fall in the productivity of factor inputs, labour productivity changes do not lead to changes in employment. Going to less standard utility and production functions is possible but this would be a solution reliant on special cases in which the labour quantity did change, and so such a direction is not particularly satisfactory.

One aspect of the productivity change within the model that it viewed as being reasonable relative to the data is that the real wage does rise and fall as productivity rises and falls, making the changes 'procyclic'. Evidence is still mixed on this, but real wage rates have been found to be procyclic. This makes attractive the procyclic nature of the model's real wage change as a result of productivity changes. But the fixity of the employment level of labour is not attractive.

Clearly during recessions the employment level drops and this leads to policy issues of how best to meet the needs of those not employed. During large crisis-type recessions, such as the 1930s international depression or the recent 2007–09 global deep recession, the employment policy becomes a central issue. Therefore it is useful if the representative agent model can simulate the type of recessions or depressions that are experienced, both in 'normal' business cycles and in crisis periods.

3.2.1 Internal versus external labour margins

The lack of the change in the equilibrium employment rate when there is a productivity increase in goods sector production makes it hard to explain business cycles with the standard device used to explain business cycles: goods sector productivity changes. And this constancy of the equilibrium labour quantity is found also in the more complete dynamic model of Part 4.

The idea that the time worked per day stays at 8 hours, or the time per week stays at 40 hours, over the business cycle is consistent empirically with the labour quantity per agent not changing in equilibrium. Yet the total labour employment rate does move up and down in the business cycle. How to rectify this seeming paradox is a central issue of explaining business cycles with the standard macroeconomic model.

One view of this is that the 'internal margin' of labour versus leisure does not change over the business cycle but rather the 'external margin' does change. This means that the decision to work or not can change over the business cycle. People choosing to enter the labour market during the upswing, but to stay out of the labour market when the wage rate is lower during the downswing, manifests the idea of how the external margin works.

A decision to stay out of the labour market can be interpreted as implying that the individual chooses instead to be only a part of the non-market sector, such as the home or education sector. Therefore a way to discuss the external labour margin is in terms of the 'labour force participation rate'. This rate tells us how much of the labour is actively participating in the labour market, rather than being devoted instead to the non-market sector.

Being able to explain the change in the labour market participation rate is viewed as one way to explain how a business cycle occurs, in that this perspective is able to explain changes in the overall employment of labour. A way to interpret this within our analysis here is by changing the time endowment available for work and leisure. The time endowment is the 'external margin' of the consumer's decision between work and leisure, but in our analysis this margin is exogenously given.

A standard interpretation of a decrease in the time endowment is that more time is devoted to non-market activity and less is left for market activity. This decrease is what happens in the economic downturn when the labour force participation rate drops and more people 'work' in the non-market home or education sector. It turns out that adding this time endowment change to a productivity change enables an explanation of the business cycle that is consistent with facts about wage rate, labour employed and output changes. Such a change in the time endowment, and subsequent business cycle explanation, is also consistent with Part 5 in which this time endowment change becomes endogenous by including human capital along with physical capital.

3.2.2 Time endowment increase

A second important comparative static experiment besides the productivity change is to examine the effects of a change in the representative agent's time endowment T. The time endowment is exogenous in the model and it indicates the amount of resources available to the consumer for work and leisure. Allowing for a change in T is an abstraction that allows for other uses of time such as education to change, so that what is left for labour and leisure also changes.

Consider the results of years of education in primary, secondary and then tertiary schools. It is well known that increased education is linked with higher future wage earning. But during the education period the time available for work and leisure is greatly reduced. Anyone getting educated still has the same amount of total raw time as everyone else, but education uses up time left over for labour and leisure.

If more time is spent in education or child-rearing, which is another form of educating the next generation, then less time is left for labour and leisure and the time available for this goes down. Therefore a decrease in the exogenous time endowment is also analogous to an increase in education time. Education time is studied in Chapter 12 in the context of 'human capital', but it can be incorporated exogenously within the labour–leisure analysis of this chapter in terms of changing the endowment of time.

3.2.3 Example 3.1

Consider Example 2.1 in which the time endowment is $T = 1$. And now let the time endowment T rise 5% to 1.05, while letting the other parameters remain as in Example 2.1 at $\gamma = \frac{1}{3}$, $A_G = 1$ and $\alpha = 0.5$.

Centralised problem

Instead of equation (2.9), the new representative agent problem is

$$\text{Max}_l \; u = \ln\left(l^\gamma\right) + \alpha \ln\left(1.05 - l\right)$$

$$= \ln\left(l^{\frac{1}{3}}\right) + 0.5 \ln\left(1.05 - l\right),$$

with the equilibrium condition:

$$\frac{(l)^{-\frac{2}{3}}}{3l^{\frac{1}{3}}} - 0.5\left(\frac{1}{1.05 - l}\right) = 0, \tag{3.1}$$

$$l = 0.42. \tag{3.2}$$

The solution for the labour quantity is $l = 0.42$. The 5% time endowment increase raises the labour employed in equilibrium to 0.42 from 0.40 when the time endowment equals 1. This is an increase of $\frac{0.02}{0.4} = 0.05$, or 5% of labour.

The rest of the equilibrium is that

$$c = l^\gamma = 0.42^{\frac{1}{3}} = 0.74889,$$

$$x = 1.05 - 0.42 = 0.63,$$

and utility is

$$u(c, x) = \ln\left(l^{\frac{1}{3}}\right) + 0.5 \ln\left(1.05 - l\right)$$

$$= \ln 0.74889 + 0.5 \ln 0.63 = -0.52018. \tag{3.3}$$

The utility level is higher than the value of -0.56058 in Example 2.1 when the time endowment is 1.

The production curve for graphing in $(c : x)$ space is

$$c = \left(1.05 - x\right)^{\frac{1}{3}}, \tag{3.4}$$

instead of

$$c = \left(1 - x\right)^{\frac{1}{3}}. \tag{3.5}$$

And solving for c from the utility level curve of equation (3.3),

$$c = \frac{e^{-0.5201}}{x^{0.5}}, \tag{3.6}$$

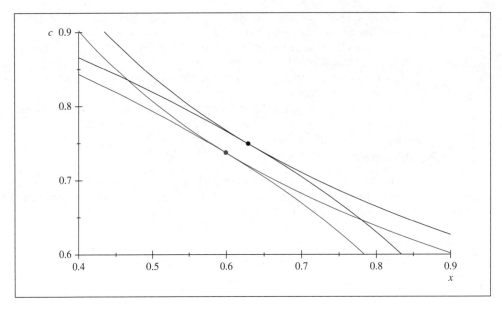

Figure 3.1 A 5% increase in time endowment in Example 3.1 in black compared to Example 2.1 in blue

the utility level curve also shifts upwards from its previous equation of

$$c = \frac{e^{-0.56058}}{x^{0.5}}. \tag{3.7}$$

Figure 3.1 graphs equations (3.4) and (3.6) in black for the new general equilibrium of Example 3.1, along with equations (3.5) and (3.7) for comparison to the baseline equilibrium of Example 2.1.

Decentralised problem

Consider the same example in terms of the consumer and firm decentralised problems, so that the changes in supply and demand can be discovered. The consumer problem is

$$\text{Max } L = \ln \left(w l^s + \Pi \right) + 0.5 \ln(1.05 - l^s), \tag{3.8}$$
$$\quad l^s$$

with the equilibrium condition of

$$\frac{w}{w l^s + \Pi} - \frac{0.5}{1.05 - l^s} = 0.$$

This implies the labour supply, consumption goods demand, and leisure functions of

$$\frac{1.05}{0.5} - \frac{\Pi}{w} = l^s \left(1 + \frac{1}{0.5} \right),$$

$$l^s = \frac{2.10}{3} - \frac{\Pi}{3w} = 0.7 - \frac{\Pi}{3w}.$$

$$c^d = w l^s + \Pi = w \left(\frac{2.10}{3} - \frac{\Pi}{3w} \right) + \Pi,$$

$$= 0.7w + \frac{2}{3}\Pi.$$

$$x = 1.05 - l^s = 1.05 - \frac{2.10}{3} + \frac{\Pi}{3w},$$

$$= 0.35 + \frac{\Pi}{3w}.$$

The firm problem is unaffected by the time endowment change, with output given by

$$y = A_G \left(l^d\right)^{\gamma} = \left(l^d\right)^{\frac{1}{3}},$$

and the profit maximisation problem equal to

$$\underset{l^d}{\text{Max}} \ \Pi = \left(l^d\right)^{\frac{1}{3}} - wl^d. \tag{3.9}$$

The equilibrium is

$$\frac{1}{3} \left(l^d\right)^{-\frac{2}{3}} = w, \tag{3.10}$$

$$l^d = \left(\frac{1}{3w}\right)^{1.5}. \tag{3.11}$$

Inversely, the labour demand as solved for w is

$$w = \frac{1}{3 \left(l^d\right)^{\frac{2}{3}}}.$$

This gives the supply of goods and profit as a function of w:

$$c^S = \left(\frac{1}{3w}\right)^{\frac{1.5}{3}} = \left(\frac{1}{3w}\right)^{0.5}, \tag{3.12}$$

$$\Pi = c^S - wl^d,$$

$$= \left(\frac{1}{3w}\right)^{0.5} - w \left(\frac{1}{3w}\right)^{1.5} = \left(\frac{1}{3}\right)^{0.5} w^{-0.5} - \left(\frac{1}{3}\right)^{1.5} w^{-0.5},$$

$$= \left(\frac{1}{3w}\right)^{0.5} \left(1 - \frac{1}{3}\right), \tag{3.13}$$

$$= \frac{2}{3\sqrt{3w}} = \frac{0.3849}{\sqrt{w}}. \tag{3.14}$$

Now the consumer demand can be expressed with the equilibrium profit $\Pi = \frac{2}{3\sqrt{3w}}$ substituted in:

$$c^d = 0.7w + \frac{2}{3}\Pi = 0.7w + \frac{4}{9\sqrt{3w}}.$$

And, focusing on the labour market, the supply of labour can be found as a function of w by substituting in the firm profit Π:

$$l^s = 0.7 - \frac{\Pi}{3w}, \tag{3.15}$$

$$= 0.7 - \frac{2}{9\sqrt{3}w^{1.5}}. \tag{3.16}$$

Inversely, for graphing purposes, this is

$$w = \left(\frac{2}{\left(0.7 - l^s\right) 9\sqrt{3}}\right)^{\frac{2}{3}}. \tag{3.17}$$

The labour demand is

$$w = \frac{1}{3 \left(l^d\right)^{\frac{2}{3}}}. \tag{3.18}$$

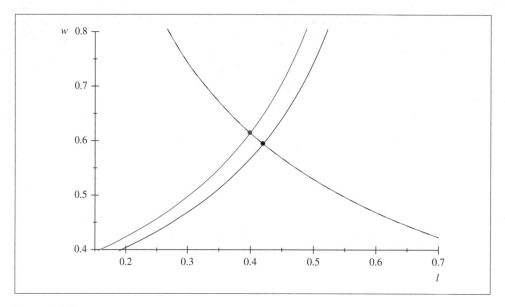

Figure 3.2 The labour market with a 5% time endowment increase in Example 3.1

With $T = 1$, the only change to the labour supply is that instead of the parameter 0.7 in the labour supply equation (3.17), there is $\frac{2}{3}$. The labour supply is

$$w = \left(\frac{2}{\left(\frac{2}{3} - l^s\right) 9\sqrt{3}} \right)^{\frac{2}{3}},$$

while the labour demand is the same as in equation (3.18).

Figure 3.2 graphs the supply and demand of labour in equations (3.17) and (3.18), in black, as compared to Example 2.1, in blue, when the time endowment is 1 instead of 1.05. The labour demand is the same in both Examples 2.1 and 3.1, indicated by the dashed blue and black curve. The time increase shifts out supply and causes the wage rate to fall and the employment rate to rise. The wage falls from 0.614 to 0.594 while the employment rises from 0.4 to 0.42.

The equilibrium wage is found quantitatively by setting labour supply to labour demand:

$$l^s = 0.7 - \frac{2}{9\sqrt{3}w^{1.5}} = \left(\frac{1}{3}\right)^{1.5} \frac{1}{w^{1.5}} = l^d; \tag{3.19}$$

$$w = \left(\frac{\left(\frac{1}{3}\right)^{1.5} + \frac{2}{9\sqrt{3}}}{0.7} \right)^{\frac{2}{3}} = \left(\frac{\left(\frac{1}{3}\right)^{1.5} + 0.1283}{0.7} \right)^{\frac{2}{3}}, \tag{3.20}$$

$$= 0.594; \tag{3.21}$$

$$l^s = 0.7 - \frac{2}{9\left(0.594\right)^{1.5}} \frac{1}{\sqrt{3}} = 0.420 = \left(\frac{1}{3}\right)^{1.5} \frac{1}{\left(0.594\right)^{1.5}} = l^d. \tag{3.22}$$

This shows also that the equilibrium labour supplied and demanded at this wage of $w = 0.594$ is $l = 0.420$.

In comparison, when $T = 1$, and setting supply equal to demand, the labour equilibrium is 0.4 and the wage is 0.614:

$$\left(\frac{2}{\left(\frac{2}{3} - l^s\right) 9\sqrt{3}} \right)^{\frac{2}{3}} = \frac{1}{3 \left(l^d\right)^{\frac{2}{3}}},$$

$$l = \frac{\frac{2}{3} 9 \left(3\right)^{0.5}}{9 \left(3\right)^{0.5} + 3^{1.5} 2} = 0.4$$

$$w = \frac{1}{3 \left(0.4\right)^{\frac{2}{3}}} = 0.614.$$

The time endowment increase effectively increases the labour supply. This happens for example when students leave school and have more time for work and leisure. Exogenous changes in time T can therefore be a reflection of changes in education time. This is the view expanded upon when the economy's growth rate is made endogenous starting in Chapter 12.

3.2.4 Economic expansion and contraction

Consider combining a labour productivity increase with an increase in the endowment of time, a combination of the two comparative static experiments conducted in Chapter 2. In particular, let both the goods productivity parameter A_G and the time endowment of 1 rise by 5%. The wage rate will rise if the productivity effect towards a higher wage is stronger than the time endowment effect towards a lower wage rate. And the quantity of labour will certainly rise since the productivity increase leaves the equilibrium labour unchanged while the time endowment increase causes the labour employed to rise.

If the wage rises and the quantity of labour rises, this would be what is thought to be typical of economic expansions. In reverse, a falling wage rate and employment rate would be typical of a contraction. An example of this is found by letting the goods productivity and time endowment decrease by 5%.

3.2.5 Example 3.2: Expansion

Using the decentralised consumer and firm problem allows the shifts in the labour supply and demand functions to be seen. Example 3.1 allows the time endowment to increase by 5%, from $T = 1$ in Example 2.1, to $T = 1.05$, given that $\gamma = \frac{1}{3}$, $A_G = 1$, and $\alpha = 0.5$. This example will be extended here by also increasing the goods productivity by 5%, from $A_G = 1$ to $A_G = 1.05$.

The consumer side is affected by the change in A_G only in that the profit Π from the firm will be different. Therefore the consumer demand in terms of w and Π is again

$$c^d = w l^s + \Pi = 0.7w + \frac{2}{3}\Pi.$$

And labour supply is again

$$l^s = 0.7 - \frac{\Pi}{3w}.$$

The firm problem is unaffected by the time endowment change, but affected by the A_G change. With output now given by

$$y = A_G \left(l^d\right)^\gamma = 1.05 \left(l^d\right)^{\frac{1}{3}},$$

the profit maximisation problem is

$$\underset{l^d}{\text{Max}} \; \Pi = 1.05 \left(l^d\right)^{\frac{1}{3}} - w l^d. \tag{3.23}$$

The equilibrium condition and labour demand of the firm are

$$\frac{1}{3} \left(1.05\right) \left(l^d\right)^{-\frac{2}{3}} = w, \tag{3.24}$$

$$l^d = \left(\frac{1.05}{3w}\right)^{1.5}. \tag{3.25}$$

Solved for w, labour demand is also

$$w = \frac{1.05}{3 \left(l^d\right)^{\frac{2}{3}}}. \tag{3.26}$$

The supply of goods and profit are:

$$c^s = y = A_G \left(l^d\right)^\gamma = 1.05 \left(\frac{1.05}{3w}\right)^{\frac{1.5}{3}} = \frac{\left(1.05\right)^{1.5}}{\sqrt{3w}}; \tag{3.27}$$

$$\Pi = c^s - w l^d,$$
$$= \frac{\left(1.05\right)^{1.5}}{\sqrt{3w}} - w \left(\frac{1.05}{3w}\right)^{1.5} = \frac{\left(1.05\right)^{1.5}}{3^{0.5}\sqrt{w}} - \frac{\left(1.05\right)^{1.5}}{3^{1.5}\sqrt{w}},$$
$$= \frac{\left(1.05\right)^{1.5}}{3^{0.5}\sqrt{w}} \left(1 - \frac{1}{3}\right) = \frac{2\left(1.05\right)^{1.5}}{3\sqrt{3w}} = \frac{2\left(1.05\right)^{1.5}}{3^{1.5}\sqrt{w}}, \tag{3.28}$$

$$= \frac{0.41413}{\sqrt{w}}. \tag{3.29}$$

The demand for goods as a function of only w is

$$c^d = 0.7w + \frac{2}{3}\Pi = 0.7w + \frac{2}{3}\frac{2\left(1.05\right)^{1.5}}{3^{1.5}\sqrt{w}},$$
$$= 0.7w + \frac{0.27608}{\sqrt{w}}.$$

The supply of labour is now

$$l^s = 0.7 - \frac{\Pi}{3w} = 0.7 - \left(\frac{1}{3w}\right)\frac{2\left(1.05\right)^{1.5}}{3^{1.5}\sqrt{w}}, \tag{3.30}$$

$$= 0.7 - \frac{0.13804}{w^{1.5}}. \tag{3.31}$$

Inversely, labour supply is

$$w = \left(\frac{0.13804}{0.7 - l^s}\right)^{\frac{2}{3}}. \tag{3.32}$$

The equilibrium wage is found by setting labour supply to labour demand:

$$l^S = 0.7 - \frac{0.13804}{w^{1.5}} = \left(\frac{1.05}{3w}\right)^{1.5} = l^d, \tag{3.33}$$

$$0.7 = \frac{1}{w^{1.5}}\left(\frac{1.05^{1.5}}{3^{1.5}} + 0.13804\right), \tag{3.34}$$

$$w = \left(\frac{\frac{1.05^{1.5}}{3^{1.5}} + 0.13804}{0.7}\right)^{\frac{2}{3}} = 0.62407. \tag{3.35}$$

The equilibrium wage is higher than the $w = 0.614$ when $A_G = T = 1$, as in Example 2.1, so the increase in A_G increases the wage rate. This is a fractional increase of $\frac{0.62407 - 0.614}{0.614} = 0.0164$, or 1.64%.

The labour employment at $w = 0.62407$ is the same as in Example 3.1 at $l = 0.42$, so that the increase in A_G does not affect employment:

$$l^S = 0.7 - \frac{0.13804}{w^{1.5}} = 0.7 - \frac{0.13804}{(0.62407)^{1.5}} = 0.42$$

$$0.42 = \left(\frac{1.05}{3(0.62407)}\right)^{1.5} = \left(\frac{1.05}{3w}\right)^{1.5} = l^d.$$

Relative to the equilibrium in which $A_G = T = 1$, and $l = 0.4$, employment is fractionally higher by $\frac{0.02}{0.4} = 0.05$, or 5%.

Figure 3.3 graphs the new equilibrium when $A_G = T = 1.05$, of equations (3.26) and (3.32), in black, and the initial supply and demand when $A_G = T = 1$ in blue.

The graph shows that the supply of labour pivots out, with the higher productivity and time endowment, rather than shifting back as it does when there is only a productivity

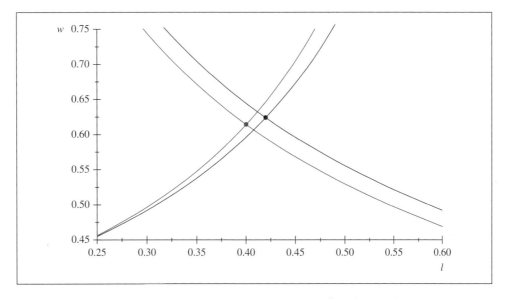

Figure 3.3 Expansion with a 5% increase in time endowment T and in goods productivity A_G in Example 3.2

increase. This is because the time endowment increase shifts out the supply curve by more than the productivity increase raises profit and shifts it back.

Employment is the same as in Example 3.1 when only the time endowment increases, because the productivity increase alone causes exactly offsetting substitution and income effects that yield no change in labour supply. So the two changes occurring simultaneously only see a change in labour from the time endowment increase. And now the wage rate rises, rather than falling as with only a time endowment increase. The wage rise is because the productivity effect dominates the labour supply increase from the time endowment increase. The outcome of the rise in both the wage rate and in the quantity of employment is consistent with our notions of a business cycle expansion.

3.2.6 Example 3.3: Contraction

Starting again with the economy in Example 2.1, with $A_G = T = 1$, let these fall by 5% to $A_G = T = 0.95$. The consumer problem is

$$\text{Max}_{l^s} \; u = \ln\left(wl^s + \Pi\right) + 0.5\ln(0.95 - l^s), \tag{3.36}$$

with the equilibrium condition of

$$\frac{w}{wl^s + \Pi} - \frac{0.5}{0.95 - l^s} = 0.$$

Using this condition to get the labour supply as a function of w and Π,

$$\frac{0.95}{0.5} - \frac{\Pi}{w} = l^s\left(1 + \frac{1}{0.5}\right),$$

$$l^s = \frac{1.9}{3} - \frac{\Pi}{3w} = 0.63333 - \frac{\Pi}{3w}.$$

$$c^d = wl^s + \Pi = w\left(0.63333 - \frac{\Pi}{3w}\right) + \Pi,$$

$$= (0.63333)\, w + \frac{2}{3}\Pi.$$

The firm problem is

$$\text{Max}_{l^d} \; \Pi = 0.95\left(l^d\right)^{\frac{1}{3}} - wl^d, \tag{3.37}$$

with the equilibrium of

$$l^d = \left(\frac{0.95}{3w}\right)^{1.5}, \tag{3.38}$$

$$c^s = (0.95)\left(\frac{0.95}{3w}\right)^{\frac{1.5}{3}}, \tag{3.39}$$

$$\Pi = c^s - wl^d, \tag{3.40}$$

$$= (0.95)\left(\frac{0.95}{3w}\right)^{\frac{1.5}{3}} - w\left(\frac{0.95}{3w}\right)^{1.5}, \tag{3.41}$$

$$= \frac{2\,(0.95)^{1.5}}{3^{1.5}\sqrt{w}} = \frac{0.35640}{\sqrt{w}}. \tag{3.42}$$

This gives the consumer demand for goods as a function of only the wage rate:

$$c^d = (0.63333) \, w + \left(\frac{2}{3}\right) \frac{0.35640}{\sqrt{w}}. \tag{3.43}$$

Substituting the firm's profit back into the consumer's supply of labour function,

$$l^s = 0.63333 - \frac{\Pi}{3w} = 0.63333 - \frac{\left(\frac{0.35640}{\sqrt{w}}\right)}{3w},$$

$$= 0.63333 - \frac{0.1188}{w^{1.5}}. \tag{3.44}$$

The labour market clearing condition,

$$l^s = 0.63333 - \frac{0.1188}{w^{1.5}} = \left(\frac{0.95}{3w}\right)^{1.5} = l^d,$$

implies the equilibrium wage:

$$0.63333 - \frac{0.1188}{w^{1.5}} = \left(\frac{0.95}{3w^{1.5}}\right)^{1.5},$$

$$0.63333 = \frac{1}{w^{1.5}} \left(\frac{(0.95)^{1.5}}{3^{1.5}} + 0.1188\right), \tag{3.45}$$

$$w = \left(\frac{\frac{0.95^{1.5}}{3^{1.5}} + 0.1188}{0.63333}\right)^{\frac{2}{3}} = 0.6036. \tag{3.46}$$

And the equilibrium quantity of employment is 0.38:

$$l^s = 0.63333 - \frac{0.1188}{(0.6036)^{1.5}} = 0.38 = \left(\frac{0.95}{3\,(0.6036)}\right)^{1.5} = l^d. \tag{3.47}$$

A wage of 0.6036 and employment of 0.38 compare to 0.614 and 0.40 when $A_G = T = 1$. Thus the wage rate falls by $\frac{0.614-0.6036}{0.614} = 0.01694$, or 1.69%; employment falls by $\frac{0.02}{0.40} = 0.05$, or 5%. The fall in the wage rate and the employment is typical of recessions.

The labour supply and labour demand equations are

$$w = \left(\frac{0.1188}{0.63333 - l^s}\right)^{\frac{2}{3}}, \tag{3.48}$$

$$w = \frac{0.95}{3\,(l^d)^{\frac{2}{3}}}. \tag{3.49}$$

Figure 3.4 graphs equations (3.48) and (3.49) in black, along with the initial equilibrium with $A_G = T = 1$ in blue.

The graph shows that the supply of labour pivots back while the labour demand shifts down, with the result of a lower wage and employment as is typical with an economic contraction.

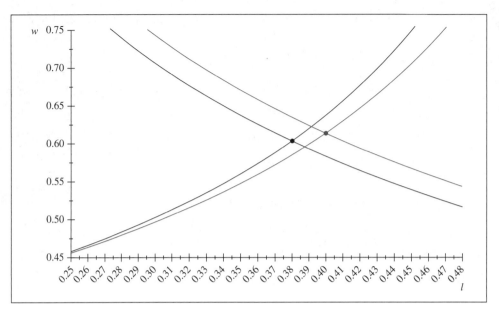

Figure 3.4 Contraction with a 5% decrease in time endowment T and in goods productivity A_G in Example 3.3

3.3 Unemployed labour

The labour movements as seen over a typical business cycle are shown above in a so-called 'flexible price' model, in which the wage rate can adjust to its equilibrium value. Some recessions are more severe. They create decreases in employment that in a sense are not normal. These undesirable employment decreases can be a type of crisis unemployment situation, as in the 1930s, and even as in the high unemployment found in the 2007–09 recession.

Keynes's *General Theory* has been interpreted as suggesting that the labour market may not be clearing in that the wage rate cannot adjust downwards sufficiently. In modern specifications of aggregate economies this has been modelled by assuming fixed or inflexible wages and prices. Such an approach can also be taken in our simple economy as a means of simulating crisis periods.

The simplest approach to this is to assume that for some reason the wage rate is fixed. This might be because of efficient contracts that fix the wage and allow the employment rate to vary instead. Or it may be that wage contracts are imperfect and do not build in the expectations of crisis situations within the labour market, and as a result they inefficiently keep the wage fixed relative to contracts that had been able to foresee the possibility of crisis situations. In such a crisis, a fixed wage might result because labour unions refuse unexpected wage reductions, even at the cost of facing unemployment. Then the fixed wage ends up acting like an implicit tax that creates a wedge between the supply and demand price of labour.

In order to explain more extreme decreases in the employment of labour, the analysis assumes a fixed wage in combination with a 5% decrease in the productivity level and time endowment. The 5% simultaneous decrease is shown in the last section to cause employment to fall by 5%; now the fall will be shown to be substantially bigger if the wage rate is fixed.

The standard utility function will be assumed, of

$$u = \ln c + \alpha \ln x.$$

And production is given again in a general form as

$$y = Al^{\gamma}.$$
(3.50)

Implicitly again it is assumed that capital is fixed at $k = 1$. The problem will be stated in decentralised form, with consumer and firm problems, so that the role of the wage rate w is made explicit.

3.3.1 Example 3.4: A fixed wage during a contraction

The example economy will therefore be similar to Example 3.3 except that now the wage is fixed at $w = \overline{w}$, where $\overline{w}$ is the value in the initial equilibrium before the 5% decrease in productivity and time endowment. The initial parameter values are as in Example 2.1: $\gamma = \frac{1}{3}$, $\alpha = 0.5$, $A_G = 1$ and $T = 1$. And given that

$$w = \overline{w} = 0.614,$$

assume that there occurs a 5% drop in goods productivity and time endowment, as in Example 3.3, such that $A_G = T = 0.95$. The consumer and firm problems, and the equilibrium supply and demand functions, are the same as in Example 3.3, but the fixity of the wage rate at its previous equilibrium value means that markets will not clear

3.3.2 Excess labour supply and goods demand

The labour market clearing condition will not result in an equilibrium between supply and demand, since the wage is kept fixed at its old equilibrium level of 0.614. From equations (3.38) and (3.44),

$$l^s = 0.63333 - \frac{0.1188}{(\overline{w})^{1.5}} = 0.63333 - \frac{0.1188}{(0.614)^{1.5}} = 0.38641,$$

$$l^d = \left(\frac{0.95}{3\overline{w}}\right)^{1.5} = \left(\frac{0.95}{3(0.614)}\right)^{1.5} = 0.37038.$$

The quantity of labour supplied at the fixed wage is 0.38641 while the quantity demanded is 0.37038. This means there is an excess supply of labour equal to

$$l^s - l^d = 0.38641 - 0.37038 = 0.01603,$$

at the given wage. This would be the fraction $\frac{0.01603}{0.37038} = 0.04328$, or 4.3% of the actual employment rate. Such an excess supply is sometimes called 'surplus labour' in the unemployment literature. The surplus labour is also thought of as being involuntarily unemployed. Or sometimes this is thought of as the amount of unemployment above the 'structural' and 'frictional' amount of the 'normal' unemployment rate.

Figure 3.5 adds the fixed wage $\overline{w} = 0.614$ to Figure 3.3, to illustrate Example 3.4. The excess supply of labour is the difference between the black labour supply and labour demand curves at the wage of $\overline{w} = 0.614$, which is an amount equal to 0.016. Surplus labour is one way that the concept of 'unemployment' can be defined in a rigorous way.

The amount of labour actually employed in this fixed wage situation will be that which is demanded at the given wage rate, rather than the higher amount that is supplied. Therefore 0.37 is the equilibrium amount of labour, given the fixed wage. This means that the labour employment drops from 0.40 down to 0.37, a decrease of $\frac{0.4-0.37}{0.4} = 0.075$, or a

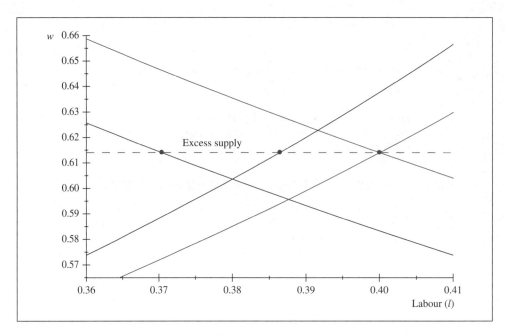

Figure 3.5 Excess labour supply with a fixed wage and deeper contraction in Example 3.4

50% bigger decrease of a 7.5% drop in employment, as compared to the flexible wage equilibrium of $l = 0.38$ in Figure 3.5.

Such a drop in employment, by 7.5% in this example, occurs infrequently and really only in our biggest recessions/depressions. It would be as if the official unemployment rate of, say, 4% rose to 11.5%. The fixity of the wage rate thereby is one way to explain how an otherwise mild drop in productivity and time endowment of 5% translates into a bigger percentage drop in employment, while under flexible wages the employment decrease would be only 5%.

One symptom of the excess supply of labour is a rationing of jobs, and 'queuing' in employment centres. This rationing would also occur in goods markets if the wage rate is fixed. Just as the labour market does not clear, with an excess supply of labour, the goods market also does not clear, this time with an excess demand for goods. To see this, simply substitute in $\overline{w} = 0.614$ into the supply and demand for consumption goods. From equations (3.39) and (3.43),

$$c^s = (0.95)\left(\frac{0.95}{3\overline{w}}\right)^{\frac{1.5}{3}} = (0.95)\left(\frac{0.95}{3(0.614)}\right)^{\frac{1.5}{3}} = 0.68225,$$

$$c^d = (0.633)\,\overline{w} + \frac{2(0.3564)}{3\sqrt{\overline{w}}} = (0.633)(0.614) + \frac{2(0.3564)}{3\sqrt{0.614}} = 0.69209.$$

The demand for consumption is 0.69209 while the supply is 0.68225, giving an excess demand of

$$c^d - c^s = 0.69209 - 0.68225 = 0.00984,$$

which is a fraction of actual consumption equal to $\frac{0.00984}{0.68225} = 0.0144$, or 1.44%.

Rationing of the goods market manifests through queuing to buy goods, or in a myriad of other ways. The 1930s US depression may have had both goods and labour market rationing. And if this postulated theory of a fixed-wage type of recession is accurate, then such labour and goods rationing should be in evidence. It is not at all clear that the 2007–09 recession exhibited such symptoms. Nor is it clear that any other recession since the 1930s has clearly exhibited such rationing. The oil rationing of the 1970s was not part of a widespread rationing of goods, as much of it was a problem within just one commodity market in which contractual relations broke down. The 1970s oil crisis is discussed in Chapter 20 in terms of contracts being violated because inflation made contracted nominal oil prices too low.

3.4 A goods tax

Sometimes during an economic contraction the government seeks to lower tax rates as a way to induce some expansion that can offset the contraction. Decreasing tax rates can increase the equilibrium employment and output, but this is difficult to enact during a recession when the demand for government spending can increase. For example, the financing of government unemployment systems requires raising revenue through taxation. For an unemployment system that has adequate funds to cover payouts during a recession, there is no unfunded government expenditure that needs to be financed. But for large drops in employment, the unemployment insurance fund may be inadequate and additional government spending may be required that needs to be financed by new taxes either now or in the future.

Perhaps more important than cyclical changes in the tax rates as a means of fighting recessions, which are used only infrequently as government policy, is how tax rates affect long run employment, output and economic growth. And so the total level of government taxation to cover the spending becomes an issue of the efficacity of the government policy in a broad sense. Generally, the higher government taxation is as a share of aggregate output, the greater will be the disincentives to productive activity.

Spending has to be financed by some form of taxation. And in practice, there is no such availability of a tax that does not distort the incentives of the representative agent. Arguably, all taxation is distortionary. In our labour–leisure economy, there is a similar distortion to incentives from either a tax on goods purchases, or on labour income, that is used to finance the payment of government spending. This spending may be in the form of benefits that are often called 'income transfers'. This transfer can be viewed in part as the unemployment benefit.

With a perfect unemployment system, with no 'moral hazard', there is no distortion from the transfer of the benefits. Moral hazard here refers to the decrease in the incentive to work when receiving unemployment benefits. When there is no moral hazard, there is no bigger incentive to avoid work. An unemployment benefit payout simply covers missing income when not employed, as in a perfect insurance system. But with the income benefits being treated in part by potential workers as a permanent benefit, the transfer itself is also distortionary in that the extra income shifts back the supply of labour. People on a permanent income subsidy do not want to work as hard.

Legally people who collect unemployment benefits are often restricted from any work at all. But many still work without reporting the activity. So the analysis simply assumes that there are no legal restrictions at all and looks at how the extra income transfer affects the supply of labour. Such a permanent unemployment transfer has long been referred to as the 'dole' in the UK, Australia and New Zealand.

The analysis treats all of the benefits being paid as a permanent income transfer, and finances the expenditure with a tax. Assume that the agent receives a government transfer G as additional income, which is paid for through a value added (proportional sales) tax on consumption goods, denoted by τ_c. This makes the cost of goods to the consumer

$c\left(1+\tau_c\right)$, instead of just c when there is no tax. And it increases consumer income to $wl^s + \Pi + G$.

The consumer's budget constraint with the tax and transfer becomes

$$\left(1+\tau_c\right)c^d = wl^s + \Pi + G. \tag{3.51}$$

The government budget constraint is that the transfer payments equal the tax receipts, or

$$G = \tau_c c^d. \tag{3.52}$$

Clearly if G in the budget constraint (3.51) is substituted with $\tau_c c^d$ from equation (3.52), then the consumer gets back the budget constraint when there is no tax at all: $c^d = \Pi + wl^s$. This means that in equilibrium the tax and income transfer leaves the consumer's net income unchanged.

However the consumer maximises utility before the income transfer can wash out the tax effect. Only as an equilibrium condition does this occur. This means that the tax will appear in the consumer's equilibrium marginal conditions and so distort decisions, despite eventually getting the tax revenue back as a transfer.

As a result, there is both a substitution type and income type effect of the tax. The substitution effect is seen in the tax 'distortions' to the consumer's marginal rate of substitution; the income effect is from the transfer G. The marginal rate of substitution between goods and leisure will be shown in the following example now to be equal to

$$MRS_{c,x} = \frac{\frac{\alpha}{x}}{\frac{1}{c^d}} = \frac{w}{1+\tau_c},$$

instead of simply w when there is no tax. The tax distorts allocation by raising the 'shadow price' of consumption to $1 + \tau_v$ from 1, thereby causing a goods to leisure substitution. Working time goes down by this distortive substitution effect. And the income effect will cause labour supply to shift back.

3.4.1 Example 3.5: Goods tax and transfer

Consider the decentralised consumer and firm problems so that the wage rate is explicit, while assuming the same log utility and Cobb–Douglas specifications. The same parameterisation will be used as in Examples 2.3 and 2.5, with $A_G = 1$, the time endowment equal to 24, $\gamma = 0.5$ and $\alpha = 1$. The tax rate will be specified at 20%, with the idea that a country's government expenditure is usually 20% or more of aggregate output. Then the example will show the effect of both the unemployment insurance spending along with other government taxes and income transfers.

The consumer has the log utility function of

$$u = \ln c^d + \ln x,$$

and time allocation,

$$24 = x + l^s.$$

When the consumer solves the optimisation problem, the profit Π and the income transfer G are kept as exogenous factors since the consumer just considers these as 'lump sum' income transfers and does not know exactly how they are derived. Once first-order conditions are obtained, the consumer knows the other equilibrium conditions of the constraints, in equations (3.51) and (3.52), and these can be substituted into the other conditions to get supply and demand.

The consumer budget constraint can be solved for c^d from equation (3.51), as

$$c^d = \frac{wl^s + \Pi + G}{1 + \tau_c},$$ (3.53)

and substituted in for goods demanded c^d in the utility function. The consumer problem is

$$\text{Max } u = \ln\left(\frac{wl^s + \Pi + G}{1 + \tau_c}\right) + \ln(24 - l^s),$$

with the equilibrium condition:

$$\frac{\frac{w}{1+\tau_c}}{\frac{\Pi + wl^s + G}{1 + \tau_c}} - \frac{1}{24 - l^s} = 0.$$

Rearranged in terms of the marginal rate of substitution between goods and leisure, this is

$$\frac{w}{1 + \tau_c} = \frac{\frac{1}{24 - l^s}}{\frac{1}{\frac{\Pi + wl^s + G}{1 + \tau_c}}} = \frac{\frac{1}{x}}{\frac{1}{c}} = \frac{\frac{\partial u(c,x)}{\partial x}}{\frac{\partial u(c,x)}{\partial c^d}}.$$

Solving the equilibrium condition for l^s gives the equilibrium labour supply,

$$l^s = 12 - \left(\frac{\Pi + G}{2w}\right).$$ (3.54)

Equation (3.54) shows that the transfer G acts as an income effect that shifts back the labour supply. The demand for goods is found by substituting in the labour supply l^s into the solution for c^d as derived from the budget constraint:

$$c^d = \frac{0.5\left(24w + \Pi + G\right)}{1 + \tau_c}.$$ (3.55)

The solution for profit comes from the firm problem, which is identical to that of Example 2.5.

The firm is assumed to have the production function:

$$c^s = \left(l^d\right)^{0.5},$$ (3.56)

as in Example 2.5, but now collects the tax revenue and gives it to the government. This means that revenue is now $(1 + \tau_c)\, c^s$, while the firm's cost includes not only the wage payments of wl^d but also the tax payments to the government of $\tau_c c^s$. This makes the profit of revenues minus cost equal to

$$\Pi = \left(1 + \tau_c\right) c^s - wl^d - \tau_c c^s$$
$$= c^s - wl^d.$$

This is the same profit function as before, since the tax receipts and transfer of tax back to the government nets out to zero. The profit maximisation problem is again

$$\text{Max } \Pi = \left(l^d\right)^{0.5} - wl^d,$$ (3.57)

with the equilibrium condition of

$$0.5\left(l^d\right)^{-0.5} - w = 0,$$

and the labour demand, goods supply and profit as in equations (2.36) to (2.38) are:

$$l^d = \frac{1}{4w^2},$$ (3.58)

$$c^S = \frac{0.5}{w},$$ (3.59)

$$\Pi = \frac{1}{4w}.$$ (3.60)

The profit can be substituted back into the consumer's demand for goods,

$$c^d = \frac{0.5\left(24w + \frac{1}{4w} + G\right)}{1 + \tau_c},$$ (3.61)

and supply of labour,

$$l^S = 12 - \left(\frac{\frac{1}{4w} + G}{2w}\right).$$ (3.62)

To get to a final form of the consumer's consumption goods demand, as a function of only the real wage w and the tax rate τ_c, requires using the government budget constraint to substitute $G = \tau_v c^d$ into equation (3.61), and then solving for c^d in terms of only w and τ_c:

$$c^d = \frac{w12 + \frac{1}{8w}}{1 + \frac{\tau_c}{2}}.$$ (3.63)

This shows clearly how an increase in the tax rate τ_c can lower consumer demand for goods; $\frac{\partial c^d}{\partial \tau_c} < 0$. Thus the consumer demand for goods is shifted back, while the firm's goods supply function is unchanged, implying a decrease in the equilibrium relative price of goods to labour, $1/w$, or an increase in the equilibrium real wage w.

With $\tau_c = 0.2$, the inverted supply of goods of equations (3.59), solved in terms of $\frac{1}{w}$, is

$$\frac{1}{w} = \frac{c^S}{0.5}.$$ (3.64)

For demand the equation (3.63) can only be solved for $\frac{1}{w}$ in terms of a 'quadratic' expression. The quadratic in $\frac{1}{w}$ is

$$\left(\frac{1}{w}\right)^2 - \left[\left(1 + \frac{\tau_c}{2}\right) 8c^d\right]\left(\frac{1}{w}\right) + 96 = 0.$$

Using a standard solution for a quadratic that $\frac{1}{w} = \frac{-B - \sqrt{B^2 - 4AC}}{2a}$, where $A = 1$, $B = -\left(1 + \frac{\tau_c}{2}\right) 8c^d$ and $C = 96$, then

$$\frac{1}{w} = \frac{\left(1 + \frac{\tau_c}{2}\right) 8\left(c^d\right) - \sqrt{\left(\left(1 + \frac{\tau_c}{2}\right) 8\right)^2 \left(c^d\right)^2 - 4\left(96\right)}}{2}.$$ (3.65)

Figure 3.6 graphs the goods supply and demand equations (3.64) and (3.65) of Example 3.5 in black, along with the baseline with zero tax as in Example 2.5 in blue. The supply curve is the same in both cases and so is in dashed blue and black.

A positive tax rate shifts back goods demand relative to the case of no taxes, while supply remains the same. This causes a lower relative price of goods, $\frac{1}{w}$, a lower equilibrium goods demand c^d, and a higher real wage w.

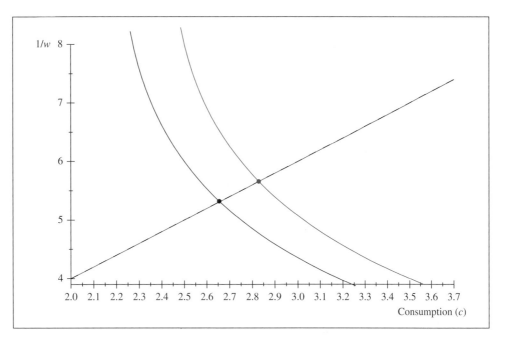

Figure 3.6 A 20% tax on goods with income transfer in Example 3.5

3.4.2 Labour market

The goods tax and income transfer also affects the labour market. Substituting in for G in the labour supply equation (3.62), gives that

$$l^s = 12 - \frac{1}{8w^2} - \frac{\tau_c c^d}{2w}. \tag{3.66}$$

Equation (3.66) contains c^d and so is not in final form of a labour supply function that depends upon only the real wage and the exogenous tax rate τ_c. To substitute in for c^d, consider that since in equilibrium there is market clearing, and so goods supply equals demand, $c^s = c^d$, then either c^d or c^s can be used in equation (3.66). Substituting in $c^s = \frac{1}{2w}$ from equation (3.59) gives that

$$l^s = 12 - \frac{1}{8w^2} - \frac{\tau_c}{4w^2}. \tag{3.67}$$

As the tax rate τ_c goes up, it makes l^s in equation (3.67) lower, resulting in a shift back of the labour supply. This means that the higher the tax is, the lower is the employment of labour.

With $\tau_c = 0.2$, the inverted supply and demand equations are

$$l^s = 12 - \frac{1}{8w^2} - \frac{\tau_c}{4w^2},$$

$$w = \sqrt{\frac{1.40}{8\left(12 - l^s\right)}}, \tag{3.68}$$

$$w = \frac{1}{2\sqrt{l^d}}. \tag{3.69}$$

Figure 3.7 graphs the supply and demand for labour with $\tau_c = 0.2$ of equations (3.68) and (3.69) in the black curves, and with the $\tau_c = 0$ equilibrium of Example 2.5 in blue.

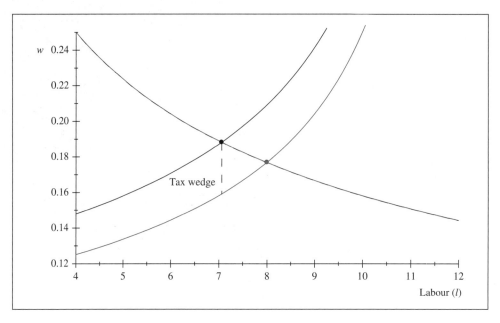

Figure 3.7 Labour market with goods tax $\tau_c = 0.2$ and income transfer in Example 3.5

The tax shifts back the supply curve and leaves unchanged the demand curve. The result is to increase the real wage, and reduce equilibrium employment.

Solving analytically for the wage rate follows from setting the supply of labour equal to the demand for labour:

$$l^s = 12 - \frac{1}{8w^2} - \frac{\tau_c c^d}{2w} = \frac{1}{4w^2} = l^d,$$

and solving for the w:

$$w = \sqrt{\frac{3 + 2\tau_c}{96}} = \sqrt{\frac{3 + 2\,(0.2)}{96}} = 0.18819. \tag{3.70}$$

It shows that the real wage is an increasing function of the tax rate. The higher the tax τ_c, the higher will be the 'before-tax' real wage. A higher real wage reduces the demand for labour, and the equilibrium labour employed.

With $\tau_c = 0.2$, $w = 0.188$, by equation (3.70), which is higher than when $\tau_v = 0$ and $w = 0.17678$. Employment of labour is $l = \frac{1}{4(0.18819)^2} = 7.0591$ versus $\frac{1}{4(0.17678)^2} = 8.0$ when $\tau_c = 0$, a decrease of $\frac{8 - 7.0591}{8} = 0.11761$, or 11.8%. Even given the simplicity of the model, this magnitude of the effect on employment may be plausible although this example is meant to be illustrative.

The equilibrium consumption at the wage of $w = 0.188$ is

$$c^d = \frac{(0.18819)\,12 + \frac{1}{8(0.18819)}}{1 + \frac{0.2}{2}} = 2.6568, \tag{3.71}$$

and equilibrium utility is

$$u = \ln c + \ln\,(24 - l) = \ln 2.6568 + \ln\,(24 - 7.0591) = 3.8069,$$

$$c = \frac{e^{3.8069}}{(24 - l)} = \frac{45.011}{24 - l}. \tag{3.72}$$

This compares to the zero tax equilibrium of $x = 16$,

$$c^d = (0.17678) \, 12 + \frac{1}{8 \, (0.17678)} = 2.8285, \tag{3.73}$$

and

$$u = \ln c + \ln (24 - l) = \ln 2.8285 + \ln (16) = 3.8123,$$

$$c = \frac{e^{3.8123}}{(24 - l)} = \frac{45.254}{24 - l}. \tag{3.74}$$

3.4.3 After tax wage rate and tax wedge

There is also the concept of the 'after tax' wage rate, or net of tax wage rate. The wage rate in the last example was found to rise in equilibrium because of the tax to $\sqrt{\frac{3+2\tau_c}{96}}$ instead of $\sqrt{\frac{3}{96}}$. But the amount of labour hours dropped from 8 hours to 7.06. The 'tax wedge' is the difference between (a) the equilibrium wage rate when there is a tax of $\tau_c = 0.2$ and (b) the wage rate that would induce only 7.06 of labour time in the equilibrium labour supply function when the tax is zero. This wedge is measured as the vertical difference in Figure 3.7 between the zero tax labour supply curve and the 20% tax labour supply curve, when $l^s = 7.06$, as given by the dashed black vertical line.

To compute the wage that would induce 7.06 with the original supply curve, let

$$7.06 = l^s = 12 - \frac{1}{8w^2},$$

$$w = \sqrt{\frac{1}{8 \, (12 - 7.0591)}} = 0.15906,$$

and solve for w. This gives the 'after tax' wage rate of $w = 0.159$, making the 'tax wedge' equal to

$$0.188 - 0.159 = 0.029.$$

The tax wedge is $\frac{0.029}{0.159} = 0.18$, or 18% of the equilibrium wage when there is a 20% goods tax. The after tax wage that the consumer is getting is less than the zero-tax wage of 0.177, a lower real wage, and this is one way to understand why less labour is being supplied. The new equilibrium wage is indeed higher at 0.188, but 0.029 of this is just due to payment of the tax, and only 0.159 is left to the consumer.

3.4.4 General equilibrium tax wedge

Tax analysis suggests the idea that there are good wage increases, such as when productivity increases, and tax-induced increases in the equilibrium wage, such as here when the after-tax wage rate is actually made lower by the tax. These tax wedges can also be seen in general equilibrium, with just the production function and utility level curve.

Figure 3.8 shows the dashed black utility level curve when $\tau_c = 0.20$, of equation (3.72), along with the black level curve with no tax, of equation (3.74), and the blue production function of equation (3.56) that is unaffected by the tax.

Production possibilities are not altered; only the utility level is lowered by the tax. The zero tax black utility curve is tangent to the blue production function at the zero tax equilibrium. The dashed black utility curve intersects the blue production function at two points. The lower intersection point is the equilibrium with the 20% tax.

The 'tax wedge' in the general equilibrium $(c : x)$ dimensions is seen by the lower intersection of the dashed black utility curve with the production function at which $x = 16.93$

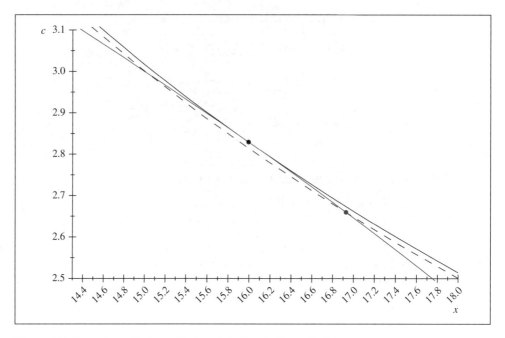

Figure 3.8 General equilibrium with tax distortion in Example 3.5

for $\tau_c = 0.20$. The wage rate paid by the firm equals the (negative of the) slope of the production function at $x = 16.93$, or $w = 0.188$. And this is higher than the (negative of the) slope of the utility level curve at $x = 16.93$, which is the marginal rate of substitution between leisure and goods, equal to the after-tax wage of $w = 0.159$. Note that the upper intersection point of the dashed black utility level curve represents the equilibrium when there is a subsidy rather than a tax on goods.

3.5 Zero government transfer

In the budget constraint when the tax revenue is transferred back to the consumer, from equation (3.51) it is true that

$$c^d = wl^s + \Pi - \tau_c c^d + G. \tag{3.75}$$

Defining the taxes paid as $\hat{T}$, where

$$\hat{T} \equiv \tau_c c^d,$$

and using that output $y = wl^s + \Pi$, then in equilibrium

$$c^d = y - \hat{T} + G. \tag{3.76}$$

So when the government transfers back the money, then $\hat{T} = G$ and

$$c^d = y.$$

There is no addition of government expenditure in this equation because the income transfer and the taxes cancel out the budget constraint.

3.5.1 $C + G = Y$

Suppose that the government does not transfer back the tax income to the consumer but rather uses it all up in some form of spending. Then there is a sense in which the output is divided between the consumer and the government. In this case, the consumer gets no transfer G so that

$$c^d = wl^s + \Pi - \tau_c c^d = y - \hat{T}. \tag{3.77}$$

Add G to each side of this budget constraint equation to get that

$$c^d + G = y - \hat{T} + G, \tag{3.78}$$

and given that $G = \hat{T}$, this becomes

$$c^d + G = y. \tag{3.79}$$

Therefore this well-known type of identity in national accounts (investment is included once that is part of the model as in Part 4) applies here only to that part of government spending that is not transferred back to the consumer as income.

3.5.2 Example 3.6

This example uses the exact same economy as in Example 3.5, except that the transfer G equals zero. The goods market equilibrium can be graphed when there is no income transfer but there are taxes and government spending. Instead of equation (3.61), we now have

$$c^d = \frac{0.5\left(24w + \frac{1}{4w}\right)}{1 + \tau_c}. \tag{3.80}$$

Solving for $\frac{1}{w}$ in terms of a quadratic, the demand function with no transfer is

$$\frac{1}{w} = \frac{(1 + \tau_c)\,8\,(c^d) - \sqrt{((1 + \tau_c)\,8)^2\,(c^d)^2 - 4\,(96)}}{2}, \tag{3.81}$$

while supply remains at

$$\frac{1}{w} = \frac{c^s}{0.5}. \tag{3.82}$$

With $\tau_c = 0.2$, a concept of the excess relative price for goods can be defined. Denoting this by $E\,(c)$ and using s and d superscripts, then the demand price $\left(\frac{1}{w}\right)^d$ of equation (3.81) minus the supply price $\left(\frac{1}{w}\right)^s$ of equation (3.64) is zero in equilibrium since the equilibrium c clears the market. This makes $E\,(c)$, from equations (3.64) and (3.81), equal to

$$E\,(c) = \left(\frac{1}{w}\right)^d - \left(\frac{1}{w}\right)^s = \frac{c}{0.5} - \frac{(1 + 0.2)\,8\,(c^d) - \sqrt{((1 + 0.2)\,8)^2\,(c)^2 - 4\,(96)}}{2} = 0. \tag{3.83}$$

Figure 3.9 graphs equations (3.83) to show that at $c = 2.5126$, $E\,(c) = 0$, which implies that the equilibrium relative price is

$$\frac{1}{w} = \frac{c^s}{0.5} = \frac{2.5126}{0.5} = 5.0252.$$

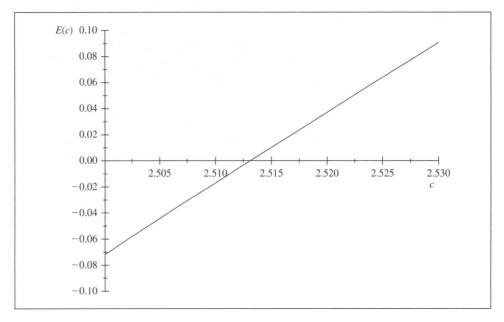

Figure 3.9 Zero excess relative price at equilibrium $c = 2.51$ in Example 3.6

If c were lower than 2.5126, then the demand price $\left(\frac{1}{w}\right)^d$ would be less than the supply price $\left(\frac{1}{w}\right)^s$, and less goods would be supplied. If c were higher than 2.5126, then the supply price would be less than the demand price and more goods would be demanded, driving up the supply price and forcing the equilibrium back towards $c = 2.5126$.

The total output is this consumption of $c = 2.5126$ plus the government spending. Since $c + G = y$, and $G = \tau_v c$, then

$$c + G = c + \tau_c c = c \left(1 + \tau_c\right) = y,$$

and if the consumption function of equation (3.80) is multiplied by $\left(1 + \tau_c\right)$, then

$$c \left(1 + \tau_c\right) = y = 0.5 \left(24w + \frac{1}{4w}\right), \tag{3.84}$$

which is the original consumption function when there is no tax and no government spending. The equivalence of the total aggregate output demand to the original consumption demand function is due to the fact that the government consumes the fraction $\tau_v = 0.2$ of output. The output is demanded by both the consumer and the government.

3.5.3 Goods market

Figure 3.10 graphs equations (3.81) and (3.82) of Example 3.6 in black, the consumer aggregate supply and demand for output when there is no government transfer, as compared to the blue aggregate demand of Example 3.5 when the taxes are transferred back in full. Aggregate supply is the same in both cases, given by the dashed blue and black line. The total output aggregate demand including the government consumption of tax revenue is given by the dashed black demand curve.

This makes it clear that when the taxes are used up with no transfer, then consumer demand is shifted back by even more than when the taxes are transferred back as income. And the additional dashed black curve then accounts for the total output demand as the

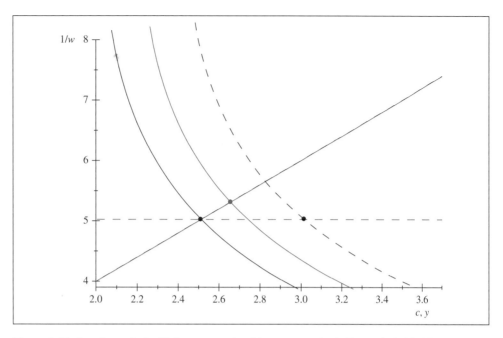

Figure 3.10 Goods market with tax on goods with zero transfer in Example 3.6 in black, with transfer of Example 3.5 in blue, and zero transfer output *y* in dashed black

government uses up the tax revenue; it also determines the relative price as the same as the zero tax price of $\frac{1}{w} = \frac{1}{0.177} = 5.65$.

With the government consuming the taxes, this amount is $G = \tau_c c^d = (0.2)(2.51226) = 0.50245$, which is given in the graph by the horizontal distance at $\frac{1}{w} = 5.0252$ (dashed blue line) between the consumer's equilibrium $c = 2.51$ and the total output aggregate demand of $y = 2.51226 + 0.50245 = 3.0147$ along the dashed black curve. This is about one-fifth of the consumption, used up in government spending G.

3.5.4 Labour market

In the labour market, if the government transfer is zero, then remembering that the firm equations are unaffected by the tax and transfer, it requires only recomputing the consumer's labour supply with $G = 0$. From equation (3.67), with $G = 0$, the labour supply and demand are

$$l^s = 12 - \frac{1}{8w^2},$$

$$w = \sqrt{\frac{1}{8(12 - l^s)}}; \tag{3.85}$$

$$w = \frac{1}{2\sqrt{l^d}}. \tag{3.86}$$

This gives the original labour supply when there was no tax and income transfer, and the same labour demand throughout. This means that labour supply is shifted out relative to when the income transfer is positive.

Figure 3.11 graphs equations (3.85) and (3.86) of Example 3.6 in the black supply and demand curves. The blue supply curve is provided for comparison, for when $\tau_c = 0.2$ and

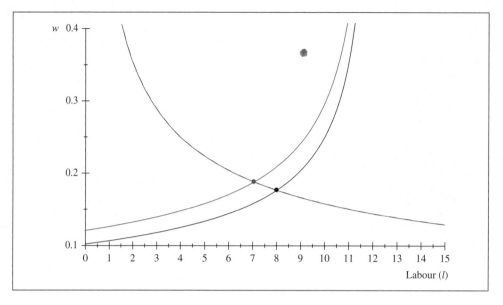

Figure 3.11 Labour market with a goods tax and zero transfer in Example 3.6

the tax revenue is fully transferred back as in Example 3.5. The demand is the same in both cases.

Figure 3.11 shows that the lack of a transfer creates a negative income effect that shifts out the supply of labour so that $l = 8$, as when there is no tax at all. In other words, the consumer works just as hard as when there is no tax, and gets the same wage as when there is no tax, but now the consumer gets less goods to consume since the government is consuming G instead of transferring it back.

3.6 Labour tax

Goods and labour taxes have very similar effects on the equilibrium. For the tax on goods, the marginal rate of substitution between goods and leisure is $\frac{\frac{\partial u}{\partial x}}{\frac{\partial u}{\partial c^d}} = \frac{w}{1+\tau_c}$. Consider if a proportional tax is put on labour income instead of on the purchase price of goods, equal to τ_l of labour income, so that the consumer receives $wl^s(1 - \tau_l)$ instead of wl^s in wages. The goods price is still just 1. The marginal rate of substitution is now

$$\frac{\frac{\partial u}{\partial x}}{\frac{\partial u}{\partial c^d}} = \frac{w\left(1 - \tau_l\right)}{1}.$$

The tax on labour income causes the same type of substitution from goods to leisure as does the tax on goods.

3.6.1 Example 3.7

Assume the same parameters as in Examples 2.5 and 3.5: $T = 24$, $\alpha = 1$, $A_G = 1$ and $\gamma = 0.5$. But now let there be a proportional tax on labour income of τ_l so that the net income for spending on consumption goods is

$$c^d = \left(1 - \tau_l\right) wl^s + \Pi + G, \tag{3.87}$$

where G is the transfer of income from the government:

$$G = \tau_l w l^s.$$

The consumer problem is

$$\text{Max}_{l^s} \ u = \ln\left[(1 - \tau_l)\, w l^s + \Pi + G\right] + \ln\left(24 - l^s\right). \tag{3.88}$$

The first-order equilibrium condition is

$$\frac{(1 - \tau_l)\, w}{(1 - \tau_l)\, w l^s + \Pi + G} - \frac{1}{24 - l^s} = 0. \tag{3.89}$$

And the labour supply is solved as

$$l^s = \frac{24 + \Pi + G}{2\,(1 - \tau_l)\, w}. \tag{3.90}$$

The firm problem is exactly the same as when the tax was on goods, and also when there was no tax at all:

$$\text{Max}_{l^d} \ \Pi = \sqrt{l^d} - w l^d. \tag{3.91}$$

The equilibrium condition is

$$0.5\left(l^d\right)^{-0.5} - w = 0; \tag{3.92}$$

the demand for labour and profit is

$$l^d = \frac{1}{4w^2}; \tag{3.93}$$

$$\Pi = \frac{1}{4w}. \tag{3.94}$$

Going back to the labour supply of equation (3.90), and substituting into the labour supply that $\Pi = \frac{1}{4w}$ and that $G = \tau_l w l^s$, the supply of labour as a function of only w is

$$l^s = 24\left(\frac{1 - \tau_l}{2 - \tau_l}\right) - \frac{1}{4w^2\,(2 - \tau_l)}. \tag{3.95}$$

Labour demand is unchanged by the tax:

$$l^d = \frac{1}{4w^2}. \tag{3.96}$$

Assume $\tau_l = 0.2$. Solved for w the supply and demand functions are

$$w = \frac{1}{2\left[\sqrt{19.2 - 1.8\,(l^s)}\right]}, \tag{3.97}$$

$$w = \frac{1}{2\sqrt{l^d}}. \tag{3.98}$$

Figure 3.12 graphs the labour market equations (3.97) and (3.98) of Example 3.7 in black, and zero tax equilibrium of Example 2.5 in blue. It shows the shift back in labour supply from the blue to the black curve while labour demand is unchanged by the tax. The shift back in the labour supply, and no change in labour demand, is very similar to when there is a goods tax and income transfer. Therefore in this economy the taxes have a similar economic effect.

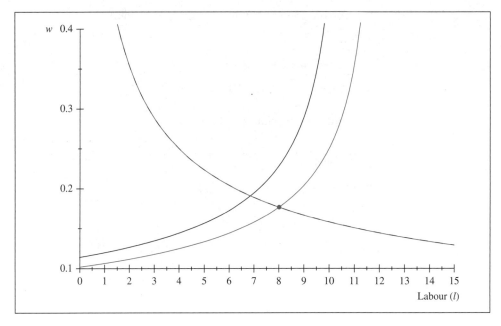

Figure 3.12 Labour market with labour tax and transfer in Example 3.7

To find the equilibrium wage quantitatively, set the supply of labour equal to the demand of

$$l^d = \frac{1}{4w^2} = 24\left(\frac{1-\tau_l}{2-\tau_l}\right) - \frac{1}{4w^2\left(2-\tau_l\right)} = l^s, \tag{3.99}$$

giving the equilibrium wage as a function of the tax rate τ_l:

$$w = \sqrt{\frac{1}{96}\left(\frac{3-\tau_l}{1-\tau_l}\right)}. \tag{3.100}$$

With $\tau_l = 0.2$, the equilibrium wage rate is $w = 0.191$. This compares to $w = 0.177$ when there is no tax. Thus the 20% tax rate causes the real wage to rise by 8%.

In the goods market, consumption goods demand is found by substituting in the labour supply function, the firm's profit and the government transfer into the consumer's budget constraint. With just the transfer of $G = \tau_l w l^s$ substituted in,

$$c^d = \left(1 - \tau_l\right) w l^s + \Pi + \tau_l w l^s,$$
$$= w l^s + \Pi.$$

And with the equilibrium l^s and Π substituted in,

$$c^d = w\left[24\left(\frac{1-\tau_l}{2-\tau_l}\right) - \frac{1}{4w^2\left(2-\tau_l\right)}\right] + \frac{1}{4w}; \quad \frac{\partial c^d}{\partial \tau_l} < 0 \text{ with } \tau_l = 0.2.$$

Therefore, just as a positive tax $\tau_l = 0.2$ shifts back labour supply, it also shifts back consumption goods demand, while leaving goods supply unchanged. Therefore the relative price of goods to leisure, $\frac{1}{w}$, falls in the goods market, and w rises in the labour market.

3.6.2 Comparison of taxes

Comparing the goods tax and the labour tax, consider that when there is a goods tax, as in the preceding section, the wage distortion to the marginal rate of substitution between goods and leisure is $\frac{1}{1+\tau_v}$, while with a labour tax this is now $\frac{1-\tau_l}{1}$. For $\tau_v = 0.2$, this distortion is $\frac{1}{1+\tau_v} = \frac{1}{1.2} = 0.833$. To have the same magnitude of the marginal distortion with the labour tax, set $\tau_l = 0.177$, so that

$$\frac{1-\tau_l}{1} = 1 - 0.177 = 0.833 = \frac{1}{1+\tau_c}.$$

Now consider that with $\tau_l = 0.177$, so that the marginal distortion is the same as a goods tax rate of $\tau_c = 0.2$, the equilibrium wage from equation (3.100) is $w = 0.189$; this 0.189 is very close to the wage rate when $\tau_c = 0.2$, and $w = 0.188$. This shows that when the marginal distortion is quantitatively the same, the goods and labour taxes are not only similar qualitatively in terms of the same type of shifts in the supply and demand curves, but also are almost identical quantitatively in terms of their impact on the economy.

3.7 Regulation and implicit taxes

Regulations work much the same way as do taxes within the analysis, with the difference being that regulations act as implicit taxes, not explicit ones. The tax revenue from an explicit tax is collected by the government, while the tax revenue from a regulation, which acts as an implicit tax, is not collected by the government. Rather these are typically called 'rents', and are equal in magnitude analytically to the amount of tax revenue that would be collected if it were an explicit tax rather than a regulation. Rather than going to the government these rents can go to anyone, such as those passing the legislation, the members of the government, or to those working to have the legislation implemented, such as the unions. And rather than being in tangible form, the rents often are just 'power' yielded to people who are involved in implementing such protective legislation.

3.7.1 Rents and corruption

Analytically, economists consider that these rents get 'used up' in this way and they are therefore not redistributed back to the agent, although some part of them may in some sense get back to the agent. For example, corruption can be thought of as the explicit payment of the rents to people involved in implementing the regulation. Therefore the analysis of regulation can be done with no explicit transfer of the rents or with some transfer of the rents.

With zero redistribution of rents, it becomes analogous to when the government transfer is zero, or $G = 0$. More generally, implicit taxes include monopoly distortions, regulations and other restrictions, and it can be that the firm instead collects the implicit tax revenue. Some part of this revenue may get paid out to others as corruption payments for getting the distortion imposed. In the representative agent model, this means the consumer may get some of the firm's corruption payments as income transfers. Or the corruption income may get paid out by the firm and 'burned up' so that no one gets the tax revenue.

Assume that the consumer has some of the rents indirectly transferred back from the firm. Denote these additional rents as Π_{cr}, for 'consumer rents'. And assume the economy as in Example 3.5, except with no government collection of the tax revenue and no government transfer. Let the implicit tax of the regulation be denoted τ and let this be an implicit tax on the purchase of goods. Therefore the consumer gets the normal profit from owning the firm, gets wage income from working, and gets the transfer Π_{cr}; the budget constraint is

$$\left(1+\tau\right) c^d = \Pi + w l^s + \Pi_{cr}.$$

The consumer problem is now:

$$\underset{l^s}{\text{Max}}\; u = \ln\left(\frac{\Pi + w l^s + \Pi_{cr}}{1+\tau}\right) + \ln(24 - l^s).$$

The solution is

$$c^d = \frac{w12 + \frac{\Pi + \Pi_{cr}}{2}}{1+\tau},$$

and

$$l^s = 12 - \left(\frac{\Pi + \Pi_{cr}}{2w}\right). \tag{3.101}$$

On the firm side, denote by Π_{fr} the rents that the firm must pay out to the consumer in return for having the implicit tax distortion imposed. In equilibrium, this is equal to some fraction $\eta \in [0, 1]$ of the total implicit tax revenue τc^s. Therefore, in equilibrium

$$\Pi_{fr} = \eta \tau c^s. \tag{3.102}$$

If there is a competitive market for the rents from the implicit tax imposition, then $\eta = 1$ and $\Pi_{cr} = \Pi_{fr}$, and all of the rents are distributed from the firm back to the consumer, just as in the case when the government was collecting the rent. However, if no rents need to be paid out, then $\eta = 0$, and this is as in the case when $G = 0$. So in general, this makes the firm problem:

$$\underset{l^d}{\text{Max}}\; \Pi = \left(1+\tau\right) c^s - w l^d - \Pi_{fr}, \tag{3.103}$$

subject to the constraint (3.102) and the production technology $c^s = \sqrt{l^d}$. Or substituting in the constraints, the firm problem is

$$\underset{l^d}{\text{Max}}\; \Pi = \left(1+\tau\right) \sqrt{l^d} - w l^d - \eta \tau \sqrt{l^d} \tag{3.104}$$

$$= \left[1 + \tau\left(1 - \eta\right)\right] \sqrt{l^d} - w l^d. \tag{3.105}$$

The equilibrium supply and demand are exactly as in the case with a tax and dole administered by the government for the case when $\eta = 1$. The smaller η is, the less is the transfer back to the consumer, and the less is the income effect that shifts back the consumer's supply of labour. But the new firm equilibrium is a bit more complicated.

3.7.2 Economics of regulation

There are therefore several cases that could be considered within the analysis:

1. Monopoly rents collected by firm and distributed back to consumer indirectly only through firm profits. Here $\eta = 0$ and $\Pi_{fr} = \Pi_{cr} = 0$ for consumer and firm so that all of the implicit tax revenue gets collected by the firm and transferred to the consumer ultimately as owner of the monopoly. The tax τ in this case is a function of the price elasticity of demand for the consumption good and represents the so-called price 'mark-up', as in standard microeconomic theory. Such a monopoly mark-up is incorporated in a class of advanced macroeconomic models through the use of an intermediate goods sector, or directly as a simple monopoly mark-up.
2. Efficient regulation whereby rents are collected by the firm and given back to the consumer through competitive payments for the rents. Here $\eta = 1$, and $\Pi_{fr} = \tau c^s = \Pi_{cr}$.

This is the same solution as with a government collecting explicit tax revenue and giving it back to the consumer, and so it reduces down to the same as an explicit tax, similar to what was studied above. Of course this case can also be called efficient 'corruption', but what is missing here in the single agent model is that corruption typically involves both the amount of the redistribution but also that different agents get different amounts of the payback.

3. Inefficient regulation whereby rents are collected by the firm and paid out by the firm, but no one gets the rents; they are burned up in the process of competing for the rents. Here for the firm, $\eta = 1$ and $\Pi_{fr} = \tau c^s$, but for the consumer $\Pi_{cr} = 0$. More generally, the rent that reaches the consumer Π_{cr} is some fraction of the rent paid out by the firm, or $\Pi_{cr} = \eta_c \Pi_{fr}$, where $\eta_c \leq 1$. Therefore η_c is the consumer's fraction of firm rents that are paid out.

3.8 Applications

3.8.1 Moral hazard

The chapter has presented an analysis of how business cycles can occur in both normal and crisis situations. Thereby it has so established how the employment rate can fall in expected ways and how unemployment in terms of surplus labour can arise, which may be rather unexpected. Giving the means by which such business cycles occur makes it easier to go on to consider what policy might be used to confront the business cycle changes in employment.

Employment changes occurring with flexible prices are predictable in some sense, and so unemployment insurance systems can be put in place to cover such loss of employment. This unemployment insurance may be sculpted into the actual private contract of employees with firms, or it may otherwise be provided by government programmes designed for this purpose. The economic analysis of such insurance is left to Part 6 of the text, in Chapter 15. The upshot is that when such employment change is expected, it is possible that it can be fully insured so that labour income is smoothed across time.

However there are problems with unemployment insurance in terms of distorting incentives to work. Rather than business cycle unemployment, such incentive distortion can cause the long term structural unemployment of those who choose to live on government benefits rather than work.

If workers can forever receive unemployment benefits, then they have less incentive to find work. This lowers the probability of getting work and this lower probability of 'being employed' causes what is called 'moral hazard'. A policy induces moral hazard when the nature of the policy causes the probability of the bad state to increase.

If the government unemployment insurance policy acts as a permanent subsidy to unemployment, it typically causes more long-term unemployment. This is widely accepted as why 'dole', or 'welfare', cultures arise. Of course, the presumption of government policy is that only a very limited form of work, or none at all, is supposed to be done when unemployed and collecting unemployment benefits. But many such people still work, but by less than if they were not collecting the benefits. Such a scenario causes the long term employment rate to be lower, and the 'official' unemployment rate to be higher.

3.8.2 Unemployment benefits as insurance

Historically, unemployment insurance systems were very strict in paying out funds to the unemployed according to how long the employee had worked, and such payouts were always for a strictly limited time. However, during the Depression of the 1930s, economists such as Nobel Laureate (1977) James Meade, in his 1937 book *Economic Analysis and Policy*, suggested that the payments from the UK's then-existing Unemployment Insurance Scheme should be made more 'generous' and without limits. The stated idea was that taxes paid in to the government during good times would approximately be balanced by government payouts during bad times. And during times of large payouts, the government insurance fund would experience deficits which would be funded by government borrowing; during good times this debt would be paid back by surpluses to the insurance fund.

A natural balancing of benefit payouts against tax intakes over the business cycle was a reasonable idea at the time, but there is a flaw in this logic that has now been understood. In particular, work incentives get distorted so that the employment rate does not return to its undistorted level. This gets insurance funds stuck in a perpetual deficit that is unfunded and that must be financed with general Treasury funding. Such a breakdown of the insurance system is thought to be likely if workers get unrestricted unemployment benefits for an unlimited time, or 'duration'.

Research has focused on the moral hazard of unlimited duration benefits, with the main finding that unemployment benefits should not be of unlimited duration, as this breaks down the insurance element of the system. The result has seen for example that the US, UK, Australia and New Zealand have all reformed their government unemployment insurance systems by instituting limited durations and other restriction on benefits, so as to try to eliminate the moral hazard problem. When this problem is eliminated, an unemployment insurance system can work exactly as insurance for the bad times of no work income, without distorting the incentive to get back to the good times of having employment.

3.8.3 Taxes and employment policy

An employment policy of a tax-financed income transfer, with the tax on either goods purchases or labour income, causes the labour supply to shift back and employment to fall. A perfect insurance system with no moral hazard in contrast would not result in such a shift back in labour supply on a permanent basis. It is the income effect of the transfer that causes the labour to shift back, and this disincentive to work would not exist with a perfect insurance system.

However benefits of all types that are permanent transfers from the government to the consumer have the same effect of shifting back the supply of labour. Thus the broader interpretation of the tax and transfer analysis is that a wide variety of programmes within a country's social welfare system can have the disincentive effect on the supply of labour.

Still, a country with a large welfare system does not necessarily have a larger disincentive to work in that it may be more efficient at eliminating moral hazard type problems. Therefore an efficient social welfare system may have less disincentive to work than a less efficient social welfare system even if the efficient one is bigger in terms of the magnitude of the taxes and the transfer. The important aspect of the benefit programme is not just its size but its efficiency in terms of not inducing moral hazard.

Zero income transfer

Of course, with $G = 0$, taxes on goods purchases and labour income still have disincentive effects even if all of the taxes are spent by the government and completely used up in the process, with zero resulting transfer to the consumer. For the goods tax, τ_c, it is shown above that if the tax proceeds are used up, then the labour market is not affected, but the goods market sees a shift back in the consumer's demand for goods. For the labour tax τ_l, if $G = 0$, it can be shown that the labour supply is shifted out as the tax rate goes up, while the goods demand is unaffected by the tax. This means that the consumer ends up working more, but gives part of the income to the government, which in effect then uses it up.

Tax reduction as policy

Reducing the tax rate on goods purchases or labour income would indeed have stimulative effects, in the opposite direction of how a tax reduces incentives, but only if the level of government spending also falls. If government spending remains at the same level, then somehow the spending must be financed. Even a temporary reduction in tax rates, designed to stimulate for example employment in the short run, must be offset by higher future taxes if the level of government spending does not change. For this reason in part, temporary reductions in tax rates are not perceived as the most efficacious way to stimulate employment. Rather long term reductions in the tax rate levels are useful but again only if the government can gradually become more efficient over time and so require less spending as a percentage of national income.

3.8.4 Regulation of airlines, oil and pollution

Many policies of economic regulation fit into the chapter's regulation analysis. For example, before airline deregulation in the 1970s, airline prices were very uniformly set and entry into the industry was limited. This increased the price of the air tickets to consumers. But some of the rents were transferred back to the consumer in terms of luxurious meal service and little crowding at airports. Once the airline industry was deregulated, competition eventually saw the entry of low cost carriers that forced down prices dramatically, thereby all but eliminating the implicit tax τ that airlines could add on to the price of tickets.

Oil policy in the US has often forced the price of oil to be below the world market price within US domestic markets by putting a ceiling on the sales price that can be charged for old oil wells in the US. This makes the tax τ equal to a negative amount so that it is in effect a subsidy for oil, and for US goods produced with oil such as large automobiles. Of course this policy put the US auto industry at a competitive disadvantage in the world market, in which other countries had to manufacture autos suited for the world oil price.

Analysing this oil regulation is difficult because it is intertwined across industries. For example, perhaps this means that the amount of rents paid out by oil firms and industries using oil is zero, rather than some positive amount. And consider the 1970s petrol rationing. In particular, when there is insufficient supply caused by the price being below the world price, then the consumer must queue, in order to get petrol at a petrol station. And in this case the transfer of rents Π_{cr} becomes as if the amount of Π_{cr} is a negative quantity, so that rents are taken away from the consumer even while paying a low price. And the amount or rents used up during rationing can be as much as the subsidy to the price of oil, so that $\Pi_{cr} = \tau c^s$, where $\tau < 0$. This is one interpretation of what happened during the US oil crisis of the 1970s when people queued at petrol stations to get petrol.

Regulations can play a role other than just the redistribution of rents; these other roles can positively add to the value of output: for example by helping to establish standards of safety, pollution and other areas in which it is difficult to enforce property rights without some regulation. In this case the effect of such policies might be seen as increasing the marginal product of labour. More generally, such productive regulation offsets a social externality that acts as an implicit tax on society. Then the externality itself is the tax in an analytic sense, and the regulation can act to decrease the magnitude of the tax or eliminate the tax altogether. Costs of such beneficial regulation do exist however, and these need to be balanced against benefits of reducing the magnitude of externalities. For example, establishing a market for trading excess industrial emissions can be a way to regulate pollution in a way that minimises the cost of the regulation itself.

3.9 Questions

1. Use comparative statics of the baseline log utility model with Cobb–Douglas production to explain business cycle changes in employment. Can this be done using only changes in A_G?

2. How do offsetting income and substitution effects from a change in A_G affect the ability to explain a business cycle?

3. What is the effect in terms of the supply and demand for goods and labour from changing the amount of time endowed to the consumer?

4. How can the time endowment be viewed in terms of the labour force participation rate?

5. Find the effect on employment if in Example 3.2 the increase in both A_G and T were by 10% instead of 5%.

6. What is the difference between an equilibrium employment level that has fallen from changes in endowments, versus an excess supply of labour at a fixed wage?

7. Let $\gamma = \frac{2}{3}$ in Example 3.1, instead of $\gamma = \frac{1}{3}$. Show that this gives a bigger change in employment, during an expansion that is generated by a 5% increase in A_G and in the time endowment T, as compared to when $\gamma = \frac{1}{3}$.

8. In Example 3.5, let the tax rate rise to $\tau_c = 0.30$, instead of $\tau_c = 0.20$. Find the equilibrium supply and demand for goods and labour, and graph the goods and labour markets, both when $\tau_c = 0.30$ and $\tau_c = 0.20$. Find the equilibrium wage rate and labour employment with $\tau_c = 0.30$.

9. How do taxes on goods and taxes on labour differ in terms of their effect on the equilibrium?

10. Compare the tax revenue from the goods tax in Example 3.5 to the tax revenue from the labour tax in Example 3.6.

11. How can economic regulation have the same effect as a labour or goods tax?

12. How can an unemployment insurance system be designed to be perfectly efficient with no ensuing shift back in the supply of labour?

3.10 References

Becker, Gary S., 1957, *The Economics of Discrimination*, The University of Chicago Press, Chicago, 2nd edition, 1971.

Harberger, Arnold C., 1974, *Taxation and Welfare*, Little Brown, Boston.

Hicks, J. R., 1937, 'Mr. Keynes and the "Classics"; A Suggested Interpretation', *Econometrica*, 5(2) (April): 147–159.

Keynes, John, M., 1936, *The General Theory of Employment, Interest, and Money*; 1964 edition, Harcourt Brace Jovanovich, New York.

Meade, James, 1937, *Economic Analysis and Policy*, 2nd edition, Oxford University Press, Oxford.

Posner, Richard A., 1973, *Economics of Law*, Little Brown, Boston; 7th edition, 2007, *Economic Analysis of Law*, Aspen.

Ricardo, David, 1817, *The Principles of Political Economy and Taxation*; 3rd edition, 1821, by John Murray, London.

Samuelson, Paul Anthony, 1951, *Economics: An Introductory Analysis*, 2nd edition, McGraw-Hill, New York.

CHAPTER ④

Trade in labour and goods markets

4.1 Introduction and summary

The chapter specifies two representative agents. They have the same utility function and are different only in terms of their labour productivity. The two-agent model is the simplest case of a heterogeneous agent model. The two agents, denoted by A and B, represent two different countries, or even cultures within a country. Initially there is only one agent of each type, A and B, but this is expanded to any number of each type. Each agent A and agent B solve their own consumer and firm problems.

The agents first exist in autarky, which means they each produce and consume independent of the other. The autarky equilibrium is found and characterised by different wage rates in each country. When trade is allowed, a new world market clearing condition is specified that results in a single world equilibrium wage rate. Trade results with the less productive agent supplying labour to the more productive agent, and receiving goods in return. Utility for each agent increases as a manifestation of the gains from trade.

The outcome of trade is that the agents specialise in what they are better in, or in their comparative advantage. The less productive agent is better in supplying labour, and so does more of this when trade opens up, while the more productive agent is better at producing goods more easily rather than supplying labour, and so works less, employs the other agent, and produces more goods.

The trade patterns are shown both in the goods and labour markets, and in the general equilibrium goods and leisure dimensions. Trade triangles are found which show the excess demand for goods and supply of labour by the less productive agent and the excess supply of goods and demand for labour by the more productive agent. With a single agent of each type, the agent's excess supply equals the other agent's excess demand within each market.

With different numbers of agents of each type, the world equilibrium wage is different, the trade triangles become altered for each agent, even though the supply and demand functions by each agent as a function of the wage are unaltered. The agent with more numbers relative to the other has a smaller trade triangle per agent, while the total excess supply for each good and labour is still equal to the total excess demand.

Examples include education, immigration restrictions and taxes. And further applications are made to trade laws and treaties, immigration waves and globalisation.

4.1.1 Building on the last chapters

Example 2.5 of Chapter 2 is expanded in Example 3.5 to include taxes in the last chapter. Now the same Examples 2.5 and 3.5 specifications are used for agent A, meaning that the resulting supply and demand functions have already been derived. The agent B specification is a modification of the agent A economy that was already specified in Chapter 2 when productivity was doubled in Example 2.6. This makes familiar the economy of each agent. The market clearing condition of this chapter is a modification of the market clearing condition used to find the real wage in the last chapter as well as in Chapter 2. The goods and labour markets now involve two supply and two demand functions that aggregate together to get the market equilibrium. And the tax application of this chapter in Example 4.6 is an extension to two agents of Example 3.5.

4.1.2 Learning objective

The aim is to see how to apply the single representative agent model to two different agents who trade goods and time rather than existing in isolation. This requires understanding the key mechanism that the real wage plays in inducing world trade, with the wage lower for the less productive agent than for the more productive agent in autarky, but then equal for both agents at an intermediate level under trade. Equilibrium excess goods and labour need to be understood now as equilibrium trade flows, as opposed to such excess that results from fixed prices as in the last chapter. It becomes important to see that under trade each agent's production function is tangent to the budget line at a different place than the utility level curve is tangent to the budget line, thereby establishing the trade flows, such as a quantity of goods supplied (firm) that is different from the quantity of goods demanded (consumer) for each agent. Visualising the trade flows in markets and in general equilibrium allows for realisation of the breadth of this paradigm for explaining long term trends such as education, globalisation and immigration.

4.1.3 Who made it happen?

Eli Heckscher, in 1919, and Bertil Ohlin (Nobel Laureate 1977), in 1933, pioneered the modern framework of trading goods using comparative advantage. They use a two-good framework that in this chapter is simplified even further to goods and leisure. Key to their analysis was a difference in factor prices in autarky, and Heckscher wrote that absolute factor price equalisation was 'an inescapable consequence of trade' when countries have similar technologies. This was extended into a full general equilibrium model by Stolper and Samuelson (1941). Then Paul A. Samuelson (1948, 1949) proved that the wage rate would be equalised across countries, in his 'factor price equalisation theorem'.

The Heckscher–Ohlin theorem is that trade patterns arise when there are different endowments of resources with the same preferences of consumers. In this chapter, the greater productivity of goods production can be thought of as a greater endowment of goods, which do indeed lead to trade arising. Stolper and Samuelson (1941) consider the effect of protectionist trade policy designed to protect workers' wages. Such an application in terms of immigration restrictions is also considered in this chapter.

4.2 Two-agent model

The same utility and production functions of Chapters 2 and 3 are assumed for both agents. The difference is that one agent will have a higher marginal product of labour by virtue of a production function that is pivoted upward compared to the other agent. These two agents can be thought of as being the representative agents of two different countries, A and B. The A and B are used as subscripts on endogenous variables to indicate each agent's equilibrium.

With no trade, or 'autarky', the real wage will be independent of the other country. There is a different equilibrium relative price in each country, with a separate market clearing condition in each country. And the world consumption is just the simple sum of goods consumption by agent A and by agent B.

4.2.1 Example 4.1: Autarky

Let the parameters of the log utility and Cobb–Douglas production function be $\alpha = 1$ and $\gamma = 0.5$, with the time endowment of $T = 24$, as in Examples 2.5 and 2.6. This makes utility for both agents,

$$u_A = \ln c_A^d + \ln \left(24 - l_A^s\right),$$
$$u_B = \ln c_B^d + \ln \left(24 - l_B^s\right).$$

Let the A agent have the production function with $A_G = 1$, as in Example 2.5:

$$c_A = \sqrt{l_A},$$

while the B agent has the higher productivity function with $A_G = 2$, as in Example 2.6:

$$c_B = 2\sqrt{l_B}.$$

The no trade, or 'autarky', equilibrium has already been derived since these specifications are the same as in Example 2.5 for A, and the same as in Example 2.6 for B. This equilibrium for A is $l_A = 8$ and $c_A = \sqrt{8}$, with a marginal product of labour equal to $w_A = \frac{0.5}{\sqrt{8}} = 0.17678$ and for B the equilibrium is given by $l_B = 8$ and $c_B = 2\sqrt{8}$, with a marginal product of labour that is twice the level of A, at $w_B = \frac{1}{\sqrt{8}} = 0.35355$.

To derive the supply and demand for goods and labour as functions of w requires setting out the consumer and firm problems. And then with free trade a single equilibrium wage can be found from the world market clearing condition.

4.3 Decentralised problems

Gains from trade are possible exactly because of the differences in autarky relative prices. With free mobility of labour, the real wage will be the same in both countries as the result of establishing a single market across both countries, through trade of goods and labour that acts to cause the marginal products of labour to converge to just one value. Market clearing means one world market clearing condition with one relative price that prevails in both countries.

Trade patterns emerge that are based in comparative advantage. And the different productivities of labour imply that the two agents get a different amount of income. This is the basis for income differentials across or among nations. Such free trade is established by laws, international agreements, and de facto by the process of evolving regional competition.

With free trade, the demand and supply functions will be the same as were derived for autarky, and they will depend on the real wage, but now the real wage will end up being one that is intermediate between the autarky wage of A and the autarky wage of B. The amount supplied and demanded will therefore end up being different, even though the supply and demand functions are the same.

The equilibrium wage is again found by setting supply equal to demand. The new world market clearing conditions sum up the supplies of both agents and set that equal to the demands. The goods clearing condition is

$$c_A^d + c_B^d = c_A^s + c_B^s; \tag{4.1}$$

and the labour market clearing condition is

$$l_A^d + l_B^d = l_A^s + l_B^s. \tag{4.2}$$

Either one can be used to find the equilibrium wage w. The equilibrium demand and supply functions follow from the consumer and firm problems for each agent.

4.3.1 Example 4.2: Autarky

First consider the economies without the world market clearing conditions, so that there is no trade. Assume the same parameters of Example 4.1: $\alpha = 1$ and $\gamma = 0.5$, $T = 24$, again as in Examples 2.5 and 2.6.

Consumer problems: agents A and B

For agent A, the utility maximisation problem is

$$\underset{c_A^d, l_A^s}{\text{Max}} \ u = \ln c_A^d + \ln \left(24 - l_A^s \right),$$

subject to

$$c_A^d = \Pi_A + w l_A^s.$$

More simply, to make the problem involve only taking the derivative with respect to labour supply, use the budget constraint to solve for c_A^d and substitute in for c_A^d in the utility function:

$$\underset{l_A^s}{\text{Max}} \ u = \ln \left(\Pi_A + w l_A^s \right) + \ln \left(24 - l_A^s \right).$$

The first-order equilibrium condition is

$$\frac{\partial L}{\partial l_A^s} = \frac{w}{\Pi_A + w l_A^s} + \frac{(-1)}{24 - l_A^s} = 0.$$

This reduces to

$$l_A^s = 12 - \frac{\Pi_A}{2w}. \tag{4.3}$$

When the profit is substituted in from the agent A firm problem's solution, then this would give the supply of labour function for agent A.

The equilibrium for goods, c_A^d, follows by substituting the equilibrium supply of labour into the budget constraint:

$$c_A^d = \Pi_A + w l_A^s = \Pi_A + w \left(12 - \frac{\Pi_A}{2w} \right) = 12w + \frac{\Pi_A}{2}. \tag{4.4}$$

For agent B, the utility maximisation problem is identical. In one unknown variable l_B^s it is

$$\underset{l_B^s}{\text{Max}} \ u = \ln \left(\Pi_B + w l_B^s \right) + \ln \left(24 - l_B^s \right).$$

The first-order equilibrium condition is

$$\frac{\partial L}{\partial l_B^s} = \frac{w}{\Pi_B + w l_B^s} + \frac{-1}{24 - l_B^s} = 0.$$

This reduces to

$$l_B^s = 12 - \frac{\Pi_B}{2w}. \tag{4.5}$$

The equilibrium goods demand c_B^d follows from substituting in l_A^s from equation (4.5) into the budget constraint:

$$c_B^d = \Pi_A + w l_A^s = \Pi_A + w \left(12 - \frac{\Pi_B}{2w} \right) = 12w + \frac{\Pi_B}{2}.$$

(4.6)

The consumer's labour supply and goods demand have the same functional form for both agents A and B. But the profit distribution to consumer A and to consumer B are different, as seen from the firm problem.

Firm problems: agents *A* and *B*

On the producer side, the profit maximisation problem for each agent A and B yields the demand for labour, the supply of goods, and the profit, all as a function of the real wage, for each agent A and B. Agent A sets profit, Π_A, equal to revenues, c_A^s, minus costs, $w n_A^d$. Then the agent maximises with respect to goods, c_A^s, and labour, l_A^d, profit subject to the production constraint. Making the problem a one-step derivative, and taking agent A first, substitute the production function into the profit function, and maximise profit with respect to labour n_A^d only:

$$\text{Max}_{l_A^d} \; \Pi_A = \sqrt{l_A^d} - w l_A^d.$$

The equilibrium condition is

$$\frac{\partial \Pi_A}{\partial l_A^d} = 0.5 \left(l_A^d \right)^{-0.5} - w = 0.$$

The solution for the demand for labour is

$$l_A^d = \frac{1}{4w^2}.$$

(4.7)

Substituting the labour demand back into the production function yields the supply of goods:

$$c_A^s = \sqrt{l_A^d} = \sqrt{\frac{1}{4w^2}} = \frac{1}{2w}.$$

(4.8)

Finally, on the producer side, total profit is

$$\Pi_A = c_A^s - w l_A^d = \frac{1}{2w} - \frac{w}{4w^2} = \frac{1}{4w}.$$

(4.9)

Similarly for each agent B, the one-step profit maximisation problem, with the higher productivity output function, $c_B^s = 2\sqrt{l_B^d}$, is

$$\text{Max}_{l_B^d} \; \Pi_B = 2\sqrt{l_B^d} - w l_B^d.$$

The equilibrium condition is

$$\frac{\partial \Pi_B}{\partial l_B^d} = \left(l_B^d \right)^{-0.5} - w = 0.$$

The solution is

$$l_B^d = \frac{1}{w^2},$$

(4.10)

$$c_B^s = 2\sqrt{l_B^d} = 2\sqrt{\frac{1}{w^2}} = \frac{2}{w},$$

(4.11)

$$\Pi_B = 2\sqrt{l_B^d} - w l_B^d = \frac{2}{w} - \frac{w}{w^2} = \frac{1}{w}.$$

(4.12)

Supply of labour, demand for goods

The supply of labour is found by substituting $\Pi_A = \frac{1}{4w}$, from equation (4.9) above, into the labour supply in equation (4.3), giving it as a function of the real wage:

$$l_A^s = 12 - \frac{1}{8w^2}. \tag{4.13}$$

For agent B, substitute in $\Pi_B = \frac{1}{w}$ from equation (4.12) above, into the labour supply in equation (4.5):

$$l_B^s = 12 - \frac{1}{2w^2}. \tag{4.14}$$

Substituting in the profit for each A and B into the consumption functions in equations (4.4) and (4.6) gives that

$$c_A^d = 12w + \frac{\Pi_A}{2} = 12w + \frac{1}{8w}, \tag{4.15}$$

and

$$c_B^d = 12w + \frac{\Pi_B}{2} = 12w + \frac{1}{2w}. \tag{4.16}$$

The supply curves for labour, and demand curves for goods, for each A and B agents, are positive functions of the real wage w: $\frac{\partial l_A^s}{\partial w} > 0$; $\frac{\partial l_B^s}{\partial w} > 0$; $\frac{\partial c_A^d}{\partial w} > 0$; $\frac{\partial c_B^d}{\partial w} > 0$. The opposite holds for the demand for labour and supply of goods: $\frac{\partial l_A^d}{\partial w} < 0$; $\frac{\partial l_B^d}{\partial w} < 0$; $\frac{\partial c_A^s}{\partial w} < 0$; $\frac{\partial c_B^s}{\partial w} < 0$.

The no-trade autarky equilibrium can be graphed in goods and labour markets using the supply and demand functions solved in terms of $\frac{1}{w}$ and w. From equations (4.7) and (4.3), (4.10) and (4.5), and (4.13) to (4.16), the inverted supply and demand equations are

$$Goods_A: \quad \frac{1}{w} = 2c_A^s, \tag{4.17}$$

$$Goods_A: \quad \frac{1}{w} = 4c^d - 4\sqrt{\left(c_A^d\right)^2 - 6}. \tag{4.18}$$

$$Labour_A: \quad w = \frac{1}{2}\sqrt{\frac{1}{l_A^d}}, \tag{4.19}$$

$$Labour_A: \quad w = \sqrt{\frac{1}{8\left(12 - l_A^s\right)}}. \tag{4.20}$$

$$Goods_B: \quad \frac{1}{w} = \frac{c_B^s}{2}, \tag{4.21}$$

$$Goods_B: \quad \frac{1}{w} = c_B^d - \sqrt{\left(c_B^d\right)^2 - 24}. \tag{4.22}$$

$$Labour_B: \quad w = \sqrt{\frac{1}{l_B^d}}, \tag{4.23}$$

$$Labour_B: \quad w = \sqrt{\frac{1}{2\left(12 - l_B^s\right)}}. \tag{4.24}$$

Note that the consumption demand for A in terms of $\frac{1}{w}$ was found in Example 2.5. For B, the consumption demand in terms of $\frac{1}{w}$ is found from a different quadratic equation in $\frac{1}{w}$:

$$c_B^d = 12w + \frac{1}{2w},$$ (4.25)

$$0 = \left(\frac{1}{w}\right)^2 - 2c_B^d \frac{1}{w} + 24 = 0.$$ (4.26)

This is again a quadratic of $A\left(\frac{1}{w}\right)^2 + B\frac{1}{w} + C = 0$, but now with $A = 1$, $B = -2c^d$, and $C = 24$. Using the general solution formula for quadratics of $\frac{1}{w} = \frac{-B-\sqrt{B^2-4AC}}{2A}$, equation (4.27) results:

$$\frac{1}{w} = \frac{2c^d - \sqrt{4\left(c^d\right)^2 - 4\left(24\right)}}{2} = c^d - \sqrt{\left(c^d\right)^2 - 24}.$$ (4.27)

Markets

Figure 4.1 graphs the goods market of equations (4.17) and (4.18) for A in black and equations (4.21) and (4.22) for B in blue. The relative price for A is the dashed black horizontal line, and the relative price for B is the dashed blue horizontal line, so that the equilibrium price $\frac{1}{w}$ is higher for A than for B, and the output is lower for A than for B.

Figure 4.2 graphs the labour market equations (4.19) and (4.20) for A in black and (4.23) and (4.24) for B in blue. The dashed black horizontal line is the wage for A, and the dashed blue horizontal line is the wage for B. Both employ 8 hours.

The general equilibrium graph is the same as in Figure 2.14, but with the interpretation that the upper utility equilibrium is that of agent B, and the lower utility equilibrium is that of A. This will be redrawn below when trade is allowed.

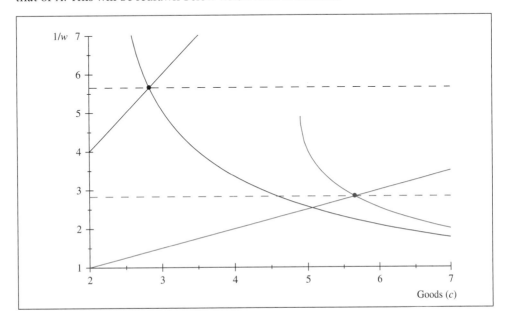

Figure 4.1 The goods market under autarky in Example 4.1 for A in black and B in blue

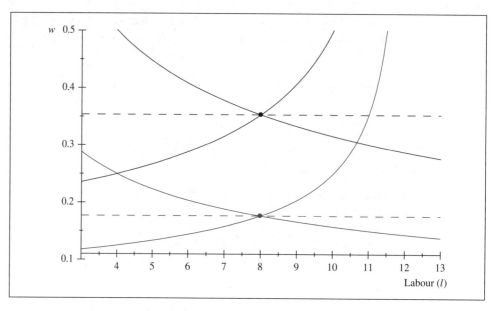

Figure 4.2 The labour market under autarky in Example 4.1 for A in black and for B in blue

4.3.2 Example 4.3: Trade

Assume the same economies for A and B as in Examples 4.1 and 4.2, except that now add in the market clearing condition that is the manifestation of allowing trade to occur in goods and labour. Bringing together supply and demand curves for labour and goods finds the equilibrium labour and goods for each agent as a function of the real wage. To find this equilibrium wage, that equates supply and demand for both agents, requires 'horizontally summing' the curves when the price is on the vertical axis of the graph and the quantity on the horizontal axis.

The full solution of the economy requires using either of the market clearing conditions of equations (4.1) and (4.2), determining the market wage rate w, and then finding all of the quantities; $c_A^d, c_B^d, c_A^s, c_B^s, l_A^d, l_B^d, l_A^s, l_B^s, \Pi_A$ and Π_B.

Using the market for labour in equation (4.2), set the total equilibrium quantity of labour supplied equal to the total equilibrium quantity of labour demanded, using equations (4.7), (4.10), (4.13), and (4.14), and solve for the real wage:

$$l^d = l_A^d + l_B^d = \frac{1}{4w^2} + \frac{1}{w^2} = 12 - \frac{1}{8w^2} + 12 - \frac{1}{2w^2} = l_A^s + l_B^s = l^s,$$

$$24 = \frac{1}{4w^2} + \frac{1}{8w^2} + \frac{1}{w^2} + \frac{1}{2w^2} = \frac{1}{w^2}\left(\frac{1}{4} + \frac{1}{8} + 1 + \frac{1}{2}\right) = \frac{15}{8}\frac{1}{w^2},$$

$$w = \sqrt{\frac{15}{8}\frac{1}{24}} = 0.2795.$$

Solving for w gives the equilibrium real wage as $w = 0.28$.

The same result is found from the goods market:

$$c_A^d + c_B^d = 12w + \frac{1}{8w} + 12w + \frac{1}{2w} = \frac{1}{2w} + \frac{2}{w} = c_A^s + c_B^s,$$

$$24w = \frac{1}{w}\left(2.5 - \frac{5}{8}\right) = \frac{1.875}{w},$$

$$w = \sqrt{\frac{1.875}{24}} = 0.2795.$$

Table 4.1 Equilibrium with free trade; $w = 0.28$

Equilibrium	Agent A	Agent B
Labour demand	$l_A^d = \dfrac{1}{4w^2} = 3.2$	$l_B^d = \dfrac{1}{w^2} = 12.8$
Labour supply	$l_A^s = 12 - \dfrac{1}{8w^2} = 10.4$	$l_B^s = 12 - \dfrac{1}{2w^2} = 5.6$
Profit	$\Pi_A = \dfrac{1}{4w} = 0.89$	$\Pi_B = \dfrac{1}{w} = 3.57$
Goods supply	$c_A^s = \dfrac{1}{2w} = 1.80$	$c_B^s = \dfrac{2}{w} = 7.14$
Goods demand	$c_A^d = 12w + \dfrac{1}{8w} = 3.80$	$c_B^d = 12w + \dfrac{1}{2w} = 5.14$
Utility	$\ln c_A^d + \ln\left(24 - l_A^s\right) = 3.95$	$\ln c_B^d + \ln\left(24 - l_B^s\right) = 4.55$

Substituting the equilibrium wage back into the supply, demand and profit functions gives all of the equilibrium variables in the economy, plus the utility levels. Table 4.1 summarises these functions and the equilibrium quantities and utility level.

4.3.3 Market for goods

The world market supply and demand for goods are found by adding separately each the goods demand, and the goods supply, and inverting each to solve for $\frac{1}{w}$ so they can be graphed. For Example 4.3,

$$c^d = c_A^d + c_B^d = 12w + \frac{1}{8w} + 12w + \frac{1}{2w} = 24w + \frac{5}{8w},$$

$$\frac{1}{w} = \frac{4}{5}c^d - \frac{4}{5}\sqrt{\left(c^d\right)^2 - 60}; \tag{4.28}$$

$$c^s = c_A^s + c_B^s = \frac{1}{2w} + \frac{2}{w} = \frac{2.5}{w},$$

$$\frac{1}{w} = \frac{c^s}{2.5}. \tag{4.29}$$

Figure 4.3 graphs the market demand and supply of equations (4.28) and (4.29) in the dashed black curves, with the country supply and demand for A and B in the solid black and blue curves respectively. The dashed blue line at $\frac{1}{w} = \frac{1}{0.27951} = 3.5777$ is the world market clearing wage equilibrium relative price.

Relative to autarky, the relative price of goods falls for agent A and rises for agent B. Agent A demands excess goods while agent B supplies excess goods. And this leads to the trade patterns. There is an excess demand for goods by agent A that exactly equals an excess supply of goods by agent B, at the equilibrium relative price.

In Figure 4.1 the excess demand is given by the horizontal difference between supply and demand curves of agent A at $\frac{1}{w} = 3.5778$, and is equal to

$$Excess\ demand_A:\ c_A^d - c_A^s = 3.80 - 1.80 = 2.0, \tag{4.30}$$

$$Excess\ supply_B:\ c_B^s - c_B^d = 7.14 - 5.14 = 2.0. \tag{4.31}$$

4.3.4 Market for labour

The market for labour is graphed by plotting the supply and demand functions for each agent, and then plotting the horizontal sum of the supplies and the sum of the demands. The separate market labour demand and labour supply functions, and their inverses in

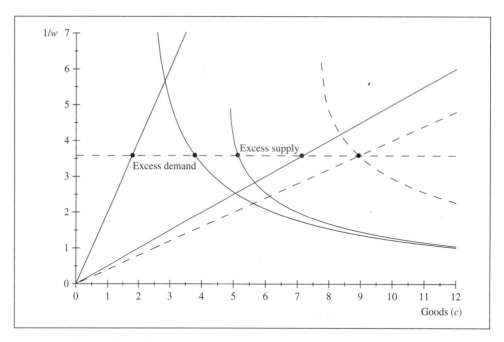

Figure 4.3 The goods market under free trade in Example 4.3

terms of w, are given for Example 4.2 by

$$l^d = l^d_A + l^d_B = \frac{1}{4w^2} + \frac{1}{w^2} = \frac{5}{4w^2},$$

$$w = \sqrt{\frac{5}{4l^d}}; \tag{4.32}$$

$$l^s = l^s_A + l^s_B = 12 - \frac{1}{8w^2} + 12 - \frac{1}{2w^2} = 24 - \frac{5}{8w^2},$$

$$w = \sqrt{\frac{5}{8\,(24 - l^s)}}. \tag{4.33}$$

Figure 4.4 graphs equations (4.32) and (4.33), in dashed black, along with the individual country supply and demand for labour, in solid black for A and in blue for B, and the world wage rate in dashed blue.

The excess supply of labour by agent A and the excess demand for labour by agent B can be seen as the horizontal difference between supply and demand at the given wage. With one agent of each type, again in the labour market the excess supply equals the excess demand:

$$\textit{Excess supply}_A: \ l^s_A - l^d_A = 10.4 - 3.2 = 7.2, \tag{4.34}$$

$$\textit{Excess demand}_B: \ l^d_B - l^s_B = 12.8 - 5.6 = 7.2. \tag{4.35}$$

Figure 4.4 shows how the real wage rises for agent A, how the quantity of labour supplied rises while the quantity demanded falls, and how these represent movements along the individual supply and demand curves. The real wage facing agent B falls, the quantity of labour supplied falls while the quantity of labour demanded rises; and these also represent movements along the individual supply and demand curves.

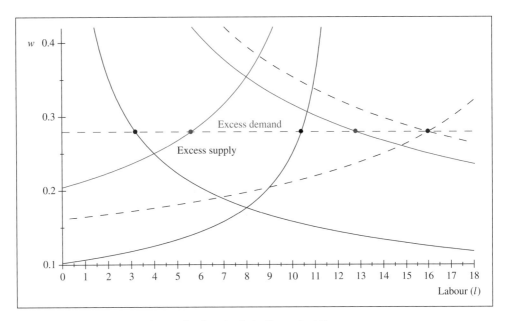

Figure 4.4 The labour market under free trade in Example 4.3

4.3.5 General equilibrium representation

The goods and labour markets can also be shown in general equilibrium, here in $(c : x)$ dimensions. Figure 4.5 graphs the free trade parallel market (consumer budget) lines, in dashed blue, with the equilibrium real wage as the slope of the market lines; the autarky lower-level utility curves, in black (A) and blue (B), and the free trade higher-level utility curves, in dotted black (A) and dashed black (B); and the production functions in black (A) and blue (B).

The lower dashed blue budget line for A is given by equation (4.36):

$$c_A^d = wl_A^s + \Pi_A,$$

$$\Pi_A = \frac{1}{4w} = \frac{1}{4(0.28)} = 0.894,$$

$$c_A^d = wl_A^s + 0.894 = (0.28)(24 - x_A) + 0.894. \tag{4.36}$$

The upper dashed blue budget line for B is given by equation (4.37):

$$c_B^d = wl_B^s + \Pi_B,$$

$$\Pi_B = \frac{1}{w} = \frac{1}{(0.28)} = 3.578,$$

$$c_B^d = wl_B^s + 3.578 = (0.28)(24 - x_B) + 3.578. \tag{4.37}$$

The production functions for A and B are

$$c_A^s = \sqrt{l_A^d} = \sqrt{(24 - x_A)},$$

$$c_B^s = 2\sqrt{l_B^d} = 2\sqrt{(24 - x_B)}.$$

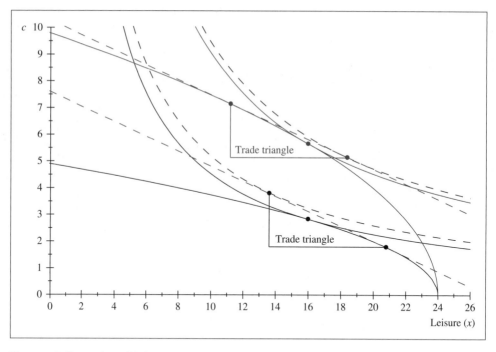

Figure 4.5 General equilibrium goods and labour markets under free trade in Example 4.3

And the Figure 4.5 lower level utility curves under autarky are given by equations (4.38) and (4.39):

$$u_A = \ln c_A^d + \ln\left(24 - l_A^s\right) = \ln 2.828 + \ln\left(24 - 8\right) = 3.8123,$$

$$c_A^d = \frac{e^{3.8123}}{24 - l_A^s} = \frac{e^{3.8123}}{x_A}; \tag{4.38}$$

$$u_B = \ln c_B^d + \ln\left(24 - l_B^s\right) = \ln 5.6569 + \ln\left(24 - 8\right) = 4.5055,$$

$$c_B^d = \frac{e^{4.5055}}{24 - l_B^s} = \frac{e^{4.5055}}{x_B}. \tag{4.39}$$

And the higher level utility curves under free trade are given by equations (4.40) and (4.41):

$$u_A = \ln c_A^d + \ln\left(24 - l_A^s\right) = \ln 3.8013 + \ln\left(24 - 10.4\right) = 3.9454,$$

$$c_A^d = \frac{e^{3.9454}}{24 - l_A^s} = \frac{e^{3.9454}}{x_A}; \tag{4.40}$$

$$u_B = \ln c_B^d + \ln\left(24 - l_B^s\right) = \ln 5.143 + \ln\left(24 - 5.6\right) = 4.55,$$

$$c_B^d = \frac{e^{4.55}}{24 - l_B^s} = \frac{e^{4.55}}{x_B}. \tag{4.41}$$

The increase in the utility level for each agent exactly equals what in trade theory is called the 'gains from trade'.

Figure 4.5 also indicates the 'trade triangles' each for A (lower black one) and for B (higher blue one). The horizontal and vertical sides of the triangles indicate the trade flows in terms of the excess demand for goods (vertical side, lower triangle), the excess supply of goods (vertical side, higher triangle), the excess supply of labour (horizontal side, lower triangle), and the excess demand for labour (horizontal side, higher triangle). These quantities of the sides of the triangles are the amounts traded, and are given in equations (4.30), (4.31), (4.34) and (4.35).

4.3.6 Trade flows

For each agent, the general equilibrium trade triangle occurs between the trade equilibrium tangency points, between where the higher trade utility curve is tangent to the market (budget) line, and the production curve is tangent to the market (profit) line. The lower productivity agent A consumes more than that produced by working part of the time as self-employed and part of the time for B ('exporting' the excess labour supply). Agent A uses the wages earned from agent B to buy more goods (importing the excess demand of goods) than those that have been self-produced. Agent B produces more than consumed, and pays for the imported labour with the excess goods (that are exported).

The gains from trade result when the two countries, or two agents in one country, rather than living in isolation (or cultural segregation), fully interact, create free trade in labour, and so establish a common price of labour w. In contrast is autarky (no trade): each consumer's labour demand equals the labour supply, each firm's goods demand equals the goods supply, and the real wage w (given by the slope of the production function) is higher for the more productive group B than the less productive group A. The wage differential represents a cost of 'segregation'. Moving to free trade, the wage differential disappears, with the wage rate rising for agent A and falling for agent B.

The gains from trade manifest as increases in utilities for each agent of group A and group B, as 'trade triangles' open up relative to the autarky equilibrium. The excess labour supply and excess goods demand comprise two sides of the triangle for agent A; the excess labour demand and excess goods supply comprise two sides of the triangle for agent B. The splitting of supply from demand, for goods and labour, for each agent A and B, creates trade and increases utility.

Ending autarky isolation (segregation) through trade induces each group to specialise in what they do best, either in goods (A) or leisure (B). Under trade, agent A increases the supply of labour, increases the consumption of goods, and decreases leisure, while agent B decreases the supply of labour, decreases the consumption of goods, and increases leisure.

Notice that agents do not even have to move in order to work for another country. Witness the so-called 'outsourcing' of jobs to India that has been enabled in the last decade due to computer technology advances. Such job centres in India perform work for international companies based in the US and UK so that the labour in India is being provided to the higher productivity country without businesses having to physically relocate to the other countries.

4.3.7 Marginal productivity theory of income distribution

The general equilibrium clarifies how the more productive agent has a higher consumption of goods and of leisure, and thus agent B has a higher income 'class' than agent A. Also agent A works for agent B and only engages in a little bit of self-production, while agent B works only on self-production and employs agent A. This reinforces the notion that this theory of two agents of different productivities who engage in trade with each other represents a theory of the income distribution amongst 'labour' and 'capitalist' classes. Of course, capital is not yet introduced in the model, but the more productive agent is similar to a capitalist in the sense that agent A works for agent B's firm.

Such a theory also provides a basis for Veblen's 'A Theory of the Leisure Class'. Veblen is associated with the 'Institutional' school of economics. But mathematically even this simple theory of trade, when applied to two different classes within a culture, produces

Veblen's observation that the higher income class takes more leisure. The difference is that here there is no negative connotation to having higher income and taking more leisure. The only 'normative' suggestion from the theory is that education may be the most important factor in equalising income across classes in that with greater education tends to come greater marginal productivity.

4.4 Multiple heterogeneous agents

The example with two types of agents, one more productive than the other, who trade in open markets presents a paradigm of the trade between lower wage developing countries and high wage developed countries. Or within a country it represents a two-class society of blue collar versus white collar workers. From this perspective, the difference between developing and developed, between labour and 'capitalists' becomes the difference in productivity.

This can be extended to include any number of each type of the agents. This allows for analysis of changes in income distribution, such as from education increases, immigration restrictions, or the tax-financed dole, as is studied below. And the only change in the mathematical analysis of the equilibrium is that the market clearing condition changes to allow for the different number of agents. The supply and demand functions for each type of agent remain the same.

4.4.1 Example 4.4: More *B* than *A*

In particular, suppose there are 400 identical *A* agents in country *A* and 600 identical *B* agents in country *B*. The aggregate goods demand of both countries c^d, equals the weighted sum of goods consumption in each country, and the aggregate supply of goods, c^s, equals the similarly weighted sum of the goods supply by each agent. With the same relation for the labour market, this gives the new market clearing conditions,

$$c^d = 400c_A^d + 600c_B^d = 400c_A^s + 600c_B^s = c^s; \qquad (4.42)$$

$$l^d = 400l_A^d + 600l_B^d = 400l_A^s + 600l_B^s = l^s; \qquad (4.43)$$

Again the object is to solve numerically for $c_A^d, c_B^d, c_A^s, c_B^s, l_A^d, l_B^d, l_A^s, l_B^s, \Pi_A$ and Π_B, and for the real wage w. To solve for the wage, consider again using the labour market. Then from equation (4.43), and using the supply and demand functions in Table 4.1,

$$400\left(\frac{1}{4w^2}\right) + 600\left(\frac{1}{w^2}\right) = 400\left(12 - \frac{1}{8w^2}\right) + 600\left(12 - \frac{1}{2w^2}\right), \qquad (4.44)$$

$$w = \sqrt{\frac{8400}{1000\,(12)\,8}} = 0.2958. \qquad (4.45)$$

Solving for the wage w in equation (4.44) gives that $w = 0.2958$.

Substituting the equilibrium wage $w = 0.2958$ back into the supply, demand and profit functions of Table 4.1 gives all of the unknown choice variables in the economy. Table 4.2 presents these results.

Note the differences between what each agent *A* sells in labour and what each agent *B* buys in labour. If there are an equal number of each agent *A* and *B*, say 500 of each, these numbers of labour sold and bought would be equal. But because of the unequal numbers of agent *A* and *B*, 400 and 600 in the example, the numbers differ. However in aggregate,

Table 4.2 Equilibrium with free trade, multiple agents; $w = 0.2958$

Equilibrium	Agent A	Agent B
Labour demand	$l_A^d = \dfrac{1}{4w^2} = 2.86$	$l_B^d = \dfrac{1}{w^2} = 11.43$
Labour supply	$l_A^s = 12 - \dfrac{1}{8w^2} = 10.57$	$l_B^s = 12 - \dfrac{1}{2w^2} = 6.29$
Profit	$\Pi_A = \dfrac{1}{4w} = 0.85$	$\Pi_B = \dfrac{1}{w} = 3.38$
Goods supply	$c_A^s = \sqrt{l_A^s} = 1.69$	$c_B^s = 2\sqrt{l_B^s} = 6.77$
Goods demand	$c_A^d = \Pi_A + w l_A^s = 3.97$	$c_B^d = \Pi_B + w l_B^s = 5.24$
Utility level	$\ln(3.97) + \ln(24 - 10.57) = 3.98$	$\ln(5.24) + \ln(24 - 6.29) = 4.53$

the labour supplied by all of the A agents to the B agents equals the labour bought by the B agents from the A agents. The total labour supplied (and demanded) equals

$$400 l_A^d + 600 l_B^d = 8000.$$

The aggregate goods consumption (and goods supplied) is

$$400 c_A^d + 600 c_B^d = 4732.$$

4.4.2 Trade flows

The excess demand is given by the horizontal difference between supply and demand curves of agent A at $w = 0.2958$, and the excess supply is the horizontal difference between supply and demand of agent B at $w = 0.2958$:

$$\text{Excess demand}_A: \quad c_A^d - c_A^s = 3.97 - 1.69 = 2.28, \tag{4.46}$$
$$\text{Excess supply}_B: \quad c_B^s - c_B^d = 6.77 - 5.25 = 1.52. \tag{4.47}$$

The total excess demand for goods equals the total excess supply of goods:

$$400 \left(c_A^d - c_A^s \right) = 400 \left(2.2819 \right) = 912.8,$$
$$600 \left(c_B^s - c_B^d \right) = 600 \left(1.5214 \right) = 912.8.$$

The excess labour supply and demand by A and B are

$$\text{Excess supply}_A: \quad l_A^s - l_A^d = 10.57 - 2.86 = 7.71, \tag{4.48}$$
$$\text{Excess demand}_B: \quad l_B^d - l_B^s = 11.43 - 6.29 = 5.14. \tag{4.49}$$

The total excess demand for labour equals the total excess supply of labour:

$$600 \left(l_B^d - l_B^s \right) = 600 \left(5.1433 \right) = 3086;$$
$$400 \left(l_A^s - l_A^d \right) = 400 \left(7.7142 \right) = 3086.$$

Using the last row of Table 4.2, utility level curves for graphing in $(c : x)$ dimensions are given by

$$c_A^d = \frac{e^{3.98}}{24 - l_A^s} = \frac{e^{3.98}}{x_A}; \tag{4.50}$$

$$c_B^d = \frac{e^{4.53}}{24 - l_B^s} = \frac{e^{4.53}}{x_B}. \tag{4.51}$$

The budget constraint for agent A is

$$c_A^d = wl_A^s + \Pi_A,$$

$$\Pi_A = \frac{1}{4w} = \frac{1}{4(0.2958)} = 0.84517,$$

$$c_A^d = wl_A^s + 0.84517 = (0.2958)(24 - x_A) + 0.84517. \qquad (4.52)$$

The budget line for B is

$$c_B^d = wl_B^s + \Pi_B,$$

$$\Pi_B = \frac{1}{w} = \frac{1}{(0.2958)} = 3.3807,$$

$$c_B^d = wl_B^s + 3.3807 = (0.2958)(24 - x_B) + 3.3807. \qquad (4.53)$$

Figure 4.6 graphs the utility level curves and budget lines under trade of equations (4.50), (4.51), (4.52) and (4.53) for agents A and B as in Figure 4.5. Also drawn are the production functions and autarky equilibrium of Example 4.3; this is unchanged here. The trade triangles are indicated to show the trade flows of equations (4.46), (4.47), (4.48) and (4.49).

With trade, the goods distribution finds A agents consuming less than B agents, and with lower utility levels for each A as compared to each B. But as compared to autarky with no trade, the equilibrium with trade shows that per capita consumption of group A rises from 2.83 to 3.97, while working time rises, and each A utility level rises from 3.8 to 3.98. Per capita consumption for group B falls from 5.66 to 5.23, but leisure rises from 16 to 17.71, so that utility rises from 4.51 to 4.53. Notice that while everyone gains, the lower productivity class experiences the larger percentage increase in utility. And further, the per capita consumption of goods difference between the groups narrows. This means the 'income gap', measured through goods consumption, is less.

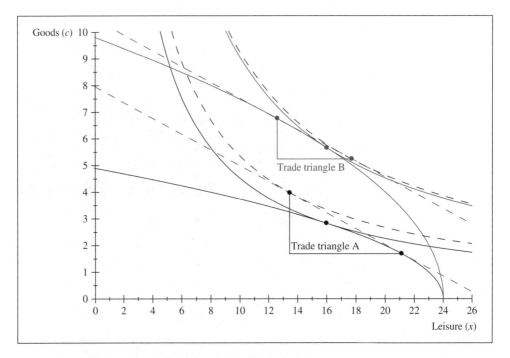

Figure 4.6 Multiple agents under free trade in Example 4.4

Several differences are apparent in Figure 4.6 as compared to Figure 4.5. The blue trade triangle of agent B is smaller than the black trade triangle of agent A. This is because there are 600 of B and only 400 of A. The total excess supply and demand of goods is equal as is the total excess supply and demand of labour. Also the increase in utility from trade, the 'gains from trade', are higher for agent A than for B, as seen by the bigger shift up in utility for A than for B. This is because the smaller number of agent A each have a larger trade triangle and so a bigger increase in utility per agent, while the larger number of agent B each have a smaller trade triangle and so a smaller increase in utility per agent.

4.5 Changes in the distribution of income

The distribution of income can be changed in numerous ways, which can end up increasing or decreasing barriers between different countries or socio-economic groups within a country. World trade policies or domestic government policies can alter the market equilibrium so as to move closer towards free trade or to put up additional barriers to trade. And in this sense such policies can be either 'proactive' or 'defensive', if in effect they either decrease or increase barriers, or discrimination, amongst countries or cultural groups. And policies can increase or decrease the total amount of goods to be distributed in the process of inducing a redistribution.

4.5.1 Example 4.5: Education increase

An increase in education results in a redistribution of income for agents engaged in trade. This can be seen within a specific example economy. Such an experiment can be conducted with little change in the equilibrium conditions given certain assumptions. In particular, it will be assumed that some agents become more productive without any additional cost to the economy.

Taking the Example 4.4 specification of 400 A agents and 600 B agents, with A agents having the production function $c = \sqrt{l}$ and B agents having the production function $c = 2\sqrt{l}$, suppose now that 100 of the 400 A agents obtain education (at no cost) that raises their productivity level to that of the B agents. Then of the 1000 agents, only 300 are now of group A and 700 are now of group B.

The change in the mix of agents leaves unchanged all of the first-order conditions that give the supply and demand for goods and labour by each agent. Only the labour market clearing condition, that determines the real wage, needs recomputation. The market clearing equation (4.44) now becomes

$$300\left(\frac{1}{4w^2}\right) + 700\left(\frac{1}{2w^2}\right) = 300\left(12 - \frac{1}{8w^2}\right) + 700\left(12 - \frac{1}{2w^2}\right).$$

Solving for the equilibrium wage, it is $w = 0.31$, which is higher than $w = 0.30$ when there is a 400/600 mix of agents. Similarly individual consumption for each agent, c_A^d and c_B^d, as well as aggregate consumption,

$$c^d = 300c_A^d + 700c_B^d$$

can be computed, using Tables 4.1 or 4.2. Individual consumption of each agent rises, to $c_A^d = 4.12$, and $c_B^d = 5.33$, while aggregate consumption rises to 4969.

The trade triangles change in a way similar to Example 4.4 compared to Example 4.3. In Example 4.3, with one agent A and one agent B, this is the same for the equilibrium wage as if there were 500 of A and 500 of B. And so in Example 4.4, going from one of each agent to 400/600, is similar to going from 500/500 of A/B to 400/600 of A/B. In Example 4.4, the trade triangle shrinks for agent B and gets bigger for A. This also happens here in Example 4.5 compared to Examples 4.3 and 4.4. The trade triangle further shrinks for each agent B and gets bigger for each agent A.

However it is true that the actual utility level for each B decreases, even though consumption for each B increases. For A, the transformation of the 100 agents not only raises the consumption of each of these 100, but also that of the remaining 300 A agents. Consequently for income distribution, in terms of goods consumption, are that the percentage increase in consumption for each A agent is 3.8%, while the percentage increase for the B agent is 1.669%, so that the income gap between the two groups actually narrows.

One important qualification is that the cost of the education, which here is assumed to be zero, would decrease these consumption increases, in a way that depends on how the costs are recouped. Assuming the cost is borne equally by all agents, and that it was not so high as to offset all the gains, then rising consumption results, and the narrowing distribution of income would be maintained.

Such an education policy here would be classified as proactive, barrier lowering, or discrimination decreasing, in that aggregate consumption rises, each individual consumption rises, and the income gap between groups narrows. Welfare wise, a weighting of utilities by agent numbers shows a total utility gain, but B agents are each worse off. This welfare difference suggests why more productive groups may not favour expanding education levels of less productive classes or countries.

4.5.2 Example 4.6: Immigration restrictions

Consider another example of redistributive policy that is more of the defensive type rather than the proactive type: immigration restrictions. Suppose that from the original 400/600 mix of A/B agents, 100 of the A agents are either precluded from entering the country or are deported because of an illegal alien status, leaving a 300/600 mix in one country and 100 of agent A in the other. To see the change in the real wage, consumption and the distribution of income requires a similar analysis to the previous education example.

The labour market clearing condition for the country with the 300/600 mix becomes

$$300 \left(\frac{1}{4w^2} \right) + 600 \left(\frac{1}{w^2} \right) = 300 \left(12 - \frac{1}{8w^2} \right) + 600 \left(12 - \frac{1}{2w^2} \right)$$

and the real wage rises from $w = 0.2958$ with a 400/600 mix to $w = 0.3062$ for the 300/600 mix. The wage increase raises per capita consumption by 2.8% and 1.5%, to 4.08 and 5.31, respectively for each agent of group A and B. Such real wage and consumption increases may explain why unions support immigration restrictions.

However, aggregate consumption of the 300/600 falls to 4409 from 4732, a 6.8% decrease. Also, if enforcement of the immigration law requires a bureaucracy and policing, then the associated costs, just as there would be costs of education, make the decrease in aggregate consumption even greater. So-called positive 'spillover' effects from more people are also decreased with the restrictions.

The focus on the $300 + 600 = 900$ remaining citizens only tells a part of the total economic story. The barred 100 A agents still exist, although elsewhere. Continuing to assume there are only 1000 agents, then the excluded 100 would have to exist in 'autarky', in a no-trade environment, where they produce and consume their output. These 100 work 8 hours, $l^* = 8$, and consume 2.83, $c^* = \sqrt{8}$; their real wage equals their marginal product of labour, $0.5 \, (l^*)^{-0.5} = 0.177$.

Now accounting for all 1000 of the agents once again, the average real wage, weighted by agent numbers across the entire two-country region, is $900(0.3062) + 100(0.177) = 0.2932$, a decline from the wage level of $w = 0.2958$ when there was an integrated 400/600 mix. The average per capita consumption of the 400 A agents, $[(300 \cdot 4.08) + (100 \cdot 2.83)]/ 400 = 3.76$, also a decline from 3.97 for 400 A agents within the 400/600 integrated mix. And aggregate consumption for the entire 1000 agents, which equals $100(2.83) + 300(4.08) + 600(5.31) = 4693$, declines from 4732 in the integrated economy. Such immigration restrictions, or any policy that partitions off separate groups, in this example economy reduces average wages, consumption and average utility levels.

Trade triangles for each class are affected. As in Example 4.5, real wages in the restricting country also rise. The less productive class finds each labourer induced into working more, with a growing trade triangle, while the more productive class each works less, with a shrinking trade triangle.

A broader policy analysis emerges: keeping countries or groups separated reduces utility. Globally, a policy of restricting trade reduces welfare for these reasons. Domestically, such a policy may be one that establishes a 'welfare' system that induces particular groups to live in separate housing, shop at separate stores, and go to separate schools. Despite the stated motives, such policies are 'defensive', discriminatory and segregating.

4.6 Taxes and two classes of agents

The policy of income redistribution through a tax-financed income transfer was analysed in a single representative agent context in Section 2.6. This showed how the labour supply and goods demand were shifted back by the tax and transfer policy. The same type of result also holds when two agents are specified, with a tax on one agent and a transfer to the other agent. But now the shift in labour supply and goods demand is seen when the aggregate labour supply and goods demand involves summing the supply and demand of two agents. And with two agents there is an income redistribution within the heterogeneous agent case that does not exist in the single representative agent.

4.6.1 Example 4.7: Tax both and transfer to A

Consider Example 3.5, in which there is a goods tax, and income transfer of the tax revenue, with a single representative agent in combination with Example 4.4 in which there are 400 A and 600 B. And now consider that the tax revenue is transferred back only to the 400 of agent A, and none to the 600 B. The transfer to the A agents is financed by a value-added tax, τ_c, on goods purchases, by both A and B agents. Therefore this is an income redistribution policy, sometimes called a 'welfare system'.

Expenditure now equals $(1 + \tau_c) c_A^d$ instead of c_A^d, and $(1 + \tau_c) c_B^d$ instead of c_B^d, because of the tax. Income for the A agents increases by the income transfer G, for each A agent, while each B gets no transfer. This makes the budget constraints:

$$(1 + \tau_c) c_A^d = \Pi_A + w l_A^s + G,$$
$$(1 + \tau_c) c_B^d = \Pi_B + w l_B^s,$$

while the government budget constraint requires that the G payments to each of the 400 A agents equals the tax revenues from all 1000 agents:

$$400G = \tau_c 400 c_A^d + \tau_c 600 c_B^d. \tag{4.54}$$

The tax and transfer leaves unchanged the firm demand for labour, as a function of the real wage, for each A and B agent. The supply of labour for B also remains the same function as when there is no tax and transfer. However the labour supply curve for agent A is shifted back by the income transfer:

$$l_A^s = 12 - \frac{1}{8w^2} - \frac{G}{2w}.$$

This shifts back each agent A's supply curve of labour, shifts back the aggregate labour supply curve, and forces up the real wage.

Solving for the real wage now involves not only the labour market clearing condition,

$$400\left(\frac{1}{4w^2}\right) + 600\left(\frac{1}{w^2}\right) = 400\left(12 - \frac{1}{8w^2} - \frac{G}{2w}\right) + 600\left(12 - \frac{1}{2w^2}\right), \qquad (4.55)$$

but also the government budget constraint. Substituting in for consumption, c_A^d and c_B^d, the government budget constraint in equation (4.54) reduces down to an equation in the unknowns G, w, and τ_c:

$$G = \tau_c\left[\frac{1}{4w} + \frac{1.5}{w} + w\left(12 - \frac{1}{8w^2}\right) + (1.5)w\left(12 - \frac{1}{2w^2}\right)\right]. \qquad (4.56)$$

With a 12.5% value-added tax, for example (New Zealand), set $\tau_c = 0.125$. Then the two equations (4.55) and (4.56) are in the two unknowns, G and w, and they imply that $w = 0.3077$, and $G = 1.42$. Writing w for any tax rate, by solving the two equations (4.55) and (4.56) for w as a function of τ_c, gives that

$$w = \sqrt{\left(\frac{7}{2.5}\right)\frac{(3 + 2\tau_c)}{96}}.$$

This shows that the higher the tax, the higher the real wage. As the transfer rises, so does the tax, by the government budget constraint, and so does the real wage. This is the same type of result as found with just one representative agent, in Example 3.5.

The rise in the real wage, rather than being due to a productivity increase on market segregation, as in the education or immigration restriction examples, is due instead to the tax 'wedge'. The average price for labour paid by producers goes up, while the average real wage received after taxes goes down. The real wage increase is for the 'gross', 'before-tax', wage.

A reflection of the 'after-tax' wage going down is seen in the decrease in aggregate consumption. This is found by computing the individual consumption of goods, $c_A = 4.27$ and $c_B = 4.73$, and weighting them to get an aggregate: $c^d = 400(4.27) + 600(4.73) = 4546$. This aggregate consumption is down from 4732 when the tax rate is zero. The resulting goods distribution finds A agents gaining 7.1% from 3.97 to 4.27 per capita but B agents losing 10% from 5.24 to 4.73 per capita. The income transfer accomplishes a redistribution from B agents to A agents at the cost of lower average consumption. To the extent that A agents are effectively prohibited from working, as some unemployment compensation schemes demand, the average consumption would be even lower.

4.6.2 As an unemployment/welfare system

The income transfer as described here subsidises unemployment, if the A agents in the example are those who declare themselves to be unemployed and so receive the transfer as a result. A less permanent transfer for unemployment, with more 'insurance' features, would subsidise unemployment less and act more to smooth income across different uncertain states of nature.

Perhaps the main problem with the income transfer is that, if work restrictions are enforced, it can create an underclass, 'depreciate' the agents' 'human capital' and segregate classes of people within a society. People on welfare often still work, but generally do so in the underground, or even criminal, economy so as to maintain their benefits. In this vein, the transfer can increase barriers, and discriminate amongst people, especially against those receiving it. A permanent, long term, transfer stands as a defensive policy that lowers aggregate consumption, in order to achieve a redistribution that may have limited justification.

4.7 Applications

Goods and labour are traded pervasively across national boundaries. In Canada and Mexico, many workers and their earnings freely move back and forth from the United States, as aided by the North American Free Trade Agreement. So also for countries of the European Union and other regions. Formal laws or free trade agreements greatly facilitate such movement of resources.

4.7.1 UK's Magna Carta 1297, Australia's ASEAN FTA 2009 and globalisation

The Magna Carta (Great Charter) of 1297 remains part of the statutory law of England and Wales. Consisting of 39 clauses, number 9 provides for the free movement of goods in all ports and cities of Britain:

> The city of London and ... all other Cities, Boroughs, Towns, and the Barons of the Five Ports, and all other Ports, shall have all their liberties and free customs.

This established free trade within Britain. And it included free trade with all those entering Britain to conduct trade, by clause 30:

> All Merchants ... shall have their safe and sure Conduct to depart out of England, to come into England, to tarry in, and go through England, as well by Land as by Water, to buy and sell without any manner of evil Tolts, by the old and rightful Customs, except in Time of War.

At the same time, free trade of ideas was established in clause 1, by allowing freedom of the Church, while due process of law for individuals was guaranteed by clause 29.

The establishment of an internal market with the free trade of goods and labour was put into law when the English King signed the Magna Carta. It enabled specialisation of labour that led to the rise of the Medieval Craft Guilds. This was a prominent feature of the establishment of a British labour market, with apprentices and journeymen, the latter being day labourers who received a wage, while the former were acting more as unpaid trainees. Masters were at the top as the experienced, or skilled, labour. As in our analysis, the Guild labour divisions can be thought of as the less skilled workers with lower productivity and the more skilled with higher productivity.

The Magna Carta is often cited as the basis for the US Constitution as well, and the freedom of trade is a crucial part of this constitutional development. Establishing free trade agreements (FTAs) has continued to this day. Regional trade agreements are now the most common form of these taking place. The North Atlantic FTA of 1994 joined the markets of the US, Canada and Mexico. The European Union started as a free trade agreement in coal, became the EU in 1993 with the Maastricht Treaty, and now has established a single internal market amongst 27 EU nations with few restrictions on labour movement.

Australia signed an FTA in February 2009 with the Association of South-East Asian Nations (ASEAN) group of nations to establish free trade over time in more than 90% of the goods traded in the region. This shows that FTAs continue to be established in order to foster greater inter-regional competition, with the result of causing greater integration of markets internationally, and of creating the manifestation of what is called 'globalisation'.

4.7.2 Immigration waves and rural–urban migration

The first large labour movement in Europe after the demise of the Soviet Union, and the fall of the Berlin Wall that separated East from West Berlin, was from East Germany to West Germany as Germany became once again a unified nation. In this sense Germany opened up free trade in labour and goods within their internal market. With more productive technology in Western Germany, people were happy to be able to finally go from East to West Germany and earn higher incomes and have a better lifestyle. This raised income levels across Germany on average but there were many problems with the decline of the East German infrastructure and manufacturing that were addressed through many years of subsidies aimed at rebuilding East Germany.

Allowing the Eastern European workers into the UK, starting in 2004 with the new EU Accession Treaty, has allowed not only the trade of goods but also much greater immigration. This creates a force that puts downward pressure on the real wage and allows greater gains from trade. When the UK economy entered recession after the bank crisis of 2008, the UK wage rate fell for these workers and many went back to Eastern Europe. As the EU expands eastwards, and as more countries allow for immigration from the new EU countries, as Switzerland recently did, the labour market becomes more integrated with the result of a tendency towards greater wages equalisation across the region.

Several countries were largely populated by immigration waves, such as the UK, US, Australia and New Zealand. And this resulted despite some countries having, in effect, 'White-only' policies of immigration such as in the Australasian countries of Australia and New Zealand up until the 1960s. Such restrictions were eliminated gradually until now Asians are the biggest immigrant group to both of these nations. This helps to integrate Australasia within the Asia economy, adding a huge dimension to its historical reliance on US and European trade.

Similarly, one of the greatest events of modern society is the mass migration from rural areas into cities. As the education and productivity of people rise, they seek out higher wages that are available in the cities. As China, for example, opens up towards having free trade with the world economy, wages rise in the cities and workers move from rural areas to urban areas. At the same time more productive technology is adopted in the agriculture sector so that less workers are necessary in order to produce an even higher amount of produce. Therefore a massive influx into China's cities is now occurring. This happens in nearly every country at some point in its history as the economy develops and becomes more open to trade. For the US, agricultural rural labour was at one time 50% of the labour supply while now its stands as low as 3%.

4.8 Questions

1. If two groups of representative consumers have the same utility function, depending on goods and leisure, but different marginal products of labour, then
   (a) profit maximisation determines each group's demand for labour;
   (b) utility maximisation determines each group's demand for goods;
   (c) the real wage depends on each group's supply of labour;
   (d) all of the above.

2. To find the equilibrium distribution of income between two groups of economic agents, with identical utility functions of goods and leisure, but with different goods production functions that depend only on time, should we
   (a) for each group, maximise the utility subject to the budget constraint, to find the demand for goods and leisure;
   (b) for each group, maximise profit subject to the production technology to find the demand for labour;
   (c) set the total quantity of labour supplied equal to the total quantity of labour demanded to find the real wage;
   (d) all of the above.

3. With two groups of consumers, each with the same utility function of goods and leisure but one more productive than the other, living in autarky means that
    (a) utility levels are higher for each individual compared to free trade;
    (b) goods produced by each individual are the goods consumed by each individual;
    (c) trade of labour between groups takes place;
    (d) all of the above.
4. Deducing from an economy that consumes only goods and leisure and produces goods with only labour time, a net inflow of labour, through migration from South Pacific islands to Auckland, implies
    (a) a higher real wage in Auckland than in the islands;
    (b) an export of labour from Auckland to the islands;
    (c) a lower consumption per capita in Auckland than in the islands;
    (d) all of the above.
5. In a representative consumer economy with free trade, and with two groups of consumers that have identical utility functions of goods and leisure but different productivities of labour, an increase in education of the less productive group increases that group's productivity of labour. This also causes
    (a) the economy's real wage to increase;
    (b) the economy's average per capita consumption to decrease;
    (c) the quantity of labour supplied to decrease;
    (d) all of the above.
6. An income transfer to one agent that is financed by a value-added tax on consumption goods purchases of both agents, as in Example 4.7, causes
    (a) the aggregate demand for labour to shift out;
    (b) the aggregate supply of goods to shift out;
    (c) the aggregate supply of labour to shift back;
    (d) all of the above.
7. True, false, uncertain; explain. Public education increases utility levels because it raises the real wage.
8. Indicate how two classes of entrepreneurs generally divide their equilibrium working time l^s and output c^s, if they all have utility from goods c^d and work l^s, equal to $\ln c^d + \ln(24 - l^s)$, and if class A has the production function $c_A^s = \sqrt{l_A^d}$, and class B has the technology $c_B^s = 2\sqrt{l_B^d}$.
9. For the income distribution between two groups of people, A and B, with identical utility functions, $\ln(c) + \ln(24 - l)$, and with production functions $c_A^s = \sqrt{l_A^d}$, and $c_B^s = 2\sqrt{l_B^d}$, respectively,
    (a) indicate who consumes more, and indicate the income source for the consumption of each person in group A and B.
    (b) Do you think this model explains differences in income classes within nations? Why or why not?
    (c) How would you as reformer best close the gap in consumption?
10. Modify Example 4.3 by assuming that agent B has the production function $c_B^s = 3\sqrt{l_B}$ instead of $c_B^s = 2\sqrt{l_B}$. Find the equilibrium wage rate in the world economy under trade. Then find the quantities of the trade flows.
11. For Example 4.7, assume instead that the goods tax falls only on purchases of the agent B, while the tax revenue transfer continues to go only to agent A. Find the new equilibrium wage, and the supply and demand functions for each agent A and B. Find the aggregate supply and demand functions, and graph them. Describe how the tax and the income transfer shift the supply and demand functions.
12. Assume a regional economy that is composed of a country restricting immigration and a country with a number of prospective immigrants that are prohibited from immigrating to the other country. How do immigration restrictions affect the average real wage and average consumption of this regional economy and within each country?

13. Explain a possible rationale for the now current policy in several countries of allowing into the country only those immigrants who have some combination of high skills or high income. This is sometimes called a points system of immigration qualification. How does the country's social welfare system relate to the decision of who to allow into the country? What are the advantages of allowing in low skilled workers?

4.9 References

Heckscher, E., 1919, 'The Effect of Foreign Trade on the Distribution of Income', *Ekonomisk Tidskriff,* pp. 497–512. Translated as chapter 13 in *American Economic Association, Readings in the Theory of International Trade,* Philadelphia: Blakiston, 1949, pp. 272–300.

Jones, Ronald W., 2008, 'Heckscher–Ohlin Trade Theory', *The New Palgrave Dictionary of Economics,* 2nd edition, Steven N. Durlauf and Lawrence E. Blume (editors), Palgrave Macmillan.

Ohlin, B., 1933, *Interregional and International Trade,* Harvard University Press, Cambridge.

Samuelson, P., 1953, 'Prices of factors and goods in general equilibrium', *Review of Economic Studies,* 21: 1–20.

Samuelson, P., 1971, 'Ohlin was Right', *Swedish Journal of Economics,* 73: 365–384.

Stolper, W. and P. Samuelson, 1941, 'Protection and Real Wages', *Review of Economic Studies,* 9: 58–73.

PART 3

CAPITAL AND GOODS MARKETS

CHAPTER 5

Savings and investment

5.1 Introduction

5.1.1 Summary

Goods output can be thought of as being divided between consumption and savings. And the savings then goes to firms which use it for investment. In this way the consumer subtracts capital from what could be consumed today in order to yield more consumption in the next period. And this then defines the composition of the capital market.

For the consumer and firm this capital is thought of as capital savings and capital investment respectively, and this is what makes for the capital supply and capital demand. This chapter examines the investment–savings decision within the general equilibrium when there are only two periods, the current and next period, and the initial output is given exogenously. There is consumption in the current period and in the next period, and a decision of how much to save and invest only in the current period. All capital gets used up in the production process, so in the next period the goods consumption is equal to the output produced using the capital.

This intertemporal problem has the result that the consumer can smooth consumption across time through capital usage. Labour is assumed to be fixed at 1 so that the focus is only on the savings–investment decision. First the savings–investment decision is presented in the centralised general equilibrium for the representative agent. Then the problem is decentralised into consumer and firm problems to bring out the explicit price, the interest rate for capital r. The budget constraints for the consumer for each of the two periods are shown equivalently in the form of a wealth constraint. And then the chapter sets out the demand and supply within capital and goods markets, and the general equilibrium with both of these markets, with comparative statics and applications.

5.1.2 Building on the last chapters

The last chapter finished Part 2 on labour theory and intratemporal substitution between goods and leisure. This chapter applies the same tools of Part 2 now to capital theory and the intertemporal substitution between goods over two periods of time. Instead of the goods–leisure choice, there is now the choice between consumption today and consumption tomorrow. It is a two-dimensional problem just as was the goods–leisure choice.

The mathematical form of the consumer's budget constraints in this chapter's savings–investment analysis is almost identical to the mathematical form of the consumer's budget constraint in Part 2. In Part 2 there is an allocation of time constraint, with a given time endowment. In this chapter there is an allocation of goods between consumption and investment with a given goods/income endowment. The second constraint on the consumer's consumption is also very similar to Part 2. In Part 2 the constraint is that consumption equals labour wage income plus profits. In this chapter the constraint is that consumption equals capital savings income plus profit.

Separating the problem into its consumer and firm components allows the savings and investment behaviour to be shown as a function of the marginal product of capital, while in Part 2 the relevant margin is the marginal product of labour. The consumer problem is analogous to the labour theory of Chapter 2, with utility maximisation subject to the budget constraint, and the firm maximisation of profit subject to the production function. The consumer constraints and the firm's profit are the same 'market line' similar to the labour theory, although now the market line is different.

5.1.3 Learning objective

The student conceptualises how capital is saved and invested in order to increase consumption in the next period. This comprises the key step of intertemporal consumption smoothing, seen both in the centralised general equilibrium and decentralised into separate consumer and firm problems. The focus is on understanding the intertemporal consumption margin in a simple framework so that this margin can be understood in later chapters when both labour–leisure and savings–investment decisions are made simultaneously. This margin is key to determining the growth rate of the economy.

5.1.4 Who made it happen?

The history of the theory of capital use for savings and investment goes back to Adam Smith's *Wealth of Nations* (1776). The division of output into current consumption and capital used to create output in the future is discussed in his Book 2, Chapter 1 'Of the Division of Stock':

> *The general stock of any country … naturally divides itself into … that portion which is reserved for immediate consumption, and … fixed capital…and circulating capital … that … affords a revenue or profit.*

In the late 1800s, capital theory began to take shape mathematically. Eugen Bohm-Bawerk's 1888 *The Positive Theory of Capital* describes capital as something instrumental to producing output, and Irving Fisher's work, such as his 1896 *Appreciation and Interest*, 1907 *The Rate of Interest* and 1930 *Theory of Interest*, showed first the general equilibrium intertemporal optimisation problem, using two periods of time. Frank P. Ramsey's 1928 article 'A Mathematical Theory of Saving' presented the modern general equilibrium theory of capital accumulation, over all future time. Fisher's 1930 *Theory of Interest* builds on this by more fully developing the consumer and the producer sides of the problem with utility level curves tangent to the production function at the optimum. Knut Wicksell's (1901) *Lectures on Political Economy* makes capital a factor used in the production of current output, along with labour as the other input.

Thus the development of capital theory turned away from early emphasis on land, labour and capital as factors of production to just labour and capital. Within this framework, the 1950s and 1960s saw the marginal productivity theory of capital directed towards savings and investment as the means to smooth consumption optimally over time. Milton Friedman's 1957 *Theory of the Consumption Function* presented the permanent income hypothesis of consumption whereby the consumer plans consumption on the basis of the perceived permanent income stream. Friedman used the two-period intertemporal margin to present his ideas, as did Irving Fisher. This focus on the intertemporal margin and the permanent income remains a foundation of current savings theory. Extended over time dynamically, this consumption–savings theory was used by economists such as Robert Solow (1956) to explain economic growth in a way that is still the standard today.

5.2 Representative agent intertemporal economy

Now the representative agent maximises utility subject to the production function whereby capital is the current period input and goods for consumption is the second period output. Here the only given is the endowment of income in the current period, denoted by y_0. And this is divided into current consumption, denoted by c_0, and capital investment, denoted by k_1. This gives an allocation of goods constraint, instead of an allocation of time constraint in Part 2 on labour decisions.

Note that here it is assumed that capital gets fully used up in the production process. This assumption makes the two-period analysis somewhat simpler to present. This assumption is relaxed, so that there is still some of the capital left at the end of the period, starting in Part 4, which extends forward the number of time periods over which the savings and investment take place. An alternative assumption of zero depreciation is presented in the Appendix A5 to show that this gives a solution that is too complex for presentational purposes.

The representative agent's utility function depends on consumption of goods this period c_0, and consumption of goods next period, denoted by c_1:

$$u \equiv u\left(c_0, c_1\right). \tag{5.1}$$

The given current period supply of goods y_0 is divided between goods consumption today and investment of capital (for goods consumption tomorrow):

$$y_0 = c_0 + k_1.$$

Production possibilities allow the transformation of capital into higher income tomorrow. The capital used for this transformation is k_1. With next period's supply of goods denoted y_1, the production function is

$$y_1 = f\left(k_1\right).$$

Because this is a limited two-period problem, there is investment only in period 0. Further, the capital depreciates fully and so the only goods available for consumption in period 1 are those produced in the production function. Therefore the next period consumption of goods, c_1, equals the supply of goods y_1:

$$c_1 = y_1.$$

Given y_0 as exogenously known, the agent's problem is to maximise utility with respect to goods consumption, investment and next period output, or c_0, c_1, k_1 and y_1,

$$\operatorname*{Max}_{c_0, c_1, k_1, y_1} u\left(c_0, c_1\right)$$

subject to goods and production constraints:

$$y_0 = c_0 + k_1;$$
$$y_1 = f\left(k_1\right);$$
$$c_1 = y_1.$$

The problem can be reduced to a problem in any one of the variables, for example k_1, by substituting the constraints back into the utility function. To do this, use the constraints to write current period consumption as

$$c_0 = y_0 - k_1,$$

and next period consumption as

$$c_1 = f\left(k_1\right).$$

Then the one-step problem is

$$\underset{k_1}{\text{Max}} \; u\left[y_0 - k_1, f\left(k_1\right)\right].$$

Taking the derivative of $u\left(c_0, c_1\right)$ with respect to k_1 (by the 'chain rule'), and setting the derivative equal to zero yields the equilibrium condition from which to solve for k_1:

$$\frac{\partial u\left(c_0, c_1\right)}{\partial c_0} \frac{\partial \left(y_0 - k_1\right)}{\partial k_1} + \frac{\partial u\left(c_0, c_1\right)}{\partial c_1} \frac{\partial \left[f\left(k_1\right)\right]}{\partial k_1} = 0.$$

Rearranging algebraically gives the well-known tangency condition

$$\frac{\partial f\left(k_1\right)}{\partial k_1} = \frac{\frac{\partial u\left(c_0, c_1\right)}{\partial c_0}}{\frac{\partial u\left(c_0, c_1\right)}{\partial c_1}}. \tag{5.2}$$

This says that the marginal product of capital, $MP_k \equiv \frac{\partial f\left(k_1\right)}{\partial k_1}$, equals the marginal rate of substitution between current and future consumption, $MRS_{c_0,c_1} \equiv \frac{\frac{\partial u\left(c_0,c_1\right)}{\partial c_0}}{\frac{\partial u\left(c_0,c_1\right)}{\partial c_1}}$:

$$MP_k \equiv \frac{\partial f\left(k_1\right)}{\partial k_1} = \frac{\frac{\partial u\left(c_0,c_1\right)}{\partial c_0}}{\frac{\partial u\left(c_0,c_1\right)}{\partial c_1}} \equiv MRS_{c_0,c_1}.$$

5.2.1 Log utility and Cobb–Douglas production

Suppose the utility function with the natural log function is

$$u = \ln c_0 + \beta \ln c_1,$$

where β is a parameter of 'time preference'. This parameter indicates how much future consumption is discounted relative to current consumption; with perfect patience this parameter equals one and the agent does not discount future consumption at all. An agent that cares less about goods consumed next period, than those consumed today, has $\beta < 1$. With this log utility function (and using that $\frac{\partial \ln z}{\partial x} = \frac{\partial z / \partial x}{z}$, the marginal rate of substitution between c_0 and c_1 is

$$MRS_{c_0,c_1} \equiv \frac{\frac{\partial \ln c_0}{\partial c_0}}{\beta \frac{\partial \ln c_1}{\partial c_1}} = \frac{\frac{1}{c_0}}{\frac{\beta}{c_1}},$$

so that the rate of time preference is explicit rather than buried within the general utility function of equation (5.1). The explicit role of the time discount β is standard.

With a Cobb–Douglas production function, with t subscripts indicating the time period, assume

$$y_t = A_G l_t^{\gamma} k_t^{1-\gamma},$$

where $\gamma \in \left(0, 1\right)$ is the same Cobb–Douglas parameter as in Part 2 of the text. But now the labour supply is assumed to be inelastically supplied at $l_t = 1$, and production occurs only at time $t = 1$, so that

$$y_1 = A_G k_1^{1-\gamma},$$

and equation (5.2) becomes

$$A_G \left(1 - \gamma\right) k_1^{-\gamma} = \frac{\partial f}{\partial k_1} = \frac{\frac{\partial u(c_0, c_1)}{\partial c_0}}{\beta \frac{\partial u(c_0, c_1)}{\partial c_1}} = \frac{\frac{1}{c_0}}{\frac{\beta}{c_1}}. \tag{5.3}$$

5.2.2 Example 5.1

A particular specification of the utility and production function is now given by assuming values of the parameters, the procedure known as calibrating the model so that it can fit certain facts. The aim here will be a simple one: to calibrate the model so that consumption shows a reasonable growth rate over time, of around 2.5%.

Assume that $\beta = 0.98$, $\gamma = 0.5$, and $A_G = 12$. Then the problem is to maximise utility,

$$u = \ln c_0 + \left(0.98\right) \ln c_1, \tag{5.4}$$

subject to the constraints of

$$c_1 = y_1 = 12\sqrt{k_1}.$$

And assume that $y_0 = 100$, so that the goods constraint is

$$100 = c_0 + k_1.$$

Substituting for c_0 and c_1 in terms of k_1, by using the constraints, the simple one-step problem is to maximise

$$\underset{k_1}{\text{Max}}\, u\left(c_0, c_1\right) = \ln\left(100 - k_1\right) + \left(0.98\right) \ln\left(12\sqrt{k_1}\right).$$

The equilibrium condition is

$$\frac{\partial u\left(c_0, c_1\right)}{\partial k_1} = 0; \tag{5.5}$$

$$-\frac{1}{100 - k_1} + \frac{\left(0.98\right)\left(0.5\right) 12 k_1^{-0.5}}{12 k_1^{0.5}} = 0. \tag{5.6}$$

Solving algebraically equation (5.5) for k_1 gives that

$$k_1 = \frac{\left(98\right)\left(0.5\right)}{1 + \left(0.98\right)\left(0.5\right)} = 32.886. \tag{5.7}$$

Substituting the solution for k_1 into the constraints implies that

$$c_1 = 12\sqrt{32.886} = 68.816, \tag{5.8}$$

and

$$c_0 = 100 - 32.886 = 67.114. \tag{5.9}$$

5.2.3 Growth and welfare

Having calculated the consumption over time, the growth rate of consumption can be directly computed. Define the growth rate g using the ratio of consumption:

$$1 + g = \frac{c_1}{c_0} = \frac{68.82}{67.11} = 1.0255,$$

the growth rate is $g = 0.0255$, or about 2.55%. This value is close to the target value of a 2.5% growth rate of consumption.

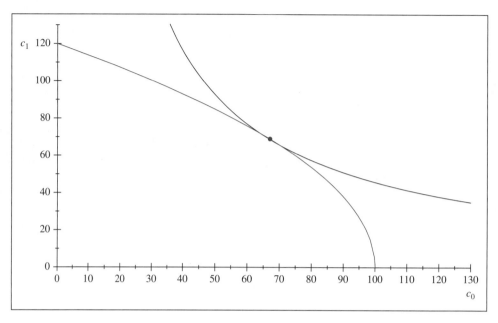

Figure 5.1 Intertemporal consumption and investment in Example 5.1

The welfare of the agent is given by the utility level. Utility at the equilibrium is given by

$$u = \ln 67.114 + (0.98) \ln (68.816) = 8.3532. \tag{5.10}$$

5.2.4 Graphically

In this example, the investment process allows a smoothing of consumption, with a little more consumed next period, 68.82, than in the current period, 67.11. Figure 5.1 graphs the equilibrium in $(c_0 : c_1)$ space, with the utility level curve in black and the production function in blue. To graph the utility level curve at the equilibrium, from equation (5.10), c_1 is solved as a function of c_0, giving that

$$c_1 = \left(\frac{e^u}{c_0}\right)^{\frac{1}{\beta}} = \left(\frac{e^{8.3532}}{c_0}\right)^{\frac{1}{0.98}}. \tag{5.11}$$

And the production function is graphed as

$$c_1 = 12\sqrt{k_1} = 12\sqrt{100 - c_0}. \tag{5.12}$$

5.3 Productivity change

Suppose that the marginal product of capital doubles for every level of k_1. This happens when the production function parameter A_G doubles in its parameterised value. Then the production function pivots up, the slope becomes steeper for every k_1, and the equilibrium level of utility rises.

5.3.1 Example 5.2

Assume the same parameterisation as in Example 5.1, of $\beta = 0.98$, $\gamma = 0.5$, and $A_G = 12$, and then let the capital productivity double by increasing A_G from 12 to 24. Then the production function of Example 5.1 changes from $y_1 = 12\sqrt{k_1}$ to $y_1 = 24\sqrt{k_1}$. The problem now is

$$\underset{k_1}{\mathrm{Max}}\, u = \ln\left(100 - k_1\right) + (0.98)\ln\left(24\sqrt{k_1}\right).$$

The equilibrium condition is equivalent to equation (5.5), since the term 24 drops out:

$$-\frac{1}{100 - k_1} + \frac{(0.98)(0.5)\,24k_1^{-0.5}}{24k_1^{0.5}} = 0. \tag{5.13}$$

So the solution for capital k_1 is the same:

$$k_1 = \frac{(98)(0.5)}{1 + (0.98)(0.5)} = 32.89.$$

But the next period consumption doubles:

$$c_1 = 24\sqrt{32.89} = 137.64.$$

Current consumption remains at

$$c_0 = 100 - 32.89 = 67.11.$$

And utility now rises to

$$u = \ln 67.11 + (0.98)\ln\left(137.64\right) = 9.03.$$

Figure 5.2 graphs the new equilibrium in dashed black and dashed blue with the original equilibrium again in black and blue. The equation for the new equilibrium utility level curve is given by

$$c_1 = \left(\frac{e^u}{c_0}\right)^{\frac{1}{\beta}} = \left(\frac{e^{9.03}}{c_0}\right)^{\frac{1}{0.98}}. \tag{5.14}$$

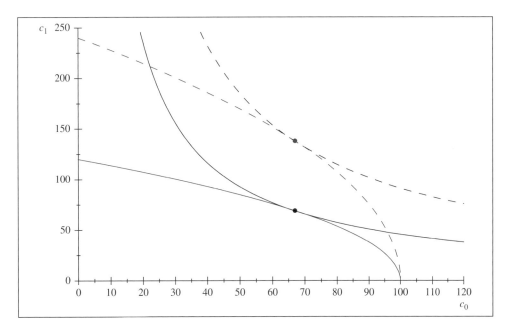

Figure 5.2 Intertemporal consumption with doubling of productivity in Example 5.2

And the production function is graphed as

$$c_1 = 24\sqrt{\left(100 - c_0\right)}.$$

The substitution and income effects of the capital productivity increase offset each other and leave capital investment unchanged; but next period consumption rises.

5.3.2 Substitution and income effects

The change in equilibrium from the productivity increase decomposes into substitution and income effects. Figure 5.3 shows the substitution effect as the change in the production function from the lower dashed blue curve to the black curve, with both tangent to the dashed black utility level curve; the utility level is the same but the relative price has increased as evident in the steeper slope of the black curve tangency point with the dashed black utility curve as compared to the original equilibrium tangency point. Then the shift upwards from the black substitution curve to the final blue production function is the positive income effect, which keeps the relative price at the tangency points the same while letting utility increase.

Figure 5.3 shows that when the slope of the production function gets steeper, while the utility level remains the same, then the consumer substitutes towards more future consumption c_1 and less current consumption c_0. With current consumption down, and income y_0 the same, then investment goes up.

The income effect shows how both current consumption c_0 and future consumption c_1 increase when utility increases. The positive income effect on both c_0 and c_1 follows since both are 'normal' goods, meaning that consumption increases with a positive income effect. Because current consumption rises, and endowed income is fixed at y_0, the income effect acts to push investment down. With the substitution effect increasing and the income effect decreasing investment, the net effect is indeterminate a priori. In Example 5.2, the effects offset each other exactly. And this exact offset is true with any log utility and Cobb–Douglas production combination.

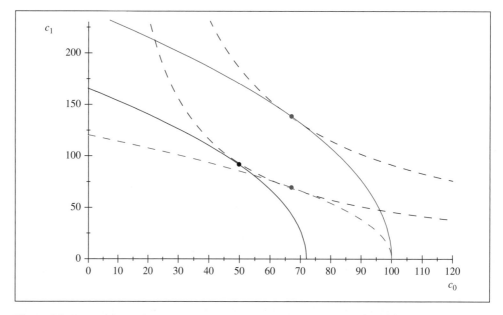

Figure 5.3 Substitution effect from doubling of capital productivity in Example 5.2

5.4 Consumer and firm problems

Implicit in the representative agent general equilibrium is that the slope of the tangency point between utility and the production function represents the market interest rate on capital. This is brought out explicitly by decentralising the problem into consumer and firm problems. Only through an implicit freely determined interest rate can the capital market reach its undistorted equilibrium. And this interest rate is made explicit by decentralising the problem into consumer and goods producer problems.

Denote the real rental rate of interest on capital by r. The consumer rents the savings to the firm to use as investment at the rate r. In addition, the economy needs to use up the capital at the end of the second period, since it is a two-period problem and any left-over capital would be a waste. Here this happens automatically since the capital is consumed in full in the production process, given its 100% depreciation rate. Therefore the total cost of capital that the firm incurs and must repay the consumer is not only the rental rate r but also the capital itself, so that the gross interest rate on capital is $1 + r$. Total amount of capital to be repaid is $(1 + r) k_1$.

Notationally, the consumer's supply of capital, which is also the consumer savings, is denoted by k_1^s. The firm's demand for capital, or investment, is denoted by k_1^d. For the consumer's demand for current and next period consumption, similar notation will be used, of c_0^d and c_1^d. And the firm's supply of next period consumption is c_1^s, which is equal to firm output y_1. Current period output is again given exogenously at y_0. Market clearing implies that

$$k_1^s = k_1^d, \tag{5.15}$$
$$c_1^d = c_1^s = y_1.$$

With the same natural log utility function,

$$u = \ln c_0^d + \beta \ln c_1^d,$$

we state the current period goods constraint as consumption being equal to endowed income minus capital investment:

$$c_0^d = y_0 - k_1^s. \tag{5.16}$$

Next period consumption expenditures are set equal to income. The income comes in two forms. Profit from the firm is distributed to the consumer, since the consumer owns the firm; denote this profit as Π_1. Also the consumer lends, or rents, capital savings to the firm, earning an interest rate r per unit of capital. And since the capital gets used up in production, with a depreciation rate of 100%, the consumer must also be compensated for the quantity of the capital that is lent. The rental income is then $r k_1^s$ and the quantity of capital received back is k_1^s, making the rest of the income, besides profit, equal to $k_1^s (1 + r)$. The budget constraint is

$$c_1^d = \Pi_1 + k_1^s (1 + r). \tag{5.17}$$

Note that these two budget constraints for each period can be combined to give a single 'wealth constraint' over time. Dividing the constraint in equation (5.17) through $1 + r$, solving the current period constraint in equation (5.16) for k_1^s and substituting with this into equation (5.17), gives a wealth form:

$$\frac{c_1^d}{1 + r} = \frac{\Pi_1}{1 + r} + k_1^s;$$
$$k_1^s = y_0 - c_0^d;$$
$$c_0^d + \frac{c_1^d}{1 + r} = y_0 + \frac{\Pi_1}{1 + r}.$$

The 'present discounted sum' of the consumption stream is equal to the present discounted sum of the income stream, where Π_1 is the next period income. Denoting these values of wealth by W, the wealth constraint is

$$W \equiv y_0 + \frac{\Pi_1}{1+r} = c_0^d + \frac{c_1^d}{1+r}. \tag{5.18}$$

Thus the consumer problem could be written either using the two constraints for each period, or just the single wealth constraint. These are equivalent approaches. Here the two constraints for each period will still be used.

The consumer problem can be written as

$$\underset{c_0, c_1, k_1^s}{\text{Max}} \ u = \ln c_0^d + \beta \ln c_1^d$$

subject to

$$c_0^d = y_0 - k_1^s, \tag{5.19}$$

and

$$c_1^d = \Pi_1 + k_1^s \left(1 + r\right). \tag{5.20}$$

Or substituting the constraints into the utility function, the one-step problem in just one unknown, k_1^s, is

$$\underset{k_1^s}{\text{Max}} \ u = \ln \left(y_0 - k_1^s\right) + \beta \ln \left[\Pi_1 + \left(1 + r\right) k_1^s\right].$$

Differentiating with respect to k_1^s and setting the derivative equal to zero, yields the equilibrium condition:

$$\frac{\beta \left(1 + r\right)}{\Pi_1 + k_1^s \left(1 + r\right)} - \left(\frac{1}{y_0 - k_1^s}\right) = 0.$$

The supply of capital can now be solved as a function of the interest rate r, the endowment y_0, and the profit Π_1:

$$k_1^s = \frac{y_0 \beta}{1 + \beta} - \frac{\Pi_1}{\left(1 + \beta\right) \left(1 + r\right)}. \tag{5.21}$$

The firm problem is to maximise profit in the next period, Π_1, where the revenues are next period's output, $c^s = y_1 = f\left(k_1^d\right)$, and costs are the costs of capital equal to the quantity of capital borrowed, k_1^d, that must be paid back, and the interest on the capital, rk_1^d. It is assumed that there is no leisure time, and that all labour is supplied inelastically to the firm, so that the focus is on the savings–investment decisions. This means that profit will be a positive amount that can be viewed as a return to the fixed labour factor. The consumer owns the firm and receives this profit.

Putting the revenues and capital cost of production together into the profit function, the firm problem is to maximise profit with respect to the capital stock,

$$\underset{k_1^d}{\text{Max}} \ \Pi_1 = y_1 - \left(1 + r\right) k_1^d,$$

subject to the Cobb–Douglas production function,

$$y_1 = f\left(k_1^d\right) = A_G \left(k_1^d\right)^{1-\gamma}.$$

The one-step problem, with the constraint substituted into the profit function, is

$$\text{Max } \Pi_1 = A_G \left(k_1^d \right)^{1-\gamma} - \left(1 + r \right) k_1^d. \tag{5.22}$$
$$k_1^d$$

Differentiating with respect to k_1^d and setting the derivative to zero, gives that the marginal product of capital, denoted by $MP_k \equiv \frac{\partial f\left(k_1^d \right)}{\partial k_1^d}$, is equal to $1 + r$:

$$\frac{\partial f\left(k_1^d \right)}{\partial k_1^d} = \left(1 - \gamma \right) A_G \left(k_1^d \right)^{-\gamma} = 1 + r. \tag{5.23}$$

5.4.1 Example 5.3

Let the production function be parameterised as in Example 5.1, with $A_G = 12$, and $\gamma = 0.5$, so that

$$y_1 = 12 \left(k_1^d \right)^{0.5};$$

also assume that $y_0 = 100$ and $\beta = 0.98$ on the consumer side.

The equilibrium condition in equation (5.23) implies that

$$\left(0.5 \right) 12 \left(k_1^d \right)^{-0.5} = 1 + r. \tag{5.24}$$

And the interpretation of this condition is that the marginal product of capital is equal to the gross interest rate (net is r, and gross is $1 + r$). The marginal product can be written as $\frac{(0.5)12}{(k_1^d)^{0.5}}$, and in this way it is clear that as the capital investment goes up, the marginal product goes down, implying what is called a 'diminishing marginal product' of capital. It means that as the capital stock goes up, the rental rate on capital r goes down.

The equilibrium condition (5.24) can be written by solving for the capital investment, so as to give the capital demand function:

$$k_1^d = \frac{36}{\left(1 + r \right)^2}. \tag{5.25}$$

Substituting for $k_1^d = 36/(1+r)^2$ and $f\left(k_1^d \right) = 12\sqrt{k_1^d}$ into the profit function in equation (5.22) gives the equilibrium profit:

$$\Pi_1 = 12 \sqrt{\frac{36}{\left(1 + r \right)^2}} - \frac{36 \left(1 + r \right)}{\left(1 + r \right)^2} = \frac{36}{1 + r}. \tag{5.26}$$

And substituting in the equilibrium demand for capital into the production function gives the equilibrium supply of period 1 output:

$$y_1 = 12 \sqrt{\frac{36}{\left(1 + r \right)^2}} = \frac{72}{1 + r}. \tag{5.27}$$

This gives the firm's demand for capital and supply of goods, both as decreasing functions of the real interest rate r. In equations (5.25) and (5.27), $\frac{\partial k_1^d}{\partial r} < 0$, and $\frac{\partial y_1}{\partial r} < 0$. When the rental cost of capital is higher, the capital demand and output supply are lower.

Finding the equilibrium interest rate requires employing a market clearing condition, either in the capital market or in the goods market. To use the capital market, the consumer's supply of capital must be solved as a function of only the interest rate r and the exogenous parameters, and then this supply is set equal to the firm's demand for capital.

The consumer's supply of capital can be found as a function of r by substituting into the consumer supply in equation (5.21) for the profit Π_1, from the firm problem in equation (5.26):

$$k_1^s = \frac{y_0 \beta}{1 + \beta} - \frac{\Pi_1}{(1 + \beta)(1 + r)} = \frac{y_0 \beta}{1 + \beta} - \left(\frac{1}{1 + \beta}\right) \frac{36}{(1 + r)^2}. \qquad (5.28)$$

Use the firm's demand for capital in equation (5.25), the supply of capital in equation (5.28), and the market clearing condition of equation (5.15), to present one equation in the real interest rate r:

$$k_1^d = \frac{36}{(1 + r)^2} = \frac{y_0 \beta}{1 + \beta} - \left(\frac{1}{1 + \beta}\right) \frac{36}{(1 + r)^2} = k_1^s. \qquad (5.29)$$

Solving for r,

$$r = \sqrt{\frac{36(2 + \beta)}{y_0 \beta}} - 1. \qquad (5.30)$$

With $y_0 = 100$ and $\beta = 0.98$, the solution for r is

$$r = \sqrt{\frac{36(2.98)}{98}} - 1 = 0.0463. \qquad (5.31)$$

The market interest rate 4.63%.

The rest of the equilibrium is given by substituting the equilibrium r into the variables that are dependent on r:

$$k_1^d = \frac{36}{(1 + r)^2} = \frac{36}{(1.0463)^2} = 32.89;$$

$$k_1^s = \frac{98}{1.98} - \left(\frac{1}{1.98}\right) \frac{36}{(1 + r)^2},$$

$$= \frac{98}{1.98} - \left(\frac{1}{1.98}\right) \frac{36}{(1.0463)^2} = 32.89.$$

$$y_1 = \frac{72}{1 + r} = \frac{72}{1.0463} = 68.81. \qquad (5.32)$$

$$\Pi_1 = \frac{36}{1 + r} = \frac{36}{1.0463} = 34.41. \qquad (5.33)$$

$$c_0^d = 100 - k_1^s = 67.12. \qquad (5.34)$$

$$y_1 = c_1^d = \Pi_1 + k_1^s(1 + r), \qquad (5.35)$$

$$= 34.41 + 32.88(1.0463) = 68.81. \qquad (5.36)$$

The growth rate of consumption is

$$1 + g = \frac{c_1}{c_0} = \frac{68.82}{67.11} = 1.0255,$$

and the utility level in equilibrium is

$$u = \ln 67.12 + 0.98 \ln 68.81 = 8.35.$$

These decentralised equilibria are the same as in the centralised representative agent problem above in Example 5.1.

Also, the equilibrium amount of investment and savings is 32.88, out of a total given initial income of 100. Therefore it is immediate that the rate of savings is 32.88/100, or 33%.

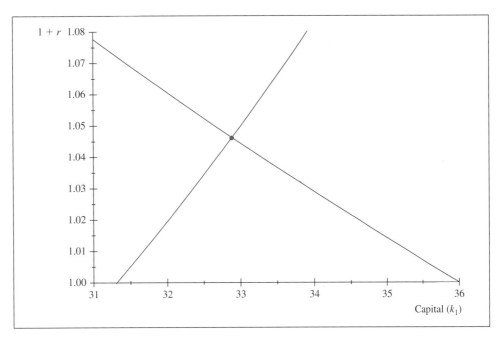

Figure 5.4 Savings and investment: aggregate supply and demand for capital in Example 5.3

5.4.2 Capital market

For Example 5.3, from the capital supply and demand of equations (5.25) and (5.28), the interest rate can be solved for and graphed. Figure 5.4 graphs the inverse demand equation of

$$1 + r = \frac{6}{\left(k_1^d\right)^{0.5}}, \tag{5.37}$$

and the inverse supply equation of

$$1 + r = \frac{6}{\left(y_0\beta - (1 + \beta) k_1^s\right)^{0.5}}. \tag{5.38}$$

Demand for capital is downward-sloping and supply is upward-sloping, with the equilibrium of $1 + r = 1.0463$ and $k_1 = 32.88$, when $y_0 = 100$ and $\beta = 0.98$.

5.4.3 Goods market

The consumer demand for goods consumption in the current period can also be graphed. The demand is given by substituting for k_1^s in equation (7.20), using equation (5.28):

$$c_0 = y_0 - k_1^s = 100 - \left(\frac{100\,(0.98)}{1.98} - \frac{\left(\frac{1}{1.98}\right)36}{(1 + r)^2}\right), \tag{5.39}$$

$$c_0 = 50.51 + \frac{18.18}{(1 + r)^2}. \tag{5.40}$$

This shows that as the interest rate rises, the consumer consumes less (and saves more). It is a residual of the supply of savings. Here the price of current consumption is $1 + r$.

The next period consumption is demanded by the consumer, through c_1 in equation (5.20), and supplied by the firm, through y_1 as in the production function. Taking the demand first, rewrite equation (5.20) with the profit and supply of capital substituted in from equations (5.26) and (5.28):

$$c_1^d = \Pi_1 + k_1^s (1+r),$$ (5.41)

$$c_1^d = \frac{36}{1+r} + \left(\frac{100 (0.98)}{1.98} - \frac{\left(\frac{1}{1.98} \right) 36}{(1+r)^2} \right) (1+r),$$

$$c_1^d = 49.49 (1+r) + \frac{17.82}{1+r}.$$ (5.42)

The supply function for output is given by equation (5.27) as

$$c_1^s = y_1 = \frac{72}{1+r}.$$ (5.43)

At $1+r = 1.0463$, in equilibrium by equations (5.39) and (5.43), $c_1 = y_1 = 68.81$, $c_0 = 67.12$, so that there is somewhat more consumption in the second period than in the first, which gives a smoothing of consumption intertemporally; the utility level is $u = \ln 67.12 + (0.98) \ln 68.81 = 8.35$.

To graph the supply and demand for c_1 in the typical way with the relative price on the vertical axis, the equations need to be inverted by solving them for $\frac{1}{1+r}$, the relative price. For demand,

$$c_1^d = 49.49 (1+r) + \frac{17.82}{1+r} = \frac{49.49}{\left(\frac{1}{1+r} \right)} + 17.82 \left(\frac{1}{1+r} \right)$$

$$0 = 17.82 \left(\frac{1}{1+r} \right)^2 - c_1^d \left(\frac{1}{1+r} \right) + 49.49.$$ (5.44)

Solving for $\frac{1}{1+r}$ from equation (5.44) requires using the quadratic solution to the equation $A \left(\frac{1}{1+r} \right)^2 + B \left(\frac{1}{1+r} \right) + C = 0$, with $A = 17.82$, $B = -c_1^d$, and $C = 49.49$. This solution is given by

$$\frac{1}{1+r} = \frac{-B - \sqrt{B^2 - 4AC}}{2A} = \frac{c_1^d - \sqrt{\left(c_1^d \right)^2 - 4 (17.82) (49.49)}}{2 (17.82)}.$$ (5.45)

The inverted supply equation is

$$\frac{1}{1+r} = \frac{c_1^s}{72}.$$ (5.46)

Figure 5.5 graphs the demand and supply for goods consumed next period in equations (5.45) and (5.46). The price of the future consumption is described as the relative price of future to current consumption, or the ratio $\frac{1}{1+r}$, with demand downward sloping and supply upward sloping. The relative price is less than one, at $\frac{1}{1+r} = \frac{1}{1.0463} = 0.956$.

5.4.4 General equilibrium

The equilibrium in the capital market and the goods consumption market can be represented graphically. In Figure 5.6, compared to the general equilibrium in Figure 5.1, now the budget line is also drawn in, and the production function is slightly different. This graph includes the same blue production function of equation (5.12), the same black

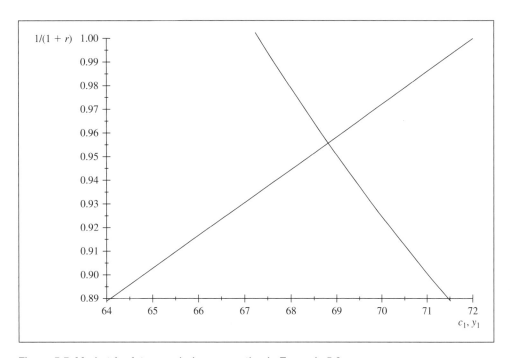

Figure 5.5 Market for future period consumption in Example 5.3

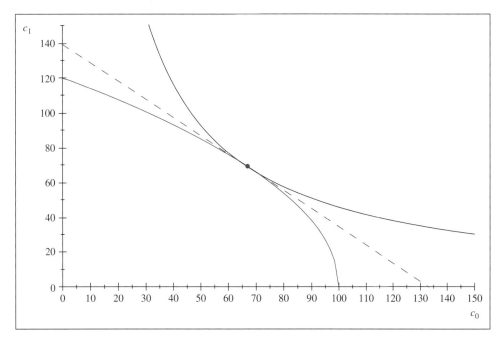

Figure 5.6 General equilibrium intertemporal consumption with market line in Example 5.3

utility level curve of equation (5.11), and the dashed blue market line (or profit line). The market line is found from the consumer's next period budget constraint, using the solutions for the profit Π and the interest rate r, and that $k_1 = 100 - c_0$, to get that

$$c_1^d = \Pi_1 + k_1^s (1+r),$$

$$c_1 = \frac{36}{1.0463} + (100 - c_0)(1.0463).$$

5.4.5 Growth rate implications

Having the solutions for the current and next period consumption, the growth rate in the economy can be computed. Again define the growth rate g as the percentage change in consumption over time, in this case from the current to the future period, or

$$1 + g \equiv \frac{c_1}{c_0}.$$

In the example economy with log utility and $y_1 = 12\sqrt{k_1^d}$, the equilibrium ratio of consumption is given as $1 + g = \frac{c_1}{c_0} = \frac{68.81}{67.12} = 1.025$. This means the economy goods consumption grows by 2.5% over the two periods, so that $g = 0.025$. The long term historical average growth rates in industrialised nations are close to this amount.

5.5 Capital productivity

When productivity increases, as happens in the upswing of the business cycle and over time with growth, the demand and supply curves for both capital and next period consumption are affected. Such a productivity increase is evaluated in general equilibrium in Example 5.2. Now it is seen when the economy is decentralised into consumer and goods producer, so that the effect on the supply and demand for capital and goods can be determined.

5.5.1 Example 5.4

Suppose that the productivity factor A_G increases by 5% from 12 to $12(1.05) = 12.6$, and that all other parameters are as in Example 5.3: $\gamma = 0.5$, $y_0 = 100$ and $\beta = 0.98$.

The production function for next period output becomes

$$y_1 = 12.6\sqrt{k_1^d}.$$

The consumer supply of capital and demand for future consumption is affected only by an increase in profit Π_1. The new profit is found on the firm side, along with the new demand for capital, and supply of future consumption.

The new one-step firm profit maximisation problem is

$$\underset{k_1^d}{\text{Max}} \; \Pi_1 = 12.6\sqrt{k_1^d} - (1+r)k_1^d, \tag{5.47}$$

with the equilibrium condition,

$$(0.5)\,12.6\left(k_1^d\right)^{-0.5} = 1 + r.$$

The capital demand is therefore

$$k_1^d = \frac{(6.3)^2}{(1+r)^2} = \frac{39.69}{(1+r)^2}, \tag{5.48}$$

and profit is

$$\Pi_1 = 12.6\sqrt{\frac{39.69}{(1+r)^2}} - \frac{39.69\,(1+r)}{(1+r)^2} = \frac{39.69}{1+r}. \tag{5.49}$$

The supply of next period goods y_1 is

$$y_1 = 12.6\sqrt{\frac{39.69}{(1+r)^2}} = \frac{79.38}{1+r}. \tag{5.50}$$

The inverted capital demand is

$$k_1^d = \frac{39.69}{(1+r)^2},$$

$$1+r = \sqrt{\frac{39.69}{k_1^d}}. \tag{5.51}$$

On the consumer side, again with $y_0 = 100$ and $\beta = 0.98$, the supply of capital is now

$$k_1^s = \frac{y_0\beta}{1+\beta} - \frac{\Pi_1}{(1+\beta)(1+r)}, \tag{5.52}$$

$$= 49.49 - \frac{\left(\frac{39.69}{1+r}\right)}{1.98\,(1+r)} = 49.49 - \frac{20.045}{(1+r)^2}, \tag{5.53}$$

and its inverted form for graphing is

$$1+r = \sqrt{\frac{20.045}{49.49 - k_1^s}}. \tag{5.54}$$

The demand for future consumption is

$$c_1^d = \Pi_1 + k_1^s(1+r), \tag{5.55}$$

$$= \frac{39.69}{1+r} + \left(49.49 - \frac{20.045}{(1+r)^2}\right)(1+r). \tag{5.56}$$

The simpler form of this is

$$c_1^d = 49.49\,(1+r) + \frac{19.645}{1+r}. \tag{5.57}$$

For the inverted next period consumption demand equation,

$$c_1^d = 49.49\,(1+r) + \frac{19.645}{1+r} = \frac{49.49}{\left(\frac{1}{1+r}\right)} + 19.645\left(\frac{1}{1+r}\right),$$

$$0 = 19.645\left(\frac{1}{1+r}\right)^2 - c_1^d\left(\frac{1}{1+r}\right) + 49.49. \tag{5.58}$$

The quadratic solution to the equation $A\left(\frac{1}{1+r}\right)^2 + B\left(\frac{1}{1+r}\right) + C = 0$, with $A = 19.645$, $B = -c_1^d$, and $C = 49.49$, is given by

$$\frac{1}{1+r} = \frac{-B - \sqrt{B^2 - 4AC}}{2A} = \frac{c_1^d - \sqrt{\left(c_1^d\right)^2 - 4\,(19.645)\,(49.49)}}{2\,(19.645)}. \tag{5.59}$$

The inverted supply of next period consumption equation is

$$c_1^s = \frac{79.38}{1+r},$$

$$\frac{1}{1+r} = \frac{c_1^s}{79.38}. \tag{5.60}$$

5.5.2 Graphically

Figure 5.7 graphs the new demand and supply in the capital market of Example 5.4, in equations (5.51) and (5.54), by the black curves and the original lower productivity equilibrium of Example 5.3, in equations (5.37) and (5.38) given in the blue curves.

The supply of savings by the consumer shifts back, due to the income effect of the increase in profit received by owning the firm. And the demand for capital shifts out, due to greater capital productivity. The interest rate rises and the capital investment k_1 does not change as the income and substitution effects exactly offset each other.

Figure 5.8 graphs the market for future consumption of equations (5.59) and (5.60) in black with the Example 5.3 equilibrium of equations (5.45) and (5.46) given in blue. The demand for future consumption shifts out and up, and the supply of future consumption shifts out and down, with the price of future consumption, $\frac{1}{1+r}$, falling from $\frac{1}{1.0463} = 0.956$ to $\frac{1}{1.0986} = 0.91$.

To find the exact interest rate, set the supply of capital equal to the demand and solve for $1+r$:

$$k_1^s = 49.49 - \frac{20.045}{(1+r)^2} = \frac{39.69}{(1+r)^2} = k_1^d.$$

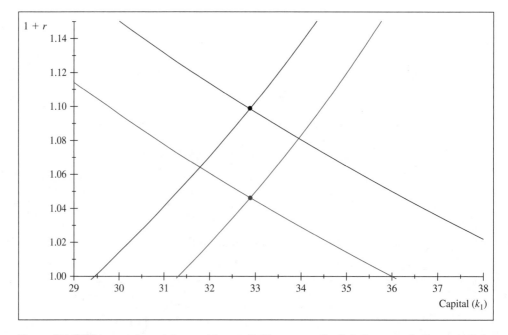

Figure 5.7 Shift in supply and demand for capital from a productivity increase in Example 5.4

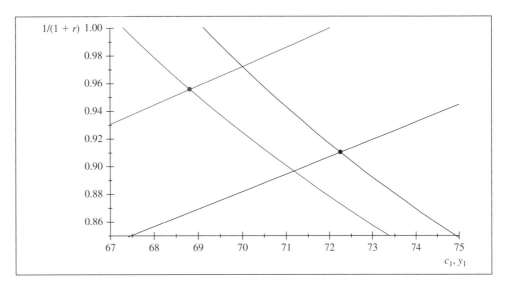

Figure 5.8 Market for future period consumption with 5% productivity increase in Example 5.4 (black) versus Example 5.3 (blue)

The solution for $1 + r$ is found to be

$$1 + r = \sqrt{\frac{(39.69 + 20.045)}{49.49}} = 1.0986,$$

so that r is approximately 10%. And equilibrium capital stays at

$$k_1 = \frac{39.69}{(1.0986)^2} = 32.885,$$

while next period output rises to

$$y_1 = 12.6\sqrt{k_1^d} = 12.6\sqrt{32.885} = 72.255.$$

In actual economies, the productivity of capital can jump significantly during times of epoch innovation, as some argue the computer age heralded, or the railroads did more than a century ago. On a year to year basis, absent such epoch productivity jumps, the productivity growth is typically just a fractional increase such as the 5% increase of this example. The fractional increase in the marginal productivity of capital is thought to be a characteristic feature of the business cycle, during the expansion phase when real interest rates do indeed tend to rise.

Comparative statics within the savings–investment problem involve seeing how changes in the exogenously given parameters of the problem affect the supply of savings, the demand for investment, and the equilibrium interest rate, as well as the amount consumed in the current and future periods. One exogenous parameter was already studied by allowing the marginal productivity of the capital A_G to increase. One of the other main parameters is the exogenously given amount of income in the initial period, $y_0 = 100$.

5.6 Current period income endowment

An increase in the capital productivity is shown to raise the real interest rate. At the same time, the quantity of capital investment does not change. During a business cycle, when productivity rises and falls, capital investment does fluctuate. The problem with the two-period model and an increase in capital productivity is that the initial period income is left unaffected by the productivity increase to the next period output.

Consider the comparative static experiment: that of increasing the current period income endowment y_0. This y_0 can be interpreted as including exogenous labour income that increases, such as when the time endowment increases. Here there is no time so the change in y_0 is simply an exogenous change in the income endowment.

Increasing y_0 leads to more consumption and investment in the current period and more consumption in the next period. And it causes the real interest rate to fall. This can be shown from both the centralised representative agent problem and from the decentralised consumer and firm problems.

5.6.1 Example 5.5

Consider the centralised economy of Example 5.1. Keep all of the parameters the same, except that now let y_0 rise by 5% to 105. Using equation (5.7) by substituting in $y_0 = 105$ instead of $y_0 = 100$, the solution is

$$k_1 = \frac{105 \, (0.98) \, (0.5)}{1 + (0.98) \, (0.5)} = 34.53.$$

The savings rate of $\frac{k_1}{y_0} = \frac{34.53}{105} = 0.3289$ does not change from when $y_0 = 100$. But the quantity of capital investment does rise.

Current period consumption from equation (5.9) also rises to

$$c_0 = 105 - 34.53 = 70.47.$$

And next period consumption from equation (5.8) rises by less to

$$c_1^s = y_1 = 12\sqrt{k_1} = 12 \, (34.53)^{0.5} = 70.52,$$

for a lower growth rate near to zero, of $g = \frac{c_1}{c_0} - 1 = \frac{70.52}{70.47} - 1 = 0.0007$.
Utility is

$$u = \ln \left(105 - k_1 \right) + (0.98) \ln \left(12\sqrt{k_1} \right),$$
$$u = \ln \left(105 - 34.53 \right) + (0.98) \ln \left(12\sqrt{34.53} \right) = 8.4259,$$
$$c_1^d = \left(\frac{e^u}{c_0} \right)^{\frac{1}{\beta}} = \left(\frac{e^{8.4259}}{c_0} \right)^{\frac{1}{0.98}}.$$

And the production function is graphed as

$$c_1^s = 12\sqrt{k_1} = 12\sqrt{105 - c_0}. \tag{5.61}$$

Figure 5.9 graphs the Example 5.5 utility level curve in dashed black and production in dashed blue, and the Example 5.1 utility in black and production in blue.

The current income increase acts to shift out the production curve and the utility level, with an increase in the amount of capital supplied to the market, a lower interest rate and a lower growth rate of consumption. This can be checked by looking at the decentralised market for capital.

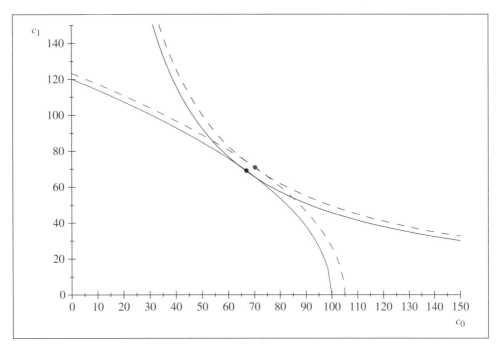

Figure 5.9 General equilibrium intertemporal consumption with current income increase in Example 5.5 (dashed black and dashed blue) compared to Example 5.1

5.6.2 Decentralised problem

The consumer supply of capital in Example 5.1, from equation (5.21), is dependent on y_0 and given by

$$k_1^s = \frac{y_0 \beta}{1 + \beta} - \frac{\Pi_1}{(1 + \beta)(1 + r)}. \tag{5.62}$$

The firm demand for capital and profit are each independent of y_0 and so in Example 1 remain unchanged at

$$k_1^d = \frac{36}{(1 + r)^2}; \tag{5.63}$$

$$\Pi_1 = \frac{36}{1 + r}. \tag{5.64}$$

The inverse capital demand is given as

$$1 + r = \frac{6}{\sqrt{k_1^d}}. \tag{5.65}$$

Substituting in the expression for profit, the consumer capital supply as a function of r is therefore

$$k_1^s = \frac{y_0 \beta}{1 + \beta} - \frac{\frac{36}{1+r}}{(1 + \beta)(1 + r)}, \tag{5.66}$$

$$= \frac{1}{1 + \beta}\left[y_0 \beta - \frac{36}{(1 + r)^2} \right]. \tag{5.67}$$

When y_0 increases from 100 to 105, the consumer supply of capital shifts out while the firm demand is unchanged. The new consumer supply, and its inverse, with the calibration of $\beta = 0.98$, is

$$k_1^s = \frac{1}{1.98}\left[105\,(0.98) - \frac{36}{(1+r)^2}\right], \tag{5.68}$$

$$1 + r = \left(\frac{36}{105\,(0.98) - 1.98k_1^s}\right)^{0.5}. \tag{5.69}$$

To find the equilibrium interest rate, set supply equal to demand, and solve for r:

$$k_1^s = \frac{1}{1.98}\left[105\,(0.98) - \frac{36}{(1+r)^2}\right] = \frac{36}{(1+r)^2} = k_1^d, \tag{5.70}$$

$$\frac{102.9}{1.98} = \frac{36}{(1+r)^2}\left(1 + \frac{1}{1.98}\right), \tag{5.71}$$

$$(1+r)^2 = \frac{36}{\frac{102.9}{1.98}}\left(1 + \frac{1}{1.98}\right), \tag{5.72}$$

$$1 + r = \left[\frac{36}{\frac{102.9}{1.98}}\left(1 + \frac{1}{1.98}\right)\right]^{0.5} = 1.021; \tag{5.73}$$

$$k_1^d = \frac{36}{(1+r)^2} = \frac{36}{(1.021)^2} = 34.534. \tag{5.74}$$

The interest rate does indeed fall as the capital supply shifts out and capital investment rises to 34.534.

Figure 5.10 graphs the change in equilibrium from the 5% increase in y_0, with the initial equilibrium supply curve of Example 5.3, equation (5.38), in blue and the new supply and

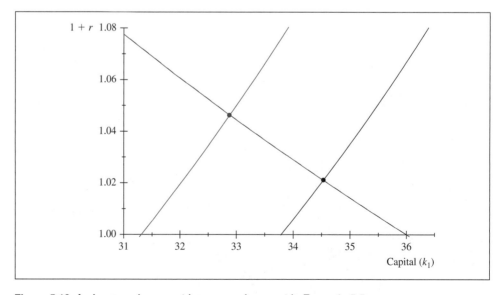

Figure 5.10 An increase in current income endowment in Example 5.5

demand of equations (5.65) and (5.69) of Example 5.5 in black. The demand curve is the same in both examples, now in dashed black and blue.

The fact that the savings rate does remain the same when the current income is increased verifies the sense in which the consumer treats the income as a permanent income increase. More is saved and invested, more is consumed both now and in the next period, but the consumer's savings behaviour does not change in that the rate of savings remains the same.

The demand for future consumption, using equation (5.68) for k_1^s, is

$$c_1^d = \Pi_1 + k_1^s (1 + r),\tag{5.75}$$

$$c_1^d = \frac{36}{1+r} + \left(\frac{105\,(0.98)}{1.98} - \frac{36}{1.98\,(1+r)^2}\right)(1+r),\tag{5.76}$$

$$c_1^d = 51.97\,(1+r) + \left(\frac{1}{1+r}\right)36\left(1 - \frac{1}{1.98}\right).\tag{5.77}$$

Inversely written by solving for $\frac{1}{1+r}$,

$$c_1^d = \frac{51.97}{\left(\frac{1}{1+r}\right)} + 36\left(1 - \frac{1}{1.98}\right)\left(\frac{1}{1+r}\right),$$

$$0 = 36\left(1 - \frac{1}{1.98}\right)\left(\frac{1}{1+r}\right)^2 - c_1^d\left(\frac{1}{1+r}\right) + 51.97.\tag{5.78}$$

The quadratic solution to the equation $A\left(\frac{1}{1+r}\right)^2 + B\left(\frac{1}{1+r}\right) + C = 0$, with $A = 17.818$, $B = -c_1^d$, and $C = 51.97$, is given by

$$\frac{1}{1+r} = \frac{-B - \sqrt{B^2 - 4AC}}{2A} = \frac{c_1^d - \sqrt{\left(c_1^d\right)^2 - 4\,(17.818)\,(51.97)}}{2\,(17.818)}.\tag{5.79}$$

The inverted supply of next period consumption equation is as in Example 5.3:

$$\frac{1}{1+r} = \frac{c_1^s}{72}.\tag{5.80}$$

Figure 5.11 graphs the market for future consumption in equations (5.79) and (5.80) in black, along with the baseline equilibrium consumption demand of Example 5.3 in blue, in which $y_0 = 100$. Supply is unchanged from Example 5.3 as the time endowment does not affect it; this appears in dashed blue-black.

Thus the demand shifts out and the relative price $\frac{1}{1+r}$ rises, as r falls. Both current and future consumption rise. This can be seen by also computing c_0, the current consumption, as

$$c_0 = y_0 - k_1^d = 105 - \frac{36}{(1.021)^2} = 70.466,$$

$$c_1 = \frac{72}{1.021} = 70.519,$$

as compared to $c_0 = 67.11$ and $c_1 = 68.81$ of Example 5.3.

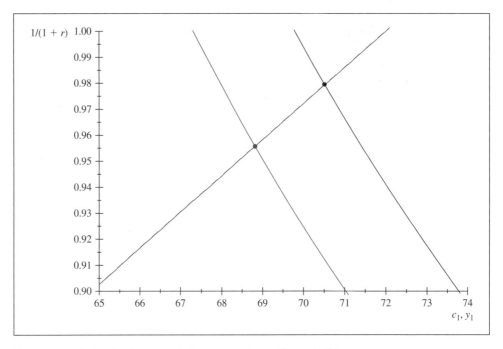

Figure 5.11 Market for future period consumption in Example 5.5

The general equilibrium representation of the increase in income endowment can be seen relative to Example 5.3. The budget line, production function and utility level are now

$$c_1^d = \Pi_1 + k_1^s (1+r) = \frac{36}{1.021} + (105 - c_0)(1.021);$$

$$c_1^d = \left(\frac{e^u}{c_0}\right)^{\frac{1}{\beta}} = \left(\frac{e^{8.4259}}{c_0}\right)^{\frac{1}{0.98}};$$

$$c_1^s = 12\sqrt{k_1} = 12\sqrt{105 - c_0}.$$

Figure 5.12 graphs this Example 5.5 equilibrium, showing that the production function and utility level curve shift out while the budget line pivots out, with a slightly flatter slope of $-(1+r) = -1.021$.

5.7 Applications

5.7.1 Savings rate, permanent income and debt crisis

Figure 5.13 shows how US National Income and Product Account personal savings rate fell dramatically from around 11% in 1983 until in 2000 the rate was less than 1%. The UK, Australia and Canada all experienced the same drop. And while this fall in the savings rate corresponded to a rise in the output growth rates from the low growth period of the 1970s, it has fallen to exceedingly low levels since 2000.

A very low savings rate has been a policy issue at times, with concerns about what would be the consequences. One prominent explanation of the low rate is that it is the

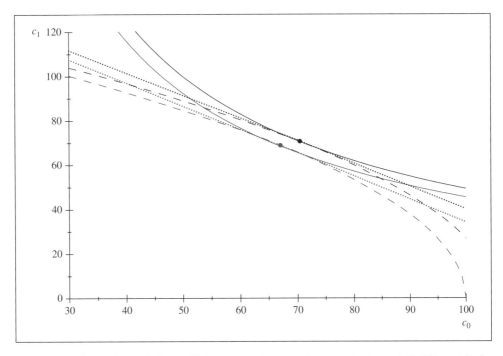

Figure 5.12 General equilibrium with income endowment increase in Example 5.5 (three black lines) compared to Example 5.3 (three blue lines)

consequence of a 'wealth effect', or a result of a rising permanent income stream that households faced. In particular, as the value of the market equity in corporations and home equity through house ownership rose dramatically during the 1990s, households felt that their permanent income was rising. This permanent income is what the consumer could reasonably expect to have on average every year on into the future, and it rose because the expected interest earnings from the higher wealth in national equity also rose. And as permanent income was expected to rise even more, less needed to be saved.

This theory that consumption is based not on current income so much as upon the expected permanent income came from Milton Friedman who formalised the theory in a 1957 book called *A Theory of the Consumption Function*. The theory is typically called the permanent income hypothesis of consumption. Its application here might be viewed more easily by focusing on the consumption rate, which is defined as one minus the savings rate. The consumption rate is defined as current consumption divided by current income. And this does not capture whether the future income is believed to be rising. When future income is higher, and consumption in fact depends on the expected permanent income, which is also defined as the present discounted value of the stream of future income, then current consumption rises even if current income has not yet risen by as much as permanent income. This makes the consumption rate rise, and the savings rate fall. And this links the rise in wealth, which implies a rise in permanent income, to the fall in the savings rate.

The permanent income explanation of the fall in the savings rate implies that really it is not at all a worry in a policy sense, as long as the expectations of rising permanent income are realised. Yet there was a dark underside to this fall in savings rate and rise in consumption: many houses were bought by borrowing money which the new owners thought they could pay back because of their rising equity wealth. The collapse in the stock market value in 2007 and 2008 left many house owners with little wealth. Combined

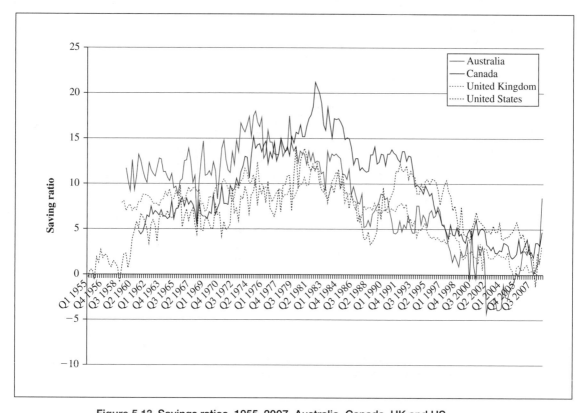

Figure 5.13 Savings ratios, 1955–2007, Australia, Canada, UK and US
Sources: Australian Bureau of Statistics, Statistics Canada, Office for National Statistics (UK), Federal Reserve (US)

with a deep recession that led to much unemployment, many houses were foreclosed and repossessed by banks that issued the loans. This was such a serious sequence of events that the US passed legislation in February 2009 to try to decrease the number of bank foreclosures on house mortgage loans. So what started as a simple economic response to rising wealth, this being a low savings rate, became an urgent policy issue once the wealth collapsed and the debt undertaken could not be repaid.

5.8 Questions

1. Assume that a representative agent can allocate current period income to current period consumption, or to investment that produces next period consumption, via a production function that depends only on the quantity invested. With utility depending on current and next period consumption, the agent

   (a) sets $1 + r$ equal to the marginal product of capital, with r the interest rate;

   (b) sets $1 + r$ equal to the marginal rate of substitution between current and next period consumption;

   (c) sets the marginal rate of substitution between current and next period consumption equal to the marginal product of capital;

   (d) all of the above.

2. A representative agent that chooses in equilibrium to set aside income as investment and then transforms the invested capital into next period consumption through a production function will

   (a) have a lower consumption next period than if no investment took place;
   (b) produce at a tangency point between the indifference curve and the production function;
   (c) have the same level of utility as when no investment is made;
   (d) all of the above.

3. The equilibrium marginal rate of substitution between current and future consumption, for a representative consumer

   (a) equals the slope of the indifference curve;
   (b) equals the marginal product of capital;
   (c) describes an aspect of the tangency point between a utility level curve and the production possibility curve;
   (d) all of the above.

4. A representative agent consumer of current and next period consumption, c_0 and c_1 (c_1 also equals next period income here), and producer of next period income through investment k_1 in a Cobb–Douglas production function, finds that an increase in the marginal product of capital, while keeping log utility constant,

   (a) increases current consumption c_0;
   (b) decreases investment k_1;
   (c) increases next period income;
   (d) all of the above.

5. For a representative consumer with log utility depending on current and future period consumption, an increase in the marginal product of capital causes investment to

   (a) increase by the substitution effect when the marginal product of capital increases;
   (b) increase by the income effect;
   (c) always increase as the net effect of both substitution and income effects;
   (d) all of the above.

6. A representative agent with the problem of maximising utility, $u = \ln c_0 + \beta \ln c_1$, subject to the constraints, and with respect to c_0 and c_1, can reduce the problem to just one unknown variable by

   (a) solving from the constraints for k_1 and then substituting in for c_0 in the production function;
   (b) solving from the constraints for y_0 and then substituting in for c_1 in the utility function;
   (c) solving from the constraints for both c_0 and c_1 in terms of k_1 and then substituting these in the utility function;
   (d) all of the above.

7. In Example 5.3, except that now $y_0 = 50$, find the equilibrium consumption in the current period c_0, the next period c_1, the output in period 1, y_1, and the investment in period 0, k_1, for the consumer with utility $u(c_0, c_1) = \ln c_0 + \beta \ln c_1$, and subject to investment $y_1 = 12\sqrt{k_1}$, the social resources $y_0 = c_0 + k_1$, $c_1 = y_1$, and where $y_0 = 50$ and $\beta = 0.98$.

8. Given the consumer's utility $u = \ln c_0 + \beta \ln c_1$, and that $y_0 = 100$, $y_0 = c_0 + k_1$, $c_1 = y_1$, and $\beta = 0.98$, now suppose that $y_1 = 14\sqrt{k_1}$:

   (a) Find the equilibrium c_0, c_1, k_1, and utility level u;
   (b) and graph the general equilibrium in $(c_0 : c_1)$ space.
   (c) Find the equilibrium supply and demand functions for capital and for future consumption, and find the equilibrium interest rate;
   (d) and graph these supply and demand functions for goods and capital in price–quantity space.
   (e) Compare this equilibrium to when $y_1 = 12\sqrt{k_1}$ in Example 5.3.

9. Suppose in Example 5.5 that the goods endowment y_0 equals 120 instead of 100, and all other specifications are the same:
   (a) Find the equilibrium c_0, c_1, k_1, and utility level u;
   (b) and graph the general equilibrium in $(c_0 : c_1)$ space.
   (c) Find the equilibrium supply and demand functions for capital and for future consumption, and find the equilibrium interest rate;
   (d) and graph these supply and demand functions for goods and capital in price–quantity space.
   (e) Compare this equilibrium to when $y_0 = 100$ in Example 5.5.

5.9 References

Bohm-Bawerk, Eugen, 1888, *The Positive Theory of Capital;* translated by William A. Smart, Macmillan and Co., London, 1891.

Fisher, Irving, 1896, *Appreciation and Interest,* New York: Macmillan.

Fisher, Irving, 1906, *The Nature of Capital and Income,* New York: Macmillan.

Fisher, Irving, 1907, *The Rate of Interest,* New York: Macmillan.

Fisher, Irving, 1930, *Theory of Interest,* New York: Macmillan.

Friedman, Milton, 1957, *A Theory of the Consumption Function,* Princeton: Princeton University Press for NBER.

Friedman, Milton, 1976, *Price Theory,* Aldine Publishing Company, Chicago.

Ramsey, Frank, 1928, 'A Mathematical Theory of Saving', *The Economic Journal* 38(152) (December): 543–559.

Smith, Adam, 1776, *An Inquiry into the Nature and Causes of The Wealth of Nations; The Cannan edition,* The University of Chicago Press, Chicago, 1976.

Solow, Robert M., 1956, 'A Contribution to the Theory of Economic Growth', *Quarterly Journal of Economics* 70(1): 65–94.

Wicksell, Knut, 1901, *Lectures on Political Economy*. Vol. 1. Translated by E. Classen. London: Routledge and Kegan Paul, 1934.

5.10 Appendix A5: Alternative two-period formulations

An alternative way to present the capital savings–investment problem in a two-period setting is to allow for no depreciation. This means that after the production process, the capital still remains. And since there are only two periods, then the consumer must 'eat' the capital at the end of the second period, which is period 1 in our notation.

The form of this problem with no depreciation has the advantage that zero depreciation is closer to the full dynamic problem set out in Part 4, in that there the depreciation rate is typically calibrated to be much closer to zero than to one. More generally the depreciation rate can be made here to be any value between zero and one, but that does complicate notation.

In the alternative with zero depreciation, the consumer has to eat the remaining capital at the end of the second period. It will become apparent that the problem using this approach has a solution that is not easily computed. This appendix sets out the problem and shows that there is no simple solution, which is why the alternative of zero depreciation is used throughout Part 3.

Utility is again the natural log function as

$$u = \ln c_0 + \beta \ln c_1.$$

The given current period supply of goods y_0 is again divided between goods consumption today and investment of capital (for goods consumption tomorrow):

$$y_0 = c_0 + k_1,$$

and output is again

$$y_1 = A_G k_1^{1-\gamma}.$$

But now consumption in the second period is not just y_1, but rather y_1 plus the un-depreciated capital k_1:

$$c_1 = y_1 + k_1,$$
$$c_1 = A k_1^{1-\gamma} + k_1.$$

Investing the capital k_1 and having a yield on it of the output $A k_1^{1-\gamma}$, plus getting back the capital k_1, is a reasonable way to formulate the problem, but computationally difficult. To see this consider the representative agent problem:

$$\max_{k_1} \ln\left(y_0 - k_1\right) + \beta \ln\left(A k_1^{1-\gamma} + k_1\right).$$

Taking the derivative with respect to k_1,

$$-\frac{1}{y_0 - k_1} + \frac{\beta \left[1 + \left(1 - \gamma\right) A k_1^{-\gamma}\right]}{A_G k_1^{1-\gamma} + k_1} = 0, \tag{5.81}$$

or in terms of the marginal product of capital being equal to the marginal rate of intertemporal substitution of goods,

$$1 + \frac{\partial f\left(k_1\right)}{\partial k_1} = 1 + A_G \left(1 - \gamma\right) k^{-\gamma} = \frac{\frac{1}{y_0 - k_1}}{\frac{\beta}{A k_1^{1-\gamma} + k_1}} = \frac{\frac{1}{c_0}}{\frac{\beta}{c_1}}. \tag{5.82}$$

The difference here from equation (5.3) is that now it is $1 + \frac{\partial f(k_1)}{\partial k_1}$, instead of just $\frac{\partial f(k_1)}{\partial k_1}$, in the intertemporal equilibrium condition. This ends up making it difficult to solve for k_1.

Consider the same calibration, where $\beta = 0.98$, $\gamma = 0.5$, $y_0 = 100$, and $A_G = 12$. Then the equilibrium condition (5.82) can be rewritten as

$$(0.98) \left[1 + (0.98)(0.5)(12) k_1^{-0.5}\right] (100 - k_1) = (12) k_1^{0.5} + k_1. \tag{5.83}$$

There is no simple analytic solution for k_1 for $\gamma \in \left(0, 1\right)$, making the rest of the solution equally difficult.

For this reason, the two-period problem in Part 3 is formed with no capital left over after production. In Part 4, this assumption is relaxed in the infinite horizon dynamic problem. However note that the two-period problem in Part 3 is not an exact special case of the infinite horizon problem of Part 4 because this is not easily solvable. The way in which the two-period problem is formulated in Part 3, with complete depreciation, makes the marginal product of capital $A_G \left(1 - \gamma\right) k^{-\gamma}$ equal to $1 + r$. This allows r to be interpreted as the interest rate on capital.

In Part 4, at time t the gross marginal product of capital is equal to $1 + r_t - \delta_k$, where δ_k is the depreciation rate; therefore in the special case of $\delta_k = 1$, this reduces to r_t, rather than $1 + r$ as in Part 3. The Part 3 formulation has the advantage of its analytic solution, although it is not strictly a special case of the Part 4 formulation. It allows the fundamentals of intertemporal consumption smoothing to be set out, with a complete formulation of the dynamic problem following in Part 4.

Another alternative way of formulating the two-period problem that is more complete but again more complex conceptually is to follow for example Friedman (1976). He reduces the infinite horizon into the two periods by using the current consumption versus the stream of infinite future consumption, rather than just the next period's consumption.

The price of the future infinite stream is $\frac{1}{r} = \frac{1}{1+r}\left(1 + \frac{1}{1+r} + \frac{1}{\left(1+r\right)^2} + \cdots\right) = \frac{1}{1+r}\frac{1}{1-\frac{1}{1+r}}$,

the discounted price of an infinite stream of one dollar of future income. Thus $\frac{1}{r}$ is the relative price, while in the simpler two-period framework the discounted price of next period's one dollar of income is instead $\frac{1}{1+r}$.

CHAPTER 6

Capital policy and business cycles

6.1 Introduction

There are two prominent issues in policy with respect to capital investment. One is that over the business cycle, the capital investment fluctuates quite a bit. In an economic downturn, the equilibrium investment can fall so much as to be a concern in terms of overall employment of resources. And within business cycles, there are occasional dramatic decreases in investment, during crisis periods.

The other type of policy is how investment is affected by taxes needed to pay for government expenditure. This is more of a long term feature of capital investment than a business cycle concern. However, tax changes can also be used during the business cycle to affect aggregate output levels.

The chapter will analyse how business cycles can be shown in the two-period capital framework, through changes in productivity and the income endowment. Then the effect of fixed prices, in terms of the interest rate, is analysed to show how an 'excess supply of capital' can be envisioned within the framework. And last the effect of capital taxes on the equilibrium is shown. In doing so, the chapter is able to present a view of policy issues John M. Keynes raised in his famous *General Theory*; these issues remain an active interest of capital policy.

6.1.1 Building on the last chapters

The same analysis developed in the last chapter, of two-period consumption with capital investment, is applied to show a business cycle in capital with simple comparative statics. This is done as in Chapter 3 for labour by also assuming a 5% increase in endowment and in productivity. Here the endowment is a current period income endowment and the productivity is for capital production, rather than the time endowment in Chapter 3 and the labour productivity.

Unemployed capital is defined within the economy of the last chapter, with a fixed price assumed and excess capital resulting. This is similar to how unemployed labour was defined in Chapter 3 with a fixed price and excess labour, as based on the Chapter 2 economy. The tax analysis also uses the last chapter's structure of the capital investment problem, with the addition of a tax. And again it is parallel to how a tax on labour was added in Chapter 3 using the same framework as in Chapter 2.

6.1.2 Learning objective

You are challenged to formulate the changes in supply and demand in goods and capital markets, along with the general equilibrium representation in terms of current and future consumption, that represent an economic expansion and contraction. Also the concept of surplus capital and its connection to Keynes's *General Theory* is presented for understanding the importance of occasional large decreases in investment. Here it is necessary to see that only a change in productivity of investment is insufficient to generate the cycle; it is also necessary to add a change in the income endowment. Finally, how the marginal distortion of taxes on capital affects output, even when the tax revenue is returned to the consumer, is a study of how taxes distort investment.

6.1.3 Who made it happen?

John Maynard Keynes's most famous writing is his 1936 book *The General Theory of Employment, Interest, and Money*. You might be surprised to learn that the only graphical figure in the entire book (in Chapter 14) is one of the capital market, similar to Figure 5.10. Keynes uses the supply and demand in the capital market to illustrate a decrease in the interest rate that is caused by the supply of capital shifting out by more than does the demand for capital; this also occurs in Figure 5.10, from an increase in y_0, although here demand does not shift out at all. But in our approach this is the result of shifting an exogenous parameter in a mathematical general equilibrium model. Keynes's analysis in contrast is a theoretical diagram of what might happen in the capital market.

Keynes is representing the classical interest rate theory, but at the same time in the 1936 text is arguing that the interest rate is determined in the money market rather than in the capital market. Modern analysis no longer makes this distinction in general, although it can arise as an exception such as when discussing interest rate targeting in monetary policy. Generally, modern analysis accepts that the capital market does indeed set the price of capital, this being the real interest rate. And if there is short run monetary policy, this is still conducted within the realm of capital markets.

Fundamentally what Keynes wrote about was the concern that during crisis periods there would somehow be too much of a supply of capital relative to the demand for capital, so that some of the capital supplied simply went unused. He took this idea very far. First he developed this idea at length in his also famous 1930 *Treatise of Money, Volume I*, where he argued that the quantity of savings and investment are not equalised over the business cycle. Rather the quantity of savings exceeds investment in a downturn and the quantity of investment exceeds the quantity of savings in the upturn. In the *General Theory* Keynes calls the equality of investment and savings 'the old fashioned view', although at the same time he calls a difference in the quantity of investment and savings 'an optical illusion' (Chapter 7). Interpreting such descriptive analyses can be confusing and this is why the micro-founded mathematical approach to economics is the modern approach in which there is less ambiguity about the results.

One way to approach the idea of excess savings is given by diagrams of the capital market in which there is a so-called 'liquidity trap'. However Keynes (1936) writes in Chapter 15 that 'I know of no example of it hitherto', and this includes the Great Depression period of the early 1930s, in which the interest rate could become such that it could no longer be affected by monetary policy. Without describing for the student in detail the role of monetary policy at this point in the text, except to say that it involves trying to increase the supply of (money) capital so as to lower the real interest rate, it is here that Keynes's definition of a liquidity trap appears: being that an increase in the supply of capital has no effect on the real interest rate.

A way to illustrate this is with a graph such as in Figure 5.10. Should the supply of capital curve somehow be nearly horizontal at some low interest rate, then any further increase or shift out in the supply of capital (such as through monetary policy), while keeping the demand function for capital unchanged, will have no effect since it would involve simply extending the horizontal supply of capital curve. From this logic, the only way left to increase the quantity of capital invested and saved in equilibrium is to increase the demand for capital, and so shift out the investment curve. This liquidity trap concept describes a way in which there can exist 'excess savings' that are not being turned into investment, or at least that is the general idea.

The idea of a fixed interest rate that yields an excess supply of capital during a recession is developed in this chapter. Keynes's solution to the excess capital supply is to somehow increase the demand for capital. And in particular, one solution is to engage the government for taking on this task of increasing the demand for capital. As put forth by Keynes (Chapter 12, p. 164):

> For my own part I am now somewhat sceptical of the success of a merely monetary policy directed towards influencing the rate of interest. I expect to see the State, which is in a position to calculate the marginal efficiency of capital-goods on long views and on the basis of the general social advantage, taking an ever greater responsibility for directly organizing investment.

The idea here is that the quantity of investment cannot be increased by increasing the supply of capital, when there is some sort of 'liquidity trap', and so the government should itself directly conduct investment that shifts out the demand for investment and so lead to more investment. The end goal is to have more capital invested in equilibrium and so have greater economic activity. And this became a foundation of the later school of Keynesian economics.

The Great Depression in the US also coincided with a collapse of the financial sector that acts as the main intermediary between the consumer's savings and the firm's investment. And many economists have pointed to that as the root cause of the severity of the Great Depression. In modern times, during similar periods of great crisis, such as the international banking sector collapse of 2007–09, governments have turned to so-called Keynesian policies of increasing government spending and investment in infrastructure and education and health systems. But it is also generally realised that, as in the 'Lost Decade' of slow growth in Japan during the 1990s, the financial sector has to be put back on a sound basis in order for an economic recovery to ensue. And such bank reform was perhaps even more paramount in international government policy during the 2007–09 crisis. Banking intermediation is further discussed in Chapter 16.

6.2 Business cycles and investment

Over the business cycle, investment rises in economic expansions and falls in economic contractions. A common way to view business cycles is in terms of changes in the productivity of factor inputs. The Chapter 5 analysis of capital shows that when there is an increase in the productivity of capital, the marginal product of capital rises but the actual amount of investment remains unchanged. This is because the substitution effect towards more investment when the marginal product rises is offset exactly by the income effect of a higher return on capital. These offsetting effects are common with standard utility and production functions, but they present a puzzle in explaining business cycles, and therefore in trying to understand the policy issues presented by business cycle fluctuations in investment.

The business cycle however can be explained in terms of another comparative static change also examined in Chapter 5. The lack of a change in investment with a productivity change can be overcome by combining such a change with a change in the given current period income. When current income increases, the supply of capital shifts out while the demand remains the same.

6.2.1 Economic expansions and contractions

Therefore if capital productivity increases and at the same time the current income increases, then what happens is that the real interest rate is pushed up by the productivity increase, while the current income increase pushes down the real interest rate. At the same time, the productivity increase causes no change in investment while the current income increase causes investment to rise. This means that it is possible to formulate the changes in the exogenous productivity and the current income so that both the real interest rate and the quantity of investment rise, as is characteristic of a business cycle expansion.

A decrease in capital productivity combined with a decrease in current income can be specified so as to have the opposite effect. In particular, the real interest rate can fall while at the same time the quantity of capital investment increases. This would be typical of business cycle contractions of economic activity: a procyclic real interest rate and a procyclic quantity of investment.

6.2.2 Example 6.1: Expansion

Consider a variation of Example 5.3, which presents the baseline decentralised problems of the consumer and the firm. Now let both the goods productivity and the goods endowment increase by 5%.

Initially assume the same specification of the economy, with log utility and Cobb–Douglas production, as in Example 5.3, with $\beta = 0.98$, $y_0 = 100$, and $A_G = 12$. The supply and demand for capital in this specification are

$$k_1^s = \frac{y_0 \beta}{1+\beta} - \frac{\Pi_1}{(1+\beta)(1+r)} = \frac{y_0 \beta}{1+\beta} - \left(\frac{1}{1+\beta}\right)\frac{36}{(1+r)^2}, \tag{6.1}$$

$$k_1^d = \frac{36}{(1+r)^2}, \tag{6.2}$$

while profit is given by

$$\Pi_1 = 12 \left[\frac{36}{(1+r)^2}\right]^{0.5} - \frac{36(1+r)}{(1+r)^2} = \frac{36}{1+r}. \tag{6.3}$$

Now let both A_G and y_0 simultaneously increase by 5%. Then $A_G = 12.6$ and $y_0 = 105$.

To determine the new equilibrium, consider the firm side, which is affected only by the increase in A_G, as can be seen by looking at its equilibrium condition. The firm equilibrium condition, that sets the marginal product of capital equal to $1 + r$ in equation (5.24), is now instead

$$(0.5)(12.6)\left(k_1^d\right)^{-0.5} = 1+r, \tag{6.4}$$

$$k_1^d = \frac{39.69}{(1+r)^2}. \tag{6.5}$$

This gives a firm profit of

$$\Pi_1 = 12.6 \left[\frac{39.69}{(1+r)^2}\right]^{0.5} - \frac{39.69(1+r)}{(1+r)^2} = \frac{39.69}{1+r}. \tag{6.6}$$

The consumer supply of capital is affected by the changes in both A_G and y_0. The change in A_G causes a higher profit transfer from the firm. The change in y_0 causes a direct income effect also. The supply function now is

$$k_1^s = \frac{105\,(0.98)}{1.98} - \frac{39.69}{(1.98)\,(1+r)^2}. \tag{6.7}$$

And the equilibrium interest rate is found by setting supply equal to demand:

$$\frac{105\,(0.98)}{1.98} - \frac{39.69}{(1.98)\,(1+r)^2} = \frac{39.69}{(1+r)^2}. \tag{6.8}$$

This allows for the solution of the real interest rate:

$$r = \left(\frac{39.69\,(2+\beta)}{105\,(\beta)}\right)^{0.5} - 1;$$

$$= \left(\frac{39.69\,(2.98)}{105\,(0.98)}\right)^{0.5} - 1 = 0.0721. \tag{6.9}$$

The new equilibrium shows that indeed the real interest rate increases from 0.0463 to 0.0721, the kind of movement that is seen during business cycle upturns. The quantity of capital also increases from 32.89 to 34.531:

$$k_1^s = \frac{105\,(0.98)}{1.98} - \frac{39.69}{(1.98)\,(1.0721)^2} = 34.531 = \frac{39.69}{(1.0721)^2} = k_1^d.$$

The investment rate relative to current income stays the same at $\frac{34.531}{105} = 0.3289$, but the quantity of investment increases.

The rest of the equilibrium is

$$y_1 = \frac{12.6\,(39.69)^{0.5}}{1.0721} = 74.042, \tag{6.10}$$

$$\Pi_1 = \frac{39.69}{1.0721} = 37.021, \tag{6.11}$$

$$c_0^d = 105 - k_1^s = 105 - 34.531 = 70.469, \tag{6.12}$$

$$y_1 = c_1^d = \Pi_1 + k_1^s\,(1+r), \tag{6.13}$$

$$= 37.021 + 34.531\,(1.0721) = 74.042. \tag{6.14}$$

Utility is

$$u = \ln c_0^d + \beta \ln c_1^d = \ln 70.469 + 0.98 \ln 74.042 = 8.4737,$$

$$c_1 = \left(\frac{e^u}{c_0}\right)^{\frac{1}{\beta}} = \left(\frac{e^{8.4737}}{c_0}\right)^{\frac{1}{0.98}}.$$

The growth rate of consumption is therefore

$$1 + g = \frac{c_1}{c_0} = \frac{74.042}{70.469} = 1.0507,$$

as compared to a previous growth rate of $g = 0.0255$ before the two simultaneous comparative static changes. Again such a growth rate increase is typical of economic expansions.

In the capital market, the shift in the supply and demand for capital can be demonstrated with the 5% increase in goods productivity and the income endowment. The capital supply equation and its inverse are

$$k_1^s = \frac{y_0 \beta}{1+\beta} - \frac{\Pi_1}{(1+\beta)(1+r)} = \frac{105\,(0.98)}{1.98} - \frac{39.69}{(1.98)(1+r)^2}; \tag{6.15}$$

$$1 + r = \left(\frac{39.69}{\left(105\,(0.98) - (1.98)\,k_1^s \right)} \right)^{0.5}. \tag{6.16}$$

The capital demand and its inverse are

$$k_1^d = \frac{39.69}{(1+r)^2},$$

$$1 + r = \left(\frac{39.69}{k_1^d} \right)^{0.5}. \tag{6.17}$$

Figure 6.1 graphs the new supply and demand of equations (6.16) and (6.17) in black, after the 5% increase in A_G and y_0, along with the initial equilibrium in blue. Supply and demand shift out causing a higher interest rate and investment, as in an economic expansion.

In general equilibrium, Figure 6.2 graphs the following new budget line, utility level curve, and production function, in three black lines, with the initial equilibrium of Example 5.3 in three blue lines.

$$c_1^d = \Pi_1 + k_1^s\,(1+r) = \frac{39.69}{1.0721} + (105 - c_0)\,(1.0721);$$

$$c_1^d = \left(\frac{e^u}{c_0} \right)^{\frac{1}{\beta}} = \left(\frac{e^{8.4737}}{c_0} \right)^{\frac{1}{0.98}};$$

$$c_1^s = 12.6\sqrt{k_1^d} = 12.6\,(105 - c_0)^{0.5}.$$

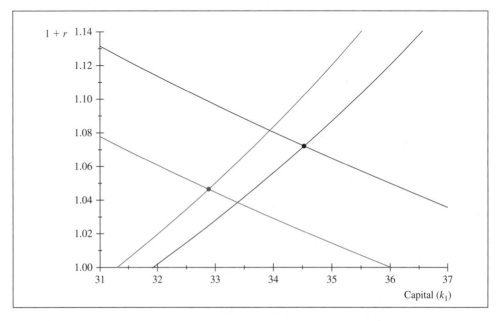

Figure 6.1 Capital market with 5% increase in goods productivity and income endowment (black) in Example 6.1 versus Example 5.3 (blue)

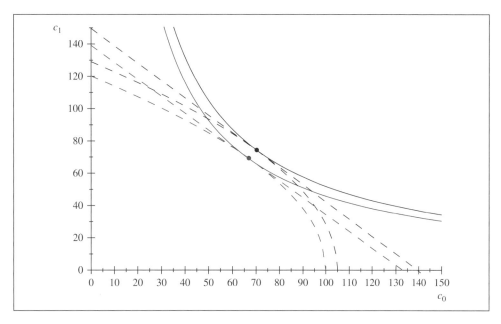

Figure 6.2 Economic expansion in Example 6.1 (three black lines) compared to baseline Example 5.3 (three blue lines)

The production function and utility level curve shift up while the budget line pivots up with a steeper, more negative, slope of $-(1+r) = -1.0721$.

6.2.3 Example 6.2: Contraction

Starting with the baseline of Example 5.3, now let goods productivity and the income endowment fall by 5% from the baseline values so that $A_G = 11.4$ and let $y_0 = 95$. The new supply and demand for capital are given by

$$k_1^s = \frac{95\,(0.98)}{1.98} - \frac{\Pi_1}{(1.98)\,(1+r)}, \tag{6.18}$$

$$k_1^d = \left[\frac{(0.5)\,(11.4)}{(1+r)}\right]^2 = \frac{32.49}{(1+r)^2}. \tag{6.19}$$

The solution for profit comes from the firm problem:

$$\Pi_1 = 11.4\left[\frac{[(0.5)\,(11.4)]^2}{(1+r)^2}\right]^{0.5} - \frac{32.49\,(1+r)}{(1+r)^2} = \frac{32.49}{1+r}. \tag{6.20}$$

This makes the market clearing condition for the equilibrium of capital supply and demand as a function of r:

$$k_1^s = \frac{95\,(0.98)}{1.98} - \frac{32.49}{(1.98)\,(1+r)^2} = \frac{32.49}{(1+r)^2} = k_1^d.$$

The equilibrium interest rate is

$$1+r = \left(\frac{32.49\,(2+\beta)}{95\,(\beta)}\right)^{0.5},$$

$$= \left(\frac{32.49\,(2.98)}{95\,(0.98)}\right)^{0.5} = 1.0198. \tag{6.21}$$

The result shows that the interest rate falls from 0.0463 to 0.0198, or to about 2%. This is a realistic level of the real interest rate in a recession.

The equilibrium capital is

$$k_1^s = \frac{95\,(0.98)}{1.98} - \frac{32.49}{(1.98)\,(1.0198)^2} = 31.24 = \frac{32.49}{(1.0198)^2} = k_1^d.$$

The capital equilibrium at 31.24 marks a reduction from the initial equilibrium in Example 3.5 when $k_1 = 32.89$. Thus the quantity of capital investment has fallen.

The rest of the equilibrium is

$$y_1 = \frac{11.4\,(32.49)^{0.5}}{1.0198} = 63.72, \tag{6.22}$$

$$\Pi_1 = \frac{32.49}{1.0198} = 31.86, \tag{6.23}$$

$$c_0^d = 95 - k_1^s = 95 - 31.24 = 63.76, \tag{6.24}$$

$$y_1 = c_1^d = \Pi_1 + k_1^s\,(1+r),$$

$$y_1 = 31.86 + 31.24\,(1.0198) = 63.72. \tag{6.25}$$

The utility level in contraction is

$$u = \ln c_0^d + \beta \ln c_1^d = \ln 63.76 + 0.98 \ln 63.72 = 8.2265,$$

$$c_1 = \left(\frac{e^u}{c_0}\right)^{\frac{1}{\beta}} = \left(\frac{e^{8.2265}}{c_0}\right)^{\frac{1}{0.98}}.$$

The growth rate of consumption falls slightly negative:

$$1+g = \frac{c_1}{c_0} = \frac{63.72}{63.76} = 0.999,$$

and so $g = -0.001$, or a negative 0.1%. Again this is how typical downswings occur. The growth rate turns negative, but usually not by too much. This example has the growth rate just barely turning negative.

The contraction can be seen in the capital market and in general equilibrium. With the 5% decrease in goods productivity and the income endowment, the capital supply equation and its inverse are

$$k_1^s = \frac{y_0 \beta}{1+\beta} - \frac{\Pi_1}{(1+\beta)\,(1+r)} = \frac{95\,(0.98)}{1.98} - \frac{32.49}{(1.98)\,(1+r)^2}, \tag{6.26}$$

$$1+r = \left(\frac{32.49}{\Big(95\,(0.98) - (1.98)\,k_1^s\Big)}\right)^{0.5}, \tag{6.27}$$

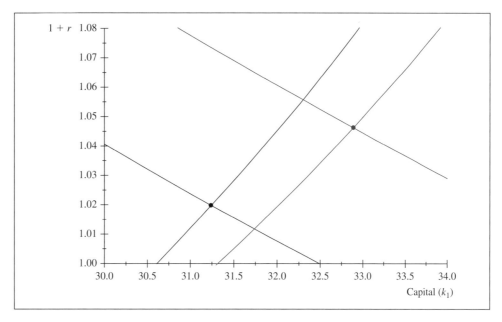

Figure 6.3 Capital market with 5% decrease in goods productivity and income endowment (black) in Example 6.2 versus Example 5.3 (blue)

and the capital demand and its inverse are

$$k_1^d = \frac{32.49}{(1+r)^2},$$

$$1+r = \left(\frac{32.49}{k_1^d}\right)^{0.5}. \tag{6.28}$$

Figure 6.3 graphs the new supply and demand of equations (6.27) and (6.28) in black, after the 5% decrease in A_G and y_0, along with the initial equilibrium of Example 3.5 in blue. Supply and demand shift back, the interest rate falls, and investment also falls, as in an economic contraction.

In general equilibrium, Figure 6.4 graphs the initial equilibrium of Example 5.3 in three blue lines, and the new budget line, utility level curve, and production function of Example 6.2, in three blue lines, as given in the following equations:

$$c_1^d = \Pi_1 + k_1^s (1+r) = \frac{32.49}{1.0198} + (95 - c_0)(1.0198),$$

$$c_1^d = \left(\frac{e^u}{c_0}\right)^{\frac{1}{\beta}} = \left(\frac{e^{8.2265}}{c_0}\right)^{\frac{1}{0.98}},$$

$$c_1^s = 11.4\sqrt{k_1^d} = 11.4\left(95 - c_0\right)^{0.5}.$$

The new production function, utility level curve and budget line all shift down, with a new tangency at a flatter, less negative, slope of $-(1+r) = -1.0198$. Less current consumption and investment result while the interest rate and consumption growth rate fall, as in a recession.

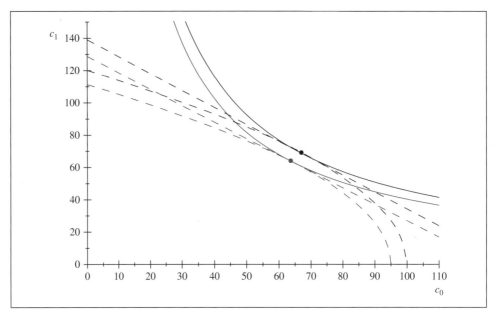

Figure 6.4 Economic contraction in Example 6.2 (three black lines) compared to baseline Example 5.3 (three blue lines)

6.3 Unemployed capital

Typical economic expansions and contractions have been explained in terms of simultaneous equal-proportionate increases in the capital productivity and the current income endowment. This causes procyclic changes in the real interest rate and in the quantity of investment, as is typical of business cycles.

During crisis periods of recession, which occur occasionally, the decrease in the quantity of investment may be more extreme. And Keynes's (1936) concept of excess, unused capital may be a more realistic possibility. This surplus capital can be thought of in our analysis by assuming price rigidity on behalf of the real interest rate. In doing this, the analysis is a paradigm comparable to the 'liquidity trap' of Keynes, in which the interest rate cannot fall any further for some reason. And although Keynes was referring to the nominal interest rate rather than the real interest rate, the fixed price view is still analogous in that it results in the excess capital being supplied. Keynes emphasised surplus capital being supplied in both his 1930 *Treatise on Money*, and his inclusion in his 1936 *General Theory* of a defence of the excess capital postulated in his *Treatise*.

A fixed interest rate is an alternative explanation of business cycles. Samuelson (1951) felt the concept of unemployed resources should be reserved for the analysis of crisis periods, which he called 'depression economics'. Therefore he shifted his 1951 second edition away from his 1948 first edition emphasis on 'the problem of mass unemployment'. Surprisingly, rigid prices have come to be used in modern analysis for all business cycles, as an alternative to the type of relative price flexibility that is used in the previous explanation of the business cycle through the simultaneous change in productivity and current income.

6.3.1 Example 6.3: Fixed price

Assume that for some reason, be it a liquidity trap or another reason, the interest rate cannot fall, and is fixed at

$$r = \bar{r}.$$

And also assume as in the flexible price explanation of the business cycle that both the capital productivity and the current income fall by 5%. Then it can be shown that there is an excess supply of capital.

To see this use Example 5.3 as the starting point, with $A_G = 12$, $y_0 = 100$, and $\beta = 0.98$. Then, as in Example 6.2, let $A_G = 11.4$ and at the same time let $y_0 = 95$. And crucially in addition, keep r fixed at the previous equilibrium value of 0.0463.

The capital demand from Example 6.2 is now given by

$$k_1^d = \frac{32.49}{\left(1+r\right)^2},$$

but with r fixed at

$$\bar{r} = 0.0463,$$

the equilibrium capital demand is

$$k_1^d = \frac{32.49}{\left(1.0463\right)^2} = 29.68.$$

Meanwhile the equilibrium capital supply from Example 6.2 is given by

$$k_1^s = \frac{95\left(0.98\right)}{1.98} - \frac{32.49}{\left(1.98\right)\left(1+r\right)^2}; \tag{6.29}$$

but with r fixed at 0.0463, the supply is

$$k_1^s = \frac{95\left(0.98\right)}{1.98} - \frac{32.49}{\left(1.98\right)\left(1.0463\right)^2} = 32.03.$$

The equilibrium with a fixed price and excess capital in the face of a 5% productivity and current income decrease can be graphed. Starting from the supply function,

$$1+r = \left(\frac{\frac{36}{(1.98)}}{\left(\frac{100(0.98)}{1.98} - k_1^s\right)}\right)^{0.5}, \tag{6.30}$$

which is the original equilibrium capital supply of Example 5.3; the new capital supply with the decrease in productivity and current income is given by

$$1+\bar{r} = \left(\frac{\frac{32.49}{(1.98)}}{\left(\frac{95(0.98)}{1.98} - k_1^s\right)}\right)^{0.5}. \tag{6.31}$$

The original capital demand of Example 5.3 is

$$1+r = \frac{6}{\left(k_1^d\right)^{0.5}}, \tag{6.32}$$

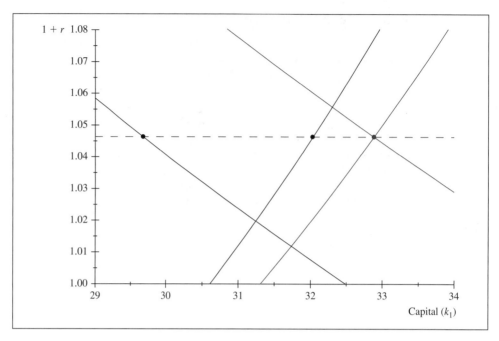

Figure 6.5 Deeper recession with a fixed interest rate in Example 6.3

and the new capital demand in recession, with fixed r, is

$$1 + \bar{r} = \left(\frac{32.49}{k_1^d} \right)^{0.5}. \tag{6.33}$$

Figure 6.5 graphs the fixed price recession equations (6.31) and (6.33) in black, and the Example 5.3 supply and demand of equations (6.30) and (6.32) in blue.

6.3.2 Excess capital supply and goods demand

The equilibrium has the supply of capital greater than demand at the given price. The amount of capital that will be employed is the amount demanded at the price, leaving the excess supply to be unemployed. This means that the equilibrium capital employed is the demand amount of 29.68. And the excess is

Excess capital supply: $k_1^s - k_1^d = 32.03 - 29.68 = 2.35.$

Relative to the original equilibrium quantity of capital of 32.89, this is $\frac{2.35}{32.89} = 0.071$, or 7% of the capital unemployed.

Figure 6.6 graphs the same equilibrium as Figure 6.5 but adds in the dashed black vertical lines to indicate the magnitude of the excess supply of capital as the horizontal difference between these two dashed black lines.

The fixed interest rate leads to a crisis-type drop in the employment of capital, and a bigger drop in future consumption. This brings up questions of what policy might be used to offset such crisis decreases. Tax changes are sometimes used as policy tools, as another way to get out of recession, although these tools are perhaps best used for increasing the long term efficiency of government by moving towards lower tax rates over time. The next section examines the effect of a capital tax.

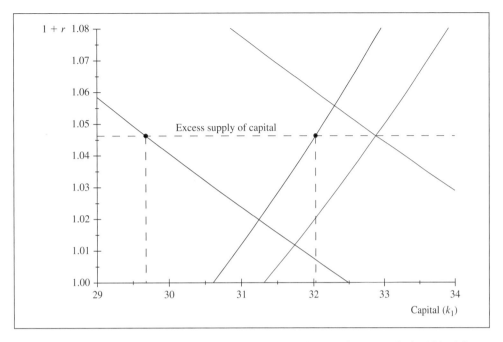

Figure 6.6 Excess capital supply indicated by horizontal distance between dashed black lines in Example 6.3

6.4 A tax on capital income

Suppose government spending is paid for by issuing a proportional tax on capital income that the consumer receives. Denoting this tax by τ_k, it is levied on all capital income, including the principal, which is equal to $(1+r)\,k_1$ in the decentralised economy in this chapter with the consumer and firm problems separately laid out.

Note that if the capital tax is alternatively postulated to be levied only upon the interest rk_1, the economic effects are similar: the supply of capital shifts back and the demand for next period consumption also shifts back. The assumption that the tax is levied only on interest income rk_1 instead of the gross capital income of $(1+r)\,k_1$ is used later in the text's chapter on growth. However such an assumption here does not lead to an analytic solution for the interest rate in our example economy. The assumption that the tax falls on gross capital income is used instead in this two-period framework because it does provide an analytic solution for the interest rate, and yields the same qualitative economic analysis of a capital tax.

The tax is levied on the consumer's income rather than the firm's. This makes the firm's problem unchanged; only the consumer's problem is altered. And it is important to note that if the tax is levied on the firm instead of the consumer, the intermediate analysis is different but the equilibrium results of the tax end up the same: it does not matter in a competitive market whether the tax is issued on the consumer or firm side.

6.4.1 Budget constraints

The tax on capital income makes the consumer's after-tax capital income equal to $(1+r)\,k_1\,(1-\tau_k)$. Including the profit Π_1 and the tax transfer T, this makes the consumer's second period consumption budget constraint:

$$c_1 = \Pi_1 + k_1^s \left(1+r\right)\left(1-\tau_k\right) + T. \tag{6.34}$$

The government budget constraint is given by

$$T = \tau_k \left(1+r\right) k_1. \tag{6.35}$$

6.4.2 Example 6.4

Assume that specification of the full economy is the same as in Example 5.3, with the addition of the capital tax as in equations (6.34) and (6.35). Then $\beta = 0.98$, $y_0 = 100$, and assume a tax rate of $\tau_k = 0.1$. The consumer problem is

$$\underset{k_1^s}{\text{Max }} u = \ln\left(y_0 - k_1^s\right) + \beta \ln\left[\Pi_1 + k_1^s \left(1+r\right)\left(1-\tau_k\right) + T\right].$$

From the equilibrium conditions of the consumer,

$$\frac{-1}{y_0 - k_1^s} + \beta \frac{\left(1+r\right)\left(1-\tau_k\right)}{\Pi_1 + k_1^s \left(1+r\right)\left(1-\tau_k\right) + T} = 0.$$

Substitute in from the government budget constraint that $T = \tau_k \left(1+r\right) k_1$:

$$\frac{-1}{y_0 - k_1^s} + \beta \frac{\left(1+r\right)\left(1-\tau_k\right)}{\Pi_1 + k_1^s \left(1+r\right)} = 0.$$

This gives the supply of capital as a function of profit:

$$k_1^s = \frac{y_0\beta \left(1+r\right)\left(1-\tau_k\right) - \Pi_1}{\left(1+r\right)\left(1+\beta\left(1-\tau_k\right)\right)}.$$

With the firm production function of

$$y_1 = 12 \left(k_1^d\right)^{0.5},$$

the equilibrium condition is

$$\left(0.5\right) 12 \left(k_1^d\right)^{-0.5} = 1+r, \tag{6.36}$$

with demand

$$k_1^d = \frac{36}{\left(1+r\right)^2}. \tag{6.37}$$

And profit is

$$\Pi_1 = 12\sqrt{k_1^d} - k_1^d \left(1+r\right), \tag{6.38}$$

$$\Pi_1 = 12\sqrt{\frac{36}{\left(1+r\right)^2}} - \left(\frac{36}{\left(1+r\right)^2}\right)\left(1+r\right) = \frac{36}{1+r}. \tag{6.39}$$

Substituting in the profit from the firm problem, which is unchanged, gives the solution for the supply of capital in terms of the interest rate and the exogenous parameters:

$$k_1^s = \frac{y_0\beta \left(1+r\right)\left(1-\tau_k\right) - \frac{36}{1+r}}{\left(1+r\right)\left(1+\beta\left(1-\tau_k\right)\right)}. \tag{6.40}$$

The supply in terms of the calibration of the example is

$$k_1^s = \frac{100\,(0.98)\,(1+r)\,(1-0.1) - \frac{36}{1+r}}{(1+r)\,(1.98\,(1-0.1))}. \tag{6.41}$$

And the inverse when solved for $1+r$ is

$$1+r = \left(\frac{36}{100\,(0.98)\,(1-0.1) - k_1^s\,(1.98\,(1-0.1))} \right)^{0.5}. \tag{6.42}$$

Demand for capital written in its inverse form is again

$$1+r = \frac{36}{\left(k_1^d\right)^2}. \tag{6.43}$$

Figure 6.7 graphs equations (6.42) and (6.43) of Example 6.4 in black, along with the zero tax supply of capital, in blue, from Example 5.3, or in Example 6.4 with $\tau_k = 0$. The demand curve of equation (6.43) does not change with the tax rate but the supply curve shifts back with a positive tax rate.

The capital tax increases the equilibrium interest from $r = 0.0463$ to $r = 0.0656$. As with the tax on labour income, the tax shifts back savings and causes a higher equilibrium price even though the tax revenue is transferred back to the consumer. The shift in savings is purely a substitution distortion whereby the capital tax makes the price of future consumption higher and so discourages savings. Implicit taxes on capital, through regulations and other restrictions, have the same type of economic effect.

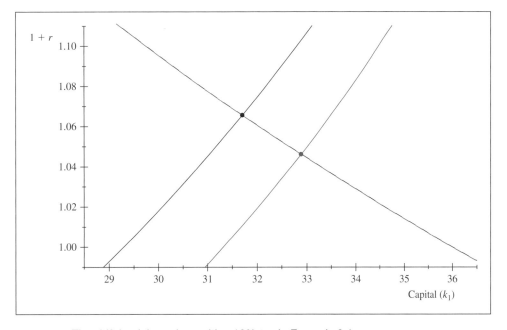

Figure 6.7 The shift back in savings with a 10% tax in Example 6.4

Setting equal the quantity of capital supplied and demanded as a function of r gives the solution for the interest rate:

$$\frac{100\,(0.98)\,(1+r)\,(1-0.1) - \frac{36}{1+r}}{(1+r)\,(1.98\,(1-0.1))} = \frac{36}{(1+r)^2},$$

$$1+r = \left(\frac{(1.98\,(1-0.1))\,36 + 36}{100\,(0.98)\,(1-0.1)}\right)^{0.5} = 1.0656.$$

The equilibrium capital at $\tau_k = 0.1$ is $k_1^d = \frac{36}{(1.0656)^2} = 31.704.$

And in general form, for any tax rate τ_k,

$$1+r = \left(\frac{(1.98\,(1-\tau_k))\,36 + 36}{100\,(0.98)\,(1-\tau_k)}\right)^{0.5}.$$

With a tax rate of $\tau_k = 0.05$, the equilibrium interest rate rises from 0.0463, when $\tau_k = 0$, up to $r = 0.0555$ or 5.55%. Or if $\tau_k = 0.2$, then $r = 0.0893$ or 8.93%.

In the market for future consumption, the supply of future consumption is unaffected by the tax and remains at

$$c_1^s = 12\sqrt{k_1^d} = 12\sqrt{\frac{36}{(1+r)^2}} = \frac{72}{1+r},$$

$$1+r = \frac{72}{c_1^s}. \tag{6.44}$$

The demand for future consumption, using equation (6.41) for k_1^s, is

$$c_1^d = \Pi + k_1^s\,(1+r) = \frac{36}{1+r} + k_1^s\,(1+r),$$

$$c_1^d = 36\left(\frac{1}{1+r}\right) + \frac{100\,(0.98)\,(1+r)\,(1-0.1) - \frac{36}{1+r}}{(1.98\,(1-0.1))},$$

$$0 = 36\left(1 - \frac{1}{(1.98\,(1-0.1))}\right)\left(\frac{1}{1+r}\right)^2 - c_1^d\left(\frac{1}{1+r}\right) + \frac{100\,(0.98)\,(1-0.1)}{(1.98\,(1-0.1))},$$

$$0 = 15.798\left(\frac{1}{1+r}\right)^2 - c_1^d\left(\frac{1}{1+r}\right) + 49.495.$$

The quadratic solution to the equation $A\left(\frac{1}{1+r}\right)^2 + B\left(\frac{1}{1+r}\right) + C = 0$, with $A = 15.798$, $B = -c_1^d$, and $C = 49.495$, is given by

$$\frac{1}{1+r} = \frac{-B - \sqrt{B^2 - 4AC}}{2A} = \frac{c_1^d - \sqrt{\left(c_1^d\right)^2 - 4\,(15.798)\,(49.495)}}{2\,(15.798)}. \tag{6.45}$$

Figure 6.8 graphs the supply and demand for future consumption under the 10% tax of Example 6.4 in equations (6.44) and (6.45), in black, along with the Example 5.3 zero tax demand function, in blue. Supply is not affected by the tax, but demand shifts back and less future consumption results.

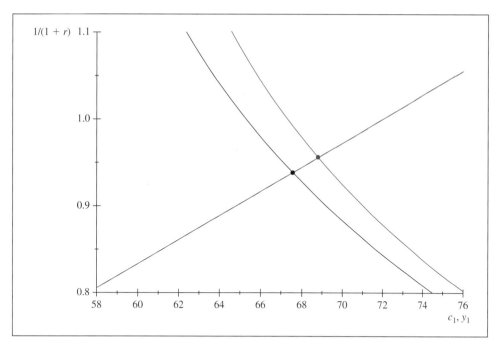

Figure 6.8 Future period consumption with 10% tax in Example 6.4

The equilibrium relative price is $\frac{1}{1+r} = \frac{1}{1.0656} = 0.93844$, and the equilibrium future goods consumption is $c_1^s = \frac{72}{1+r} = \frac{72}{1.0656} = 67.568$, instead of $\frac{72}{1.0463} = 68.814$ with no tax.

The general effect of the tax can also be found. The utility level curve is found from the utility function:

$$u = \ln\left(100 - k_1^s\right) + 0.98 \ln\left(c_1^d\right),$$
$$u = \ln\left(100 - 31.704\right) + 0.98 \ln\left(67.568\right) = 8.3527,$$
$$c_1^d = \left(\frac{e^u}{c_0}\right)^{\frac{1}{\beta}} = \left(\frac{e^{8.3706}}{c_0}\right)^{\frac{1}{0.98}}.$$

The production function is the same at

$$c_1^s = 12\sqrt{k_1^d} = 12\left(100 - c_0\right)^{0.5},$$

and the budget line is

$$c_1^d = \Pi_1 + k_1^s\left(1 + r\right) = \frac{36}{1.0656} + \left(100 - c_0\right)\left(1.0656\right).$$

The utility level falls only slightly from the zero tax equilibrium, from $u = 8.3532$ to 8.3527 with $\tau_k = 0.1$. Therefore the tax wedge is difficult to discern in a general equilibrium graph, although it is still there. The budget line intersects the production function rather than being tangent to it, while the utility level curve remains tangent to the budget line at the equilibrium. The tax causes current consumption to rise, since the net interest return after the tax is lower, and the consumer saves less. At the same time, future consumption is lower since less capital is invested.

6.5 Capital policy alternatives

It is indeed a shortcut to use a fixed interest rate to explain crisis drops in investment demand. It would be better to explain the problem by analysing what might be wrong in the capital markets themselves: the bank industry for example was failing in both the 1930s and in 2007–09. Therefore it is more a failure of insurance and consumption smoothing, including government insurance, than a fixity of prices. This will be taken up in Part 5 and an analysis of aggregate risk is provided as a possible reason for the failure of adequate insurance. Unexpected changes to banking productivity can *de facto* be counted as aggregate risk. A priori, and ideally, it would have been possible to expect such shocks and so internalise such risk into markets. And this then becomes the aim of policy solutions.

Tax cuts might be used during recessions or worse crises, but are best only if they can be sustained. Another alternative is to borrow from future generations and so spend more government money now. Keynes argued that the government must step in and do the investment itself so as to soak up the excess supply of capital and employ it. But such investment is spending that needs to be repaid eventually. Markets know this and build in expectations of future taxes either in terms of inflation or explicit taxes.

6.6 Applications

6.6.1 Capital market regulation, usury and economic science

An important historical role has been played by restrictions on paying interest on capital. Roman Emperor Constantine I in AD 325 prohibited the charging of interest on loans, a practice then known as usury. This was significant because it was part of the first uniform Christian doctrine, called the First Council of Nicea. Ancient China prohibited charging interest as does early and current Islamic law. While usury is sometimes meant to imply the charging of excessive interest, the prohibition nonetheless has actually applied to the charging of any interest at all in these examples.

In Western nations, such prohibitions on interest have extended to national laws, such as article 10 of the original British Magna Carta of 1215. The Magna Carta became part of the common law code of England and Wales. By the final version of the Magna Carta of 1297, which is still part of the law code of England and Wales, the usury prohibition was repealed. Rather than being part of the formal law, usury restrictions became religious doctrines that dictated standards of morality. For example, in the 14th century in Western society, charging interest was deemed heresy to the Church by Pope Clement V. And as late as 1745, when Pope Benedict XIV published his codification of church doctrine called *Vix Pervenit: On Usury and Other Dishonest Profit*, charging interest on loans remained religiously forbidden.

Adam Smith combated the misperceptions on restricting the charging of interest on capital in his 1776 *Wealth of Nations*. In the process, many believe he began modern economics. Smith described how the market for interest is determined by supply and demand. And he clarified that any attempt to regulate the market rate of interest will not likely prevail, as the market will get around the restriction. For example (p. 380 Book II Chapter 4):

> Notwithstanding the Edict of 1766, by which the French king attempted to reduce the rate of interest from five to four percent, money continued to be lent in France at five percent, the law being evaded in several different ways.

The Wealth of Nations gave birth to modern economics in part by establishing the principles of the capital market. This is a major accomplishment given the religious intolerance of usury that held firmly even at that time.

Analytically, the effects of laws against usury are that they act as restrictions which implicitly impose a tax on capital. This can be represented in the two-period intertemporal consumption analysis. Consider usury restrictions as an implicit tax on capital investment, that leaves unchanged the production possibilities themselves. For example, if no interest were allowed to be paid, so that $r = 0$ to savers, then consumers substitute towards more current consumption and towards less investment. While consumers face a zero price, the firm investing capital faces an effectively higher price of capital, due to the decreased supply by consumers. The usury laws drive a tax wedge between consumer-suppliers and producer-demanders.

Figure 6.8 suggests an analysis for the difference in wealth between the modern 'Western' nations and the traditional 'Eastern' nations. Implicit taxes on capital through usury laws still existing in Eastern nations, while the Western nations have been fully allowing unrestricted market interest rates on capital, can over several centuries result in much less investment and the accumulation of wealth in the East as compared to the West. This is a very broad way to view one reason for less development in the Middle East as a region.

However in recent decades Islamic banking has become very sophisticated and now provides vehicles for allowing profits on capital that in Western nations are viewed as interest on capital. This allows for the implicit tax on capital to be reduced. As a result, and combined with income from successful oil and gas industries, such nations have recently been building huge capital infrastructures, as in Dubai.

Still Islamic banking is not something that can be readily spread in Western economies, with the result that religious led countries still end up implicitly taxing their capital markets. For example Messmann (2010) argues that European Union laws make unlikely the effective application of Islamic banking provisions within the EU. Instituting Islamic law requires restructuring all loans, such as automobile financing, in complicated ways that can involve automobile repurchase agreements. Because of EU restrictions, services for the automobile would have to be supplied and this would end up as the responsibility of the bank, which may make the whole set-up unworkable.

6.7 Questions

1. How can a business cycle be described using the analysis of this chapter?
2. In Example 6.1, assume that the income endowment y_0 and the productivity factor $A_G = 12$ increase during an expansion by 10% instead of 5%.
   (a) Find the equilibrium supply and demand as functions of $1 + r$, and graph the functions in both goods and capital markets.
   (b) Find the equilibrium interest rate $1 + r$.
   (c) Find all of the equilibrium quantities of the economy, and the utility level.
   (d) Describe how the economy compares to when there is no increase in endowment or productivity; how do supply and demand shift in each market with the increases?
3. Define an excess supply of capital, and define unemployed capital. Compare these to an equilibrium decrease in capital investment during a flexible price decrease in endowment and productivity as in Example 6.2.
4. In Example 6.3 with a fixed price, let the decrease in goods endowment and productivity be 10% instead of 5%.
   (a) Find the quantity of the excess supply of capital.
   (b) Graph the excess quantity of capital.

    (c) Indicate how utility decreases given the fixed price, as compared to when the price is flexible, when the goods endowment and productivity both fall by 10%.

5. In Example 6.4, a tax on the interest from capital causes
    (a) a decrease in next period consumption;
    (b) a decrease in next period income;
    (c) an increase in current period consumption;
    (d) all of the above.

6. In a representative consumer economy with Cobb–Douglas production and where log utility depends on current and future period consumption, imposing laws against usury, as occurs for example under Islamic religious law, causes
    (a) current period consumption to rise;
    (b) future period consumption to fall;
    (c) utility to fall;
    (d) all of the above.

7. In Example 6.4, let the tax on capital income be 20% instead of 10%.
    (a) Find the supply and demand functions as a function of the interest rate for both goods and labour markets.
    (b) Graph the supply and demand and determine the equilibrium interest rate.
    (c) Find the change in utility caused by the tax.
    (d) Define and find the tax wedge in the economy in terms of the difference between the equilibrium interest rate with the 20% tax, and that rate along the original no-tax supply of capital at the equilibrium quantity of capital that prevails with the 20% tax. (Hint: see the labour tax wedge in Chapter 3.)

8. How do usury laws affect investment levels in Islamic countries?

6.8 References

Keynes, John Maynard, 1930, *A Treatise on Money*, Volume 1, Macmillan and Co., London.

Keynes, John Maynard, 1936, *The General Theory of Employment, Interest, and Money*, Harcourt Brace Jovanovich, first Harbinger edition, 1964.

Messmann, Stefan, 2010, *Islamic Banking and Finance – Transplantable Models from Malaysia to the EU?*, in press.

Samuelson, Paul Anthony, 1951, *Economics: An Introductory Analysis*, second edition, McGraw-Hill, New York.

Smith, Adam, 1776, *An Inquiry into the Nature and Causes of The Wealth of Nations; The Cannan edition*, The University of Chicago Press, Chicago, 1976.

CHAPTER (7)

Trade in physical capital markets

7.1 Introduction

The chapter shows trade in the capital market with two-agents of different marginal productivity. In autarky with no trade, the interest rates are different in each country and the savings equals the investment in each country. With trade allowed, a world market clearing condition in capital establishes a world interest rate in equilibrium that is in-between the two autarky rates. Trade patterns emerge with savings and investment no longer equal within each country, but with global savings equal to global investment.

First a partial equilibrium 'small open' endowment economy is presented to illustrate the issues of borrowing and lending capital. This shows one side of the borrowing or lending, while in general equilibrium it naturally arises that one agent is the borrower and the other the lender. However the interest rate is given exogenously in the simpler partial equilibrium while it is the fundamental adjustment mechanism in the general equilibrium.

In general equilibrium, factor price equalisation occurs through the two different interest rates under autarky becoming equal under trade in which a world market clearing condition is introduced. This sets total supply of both agents equal to total demand for both agents. From either market clearing in goods, or in capital, the world interest rate can be found. The less productive agent finds the equilibrium interest rate higher than in autarky and so lends capital in equilibrium. The more productive agent finds the world interest rate lower than in autarky and so borrows capital from the less productive agent.

Trade patterns are identified on the basis of comparative advantage. The more productive agent borrows and invests capital supplied by the less productive agent. Therefore the more productive agent specialises in future period consumption while the less productive agent specialises in current period consumption. The trade flows that comprise this comparative advantage are identified in both the goods and capital markets and in the general equilibrium with both current and future consumption. In general equilibrium these patterns are called trade triangles. Application of trade in capital is made to several global issues.

7.1.1 Building on the last chapters

The small open economy at the beginning of the chapter is a warm-up model not found in the previous chapters. This is because it assumes a constant interest rate and so is not a general equilibrium model. This exception is made because it is a very commonly used analysis, and because it serves to help indicate how borrowing and lending of capital occur.

The trade between agents of this chapter is built upon in Example 5.3, and the baseline model of the last chapter's Examples 6.1, 6.2, 6.3 and 6.4, in that the baseline specification of these examples is the same for the less productive agent. The more productive agent has the same technology as in Question 8 of Chapter 5, with a higher productivity of capital than in Example 5.3. The other parameters of the last chapter are all the same in this chapter. Therefore only the more productive agent is a new specification. This allows the autarky equilibrium of the less productive agent to be already known, and only the second agent equilibrium must be computed.

Trade with a market clearing condition is then the new part of the chapter relative to the last chapter, although this is the same concept of the market clearing condition with labour as in Chapter 4. The excess supply of goods and capital is set out as in Chapter 4, and so are the trade triangles in the general equilibrium graph in dimensions of current and future consumption.

7.1.2 Learning objective

The student is challenged to get a glimpse of how international capital flows take place. The complications of the normal financial instruments of such borrowing are all avoided until later chapters and instead the simple trade flows based on comparative advantage are set out. The main concept to be grasped is that countries with higher capital productivity will import capital from less productive countries, although this is seen only in a two-agent economy. Borrowing capital, rather than having some negative connotation, is simply part of international trade based on investment opportunities.

7.1.3 Who made it happen?

Keynes in his 1930 *Treatise on Money* discusses credit cycles having to do with business cycles but also in the same treatise discusses the borrowing and lending of capital that we set out in this chapter, although without the general equilibrium mathematical development. The concept that capital savings is not necessarily equal to capital investment is an old concept based on the existence of trade in capital.

A more modern development to highlight the trade in capital is the Feldstein and Horioka 1980 study of how savings and investment tend to move together rather closely, indicating less trade in capital than we might think would occur. Obstfeld and Rogoff in their 1996 *Foundations in International Macroeconomics* popularised a general equilibrium approach to such capital trade. And in the business cycle setting internationally, a large literature analyses the trade between nations using such differences in productivities, for example Backus, Kehoe and Kydland (1992) and Robert Kollmann (1996).

7.2 Two-period 'small open' endowment economy

One side of the trade can be examined in terms of borrowing and lending capital. This becomes part of the general equilibrium with two agents. But in the so-called 'small open economy' model, with a given interest rate, the output can also be taken as being given. In the two-agent general equilibrium the output is produced by each agent/country. Here the income of the agent is assumed to be given along with the interest rate, so the only decision is whether to borrow or lend. Assuming the income of the agent is the same as assuming an 'endowment' economy, where output is somehow exogenously endowed.

An endowment economy here means that the income each period is given to the consumer as an exogenous known amount. Therefore the production by the firm is not part of the economy. This makes the model a partial equilibrium and not a general equilibrium model because production is not specified. It is used in international macroeconomics with the reasoning that for small countries, the world interest rate will not be affected by their actions, and so can be taken as given.

There are two periods in which to consume, with savings of the consumer determining how much is consumed in each period. Let c_0 denote consumption in the current period and c_1 consumption in the next period; let the income endowment be denoted by y_0 and y_1; and let r be the real interest rate.

Let the consumer's utility function, as in Chapters 4 and 5, take the log form,

$$u(c_0, c_1) \equiv \ln c_0 + \beta \ln c_1,$$

where β is the discount factor for future income, where $0 < \beta < 1$.

7.2.1 Wealth constraint

The wealth constraint sets the discounted value of expenditures on consumption equal to the discounted value of the income stream:

$$c_0 + \frac{c_1}{1+r} = y_0 + \frac{y_1}{1+r}. \tag{7.1}$$

This constraint is the same as equation (5.18), if the next period income endowment is defined as the profit received next period, $y_1 \equiv \Pi_1$. In other words, the endowed income next period can be compared to the profits earned in a more general economy in which the interest rate r is endogenously determined. But in this simpler economy r is exogenously given as the 'world' interest rate that a small country faces.

Once y_0 and y_1 are exogenously specified, and given r, the value of the income stream can more simply be given in terms of a single present discounted value. Defining wealth W again as the discounted value of the income stream, then

$$W \equiv y_0 + \frac{y_1}{1+r} = c_0 + \frac{c_1}{1+r}.$$

7.2.2 Example 7.1: Lender

Let $(y_0, y_1) = (100, 0)$ so that wealth equals

$$W = y_0 + \frac{y_1}{1+r} = 100 + \frac{0}{1+r} = 100.$$

Therefore the wealth constraint reduces to

$$c_0 + \frac{c_1}{1+r} = 100. \tag{7.2}$$

Given $W = 100$, and the log utility specification,

$$u = \ln c_0 + \beta \ln c_1,$$

the only other parameters to specify are the discount factor β and the interest rate r. Let $\beta = 0.98$ and $r = 0.10$.

Solving for

$$c_0 = 100 - \frac{c_1}{1+r},$$

from the wealth constraint and substituting this in for c_0 in the utility function, the maximisation problem in only the variable c_1 is

$$\underset{c_1}{\text{Max}}\, u = \ln\left(100 - \frac{c_1}{1.1}\right) + 0.98 \ln c_1.$$

Take the derivative of utility with respect to c_1,

$$\frac{\partial u}{\partial c_1} = \frac{-\left(\frac{1}{1.1}\right)}{100 - \frac{c_1}{1.1}} + \frac{0.98}{c_1} = 0,$$

$$c_1 = \frac{(110)\,0.98}{(1+0.98)} = 54.44.$$

With $c_1 = 54.44$, substitute c_1 back into the wealth constraint,

$$c_0 = 100 - \frac{54.44}{1.1} = 50.509,$$

and so $c_0 = 50.51$.

The result is that there is more future consumption than present consumption $c_1 > c_0$. This happens when the interest rate is greater than the rate of time preference. Here with the consumer discount factor $\beta = 0.98$, the related 'rate of time preference' is defined as $\beta = \frac{1}{1+\rho}$. So with $\beta = 0.98$, then $\rho = \frac{1}{\beta} - 1 = \frac{1}{0.98} - 1 = 0.0204$. More future consumption results when

$$r > \rho,$$

which occurs in Example 7.1. This is because the market's time preference rate of r is more than the consumer's own time preference rate of ρ, and so the consumer saves more today in order to take advantage of the relatively high r and so consumes more tomorrow.

Utility in the example is given by

$$u = \ln(50.509) + 0.98 \ln(54.44) = 7.8393,$$

$$e^u = (c_0)(c_1)^{0.98},$$

$$c_1 = \left(\frac{e^u}{c_0}\right)^{\frac{1}{0.98}} = \left(\frac{e^{7.8393}}{c_0}\right)^{\frac{1}{0.98}}. \tag{7.3}$$

The consumer is endowed with positive current income of $y_0 = 100$ and zero future income of $y_1 = 0$. This make the consumer a lender, consuming only about half of current income and lending the rest until next period. Lending out current income in order to receive some future consumption acts to smooth the consumption stream over time. By lending and smoothing consumption the consumer raises the utility level. The amount lent is the given current income minus current consumption, of

Lending: $y_0 - c_0 = 100 - 50.509 = 49.491$.

The wealth constraint can be graphed by solving for c_1:

$$c_1 = (1+r)(W - c_0),$$
$$c_1 = (1.1)(100 - c_0). \tag{7.4}$$

Figure 7.1 graphs equations (7.3) and (7.4), with the utility level as the black curve, and the wealth constraint in blue.

The equilibrium occurs at the tangency, and the endowment point is the black point on the horizontal axis at $(y_0, y_1) = (100, 0)$. Lending is the difference on the horizontal axis between the endowment point and the equilibrium c_0.

7.2.3 Example 7.2: Interest rate increase

Assume again that $\beta = 0.98$ and $(y_0, y_1) = (100, 0)$, with $W = y_0 + \frac{y_1}{1+r} = 100 + \frac{0}{1+r} = 100$. Suppose the interest rate rises from $r = 0.1$ to $r = 0.12$, a 20% increase. Then the

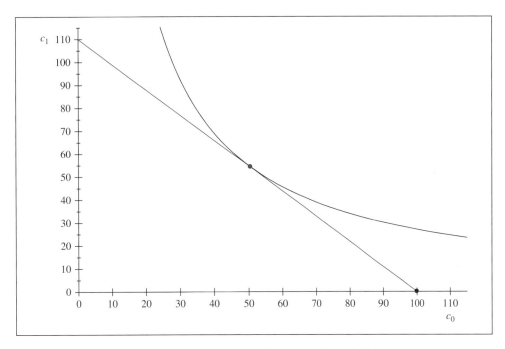

Figure 7.1 Small open economy equilibrium with lending in Example 7.1

consumer maximisation problem is

$$\underset{c_1}{\text{Max}}\, u = \ln\left(30 - \frac{c_1}{1.12}\right) + 0.98\ln(c_1).$$

The equilibrium condition becomes

$$\frac{\partial u}{\partial c_1} = \frac{-\frac{1}{1.12}}{100 - \frac{c_1}{1.12}} + \frac{0.98}{c_1} = 0,$$

$$c_1 = \frac{(112)\,0.98}{(1+0.98)} = 55.43.$$

The fractional increase in c_1 is $\frac{55.434-54.44}{54.44} = 0.0183$, or 1.83%. Current consumption is unchanged at

$$c_0 = 100 - \frac{c_1}{1.12} = 100 - \frac{55.43}{1.12} = 50.509.$$

This is because the substitution effect towards less current consumption, with a lower price of future consumption given by $\frac{1}{1+r} = \frac{1}{1.12}$, is offset exactly by the positive income effect on current consumption of earning more on what is lent out since the interest rate is higher. The utility level now is

$$u = \ln 50.509 + 0.98\ln 55.43 = 7.857,$$

$$c_1 = \left(\frac{e^u}{c_0}\right)^{\frac{1}{0.98}} = \left(\frac{e^{7.857}}{c_0}\right)^{\frac{1}{0.98}}. \tag{7.5}$$

And the budget line, or wealth constraint, can be graphed by solving for c_1:

$$c_1 = (1+r)(W-c_0),$$
$$c_1 = (1.12)(100-c_0). \tag{7.6}$$

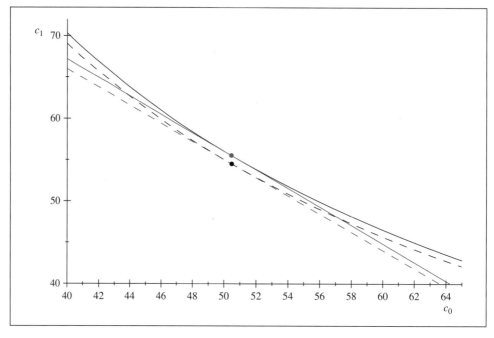

Figure 7.2 Lender better off with interest rate increase in Example 7.2

Figure 7.2 graphs equations (7.5) and (7.6) in solid black and blue, along with the lower equilibrium of Example 7.1, which is graphed in dashed black and dashed blue.

The interest rate increase causes future consumption to rise while keeping current consumption unchanged.

7.2.4 Consumption smoothing and time preference

Examining the equilibrium conditions in Examples 7.1 and 7.2, the general result for future consumption is

$$c_1 = (1+r) \left(\frac{\beta}{1+\beta} \right) W. \tag{7.7}$$

Substituting this into the budget constraint gives the general result for current consumption:

$$W = c_0 + \frac{c_1}{1+r},$$

$$W = c_0 + \frac{(1+r) \left(\frac{\beta}{1+\beta} \right) W}{1+r},$$

$$c_0 = W - \left(\frac{\beta}{1+\beta} \right) W,$$

$$c_0 = \frac{W}{1+\beta}.$$

Current consumption is independent of the interest rate because with log utility the substitution and income effects of changes in r go in opposite directions, exactly offsetting each other. Future consumption rises with the interest rate. And both current and next period consumption rise with the increases in wealth W.

An increase in the discount factor β means moving it towards 1. This means that the consumer is more patient with getting consumption in the future instead of today. And this leads to a decrease in current consumption and an increase in next period consumption. If $\beta = 1$, this would be viewed as an extreme case of infinite patience: the consumer would not care at all if consumption was this period or next period. Generally $\beta = 1$ is ruled out as inadmissible because it gives rise to unbounded wealth. And so the restriction is that $\beta < 1$.

The role of time preference can be seen a bit more clearly by again defining $\beta \equiv \frac{1}{1+\rho}$, where ρ is called the rate of time preference, while β is the time discount factor. These are similar to the real rate of interest r, and the rate at which future income is discounted to its present value, which is $\frac{1}{1+r}$. But now the discount rate and rate of time discount are a part of the consumer's preferences, or utility function, and these end up determining the consumer will save given the market rate of interest r.

The relation between time preference and the market rate of interest can be seen clearly in the simple economy of this section. The consumer's current and future consumption can be restated using $\beta \equiv \frac{1}{1+\rho}$ as

$$c_0 = \frac{W}{1+\beta} = \left(\frac{1+\rho}{2+\rho}\right) W, \tag{7.8}$$

and

$$c_1 = (1+r)\left(\frac{\beta}{1+\beta}\right) W = \left(\frac{1+r}{2+\rho}\right) W. \tag{7.9}$$

As the simplest case, consider when

$$r = \rho;$$

then there will be no growth in consumption over time since $c_0 = c_1$:

$$c_0 = c_1 = \frac{1+\rho}{2+\rho} W. \tag{7.10}$$

This is when there is perfect consumption smoothing over time.

A perfectly patient saver is said to have zero time preference and so is perfectly indifferent to consuming today or tomorrow. This means that $\rho = 0$ $(\beta = 1)$ and for this case, and with $r = \rho$, then by equation (7.10) consumption each period is one half of wealth: $c_0 = c_1 = \frac{1}{2}W$.

When the interest rate is greater than time preference, or $r > \rho$, then current consumption is less than future consumption:

$$c_0 = \left(\frac{1+\rho}{2+\rho}\right) W < \left(\frac{1+r}{2+\rho}\right) W = c_1. \tag{7.11}$$

Now the consumption is growing over time. And this is why we think of the case with $r > \rho$ in general as when the economy will be growing. Consumption growth requires that $r > \rho$.

7.2.5 Example 7.3: Borrower

An equilibrium borrower will have an endowment of future income but not so much current income. Consider for the same log utility, the case when $(y_0, y_1) = (0, 100)$, with $\beta = 0.98$ and $r = 0.10$. Wealth equals

$$W = y_0 + \frac{y_1}{1+r} = 0 + \frac{100}{1+0.1} = 90.909,$$

making the wealth constraint

$$c_0 + \frac{c_1}{1.1} = 90.909, \tag{7.12}$$

$$c_0 = 90.909 - \frac{c_1}{1.1}. \tag{7.13}$$

The consumer problem is similar to Examples 7.1 and 7.2:

$$\text{Max } u = \ln\left(90.909 - \frac{c_1}{1.1}\right) + 0.98 \ln c_1.$$

$$\frac{\partial u}{\partial c_1} = \frac{-\left(\frac{1}{1.1}\right)}{90.909 - \frac{c_1}{1.1}} + \frac{0.98}{c_1} = 0,$$

$$c_1 = \frac{(90.909)(1.1)\,0.98}{(1+0.98)} = 49.495,$$

$$c_0 = W - \frac{c_1}{1+r} = 90.909 - \frac{49.495}{1.1} = 45.914.$$

Borrowing is the income endowment in the current period of 0 minus the equilibrium consumption c_0:

Lending: $y_0 - c_0 = 0 - 45.9 = -45.9$.

A negative amount of lending is the same as a positive amount of borrowing, of 45.9.
Utility and the budget line are given by

$$u = \ln 45.914 + 0.98 \ln 49.495 = 7.6506,$$

$$c_1 = \left(\frac{e^u}{c_0}\right)^{\frac{1}{0.98}} = \left(\frac{e^{7.6506}}{c_0}\right)^{\frac{1}{0.98}}, \tag{7.14}$$

$$c_1 = (1+r)(W - c_0),$$
$$c_1 = (1.1)(90.91 - c_0). \tag{7.15}$$

Figure 7.3 graphs the utility level curve of equation (7.14) and the budget constraint of equation (7.15), in black and blue. The black endowment point on the vertical axis is at $(y_0, y_1) = (0, 100)$.

7.2.6 Example 7.4: Borrower with interest increase

Take the same assumptions of Example 7.3 but now allow an interest rate increase. Then the consumer who is borrowing must pay a higher price for the borrowing and the utility level falls. Let $(y_0, y_1) = (0, 100)$, with $\beta = 0.98$ and now let the interest rate rise to $r = 0.12$. Wealth falls somewhat to

$$W = y_0 + \frac{y_1}{1+r} = 0 + \frac{100}{1+0.12} = 89.286,$$

and the wealth constraint and consumer problem are

$$c_0 + \frac{c_1}{1.12} = 89.286, \tag{7.16}$$

$$\text{Max } u = \ln\left(89.286 - \frac{c_1}{1.12}\right) + 0.98 \ln c_1.$$

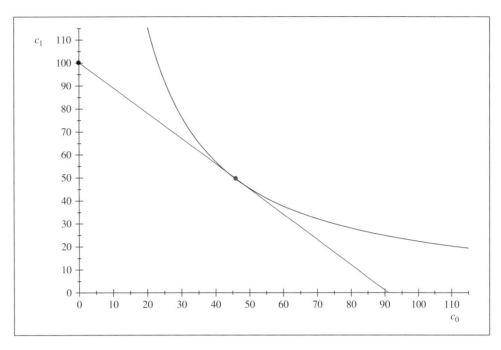

Figure 7.3 Small open economy equilibrium with borrowing in Example 7.3

$$\frac{\partial u}{\partial c_1} = \frac{-\left(\frac{1}{1.12}\right)}{89.286 - \frac{c_1}{1.1}} + \frac{0.98}{c_1} = 0,$$

$$c_1 = \frac{(89.286)(1.12)\,0.98}{(1 + 0.98)} = 49.495,$$

$$c_0 = W - \frac{c_1}{1 + r} = 89.286 - \frac{49.495}{1.12} = 45.094.$$

Future consumption is unchanged because the interest rate increase is offset by the wealth decrease. But current consumption falls.

Borrowing equals current consumption, thereby falling by the same amount as current consumption, to

Lending: $y_0 - c_0 = 0 - 45.094 = -45.094$.

Utility is

$$u = \ln 45.094 + 0.98 \ln 49.495 = 7.6326,$$

$$c_1 = \left(\frac{e^u}{c_0}\right)^{\frac{1}{0.98}} = \left(\frac{e^{7.6326}}{c_0}\right)^{\frac{1}{0.98}}, \tag{7.17}$$

and the budget line is

$$c_1 = (1 + r)(W - c_0),$$
$$c_1 = (1.12)(89.286 - c_0). \tag{7.18}$$

Figure 7.4 graphs the new utility level curve and budget constraint of equations (7.17) and (7.18), in solid black and blue, compared to the Example 7.3 equilibrium with $r = 0.1$ in dashed black and dashed blue.

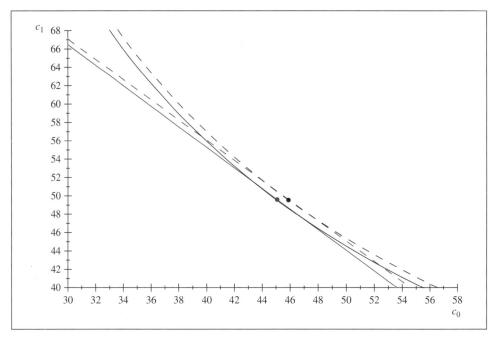

Figure 7.4 Interest rate increase with borrowing in Example 7.4

The budget line pivots down, giving a lower utility level for the borrower, with less current but the same future consumption.

7.3 Two-agent general equilibrium

A decentralised two-agent model allows for representation of a world economy engaging in trade in capital whereby the interest rate is endogenously determined. The same designation of agents as A and B is made, as in Chapter 4, and again these will be used as subscripts. And the agents have the same utility function, the same endowment of current period income y_0, and differ only by productivity in transforming investment into future income, similar to the approach of Chapter 4. The A and B consumers supply capital and demand goods, and as firms they demand capital and supply goods. The consumers have the same current and next period goods constraints as in Chapters 5 and 6, but now have new market clearing conditions, similar to Chapter 4.

The key component in the analysis of the two agents trading capital is the difference in the productivity of each agent in using capital investment to produce output in the following period. This represents a broad array of possibilities for why such productivity differences may exist. For example, there may be differences in the overall infrastructure of the country that makes its capital investment productivity less than more developed countries. This then suggests the developing versus developed country analysis. Or it may be that some countries are less financially developed than others and that this gives rise to a lower capital productivity. This suggests some Asian countries with historic prohibitions on capital interest, such as in the Middle East versus financial centres such as in London, New York and Hong Kong. Or the political system of governance in the country may be very unstable and this can cause an expected capital productivity that is less than in more stable countries such as long-standing democracies. This suggests for example the African countries versus the Western countries.

7.3.1 **Example 7.5: Decentralised autarky**

First the supply and demand of each agent A and B are examined with no trade allowed, giving an 'autarky' equilibrium of each country existing independently.

Again assuming that $\beta = 0.98$ and $y_0 = 100$, let there be just one agent A and one agent B, both with the same log utility function,

$$u\left(c_0^d, c_1^d\right) = \ln c_0^d + \beta \ln c_1^d.$$

Agent A has the same production function as in Example 5.3, with $A_G = 12$:

$$c_{1A}^s = y_{1A} = 12\sqrt{k_{1A}^d},$$

and let agent B be more productive, with $A_G = 14$ and the production function

$$c_{1B}^s = y_{1B} = 14\sqrt{k_{1B}^d}.$$

The new market clearing condition for capital is

$$k_{1A}^d + k_{1B}^d = k_{1A}^s + k_{1B}^s; \tag{7.19}$$

and the market clearing condition for next period's demand and supply of consumption goods is

$$c_{1A}^d + c_{1B}^d = y_{1A} + y_{1B}.$$

The consumer problem for agent A can be written as

$$\operatorname*{Max}_{c_{0A}, c_{1A}, k_{1A}^s} u = \ln c_{0A}^d + \beta \ln c_{1A}^d$$

subject to

$$c_{0A}^d = y_{0A} - k_{1A}^s, \tag{7.20}$$

and

$$c_{1A}^d = \Pi_{1A} + k_{1A}^s \left(1 + r\right). \tag{7.21}$$

The one-step problem in k_{1A}^s, is

$$\operatorname*{Max}_{k_{1A}^s} u = \ln\left(y_0 - k_{1A}^s\right) + \beta \ln\left[\Pi_{1A} + \left(1 + r\right) k_{1A}^s\right].$$

The equilibrium condition is

$$\frac{\beta\left(1 + r\right)}{\Pi_{1A} + k_{1A}^s\left(1 + r\right)} - \left(\frac{1}{y_{0A} - k_{1A}^s}\right) = 0.$$

And the supply of capital is

$$k_{1A}^s = \frac{y_0\beta}{1 + \beta} - \frac{\Pi_{1A}}{\left(1 + \beta\right)\left(1 + r\right)}. \tag{7.22}$$

For agent B, the capital supply is the same functional form:

$$k_{1B}^s = \frac{y_0\beta}{1 + \beta} - \frac{\Pi_{1B}}{\left(1 + \beta\right)\left(1 + r\right)}. \tag{7.23}$$

The profit for each A and B will be different, coming from the firm problem. The agent A firm problem is

$$\operatorname*{Max}_{k_{1A}^d} \Pi_{1A} = 12\sqrt{k_{1A}^d} - \left(1 + r\right) k_{1A}^d. \tag{7.24}$$

From Example 5.3, the firm equilibrium for agent A is already known as functions of r. The capital demand is

$$k_{1A}^d = \frac{36}{(1+r)^2}. \tag{7.25}$$

The resulting profit is

$$\Pi_{1A} = 12\sqrt{\frac{36}{(1+r)^2}} - \frac{36(1+r)}{(1+r)^2} = \frac{36}{1+r}. \tag{7.26}$$

And the supply of next period goods is

$$c_{1A}^s = y_{1A} = 12\sqrt{\frac{36}{(1+r)^2}} = \frac{72}{1+r}. \tag{7.27}$$

Substituting the profit back into the consumer supply of capital gives that

$$k_{1A}^s = \frac{y_0\beta}{1+\beta} - \frac{\left(\frac{36}{1+r}\right)}{(1+\beta)(1+r)}, \tag{7.28}$$

$$k_{1A}^s = \frac{(100)\,0.98}{1+0.98} - \frac{\left(\frac{36}{1+r}\right)}{(1+0.98)(1+r)}. \tag{7.29}$$

Also, now having profit and the supply of capital, the agent A demand for next period consumption is

$$c_{1A}^d = \Pi_{1A} + k_{1A}^s(1+r),$$

$$c_{1A}^d = \frac{36}{1+r} + (1+r)\frac{(100)\,0.98}{1+0.98} - \frac{36}{(1+0.98)(1+r)}. \tag{7.30}$$

Agent B has a somewhat different demand for capital, profit, and supply of goods because $A_G = 14$. The firm problem is

$$\underset{k_{1B}^d}{\text{Max }} \Pi_{1B} = 14\sqrt{k_{1B}^d} - (1+r)\,k_{1B}^d, \tag{7.31}$$

with the equilibrium condition

$$\frac{\partial f\left(k_{1B}^d\right)}{\partial k_{1B}^d} = (0.5)\,14\left(k_{1B}^d\right)^{-0.5} = 1+r. \tag{7.32}$$

The resulting demand function is

$$k_{1B}^d = \frac{49}{(1+r)^2}, \tag{7.33}$$

and the profit becomes

$$\Pi_{1B} = 14\sqrt{\frac{49}{(1+r)^2}} - \frac{49(1+r)}{(1+r)^2} = \frac{49}{1+r}. \tag{7.34}$$

The supply of next period goods y_{1B} is

$$c_{1B}^s = y_{1B} = 14\sqrt{k_{1B}^d} = 14\sqrt{\frac{49}{(1+r)^2}} = \frac{98}{1+r}. \tag{7.35}$$

For agent B, the capital supply is the same functional form:

$$k_{1B}^s = \frac{y_0\beta}{1+\beta} - \frac{\left(\frac{49}{1+r}\right)}{(1+\beta)(1+r)},$$ (7.36)

$$k_{1B}^s = \frac{(100)\,0.98}{1+0.98} - \frac{\left(\frac{49}{1+r}\right)}{(1+0.98)(1+r)}.$$ (7.37)

Agent B demand for next period consumption comes from the budget constraint with profit and capital supply substituted in:

$$c_{1B}^d = \Pi_{1B} + k_{1B}^s(1+r),$$

$$c_{1B}^d = \frac{49}{1+r} + (1+r)\frac{(100)\,0.98}{1+0.98} - \frac{49}{(1+0.98)(1+r)}.$$ (7.38)

7.3.2 Capital market

The Example 7.5 equilibrium of each agent/country living in autarky can be illustrated in the capital and goods markets, as well as in general equilibrium $(c_1 : c_0)$ space. Consider the capital market, and invert the capital supply and demand for each agent so that it is solved for $1+r$:

$$k_{1A}^d = \frac{36}{(1+r)^2},$$

$$1+r = \frac{6}{\sqrt{k_{1A}^d}};$$ (7.39)

$$k_{1B}^d = \frac{49}{(1+r)^2},$$

$$1+r = \frac{7}{\sqrt{k_{1B}^d}};$$ (7.40)

$$k_{1A}^s = \frac{(100)\,0.98}{1+0.98} - \frac{\left(\frac{36}{1+r}\right)}{(1+0.98)(1+r)},$$ (7.41)

$$1+r = \sqrt{\frac{36}{(1+0.98)\left(\frac{(100)0.98}{1+0.98} - k_{1A}^s\right)}};$$ (7.42)

$$k_{1B}^s = \frac{(100)\,0.98}{1+0.98} - \frac{\left(\frac{49}{1+r}\right)}{(1+0.98)(1+r)},$$ (7.43)

$$1+r = \sqrt{\frac{49}{(1+0.98)\left(\frac{(100)0.98}{1+0.98} - k_{1B}^s\right)}}.$$ (7.44)

Figure 7.5 graphs the capital demand and supply equations (7.39), (7.40), (7.42) and (7.44), with agent A in black and agent B in blue.

The equilibrium interest rate under autarky for agent A is $1+r = 1.0463$, as in Example 5.3, for A.

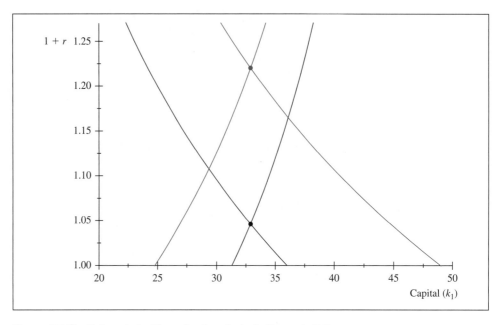

Figure 7.5 Capital market with no-trade autarky in Example 7.5

To find the exact B interest rate, set capital supply equal to demand. From equations (7.33) and (7.37), the B interest rate is $1 + r = 1.2207$:

$$k_{1B}^d = \frac{49}{(1+r)^2}$$

$$= \frac{(100)\,0.98}{1 + 0.98} - \frac{\left(\frac{49}{1+r}\right)}{(1 + 0.98)\,(1 + r)} = k_{1B}^s,$$

$$1 + r = \sqrt{\frac{49\left(1 + \frac{1}{1.98}\right)}{\frac{(100)0.98}{1+0.98}}} = 1.2207.$$

And both A and B have an equilibrium capital of

$$k_{1A}^d = \frac{36}{(1+r)^2} = \frac{36}{(1.0463)^2} = 32.884,$$

$$k_{1B}^d = \frac{49}{(1+r)^2} = \frac{49}{(1.2207)^2} = 32.884,$$

since a higher marginal productivity of capital, as B has relative to A, causes offsetting income and substitution effects to keep the capital stock at 32.884. And this gives the current consumption equilibria of

$$c_{0A}^d = y_0 - k_{1A}^d = 100 - 32.884 = 67.116,$$

$$c_{0B}^d = y_0 - k_{1B}^d = 100 - 32.884 = 67.116.$$

7.3.3 Goods market

The market for next period consumption can be graphed from the supply and demand for c_1, inversely solved for $\frac{1}{1+r}$, from equations (7.27), (7.30), (7.35) and (7.38):

$$\frac{1}{1+r} = \frac{c_{1A}^s}{72}; \tag{7.45}$$

$$c_{1A}^d = \frac{36}{1+r} + (1+r)\frac{(100)\,0.98}{1+0.98} - \frac{36}{(1+0.98)\,(1+r)},$$

$$0 = \left(36 - \frac{36}{(1+0.98)}\right)\frac{1}{(1+r)^2} - c_{1A}^d\left(\frac{1}{1+r}\right) + \frac{98}{1.98}; \tag{7.46}$$

$$\frac{1}{1+r} = \frac{c_{1B}^s}{98}; \tag{7.47}$$

$$c_{1B}^d = \frac{49}{1+r} + (1+r)\frac{(100)\,0.98}{1+0.98} - \frac{49}{(1+0.98)\,(1+r)},$$

$$0 = \left(49 - \frac{49}{(1+0.98)}\right)\frac{1}{(1+r)^2} - c_{1B}^d\left(\frac{1}{1+r}\right) + \frac{98}{1.98}. \tag{7.48}$$

Equations (7.46) and (7.48) are quadratic equations in $\frac{1}{1+r}$, with the form of $A\left(\frac{1}{(1+r)^2}\right)^2 +$ $B\left(\frac{1}{1+r}\right) + C = 0$. With $A = 36\left(1 - \frac{1}{(1+0.98)}\right)$, $B = -c_{1A}^d$ and $C = \frac{(100)0.98}{1+0.98}$ for equation (7.46), the agent A demand equation for graphing is

$$\frac{1}{1+r} = \frac{-B - \sqrt{B^2 - 4AC}}{2A} = \frac{c_{1A}^d - \sqrt{\left(c_{1A}^d\right)^2 - 4\,(36)\left(1 - \frac{1}{(1+0.98)}\right)\left(\frac{(100)0.98}{1+0.98}\right)}}{2\,(36)\left(1 - \frac{1}{(1+0.98)}\right)}. \tag{7.49}$$

And for agent B, with $A = 49\left(1 - \frac{1}{(1+0.98)}\right)$, $B = -c_{1B}^d$ and $C = \frac{(100)0.98}{1+0.98}$ for equation (7.48), the demand equation for graphing is

$$\frac{1}{1+r} = \frac{-B - \sqrt{B^2 - 4AC}}{2A} = \frac{c_{1B}^d - \sqrt{\left(c_{1B}^d\right)^2 - 4\,(49)\left(1 - \frac{1}{(1+0.98)}\right)\left(\frac{(100)0.98}{1+0.98}\right)}}{2\,(49)\left(1 - \frac{1}{(1+0.98)}\right)}. \tag{7.50}$$

Figure 7.6 graphs the supply and demand for c_1 for A in black and B in blue, from equations (7.45), (7.47), (7.49) and (7.50).

The exact next period consumption is found by using the autarky interest rates of 1.0463 and 1.2207, within either the supply or demand for goods by each agent. Using the simpler supply equations,

$$c_{1A}^s = \frac{72}{1+r} = \frac{72}{1.0463} = 68.814,$$

$$c_{1B}^s = \frac{98}{1+r} = \frac{98}{1.2207} = 80.282.$$

7.3.4 General equilibrium

The representation of both capital and goods markets in general equilibrium is created by graphing the utility level curves, the production functions and the budget lines for each

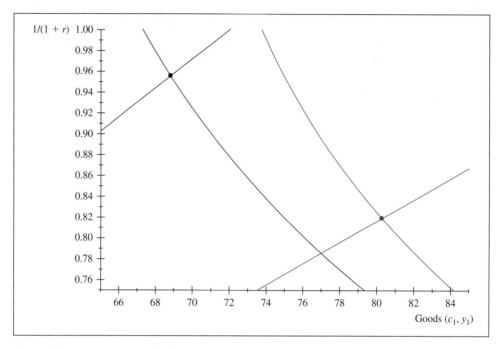

Figure 7.6 Autarky markets for future period consumption in Example 7.5

agent. Figure 5.6 of Example 5.3 already graphs the equilibrium for agent A, so it remains to add to this the equilibrium for B. The utility for A and B is

$$u_A = \ln c_{0A}^d + \beta \ln c_{1A}^d = \ln 67.116 + 0.98 \ln 68.814 = 8.3532,$$

$$c_{1A}^d = \left(\frac{e^u}{c_{0A}^d} \right)^{\frac{1}{\beta}} = \left(\frac{e^{8.3532}}{c_{0A}^d} \right)^{\frac{1}{0.98}};$$

$$u_B = \ln c_{0B}^d + \beta \ln c_{1B}^d = \ln 67.116 + 0.98 \ln 80.282 = 8.5043,$$

$$c_{1B}^d = \left(\frac{e^u}{c_{0B}^d} \right)^{\frac{1}{\beta}} = \left(\frac{e^{8.5043}}{c_{0B}^d} \right)^{\frac{1}{0.98}}.$$

The production functions are

$$c_{1A}^s = 12\sqrt{k_1} = 12\sqrt{100 - c_{0A}}, \tag{7.51}$$

$$c_{1B}^s = 14\sqrt{k_1} = 14\sqrt{100 - c_{0B}}. \tag{7.52}$$

And the budget constraints are

$$c_{1A}^d = \Pi_{1A} + k_{1A}^s \left(1 + r \right),$$

$$c_{1A}^d = \frac{36}{1.0463} + \left(100 - c_{0A}^d \right) (1.0463);$$

$$c_{1B}^d = \Pi_{1B} + k_{1B}^s \left(1 + r \right),$$

$$c_{1B}^d = \frac{49}{1.2207} + \left(100 - c_{0B}^d \right) (1.2207).$$

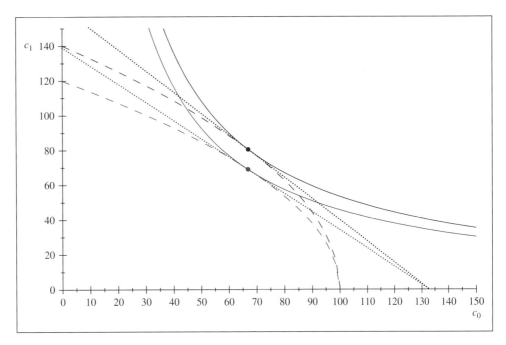

Figure 7.7 General equilibrium autarky in Example 7.5

Figure 7.7 graphs the agent A equilibrium in three blue lines, and that of agent B in three black lines. Agent B has more future consumption and a steeper slope of the budget line but the same current consumption.

7.4 Trade

In autarky, the interest rate is higher in country B than in country A. Allowing for trade by using the market clearing conditions, the interest rate for the united region becomes the intermediate of the two autarky interest rates, and the trade triangles for markets open up.

7.4.1 Example 7.6

Consider the same specification as in Example 7.5 except that now trade is allowed. The capital market clearing condition that establishes a single interest rate sets the total capital supply to the total capital demand:

$$k_{1A}^d + k_{1B}^d = k_{1A}^s + k_{1B}^s. \tag{7.53}$$

Substituting in from Example 7.5,

$$k_{1A}^d + k_{1B}^d = \frac{36+49}{(1+r)^2} = \frac{2y_0\beta}{1+\beta} - \frac{\left(\frac{36+49}{1+r}\right)}{(1+\beta)(1+r)} = k_{1A}^s + k_{1B}^s. \tag{7.54}$$

From equation (7.54),

$$1+r = \left[\frac{(36+49)(2+\beta)}{2y_0\beta}\right]^{0.5} = \left[\frac{(36+49)(2.98)}{2(98)}\right]^{0.5} = 1.1368,$$

or an interest rate of $r = 13.68\%$. This is a rise for agent A up from the autarky rate of $r = 4.63\%$. For agent B, the interest rate falls from $r = 22.07\%$ to $r = 13.68\%$.

7.4.2 Capital market

The total supply and demand for capital in Example 7.6 can be graphed by solving for each in terms of $1+r$ from equation (7.54):

$$k^d = k_{1A}^d + k_{1B}^d = \frac{36+49}{\left(1+r\right)^2},$$

$$1+r = \sqrt{\frac{36+49}{k^d}};\tag{7.55}$$

$$k^s = k_{1A}^s + k_{1B}^s = \frac{2y_0\beta}{1+\beta} - \frac{\left(36+49\right)}{\left(1+\beta\right)\left(1+r\right)^2},$$

$$1+r = \sqrt{\frac{\left(36+49\right)}{\left(1+\beta\right)\left(\frac{2y_0\beta}{1+\beta} - k^s\right)}} = \sqrt{\frac{\left(36+49\right)}{\left(1.98\right)\left(\frac{2\left(100\right)0.98}{1.98} - k^s\right)}}.\tag{7.56}$$

Figure 7.8 graphs the supply and demand for capital by A in black, by B in blue, and the total market supply and demand from both agents of equations (7.55) and (7.56) in dashed black, with the market interest rate in dashed blue.

The supply by A at $r = 0.1368$ is

$$k_{1A}^s = \frac{y_0\beta}{1+\beta} - \frac{\left(\frac{36}{1+r}\right)}{\left(1+\beta\right)\left(1+r\right)} = \frac{100\left(0.98\right)}{1.98} - \frac{36}{\left(1.98\right)\left(1.1368\right)^2} = 35.426;\tag{7.57}$$

and the supply of B is

$$k_{1B}^s = \frac{y_0\beta}{1+\beta} - \frac{\left(\frac{49}{1+r}\right)}{\left(1+\beta\right)\left(1+r\right)} = \frac{100\left(0.98\right)}{1.98} - \frac{49}{\left(1.98\right)\left(1.1368\right)^2} = 30.345.\tag{7.58}$$

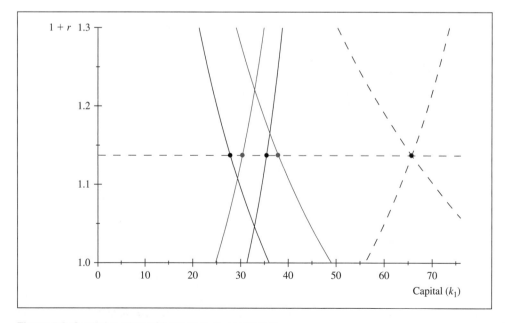

Figure 7.8 Capital market with trade in Example 7.6

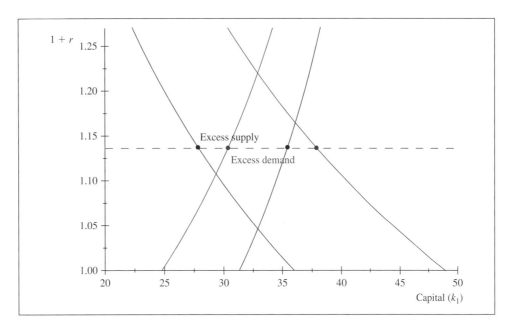

Figure 7.9 Excess supply and demand for capital with trade in Example 7.5

The demands are given by

$$k_{1A}^d = \frac{36}{(1+r)^2} = \frac{36}{(1.1368)^2} = 27.857;$$ (7.59)

and

$$k_{1B}^d = \frac{49}{(1+r)^2} = \frac{49}{(1.1368)^2} = 37.916.$$ (7.60)

Agent A has an excess supply of capital at the equilibrium interest rate that is exactly equal to the excess demand for capital of agent B at the equilibrium interest rate.

$$\text{Excess supply}_A: \ k_{1A}^s - k_{1A}^d = 35.426 - 27.857 = 7.57,$$
$$\text{Excess demand}_B: \ k_{1B}^d - k_{1B}^s = 37.916 - 30.345 = 7.57.$$

The more productive agent B is supplied capital from the less productive agent A. Agent A therefore invests capital in its own production function as well as in that of agent B, while B invests only in its own production function.

Figure 7.9 focuses on the Example 7.6 excess supply and demand for capital at the equilibrium interest rate.

7.4.3 Goods market

The total demand and supply for next period consumption can be found and graphed along with the individual country demand and supply. The total demand and supply are

$$c_1^d = c_{1A}^d + c_{1B}^d = \frac{36+49}{1+r} + (1+r)\, 2\frac{(100)\, 0.98}{1+0.98} - \frac{36+49}{(1+0.98)(1+r)},$$

$$c_1^s = c_{1A}^s + c_{1B}^s = \frac{72+98}{1+r}.$$

Inversely these are

$$0 = (36 + 49)\left(1 - \frac{1}{(1+0.98)}\right)\frac{1}{(1+r)^2} - c_1^d\left(\frac{1}{1+r}\right) + 2\frac{(100)\,0.98}{1+0.98},$$

$$\frac{1}{1+r} = \frac{c_1^s}{72+98}. \tag{7.61}$$

The demand equation is a quadratic in $\frac{1}{1+r}$, with $A = (36 + 49)\left(1 - \frac{1}{(1+0.98)}\right)$, $B = -c_{1A}^d$ and $C = 2\frac{(100)0.98}{1+0.98}$ for equation (7.46). The demand equation for graphing is

$$\frac{1}{1+r} = \frac{-B - \sqrt{B^2 - 4AC}}{2A}, \tag{7.62}$$

$$= \frac{c_1^d - \sqrt{\left(c_1^d\right)^2 - 4(36+49)\left(1 - \frac{1}{(1+0.98)}\right)2\left(\frac{(100)0.98}{1+0.98}\right)}}{2(36+49)\left(1 - \frac{1}{(1+0.98)}\right)}. \tag{7.63}$$

Figure 7.10 graphs the total supply and demand for c_1 in dashed black, from equations (7.61) and (7.62), along with the individual supply and demand from A in solid black and from B in solid blue as in Figure 7.9.

The supply of goods by each agent with $1 + r = 1.1368$ is

$$c_{1A}^s = \frac{72}{1+r} = \frac{72}{1.1368} = 63.336,$$

$$c_{1B}^s = \frac{98}{1+r} = \frac{98}{1.1368} = 86.207.$$

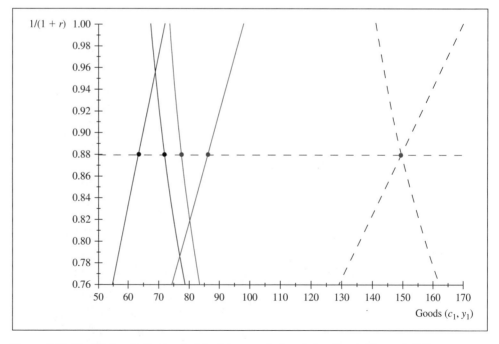

Figure 7.10 Equilibrium in the market for future period consumption in Example 7.5

The demand with $1+r = 1.1368$, given the capital supplies of equations (7.57) and (7.58), is

$$c_{1A}^d = \Pi_{1A} + k_{1A}^s \left(1+r\right)$$
$$= \frac{36}{1+r} + 35.426 \left(1+r\right),$$
$$c_{1A}^d = \frac{36}{1.1368} + 35.426 \left(1.1368\right) = 71.94. \tag{7.64}$$

And agent B has

$$c_{1B}^d = \Pi_{1B} + k_{1B}^s \left(1+r\right)$$
$$= \frac{49}{1+r} + 30.345 \left(1+r\right),$$
$$c_{1B}^d = \frac{49}{1.1368} + 30.345 \left(1.1368\right) = 77.60. \tag{7.65}$$

The excess demand of A equals the excess supply of B:

$$\text{Excess demand}_A: \ c_{1A}^d - c_{1A}^s = 71.94 - 63.336 = 8.6,$$
$$\text{Excess supply}_B: \ c_{1B}^s - c_{1B}^d = 86.207 - 77.60 = 8.6.$$

Figure 7.11 focuses in on the trade in the goods market by indicating the excess supply and demand at the equilibrium relative price of $\frac{1}{1.1368}$.

Agent A is receiving goods from B, which is the payment of B for the capital that A supplies to B. Goods are traded for capital.

Utility is now higher for each agent because of the gains from trade. The utility depends on the demand rather than the supply of next period consumption, and the supply

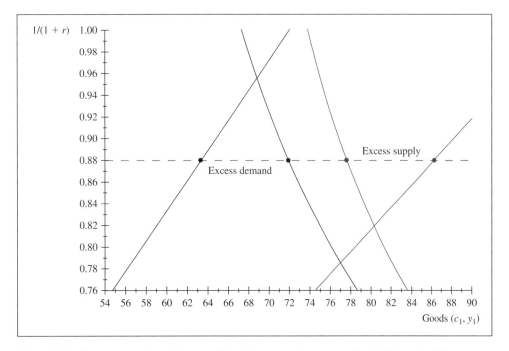

Figure 7.11 Excess supply and demand for future period consumption in Example 7.6

of capital, rather than its demand, in calculating current period consumption. Utility is given by

$$u_A = \ln c_{0A}^d + \beta \ln c_{1A}^d = \ln\left(100 - k_{1A}^s\right) + 0.98 \ln 71.94,$$

$$= \ln\left(100 - 35.426\right) + 0.98 \ln 71.94 = 8.3581,$$

$$c_{1A}^d = \left(\frac{e^u}{c_{0A}^d}\right)^{\frac{1}{\beta}} = \left(\frac{e^{8.3581}}{c_{0A}^d}\right)^{\frac{1}{0.98}}; \tag{7.66}$$

$$u_B = \ln c_{0B}^d + \beta \ln c_{1B}^d = \ln\left(100 - k_{1B}^s\right) + 0.98 \ln 77.60,$$

$$= \ln\left(100 - 30.345\right) + 0.98 \ln 77.60 = 8.5081,$$

$$c_{1B}^d = \left(\frac{e^u}{c_{0B}^d}\right)^{\frac{1}{\beta}} = \left(\frac{e^{8.5081}}{c_{0B}^d}\right)^{\frac{1}{0.98}}. \tag{7.67}$$

The market budget lines are

$$c_{1A}^d = \Pi_{1A} + k_{1A}^s\left(1+r\right),$$

$$c_{1A}^d = \frac{36}{1.1368} + \left(100 - c_{0A}^d\right)\left(1.1368\right); \tag{7.68}$$

$$c_{1B}^d = \Pi_{1B} + k_{1B}^s\left(1+r\right),$$

$$c_{1B}^d = \frac{49}{1.1368} + \left(100 - c_{0B}^d\right)\left(1.1368\right). \tag{7.69}$$

The production functions are

$$c_{1A}^s = 12\sqrt{k_1} = 12\sqrt{100 - c_{0A}}, \tag{7.70}$$

$$c_{1B}^s = 14\sqrt{k_1} = 14\sqrt{100 - c_{0B}}. \tag{7.71}$$

Figure 7.12 graphs the general equilibrium with the utility curves under trade, the budget lines under trade, and the production functions that are the same as in the autarky Example 7.5, from equations (7.66), (7.67), (7.68), (7.69), (7.70) and (7.71). Agent A is shown in three blue lines, and agent B in three black lines. Trade triangles are given in blue for A and black for B.

Comparison of the utility under autarky in Example 7.5 versus the utility with trade in Example 7.6 shows an increase in utility for each agent, and this increase is the measure of the gain from trade for each agent. However in the general equilibrium it is difficult to see the utility increase and so the autarky utility level curves have not been included in Figure 7.12. The trade triangles here reflect the same patterns that are seen in Figures 7.9 and 7.11. The horizontal sides of the trade triangles are the amounts of excess capital supply and demand seen in Figure 7.9. The vertical sides of the trade triangles are the amounts of excess next period consumption supply and demand seen in Figure 7.11.

7.5 Applications

7.5.1 Small open economies

Small open economies strictly never exist. With the globalisation of capital markets, even problems in a small economy like Brazil, Thailand, or Greece can cause world market interest rates to be affected. This is sometimes discussed in terms of 'contagion' effects, where one economy's problems spill over into others.

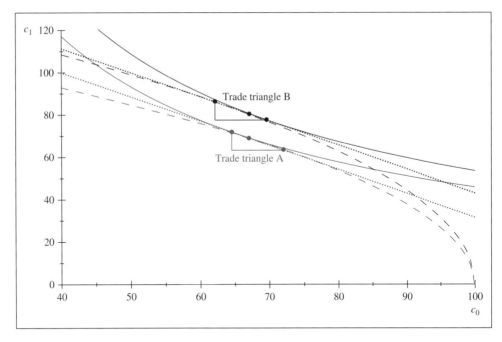

Figure 7.12 General equilibrium trade in Example 7.6

Perhaps a better way to view it is that small countries represent similar economies in particular regions. And problems in one such economy can be expected to be experienced across similar countries that make up a region. The region may not be geographically adjacent, but rather can be 'emerging markets', 'transition countries' or 'developing countries'.

Then the risk of lending capital to such countries can be understood to rise and fall together, making the assumption of fixed interest rates for small open economies rather unrealistic. Instead world interest rates are affected because of changes in investment within an entire region. General equilibrium analysis in which the interest rate is determined by all countries in the economy can better capture such regional changes.

7.5.2 Fostering capital market trade

Policies for fostering capital market trade vary as much as do the reasons for differences in the productivity of capital across countries and regions. For example the European Union (EU) addresses this in part by spending heavily on the infrastructure development of new EU members. New suburban and underground city train systems and highways are a manifestation of such spending across Eastern Europe.

Financial development has been fostered by making laws such that private banking systems can emerge. In Eastern Europe this meant restructuring formerly state-owned banks so that the bad government loans were off the banks' books. And then the banking privatisation laws had to be enacted so that the ownership of the banks could return to the private sector. This combination of restructuring and privatisation was evident almost in all former Soviet controlled countries.

Engendering democracy and stable political structures is much more difficult, as it is not easily done by a country's existing government. Rather outside events and regime changes become important in such processes and it is unclear what is the best way for neighbouring countries to push other countries in this direction. Typically it requires a broad array of events for freedom of trade in the political and social realm to emerge, which then facilitate freedom to trade economically.

7.5.3 Keynes, his revision, and the Marshall Plan

Keynes wrote against WWI war reparation payments from Germany to the Allies in his 1919 *The Economic Consequences of the Peace,* as he summarises in his 1922 *A Revision of the Treaty.* Keynes also recommended granting 'a reconstruction loan from America to Europe' (p. 162, *Revision*). And going even further in his *Revision* he wrote that the 'British Empire should waive the whole of their claims' (p. 174, *Revision*) to reparation payments from Germany and its allies. Even without Britain waiving its claim, the whole of the German reparation should be dramatically reduced to about 25% of that implied by the Treaty of Versailles that ended WWI (pp. 172–4, *Revision*). 'I should limit my Revision of the Treaty to this simple stroke of the pen' (p. 173, *Revision*).

His concern when writing in 1921 was that the restitution payments were not being made so far, that they need to be made to be seen as just, and that high reparations would weaken the ability of the German economy to survive. Rather he emphasises the making of loans and grants to help rebuild Europe as a more plausible route to 'keep the peace'.

In fact the war reparations were set by the Reparation Commission in 1921 at 132 billion gold marks, or 31.5 billion US dollars. These were only reduced in 1929, to 112 billion gold marks, or 28.4 billion US dollars. These were scheduled to be paid over time but little of it was ever paid. By 1929 the US depression had started, Germany experienced a country-wide bank run, and in the 1932 Lausanne Conference reparations were temporarily suspended. But meanwhile Hitler had begun his rise and reparations became irrelevant, and then WWII broke out.

Avoiding the same mistake of demanding payments when in fact loans were needed, the US was said to have spent some 9 billion US dollars from 1945 to 1947, in part through loans, under the so-called Truman Doctrine, and an additional 13 billion US dollars for the four years starting in 1947. This latter money was deemed the Marshall Plan, named after the US Secretary of State George Marshall, who won the Nobel Peace prize in 1953. To see the possible impact of this money, consider that Turkey and Greece were early recipients of large amounts of such postwar aid, the UK, France and Germany received the largest amounts of Marshall aid, while Russia refused such aid and acted to keep Poland from joining the Marshall Plan. This partly led to the alignment seen over the next 40 years with the Soviet bloc and Eastern Europe cut off from the 'West', while the West did indeed rebuild and prosper with Turkey and Greece as key components.

The WWI aftermath of demanding repayment, the start of WWII by bankrupt Germany, and the WWII aftermath with the granting of aid to the nations at war, illustrate how lending capital internationally can act as the means of investment that can help restore well-functioning international markets that engender peace. This is a key economic lesson from the aftermaths of the two world wars during which opposite policies were enacted, one demanding restitution payment while the other granted even more loans.

7.5.4 Soros, the Soviet Union and China

George Soros is a famous 'capitalist' who made some billions of US dollars as a successful investment banker and currency trader. He then considered philanthropy, and according to one of his books, he then 'looked around for a worthy cause', and called his foundation 'the Open Society Fund, with the objective of making open societies viable and helping to open up closed societies' (1990, pp. 6–7). Indeed he entitled his 1990 book *Opening the Soviet System*, which he wrote just as Eastern Europe was beginning to open up and it looked as if it might be possible to end the Soviet closed society system. And here he had in mind the Marshall Plan itself: 'The most glorious demonstration of the open society principle was the treatment of the defeated countries after the Second World War and the Marshall Plan in particular' (1990, pp. 140–141).

With Gorbachev still in power, Soros presciently wrote, 'We are witnessing the disintegration of a closed system as embodied by the Soviet Union' (1990, p. 88). Soros used his society to fund projects throughout Eastern Europe, including the establishment of the Open Society Institute and Central European University, now both in Budapest, and outposts of the Open Society in Russia, Poland and most of the former Soviet Union and Eastern bloc countries. This Open Society has now spread to programmes for Africa and Eurasia. Basically, Soros's efforts represent private initiatives to loan or grant capital to nations under specific conditions that help establish the institutions that can support free trade and development within the world market economy. Put differently, huge amounts of investment were needed in regions long cut off from international markets, and Soros helped provide 'seed' capital for such investment to eventually take place.

Soros views China in his 1990 book in a similar vein. It is open, but still run by a dictatorship of the Communist Party. Applying the principles of the advantages of trade in capital, versus segmenting markets and closing them off from each other, one strategy for Western nations to take towards China is to do everything possible to continue to bring China within world economic markets. To encourage trade through grants, loans and other institutional help has now been embodied in China's admittance to the World Trade Organization on 11 December 2001. The Russian Federation still awaits such admittance.

7.5.5 War versus globalisation

Consider thinking of war in terms of the income effect, and creating autarky as in a no trade equilibrium. Historically, a king in Britain could expand the kingdom through winning a battle that would effectively shift out not only his economy's current period income endowment, through acquired agricultural goods and capital hoards, but also all future consumption possibilities through the acquired production structures. Of course this is a redistribution from one economy to another. And in aggregate, wars generally shift back current and future production possibilities for all warring nations taken together regardless of boundaries, because of the used up military expenditures and loss of capital, home production and market structures.

Modern wars in Africa over natural resources may well be about obtaining future production possibilities, and certainly involve huge wastes in the process of the wars. And such regional or domestic wars make it nearly impossible for such nations to integrate within world capital markets in which the gains from trade may dwarf any gains made through war-acquired resources.

Alternatively, choosing diplomacy and international trade agreements provides a way to obtain resources peacefully, and at the fair market price. Having trade in capital, by borrowing capital and paying interest, is an alternative to war as a means for exchanging property rights over future productive capacity. Trade agreements such as GATT, the General Agreement on Tariffs and Trade, which has been reformed as the WTO, the World Trade Organization, have kept the expansion of trade as a continuing agenda.

Globalisation is exactly this expansion of trade in place of war. But for nations left out of trade agreements, denied rising capital accumulation, and without the wealth of globalisation, there is no obvious equality-trend taking place. This exclusion from world capital markets itself can give rise to war, and here the modern war with terrorism may be an apt example.

Nations engaging in terrorism, or citizens engaging in terrorism, appear to be trying to disrupt the global trade architecture that has gradually arisen. Such acts of war on nations do act to deplete resources, including priceless 'human capital', and cause greater segregation of cultures and markets at least in the short run. And it is possible that commonplace freedoms under democracies can be eroded or eliminated during wartimes, which can create an uncertain future for a resumption of such freedom to trade, economically and socially.

7.6 Questions

1. Given a 10% market rate of interest, in equilibrium a representative agent with a log utility function of current consumption c_0 and next period consumption c_1, and with a positive endowment in the next period and a zero endowment in the current period,

   (a) is a lender;

   (b) is a borrower;

   (c) stays at the endowment;

   (d) all of the above.

2. Given the wealth constraint $W = c_0 + \frac{c_1}{1+r}$, where W is wealth, c_0 current consumption, c_1 next period consumption, and r the interest rate, on a graph with c_1 the vertical and c_0 the horizontal axes,

   (a) $\frac{1}{1+r}$ is the slope of constraint;

   (b) $(W - c_0)(1 + r)$ is the horizontal axis intercept with the constraint;

   (c) $W(1 + r)$ is the vertical axis intercept with the constraint;

   (d) all of the above.

3. The 'substitution effect'

   (a) assumes that relative prices stay the same;

   (b) assumes that the level of utility stays the same;

   (c) dominates the income effect;

   (d) all of the above.

4. A representative consumer in equilibrium who lends part of the endowment of current period consumption, when faced with a doubling of the interest rate, will

   (a) increase current period consumption according to the substitution effect of the interest rate increase;

   (b) increase current period consumption according to the income effect of the interest rate increase;

   (c) increase the loans made if the income effect dominates the substitution effect, of the interest rate increase;

   (d) all of the above.

5. Assume there are two goods, current consumption, c_0, and future period consumption, c_1. Consider a hypothetical student endowment of 0 in the current period and 22,000 in the next period (when the human capital investment yields income). Assume the interest rate is 0.10 (10%).

   (a) Find the present discounted value of wealth, W, and form the 'wealth constraint' that binds the student's expenditures.

   (b) Now suppose preferences are log utility so that the student maximises $u(c_0, c_1) = \ln c_0 + (0.98) \ln c_1$ subject to the wealth constraint. Find the equilibrium c_0, c_1 and utility level.

   (c) Graph the equilibrium in part (b).

   (d) If the student borrowing rate is subsidised, graphically show the new equilibrium, and indicate the substitution and income effects on current consumption that result from the subsidy.

6. Assume a consumer with the utility function $u(c_0, c_1) = \ln c_0 + 0.98 \ln c_1$, subject to income $y_0 = 0$, $y_1 = 55$, and the budget $y_0 + \frac{y_1}{1+r} = W = c_0 + \frac{c_1}{1+r}$, where $r = 0.1$.

   (a) Find the equilibrium borrowing or lending.

   (b) Indicate the substitution and income effects on the consumer's borrowing or lending if the interest rate rises.

7. Assume the consumer's utility function is $\ln c_0 + \ln c_1$ where c_0 is the quantity of current period's consumption of goods, and c_1 is the quantity of next period's consumption of goods, and assume the wealth constraint, where W equals the present discounted value of wealth, is $W = c_0 + \frac{c_1}{1+r}$; also assume the interest rate r equals 0.1.

   (a) Let the consumption endowment for the two periods be (y_0, y_1) and assume $y_0 = 0$, $y_1 = 66$. First find the present value of the wealth W by substituting the endowed consumption into the wealth constraint and solving for W.

   (b) Find the equilibrium c_0, c_1 by maximising the utility with respect to c_0, c_1 and subject to the wealth constraint, where you have substituted in the value of W, found in part (a), into the wealth constraint.

   (c) Find the borrowing or lending of the consumer ($y_0 - c_0$ is the equilibrium lending; a negative sign means the consumer borrows rather than lends the amount).

8. For a consumer with the utility function $u(c_0, c_1) = \ln c_0 + 0.98 \ln c_1$, given the endowment in periods 0 and 1 of $(y_0, y_1) = (100, 110)$ and given the interest rate $r = 0.1$:

   (a) Find the equilibrium period 0 consumption c_0 and period 1 consumption c_1, and the equilibrium borrowing or lending.

   (b) Assume the interest rate rises to $r = 0.1$. Find the equilibrium period 0 consumption c_0 and period 1 consumption c_1, and the equilibrium borrowing or lending.

   (c) Describe the substitution and income effects of the interest rate rise on current consumption, in part (b), and indicate if either effect dominates.

9. Assume that the economy consists of two representative consumers, each with the same utility function that depends on current and future income but with different marginal productivities of capital. A move from autarky to free trade

   (a) raises the interest rate available for the less productive consumers;

   (b) causes the more productive consumer to borrow capital;

   (c) causes each group to move to a higher utility level;

   (d) all of the above.

10. Design an industrial policy for your favourite country in terms of the distribution of capital and the nature of investment capabilities (the production of future output with capital).

11. Suppose there is a representative consumer with utility $u = \ln c_0 + 0.98 \ln c_1$, with $y_0 = 100$, $y_0 = c_0 + k_1$, $c_1 = y_1$, and $y_1 = 13\sqrt{k_1}$.

    (a) Find the equilibrium c_0, c_1, y_1, k_1, u.

    (b) Suppose that investment productivity rises, so that now $y_1 = 15\sqrt{k_1}$, with all other conditions the same. Find the new equilibrium c_0, c_1, y_1, k_1, u and indicate the substitution and income effects, with respect to both the c_0 axis and the c_1 axis, of moving to the new equilibrium.

    (c) Suppose that there are two representative consumers in the economy, agent A with the production function $y_{1A} = 13\sqrt{k_{1A}}$ and agent B with the production function $y_{1B} = 15\sqrt{k_{1B}}$. Without solving the equilibrium mathematically, graphically show the equilibrium, clearly indicating the nature of the trade. Also include the autarky equilibrium on your graphs and compare to the trade equilibrium.

    (d) How might decentralised international trade in capital between these two agents decrease tensions that give rise to war?

12. Suppose the only two countries of the world, A and B, which have equal numbers of representative consumers with identical utility functions, that depend on current and next period consumption, have the production functions $y_{1A} = a\sqrt{k_1}$, $y_{1B} = 2a\sqrt{k_1}$, where k_1 is current period investment, and y_1 is next period income. Suppose each country at first lives independently in autarky, and has the exact same amount of investment, but then the countries begin trading with each other.

    (a) Graphically show both the autarky and the free trade equilibria.

    (b) Indicate what happens to the marginal product of capital and to investment in each country upon moving to free trade; indicate the nature of the trade between the countries; and indicate one gauge that illustrates the gains from trade.

13. Indicate and briefly explain the general equilibrium effect on imports of capital by a country if the world interest rate goes up.

14. True, False, Uncertain, Explain. Long periods of capital imports within trade accounts imply unfair trade.

15. True, False, Uncertain, Explain. Giving away capital to a losing nation of a war lowers income in the donor country.

16. How might decentralised international trade in capital decrease tensions that give rise to war?

7.7 References

Backus, David, K., Patrick J. Kehoe and Finn E. Kydland, 1992, 'International Real Business Cycles', *Journal of Political Economy,* University of Chicago Press, 100(4): 745–75, August.

Feldstein, M. and C. Horioka, 1980, 'Domestic Saving and International Capital Flows', *The Economic Journal,* 90: 314–329.

Keynes, John Maynard, 1919, *The Economic Consequences of the Peace,* Macmillan and Co., London.

Keynes, John Maynard, 1922, *A Revision of the Treaty,* Macmillan and Co., London.

Keynes, John Maynard, 1930, *A Treatise on Money,* Macmillan and Co., Volume I, London.

Kollmann, Robert, 1996. 'Incomplete asset markets and the cross-country consumption correlation puzzle', *Journal of Economic Dynamics and Control,* Elsevier, 20(5) (May): 945–961.

Obstfeld, Maurice and Kenneth Rogoff, 1996, *Foundations in International Macroeconomics,* The MIT Press, Cambridge.

Soros, George, 1990, *Opening the Soviet System,* Weidenfeld and Nicolson.

PART 4

MODERN *AS–AD*

CHAPTER 8

Dynamic analysis and *AS–AD*

8.1 Introduction

The labour–leisure trade-off and the two-period intertemporal consumption trade-off are combined in the standard dynamic model with an infinite horizon. The two margins again result in a similar form. Extending the time horizon from two periods to the entire horizon uses a methodology that again simplifies the problem to a two period one, even though it is an infinite horizon. This is called the recursive dynamic model. It states the representative agent problem as a function of utility today and utility from tomorrow onwards.

The recursive model uses a variable that describes what we have brought into the current period. This is called the 'state' variable. This is the capital stock as given to us at time t, so that k_t is given. Given k_t, the capital investment at $t + 1$, k_{t+1}, is a decision variable at time period t, on how much to invest. Utility is then a function of this given state k_t. And through this state variable k_t, the entire dynamic problem can be stated using only utility today and utility in the next period.

Given similar margins as before, but now fully dynamic, the traditional analysis of aggregate supply (*AS*) and aggregate demand (*AD*) is updated to the dynamic context. This gives a modern *AS–AD* dynamic framework. To derive this, first the consumer demand as a function of the wage rate, interest rate and capital stock is formulated, using the consumer budget constraint and the marginal rate of substitution between goods and leisure. Then the equilibrium of zero economic growth is combined with the intertemporal consumption margin to solve for the interest rate as a function of given parameters. This consumption demand is then added to the simple equilibrium investment demand to give the aggregate demand as a function of only the wage rate and the capital stock.

The capital stock is solved using all of the equilibrium conditions of the model, the most challenging part of the analysis. This is focused on with a separate entire chapter – Chapter 10. In this Chapter 8 the results of the equilibrium capital stock are substituted into the *AS–AD* model and then it is graphed as a function of only the wage rate. A baseline example is presented and then comparative statics are conducted with changes in the goods productivity and the time endowment. For each comparative static analysis the equilibrium capital stock is recomputed. Comparative static shifts in the supply and demand are shown in the goods market, in the general equilibrium goods–leisure graph, and in the input market graph of isoquants, isocost lines and capital to labour factor input ratios.

8.1.1 Building on the last chapters

While Part 2 analysed only the labour–leisure margin, and Part 3 only the two-period intertemporal consumption margin, here these margins are derived simultaneously while the time horizon is infinite rather than only two periods. In the last chapter, the current period capital stock is implicitly assumed to be $k_0 = 0$, while in this chapter the current period capital stock is taken to be some amount k_t.

This chapter's marginal rate of substitution between goods and leisure is exactly as in Part 2. The intertemporal consumption margin is similar to Part 3, but now there is an explicit depreciation rate which is a low value but greater than zero. The aggregate demand and supply depended upon the wage rate in Part 2, the interest rate in Part 3, and on both rates in this chapter. However the zero growth equilibrium enables the solution for the interest rate in terms of exogenous parameters, leaving the analysis again solving only for the equilibrium wage rate, given the solution for the capital stock at time t.

8.1.2 Learning objective

The challenge is to understand a dynamic formulation of *AS–AD* analysis and its comparative statics. The key to this involves the role of the capital stock. Seeing that the given period capital stock is necessary to formulate the *AS–AD* in a standard way allows for linking the static *AS–AD* framework to the dynamic *AS–AD* framework with an infinite horizon. To do this, learning to construct the consumption demand function, and then the aggregate demand from the consumption demand, is essential. The aggregate supply proves to be more straightforward in its construction in that this is done in a way similar to the static model. For *AS*, the demand for labour is substituted into the production function, leaving *AS* as a function of the capital stock, just like the *AD* curve. So both *AD* and *AS* require the equilibrium value of the capital stock before graphing them. It must be realised that changes in any exogenous parameter, which constitutes a comparative static exercise, requires recomputing the capital stock. In addition the *AS* or *AD* functions may also depend directly on the exogenous parameters being changed, so that the *AS* or *AD* may change both indirectly because of the change in the capital stock and directly because of the change in the exogenous parameters themselves.

8.1.3 Who made it happen?

Astonishingly, Frank Ramsey worked out all of the dynamic general equilibrium conditions of this chapter in his 1928 *Economic Journal* article, which Ramsey attributed to the teachings of his mentor John Maynard Keynes; Keynes in turn wrote an admiring biography of Ramsey (in Keynes, 1933). So although the dynamic theory has some complications, it is more than 80 years old and the main foundation of modern macroeconomics.

Ramsey started with a production function for aggregate output that uses labour and capital, and with the budget constraint that consumption plus savings must equal output. This is the exact same structure here. And then he derived that the marginal product of labour equals the marginal rate of substitution between goods and leisure, and that the marginal product of capital equals the percentage change in the marginal utility of consumption over time, as in the text in Parts 2 and 3.

Further, in the same 16-page article, Ramsey decentralised the problem into consumer and firm components. He did this using the same decentralising equation of this chapter that states that output is equal to the sum of the labour wage and capital rental payments. Then he derived that the wage rate equals the marginal rate of substitution between goods and leisure and that the gross interest rate net of depreciation equals the marginal rate of substitution between consumption today and consumption next period.

Ramsey went even further. He showed how analysis of the capital equilibrium also determines the economic growth rate. And here the growth rate is determined by the relation between the real rate of interest and the consumer's rate of time preference. Growth theory in this Ramsey fashion is also utilised in this chapter, with the assumption initially of zero growth. And this growth consideration allows aggregate demand and supply to be put together from the equilibrium conditions of Ramsey's famous 1928 article. Ramsey finds that there is no growth in the economy when the interest rate equals the rate of time preference plus the capital depreciation rate, as emerges directly below.

Using the recursive framework for the dynamic problem is a shorthand also developed over a long period of time, but popularised for example by Stokey, Lucas and Prescott (1989). And the consumption theory that is within the Ramsey equilibrium has also been developed over time. After Keynes (1936, p. 90) described the propensity to consume, consumption demand functions have long had a central place in macroeconomic textbooks. Milton Friedman (1957) formed the concept of consumption equalling some fraction of permanent income, which in turn could be described as the interest flow of both physical and human capital. Modern studies continue to test the permanent income hypothesis of consumption and its implications.

8.2 The recursive problem

Let $V(k_t)$ describe the maximum utility that we can get given the state k_t. This maximum utility can be described as the maximisation of current utility plus the discounted value of next period's maximum utility given that the state next period has become k_{t+1}. This is the recursive problem of the representative agent. It captures the whole infinite future by adding the complete discounted future utility at time $t+1$ onto the current period utility. This gives a simple two-period framework, at time t and $t+1$. With utility specified as a function of goods c_t and leisure x_t as before, or $u_t = u(c_t, x_t)$, the recursive utility problem can be stated as the maximisation of utility $V(k_t)$ with respect to goods c_t, leisure x_t and next period's capital k_{t+1} subject to constraints (here as yet unspecified):

$$V(k_t) = \max_{c_t, x_t, k_{t+1}} : u(c_t, x_t) + \beta V(k_{t+1}). \tag{8.1}$$

The recursive utility $V(k_t)$ can be shown to be equivalent to an infinite sequence of the stream of discounted utility. Therefore the $V(k_t)$ extends from a two-period framework to an infinite horizon. Conversely, it then is clear that it is able to state the infinite horizon in terms of just two time periods t and $t+1$. This is the useful 'trick' of the recursive approach: reducing the infinite horizon maximisation problem to a maximisation problem stated in just two time periods, t and $t+1$, where t is for any finite time $t \in [0, \infty)$.

To see this write out the recursive problem by solving for $V(k_{t+1})$ by moving up the time indexes by one in equation (8.1):

$$V(k_t) = u(c_t, x_t) + \beta V(k_{t+1}); \tag{8.2}$$
$$V(k_{t+1}) = u(c_{t+1}, x_{t+1}) + \beta V(k_{t+2}). \tag{8.3}$$

Then substituting this $V(k_{t+1})$ into equation (8.1):

$$V(k_t) = u(c_t, x_t) + \beta \left[u(c_{t+1}, x_{t+1}) + \beta V(k_{t+2}) \right]; \tag{8.4}$$
$$V(k_t) = u(c_t, x_t) + \beta u(c_{t+1}, x_{t+1}) + \beta^2 V(k_{t+2}). \tag{8.5}$$

Continue by solving for $V(k_{t+2})$ by indexing forward equation (8.1) by two periods:

$$V(k_{t+2}) = u(c_{t+2}, x_{t+2}) + \beta V(k_{t+3}).$$

Substituting this into equation (8.5),

$$V(k_t) = u(c_t, x_t) + \beta u(c_{t+1}, x_{t+1}) + \beta^2 V(k_{t+2}); \tag{8.6}$$
$$V(k_t) = u(c_t, x_t) + \beta u(c_{t+1}, x_{t+1}) + \beta^2 \left[u(c_{t+2}, x_{t+2}) + \beta V(k_{t+3}) \right]; \tag{8.7}$$
$$V(k_t) = u(c_t, x_t) + \beta u(c_{t+1}, x_{t+1}) + \beta^2 u(c_{t+2}, x_{t+2}) + \beta^3 V(k_{t+3}). \tag{8.8}$$

Then solve for $V(k_{t+3})$; the last term can continue to be solved for and substituted in for an infinite number of times. The result is that $V(k_t)$ equals the standard infinite sequence of discounted utility as in the standard dynamic problem:

$$V(k_t) = u(c_t, x_t) + \beta V(k_{t+1}) = \sum_{s=t}^{\infty} \beta^{s-t} u(c_s, x_s); \tag{8.9}$$

plus there is a so-called 'transversality condition' to ensure that the last term (there is always a last term no matter how long you expand the sequence) goes to zero so that utility is not unbounded ($\lim_{t \to \infty} \left[\beta^t V(k_t) \right] = 0$).

The recursive format recognises that the only time periods of importance, for any given consumer decision, are the current period t and the next period $t + 1$, and so reduces the problem down to just these two periods instead of using the more cumbersome infinite sequence problem. Either way the problem does deal with the whole infinite sequence of consumer decisions, but using the recursive statement allows the focus on just two periods as in our two-period capital problem of Part 3. This recursive approach is exploited famously by Stokey, Lucas and Prescott (1989).

8.3 General equilibrium representative agent problem

This framework can be fully specified by setting out the utility function, production function, and goods and time constraints faced by the representative agent, who is acting as both consumer and producer at this point. Let the current period utility be the log form as in Chapters 2 and 3:

$$u(c_t, x_t) = \ln c_t + \alpha \ln x_t. \tag{8.10}$$

Below this log utility functional form is then substituted into the recursive framework.

Let the production of the goods output y_t use both factor inputs of labour l_t and capital k_t, in a Cobb–Douglas form:

$$y_t = A_G l_t^{\gamma} k_t^{1-\gamma}, \tag{8.11}$$

where A_G is a positive parameter; this parameter is called the 'total factor productivity' since when A_G increases, the marginal product of both labour and capital increases.

The production function is the most standard one in macroeconomics. It has the particular property that the coefficient γ equals the share of labour wages in output, or $\gamma = \frac{wl}{y}$, and $1 - \gamma$ equals the share of capital rent i output, or $1 - \gamma = \frac{rk}{y}$. These properties come from the first-order conditions for the firm and are discussed in Appendix A2.

Consumption goods and investment goods are created by the production of output, where the output can costlessly take the form of either consumption c_t or investment i_t:

$$y_t = c_t + i_t. \tag{8.12}$$

Investment is, as before, the difference between output and investment. And investment is equal to savings. But now the capital is to depreciate at the rate $\delta_k \in (0, 1)$. Therefore the capital stock next period, k_{t+1}, is equal to the new investment in capital, i_t, plus the capital remaining from last period after taking into account its depreciation. This remaining capital is $k_t (1 - \delta_k)$. With $\delta_k = 0$, the capital is perfectly durable and lasts forever; with $\delta_k = 1$, the capital stock is a completely non-durable good, and only lasts for the one period. The next period capital stock is therefore given by

$$k_{t+1} = i_t + (1 - \delta_k) k_t,$$

or in terms of investment, it follows that new investment is the increment in the capital stock over the amount left over from the last period:

$$i_t = k_{t+1} - k_t \left(1 - \delta_k\right).\tag{8.13}$$

Investment, consumption and output account for the goods budget constraint, and the change in capital over time gives the first real dynamic dimension as part of an 'equation of motion' of the capital stock over time.

In Chapters 5, 6 and 7, the initial income y_0 is given, the production technology is $y_1 = Ak_1^{1-\gamma}$, and the first period constraint is that income equals consumption and investment, or $y_0 = c_0 + k_1$. So the savings/investment decision variable is the capital stock k_1. With $k_0 = 0$, and given that time $t = 0$, then equation (8.13) implies $i_0 = k_1 - k_0 \left(1 - \delta_k\right) = k_1$, so that this equation, if applied to Chapters 5–7, implies that new savings/investment i_0 and the capital k_1 are identical in that two-period special case. There is no investment in period 1 in Part 2, with the assumption that $i_1 = 0$ so that $c_1 = y_1$, because it is a two-period model; this means that the Part 2 model captures the nature of the decision for saving over time, but without being a fully dynamic model as in equation (8.13), which applies for all time t.

Current time also must still be accounted for, and here the time endowment of T is divided between work l_t and leisure x_t as in Chapters 2 and 3:

$$T = x_t + l_t.\tag{8.14}$$

The recursive problem is then stated as the maximisation with respect to the choice variables of consumption goods c_t, leisure x_t, labour time l_t, and next period's capital stock k_{t+1}, given the state variable that is the current period capital stock k_t, and given the production, goods and time constraints:

$$V\left(k_t\right) = \underset{c_t, x_t, l_t, k_{t+1}}{\text{Max}} : u\left(c_t, x_t\right) + \beta V\left(k_{t+1}\right),\tag{8.15}$$

subject to the constraints (8.11) to (8.14). Using these constraints to solve for consumption and leisure as

$$c_t = A_G l_t^\gamma k_t^{1-\gamma} - k_{t+1} + k_t\left(1 - \delta_k\right),$$

and

$$x_t = T - l_t,\tag{8.16}$$

the problem can be rewritten by substituting in from the above reduced set of two constraints directly into the recursive statement in equation (8.15). This gives a problem of choosing labour time l_t, as in Chapters 2, 3 and 4, and next period's capital stock k_{t+1}, as in Chapters 5, 6 and 7:

$$V\left(k_t\right) = \underset{l_t, k_{t+1}}{\text{Max}} : u\left(Al_t^\gamma k_t^{1-\gamma} - k_{t+1} + k_t\left(1 - \delta_k\right), T - l_t\right) + \beta V\left(k_{t+1}\right).\tag{8.17}$$

The first-order equilibrium conditions, with respect to l_t and k_{t+1}, are in respective order as follows:

$$\frac{\partial u\left(c_t, x_t\right)}{\partial c_t}\left(\gamma Al_t^{\gamma-1}k_t^{1-\gamma}\right) + \frac{\partial u\left(c_t, x_t\right)}{\partial x_t}\left(-1\right) = 0;\tag{8.18}$$

$$\frac{\partial u\left(c_t, x_t\right)}{\partial c_t}\left(-1\right) + \beta\frac{\partial V\left(k_{t+1}\right)}{\partial k_{t+1}} = 0.\tag{8.19}$$

A third equilibrium condition also exists in the recursive problem, relating to the state variable k_t. Although k_t is taken as given by the agent in choosing labour and capital investment, the agent knows that a change in the given k_t affects the utility level that is achieved at the maximum. To determine how this change affects utility, the agent also differentiates the whole problem with respect to k_t. This is called the 'envelope condition' and it is

$$\frac{\partial V(k_t)}{\partial k_t} = \frac{\partial u(c_t, x_t)}{\partial c_t} \left[(1 - \gamma) \, Al_t^\gamma k_t^{-\gamma} + (1 - \delta_k) \right]. \tag{8.20}$$

This tells us what is the marginal utility of equilibrium utility with respect to k_t, of $\frac{\partial V(k_t)}{\partial k_t}$. Equation (8.20) implies that $\frac{\partial V(k_t)}{\partial k_t}$ is the marginal utility of consumption $\frac{\partial u(c_t, x_t)}{\partial c_t}$ as factored by the gross marginal product of capital, $1 + \left[(1 - \gamma) \, Al_t^\gamma k_t^{-\gamma} - \delta_k \right]$. Note that 'gross' marginal product adds a one to the marginal product; and this here is the marginal product 'net' of depreciation, or minus the rate of depreciation.

The equilibrium can then be simplified into the same equilibrium relations found in the earlier chapters on labour and capital. From the above equation (8.20), advancing the time from t to $t + 1$, we get that

$$\frac{\partial V(k_{t+1})}{\partial k_{t+1}} = \frac{\partial u(c_{t+1}, x_{t+1})}{\partial c_{t+1}} \left[(1 - \gamma) \, Al_{t+1}^\gamma k_{t+1}^{-\gamma} + (1 - \delta_k) \right]. \tag{8.21}$$

Combining equations (8.19) and (8.21) so as to eliminate $\frac{\partial V(k_{t+1})}{\partial k_{t+1}}$, gives the result

$$\frac{\partial u(c_t, x_t)}{\partial c_t} (-1) + \beta \frac{\partial u(c_{t+1}, x_{t+1})}{\partial c_{t+1}} \left[(1 - \gamma) \, Al_{t+1}^\gamma k_{t+1}^{-\gamma} + (1 - \delta_k) \right].$$

This is the familiar condition that the intertemporal marginal rate of substitution between goods in the current and next period, or periods t and $t + 1$, is equal to the gross marginal product of capital net of depreciation:

$$MRS_{c_t, c_{t+1}} = \frac{\frac{\partial u(c_t, x_t)}{\partial c_t}}{\beta \frac{\partial u(c_{t+1}, x_{t+1})}{\partial c_{t+1}}} = 1 + (1 - \gamma) \, Al_{t+1}^\gamma k_{t+1}^{-\gamma} - \delta_k = 1 + MP_{k_{t+1}} - \delta_k. \tag{8.22}$$

The resulting equilibrium condition (8.22) has clear growth implications when simplified within a specific example economy. For the log utility function, $\frac{\partial u(c_t, x_t)}{\partial c_t} = \frac{1}{c_t}$ and $\frac{\partial u(c_{t+1}, x_{t+1})}{\partial c_{t+1}} = \frac{1}{c_{t+1}}$, and given the definition that $\beta \equiv \frac{1}{1+\rho}$, we can solve for the rate of change in the consumption over time as

$$\frac{c_{t+1}}{c_t} = \frac{1 + \left[(1 - \gamma) \, A_G l_{t+1}^\gamma k_{t+1}^{-\gamma} \right] - \delta_k}{1 + \rho}, \tag{8.23}$$

where $\left[(1 - \gamma) \, A_G l_{t+1}^\gamma k_{t+1}^{-\gamma} \right]$ is equal to the net real rate of interest when the problem is split into consumer and firm parts.

The other substitution margin comes directly from equation (8.18) and the derivatives of the log utility of equation (8.10). The marginal rate of substitution between goods and leisure is equal to the marginal product of labour:

$$MP_{l_t} = \gamma A_G l_t^{\gamma - 1} k_t^{1-\gamma} = \frac{\frac{\partial u(c_t, x_t)}{\partial x_t}}{\frac{\partial u(c_t, x_t)}{\partial c_t}} = \frac{\frac{\alpha}{x_t}}{\frac{1}{c_t}} = MRS_{x,c}. \tag{8.24}$$

This indicates that the marginal product of labour is equal to the ratio of the shadow price of leisure over the shadow price of goods. This labour marginal product is equal to the real wage when the consumer and firm problems are specified separately.

8.4 Consumer and firm problems

The general equilibrium here captures both margins from the earlier chapters on labour and capital: the substitution between goods and leisure as dependent upon the marginal product of labour, and the substitution between consumption this period and consumption next period as dependent upon the marginal product of capital. Now the separate consumer and firm problems will be examined so that an analysis of aggregate demand and supply is forthcoming. This will be done by deriving the demand and supply for goods: c_t^d and c_t^s. Also the consumer will choose how much to save through the supply of capital, while the firm will choose how much to invest through the demand for capital. And the consumer decides how much labour to supply and the goods producer how much labour to demand.

8.4.1 Consumer

The consumer now maximises the recursive utility subject to the same time constraint, and to an income constraint instead of the goods constraint. Think of the consumer as saving capital and earning a return on the capital, where the return is equal to rents from giving the capital to the firm to use. Here the consumer is directly giving capital to the firm, without going through a financial intermediary, although that is considered in later chapters. Then the consumer puts aside at time t the amount k_{t+1}^s of capital that is supplied to the firm. And the consumer receives back from the firm the original amount of capital, k_t^s, minus the amount that has depreciated, $\delta_k k_t^s$, plus the rental income of $r_t k_t^s$. This means the consumer has a capital wealth equal to k_t^s on which the net return is equal to $k_t^s (r_t - \delta_k)$.

Defining the capital savings s_t as the change in capital, $k_{t+1}^s - k_t^s (1 - \delta_k)$, then

$$s_t = k_{t+1}^s - k_t^s (1 - \delta_k). \tag{8.25}$$

Compare this to Chapters 4 and 5. There at $t = 0$ k_0 is assumed to be zero. Therefore $s_0 = k_1^s$; the capital savings is equal identically to k_1. But now in the more general case of equation (8.25), savings equals the increment of new capital supplied in the next period, k_{t+1}^s, over the amount supplied in the current period, which is $k_t^s (1 - \delta_k)$.

The budget constraint then is that consumption equals income minus savings. In particular, the consumption of goods c_t^d is equal to the wages earned from working for the firm, $w_t l_t^s$, plus the capital income from renting capital to the firm, $r_t k_t^s$, plus any profit Π_t that the firm makes and gives back to the consumer (as the owner of the firm), and finally minus the savings s_t that the consumer makes. With k_t^s denoting the supply of capital at time t, and given that $s_t = k_{t+1}^s - k_t^s (1 - \delta_k)$, this makes the budget constraint

$$c_t^d = w_t l_t^s + r_t k_t^s + \Pi_t - k_{t+1}^s + k_t^s (1 - \delta_k). \tag{8.26}$$

Notice how this combines the consumer's constraints in Chapters 2–7, for each the labour and the capital problem. The only difference is that now there is capital at the end of the period, k_{t+1}^s, while in the Chapters 4 and 5 problems there is no capital or new savings/investment at the end of the second period since it is just a two-period problem. This marks the difference in the dynamic problem relative to the two-period problem. Instead of just seeing how the economy expands between two periods, this k_{t+1}^s term allows for an additional consideration: how the economy grows over the long run time horizon. The *growth* of the economy is explored in the aggregate demand and supply analysis below.

The consumer problem can now be stated as

$$V\left(k_t^s\right) = \underset{c_t^d, x_t, l_t^s, k_{t+1}^s}{\text{Max}} : u\left(c_t^d, x_t\right) + \beta V\left(k_{t+1}^s\right), \tag{8.27}$$

subject to the time constraint (8.14) and the budget constraint (8.26). Using these two constraints, consumption and leisure can be solved for and substituted into the recursive utility problem directly:

$$V\left(k_t^s\right) = \underset{l_t^s, k_{t+1}^s}{\text{Max}} : u\left[w_t l_t^s + r_t k_t^s + \Pi_t - k_{t+1}^s + k_t^s\left(1 - \delta_k\right), T - l_t\right] + \beta V\left(k_{t+1}^s\right). \tag{8.28}$$

Now a choice problem in terms of only labour l_t^s and next period's capital stock k_{t+1}^s, the first-order equilibrium conditions are

$$\frac{\partial u\left(c_t^d, x_t\right)}{\partial c_t}\left(w_t\right) + \frac{\partial u\left(c_t^d, x_t\right)}{\partial x_t}\left(-1\right) = 0; \tag{8.29}$$

$$\frac{\partial u\left(c_t^d, x_t\right)}{\partial c_t^d}\left(-1\right) + \beta\frac{\partial V\left(k_{t+1}^s\right)}{\partial k_{t+1}^s} = 0. \tag{8.30}$$

And the envelope condition is

$$\frac{\partial V\left(k_t^s\right)}{\partial k_t^s} = \frac{\partial u\left(c_t^d, x_t\right)}{\partial c_t^d}\left[1 + r_t - \delta_k\right]. \tag{8.31}$$

The three equilibrium conditions in equations (8.29) to (8.31) can be reduced to two margins. First compute the derivatives of the log utility function of equation (8.10), $\frac{\partial u(c_t^d, x_t)}{\partial x_t} = \frac{\alpha}{x_t}$ and $\frac{\partial u(c_t^d, x_t)}{\partial c_t} = \frac{1}{c_t}$, and substitute these into the three equations. Then take the solution for $\frac{\partial V(k_t^s)}{\partial k_t^s}$ in equation (8.31) and increase its time subscript from t to $t+1$ to get the solution for $\frac{\partial V\left(k_{t+1}^s\right)}{\partial k_{t+1}^s}$; substitute this solution in for $\frac{\partial V\left(k_{t+1}^s\right)}{\partial k_{t+1}^s}$ in equation (8.30). This eliminates $\frac{\partial V(k_t^s)}{\partial k_t^s}$ and $\frac{\partial V\left(k_{t+1}^s\right)}{\partial k_{t+1}^s}$ and gives the two equilibrium conditions. Defining the rate of time preference ρ in terms of β as $\frac{1}{1+\rho} \equiv \beta$, these equations are

$$\frac{c_{t+1}^d}{c_t^d} = \frac{1 + r_t - \delta_k}{1 + \rho}, \tag{8.32}$$

$$w_t = \frac{\frac{\alpha}{x_t}}{\frac{1}{c_t^d}}. \tag{8.33}$$

8.4.2 Goods producer

The firm problem is to maximise profit Π_t subject to the production function, $y_t = A_G\left(l_t^d\right)^\gamma\left(k_t^d\right)^{1-\gamma}$. Profit is equal to the output minus the cost of labour and capital rentals, or minus $w_t l_t^d + r_t k_t^d$, making the firm problem:

$$\underset{y_t, l_t^d, k_t^d}{\text{Max}} \quad \Pi_t = y_t - w_t l_t^d - r_t k_t^d, \tag{8.34}$$

subject to

$$y_t = A_G\left(l_t^d\right)^\gamma\left(k_t^d\right)^{1-\gamma}. \tag{8.35}$$

Substituting the production function directly into the profit function for y_t, the problem can be simplified to

$$\text{Max } \Pi_t = A_G \left(l_t^d\right)^\gamma \left(k_t^d\right)^{1-\gamma} - w_t l_t^d - r_t k_t^d. \qquad (8.36)$$
$$\begin{array}{c}\scriptstyle l_t^d, k_t^d\end{array}$$

The equilibrium conditions are that the real wage and real interest rate equal their respective marginal products:

$$w_t = \gamma A_G \left(l_t^d\right)^{\gamma-1} \left(k_t^d\right)^{1-\gamma}, \qquad (8.37)$$

$$r_t = \left(1 - \gamma\right) A_G \left(l_t^s\right)^\gamma \left(k_t^d\right)^{-\gamma}. \qquad (8.38)$$

Factoring equation (8.37) by l_t^d and equation (8.38) by k_t^d, and using that $y_t = A_G \left(l_t^d\right)^\gamma \left(k_t^d\right)^{1-\gamma}$, gives that $w_t l_t^d = \gamma y_t$, and that $r_t k_t^d = \left(1 - \gamma\right) y_t$. Rewriting these reveals that γ is the share of labour wages in output and $1 - \gamma$ is the share of capital rentals in output:

$$\gamma = \frac{w_t l_t^d}{y_t}, \qquad (8.39)$$

and

$$1 - \gamma = \frac{r_t k_t^d}{y_t}. \qquad (8.40)$$

And these equilibrium conditions written as equations (8.39) and (8.40) imply that the firm's profit is zero after paying out wages and rents:

$$\Pi_t = y_t - w_t l_t^d - r_t k_t^d = y_t - \gamma y_t - \left(1 - \gamma\right) y_t = 0. \qquad (8.41)$$

Notice that the firm profit is defined so as to be identical to the consumer's budget constraint, as in Chapters 2–5. Here, because savings s_t equal investment i_t in equilibrium, then output equals consumption plus investment, or

$$y_t = c_t^s + i_t.$$

Since investment is defined like savings as

$$i_t = k_{t+1}^d - k_t^d \left(1 - \delta_k\right),$$

then

$$y_t = c_t^s + k_{t+1}^d - k_t^d \left(1 - \delta_k\right).$$

And since $y_t = w_t l_t^d + r_t k_t^d + \Pi_t$ by equation (8.34), then

$$w_t l_t^d + r_t k_t^d + \Pi_t = c_t^s + k_{t+1}^d - k_t^d \left(1 - \delta_k\right).$$

Rewriting this by solving for profit Π_t,

$$\Pi_t = c_t^s + k_{t+1}^d - k_t^d \left(1 - \delta_k\right) - w_t l_t^d - r_t k_t^d,$$

and this is the same as in the consumer's budget constraint of equation (8.26), when in equilibrium the capital market clears, so that

$$k_t^s = k_t^d,$$

and the labour market clears so that

$$l_t^s = l_t^d.$$

8.5 Aggregate demand: *AD*

The equilibrium conditions of the model allow for considerations of the goods, capital, and labour markets. First these will be considered under assumptions on zero growth and the next chapter will develop the same markets when growth occurs. The *AS–AD* analysis is developed for the given capital stock at time t, or for the given k_t.

Aggregate demand is the sum of the demand for output by the consumer for use as consumption and the demand of output by the firms to use as capital inputs in production. Starting with the consumer side, the demand for consumption goods c_t^d can be derived in the usual fashion of using the consumer's first-order conditions and budget constraint to write consumption demand as a function of prices.

The consumer's marginal rate of substitution between goods and leisure from equation (8.33) can be written in terms of leisure as

$$x_t = \frac{\alpha c_t^d}{w_t}. \tag{8.42}$$

The allocation of time constraint in equation (8.16) implies that

$$x_t = T - l_t.$$

Combining these two equations we can solve for labour time l_t as

$$l_t^s = T - \frac{\alpha c_t^d}{w_t}. \tag{8.43}$$

This labour supply can then be substituted back into the budget constraint in equation (8.26) to give that

$$c_t^d = w_t \left(T - \frac{\alpha c_t^d}{w_t} \right) + r_t k_t + \Pi_t - k_{t+1} + k_t \left(1 - \delta_k \right). \tag{8.44}$$

The consumption demand then becomes

$$c_t^d = \frac{w_t T + r_t k_t + \Pi_t - k_{t+1} + k_t \left(1 - \delta_k \right)}{1 + \alpha}. \tag{8.45}$$

Bringing together the terms in k_t gives

$$c_t^d = \frac{w_t T + \Pi_t + k_t \left(1 + r_t - \delta_k - \frac{k_{t+1}}{k_t} \right)}{1 + \alpha}. \tag{8.46}$$

8.5.1 Zero growth

The growth rate of capital over time $\frac{k_{t+1}}{k_t}$ is a component of the goods demand. The dynamic baseline model has an equilibrium at which some set of variables all grow at the same rate, while other variables such as time allocations are stationary and do not grow. The common equilibrium growth rate of the variables which grow is exogenous and the model is known as an exogenous growth model. And the equilibrium of the economy with exogenous growth is known as the 'balanced growth path' equilibrium. Here the simple case of zero growth is introduced, so that all variables are stationary in the equilibrium.

Assuming zero growth in equilibrium means that there is no change in the capital stock, so that $\frac{k_{t+1}}{k_t} = 1$. This makes the consumption demand from equation (8.46) equal to

$$c_t^d = \frac{1}{1 + \alpha} \left[w_t T + \Pi_t + k_t \left(r_t - \delta_k \right) \right]. \tag{8.47}$$

Aggregate demand for consumption goods depends on the price of labour and capital, and the consumer's wealth in the form of the given capital k_t. The price of consumption goods relative to labour is again $\frac{1}{w_t}$ as in Part 2. A rise in $\frac{1}{w_t}$ causes consumption to fall. Put differently, a rise in the real wage w_t causes consumption to rise. The effect of the interest rate represents the price of future consumption. Here the consumer is supplying capital to the firm and so is a net lender. An increase in the interest rate r_t therefore brings in more rental income $r_t k_t$; this raises consumption. Raising the fixed capital stock itself also causes a positive wealth effect that increases consumption.

Consumer demand can be further simplified when there is zero growth, since the equilibrium interest rate r_t can be solved in this case and substituted back into the consumer demand for goods. By equation (8.32) of the consumer's equilibrium conditions, which says that consumption growth is determined by the relation of the real interest rate r_t to the rate of time preference ρ, or $\frac{c_{t+1}^d}{c_t^d} = \frac{1+r_t-\delta_k}{1+\rho}$, we can determine r_t given the growth rate. With no growth in the equilibrium, not only is the capital stock stationary, but in addition none of the variables are growing over time. This means that consumption also is not growing, and so $\frac{c_{t+1}^d}{c_t^d} = 1$. Therefore it follows from equation (8.32) that

$$r_t = \rho + \delta_k. \tag{8.48}$$

This is the Ramsey (1928) equilibrium condition as well for this case of no growth.

8.5.2 Consumption demand as a fraction of permanent income

Having solved for the real interest rate in this case, consumption demand simplifies to

$$c_t^d = \frac{1}{1+\alpha}\left[w_t T + \Pi_t + \rho k_t\right]. \tag{8.49}$$

Now it is clear that the capital income that adds to consumption is equal to the flow of wealth due to the rate of time preference, that is ρk_t. And similarly the wage flow $w_t T$ and profit Π_t are the other parts of the income that provides for consumption demand.

However the profit Π_t is equal to zero in equilibrium, as in equation (8.41), making the permanent income equal simply to $w_t T + \rho k_t$. The zero profit here differs from Parts 2 and 3 of the text, in which the profit is the income residual going to the fixed factor, which is capital (fixed at one) in Part 2 and labour (fixed at one) in Part 3. Now both labour and capital are variable and there is no fixed factor or residual profit.

This means that the consumer's demand for goods is equal to a simple fraction of permanent income,

$$c_t^d = \frac{1}{1+\alpha}\left(w_t T + \rho k_t\right), \tag{8.50}$$

the basic idea of Friedman's (1957) 'permanent income theory of consumption'. And this function can be solved in terms of the relative price $\frac{1}{w_t}$ as

$$\frac{1}{w_t} = \frac{T}{c_t^d\left(1+\alpha\right) - \rho k_t}. \tag{8.51}$$

8.5.3 Permanent income and wealth

Consider defining permanent income at time t, denoted by y_{pt}, as the current time flow of the rent on labour and the rent on capital. With a wage rate of w_t each period, the income flow on the consumer's time is w_t. With k_t the capital stock and the rate of flow each period given by the interest rate net of depreciation, $r_t - \delta_k$, then the flow of income from capital is $(r_t - \delta_k)k_t$. As zero growth implies that $r_t = \rho + \delta_k$, then the capital flow is simply ρk_t. The sum of the labour income and capital income flows is then the permanent income of

$$y_{pt} \equiv w_t T + \rho k_t.$$

Similarly, the wealth W_t from the permanent income can be written as the discounted stream of permanent income. Using the consumer's time preference ρ as the discount rate of the permanent income stream, then

$$W_t = \frac{w_t T + \rho k_t}{\rho} = \frac{w_t T}{\rho} + k_t, \qquad (8.52)$$

as in Chapter 1. Put differently, wealth is the sum of the discounted value of the wage stream, $\frac{w_t T}{\rho}$, or the 'human capital', plus the physical capital k_t. And consumption is a fraction $\frac{1}{1+\alpha}$ of the permanent income flow from wealth.

Consider what determines how big is consumption as a fraction of permanent income. This depends only on the preference for leisure. With no leisure preference, so that $\alpha = 0$, then equation (8.50) indicates that consumption demand exactly equals permanent income, or

$$c_t^d = w_t + \rho k_t = y_{pt}. \qquad (8.53)$$

With preference for some positive amount of leisure, then $\alpha > 0$, and the consumption demand is not equal exactly to the full income $w_t T + \rho k_t$, but rather is a constant fraction of permanent income, as Friedman proposed (1957), and is given by

$$c_t^d = \frac{1}{1+\alpha} y_{pt},$$

where $\frac{1}{1+\alpha}$ is the fraction. The higher the preference for leisure, the less is the fraction of permanent income that is consumed each period, and the less is consumption. So here the calibration of the leisure preference α is important. If $\alpha = 0.5$, then two-thirds of permanent income is consumed, and one-third is saved. And consumption rises proportionately to any increase in permanent income.

8.5.4 Adding capital maintenance and getting *AD*

To get total output demand the investment demand needs to be added to the consumption demand. An implication of an assumed rate of growth equal to zero is that the amount of investment demanded by firms is simply equal to the capital investment needed to cover capital depreciation. This amount of capital is what is required to keep the capital stock equal to its previous level, so that depreciation is offset exactly by the new investment. To see this, write the investment as $i_t = k_{t+1}^d - k_t^d (1 - \delta_k)$, and substitute in that along the balanced growth path (BGP) $k_{t+1}^d = k_t^d$. Then

$$i_t = k_t^d - k_t^d (1 - \delta_k) = \delta_k k_t^d. \qquad (8.54)$$

Now the aggregate output demand, or the *AD* function, can be computed as the sum of the demand for goods by the consumer and the demand for capital by the firm. By equation (8.12) total aggregate output demanded (*AD*) is the sum of consumption and investment, which is found by adding the investment demand $\delta_k k_t^d$ to the consumption demand of equation (8.50). Doing this, and letting capital supply k_t^s equal capital demand k_t^d along the BGP, such that

$$k_t^s = k_t^d = k_t,$$

then the aggregate demand for output is

$$y_t^d = c_t^d + i_t = \left(\frac{1}{1+\alpha} \left[w_t T + \rho k_t \right] \right) + \delta_k k_t. \tag{8.55}$$

Simplifying, the AD function is

$$y_t^d = \frac{w_t T + k_t \left[\rho + (1+\alpha)\delta_k \right]}{1+\alpha}. \tag{8.56}$$

Aggregate demand for output is very similar to the aggregate consumption demand, with the added depreciation term the only difference. If depreciation increases, then so does aggregate demand.

Inversely the AD function can be written by solving for the relative price $\frac{1}{w_t}$, as

$$\frac{1}{w_t} = \frac{T}{y_t^d (1+\alpha) - k_t \left[\rho + (1+\alpha)\delta_k \right]}. \tag{8.57}$$

And this can be graphed in a familiar form of a downward sloping demand curve by assuming values for the parameters, and given the equilibrium value for the capital stock state variable, k_t.

8.6 Aggregate supply: AS

Aggregate supply of goods is derived from the firm's equilibrium conditions. From equation (8.37), and with a given k_t, the labour demand can be solved as

$$l_t^d = \left(\frac{\gamma A_G}{w_t} \right)^{\frac{1}{1-\gamma}} k_t. \tag{8.58}$$

This can be substituted into the production function of equation (8.11), to derive the aggregate output supply curve. This production equation is now:

$$y_t^s = A_G \left(l_t^d \right)^{\gamma} (k_t)^{1-\gamma}. \tag{8.59}$$

Note that this is equivalent to writing output simply, with the constant $\hat{A}_G \equiv A_G \cdot (k_t)^{1-\gamma}$, where k_t is given, as

$$y_t^s = \hat{A}_G \left(l_t^d \right)^{\gamma}, \tag{8.60}$$

as in Part 2.

Output rises with labour, and by substituting into the production equation (8.59) for labour from equation (8.58), the aggregate output supply, or AS, as a function of the wage is derived:

$$y_t^s = A_G (k_t)^{1-\gamma} \left(\frac{\gamma A_G}{w_t} \right)^{\frac{\gamma}{1-\gamma}} (k_t)^{\gamma} = A_G^{\frac{1}{1-\gamma}} \left(\frac{\gamma}{w_t} \right)^{\frac{\gamma}{1-\gamma}} k_t. \tag{8.61}$$

This means output supply rises with the relative price $\frac{1}{w_t}$, which is relative cost of goods to labour. Therefore the supply curve is an upward sloping function when graphed relative to the relative price and the output.

Solving for the relative price $\frac{1}{w_t}$ from the supply equation (8.61), within the same dimensions of relative price and output as for the AD function, the AS curve can be graphed from this fundamental equation of the *AS* function:

$$\frac{1}{w_t} = \frac{\left(y_t^s\right)^{\frac{1-\gamma}{\gamma}}}{\gamma A_G^{\frac{1}{\gamma}} (k_t)^{\frac{1-\gamma}{\gamma}}}. \tag{8.62}$$

8.6.1 Marginal cost of output

A way to derive the concept that $\frac{1}{w_t}$ is the relative price of aggregate output, in the sense of its relation to the marginal cost of output, is to derive the marginal cost of output directly. Total cost, denoted by TC_t, of the firm's profit maximisation is equal to the cost of labour and the cost of capital, or

$$TC_t = w_t l_t + r_t k_t.$$

Go back to the production function for output and solve for the labour demanded as

$$l_t^d = \left(\frac{y_t}{A_G}\right)^{\frac{1}{\gamma}} (k_t)^{\frac{\gamma-1}{\gamma}}.$$

Substituting this into the total cost function gives that

$$TC_t = w_t \left(\frac{y_t}{A_G}\right)^{\frac{1}{\gamma}} (k_t)^{\frac{\gamma-1}{\gamma}} + r_t k_t.$$

Using the fact that in the equilibrium r_t is a constant in exogenous growth given as $\rho + \delta_k$, and that k_t is a given amount at time t, then the marginal cost of output is the derivative of total cost with respect to output, or

$$MC_t = \frac{\partial (TC_t)}{\partial y_t} = \frac{\partial \left[w_t \left(\frac{y_t}{A_G}\right)^{\frac{1}{\gamma}} (k_t)^{\frac{\gamma-1}{\gamma}} + (\rho + \delta_k) k_t \right]}{\partial y_t},$$

$$MC_t = \frac{w_t y_t^{\frac{1-\gamma}{\gamma}}}{\gamma A_G^{\frac{1}{\gamma}} (k_t)^{\frac{1-\gamma}{\gamma}}}. \tag{8.63}$$

8.6.2 Marginal cost in terms of relative price of output

The marginal cost of output equals the price of output in equilibrium and this price has been normalised to 1 in the model throughout the text. Comparing equations (8.62) and (8.63), therefore the price of output relative to leisure/labour is 1 divided by w_t, or $\frac{1}{w_t}$, and this is just the marginal cost MC_t of equation (8.63) divided by the real wage w_t:

$$\frac{MC_t}{w_t} = \frac{1}{w_t}.$$

In microeconomic theory, for example Varian (1978, p. 22) calls the same marginal cost of equation (8.63) (except that he sets $A_G = 1$) the 'short run marginal cost', with k_t being termed a fixed factor. Here, in the zero growth equilibrium, k_t is given at time t at its equilibrium level and this *AS* function is a stationary state equilibrium which is a long run relation. There is no concept here of short run equilibrium, but rather only one of stationary equilibrium.

When a parameter of the model changes, the economy moves from one stationary equilibrium to another, and transition dynamics are the term used to describe the process of moving from one such equilibrium to another. Transition dynamics are not considered in this text, but such transition dynamics would be the basis upon which to describe short run equilibria within this model.

8.7 Baseline calibration

The model is now calibrated with a set of assumed parameters. This will be called the baseline calibration, or the baseline dynamic model.

8.7.1 Example 8.1

The baseline calibration is to assume that $\gamma = \frac{1}{3}$, $\alpha = 0.5$, and $T = 1$, as in Example 2.1, along with $\rho = 0.03$, $A_G = 0.15$ and $\delta_k = 0.03$. Note that with $r = \rho + \delta_k$, this implies that $r = 0.03 + 0.03 = 0.06$. And these parameters imply the equilibrium value of k_t is given at $k_t = 2.3148$.

The capital stock k_t cannot be set arbitrarily. Rather it is part of the endogenous variables of the model. Even though it is given to the agent at time t, the economy has evolved over time from its given initial capital stock of k_0. Generally, k_0 can be set to any value, say $k_0 = 0$. And then the economy moves along a transition path until it gets to its long run stationary equilibrium. The calculation of the transition path is difficult, and we will not do that here. However the long term equilibrium when the economy has finished its transition is well within our means. If there is no source of growth in the economy, then k_t will converge to a stationary value in the long run equilibrium with no growth. It requires all aspects of the equilibrium conditions to determine k_t and the rest of the solution. And so the k_t that we assume must be consistent with the k_t that is established in the long run equilibrium. For our given parameters, Chapter 10 gives the full solution of the economy including the derivation of k_t. The solution is that $k_t = 2.3148$.

The measure of $\gamma = \frac{1}{3}$ accords with the labour share once the human capital component has been included in the calibration, as argued in Mankiw, Romer and Weil (1992). The human capital is added in Chapter 12 with endogenous growth. Chapter 12 includes one comparative static exercise which shows a calibration that assumes instead that $\gamma = \frac{2}{3}$, but this is not preferred as it leads to a marginal cost curve that is concave to the origin rather than convex.

Then the *AD* function, as calibrated from equation (8.57), is

$$\frac{1}{w_t} = \frac{1}{y_t^d\left(1 + 0.5\right) - 2.3148\left[0.03 + \left(1.5\right)0.03\right]}, \tag{8.64}$$

and its graph in Figure 8.1 is a simple hyperbola in the form $P = \frac{1}{ay-b}$, where $P = \frac{1}{w}$, $a = 1.5$, and $b = 2.3\left(0.03 + \left(1.5\right)0.03\right) = 0.1725$.

8.7.2 *C + I = Y*

Consider how consumption and investment make up the aggregate demand. Figure 8.2 magnifies the previous graph of *AD* and adds onto it the consumption demand of equation (8.51). It graphs the aggregate demand *AD* as the black curve and the consumption demand as the blue curve. Given k_t, the horizontal difference between the curves is the investment demand, a constant fraction of the capital stock given by $\delta_k k_t$. Therefore from the vertical axis going across, for some constant relative price $\frac{1}{w}$, the output equals consumption plus investment: $y_t^d = c_t^d + i_t$.

8.7.3 Calibration of the *AS* curve

Particular parameters of the economy can be specified so that the marginal cost curve can be graphed. As in Example 8.1 assume that $\alpha = 0.5$ and $k_t = 2.3148$, and that $\gamma = \frac{1}{3}$ and

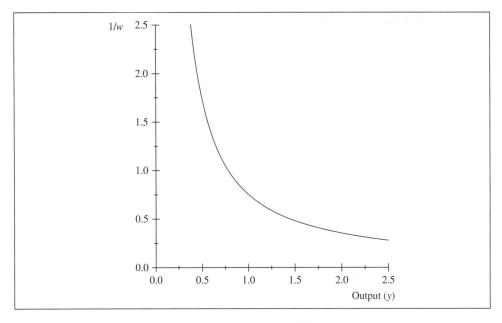

Figure 8.1 Baseline dynamic aggregate output demand *AD*

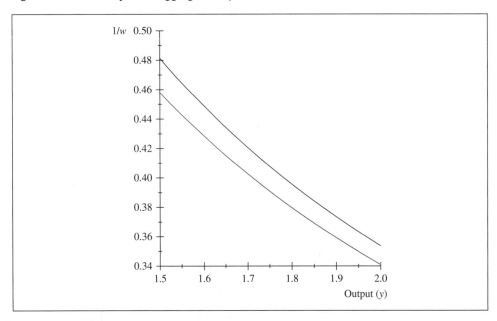

Figure 8.2 Aggregate output demand *AD* (black) and consumption demand (blue)

$A_G = 0.15$. Then the *AS* function in the example from equation (8.62) is

$$\frac{1}{w_t} = \frac{\left(y_t^s\right)^2}{\frac{1}{3}\left(0.15\right)^3\left(2.3148\right)^2},\tag{8.65}$$

which is graphed in Figure 8.3. Note that the marginal cost rises at an increasing rate with output (convex to the origin) for all $\gamma < 0.5$, remembering that $\gamma \in \left(0, 1\right)$. Here y_t is raised to the power 2.

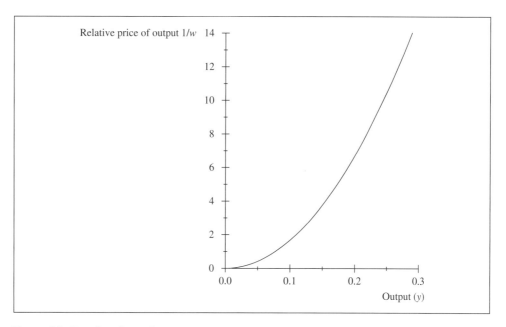

Figure 8.3 Baseline dynamic aggregate output supply AS

8.7.4 Graphical *AS–AD* equilibrium

To see the solution for w_t graphically, let us examine further the example economy with a full set of realistic parameter values given to us, as is done in calibrations of model dynamic equilibrium economies. As above, $\gamma = \frac{1}{3}$, $\rho = 0.03$, $\delta_k = 0.03$, $\alpha = 0.5$, $T = 1$, $A_G = 0.15$ and $k_t = 2.3148$. The calibrated economy implies that the *AD* curve which is given by equation (8.57) becomes

$$
\frac{1}{w_t} = \frac{T}{y_t^d\,(1+\alpha) - k_t\left[\rho + (1+\alpha)\,\delta_k\right]}
$$
$$
= \frac{1}{y_t^d\,(1.5) - 2.3148\left[0.03 + (1.5)\,0.03\right]}. \tag{8.66}
$$

For the *AS* curve, from equation (8.65) this is given by

$$
\frac{1}{w_t} = \frac{\left(y_t^s\right)^{\frac{1-\gamma}{\gamma}}}{\gamma A_G^{\frac{1}{\gamma}} (k_t)^{\frac{1-\gamma}{\gamma}}} = \frac{\left(y_t^s\right)^2}{\frac{1}{3}\left(0.15\right)^3 (2.3148)^2}. \tag{8.67}
$$

Figure 8.4 shows the graph of aggregate output demand, or the *AD* curve, of equation (8.66), as a hyperbola, and the aggregate output supply, or *AD* curve, of equation (8.67), as a curve coming from the origin, with the equilibrium price of $\frac{1}{w_t}$, seen in the blue dashed line to be around 7.2.

Conversely, $w = \frac{1}{7.2} = 0.13889$. The analytic determination of the real wage can be found by combining the *AS* and *AD* functions.

8.7.5 Equilibrium wage rate

Given the solution for the capital stock, the wage rate can be computed exactly using the solution of the economy given in Chapter 10 on the solution methodology. However the solution of the wage can also be found using the aggregate supply and demand functions. Solving for the wage rate in this way is natural in that *AS* and *AD* depend only on the real

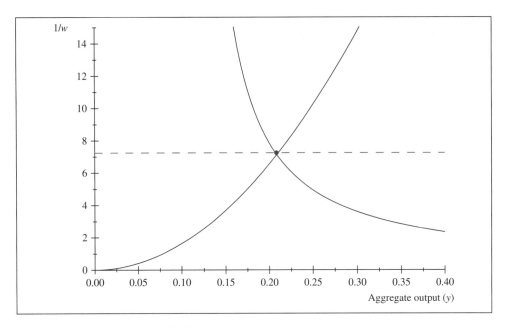

Figure 8.4 Baseline dynamic *AS–AD* equilibrium

wage rate w_t, the capital stock k_t and the output y_t, along with exogenous parameters of the model.

Setting supply of output equal to the demand for output is a market clearing condition of the model. It must be satisfied that the quantity supplied equals the quantity demanded at the equilibrium wage rate (and equilibrium capital stock). Therefore setting these equal to each other is a useful way to eliminate output from the equation and so solve for w_t. Equating aggregate output, from equations (8.56) and (8.61), it results that with AD on the left-hand side and AS on the right-hand side,

$$\frac{w_t T + k_t \left[\rho + (1 + \alpha)\, \delta_k\right]}{1 + \alpha} = A_G^{\frac{1}{1-\gamma}} \left(\frac{\gamma}{w_t}\right)^{\frac{\gamma}{1-\gamma}} k_t. \tag{8.68}$$

Given the equilibrium k_t, this equilibrium condition solves for w_t implicitly. It is not an explicit solution for w_t since w_t cannot be isolated on one side of the equation with everything else on the other side. But it still gives a solution for w_t, albeit implicitly.

Such an implicit equation in w_t has an interesting meaning, and it can be graphed to give the wage rate directly. Subtract the AS from either side of the equation (8.68) to get that

$$\frac{w_t T + k_t \left[\rho + (1 + \alpha)\, \delta_k\right]}{1 + \alpha} - A_G^{\frac{1}{1-\gamma}} \left(\frac{\gamma}{w_t}\right)^{\frac{\gamma}{1-\gamma}} k_t = 0. \tag{8.69}$$

Now call this equation (8.69) the excess demand for output, since it is the quantity demanded minus the quantity supplied at any particular wage rate. Let us use the notation of $Y(w_t; k_t)$, where

$$Y(w_t; k_t) \equiv y_t^d - y_t^s = 0$$

denotes the excess output demand of equation (8.69), at any particular wage rate w_t, given the equilibrium k_t. Then it follows that

$$Y(w_t; k_t) = \frac{w_t T + k_t \left[\rho + (1 + \alpha)\, \delta_k\right]}{1 + \alpha} - A_G^{\frac{1}{1-\gamma}} \left(\frac{\gamma}{w_t}\right)^{\frac{\gamma}{1-\gamma}} k_t = 0. \tag{8.70}$$

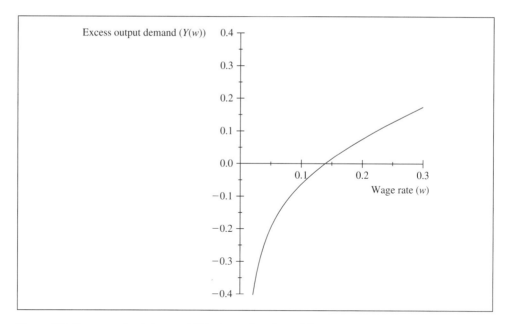

Figure 8.5 **Excess output demand** $Y(w_t)$ **as a function of the wage rate**

Given k_t, let the excess demand in this version be more simply denoted by $Y(w_t)$, and given as

$$Y(w_t) \equiv \frac{w_t + (2.3148)\left[0.03 + (1.5)\,0.03\right]}{1.5} - (0.15)^{1.5}\left(\frac{\frac{1}{3}}{w_t}\right)^{\frac{1}{2}}(2.3148) = 0.$$

The function is graphed in Figure 8.5, with excess demand $Y(w_t)$ on the vertical axis and w_t on the horizontal axis. When the $Y(w_t)$ function equals zero, there is zero excess demand, and so this value of the wage rate is the equilibrium wage rate.

Notice that this excess output demand function can be zoomed in on, as in Figure 8.6, so as to show the exact value of the wage rate at 0.13889.

At a low wage rate, for one less than 0.1389, the relative price of output $\frac{1}{w_t}$ is higher than the equilibrium of $\frac{1}{0.1389}$. Therefore at such a high price there is less demand than supply. Excess demand as a result is negative. This is what Figure 8.6 shows: low wage, high relative price, negative excess demand. For a higher wage than the equilibrium wage, the relative price of output is too low, and there is excess demand at such a price, again as in the figure: high wage, low relative price, positive excess demand. The $Y(w_t)$ function equals zero at the equilibrium wage of 0.13889 at which aggregate supply equals aggregate demand.

8.7.6 Consumption and output

Output is given as $y_t^s = A_G^{\frac{1}{1-\gamma}}\left(\frac{\gamma}{w_t}\right)^{\frac{\gamma}{1-\gamma}} k_t$, which in the baseline dynamic model, with $w_t = 0.13889$ and $k_t = 2.3148$, is

$$y_t^s = (0.15)^{1.5}\left(\frac{1}{3\,(0.13889)}\right)^{0.5} 2.3148$$

$$= 0.20832.$$

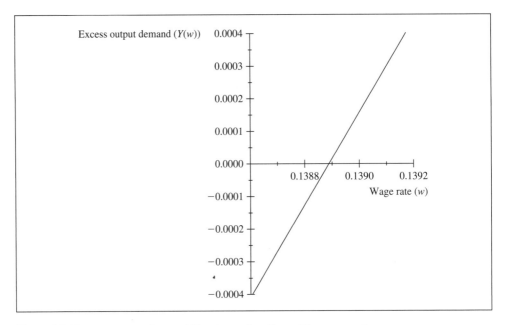

Figure 8.6 Excess output demand $Y(w_t)$ as a function of the wage rate

Similarly, consumption is given as $c_t^d = \frac{1}{1+\alpha}(w_t + \rho k_t)$. In the baseline this is

$$c_t^d = \frac{1}{1.5}\left(0.13889 + 0.03\,(2.3148)\right)$$
$$= 0.1389.$$

Consumption equals exactly the real wage rate of 0.1389.

The consumption to output ratio is

$$\frac{c^d}{y^s} = \frac{0.13889}{0.20832} = 0.667,$$

implying that two-thirds of output is consumed and one-third invested.

8.7.7 General equilibrium

Both the factor market equilibrium and production and utility level equilibrium can be graphed for the baseline Example 8.1. For the factor market consider that the goods producer equilibrium output can be computed in terms of labour and capital factors, l_t and k_t, from its profit function. With zero profit after paying factors, output is given as

$$y_t = w_t l_t + r_t k_t. \tag{8.71}$$

Using the equilibrium values of Example 8.1, this equation (8.71) provides the isocost line for a graph in factor dimension. The isocost line indicates a constant cost for given factor prices by which the capital and labour can be combined. With the equilibrium values for y_t, w_t and r_t, the equilibrium isocost line is

$$0.20832 = \left(0.13889\right) l_t + \left(0.06\right) k_t;$$
$$k_t = \frac{0.20832}{0.06} - \frac{\left(0.13889\right) l_t}{0.06};$$
$$k_t = 3.472 - 2.3148 l_t. \tag{8.72}$$

The isoquant curve indicates a constant level of output for different combinations of the inputs, similar to a utility level curve. For Example 8.1, with $y_t = 0.20832$, the goods production function implies that

$$y_t^s = A_G \left(l_t^d\right)^{\gamma} (k_t)^{1-\gamma},$$

$$0.20832 = 0.15 \left(l_t^d\right)^{\frac{1}{3}} (k_t)^{\frac{2}{3}},$$

$$k_t = \left(\frac{(0.20832)}{0.15 \left(l_t^d\right)^{\frac{1}{3}}}\right)^{\frac{3}{2}} = \frac{\left(\frac{(0.20832)}{0.15}\right)^{\frac{3}{2}}}{\left(l_t^d\right)^{\frac{1}{2}}},$$

$$k_t = \frac{1.6367}{\left(l_t^d\right)^{\frac{1}{2}}}. \tag{8.73}$$

Equations (8.72) and (8.73) are the isocost and isoquant in equilibrium that can be graphed in factor market space.

Note that $l_t = 0.5$, which can be derived from the goods production function, given the equilibrium quantity of y_t and k_t: $l_t^d = \left(\frac{0.20832}{0.15(2.3148)^{\frac{2}{3}}}\right)^3 = 0.500$. This makes the equilibrium factor input ratio

$$\frac{k_t}{l_t} = \frac{2.3148}{0.50} = 4.6296. \tag{8.74}$$

Figure 8.7 graphs equations (8.72), (8.73) and (8.74), with the black isocost, the blue isoquant, and the dashed blue input ratio as a ray from the origin.

Consumption can be expressed in terms of output minus investment using the goods production function. With a given capital stock k_t this consumption is a function only of labour, and can be graphed in c and l dimensions. The utility level curve can also be graphed in c and l dimensions by substituting in for $x_t = 1 - l_t$. In Example 8.1, in

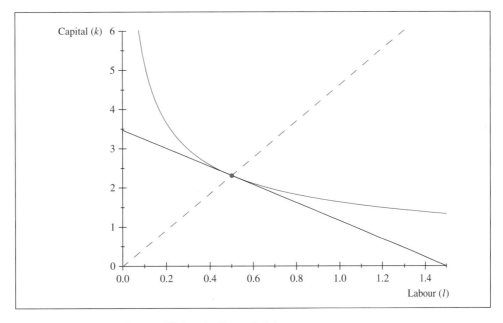

Figure 8.7 Factor market equilibrium in Example 8.1

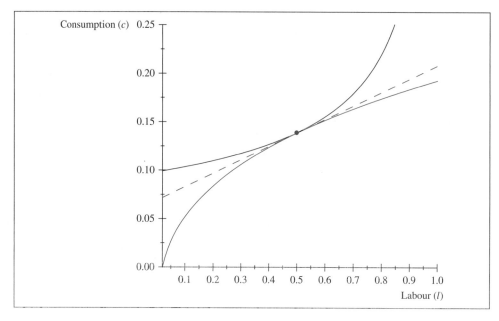

Figure 8.8 General equilibrium consumption and utility levels in **Example 8.1**

equilibrium $k_t = 2.3148$, and the consumption in terms of the production function and the utility level curve are expressed by equations (8.75) and (8.76):

$$c_t^d = y_t^s - i_t = A_G \left(l_t^d\right)^\gamma (k_t)^{1-\gamma} - \delta_k k_t,$$

$$c_t^d = (0.15) \left(l_t^d\right)^{\frac{1}{3}} (2.3148)^{\frac{2}{3}} - (0.03)(2.3148),$$

$$c_t^d = 0.26248 \left(l_t^d\right)^{\frac{1}{3}} - 0.069444; \tag{8.75}$$

$$u = \ln c_t + \alpha \ln x_t = \ln c_t + \alpha \ln \left(1 - l_t\right),$$

$$-2.3206 = \ln 0.13889 + 0.5 \ln 0.5,$$

$$-2.3206 = \ln c_t + 0.5 \ln \left(1 - l_t\right),$$

$$c_t = \frac{e^{-2.3206}}{\left(1 - l_t\right)^{0.5}}. \tag{8.76}$$

The budget line in equilibrium is

$$c_t^d = w_t l_t^s + \rho k_t^s,$$

$$c_t^d = (0.13889) \, l_t^s + (0.03)(2.3148). \tag{8.77}$$

Figure 8.8 graphs the general equilibrium, with equation (8.75) in blue, equation (8.76) in black, and the budget line (8.77) in dashed blue, in the dimensions of c_t on the vertical axis and l_t on the horizontal axis.

8.8 Productivity increase

One comparative static exercise is to examine the effect of an increase in the productivity of labour and capital in producing the output. In the goods production function, $y_t = A_G l_t^\gamma k_t^{1-\gamma}$, an increase in A_G causes the marginal productivity of both labour and capital to increase.

8.8.1 Example 8.2

To see how that affects *AS* and *AD*, let A_G increase by 5% from 0.15 to 0.1575. Other parameters are as before: $\gamma = \frac{1}{3}$, $\rho = 0.03$, $\delta_k = 0.03$, $T = 1$ and $\alpha = 0.5$. Examining the *AD* equation (8.57), it can be seen that A_G does not enter directly, but k_t does. In the solution methodology of Chapter 10, it is shown that this increase in A_G from 0.15 to 0.1575 causes k_t to increase from 2.3148 to 2.6797. This is a fractional increase of $\frac{2.6797-2.3148}{2.3148} = 0.15764$, or 15.75%.

The change in A_G and in the capital stock makes the new *AD* equation

$$\frac{1}{w_t} = \frac{1}{y_t(1.5) - 2.6797(0.03 + (1.5)0.03)}. \tag{8.78}$$

For the *AS* equation, both A_G itself and k_t enter and are changed. The new *AS* equation is

$$\frac{1}{w_t} = \frac{(y_t^s)^2}{\left(\frac{1}{3}\right)(0.1575)^3(2.6797)^2}. \tag{8.79}$$

8.8.2 Graphically

Figure 8.9 graphs equations (8.78) and (8.79) of Example 8.2 in black, along with the Example 8.1 baseline in blue.

The *AS* curve shifts out relative to the original *AS* curve when $A_G = 0.15$, to the new *AS* curve when $A_G = 0.1575$. The *AD* also shifts out from the blue to the black curve. In the new equilibrium, the relative price $\frac{1}{w_t}$ has fallen, to around 6.25, so that the real wage has risen, to around 0.1608, and output has risen as well.

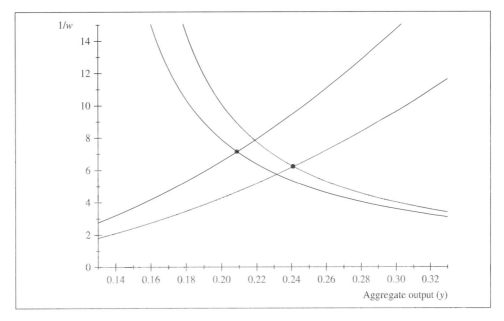

Figure 8.9 *AS–AD* equilibrium with goods productivity increase (in black) in Example 8.2, compared to the baseline (in blue) of Example 8.1

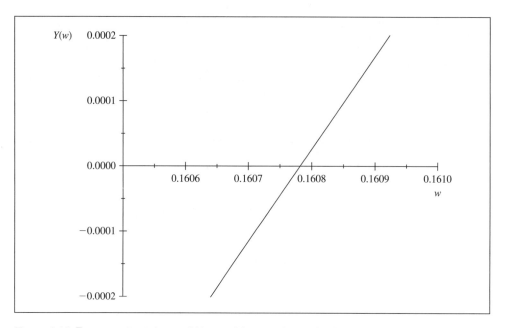

Figure 8.10 **Excess output demand** $Y(w_t)$ **with a goods productivity increase in Example 8.2**

8.8.3 Equilibrium wage

The wage rate can be computed analytically again using the market clearing condition for aggregate output. The excess demand function $Y(w_t)$ with the productivity increase is

$$Y(w_t) = \frac{w_t + (2.6797)\left[0.03 + (1.5)\,0.03\right]}{1.5} - (0.1575)^{1.5}\left(\frac{\frac{1}{3}}{w_t}\right)^{\frac{1}{2}}(2.6797) = 0.$$

Figure 8.10 graphs this $Y(w_t)$ in calibrated form, which is given as

$$Y(w_t) = \frac{0.16078 + (2.6797)\left(0.03 + (1.5)\,0.03\right)}{1.5}$$

$$- (0.1575)^{1.5}\left(\frac{\frac{1}{3}}{0.16078}\right)^{\frac{1}{2}}(2.6797) = 0.$$

The equilibrium wage rate that occurs at zero excess output demand can be seen to have a value of 0.16078, a significant increase from 0.13889 in the baseline model. Fractionally it is an increase of $\frac{0.16078-0.13889}{0.13889} = 0.1575$, or 15.75%. This is exactly the same fractional increase as in the capital stock k_t.

8.8.4 Consumption and output

Consumption is $c_t^d = \frac{1}{1+\alpha}(w_t + \rho k_t)$, which with $A_G = 0.1575$, $w_t = 0.16078$, and $k_t = 2.6797$, is

$$c_t^d = \frac{1}{1.5}\left(0.16078 + 0.03\,(2.6797)\right)$$

$$= 0.16078.$$

Consumption still exactly equals the real wage rate in this example, even after the increase in goods productivity. The consumption fractional increase is $\frac{0.16078-0.13889}{0.13889} = 0.158$, or 15.8%, the same as the increase in output.

Output is given as $y_t^s = A_G^{\frac{1}{1-\gamma}} \left(\frac{\gamma}{w_t}\right)^{\frac{\gamma}{1-\gamma}} k_t$, which with productivity rising to $A_G = 0.1575$, and with $w_t = 0.1603$, and $k_t = 2.6797$, becomes

$$y_t^s = \left(0.1575\right)^{1.5} \left(\frac{1}{3\left(0.16078\right)}\right)^{0.5} 2.6797$$

$$= 0.24117,$$

which marks a $\frac{0.24117-0.20832}{0.20832} = 0.158$ fractional increase, or 15.8% from the baseline value.

The consumption output ratio stays exactly at two-thirds. In the baseline it is $\frac{c^d}{y^s} = \frac{0.1389}{0.20832} = 0.667$ and with the productivity change, $\frac{c^d}{y^s} = \frac{0.16078}{0.24117} = 0.667$.

8.8.5 General equilibrium

Following the methodology of Example 8.1 for graphing the factor market, the isocost line is now

$$y_t = w_t l_t + r_t k_t,$$
$$0.24117 = \left(0.16078\right) l_t + \left(0.06\right) k_t,$$
$$k_t = \frac{0.24117}{0.06} - \frac{\left(0.16078\right) l_t}{0.06},$$
$$k_t = 4.0195 - 2.6797 l_t. \tag{8.80}$$

The isoquant curve is now

$$y_t^s = A_G \left(l_t^d\right)^\gamma \left(k_t\right)^{1-\gamma},$$
$$0.24117 = 0.1575 \left(l_t^d\right)^{\frac{1}{3}\gamma} \left(k_t\right)^{\frac{2}{3}},$$
$$k_t = \left(\frac{\left(0.24117\right)}{0.1575 \left(l_t^d\right)^{\frac{1}{3}}}\right)^{\frac{3}{2}} = \frac{\left(\frac{\left(0.24117\right)}{0.1575}\right)^{\frac{3}{2}}}{\left(l_t^d\right)^{\frac{1}{2}}},$$
$$k_t = \frac{1.8948}{\left(l_t^d\right)^{\frac{1}{2}}}. \tag{8.81}$$

And the factor input ratio is

$$\frac{k_t}{l_t} = \frac{2.6797}{0.50} = 5.3594. \tag{8.82}$$

Figure 8.11 graphs equations (8.80), (8.81) and (8.82) as the black isocost, dashed black isoquant, and dotted black input ratio, along with the original equilibrium in which $A_G = 0.15$, in the three blue lines.

The isocost line pivots up as the real wage rises, the isoquant shifts up as output rises, and the factor ratio pivots up as capital rises relative to a constant labour.

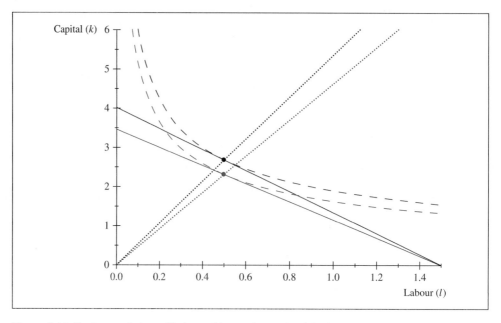

Figure 8.11 Factor market equilibrium with goods productivity increase of Example 8.2

For the general equilibrium representation of goods and labour–leisure, the consumption in terms of the production function and the utility level now are

$$c_t^d = y_t^s - i_t = A_G \left(l_t^d\right)^\gamma (k_t)^{1-\gamma} - \delta_k k_t,$$

$$c_t^d = (0.1575) \left(l_t^d\right)^{\frac{1}{3}} (2.6797)^{\frac{2}{3}} - (0.03)(2.6797),$$

$$c_t^d = 0.30386 \left(l_t^d\right)^{\frac{1}{3}} - 0.080391; \tag{8.83}$$

$$u = \ln c_t + \alpha \ln x_t = \ln c_t + \alpha \ln (1 - l_t),$$

$$-2.1743 = \ln 0.16078 + 0.5 \ln 0.5,$$

$$-2.1743 = \ln c_t + 0.5 \ln (1 - l_t),$$

$$c_t = \frac{e^{-2.1743}}{\left(1 - l_t\right)^{0.5}}. \tag{8.84}$$

The budget line in equilibrium is

$$c_t^d = w_t l_t^s + \rho k_t^s,$$

$$c_t^d = (0.16078) \, l_t^s + (0.03)(2.6797). \tag{8.85}$$

Figure 8.12 graphs the new general equilibrium, with equation (8.83) in dashed black, equation (8.84) in black, and the budget line (8.85) in dotted black, along with the original equilibrium in the three blue lines.

The production function and budget line pivot up relative to the baseline Example 8.1, and the utility level shifts up.

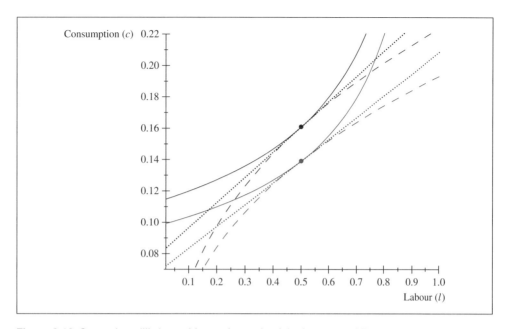

Figure 8.12 General equilibrium with goods productivity increase of Example 8.2

8.9 Time endowment increase

Increase in the time endowment causes a shift out in *AS* and *AD* similar to what occurs in Chapters 2 and 3. But now the effect also comes through the dynamically determined level of the capital stock k_t. Here it will be assumed that the time endowment T increases 5% from 1 to 1.05.

8.9.1 Example 8.3

Let the parameters be as in the baseline with $A_G = 0.15$, $\gamma = \frac{1}{3}$, $\rho = 0.03$, $\delta_k = 0.03$, $\alpha = 0.5$, and with the time endowment of $T = 1.05$. Derive the solution in terms of *AS–AD*, by considering that the allocation of time constraint in the economy is now

$$1.05 = x_t + l_t,$$

with the same marginal rate of substitution between goods and leisure, $x_t = \frac{\alpha c_t^d}{w_t}$, so that equation (8.43) now becomes

$$l_t^s = 1.05 - \frac{\alpha c_t^d}{w_t}. \tag{8.86}$$

With a zero growth rate g, and zero firm profit, the consumption demand of equation (8.44) equals

$$c_t^d = w_t \left(1.05 - \frac{\alpha c_t^d}{w_t} \right) + r_t k_t - k_{t+1} + k_t \left(1 - \delta_k \right);$$

$$c_t^d = \frac{1.05 w_t + r_t k_t - k_{t+1} + k_t \left(1 - \delta_k \right)}{1 + \alpha};$$

$$c_t^d = \frac{1}{1 + \alpha} \left(1.05 w_t + \rho k_t \right). \tag{8.87}$$

Adding depreciation to get aggregate output, gives the *AD* function:

$$y_t^d = \frac{1}{1+\alpha}\left(1.05w_t + k_t\left[\rho + \left(1+\alpha\right)\delta_k\right]\right).$$

Inverting the function to solve for $\frac{1}{w_t}$, gives instead of equation (8.57), the new *AD* function:

$$\frac{1}{w_t} = \frac{1.05}{y_t^d\left(1+\alpha\right) - k_t\left[\rho + \left(1+\alpha\right)\delta_k\right]}. \tag{8.88}$$

Aggregate supply is not affected in terms of its functional form, although the change in capital stock does shift the *AS* curve.

The capital stock can be recomputed from the solution methodology given in Chapter 10 as $k_t = 2.4306$. This means that the capital stock rises from 2.3148 to 2.4306. This is a fractional increase of $\frac{2.4306-2.3148}{2.3148} = 0.0500$, or 5%.

In calibrated form the *AS–AD* functions are

$$\frac{1}{w_t} = \frac{\left(y_t^s\right)^{\frac{1-\gamma}{\gamma}}}{\gamma A_G^{\frac{1}{\gamma}}\left(k_t\right)^{\frac{1-\gamma}{\gamma}}} = \frac{3\left(y_t^s\right)^2}{\left(0.15\right)^3\left(2.4306\right)^2}; \tag{8.89}$$

$$\frac{1}{w_t} = \frac{1.05}{y_t^d\left(1+\alpha\right) - k_t\left[\rho + \left(1+\alpha\right)\delta_k\right]} = \frac{1.05}{y_t^d\left(1.5\right) - 2.4306\left(0.03 + \left(1.5\right)0.03\right)}. \tag{8.90}$$

8.9.2 Graphically

Figure 8.13 graphs the *AS–AD* equations (8.89) and (8.89) in black along with the original baseline Example 8.1 *AS–AD* curves in blue.

The graph shows that both the *AD* and *AS* curves shift out by the same amount, so that the relative price $\frac{1}{w_t}$ is unchanged.

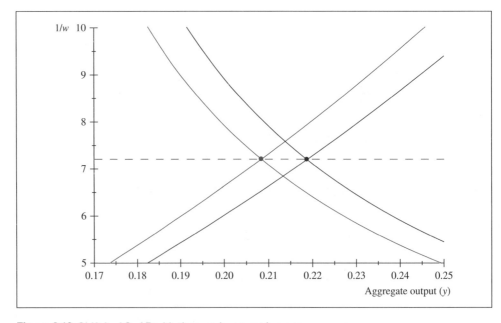

Figure 8.13 Shift in *AS–AD* with time endowment increase

In comparison, in Part 2 without capital accumulation, the time endowment increase causes only the *AD* to shift out, with a movement along the *AS* curve. While here in the dynamic model the increase in the capital stock also shifts out the *AS* curve. With *AS* also shifting out, this has the result that the increase in output is even greater. At the same time the real wage does not fall here as in Part 2.

8.9.3 Equilibrium wage

The equilibrium wage can also be determined using the excess demand equation in this example. The new excess demand, as a calibrated case of equation (8.70), is given by

$$Y(w_t) = \frac{1.05w_t + (2.4306)\left(0.03 + (1.5)\,0.03\right)}{1.5} - (0.15)^{1.5}\left(\frac{\frac{1}{3}}{w_t}\right)^{\frac{1}{2}}(2.4306) = 0.$$

Figure 8.14 graphs this $Y(w_t)$, with it zoomed in so as to determine the exact value of w_t.

It makes it clear that exactly the same equilibrium wage results as before the time endowment change, of $w = 0.13889$.

8.9.4 Consumption and output

The 5% increase in time to 1.05 causes the wage rate to stay the same and the capital stock to rise by 5%. This means that output changes from 0.208 in the baseline model to a higher value, using the demand equation for output, of

$$y_t^d = \frac{1}{1+\alpha}\left(1.05w_t + k_t\left[\rho + (1+\alpha)\,\delta_k\right]\right),$$

$$= \frac{1}{1.5}\left(1.05\,(0.1389) + 2.4306\,(0.03 + (1.5)\,0.03)\right),$$

$$= 0.21876.$$

This is a $\frac{0.21876-0.20832}{0.20832} = 0.050$ fractional increase, or 5.0%.

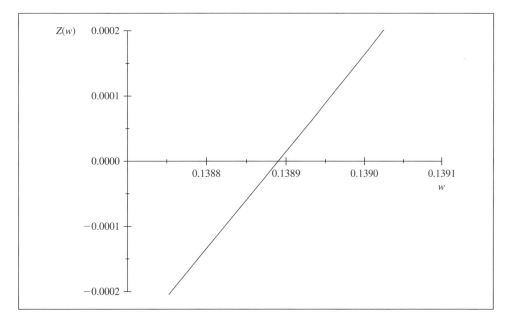

Figure 8.14 Excess output demand $Y(w_t)$ with a time endowment increase

Consumption changes from 0.01389 in the baseline to

$$c_t^d = \frac{1}{1.5}\left((1.05)\,0.1389 + 0.03\,(2.4306)\right),$$
$$= 0.1458,$$

which is a fractional increase of $\frac{0.14584-0.13889}{0.13889} = 0.0500$, or a 5% increase. Therefore the consumption to output ratio remains the same at $\frac{c^d}{y^d} = \frac{0.1389}{0.208} = 0.67 = \frac{0.14584}{0.21876} = 0.67$, or two-thirds.

8.9.5 General equilibrium

The general equilibrium comparison in input and output markets as was done in Example 8.2 is continued here, by showing the equilibrium in Example 8.3 as compared to the baseline in Example 8.1. The isocost line becomes

$$y_t = w_t l_t + r_t k_t,$$
$$0.21876 = (0.13889)\,l_t + (0.06)\,k_t,$$
$$k_t = \frac{0.21876}{0.06} - \frac{(0.13889)\,l_t}{0.06},$$
$$k_t = 3.646 - 2.3148 l_t. \tag{8.91}$$

The isoquant curve is

$$y_t^s = A_G \left(l_t^d\right)^\gamma (k_t)^{1-\gamma},$$
$$0.21876 = 0.15 \left(l_t^d\right)^{\frac{1}{3}\gamma} (k_t)^{\frac{2}{3}},$$
$$k_t = \left(\frac{(0.21876)}{0.15\left(l_t^d\right)^{\frac{1}{3}}}\right)^{\frac{3}{2}} = \frac{\left(\frac{(0.21876)}{0.15}\right)^{\frac{3}{2}}}{\left(l_t^d\right)^{\frac{1}{2}}},$$
$$k_t = \frac{1.7612}{\left(l_t^d\right)^{\frac{1}{2}}}. \tag{8.92}$$

Employment can be solved as $l_t^d = \left(\frac{0.21876}{0.15(2.4306)^{\frac{2}{3}}}\right)^3 = 0.52505.$

The factor input ratio is

$$\frac{k_t}{l_t} = \frac{2.4306}{0.52505} = 4.6293. \tag{8.93}$$

Figure 8.15 graphs equations (8.91), (8.92) and (8.93) as the black isocost, dashed black isoquant and dotted black input ratio, along with the original Example 8.1 equilibrium in which $T = 1$, in blue, dashed blue and the same dotted black ray for the input ratio.

The isocost line shifts up as $\frac{w_t}{r_t}$ remains the same since w_t stays the same while r_t is constant by the exogenous growth assumption. The isoquant shifts up as output rises, relative to the Example 8.1 baseline, and the factor ratio remains the same dotted black ray from the origin as both capital and labour rise by 5%.

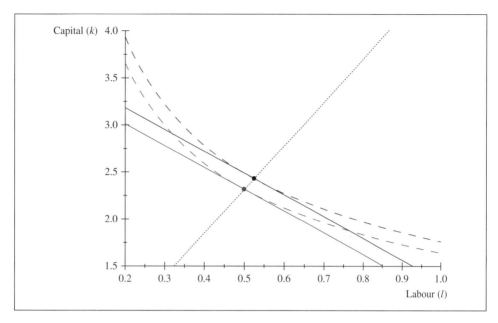

Figure 8.15 Factor market equilibrium with time endowment increase of Example 8.3

For the output market, consumption in terms of the production function, and utility with $T = 1.05$ now are

$$c_t^d = y_t^s - i_t = A_G \left(l_t^d\right)^\gamma (k_t)^{1-\gamma} - \delta_k k_t,$$

$$c_t^d = (0.15) \left(l_t^d\right)^{\frac{1}{3}} (2.4306)^{\frac{2}{3}} - (0.03) (2.4306),$$

$$c_t^d = 0.27116 \left(l_t^d\right)^{\frac{1}{3}} - 0.072918; \qquad (8.94)$$

$$u = \ln c_t + \alpha \ln x_t = \ln c_t + \alpha \ln \left(1.05 - l_t\right),$$

$$-2.2475 = \ln 0.14584 + 0.5 \ln \left(1.05 - 0.52505\right),$$

$$-2.2475 = \ln c_t + 0.5 \ln \left(1.05 - l_t\right),$$

$$c_t = \frac{e^{-2.2475}}{\left(1.05 - l_t\right)^{0.5}}. \qquad (8.95)$$

The equilibrium budget line is

$$c_t^d = w_t l_t^s + \rho k_t^s,$$

$$c_t^d = (0.13889) \, l_t^s + (0.03) (2.4306). \qquad (8.96)$$

Figure 8.16 graphs the new general equilibrium, with equation (8.96) in dashed black, equation (8.95) in black, and the budget line (8.94) in dotted black, along with the original equilibrium in the three blue lines.

The equilibrium shows only a slight increase in utility from the baseline, while in Example 8.2 the 5% productivity increase caused a much bigger utility increase. Correspondingly, the production function pivots up only somewhat. Yet this small effect accounts for an increase in the labour supply by 5%.

Note that the new black utility level curve 'crosses' the blue original level curve. Yet in utility theory, level curves do not cross. This seeming problem is just a result of graphing the diagram in goods c and labour l space. Doing it inversely in goods c and leisure x space, the utility curves would not cross. Usually such spaces interchangeably show no crossing

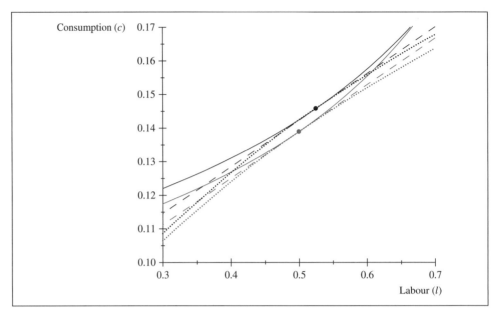

Figure 8.16 General equilibrium with time endowment increase of Example 8.3

of level curves but in this case the time endowment change affects the graph when drawn with labour on the horizontal axis.

8.10 Applications

8.10.1 Aggregate supply and demand shifts

Comparative static changes in the exogenous parameters cause shifts in aggregate supply and demand that provide the intuition for the new equilibrium relative to the original one. In fact, many such sets of changes in both *AS* and *AD* get characterised as supply changes or as demand changes, even when they typically involve shifts in both supply and demand. And the effect of the comparative static change also affects the labour market at the same time, making a broad characterisation as a supply shift or a demand shift more hazardous.

A change in goods productivity A_G causes shifts in both aggregate goods supply and demand in the same direction as the change in A_G. Supply shifts out more than demand and so this is the basis for terming this change a supply side effect, in that the net effect is more supply and demand. Yet it is clear that the increase in the consumer's permanent income from increase in A_G means that a significant demand effect is taking place as well.

A change in the consumer's time endowment causes a shift out in *AS* that is the same as the shift out in demand. Should both effects – a change in the goods endowment, through a change in A_G, and a change in time endowment – take place at the same time and in the same direction, then it would be a simplification to call the result either a demand effect or a supply effect.

An equal positive increase in both goods and time endowment would combine two effects with each component causing a shift out in both the *AD* and *AS* curves. The goods productivity increase causes *AS* to shift out by significantly more than *AD*, and the time endowment increase causes *AD* to shift out by the same as the *AS*, so overall *AS* would shift out by more than *AD*. In this sense it could be called a 'net' *AS* shift, but not only an *AS* shift.

The coincidence of both comparative static changes is plausible in a business cycle framework, a theme that is argued in the chapters ahead. They can be thought of as increases in both the goods and time endowment in an expansion and decreases in both goods and time endowment in a contraction. If indeed this is a way to characterise the business cycle, then characterising the business cycle as due only to supply shifts, as is often done, obscures what is happening in terms of aggregate demand.

8.10.2 A view of supply side economics

Our analysis shows that in Figure 8.9 an increase in productivity A_G causes a shift out of supply by more than the shift out in demand, with the real wage rising and the relative price of output falling. Arnold Harberger in his 1998 Presidential Address to the American Economics Association highlights this effect which he calls 'real cost reduction'. He views such a productivity increase of A_G as the way in which the economy continuously reduces its marginal cost, and so enables economic growth. We see this point of view exactly in that the A_G increase causes the marginal cost of output to shift down. And at the same time, since the marginal cost translates directly into the *AS* curve, the supply of goods shifts out. Harberger states that although we associate productivity increases with research and development for example, it can also be viewed as reducing costs by increasing efficiency.

The shifting out of the supply curve from the increase in A_G has given rise in part to the concept of 'supply side economics'. Here, the modern macroeconomic models focus on the change in A_G as the main force in the economy. The increase in A_G is an exogenous productivity increase that in effect increases the endowment of goods for division into consumption and investment. With output given through the production function, when A_G increases, the output exogenously jumps up for the given capital and labour inputs. And this output is the total amount of goods available at any one time period. Coming from the production function, and causing a net supply increase, it can be thought of in terms of a supply side effect. Perhaps more exact, it is an increase in the goods endowment given the production technology.

8.10.3 Say's law

The idea of focusing on the supply side in macroeconomics is not new with the modern so-called supply side economics. Rather this concept can be found in classical economics in the form of what is called 'Say's law'. Jean Baptiste Say is known for formulating the thesis that can be viewed as being also a part of our analysis. When factors cause *AS* and *AD* to shift, the market reaches a new equilibrium. When productivity increases for example, and the *AS* shifts out, then 'supply creates its own demand', as is attributed to Say. By this we mean that the decrease in marginal cost causes a fall in the relative price of output and induces the representative consumer to move along and down the *AD* curve until reaching a new equilibrium output, in this case a higher output.

8.10.4 Supply side and growth

Harberger's prescriptions for long term growth policy are to engender reductions in the marginal cost of the private sector production of goods. This is by improving national institutions that allow for the existence of the market economy, by easing trade restrictions, and minimising other taxes. All such factors might act to effectively increase A_G. Thinking about what causes changes in A_G is an important avenue for further research in the standard dynamic model.

The other traditional way to increase growth is in terms of the time endowment rather than the goods endowment. Many have focused on how increasing the infrastructure of education can increase growth. Increasing education in effect allows people to get more done with the same amount of time. This also increases productivity, albeit at the cost of reducing time available for work and leisure in the current period. So increasing education might be viewed as another type of so-called supply-side economics. This is especially true once the growth rate is made endogenous in Part 5 of the text through human capital accumulation.

8.11 Questions

1. Derive the consumer's demand for consumption in equation (8.50) by starting with the consumer's budget constraint, and substituting in from the consumer's marginal rate of substitution between goods and leisure, the intertemporal marginal rate of substitution, and using the zero growth equilibrium condition.

2. Define permanent income and describe how the consumption demand depends upon permanent income.

3. Show that given w_t, k_t, and A_G, the marginal cost MC_t of equation (8.63), $MC_t = \dfrac{w_t y_t^{\frac{1-\gamma}{\gamma}}}{\gamma A_G^{\frac{1}{\gamma}} (k_t)^{\frac{1-\gamma}{\gamma}}}$, when graphed with MC_t on the vertical axis and y_t on the horizontal axis, has a convex shape for $0 < \gamma < 0.5$, a concave shape for $0.5 < \gamma < 1$, and is linear at $\gamma = 0.5$. Recall that convexity means that MC rises at an increasing rate as y_t increases (the slope gets steeper as y_t increases); concavity means that MC rises at a decreasing rate (the slope gets flatter as y_t increases).

4. Define the balanced growth path equilibrium for the dynamic *AS–AD* model in terms of stating what variables grow at a constant rate and what variables do not grow and so are stationary at some constant value.

5. Show that when $r = \rho + \delta_k$ in stationary equilibrium then there must be a zero balanced growth path (BGP) growth rate.

6. Consider Example 8.1 and let all parameters be the same except that now $\alpha = 1$ instead of $\alpha = 0.5$. The new equilibrium capital stock is $k_t = 1.5432$.
   (a) Derive and graph the new *AD* and *AS* curves in the same $\left(\frac{1}{w_t}, y_t\right)$ space.
   (b) Determine the equilibrium wage rate.
   (c) Find the new consumption to output ratio.
   (d) Graph the new general equilibrium input and output equilibria as in Figures 8.7 and 8.8.
   (e) Summarise how having a greater preference for leisure, with α now greater than the baseline value of 0.5, affects the equilibrium.

7. As a modification to Example 8.2, let productivity increase by 10% instead of 5% so that now $A_G = 0.15 + 0.015 = 0.165$, with all other parameters the same as in Example 8.1. Given that now the new capital stock is $k_t = 3.081$:
   (a) Derive and graph the new *AD* and *AS* curves in the same $\left(\frac{1}{w_t}, y_t\right)$ space.
   (b) Determine the equilibrium wage rate.
   (c) Find the new consumption to output ratio.
   (d) Graph the new general equilibrium input and output equilibria as in Figures 8.7 and 8.8.
   (e) Summarise how an increase in goods productivity affects the entire equilibrium.

8. As a modification to Example 8.3, let the time endowment increase by 10% instead of 5% so that now $T = 1.10$, with all other parameters the same as in Example 8.1. Given that the new equilibrium capital stock is $k_t = 2.5463$:
   (a) Derive and graph the new *AD* and *AS* curves in the same $\left(\frac{1}{w_t}, y_t\right)$ space.
   (b) Determine the equilibrium wage rate.

(c) Find the new consumption to output ratio.

(d) Graph the new general equilibrium input and output equilibria as in Figures 8.7 and 8.8.

(e) Summarise how an increase in the time endowment affects the entire equilibrium.

8.12 References

Friedman, Milton, 1957, *A Theory of the Consumption Function,* Princeton: Princeton University Press for NBER.

Harberger, Arnold C., 1998, 'A Vision of the Growth Process', *American Economic Review,* 88(1): 1–32.

Keynes, John Maynard, 1933, *Essays in Biography*, Part II, Chapter 4, 'F. P. Ramsey', Harcourt Brace and Company, New York.

Keynes, John Maynard, 1936, *The General Theory of Employment, Interest, and Money,* Harcourt Brace Jovanovich, first Harbinger edition, 1964.

Mankiw, N. Gregory, David Romer and David N. Weil, 1992, 'A Contribution to the Empirics of Economic Growth', *The Quarterly Journal of Economics,* MIT Press, vol. 107(2): 407–437, May.

Ramsey, Frank, 1928, 'A Mathematical Theory of Saving', *The Economic Journal,* 38 (152, December): 543–559.

Stokey, Nancy, Robert E. Lucas, Jr. and Edward C. Prescott, 1989, *Recursive Methods in Economic Dynamics,* Harvard University Press, Cambridge.

Varian, Hal R., 1978, *Microeconomic Analysis,* W.W. Norton and Company, New York.

CHAPTER (9)

Employment

9.1 Summary/introduction

The chapter presents the labour market implications of the dynamic model. First the supply and demand for labour are derived, using the same equilibrium conditions as in Chapter 8. The labour market is graphed with the real wage on the vertical axis, this being the inverse of the goods price $\frac{1}{w_t}$. Comparative static changes in the labour market are derived in terms of changes in the goods productivity and in the time endowment.

Then the labour analysis is applied to replicate a business cycle type movement in employment. While changes in the goods productivity factor cause the wage to move in the right direction, as is consistent with the business cycle, employment does not change at all. This is because substitution and income effects exactly offset each other as in Part 2. However when a change in goods productivity is combined with a change in the time endowment, the wage and employment can be found to move in directions consistent with a basic business cycle.

While the changes in goods and time endowments replicate a normal business cycle, a more severe recession can be generated by fixing the wage rate at the same time that the goods and time endowments are decreased. This fixed price leads to an excess supply of labour as in Chapter 3, or unemployed labour. This surplus labour results in less employment than when the wage rate is flexible.

A tax on labour income is also shown to shift back the supply and demand for output, and the supply and demand for labour, resulting in less output and employment, while the wage rate remains the same. This implies that tax policy plays an important part in determining the equilibrium employment level.

9.1.1 Building on the last chapters

The last chapter presented the baseline dynamic model. This chapter uses that to derive the implications for the labour market and then to present a theory of the business cycle and of how taxes affect employment. All of the same examples of the last chapter are used in this chapter: Examples 8.1, 8.2 and 8.3 are extended in this chapter to Examples 9.1, 9.2 and 9.3.

The business cycle explanation combines Examples 9.2 and 9.3. This business cycle is a dynamic extension of the static explanation of the business cycle given in Chapter 3. The goods and time endowment changes were also combined to explain the business cycle. Now the capital stock comes into play in the dynamic explanation, as in the last chapter.

The fixed wage rate with surplus labour also echoes that analysis of Chapter 3, and causes a more severe recession. This shows that even in the dynamic analysis a similar fixed wage analysis, ad hoc as it is, can be conducted.

The tax analysis is with a labour tax as in Chapter 3, but now it is within the dynamic baseline model. However in Chapter 3, Example 3.7, the labour tax did not affect the labour demand, and it shifted back supply to cause the wage rate to rise. Here the labour tax causes both the supply and demand for labour to shift back, while the wage remains the same. The labour demand shifts here because the tax decreases the equilibrium capital stock.

9.1.2 Learning objective

The concept of equilibrium changes in employment is contrasted to unemployment caused by the market not being allowed to adjust its equilibrium wage. The challenge is to see that equilibrium changes in employment can be generated with the same simple comparative static changes in goods and time endowments, but not with a change in either the goods productivity alone, or in the time endowment alone. Then a normal recession can be shown to be much worse by assuming that the wage is fixed. And last, the concept to grasp is that tax increases also cause employment to go down and must be used cautiously in any recessionary policy. All of this needs to be viewed within the dynamic context where changes in the capital stock cause additional shifts in supply and demand not present in the static analysis of Chapter 3.

9.1.3 Who made it happen?

Wage decreases have long been expected during a recession, although many accept there are frictions that keep the wage rate from adjusting immediately. Arthur Cecil Pigou in his 1933 *Theory of Unemployment* writes (p. 252) that:

> The implication is that such unemployment as exists at any time is due wholly to the fact that changes in demand conditions are continually taking place and that frictional resistances prevent the appropriate wage adjustments from being made instantaneously.

The frictional unemployment of labour is viewed today as the result of a type of equilibrium wage adjustment that is not costless and so not instantaneous, but not the same as a fixed wage rate. The main alternative theory to the wage adjusting in equilibrium, albeit with frictions, is that the wage is fixed and cannot adjust, or can only adjust sluggishly.

That wages may change slowly because of wage contracts, and/or an unwillingness to accept lower wages, presents the idea that there can, in effect, be a fixed wage imposed on the market, thereby causing unemployment when aggregate demand falls. Recessional wage inflexibility is what Keynes describes in his famous *General Theory* (1936), in reference to what was occurring at the time during the Great Depression of the 1930s. This can cause unemployment in the sense of an excess supply of labour at a given wage rate. We show this with a fixed wage assumed.

The modern theory of business cycles has been developed by Kydland and Prescott (1982) (joint Nobel Laureates 2004) and Long and Plosser (1983) in which fluctuations in the goods productivity factor give rise to business cycles, in a body of work known as 'real business cycle theory'. However the labour employment did not move as much as in the data with this theory and many have tried to rectify this. Hansen (1985) for example allowed for another margin that compares to people deciding to enter the labour force or to leave it. This relates most closely in this chapter to the effect of the change in time endowment on employment.

9.2 Aggregate labour supply and demand

From the baseline model of Chapter 8, the labour supply can be constructed by combining the consumer's demand for goods, the marginal rate of substitution between goods and leisure, and the allocation of time constraint.

The consumer demand for goods, from equation (8.50), is a fraction of permanent income, or

$$c_t^d = \frac{1}{1+\alpha}(w_t T + \rho k_t). \tag{9.1}$$

The marginal rate of substitution between goods and leisure can be written in terms of leisure as

$$x_t = \frac{\alpha c_t^d}{w_t}.$$

The allocation of time constraint is

$$l_t^s = T - x_t.$$

Substituting in for leisure, then

$$l_t^s = T - \frac{\alpha c_t^d}{w_t}.$$

And substituting in the consumption demand

$$l_t^s = T - \frac{\frac{\alpha}{1+\alpha}(w_t T + \rho k_t)}{w_t}.$$

This is the labour supply. It can be simplified to

$$l_t^s = T - \frac{\alpha}{1+\alpha}\left[T + \left(\frac{\rho}{w_t}\right)k_t\right], \tag{9.2}$$

with leisure demand thereby given as

$$x_t = \frac{\alpha}{1+\alpha}\left[T + \left(\frac{\rho}{w_t}\right)k_t\right]. \tag{9.3}$$

Aggregate supply of goods follows directly from the firm's equilibrium conditions in Chapter 8, in particular the one setting the wage rate equal to the marginal product of labour, in equation (8.37). Rearranging this marginal productivity condition to solve for the labour quantity, the labour demand is

$$l_t^d = \left(\frac{\gamma A_G}{w_t}\right)^{\frac{1}{1-\gamma}} k_t. \tag{9.4}$$

Graphical methods can be used to solve for the wage by setting labour supply equal to labour demand. For graphing, to have the relative price of the vertical axis, the labour supply and demand can be solved in terms of w_t. For the labour supply,

$$w_t = \frac{\alpha \rho k_t}{\left(T - l_t^s\right)\left(1+\alpha\right) - \alpha T},$$

$$w_t = \frac{\alpha \rho k_t}{T - \left(1+\alpha\right)l_t^s}, \tag{9.5}$$

and for the labour demand,

$$w_t = \gamma A_G \left(\frac{k_t}{l_t^d}\right)^{1-\gamma}. \tag{9.6}$$

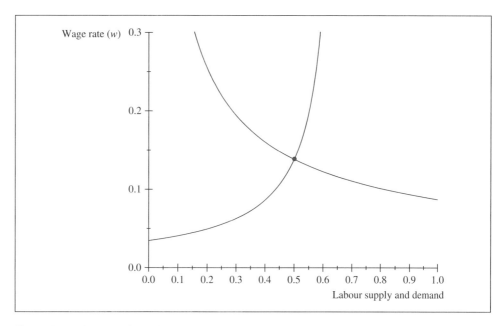

Figure 9.1 Labour market in baseline dynamic model of Example 9.1

9.2.1 Example 9.1: Labour market equilibrium

Now calibrate the economy exactly as in the baseline dynamic model of Example 8.1, with $\gamma = \frac{1}{3}$, $\alpha = 0.5$, $\rho = 0.03$, $T = 1$ and $A_G = 0.15$ and $k_t = 2.3148$. Then the labour supply is given by the equation

$$w_t = \frac{0.5 \left(0.03\right) 2.3148}{1 - \left(1.5\right) l_t^s}, \tag{9.7}$$

and the labour demand is given by

$$w_t = \frac{1}{3} \left(0.15\right) \left(\frac{2.3148}{l_t^d}\right)^{\frac{2}{3}}. \tag{9.8}$$

Figure 9.1 graphs the supply and demand for labour of equations (9.7) and (9.8). This shows the equilibrium wage to be 0.1389. And this is consistent with the equilibrium relative price in the goods market, of $\frac{1}{w} = 7.2$, since $\frac{1}{0.1389} = 7.1994$.

The labour market also can yield the equilibrium wage by setting the quantity supplied equal to the quantity demanded. From equations (9.2) and (9.4),

$$l_t^d = \left(\frac{\gamma A_G}{w_t}\right)^{\frac{1}{1-\gamma}} k_t = 1 - \frac{\alpha}{1+\alpha} \left[1 + \left(\frac{\rho}{w_t}\right) k_t\right] = l_t^s. \tag{9.9}$$

This market clearing condition in the labour market gives an implicit solution for the value of the wage w_t, given the equilibrium capital stock k_t.

9.2.2 Equilibrium wage

The market clearing in labour can be viewed in the same way as is the market clearing for goods in Chapter 8. Denote the excess demand for labour from equation (9.9) as $L\left(w_t\right)$, and define it as

$$L\left(w_t\right) \equiv l_t^d - l_t^s.$$

In equilibrium, $L(w_t) = 0$, and the wage that gives $L(w_t) = 0$ is the equilibrium wage rate, which is found from the following function for $L(w_t)$:

$$L(w) = \left(\frac{\gamma A_G}{w_t}\right)^{\frac{1}{1-\gamma}} k_t - \left(1 - \frac{\alpha}{1+\alpha}\left[1 + \left(\frac{\rho}{w_t}\right)k_t\right]\right) = 0. \tag{9.10}$$

For this calibration, with an equilibrium capital stock of $k_t = 2.3148$, this becomes

$$L(w) = \left(\frac{0.15}{3w_t}\right)^{1.5} 2.3148 - \left(1 - \frac{0.5}{1.5}\left[1 + \left(\frac{0.03}{w_t}\right)2.3148\right]\right) = 0, \tag{9.11}$$

and it is graphed in Figure 9.2. It can be seen that when the wage rate is $w_t = 0.1389$, $L(w_t)$ is equal to 0. And when the wage rate is less than the equilibrium value, there is more demand than supply, or excess demand of labour with $L(w) > 0$, while when the wage is greater than the equilibrium there is more supply than demand, or excess supply of labour with $L(w) < 0$.

The labour employment can be determined with $w = 0.1389$. Going back to equation (9.9),

$$l_t^d = \left(\frac{\gamma A_G}{w_t}\right)^{\frac{1}{1-\gamma}} k_t = 1 - \frac{\alpha}{1+\alpha}\left[1 + \left(\frac{\rho}{w_t}\right)k_t\right] = l_t^s; \tag{9.12}$$

$$0.50 = \left(\frac{0.15}{3(0.1389)}\right)^{1.5} 2.3148, \tag{9.13}$$

$$0.50 = 1 - \frac{0.5}{1.5}\left(1 + \left(\frac{0.03}{0.1389}\right)2.3148\right). \tag{9.14}$$

Both labour supply and labour demand show an equilibrium value of 0.50.

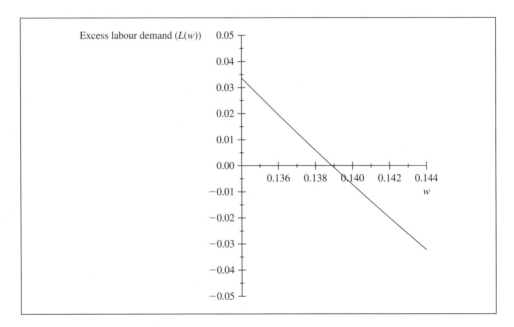

Figure 9.2 Implicit solution of the real wage from $L(w) = 0$ in Example 9.1

9.3 Productivity increase

The most important comparative static exercise is to determine how a productivity change affects the labour market. In the goods market, in Chapter 8, the increase in productivity causes a shift out in both aggregate output supply and demand, with supply shifting out more than demand, $\frac{1}{w_t}$ falling, and output rising. And in Chapter 2, the increase in A_G causes the labour supply and demand to shift up so that the real wage rose and the labour employment remains the same. Here, even though we have the more complicated dynamic model with capital accumulation, we obtain the exact same result as in Chapter 2.

9.3.1 Example 9.2

Consider the effect in the labour market of an increase of the productivity factor A_G. Assume that A_G rises 5% from 0.15 to $(0.15)(1.05) = 0.1575$, with other parameters the same at $\gamma = \frac{1}{3}$, $\alpha = 0.5$, $\rho = 0.03$ and $T = 1$. This is the same as the productivity experiment for the goods market in Example 8.2.

Examination of the labour supply given in equation (9.5) shows that A_G does not enter this equation directly. But the labour supply does depend on the equilibrium capital level k_t, and the increase in productivity causes the capital stock to rise. Chapter 10, on methodology, shows that k rises from 2.3148 to 2.6797. This causes the labour supply to shift up or backwards, since the higher capital causes an increase in permanent income and a reduced supply of labour because of this income effect.

However in equation (9.6), the productivity factor directly enters the equation positively. This means that the increase in A_G shifts out labour demand both because A_G rises and also because the capital stock rises. Figure 9.3 graphs the new supply and demand for labour with $A_G = 0.1575$ (black curves), in comparison to the baseline calibration with $A_G = 0.15$ (blue curves). The equations are for labour supply:

$$w_t = \frac{(0.03)\,2.6797}{1 - (1.5)\,l_t^s},$$ (9.15)

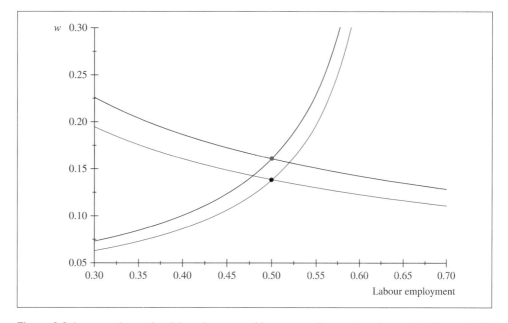

Figure 9.3 Increase in productivity raises *w* and leaves employment unchanged in Example 9.2

and for labour demand:

$$w_t = \frac{1}{3}(0.1575)\left(\frac{2.6797}{l_t^d}\right)^{\frac{2}{3}}. \tag{9.16}$$

In Figure 9.3 it can be seen that the real wage rises, while the equilibrium employment is unchanged. This is consistent with the *AS–AD* comparative static analysis.

9.3.2 Equilibrium wage

The market clearing condition for labour changes and implies the higher wage seen in Figure 9.3. With $A_G = 0.1575$ and $k_t = 2.6797$, the new $L(w_t)$ excess demand is given by

$$L(w_t) = \left(\frac{0.1575}{3w_t}\right)^{1.5}2.6797 - \left(1 - \frac{0.5}{1.5}\left[1 + \left(\frac{0.03}{w_t}\right)2.6797\right]\right) = 0. \tag{9.17}$$

Figure 9.4 graphs the excess demand and shows the wage rate to be 0.16078. This is the same wage rate found in the goods market in Example 8.2 when there is the same productivity increase.

Equilibrium employment stays at 0.50:

$$0.50 = l_t^d = \left(\frac{0.1575}{3(0.16078)}\right)^{1.5}2.6797, \tag{9.18}$$

$$0.50 = l_t^s = \left(1 - \frac{0.5}{1.5}\left(1 + \left(\frac{0.03}{0.16078}\right)2.6797\right)\right). \tag{9.19}$$

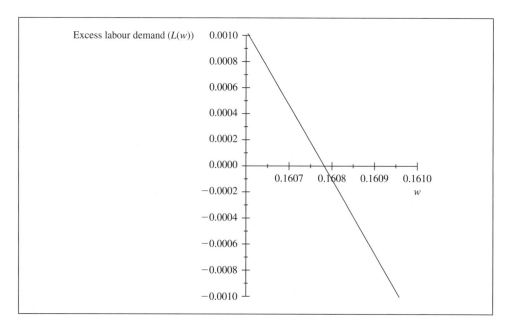

Figure 9.4 Excess demand and the real wage in Example 9.2

9.4 Time endowment increase

An increase in the endowment of time is examined in Chapters 2 and 3 for an economy without capital. There the result is that the time endowment increase causes a shift out in the supply of labour, while the labour demand is unaffected. With capital in the baseline dynamic model, the effect of increasing time also affects the capital stock, which means that both the supply and demand for labour are affected. The shift out in labour demand makes the equilibrium employment rise by more than if only the labour supply shifts out. And rather than falling as in Part 2, the wage rate ends up staying the same as the shift out in supply is the same as the shift out in demand.

9.4.1 Example 9.3

Assume all of the same parameters as in the baseline model of Example 8.1 except that T rises 5% from 1 to 1.05. This makes $T = 1.05$, $A_G = 0.15$, $\gamma = \frac{1}{3}$, $\alpha = 0.5$, $\delta_k = 0.03$ and $\rho = 0.03$. The new capital stock is shown in Chapter 10 to rise to $k_t = 2.4306$. This represents a fractional increase of $\frac{2.4306 - 2.3148}{2.3148} = 0.0500$, or 5%, the same percentage increase as in the time endowment.

The consumer demand for goods, from equation (8.50), is now the fraction of permanent income, as given by

$$c_t^d = \frac{1}{1+\alpha} \left(1.05 w_t + \rho k_t \right). \tag{9.20}$$

The marginal rate of substitution between goods and leisure is the same at

$$x_t = \frac{\alpha c_t^d}{w_t}.$$

The allocation of time constraint is

$$l_t^s = 1.05 - x_t.$$

Substituting in for leisure, this is

$$l_t^s = 1.05 - \frac{\alpha c_t^d}{w_t}.$$

Substituting in consumption demand, labour supply is

$$l_t^s = 1.05 - \frac{\frac{\alpha}{1+\alpha} \left(1.05 w_t + \rho k_t \right)}{w_t}.$$

It can be simplified to

$$l_t^s = 1.05 - \frac{\alpha}{1+\alpha} \left[1.05 + \left(\frac{\rho}{w_t} \right) k_t \right]. \tag{9.21}$$

The labour supply equation when solved for w_t is

$$w_t = \frac{\alpha \rho k_t}{1.05 - \left(1 + \alpha \right) l_t^s} = \frac{0.5 \left(0.052632 \right) 2.4306}{1.05 - \left(1.5 \right) l_t^s}. \tag{9.22}$$

Labour demand remains as

$$l_t^d = \left(\frac{\gamma A_G}{w_t} \right)^{\frac{1}{1-\gamma}} k_t, \tag{9.23}$$

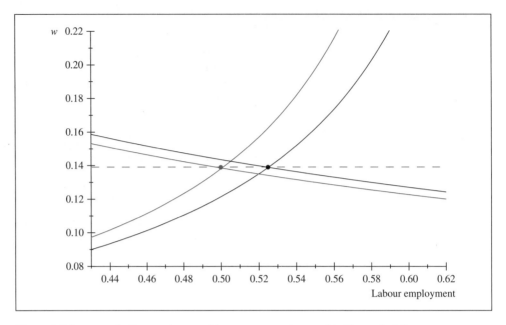

Figure 9.5 Increase in time endowment increases employment in Example 9.3

with the same inversion of

$$w_t = \gamma A_G \left(\frac{k_t}{l_t^d}\right)^{1-\gamma} = \frac{1}{3}(0.15)\left(\frac{2.4306}{l_t^d}\right)^{1-\frac{1}{3}}. \tag{9.24}$$

Figure 9.5 graphs the new equilibrium labour market in the black curves, from equations (9.22) and (9.24), with the baseline model in blue curves.

The real wage stays the same while the shift out in labour supply and in labour demand causes employment to rise from 0.5 to 0.525, a 5% increase. This is the same percentage increase seen in Part 2 for a similar experiment. However the difference from Part 2 is that here the wage rate stays the same while in Part 2 the wage rate falls.

9.4.2 Equilibrium wage

The solution for the real wage from a time endowment revision to equation (9.11) is found to be $w_t = 0.13889$:

$$L(w_t) \equiv \left(\frac{0.15}{3w_t}\right)^{1.5} 2.4306 - \left(1.05 - \frac{0.5}{1.5}\left[1.05 + \left(\frac{0.03}{w_t}\right)2.4306\right]\right) = 0,$$

as graphed in Figure 9.6.

The new labour employment is 0.525, which is found from both supply and demand for labour equations:

$$l_t^d = \left(\frac{\gamma A_G}{w_t}\right)^{\frac{1}{1-\gamma}} k_t = 1.05 - \frac{\alpha}{1+\alpha}\left[1.05 + \left(\frac{\rho}{w_t}\right)k_t\right] = l_t^s; \tag{9.25}$$

$$0.525 = \left(\frac{0.15}{3(0.13889)}\right)^{1.5}(2.4306), \tag{9.26}$$

$$0.525 = 1.05 - \frac{1}{3}\left(1.05 + \left(\frac{0.03}{0.13889}\right)(2.4306)\right). \tag{9.27}$$

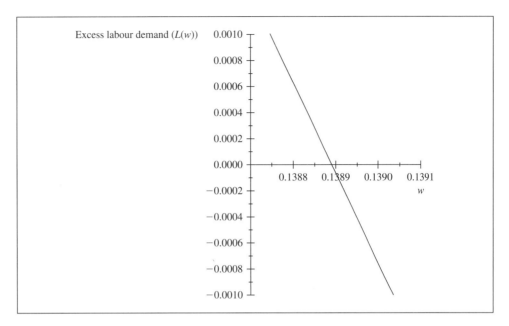

Figure 9.6 Implicit solution of the real wage in Example 9.3

This is also a 5% increase, as it is the capital stock increase and the time endowment increase that are exogenously changed.

9.5 Business cycle explanation

The business cycle expansion was explained in Part 2 by having a 5% simultaneous increase in both the goods endowment and the time endowment, through an increase in A_G and in time to 1.05 from 1. The real wage rises because of the A_G increase, but not employment, while employment rises because of the time increase, but not the real wage. Together the real wage and employment rise as in an economic expansion. The same results follow here in the dynamic baseline model of Chapter 8.

9.5.1 Example 9.4

To see this, start with the baseline calibration again, of $A_G = 0.15$, $\gamma = 0.33$, $\alpha = 0.5$, $\delta_k = 0.03$ and $\rho = 0.03$. Then assume that A_G rises 5% from 0.15 to $(0.15)(1.05) = 0.1575$. And as in the last subsection let the time endowment rise 5% to 1.05.

As shown in equation (10.53), the capital stock is now $k = 2.8137$. This is a fractional increase from the baseline of $\frac{2.8137 - 2.3148}{2.3148} = 0.21553$, or 21.6%.

The labour supply is

$$l_t^s = 1.05 - \frac{\alpha}{1+\alpha}\left[1.05 + \left(\frac{\rho}{w_t}\right)k_t\right],$$

$$l_t^s = 1.05 - \frac{0.5}{1.5}\left[1.05 + \left(\frac{0.03}{w_t}\right)2.8137\right]; \tag{9.28}$$

and labour demand is

$$l_t^d = \left(\frac{\gamma A_G}{w_t}\right)^{\frac{1}{1-\gamma}}k_t = \left(\frac{0.1575}{3w_t}\right)^{1.5}2.8137. \tag{9.29}$$

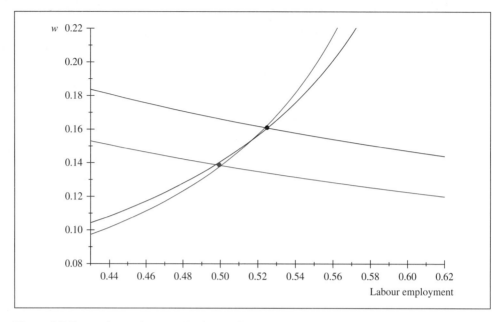

Figure 9.7 Expansionary increase in time endowment and goods productivity in Example 9.4

The inverted labour supply becomes

$$w_t = \frac{\alpha \rho k_t}{1.05 - (1+\alpha)\, l_t^s} = \frac{0.5\,(0.052632)\,2.8137}{1.05 - (1.5)\, l_t^s}, \tag{9.30}$$

and inverted labour demand is

$$w_t = \gamma A_G \left(\frac{k_t}{l_t^d}\right)^{1-\gamma} = \frac{1}{3}\,(0.1575)\left(\frac{2.8137}{l_t^d}\right)^{1-\frac{1}{3}}. \tag{9.31}$$

Figure 9.7 graphs in black the new labour supply and demand equations (9.30) and (9.31) during the expansion, in comparison to the baseline equilibrium of Example 9.1 in blue. It shows how labour supply twists out while labour demand shifts up, resulting in more employment and a higher wage rate.

The equilibrium wage rate is 0.16078, as follows from a further revision to equation (9.11) as the excess labour demand, from equations (9.28) and (9.29):

$$L\,(w_t) \equiv \left(\frac{0.1575}{3 w_t}\right)^{1.5} 2.8137 - \left(1.05 - \frac{0.5}{1.5}\left[1.05 + \left(\frac{0.03}{w_t}\right) 2.8137\right]\right) = 0,$$

which is graphed in Figure 9.8.

The new wage rate implies that labour employment is

$$l_t^d = \left(\frac{\gamma A_G}{w_t}\right)^{\frac{1}{1-\gamma}} k_t = 1.05 - \frac{\alpha}{1+\alpha}\left[1 + \left(\frac{\rho}{w_t}\right) k_t\right] = l_t^s; \tag{9.32}$$

$$0.525 = \left(\frac{(0.1575)}{3\,(0.16078)}\right)^{1.5} (2.8137), \tag{9.33}$$

$$0.525 = 1.05 - \frac{1}{3}\left(1.05 + \left(\frac{0.03}{0.16078}\right) (2.8137)\right). \tag{9.34}$$

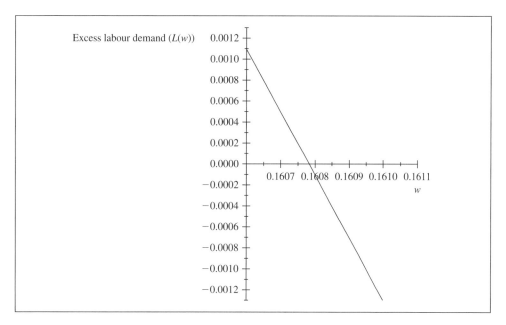

Figure 9.8 Implicit solution of the real wage in Example 9.4

This is the same employment as when there is only an increase in the time endowment, as in the last subsection.

The real wage rises significantly from 0.1389 to 0.16078, a $\frac{0.16078-0.13889}{0.13889} = 0.15761$ fractional increase, or 15.8%. Employment rises by 5%. These changes are the type that can be seen in an economic expansion, and a reverse decrease in A_G and in the time endowment down to 0.95 would cause the wage rate and employment to fall significantly. Compared to Chapter 3, the same experiment of a 5% increase in goods productivity and time endowment causes a similar percentage increase in the wage rate and employment, although the calibration is different. This means that the qualitative results are the same with a dynamic model that includes capital accumulation. Combining these two comparative static changes allows for an explanation of normal rises and falls in the labour market as consistent with our broad notion of a business cycle. A 5% decrease in the goods and time endowment, through a 5% decrease in A_G and in T, causes a reverse process with the real wage and employment falling.

The joint 5% increase in goods and time endowment causes consumption to rise from 0.01389 in the baseline to

$$c_t^d = \frac{1}{1+\alpha} \left(1.05w_t + \rho k_t\right),$$

$$= \frac{1}{1.5} \left(\left(1.05\right) 0.16078 + 0.03 \left(2.8137\right) \right) = 0.16882.$$

This is a fractional increase of $\frac{0.16882-0.13889}{0.13889} = 0.216$, or 21.6%, the same as the increase in the capital stock.

Output rises to

$$y_t^d = \frac{1}{1+\alpha} \left(1.05w_t + k_t \left[\rho + \left(1+\alpha\right) \delta_k\right]\right),$$

$$= \frac{1}{1.5} \left(\left(1.05\right) 0.16078 + \left(0.03 + \left(1.5\right) 0.03\right) \left(2.8137\right) \right) = 0.25323,$$

a fractional increase of $\frac{0.25323-0.20832}{0.20832} = 0.216$, or 21.6%, the same as consumption.

The consumption to output ratio remains at two-thirds: $\frac{c^d}{y^d} = \frac{0.1389}{0.208} = 0.67 = \frac{0.16882}{0.25323} = 0.67$.

9.5.2 Example 9.5: Contraction

Consider a symmetric business cycle contraction where the goods and time endowments fall by 5% relative to the baseline dynamic model. Then $T = 0.95$ and $A_G = 0.1425$. Chapter 10 shows that this gives a new capital stock equilibrium value of $k_t = 1.8854$.

The labour supply is

$$l_t^s = 0.95 - \frac{\alpha}{1+\alpha}\left[0.95 + \left(\frac{\rho}{w_t}\right)k_t\right],$$

$$l_t^s = 0.95 - \frac{0.5}{1.5}\left[0.95 + \left(\frac{0.03}{w_t}\right)(1.8854)\right]; \qquad (9.35)$$

labour demand is

$$l_t^d = \left(\frac{\gamma A_G}{w_t}\right)^{\frac{1}{1-\gamma}} k_t = \left(\frac{0.1425}{3w_t}\right)^{1.5}(1.8854). \qquad (9.36)$$

The inverted labour supply becomes

$$w_t = \frac{\alpha \rho k_t}{0.95 - (1+\alpha)\, l_t^s} = \frac{0.5\,(0.052632)\,1.8854}{0.95 - (1.5)\, l_t^s}, \qquad (9.37)$$

and inverted labour demand is

$$w_t = \gamma A_G \left(\frac{k_t}{l_t^d}\right)^{1-\gamma} = \frac{1}{3}\,(0.1425)\left(\frac{1.8854}{l_t^d}\right)^{1-\frac{1}{3}}. \qquad (9.38)$$

Figure 9.9 graphs the contraction equilibrium of Example 9.5 from the supply and demand equations (9.37) and (9.38), in black, along with the baseline equilibrium of Example 9.1 in blue.

Employment and the real wage fall as in a recession.

The new equilibrium wage is found from the excess labour demand equation as modified to

$$L\,(w_t) = \left(\frac{0.1425}{3w_t}\right)^{1.5} 1.8854 - \left(0.95 - \frac{0.5}{1.5}\left[0.95 + \left(\frac{0.03}{w_t}\right)1.8854\right]\right) = 0. \quad (9.39)$$

Figure 9.10 shows that this gives a wage rate of 0.1191.

The new equilibrium labour employment is 0.475.

$$l_t^d = \left(\frac{\gamma A_G}{w_t}\right)^{\frac{1}{1-\gamma}} k_t = T - \frac{\alpha}{1+\alpha}\left[T + \left(\frac{\rho}{w_t}\right)k_t\right] = l_t^s;$$

$$0.475 = \left(\frac{(0.1425)}{3\,(0.1191)}\right)^{1.5}(1.8854),$$

$$0.475 = 0.95 - \frac{1}{3}\left(0.95 + \left(\frac{0.03}{0.1191}\right)(1.8854)\right).$$

This is a decrease from 0.5, of $\frac{0.475-0.5}{0.5} = -0.05$, or a 5% decrease in employment.

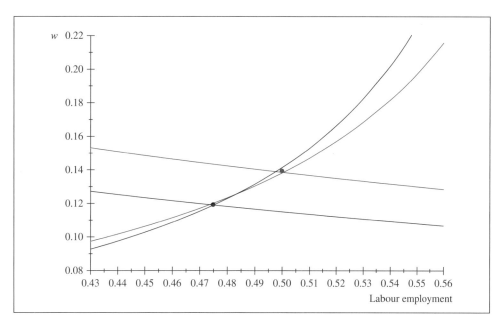

Figure 9.9 Contractionary decrease in time endowment and goods productivity in Example 9.5

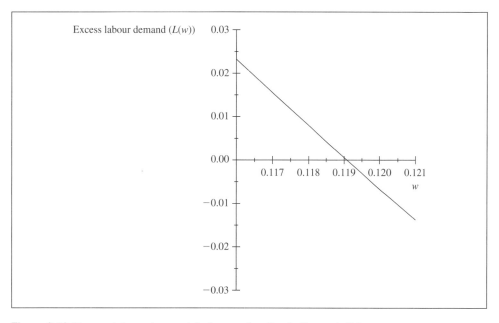

Figure 9.10 Excess labour demand during contraction in Example 9.5

9.6 Fixed wage unemployment and depressions

Occasionally there are bigger decreases in employment than that of typical recessions. The 1930s Depression had a big employment decrease, and to a lesser extent so did the 2007–10 recession. Further, the Depression was characterised as having 'excess labour supply'. To capture occasional extreme recessions, a fixed wage can be added to the model of the recession.

Labour contracts often set a wage rate that is to be applicable for several years from its onset. Such contracts can include clauses that allow employers to reduce the employment of workers during down times in the industry, such as in large cyclic manufacturing industries. For example the automobile and airplane industries undergo large cyclic swings in demand for their output that depend on the general aggregate business cycle. Such industries at various times have included wage contracts that are fixed (or indexed in a fixed fashion) which makes it so that the firms cannot reduce the wages during recessions. And instead the contracts allow for employed worker numbers to be temporarily reduced.

Such a fixity of wage rates has long been in the economics literature as a cause of unemployment, going back at least as far as John Maynard Keynes's 1936 *General Theory of Employment, Interest, and Money*. To present such theory consider again modelling a normal business cycle contraction in the dynamic model but with the wage rate fixed. An excess supply of labour results, and a dramatic decrease in employment as may occur during a depression.

Our labour market model in Chapter 3 shows that if goods and time endowment both drop moderately then the equilibrium quantity of labour employed falls by the same percentage as does the time endowment. Without assuming abnormally large decreases in the time endowment, the baseline dynamic equilibrium model is not able to reproduce a decrease in employment that characterised the 1930s Depression. Adding a fixed wage causes surplus labour and a 50% further decrease in employment. Now in the dynamic model, the same result can be found when the capital stock is arbitrarily held fixed. But allowing the capital to adjust causes the fixed wage during a contraction to result in a much bigger drop in employment.

9.6.1 Marginal productivity

Suppose now, in an 'ad hoc' fashion that is not endogenously explained within the model (so it is not micro-founded), that for some reason the real wage is fixed at $\overline{w}$. The capital stock can also be fixed, in an ad hoc fashion, or it can be allowed to reach its new flexible price equilibrium level. This then is a type of ad hoc 'short run' analysis, when the relative price of output is fixed and with the capital stock either fixed or allowed to adjust.

Consider that the marginal product of labour is given by

$$w_t = \gamma A_G \left(\frac{k_t}{l_t} \right)^{1-\gamma}. \tag{9.40}$$

With $\overline{w}$ and k_t both fixed, then when A_G falls, then l must fall in order to keep the marginal productivity condition satisfied. This can be seen by solving for l in equation (9.40):

$$l = \left(\frac{\gamma A_G}{\overline{w}} \right)^{\frac{1}{1-\gamma}} \overline{k}. \tag{9.41}$$

And if k_t adjusts, it falls during a contraction and so the drop in employment is even greater.

9.6.2 Example 9.6

Fix the real wage at its level in the baseline model, at

$$w = \overline{w} = 0.1389. \tag{9.42}$$

And let both the time T and the productivity A_G fall by 5% when the real wage is fixed at the baseline value. And let the capital stock be given at its baseline value of $k_t = 2.3148$.

Substituting in the calibrated parameters,

$$l_t = \left(\frac{(0.1425)}{3\,(0.1389)} \right)^{1.5} 2.3148 = 0.463. \tag{9.43}$$

This is a fractional decrease in employment of $\frac{0.463-0.5}{0.5} = -0.074$, or a 7.4% decrease, similar to the fixed wage result in Chapter 3. This is a 50% bigger decrease than when the wage rate is flexible, as in the contraction Example 9.5. But it does not quite represent the extremes seen in the 1930s Depression.

If the capital stock is allowed to readjust to its equilibrium value of 1.8854, then the labour employment is dramatically less at

$$l_t^d = \left(\frac{(0.1425)}{3\,(0.1389)} \right)^{1.5} (1.8854) = 0.377, \tag{9.44}$$

a fractional decrease of $\frac{0.337-0.5}{0.5} = -0.326$, or a 33% decrease.

With the labour supply given as

$$l_t^s = \left(0.95 - \frac{0.5}{1.5} \left(0.95 + \left(\frac{0.03}{0.13889} \right) 1.8854 \right) \right) = 0.498,$$

the excess supply of labour is

$$l_t^s - l_t^d = 0.498 - 0.377 = 0.121.$$

The excess is $\frac{0.498-0.377}{0.377} = 0.32095$, or 32% of the employment at the new equilibrium of $l = 0.377$. Alternatively, of the total 'labour force' of the amount supplied, of 0.498, the excess is the fraction $\frac{0.498-0.377}{0.498} = 0.24297$, or 24% which would be comparable to an unemployment figure such as during the 1930s Depression.

Figure 9.11 shows the original baseline equilibrium in blue curves and the equilibrium with the wage rate fixed and the capital stock allowed to adjust to its new equilibrium,

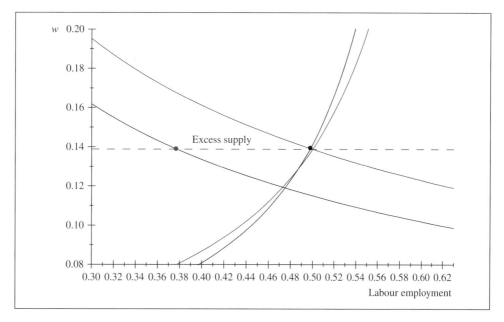

Figure 9.11 Excess labour supply with a fixed wage in Example 9.6

in Example 9.6, in black. The black supply and demand are the same equations as in Example 9.5 for when there is a contraction. The excess supply of labour at the equilibrium is given by the distance between the quantity demanded in the black demand curve at $w = 0.13889$, and the quantity supplied in the black supply curve at $w = 0.1389$.

During the Great Depression, US unemployment reached 22%, as compared to 24% in the example. This makes the model a reasonable representation of how a normal recession can instead become a full depression when the wage rate is fixed. In contrast, the other highest unemployment rates in the past 100 years in the US reached 10% in 1982 and in 2010, far below depression levels.

However, a different way to model depressions instead of a fixed wage is to allow for a specification of banking intermediation of investment in Chapter 16. Then the model produces a depression if the bank productivity falls significantly, rather than fixing the wage rate. This presents a fully micro-founded alternative to a fixed wage for explaining unusually severe recessions, or depressions.

9.7 Taxes and employment

Taxes also are a major source of decreased employment although they remain essential to finance government expenditures. Introducing taxes into the baseline model can be done in a way consistent with the approach of Chapter 3, except that now the capital is dynamically solved.

Assume that there is a tax on labour income, at a rate of τ_l. The wage income of the consumer gets reduced to $w_t (1 - \tau_l) l_t^s$ as a result, while the government has a budget constraint of

$$G_t = \tau_l w_t l_t^s. \tag{9.45}$$

The government is assumed to spend G_t in the form of a transfer that the consumer receives. Then the only result of the tax will be due to its distortion on incentives.

The consumer budget constraint with the tax is modified from equation (8.26) to

$$c_t^d = w_t (1 - \tau_l) l_t^s + r_t k_t + G_t - k_{t+1} + k_t (1 - \delta_k). \tag{9.46}$$

The equilibrium conditions are all the same except that now the marginal rate of substitution between goods and leisure is affected by the tax. Writing this margin so as to solve for x_t, it is

$$x_t = \frac{\alpha c_t}{w_t (1 - \tau_l)}. \tag{9.47}$$

The tax reduces the wage received by the consumer. The higher the tax the more the consumer substitutes from goods to leisure.

Reconstructing the *AS–AD* analysis, the *AS* is not affected by the tax. The *AD* can be constructed from equations (9.46) and (9.47), and from the time allocation constraint as solved for l_t^s, so that

$$l_t^s = T - x_t, \tag{9.48}$$

plus the assumption of a balanced growth path equilibrium growth rate of zero, whereby

$$r_t - \delta_k = \rho.$$

Substituting in the government budget constraint into the consumer budget constraint for G_t, and the time allocation for l_t^s, and the marginal rate of substitution between goods and leisure for x_t, simplifying, and substituting in $k_{t+1} = k_t$, and ρ for $r_t - \delta_k$, the consumption function emerges:

$$c_t^d = w_t \left(1 - \tau_l\right) l_t^s + r_t k_t + G_t - k_{t+1} + k_t \left(1 - \delta_k\right),$$
$$c_t^d = w_t l_t^s + r_t k_t - k_{t+1} + k_t \left(1 - \delta_k\right),$$
$$c_t^d = w_t \left(T - x_t\right) + r_t k_t - k_{t+1} + k_t \left(1 - \delta_k\right),$$
$$c_t^d = w_t \left(T - \frac{\alpha c_t}{w_t \left(1 - \tau_l\right)}\right) + r_t k_t - k_{t+1} + k_t \left(1 - \delta_k\right),$$
$$c_t^d \left(1 + \frac{\alpha}{1 - \tau_l}\right) = w_t T + r_t k_t - k_{t+1} + k_t \left(1 - \delta_k\right),$$
$$c_t^d = \frac{w_t T + r_t k_t - k_{t+1} + k_t \left(1 - \delta_k\right)}{1 + \frac{\alpha}{1 - \tau_l}},$$
$$c_t^d = \frac{w_t T + \rho k_t}{1 + \frac{\alpha}{1 - \tau_l}}. \tag{9.49}$$

Adding the investment necessary to cover depreciation on the balanced growth path, $\delta_k k_t$, the aggregate demand AD function is

$$y_t^d = \frac{w_t T + \rho k_t}{1 + \frac{\alpha}{1 - \tau_l}} + \delta_k k_t;$$

$$y_t^d = \frac{w_t T + k_t \left[\rho + \delta_k \left(1 + \frac{\alpha}{1 - \tau_l}\right)\right]}{1 + \frac{\alpha}{1 - \tau_l}}.$$

Solving for the real wage in the AD function, it can be graphed as

$$\frac{1}{w_t} = \frac{T}{y_t^d \left(1 + \frac{\alpha}{1 - \tau_l}\right) - k_t \left[\rho + \delta_k \left(1 + \frac{\alpha}{1 - \tau_l}\right)\right]}.$$

9.7.1 Example 9.7

Assuming the baseline dynamic model calibration of $A_G = 0.15$, $T = 1$, $\gamma = \frac{1}{3}$, $\alpha = 0.5$, $\delta_k = 0.03$ and $\rho = 0.03$, it remains to specify a tax rate. Let $\tau_l = 0.20$. Chapter 10 shows that the equilibrium capital stock is $k_t = 2.0576$. This is a fractional decrease of $\frac{2.3148 - 2.0576}{2.3148} = 0.111$, or 11.1%.

Then the AS–AD equations to be graphed in calibrated form are

$$\frac{1}{w_t} = \frac{1}{y_t^d \left(1 + \frac{0.5}{1 - 0.2}\right) - 2.0576 \left[0.03 + 0.03 \left(1 + \frac{0.5}{1 - 0.2}\right)\right]}, \tag{9.50}$$

and the AS which is changed only by the new capital stock of $k_t = 2.0576$:

$$\frac{1}{w_t} = \frac{\left(y_t^s\right)^{\frac{1 - \gamma}{\gamma}}}{\gamma A_G^\gamma \left(k_t\right)^{\frac{1 - \gamma}{\gamma}}} = \frac{\left(y_t^s\right)^2}{\frac{1}{3} \left(0.15\right)^3 \left(2.0576\right)^2}. \tag{9.51}$$

Figure 9.12 graphs the baseline equilibrium in blue curves, and the new equilibrium with the tax in black curves from equations (9.50) and (9.51).

The AS and AD curves both shift back, leaving the wage rate unchanged, while output significantly decreases.

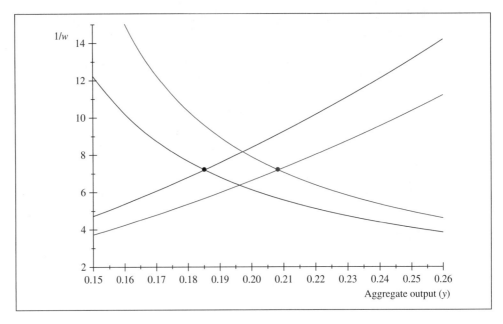

Figure 9.12 Equilibrium with a labour income tax in Example 9.7

9.7.2 Equilibrium wage

The wage rate can be solved exactly from the excess demand function of $Y(w_t) = 0$. This becomes modified to

$$
0 = Y(w_t) \equiv \frac{w_t T + k_t \left[\rho + \delta_k \left(1 + \frac{\alpha}{1-\tau_l} \right) \right]}{1 + \frac{\alpha}{1-\tau_l}} - (A_G)^{\frac{1}{1-\gamma}} \left(\frac{\gamma}{w_t} \right)^{\frac{\gamma}{1-\gamma}} k_t
$$

$$
= \frac{w_t + (2.0576) \left[0.03 + 0.03 \left(1 + \frac{0.5}{1-0.2} \right) \right]}{1 + \frac{0.5}{1-0.2}} - (0.15)^{1.5} \left(\frac{\frac{1}{3}}{w_t} \right)^{\frac{1}{2}} (2.0576).
$$

Figure 9.13 graphs the excess output demand and indeed finds the same wage as the baseline value of $w_t = 0.13889$.

9.7.3 Consumption and output

The tax shifts back the supply and demand for output, leaving the wage rate unchanged. Consumption falls to

$$
c_t^d = \frac{w_t T + \rho k_t}{1 + \frac{\alpha}{1-\tau_l}},
$$

$$
= \frac{0.13889 + 0.03 \, (2.0576)}{1 + \frac{0.5}{1-0.2}},
$$

$$
= 0.12346.
$$

This is a fractional decrease of $\frac{0.13889-0.12346}{0.13889} = 0.111$, or 11.1%, the same as the decrease in the capital stock. But the tax results in the consumption now being 11.1% less than the real wage rather than being equal to the real wage as in the baseline.

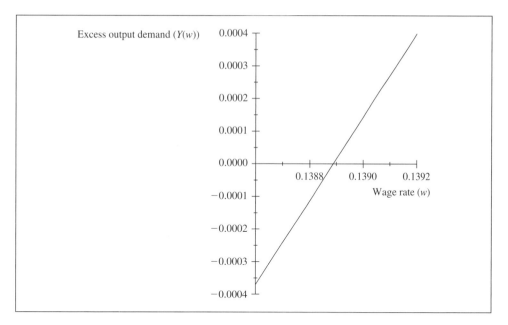

Figure 9.13 Excess output demand $Y(w_t)$ in Example 9.7

Output is

$$y_t^d = \frac{w_t T + k_t \left[\rho + \delta_k \left(1 + \frac{\alpha}{1-\tau_l} \right) \right]}{1 + \frac{\alpha}{1-\tau_l}},$$

$$= \frac{0.13889 + (2.0576) \left(0.03 + 0.03 \left(1 + \frac{0.5}{1-0.2} \right) \right)}{1 + \frac{0.5}{1-0.2}},$$

$$= 0.18519.$$

This is a fractional decrease of $\frac{0.20832 - 0.18519}{0.20832} = 0.111$, or 11.1%, the same as consumption. The consumption to output ratio remains at two-thirds: $\frac{c^d}{y^d} = \frac{0.12346}{0.18519} = 0.67$.

9.7.4 Labour market

Labour demand is not affected by the tax, just as output supply is unaffected, but the labour supply is affected, just as is output demand. Using equations (9.47), (9.48) and (9.46), the labour supply is written as

$$l_t^s = T - \frac{\alpha \left(\frac{w_t T + \rho k_t}{1 + \frac{\alpha}{1-\tau_l}} \right)}{w_t \left(1 - \tau_l \right)}. \tag{9.52}$$

Solving for the real wage, the labour supply can be written as

$$w_t = \left(\frac{\alpha \rho k_t}{\left[1 + \frac{\alpha}{1-\tau_l} \right] \left(1 - \tau_l \right) \left(T - l_t^s \right) - \alpha T} \right),$$

and the inverted labour demand is

$$w_t = \gamma A_G \left(\frac{k_t}{l_t^d} \right)^{1-\gamma}.$$

The calibrated form of labour supply and demand are

$$w_t = \left(\frac{0.5 \, (0.03) \, (2.0576)}{\left(1 + \frac{0.5}{1-0.2} \right) (1-0.2) \left(1 - l_t^s \right) - 0.5} \right),$$

$$w_t = \frac{(0.15)}{3} \left(\frac{(2.0576)}{l_t^d} \right)^{\frac{2}{3}},$$

which are graphed in Figure 9.14 in black along with the original baseline labour market equilibrium in blue.

Figure 9.14 shows how the supply and demand both shift back from the original equilibrium such that the real wage is unchanged. The employment drops from 0.5 to 0.444:

$$l_t^d = \left(\frac{(0.15)}{3 \, (0.1389)} \right)^{1.5} (2.0576) = 0.444. \tag{9.53}$$

This is a fractional decrease in employment of $\frac{0.5 - 0.44439}{0.5} = 0.111$, or 11.1%, the same as the decrease in the capital stock, in consumption and in output.

Government spending is

$$G = w_t \tau_l l_t = (0.13889) \, (0.20) \, (0.444) = 0.012333.$$

Lowering taxes stands out as a way to increase employment, capital, consumption and output. This is why tax reduction is sometimes offered as a way to deal with low employment. However this is more of a policy for the long term, rather than a way to deal with business cycles. Raising and lowering taxes to try to stabilise employment over the

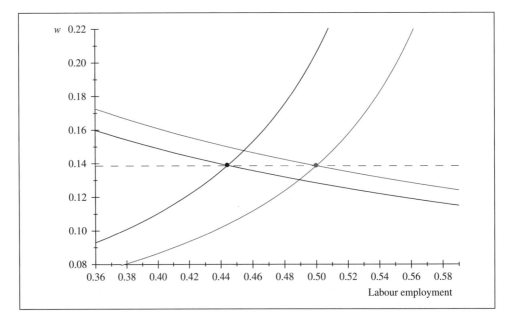

Figure 9.14 Increase in time endowment shifts out labour supply in Example 9.7

business cycle is neither practical nor wise given the uncertainty changing tax rates can create. But the analysis implies that a more efficient government that can work with lower tax rates will see higher employment and capital wealth.

9.7.5 General equilibrium

The general equilibrium comparison in input and output markets as was done in Example 8.2 is continued here, by showing the equilibrium in Example 9.7 as compared to the baseline in Example 8.1. The isocost line becomes

$$y_t = w_t l_t + r_t k_t,$$
$$0.18519 = \left(0.13889\right) l_t + \left(0.06\right) k_t,$$
$$k_t = \frac{0.18519}{0.06} - \frac{\left(0.13889\right) l_t}{0.06}. \tag{9.54}$$

The isoquant curve is

$$y_t^s = A_G \left(l_t^d\right)^\gamma (k_t)^{1-\gamma},$$
$$0.18519 = 0.15 \left(l_t^d\right)^{\frac{1}{3}} (k_t)^{\frac{2}{3}},$$
$$k_t = \left(\frac{\left(0.18519\right)}{0.15 \left(l_t^d\right)^{\frac{1}{3}}}\right)^{\frac{3}{2}} = \frac{\left(\frac{0.18519}{0.15}\right)^{\frac{3}{2}}}{\left(l_t^d\right)^{\frac{1}{2}}}. \tag{9.55}$$

The factor input ratio is

$$\frac{k_t}{l_t} = \frac{2.0576}{0.444} = 4.6342. \tag{9.56}$$

Figure 9.15 graphs the new equilibrium of equations (9.54), (9.55) and (9.56) as the black isoquant, dashed black isocost and dotted black input ratio, along with the original equilibrium.

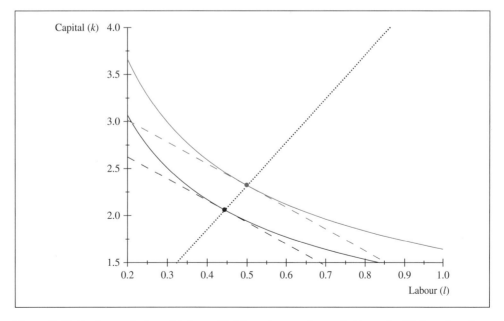

Figure 9.15 Factor market equilibrium with labour income tax τ_l, in Example 9.7 (lower) and baseline (upper)

The isocost line and isoquant shift back with the factor input ratio and factor price ratio $\frac{w_t}{r_t}$ remaining unchanged. Output is lowered by the tax.

Consumption in terms of the production function, and the utility level curve with the tax are

$$c_t^d = y_t^s - i_t = A_G \left(l_t^d\right)^{\gamma} (k_t)^{1-\gamma} - \delta_k k_t,$$

$$c_t^d = (0.15) \left(l_t^d\right)^{\frac{1}{3}} (2.0576)^{\frac{2}{3}} - (0.03) (2.0576); \tag{9.57}$$

$$u = \ln c_t + \alpha \ln x_t = \ln c_t + \alpha \ln \left(1 - l_t\right),$$

$$-2.3853 = \ln 0.12346 + 0.5 \ln \left(1 - 0.444\right),$$

$$-2.3853 = \ln c_t + 0.5 \ln \left(1.05 - l_t\right),$$

$$c_t = \frac{e^{-2.3853}}{\left(1 - l_t\right)^{0.5}}. \tag{9.58}$$

The equilibrium budget line is

$$c_t^d = w_t l_t^s \left(1 - \tau_l\right) + \rho k_t^s + G$$

$$c_t^d = (0.13889) \left(1 - 0.20\right) l_t^s + (0.03) (2.0576) + 0.012333. \tag{9.59}$$

Figure 9.16 graphs the general equilibrium goods and labour with the 20% labour income tax, from equations (9.57), (9.58) and (9.59). The production function is in black. It is cut by the dashed black utility level curve at two points, as is always the case with a tax in general equilibrium. The lower point of intersection (the blue dot) is where the equilibrium occurs of $l = 0.444$. Here the dotted black budget line is tangent to the consumer's utility level curve, but it intersects the production function. All three lines intersect at $l = 0.444$, and nowhere else.

The upper intersection of the utility curve with the production function would be the equilibrium if instead there were a subsidy to labour instead of a 20% tax. Only with a tax or subsidy does the utility level curve intersect the production function at the equilibrium, instead of being tangent to it as in an economy with no tax.

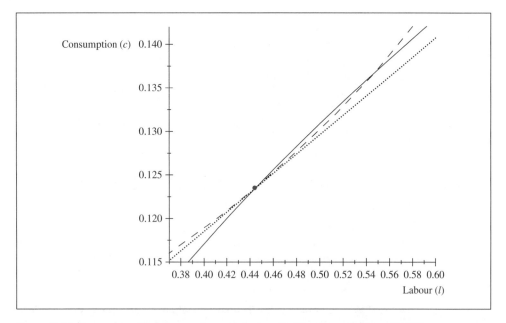

Figure 9.16 General equilibrium goods and labour with labour tax in Example 9.7

9.8 Applications

9.8.1 Hours per week, taxes and regulations

Using standard production and utility functions, we find that when marginal productivity rises then consumption rises but hours per week stay the same. Over time, with a rising productivity, the working week would be expected to stay the same on this basis. Yet international data is not consistent with a constant number of hours of work per week.

Consider the data presented in Figure 9.17. Gathered from the Economic and Social Data Service online database, it shows the average hours worked per week in the US, UK, France, Germany, Australia and Canada on an annual basis for post WWII data. The clear trend downwards is apparent in all countries but the US. Meanwhile these economies have been experiencing a trend upwards in productivity.

This creates an interesting phenomenon that our simple model cannot explain. It predicts that as productivity rises over time, the hours worked would stay stable, rather than decrease. Many explanations have been offered and this remains an area of active research. Are there extensions to the basic framework that are able to address this?

Consider the case of France. France restricted the work week to 35 hours in February 2000, under Prime Minister Lionel Jospin, the first nation to institute such a law. This was a further restriction to the 39-hour week that was instituted earlier by President Mitterrand, who was president of France from 1981 to 1995.

The idea was to allow more people to be employed, with the employed people working less, and the unemployed people thereby having a chance to work more. This idea had a long history, and for example is also found in Meade (Nobel Laureate, 1977), in his 1937 unemployment proposals as one way to reduce the unemployment rate. However, many

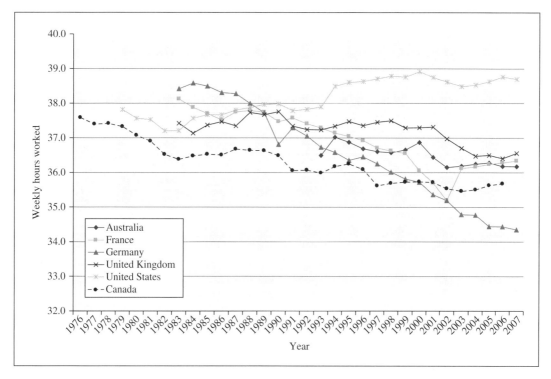

Figure 9.17 Average usual weekly hours worked on the main job

Source: OECD, Stat Extracts, Average usual weekly hours worked on the main job, annual, Organization of Economic Co-operation and Development, Paris, http://stats.oecd.org/index.aspx

have long argued that restricting the work week through law just causes labour to be less efficient because it imposes a regulation on the labour market that takes away flexibility within the labour market to adjust to different conditions. The French regulation can indeed be analysed as an implicit tax on labour that had the effect of actually causing the unemployment rate to be higher.

Jean-Pierre Raffarin, as Prime Minister of France from May 2002 to May 2005, pushed for a relaxation of the restrictions on hours, as has Nicolas Sarkozy who became France's President in May 2007. In Figure 9.17, it can be seen that France's hours dropped sharply from 2000 to 2002, and then recovered in 2003. This closely follows the legal restrictions imposed in 2000 and then relaxed in 2002.

Implicit taxes may also help explain other countries' experience with hours worked. The US, which has had a gradual increase in hours, has also seen a steady decline in union membership which has trended downwards for many years. A weakening of unions can decrease pressure for restrictions on working time. For example, the UK went in the other direction from France in the 1980s and passed legislation that decreased union power and made hours worked more competitively determined by the labour market forces. This deregulation led to the lowest unemployment rate in Europe in the 1990s and beyond, while France's unemployment rate remains stubbornly high. Germany is thought to have one of the most inflexible labour markets now in Europe, along with strong union membership; it also shows the biggest trend downwards and lowest current level of weekly hours in Figure 9.17.

A recent explanation by Ohanian, Raffo and Rogerson (2008) is that changes in tax rates over time have caused the changes in hours worked over time. They use an economic model that is very similar to the one presented here with a labour–leisure choice and standard utility and production functions. They explain falling hours with rising taxes on goods and labour, and rising hours with falling taxes. In particular, they include both explicit tax rates and implicit tax measures related to unions in their study of hours worked, including 'employment protection', 'union density' and 'measures of bargaining coordination'. All of these implicit taxes are found to be significant in explaining hours worked per week. The effect of the explicit taxes dominated the ability to explain hours worked in explaining trends. But the implicit taxes are also found to be important. And for France, the episode of the sudden fall and rise of hours worked from 2000–02 appears aptly explained by the changes in the regulations of hours worked.

9.9 Questions

1. Derive the consumer's supply of labour in equation (9.2) by starting with the consumer's marginal rate of substitution between goods and leisure, and substituting in the consumer's demand for consumption goods from the last chapter.

2. Construct the firm's demand for labour from the firm's equilibrium conditions.

3. Explain why the employment level does not change when there is an increase or decrease in the goods productivity factor A_G as in Example 9.2.

4. What features of a business cycle can you explain by changing only the goods productivity factor A_G, and what features of the business cycle can you not explain in this fashion?

5. Along the balanced growth path equilibrium with zero growth,
   (a) what happens to the employment level,
   (b) and what happens to the equilibrium wage?
   (c) How would your answers to (a) and (b) be changed if there was positive growth in the balanced growth path equilibrium?

6. An increase in the goods productivity factor A_G causes
   (a) an increase in the capital stock,

(b) a shift out in the demand for labour,

(c) a shift back in the supply of labour,

(d) all of the above.

7. When the goods productivity factor A_G increases, the capital stock increases and the supply and demand for labour are affected. Explain how the A_G factor and the capital stock k_t each separately affect the shifts in both the supply and demand for labour.

8. An increase in the time endowment causes

(a) an increase in the capital stock,

(b) a shift out in the supply of labour,

(c) a shift out in the demand for labour,

(d) all of the above.

9. Explain how an increase in the consumer's time endowment acts to increase both the equilibrium labour employment and the equilibrium amount of leisure, through shifts in the supply and demand for labour.

10. Consider Example 9.1 and let all parameters be the same except that now $\alpha = 1$ instead of $\alpha = 0.5$. The new equilibrium capital stock is $k_t = 1.5432$.

(a) Derive and graph the new supply and demand curves for labour in the same (w_t, l_t) space.

(b) Determine the equilibrium wage rate using the labour supply and demand functions.

(c) Summarise how having a greater preference for leisure, with α now greater than the baseline value of 0.5, affects the supply and demand for labour, and the equilibrium wage rate and employment level.

11. As a modification to Example 9.2, let productivity increase by 10% instead of 5% so that now $A_G = 0.15 + 0.015 = 0.165$, with all other parameters the same as in Example 8.1. Given that now the new capital stock is $k_t = 3.081$:

(a) Derive and graph the new supply and demand curves for labour in the same (w_t, l_t) space.

(b) Determine the equilibrium wage rate using the labour supply and demand functions.

(c) Summarise how having a greater productivity of goods production affects the supply and demand for labour, and the equilibrium wage rate and employment level.

12. As a modification to Example 9.3, let the time endowment increase by 10% instead of 5% so that now $T = 1.10$, with all other parameters the same as in Example 8.1. Given that the new equilibrium capital stock is $k_t = 2.5463$:

(a) Derive and graph the new supply and demand curves for labour in the same (w_t, l_t) space.

(b) Determine the equilibrium wage rate using the labour supply and demand functions.

(c) Summarise how having a greater time endowment affects the supply and demand for labour, and the equilibrium wage rate and employment level.

9.10 References

Hansen, Gary D., 1985, 'Indivisible Labor and the Business Cycle', *Journal of Monetary Economics*, Elsevier, vol. 16(3): 309–327, November.

Keynes, John Maynard, 1936, *The General Theory of Employment, Interest, and Money*, Harcourt Brace Jovanovich, first Harbinger edition, 1964.

Kydland, Finn E. and Edward C. Prescott, 1982, 'Time to Build and Aggregate Fluctuations', *Econometrica*, Econometric Society, vol. 50(6): 1345–1370, November.

Long, John B., Jr. and Charles I. Plosser, 1983, 'Real Business Cycles', *Journal of Political Economy*, University of Chicago Press, vol. 91(1): 39–69, February.

Meade, James, 1937, *Economic Analysis and Policy*, 2nd edition, Oxford University Press, Oxford.

Ohanian, Lee, Andrea Raffo and Richard Rogerson, 2008, 'Long-term Changes in Labor Supply and Taxes: Evidence from OECD Countries, 1956–2004', *Journal of Monetary Economics*, Elsevier, vol. 55(8): 1353–1362, November.

Pigou, Arthur Cecil, 1933, *The Theory of Unemployment*, London: Macmillan.

CHAPTER (10)

Dynamic *AS–AD* solution methodology

10.1 Introduction

The chapter shows how to solve the entire equilibrium of the dynamic economy with zero growth in the stationary balanced growth equilibrium. All of the equilibrium conditions of the economy must be used to find the equilibrium. Because all variables are determined simultaneously, any one variable can be solved for initially, and then this solution for the one variable can be used to solve the other variables.

Given the important role of the capital stock as the state variable of the economy, the chapter first shows how to solve for the capital stock. A closed form solution is given for the capital stock, meaning that the equilibrium conditions are used to solve for the capital stock as an explicit function of the given parameters of the economy. In this way, any comparative static change in the parameters can be easily substituted into the closed form solution for the capital stock, and the new equilibrium capital stock can be found.

The chapter proceeds to solve for the capital stock in two related ways. First the *AS* and *AD* equations are used to solve for the capital stock. This is done by setting aggregate output demand equal to aggregate output supply, so that this gives one equation in two unknowns – the capital stock and the wage rate. Then the wage rate is solved for in terms of given parameters and substituted into the *AS–AD* equation, giving one equation in the one unknown of the capital stock. Then algebra is used to solve for the capital stock.

To solve for the wage rate as a function of given parameters, the zero exogenous growth assumption is used with the consumer's intertemporal marginal rate of substitution, since this implies that the interest rate is simply the sum of the exogenously given time preference rate and the depreciation rate on capital. Then the firm's marginal product of capital condition is used. This says that the interest rate depends on the capital to labour ratio. In combination with the solution for the interest rate as the sum of the time preference and depreciation rate, this gives a solution for the capital to labour ratio. And since the wage rate, through the firm's marginal product of labour equilibrium condition, also depends upon the capital to labour ratio, the solution of the capital to labour ratio in turn gives the solution to the wage rate. When this solution for the wage rate is substituted into the *AS–AD* equation, it gives the one equation in just the one unknown of the capital stock, allowing for the capital stock solution itself.

A second approach to solving for the capital stock is presented that does not use the *AS–AD* equations, but instead starts from scratch. It simply combines the various equilibrium conditions until again the capital stock can be solved in terms of the given parameters. The same solution for the capital stock results.

The solution for the capital stock is a general solution for all of the given parameters. The chapter then substitutes in the calibrated values of the parameters for each of the examples given in Chapters 8 and 9 and finds the exact solution for the capital stock for those examples. These exact solutions are already given in Chapters 8 and 9 in the examples, but there it is not shown how these capital stock solutions are found. This chapter shows how the solutions are found. All of these solutions are the stationary state balanced growth path solutions with zero growth.

Finally the chapter shows how graphically to solve for the capital stock. This requires a four quadrant graph, with the *AS–AD* in one quadrant. The consumer demand function is also drawn into the *AS–AD* quadrant. Then the marginal rate of substitution between goods and leisure is used to form another quadrant that links to the consumption of the *AS–AD* quadrant. A third quadrant uses the firm's equilibrium ratio of the marginal product of capital to the marginal product of labour, to solve for the capital to labour ratio graphically. And the final quadrant shows the capital stock, given the capital to labour ratio, and the labour supply, of the latter two quadrants.

10.1.1 Building on the last chapters

The chapter takes all of the examples in Chapters 8 and 9 and shows how to derive the capital stock for those examples. It also adds other comparative static changes in the capital stock that are not given as examples in the previous chapters. The chapter therefore provides the full solution methodology needed to complete the analysis in Chapters 8 and 9 in a separate whole chapter so as to allow a focus on the methodology.

The previous two chapters focused on the economic analysis of goods and labour markets while being given the equilibrium value of the capital stock. This chapter ties up the analysis by showing how to solve for the capital stock. And by using the *AS–AD* equations, with aggregate output demanded set equal to aggregate output supplied, this chapter builds upon the *AS–AD* analysis as a way towards finding the full solution of the economy. It thereby provides a further use of the *AS–AD* analysis in terms of a solution methodology. This helps organize the task of finding the full equilibrium solution.

This chapter's graphical analysis builds upon the *AS–AD* graph, expanding it to four quadrants so that the capital stock itself can be found graphically. This gives a full general equilibrium analysis within a structured graph. However this is a significant extension beyond the *AS–AD* graphs. Therefore it is provided only for the baseline dynamic example and one comparative static increase in goods productivity to illustrate the idea that the capital stock can be found not only mathematically but also graphically.

10.1.2 Learning objective

Understanding how the capital stock is determined requires the realisation that all of the equilibrium conditions of the economy must be used. A trick is provided for easier learning by showing how the *AS–AD* analysis can short-cut this process by immediately getting one equation in just two unknowns. Then it requires understanding that to solve for the capital stock there needs to be only one equation in just the one unknown of the capital stock. Using the exogenous zero growth assumption then allows the steps necessary to solve for the wage rate, substitute it into the *AS–AD* equation, and so in turn solve for the capital stock.

10.1.3 Who made it happen?

The dynamic equilibrium model with capital accumulation has been around since at least Frank Ramsey. Showing the methodology for solving for the model in standard ways has been a more recent development. For example, Thomas J. Sargent's *Dynamic Macroeconomic Theory* appeared in 1987; then came the text of Nancy Stokey and Robert E. Lucas, together with Edward C. Prescott, *Recursive Methods in Economic Dynamics* in 1989; and Thomas F. Cooley (1995) edited a text *Frontiers in Business Cycle Research* that clarified the methodology and application of the modern dynamic model. More recently is Lars Ljungqvist and Thomas J. Sargent's first edition of *Recursive Macroeconomic Theory*, with a 2004 second edition. These texts have made the recursive approach a popular way of concisely stating the dynamic problem. Ohanian *et al.* (2009) provide an overview to the introduction to dynamic general equilibrium theory.

10.2 Full model solution

A full solution of the model is defined as a set of equations showing how each variable of the economy exactly depends upon the exogenous parameters of the model. Comparative statics can then be conducted by changing the exogenous parameters and seeing how every variable in the model changes.

The added complication to this scenario with the dynamic baseline model is that the so-called state variable, which is the capital stock k_t, must be solved as well. This is not a choice variable per se in that the consumer chooses k_{t+1}, not k_t. Rather k_t is given at time t to the consumer. However the 'envelope condition' of the consumer problem involves taking the derivative of recursive utility with respect to k_t, and so this is indeed another variable, albeit the current 'state variable' of the model, that must be solved.

This chapter begins with the steps taken to solve the state variable k_t. Then the other variables of the economy will be solved in turn, as functions in part of this state variable. And for every change in an exogenous parameter, there is a new equilibrium solution of the model and a new equilibrium state variable that must be solved.

What is convenient about this approach is that the state variable and all of the other variables of the economy can be solved explicitly in analytic form. Changing exogenous parameters then involves minor modifications. Further changes to the model, such as the introduction of taxes, require further modifications based on the same solution steps.

A solution for the state variable k_t shows exactly how it is a function of only the exogenous parameters. Proceeding to a solution is not a unique process. It can be done any way the student wants. There is no one avenue to the solution, but indeed only one unique solution.

Basically, deriving the solution is a matter of bringing together all of the equilibrium conditions and combining them so that finally there is only one equation in terms of one unknown variable, and the exogenous parameters of the model. One way to start is to use the *AS–AD* functions, since these have already combined several equilibrium conditions. This is just a convenient, but not unique, way. The other key step is to exploit the fact that growth is assumed to be exogenous. This greatly simplifies getting the equilibrium solution since it implies an exogenous interest rate.

10.2.1 Capital stock state variable

Consider first making use of the zero exogenous growth assumption to solve the ratio of labour to capital, $\frac{l_t}{k_t}$, in terms of exogenous parameters, from the marginal product of capital condition of the firm. This immediately gives one equation in $\frac{l_t}{k_t}$ and only exogenous parameters. Then this solution for $\frac{l_t}{k_t}$ is substituted in to the excess aggregate demand as derived from the *AS–AD* functions. Also substituting in for the wage rate using the marginal product of labour condition allows for the excess demand to be in terms of only the state variable k_t and the exogenous parameters. This allows for the solution for k_t.

Since there is no source of growth specified in the model, all variables will be stationary, or independent of time, in the long run. Since consumption is stationary, then $c_{t+1} = c_t$, and so we know from the intertemporal equilibrium condition of equation (8.32) that

$$1 = \frac{c_{t+1}}{c_t} = \frac{1 + r_t - \delta_k}{1 + \rho}. \tag{10.1}$$

It then quickly follows that r_t is constant at:

$$r_t = \rho + \delta_k. \tag{10.2}$$

Thus the zero growth equilibrium gives us a big head start since we immediately can solve for one of the variables of the model in terms of only the exogenous parameters. Because this solution is in terms of constant parameters, it follows that r_t does not change over time in its long run equilibrium and so we can write r_t as r without the time subscript should we prefer.

We also know from the firm's equilibrium condition (8.38) on the marginal product of capital that

$$\rho + \delta_k = r_t = \left(1 - \gamma\right) A_G \left(\frac{l_t}{k_t}\right)^{\gamma}. \tag{10.3}$$

Using this equation to solve for $\frac{l_t}{k_t}$ gives the solution for the labour to capital ratio $\frac{l_t}{k_t}$ as a function of given exogenous parameters:

$$\frac{l_t}{k_t} = \left[\frac{\rho + \delta_k}{\left(1 - \gamma\right) A_G}\right]^{\frac{1}{\gamma}}. \tag{10.4}$$

Now we have one equation in two unknowns. We need at least one other equation involving l_t and k_t to solve for these two variables.

We have started with the easiest starting point: exploiting the fact that there is zero growth (an assumption made implicitly or explicitly) and so realising that this implies by the intertemporal consumption equation that the solution to the interest rate is immediately given to us. In fact it is fair to interpret the zero growth model as one in which the real interest rate is an exogenous value, in that it immediately follows that it equals $\rho + \delta_k$. Then we exploited the marginal productivity of capital to get the solution for $\frac{l_t}{k_t}$.

From here, there is certainly no unique way to proceed towards the final solution: this should be understood. The equilibrium conditions can be combined in whatever sequence the student finds intuitively best. Two equal approaches are given next, with the first exploiting the AS–AD work done previously and the second starting from the beginning.

10.2.2 *AS–AD* solution approach

Probably the simplest way to proceed is to use the *AS–AD* functions that are already derived. In particular, the market clearing condition that supply equals demand in the equilibrium implies that the excess demand is zero at the equilibrium as well.

The excess demand function gives output as a function of the wage rate w_t and the capital stock k_t, and the exogenous parameters. Therefore we could add to this the solution for w_t from the marginal product of labour condition of the firm of equation (8.37). This is an equation in terms of $\frac{l_t}{k_t}$. Then the *AS–AD* equation with substitution for w_t in terms of $\frac{l_t}{k_t}$, would be one equation in terms of $\frac{l_t}{k_t}$. Then $\frac{l_t}{k_t}$ can be substituted for using equation (10.4) which gives the solution for $\frac{l_t}{k_t}$. There is then just one equation in terms of k_t.

Take the *AS–AD* equations of (8.56) for *AD* and (8.61) for *AS*, set them equal, and then subtract supply from each side of the equation to get the excess demand function $Y(w_t, k_t)$:

$$0 = y_t^d - y_t^s \equiv Y(w_t, k_t) = \frac{w_t T + k_t \left[\rho + \left(1 + \alpha\right)\delta_k\right]}{1 + \alpha} - A_G^{\frac{1}{1-\gamma}} \left(\frac{\gamma}{w_t}\right)^{\frac{\gamma}{1-\gamma}} k_t. \tag{10.5}$$

Substituting into equation (10.5) for w_t from the marginal product of labour, $w_t = \gamma A_G \left(\frac{l_t}{k_t}\right)^{\gamma-1}$, given by equation (8.37), makes the excess demand an equation in terms of k_t and l_t:

$$0 = \frac{\gamma A_G \left(\frac{l_t}{k_t}\right)^{\gamma-1} T + k_t \left[\rho + (1+\alpha)\,\delta_k\right]}{1+\alpha} - A_G^{\frac{1}{1-\gamma}} \left(\frac{(\gamma)^{\frac{\gamma}{1-\gamma}}}{(\gamma A_G)^{\frac{\gamma}{1-\gamma}} \left(\frac{l_t}{k_t}\right)^{-\gamma}}\right) k_t. \tag{10.6}$$

Now substitute in the solution for $\frac{l_t}{k_t} = \left[\frac{\rho+\delta_k}{(1-\gamma)A_G}\right]^{\frac{1}{\gamma}}$ from equation (10.4), and simplify, so that

$$0 = \frac{\gamma A_G \left(\left[\frac{\rho+\delta_k}{(1-\gamma)A_G}\right]^{\frac{1}{\gamma}}\right)^{\gamma-1} T + k_t \left[\rho + (1+\alpha)\,\delta_k\right]}{1+\alpha}$$
$$- A_G^{\frac{1}{1-\gamma}} \left(\frac{(\gamma)^{\frac{\gamma}{1-\gamma}}}{(\gamma A_G)^{\frac{\gamma}{1-\gamma}} \left(\left[\frac{\rho+\delta_k}{(1-\gamma)A_G}\right]^{\frac{1}{\gamma}}\right)^{-\gamma}}\right) k_t; \tag{10.7}$$

$$0 = \frac{\gamma A_G \left(\frac{\rho+\delta_k}{(1-\gamma)A_G}\right)^{\frac{\gamma-1}{\gamma}} T + k_t \left[\rho + (1+\alpha)\,\delta_k\right]}{1+\alpha} - \left(\frac{\rho+\delta_k}{(1-\gamma)}\right) k_t. \tag{10.8}$$

Then this gives one equation in just the one unknown k_t. This can be solved for k_t as

$$\frac{\gamma A_G \left(\frac{\rho+\delta_k}{(1-\gamma)A_G}\right)^{\frac{\gamma-1}{\gamma}} T}{(1+\alpha)\left(\frac{\rho+\delta_k}{(1-\gamma)}\right)} = k_t \left[1 - \frac{\left[\rho + (1+\alpha)\,\delta_k\right]}{(1+\alpha)\left(\frac{\rho+\delta_k}{(1-\gamma)}\right)}\right];$$

$$k_t = \frac{\frac{\gamma A_G \left(\frac{\rho+\delta_k}{(1-\gamma)A_G}\right)^{\frac{\gamma-1}{\gamma}} T}{(1+\alpha)\left(\frac{\rho+\delta_k}{(1-\gamma)}\right)}}{1 - \frac{\left[\rho+(1+\alpha)\delta_k\right]}{(1+\alpha)\left(\frac{\rho+\delta_k}{(1-\gamma)}\right)}},$$

$$k_t = \frac{T\gamma A_G \left(\frac{\rho+\delta_k}{(1-\gamma)A_G}\right)^{\frac{\gamma-1}{\gamma}}}{(1+\alpha)\left(\frac{\rho+\delta_k}{(1-\gamma)}\right) - \left[\rho + (1+\alpha)\,\delta_k\right]},$$

$$k_t = \frac{T\gamma A_G^{\frac{1}{\gamma}} \left[\frac{(1-\gamma)}{\rho+\delta_k}\right]^{\frac{1-\gamma}{\gamma}}}{(\gamma+\alpha)\left(\frac{\rho+\delta_k}{(1-\gamma)}\right) - \alpha\delta_k}. \tag{10.9}$$

The stationary k_t is constant at k, independent of time, and does not depend on the initial capital k_0. So at whatever level of k_0 the economy starts at, it ends at k. The transition dynamics of how the economy gradually builds its capital over time, if it starts with a low k_0 as is typically the case, is a subject for more advanced work. Here only the steady state equilibrium solution is studied so that the initial value of k need not be given.

The other variable solutions are given below. These follow rather easily once k_t is solved. But first is an alternative solution approach to k_t.

10.2.3 Alternative solution approach

The *AS–AD* approach above provides some structure from which to proceed to the solution. An alternative to using the *AS–AD* functions that are already derived is to start from where equation (10.4) has been derived above, but without then using the *AS–AD*. This is less structured, but is equivalent.

For example, consider using the output equation, in that output is a function of $\frac{l_t}{k_t}$ and of k_t:

$$y_t = A_G \, (l_t)^\gamma \, (k_t)^{1-\gamma} = A_G \left(\frac{l_t}{k_t}\right)^\gamma k_t.$$

And consumption is just output minus investment,

$$c_t = y_t - i_t. \tag{10.10}$$

Now we also know something about investment. When there is no growth, and capital slowly dissolves away, or depreciates, then the depreciating capital must be maintained so that capital stays constant. Therefore the investment is equal to the amount of depreciating capital or, as we noted above,

$$i_t = \delta_k k_t.$$

This $i_t = \delta_k k_t$ also results by realising that capital is constant in equilibrium and so letting $k_{t+1} = k_t$ in the capital accumulation equation,

$$k_{t+1} = k_t \left(1 - \delta_k\right) + i_t$$

also yields that $i_t = \delta_k k_t$.

Now we have the solution for investment as a function of k_t, and our production function as a function of $\frac{l_t}{k_t}$ and of k_t, and can substitute both of these functions into our consumption equation (10.10) so that

$$c_t = y_t - i_t = A_G \left(\frac{l_t}{k_t}\right)^\gamma k_t - \delta_k k_t. \tag{10.11}$$

The solution of $\frac{l_t}{k_t}$ is known but not that of k_t. This is why we have to use all of the equilibrium conditions.

From the firm side, the marginal product of labour condition of equation (8.37) is

$$w_t = \gamma \, A_G \left(\frac{k}{l}\right)^{1-\gamma}. \tag{10.12}$$

And from the consumer side, the marginal rate of substitution between goods and leisure of equation (8.42) is

$$x_t = \frac{\alpha c_t}{w_t}. \tag{10.13}$$

Leisure is by the allocation of time constraint given by

$$x_t = T - l_t,$$

so the marginal rate of substitution is also written as

$$T - l_t = \frac{\alpha c_t}{w_t}. \tag{10.14}$$

Now we have four equations, (10.4), (10.11), (10.12) and (10.14) in the four unknowns, l_t, k_t, c_t and w_t, and so can solve the full economy.

First solve for the wage w_t by putting equation (10.4) into equation (10.12):

$$w_t = \gamma A_G \left(\frac{k}{l}\right)^{1-\gamma} = \gamma A_G \left[\frac{(1-\gamma) A_G}{\rho + \delta k}\right]^{\frac{1-\gamma}{\gamma}} = \gamma A_G^{\frac{1}{\gamma}} \left[\frac{(1-\gamma)}{\rho + \delta k}\right]^{\frac{1-\gamma}{\gamma}}. \tag{10.15}$$

Now take the solution above for the wage w_t and put it into the marginal rate of substitution equation (10.14):

$$T - l_t = \frac{\alpha c_t}{w_t} = \frac{\alpha c_t}{\gamma A_G^{\frac{1}{\gamma}} \left[\frac{(1-\gamma)}{\rho + \delta k}\right]^{\frac{1-\gamma}{\gamma}}}. \tag{10.16}$$

Substitute for consumption c_t from equation (10.11) in the above equation:

$$T - l_t = \frac{\alpha c_t}{\gamma A_G^{\frac{1}{\gamma}} \left[\frac{(1-\gamma)}{\rho + \delta k}\right]^{\frac{1-\gamma}{\gamma}}} = \frac{\alpha \left[A_G \left(\frac{l_t}{k_t}\right)^{\gamma} k_t - \delta_k k_t\right]}{\gamma A_G^{\frac{1}{\gamma}} \left[\frac{(1-\gamma)}{\rho + \delta k}\right]^{\frac{1-\gamma}{\gamma}}}, \tag{10.17}$$

put the solution for $\frac{l_t}{k_t}$ into the above equation and this gives another equation in only l_t and k_t:

$$T - l_t = \frac{\alpha \left[A_G \left(\left[\frac{\rho + \delta k}{(1-\gamma) A_G}\right]^{\frac{1}{\gamma}}\right)^{\gamma} k_t - \delta_k k_t\right]}{\gamma A_G^{\frac{1}{\gamma}} \left[\frac{(1-\gamma)}{\rho + \delta k}\right]^{\frac{1-\gamma}{\gamma}}}. \tag{10.18}$$

Since $\left(\left[\frac{\rho + \delta k}{(1-\gamma) A_G}\right]^{\frac{1}{\gamma}}\right)^{\gamma}$ reduces to $\left[\frac{\rho + \delta k}{(1-\gamma) A_G}\right]$, this equation simplifies to

$$T - l_t = \frac{\alpha \left\{A_G \left[\frac{\rho + \delta k}{(1-\gamma) A_G}\right] k_t - \delta_k k_t\right\}}{\gamma A_G^{\frac{1}{\gamma}} \left[\frac{(1-\gamma)}{\rho + \delta k}\right]^{\frac{1-\gamma}{\gamma}}}. \tag{10.19}$$

What this tells us is that the solution for l_t as a function of k_t is

$$l_t = T - \frac{\alpha \left\{A_G \left[\frac{\rho + \delta k}{(1-\gamma) A_G}\right] k_t - \delta_k k_t\right\}}{\gamma A_G^{\frac{1}{\gamma}} \left[\frac{(1-\gamma)}{\rho + \delta k}\right]^{\frac{1-\gamma}{\gamma}}}. \tag{10.20}$$

Factoring out the k_t, this simplifies to

$$l_t = T - \frac{\alpha k_t \left\{A_G \left[\frac{\rho + \delta k}{(1-\gamma) A_G}\right] - \delta_k\right\}}{\gamma A_G^{\frac{1}{\gamma}} \left[\frac{(1-\gamma)}{\rho + \delta k}\right]^{\frac{1-\gamma}{\gamma}}}. \tag{10.21}$$

This is a second equation with only k and l being unknown. We can combine this with the first equation we found in k and l to get solutions for k and l. From equations (10.4) and (10.21),

$$\frac{l_t}{k_t} = \left[\frac{\rho + \delta k}{(1-\gamma) A_G}\right]^{\frac{1}{\gamma}}, \tag{10.22}$$

or

$$l_t = k_t \left[\frac{\rho + \delta_k}{\left(1 - \gamma\right) A_G} \right]^{\frac{1}{\gamma}}.$$ (10.23)

And so

$$T - \frac{\alpha k_t \left\{ A_G \left[\frac{\rho + \delta_k}{(1-\gamma) A_G} \right] - \delta_k \right\}}{\gamma A_G^{\frac{1}{\gamma}} \left[\frac{(1-\gamma)}{\rho + \delta_k} \right]^{\frac{1-\gamma}{\gamma}}} = l_t = k_t \left[\frac{\rho + \delta_k}{\left(1 - \gamma\right) A_G} \right]^{\frac{1}{\gamma}}.$$ (10.24)

If we divide the above expression through by k_t, then

$$\frac{T}{k_t} - \frac{\alpha \left\{ A_G \left[\frac{\rho + \delta_k}{(1-\gamma) A_G} \right] - \delta_k \right\}}{\gamma A_G^{\frac{1}{\gamma}} \left[\frac{(1-\gamma)}{\rho + \delta_k} \right]^{\frac{1-\gamma}{\gamma}}} = \left[\frac{\rho + \delta_k}{\left(1 - \gamma\right) A_G} \right]^{\frac{1}{\gamma}}.$$ (10.25)

This implies the solution for $\frac{T}{k_t}$:

$$\frac{T}{k_t} = \left[\frac{\rho + \delta_k}{\left(1 - \gamma\right) A_G} \right]^{\frac{1}{\gamma}} + \frac{\alpha \left\{ A_G \left[\frac{\rho + \delta_k}{(1-\gamma) A_G} \right] - \delta_k \right\}}{\gamma A_G^{\frac{1}{\gamma}} \left[\frac{(1-\gamma)}{\rho + \delta_k} \right]^{\frac{1-\gamma}{\gamma}}}.$$ (10.26)

And this expression for $\frac{T}{k_t}$ can be inverted to give the 'steady state' solution for k_t, which does not depend on time, and so can be indicated by just k:

$$k_t = k = \cfrac{T}{\left[\frac{\rho + \delta_k}{(1-\gamma) A_G} \right]^{\frac{1}{\gamma}} + \cfrac{\alpha \left\{ A_G \left[\frac{\rho + \delta_k}{(1-\gamma) A_G} \right] - \delta_k \right\}}{\gamma A_G^{\frac{1}{\gamma}} \left[\frac{(1-\gamma)}{\rho + \delta_k} \right]^{\frac{1-\gamma}{\gamma}}}}$$

$$= \cfrac{T \gamma A_G^{\frac{1}{\gamma}} \left[\frac{(1-\gamma)}{\rho + \delta_k} \right]^{\frac{1-\gamma}{\gamma}}}{\gamma A_G^{\frac{1}{\gamma}} \left[\frac{(1-\gamma)}{\rho + \delta_k} \right]^{\frac{1-\gamma}{\gamma}} \left[\frac{\rho + \delta_k}{(1-\gamma) A_G} \right]^{\frac{1}{\gamma}} + \alpha \left(\frac{\rho + \delta_k}{(1-\gamma)} - \delta_k \right)}$$

$$= \cfrac{T \gamma A_G^{\frac{1}{\gamma}} \left[\frac{(1-\gamma)}{\rho + \delta_k} \right]^{\frac{1-\gamma}{\gamma}}}{\gamma \left[\frac{\rho + \delta_k}{(1-\gamma)} \right]^{\frac{1-1+\gamma}{\gamma}} + \alpha \left(\frac{\rho + \delta_k}{(1-\gamma)} - \delta_k \right)}$$

$$= \cfrac{T \gamma A_G^{\frac{1}{\gamma}} \left[\frac{(1-\gamma)}{\rho + \delta_k} \right]^{\frac{1-\gamma}{\gamma}}}{(\gamma + \alpha) \left(\frac{\rho + \delta_k}{(1-\gamma)} \right) - \alpha \delta_k}.$$ (10.27)

This is the same solution as in equation (10.9) using *AS–AD* functions. And so the approaches are equivalent.

The solution shows for example that an increase in the goods or time endowments, through T and productivity A_G, directly causes the capital stock to rise. Various comparative static exercises are conducted below in conjunction with those examined in Chapters 8 and 9. This framework for finding comparative static changes in k_t makes it a matter of simply changing the parameters of equation (10.27). However the tax analysis presented in this chapter requires a somewhat modified re-derivation of k_t.

10.2.4 All other variables

The solution for all of the variables in the economy follows once the solution for k_t is found. Already r_t has been found:

$$r_t = \rho + \delta_k.$$

The solution for $\frac{l_t}{k_t}$ is also already given as

$$\frac{l_t}{k_t} = \left[\frac{\rho + \delta_k}{(1 - \gamma) A_G} \right]^{\frac{1}{\gamma}}.$$

Given the solution for k_t, the $\frac{l_t}{k_t}$ solution gives the equilibrium employment of

$$l_t = \left[\frac{\rho + \delta_k}{(1 - \gamma) A_G} \right]^{\frac{1}{\gamma}} k_t, \tag{10.28}$$

the wage rate solution,

$$w_t = \gamma A_G \left(\frac{l_t}{k_t} \right)^{\gamma - 1},$$

$$w_t = \gamma A_G \left[\frac{(1 - \gamma) A_G}{\rho + \delta_k} \right]^{\frac{1 - \gamma}{\gamma}},$$

$$w_t = \gamma (A_G)^{\frac{1}{\gamma}} \left[\frac{(1 - \gamma)}{\rho + \delta_k} \right]^{\frac{1 - \gamma}{\gamma}}, \tag{10.29}$$

and the output solution

$$y_t = A_G \left(\frac{l_t}{k_t} \right)^{\gamma} k_t,$$

$$y_t = A_G \left[\frac{\rho + \delta_k}{(1 - \gamma) A_G} \right] k_t.$$

Given k_t, the solution for investment is

$$i_t = \delta_k k_t,$$

and with the solution for y_t, the solution for consumption is

$$c_t = y_t - i_t,$$

$$c_t = A_G \left[\frac{\rho + \delta_k}{(1 - \gamma) A_G} \right] k_t - \delta_k k_t. \tag{10.30}$$

The last variable is leisure, and using the time allocation constraint that $x_t = T - l_t$, and the solution for l_t,

$$x_t = T - \left[\frac{\rho + \delta_k}{(1 - \gamma) A_G} \right]^{\frac{1}{\gamma}} k_t.$$

Another way to solve for x_t is to use the marginal rate of substitution between goods and leisure, and the solution for the wage rate; this solution is

$$x_t = \frac{\alpha c_t}{w_t},$$

$$x_t = \frac{\alpha \left(A_G \left[\frac{\rho + \delta_k}{(1-\gamma) A_G} \right] k_t - \delta_k k_t \right)}{\gamma (A_G)^{\frac{1}{\gamma}} \left[\frac{(1-\gamma)}{\rho + \delta_k} \right]^{\frac{1-\gamma}{\gamma}}}. \tag{10.31}$$

The equivalence of these two alternative solutions for leisure can be seen by setting them equal to each other:

$$T - \left[\frac{\rho + \delta_k}{(1-\gamma) A_G} \right]^{\frac{1}{\gamma}} k_t = \frac{\alpha A_G \left[\frac{\rho + \delta_k}{(1-\gamma) A_G} \right] k_t - \alpha \delta_k k_t}{\gamma (A_G)^{\frac{1}{\gamma}} \left[\frac{(1-\gamma)}{\rho + \delta_k} \right]^{\frac{1-\gamma}{\gamma}}}.$$

The resulting equation, when solved for k_t, in fact gives back the solution for k_t as previously derived in equation (10.9). Thus either solution of x_t is a proper and equal solution.

10.3 Baseline calibration of the solution

What is called the calibration of the model involves setting the assumed values of the exogenous parameters. And the idea is to set the exogenous parameters so that the equilibrium solution of the model gives values for the endogenous parameters that are broadly consistent with empirical evidence. In this way the model is 'calibrated' to the data.

10.3.1 Target values

A calibration can be done very specifically, for a particular country, and for a specific time period for that country. Then the average values of certain variables or ratios of variables over the period for the particular country are estimated. For example, the ratios of capital to output and of consumption to output for the US during 1949–2010 can be target values that are found empirically and used as targets to achieve in making the calibration.

Here a broad approach is taken in which the 'target values' of variables are consistent with approaches taken in research. Therefore the calibration here is really an illustration of the economy in general, rather than an empirical specification for a specific country at a specific time.

The calibration of the baseline dynamic model of Chapters 8 and 9 uses certain common target values. One of the targets is the amount of labour versus leisure. For labour hours, consider that of our waking hours of 16 hours a day, and 5 days a week, we tend to work 8 hours a day. This gives $\frac{40}{16(5)} = \frac{1}{2}$. This ignores weekends for which there are 16 hours free over the two days; this drops the labour time calculation to $\frac{40}{16(7)} = 0.357$. But if we take away 2 hours a day for normal maintenance with cooking and shopping, then there are only 14 available hours a day and we get $\frac{40}{14(7)} = 0.41$ for the fraction of time in work. If we also include 2 hours a day taken up on average for our lifetime education, then only 12 free hours a day are left for work and leisure, and working time is $\frac{40}{12(7)} = 0.48$, or almost one half. This would make leisure also about one half. Dynamic models that include education are calibrated with leisure near one half. Therefore the value $l = 0.5$ will be targeted so that also $x = 1 - l = 0.5$.

Another important value is the real interest rate r_t, since it is easy to see this in the data. A value of 0.06 is a plausible real interest rate with zero growth. Therefore $r = 0.06$ will also be used as a target value.

The share of labour income in output, which equals γ, is set equal to $\frac{1}{3}$, again following the literature that takes account of the contribution of education and human capital. And note that only if $\gamma < 0.5$ is the marginal cost curve, from equation (8.63), convex, rather than concave. Convex is how we typically specify marginal cost: rising at an increasing rate as output increases.

10.3.2 Baseline Examples 8.1 and 9.1

For the full set of parameter values, assume that $\rho = 0.03$, $\delta_k = 0.03$, $\gamma = \frac{1}{3}$, $T = 1$, $\alpha = 0.5$ and $A_G = 0.15$. First note that this immediately achieves, by equation (10.2), $r_t = \rho + \delta_k = 0.03 + 0.03 = 0.06$, one of the target values.

The resulting equilibrium value of $k = 2.3148$ follows from this calibration:

$$k = \frac{T\gamma A_G^{\frac{1}{\gamma}} \left[\frac{(1-\gamma)}{\rho+\delta_k}\right]^{\frac{1-\gamma}{\gamma}}}{(\gamma+\alpha)\left(\frac{\rho+\delta_k}{(1-\gamma)}\right) - \alpha\delta_k}; \tag{10.32}$$

$$= \frac{(1)\left(\frac{1}{3}\right)(0.15)^3\left(\frac{2}{3(0.06)}\right)^2}{\left(\frac{1}{3}+0.5\right)(0.06)(1.5) - 0.5(0.03)}; \tag{10.33}$$

$$= 2.3148. \tag{10.34}$$

Once the value of the state variable k is determined, all other variables follow. Consider our target value of labour of 0.5. Labour is determined from equation (10.4) as

$$l_t = k_t \left[\frac{\rho+\delta_k}{(1-\gamma)A_G}\right]^{\frac{1}{\gamma}} = k\left(\frac{(0.06)\,1.5}{A_G}\right)^3 \tag{10.35}$$

$$= 2.3148\left(\frac{(0.06)\,1.5}{0.15}\right)^3 = 0.50000. \tag{10.36}$$

So the target value is achieved exactly.

Output is given by

$$y_t = A_G\left(\frac{l_t}{k_t}\right)^{\gamma} k_t = (0.15)\left(\frac{0.5}{2.3148}\right)^{\frac{1}{3}}(2.3148) = 0.20833.$$

This gives a capital to output ratio of $\frac{2.3148}{0.20833} = 11.11$. This is in the high end of the range of various estimates of this for the US for example.

10.3.3 Consistency of the solution

It is worthwhile checking the solution that is found by using different ways to calculate the same variables. For example, with the values of capital and labour, the real interest rate can be calculated from the firm's equilibrium conditions. The real interest rate is

$$r = (1-\gamma)A_G\left(\frac{l_t}{k_t}\right)^{\gamma} = \left(\frac{2}{3}\right)(0.15)\left(\frac{0.5}{2.3148}\right)^{\frac{1}{3}} = 0.06.$$

This is consistent with our alternative solution for $r = 0.06$ from equation $r = \rho + \delta_k$.

The economy's wage rate, using the labour demand function, is

$$w_t = \gamma A_G \left(\frac{k}{l}\right)^{1-\gamma} = \left(\frac{1}{3}\right)(0.15)\left(\frac{2.3148}{0.5}\right)^{\frac{2}{3}} = 0.13889. \tag{10.37}$$

This can be confirmed from the labour supply function, again given that $k_t = 2.3148$ and that $l_t = 0.5$:

$$w_t = \frac{\alpha\rho k_t}{(T - l_t^s)(1+\alpha) - \alpha T},$$

$$w_t = \frac{0.5\,(0.03)\,2.3148}{(1-0.5)(1.5) - 0.5} = 0.13889. \tag{10.38}$$

10.3.4 Calibration of the full solution

All of the variables of the economy can be solved for the baseline model once k_t is solved. With

$$k = 2.3148, \tag{10.39}$$

the employment rate of l is

$$l_t = 2.3148 \left(\frac{(0.06)\,1.5}{0.15}\right)^3 = 0.50000; \tag{10.40}$$

leisure time is

$$x = 1 - l = 0.5; \tag{10.41}$$

the real wage rate is

$$w_t = \left(\frac{1}{3}\right)(0.15)\left(\frac{2.3148}{0.5}\right)^{\frac{2}{3}} = 0.13889; \tag{10.42}$$

and the real interest rate is

$$r = \rho + \delta_k = 0.06. \tag{10.43}$$

The other variables are output

$$y_t = A_G \left(\frac{l_t}{k_t}\right)^{\gamma} k_t = 0.15\left(\frac{0.5}{2.3148}\right)^{\frac{1}{3}} 2.3148 = 0.208;$$

consumption

$$c_t = y_t - i_t = A_G \left(\frac{l_t}{k_t}\right)^{\gamma} k_t - \delta_k k_t, \tag{10.44}$$

$$c_t = 0.15\left(\frac{0.5}{2.3148}\right)^{\frac{1}{3}} 2.3148 - (0.03)\,2.3148 = 0.13889; \tag{10.45}$$

and investment

$$i_t = y_t - c_t = \delta_k k_t = (0.03)\,2.3148 = 0.0694. \tag{10.46}$$

This gives a full solution to the economy.

Consumption is found to exactly equal the wage rate. The ratio of consumption to output is two-thirds.

10.4 Comparative statics of *AS–AD* analysis

Once the full analytic solution has been set out, it is straightforward to conduct a comparative static analysis. This means changing one of the exogenous parameters, and getting the new equilibrium. Since many of the analytic solutions to variables are given as functions of k_t, it is easiest to start with the new k_t solution and then to proceed to get the other variables, in order to get the new full solution.

10.4.1 Productivity change: Examples 8.2 and 9.2

In Chapter 8, the first comparative static exercise is to change the productivity of the goods sector. This change can also be thought of as changing the endowment of goods, given the production function.

In particular, Example 8.2 assumes that A_G rises 5% from 0.15 to $(0.15)(1.05) = 0.1575$. Then the new capital stock is found simply by substituting in 0.1575 for 0.15:

$$k = \frac{T\gamma A_G^{\frac{1}{\gamma}} \left[\frac{(1-\gamma)}{\rho+\delta_k}\right]^{\frac{1-\gamma}{\gamma}}}{(\gamma+\alpha)\left(\frac{\rho+\delta_k}{(1-\gamma)}\right) - \alpha\delta_k};$$

$$= \frac{(1)\left(\frac{1}{3}\right)(0.1575)^3 \left(\frac{2}{3(0.06)}\right)^2}{\left(\frac{1}{3}+0.5\right)(0.06)(1.5) - 0.5(0.03)} = 2.6797. \tag{10.47}$$

Labour time becomes

$$l_t = k_t \left[\frac{\rho+\delta_k}{(1-\gamma)A_G}\right]^{\frac{1}{\gamma}} = k\left(\frac{(0.06)\,1.5}{A_G}\right)^3 = 2.6797\left(\frac{(0.06)\,1.5}{0.1575}\right)^3 = 0.5. \tag{10.48}$$

Here labour does not rise at all, while the equilibrium wage rate rises to

$$w_t = \gamma A_G \left(\frac{k}{l}\right)^{1-\gamma} = \left(\frac{1}{3}\right)(0.1575)\left(\frac{2.6797}{0.5}\right)^{\frac{2}{3}} = 0.16078. \tag{10.49}$$

10.4.2 Time endowment change: Examples 8.3 and 9.3

A change in time endowment is relatively easy to compute. The time endowment of T is given in the equation that

$$T = x_t + l_t.$$

If T increases say by 5% from a baseline value of 1 to 1.05, then the time allocation is modified to

$$1.05 = x_t + l_t.$$

Now the solution for k_t is 5% higher, at

$$k = \frac{(1.05)\,\gamma A_G^{\frac{1}{\gamma}} \left[\frac{(1-\gamma)}{\rho+\delta_k}\right]^{\frac{1-\gamma}{\gamma}}}{(\gamma+\alpha)\left(\frac{\rho+\delta_k}{(1-\gamma)}\right) - \alpha\delta_k};$$

$$= \frac{(1.05)\left(\frac{1}{3}\right)(0.15)\left(\frac{2(0.15)}{3(0.06)}\right)^2}{\left(\frac{1}{3}+0.5\right)(0.06)(1.5) - 0.5(0.03)} = 2.4306. \tag{10.50}$$

This impacts upon the rest of the equilibrium. For labour, equation (10.21) becomes

$$l_t = 1.05 - \frac{\alpha k_t \left\{ A_G \left[\frac{\rho + \delta_k}{(1-\gamma)A_G} \right] - \delta_k \right\}}{\gamma A_G^{\frac{1}{\gamma}} \left[\frac{(1-\gamma)}{\rho + \delta_k} \right]^{\frac{1-\gamma}{\gamma}}}. \tag{10.51}$$

Since k_t rises by 5% and time rises by 5%, both terms that determine l_t rise by 5%. This means that the equilibrium employment of labour rises 5% to 0.525.

For an example of another variable, the wage rate does not change since both capital and labour rise by 5% and the wage rate depends on the capital to labour ratio:

$$w_t = \gamma A_G \left(\frac{k}{l} \right)^{1-\gamma} = \left(\frac{1}{3} \right) (0.15) \left(\frac{2.4306}{0.525} \right)^{\frac{2}{3}} = 0.13889. \tag{10.52}$$

10.5 Business cycle explanation

The business cycle explanation involves changing two parameters at the same time. It is assumed that both the goods and time endowments rise by 5% from the baseline calibration so that A_G rises to 0.1575 and T rises to 1.05, or decrease to $A_G = 0.1425$ and $T = 0.95$.

10.5.1 Example 9.4

For an expansion, with a 5% increase in A_G and T, the solution for k_t is

$$
k = \frac{(1.05) \gamma A_G^{\frac{1}{\gamma}} \left[\frac{(1-\gamma)}{\rho + \delta_k} \right]^{\frac{1-\gamma}{\gamma}}}{(\gamma + \alpha) \left(\frac{\rho + \delta_k}{(1-\gamma)} \right) - \alpha \delta_k};
$$

$$
= \frac{(1.05) \left(\frac{1}{3} \right) (0.1575)^3 \left(\frac{2}{3(0.06)} \right)^2}{\left(\frac{1}{3} + 0.5 \right) (0.06) (1.5) - 0.5 (0.03)};
$$

$$= 2.8137. \tag{10.53}$$

10.5.2 Example 9.5

For a contraction, with a 5% decrease in A_G and T, the solution for k_t is

$$
k = \frac{(0.95) \gamma A_G^{\frac{1}{\gamma}} \left[\frac{(1-\gamma)}{\rho + \delta_k} \right]^{\frac{1-\gamma}{\gamma}}}{(\gamma + \alpha) \left(\frac{\rho + \delta_k}{(1-\gamma)} \right) - \alpha \delta_k};
$$

$$
= \frac{(0.95) \left(\frac{1}{3} \right) (0.1425)^3 \left(\frac{2}{3(0.06)} \right)^2}{\left(\frac{1}{3} + 0.5 \right) (0.06) (1.5) - 0.5 (0.03)};
$$

$$= 1.8854. \tag{10.54}$$

10.6 Other comparative statics and *k*

Any one of the parameters of the economy can be changed in a comparative static fashion. Here the experiments are conducted for the depreciation rate δ_k, the preference for leisure α, the rate of time preference ρ, and the labour share in output γ. In all cases the baseline calibration is assumed except for the single change specified.

10.6.1 Depreciation rate change

Consider a rise in the depreciation rate δ_k from 0.03 to 0.04. Then k falls significantly from 2.3 to 1.5117. This is a fractional decrease of $\frac{2.3148-1.5117}{2.3148} = 0.34694$, or 35%. Therefore a 33% increase in δ_k from 0.03 to 0.04 leads to a 35% decrease in k.

$$k = \frac{T\gamma A_G \left[\frac{(1-\gamma)A_G}{\rho+\delta_k}\right]^{\frac{1-\gamma}{\gamma}}}{(\gamma+\alpha)\left(\frac{\rho+\delta_k}{(1-\gamma)}\right) - \alpha\delta_k};$$

$$= \frac{\left(\frac{1}{3}\right)(0.15)\left(\frac{2(0.15)}{3(0.07)}\right)^2}{\left(\frac{1}{3}+0.5\right)(0.07)(1.5) - 0.5(0.04)};$$

$$= 1.5117. \tag{10.55}$$

10.6.2 Leisure preference change

Suppose that α increases 20% from its baseline value of 0.5 to $\alpha = 0.6$. The state variable must be recomputed first with this one change in the model's baseline parameters:

$$k = \frac{T\gamma A_G \left[\frac{(1-\gamma)A_G}{\rho+\delta_k}\right]^{\frac{1-\gamma}{\gamma}}}{(\gamma+\alpha)\left(\frac{\rho+\delta_k}{(1-\gamma)}\right) - \alpha\delta_k};$$

$$= \frac{\left(\frac{1}{3}\right)(0.15)\left(\frac{2(0.15)}{3(0.06)}\right)^2}{\left(\frac{1}{3}+0.6\right)(0.06)(1.5) - 0.6(0.03)};$$

$$= 2.1044. \tag{10.56}$$

The new value of k is a fractional decrease of $\frac{2.3148-2.1044}{2.3148} = 0.90893$, or 9.09%. To see for example the effect on labour, go to equation (10.28) and recompute the labour time l with $\alpha = 0.6$ and $k = 2.1$. This solution does not include α and so only the capital stock will change in the equation:

$$l_t = k_t \left[\frac{\rho+\delta_k}{(1-\gamma)A_G}\right]^{\frac{1}{\gamma}} = k\left(\frac{(0.06)1.5}{0.15}\right)^3 = 2.1044\left(\frac{(0.06)1.5}{0.15}\right)^3 = 0.45455. \tag{10.57}$$

The equilibrium quantity of labour decreases by about $\frac{0.5-0.45455}{0.5} = 0.0909$, or 9.09%.

10.6.3 Time preference change

Consider increasing time preference 33% from $\rho = 0.03$ to $\rho = 0.04$. Then the new capital stock is given as

$$k = \frac{T\gamma A_G \left[\frac{(1-\gamma)A_G}{\rho+\delta_k} \right]^{\frac{1-\gamma}{\gamma}}}{(\gamma + \alpha)\left(\frac{\rho+\delta_k}{(1-\gamma)} \right) - \alpha\delta_k};$$

$$= \frac{1 \left(\frac{1}{3} \right) (0.15) \left(\frac{2(0.15)}{3(0.07)} \right)^2}{\left(\frac{1}{3} + 0.5 \right) (0.07) (1.5) - 0.5 (0.03)};$$

$$= 1.4075. \tag{10.58}$$

The capital stock falls to $k = 1.4074$. This is a decrease fractionally of $\frac{2.3148 - 1.4075}{2.3148} = 0.39196$, or 39%, even more than the percentage increase in ρ. More preference for current consumption leads to a lower capital stock.

Another experiment here is to consider the maximum capital stock in the sense that the time preference is 0. The consumer does not care whether consumption is today or in 20 years' time. With $\rho = 0$,

$$k = \frac{T\gamma A_G \left[\frac{(1-\gamma)A_G}{\rho+\delta_k} \right]^{\frac{1-\gamma}{\gamma}}}{(\gamma + \alpha)\left(\frac{\rho+\delta_k}{(1-\gamma)} \right) - \alpha\delta_k};$$

$$= \frac{1 \left(\frac{1}{3} \right) (0.15) \left(\frac{2(0.15)}{3(0.03)} \right)^2}{\left(\frac{1}{3} + 0.5 \right) (0.03) (1.5) - 0.5 (0.03)};$$

$$= 24.691. \tag{10.59}$$

In this case, with zero growth, and no preference for current over future consumption, then $r = \rho + \delta_k = 0 + 0.03$, and the capital stock is more than tenfold bigger at 24.691.

10.6.4 Labour share change

Finally consider increasing γ from $\frac{1}{3}$ to 0.5, a fractional increase of $\frac{0.5 - \frac{1}{3}}{\frac{1}{3}} = 0.5$, or 50%. The new capital stock equals

$$k = \frac{T\gamma A_G \left[\frac{(1-\gamma)A_G}{\rho+\delta_k} \right]^{\frac{1-\gamma}{\gamma}}}{(\gamma + \alpha)\left(\frac{\rho+\delta_k}{(1-\gamma)} \right) - \alpha\delta_k};$$

$$= \frac{1 \left(\frac{1}{2} \right) (0.15) \left(\frac{(0.15)}{2(0.06)} \right)}{\left(\frac{1}{2} + 0.5 \right) (0.06) (2) - 0.5 (0.03)};$$

$$= 0.89286. \tag{10.60}$$

With $k = 0.89286$, this is a fractional decrease of $\frac{2.3148 - 0.89286}{2.3148} = 0.61428$, or 61.4%. More labour intensive production of goods leads to a lower capital stock. For equilibrium employment,

$$l_t = k_t \left[\frac{\rho + \delta_k}{(1 - \gamma) A_G} \right]^{\frac{1}{\gamma}} = k \left(\frac{(0.06) \, 2}{0.15} \right)^2 = k \, (0.64),$$

(10.61)

$$l_t = 0.89286 \, (0.64) = 0.57143.$$

(10.62)

Thus the capital to labour ratio falls by two-thirds from $\frac{k_t}{l_t} = \frac{2.3148}{0.5} = 4.6296$ to $\frac{k_t}{l_t} = \frac{1}{0.64} = 1.5625$.

10.7 Unemployment with a fixed wage

Suppose the real wage is fixed at $\overline{w} = 0.1389$, the baseline solution. And suppose that there is a 5% decrease in both the goods endowment through A_G and the time endowment T.

10.7.1 Example 9.6

With $A_G = 0.1425$, and $T = 0.95$, then the equilibrium capital stock falls to

$$k = \frac{T \gamma A_G \left[\frac{(1-\gamma) A_G}{\rho + \delta_k} \right]^{\frac{1-\gamma}{\gamma}}}{(\gamma + \alpha) \left(\frac{\rho + \delta_k}{(1-\gamma)} \right) - \alpha \delta_k};$$

(10.63)

$$= \frac{0.95 \left(\frac{1}{3} \right) (0.1425) \left(\frac{2(0.1425)}{3(0.06)} \right)^2}{\left(\frac{1}{3} + 0.5 \right) (0.06) \, (1.5) - 0.5 \, (0.03)};$$

(10.64)

$$= 1.8854.$$

(10.65)

Then the change in l with w fixed but capital allowed to adjust is found from the demand for labour condition of the firm as

$$l = \left(\frac{\gamma A_G}{\overline{w}} \right)^{\frac{1}{1-\gamma}} k = \left(\frac{0.1425}{3 \, (0.13889)} \right)^{1.5} 1.8854 = 0.37708.$$

(10.66)

10.8 Taxes and employment

The solution for the economy with a tax on labour income of τ_l comes from following through the change to the marginal rate of substitution between goods and leisure, which now implies that $x_t = \frac{\alpha c_t}{w_t (1 - \tau_l)}$.

10.8.1 General solution

Proceeding now exactly to the solution, as is done above for the baseline model solution, the first equation follows unchanged:

$$\rho + \delta_k = r_t = (1 - \gamma) A_G \left(\frac{l_t}{k_t} \right)^{\gamma},$$

(10.67)

and so the labour to capital ratio $\frac{l_t}{k_t}$ is

$$\frac{l_t}{k_t} = \left[\frac{\rho + \delta_k}{(1-\gamma) A_G} \right]^{\frac{1}{\gamma}}.$$

(10.68)

Also unchanged is that output is

$$y_t = A_G \, (l_t)^{\gamma} \, (k_t)^{1-\gamma} = A_G \left(\frac{l_t}{k_t} \right)^{\gamma} k_t,$$

and that consumption equals output minus investment (the government transfer enters the consumption function as income),

$$c_t = y_t - i_t,$$

where

$$i_t = \delta_k k_t.$$

Therefore, as before,

$$c_t = y_t - i_t = A_G \left(\frac{l_t}{k_t} \right)^{\gamma} k_t - \delta_k k_t.$$

(10.69)

The marginal product of labour condition is the same:

$$w_t = \gamma A_G \left(l_t^d \right)^{\gamma - 1} \left(k_t^d \right)^{1-\gamma} = \gamma A_G \left(\frac{k}{l} \right)^{1-\gamma}.$$

(10.70)

But the marginal rate of substitution between goods and leisure is now

$$x_t = \frac{\alpha c_t}{w_t \left(1 - \tau_l \right)},$$

(10.71)

where the allocation of time constraint implies

$$x_t = T - l_t.$$

This implies that

$$T - l_t = \frac{\alpha c_t}{w_t \left(1 - \tau_l \right)},$$

(10.72)

the only change to the equations that can be brought together to solve for k_t.

As before

$$w_t = \gamma A_G \left(\frac{k}{l} \right)^{1-\gamma} = \gamma A_G^{\frac{1}{\gamma}} \left[\frac{(1-\gamma)}{\rho + \delta_k} \right]^{\frac{1-\gamma}{\gamma}},$$

(10.73)

which can be substituted into the revised time allocation relation of equation (10.72):

$$T - l_t = \frac{\alpha c_t}{w_t \left(1 - \tau_l \right)} = \frac{\alpha c_t}{\left(1 - \tau_l \right) \gamma A_G^{\frac{1}{\gamma}} \left[\frac{(1-\gamma)}{\rho + \delta_k} \right]^{\frac{1-\gamma}{\gamma}}}.$$

(10.74)

Therefore the only modification is that $\left(1 - \tau_l \right)$ enters this relation for $T - l_t$ as a factor in the denominator:

$$T - l_t = \frac{\alpha c_t}{\left(1 - \tau_l \right) \gamma A_G^{\frac{1}{\gamma}} \left[\frac{(1-\gamma)}{\rho + \delta_k} \right]^{\frac{1-\gamma}{\gamma}}} = \frac{\alpha \left[A_G \left(\frac{l_t}{k_t} \right)^{\gamma} k_t - \delta_k k_t \right]}{\left(1 - \tau_l \right) \gamma A_G^{\frac{1}{\gamma}} \left[\frac{(1-\gamma)}{\rho + \delta_k} \right]^{\frac{1-\gamma}{\gamma}}}.$$

(10.75)

Substituting in, as before, the solution for $\frac{l_t}{k_t}$,

$$T - l_t = \frac{\alpha \left[A_G \left(\left[\frac{\rho + \delta_k}{(1-\gamma) A_G} \right]^{\frac{1}{\gamma}} \right)^{\gamma} k_t - \delta_k k_t \right]}{(1 - \tau_l)\, \gamma A_G^{\frac{1}{\gamma}} \left[\frac{(1-\gamma)}{\rho + \delta_k} \right]^{\frac{1-\gamma}{\gamma}}}, \tag{10.76}$$

which simplifies to

$$T - l_t = \frac{\alpha \left\{ A_G \left[\frac{\rho + \delta_k}{(1-\gamma) A_G} \right] k_t - \delta_k k_t \right\}}{(1 - \tau_l)\, \gamma A_G^{\frac{1}{\gamma}} \left[\frac{(1-\gamma)}{\rho + \delta_k} \right]^{\frac{1-\gamma}{\gamma}}}, \tag{10.77}$$

so that

$$l_t = T - \frac{\alpha k_t \left\{ A_G \left[\frac{\rho + \delta_k}{(1-\gamma) A_G} \right] - \delta_k \right\}}{(1 - \tau_l)\, \gamma A_G^{\frac{1}{\gamma}} \left[\frac{(1-\gamma)}{\rho + \delta_k} \right]^{\frac{1-\gamma}{\gamma}}}. \tag{10.78}$$

Using the solution for $\frac{l_t}{k_t}$ again, as before,

$$l_t = k_t \left[\frac{\rho + \delta_k}{(1-\gamma) A_G} \right]^{\frac{1}{\gamma}}, \tag{10.79}$$

then

$$T - \frac{\alpha k_t \left\{ A_G \left[\frac{\rho + \delta_k}{(1-\gamma) A_G} \right] - \delta_k \right\}}{(1 - \tau_l)\, \gamma A_G^{\frac{1}{\gamma}} \left[\frac{(1-\gamma)}{\rho + \delta_k} \right]^{\frac{1-\gamma}{\gamma}}} = l_t = k_t \left[\frac{\rho + \delta_k}{(1-\gamma) A_G} \right]^{\frac{1}{\gamma}}, \tag{10.80}$$

and

$$k_t = k = \frac{T}{\left[\frac{\rho + \delta_k}{(1-\gamma) A_G} \right]^{\frac{1}{\gamma}} + \dfrac{\alpha \left\{ A_G \left[\frac{\rho + \delta_k}{(1-\gamma) A_G} \right] - \delta_k \right\}}{(1-\tau_l)\gamma A_G^{\frac{1}{\gamma}} \left[\frac{(1-\gamma)}{\rho + \delta_k} \right]^{\frac{1-\gamma}{\gamma}}}}$$

$$= \frac{T (1 - \tau_l)\, \gamma A_G^{\frac{1}{\gamma}} \left[\frac{(1-\gamma)}{\rho + \delta_k} \right]^{\frac{1-\gamma}{\gamma}}}{(1 - \tau_l)\, \gamma A_G^{\frac{1}{\gamma}} \left[\frac{(1-\gamma)}{\rho + \delta_k} \right]^{\frac{1-\gamma}{\gamma}} \left[\frac{\rho + \delta_k}{(1-\gamma) A_G} \right]^{\frac{1}{\gamma}} + \alpha \left(\frac{\rho + \delta_k}{(1-\gamma)} - \delta_k \right)}$$

$$= \frac{T (1 - \tau_l)\, \gamma A_G^{\frac{1}{\gamma}} \left[\frac{(1-\gamma)}{\rho + \delta_k} \right]^{\frac{1-\gamma}{\gamma}}}{(1 - \tau_l)\, \gamma \left[\frac{\rho + \delta_k}{(1-\gamma)} \right]^{\frac{1-1+\gamma}{\gamma}} + \alpha \left(\frac{\rho + \delta_k}{(1-\gamma)} - \delta_k \right)} = \frac{T (1 - \tau_l)\, \gamma A_G^{\frac{1}{\gamma}} \left[\frac{(1-\gamma)}{\rho + \delta_k} \right]^{\frac{1-\gamma}{\gamma}}}{\left[(1 - \tau_l)\, \gamma + \alpha \right] \left(\frac{\rho + \delta_k}{(1-\gamma)} \right) - \alpha \delta_k}. \tag{10.81}$$

Or the *AS–AD* framework could be used to find k_t when there is a labour tax.

10.8.2 Example 9.7

The calibration with the baseline parameters of $A_G = 0.15$, $T = 1$, $\gamma = 0.33$, $\alpha = 0.5$, $\delta_k = 0.03$ and $\rho = 0.03$, and assuming the tax rate of $\tau_l = 0.2$, gives the capital stock as

$$k_t = \frac{T\left(1 - \tau_l\right) \gamma A_G^{\frac{1}{\gamma}} \left[\frac{\left(1-\gamma\right)}{\rho + \delta_k}\right]^{\frac{1-\gamma}{\gamma}}}{\left[\left(1 - \tau_l\right)\gamma + \alpha\right]\left(\frac{\rho + \delta_k}{\left(1-\gamma\right)}\right) - \alpha\delta_k},$$

$$= \frac{\left(1 - 0.2\right)\frac{1}{3}\left(0.15\right)^3 \left(\frac{2}{3(0.03 + 0.03)}\right)^2}{\left(\frac{(1-0.2)}{3} + 0.5\right)\left(\frac{3(0.03 + 0.03)}{2}\right) - 0.5\left(0.03\right)} = 2.0576. \qquad (10.82)$$

This represents a decrease in the capital stock from 2.3148 when the tax rate is zero. It is a fractional decrease of $\frac{2.3148 - 2.0576}{2.3148} = 0.111$, or 11.1%.

Raising the tax rate to $\tau_l = 0.3$ further lowers the capital stock to 1.9063.

10.9 Application: capital derived graphically

The full general equilibrium solution including the capital stock can be shown graphically as an extension of the standard AS–AD graph. The AS–AD graph of output y_t against the relative price $\frac{1}{w_t}$ can be linked to the level of the capital stock. Then changes in the AS–AD can be linked to changes in the capital stock graphically. Note that this application was formulated by my longtime coauthor Michal Kejak. It shows the full dynamic model equilibrium solution including the capital stock in a four-sectioned, or quadrant, diagram. These quadrants are most easily identified in terms of northeast, southeast, southwest and northwest.

Such an extension can thus be done in four quadrants, starting with the AS–AS in the northeast quadrant as a function of the relative price $\frac{1}{w}$. The AS–AD equations are

$$AD: \frac{1}{w_t} = \frac{1}{y_t^d \left(1 + \alpha\right) - \left[\rho + \delta\left(1 + \alpha\right)\right]k_t},$$

$$AS: \frac{1}{w_t} = \frac{\left(y_t^s\right)^{\frac{1-\gamma}{\gamma}}}{\gamma A_G^{\frac{1}{\gamma}} k_t^{\frac{1-\gamma}{\gamma}}}.$$

Now add into this graph the consumption demand and supply. Consumption demand is

$$\frac{1}{w_t} = \frac{1}{c_t^d \left(1 + \alpha\right) - \rho k_t}.$$

The consumption supply is the residual of output minus the equilibrium investment, which is simply ρk_t:

$$c_t^s = y_t - \rho k_t.$$

By having c_t linked to the price $\frac{1}{w_t}$, the further link between $\frac{1}{w_t}$ and employment l_t can be established by linking consumption to labour l_t through the consumer's marginal rate of substitution between goods and leisure. This is the southeast quadrant. The margin here is

$$\frac{x}{\alpha c} = \frac{1}{w},$$

which, using that $x_t = 1 - l_t$, can be rewritten as

$$l = 1 - \frac{\alpha c}{w}.$$

Now $\frac{1}{w}$ is linked to consumption c_t, which is linked to labour l_t. Another link is between l_t and $\frac{k_t}{l_t}$. This is the southwest quadrant. It is a simple relation, in that clearly

$$l_t = \frac{k_t}{\left(\frac{k_t}{l_t}\right)}. \tag{10.83}$$

The ratio $\frac{k_t}{l_t}$ can be treated as a separate variable graphically, that links labour l_t to the capital stock k_t. This allows k_t to be identified in the graph.

The last link is between the ratio $\frac{k_t}{l_t}$ and, going full circle, the relative price $\frac{1}{w}$. This is in the northwest quadrant. A link between the capital to labour ratio $\frac{k_t}{l_t}$ and $\frac{1}{w}$ follows from the firm's equilibrium conditions. The marginal product of labour divided by the marginal product of capital gives

$$\frac{w_t}{r_t} = \frac{\gamma}{1 - \gamma} \frac{k_t}{l_t}. \tag{10.84}$$

Using $r_t = \rho + \delta_k$ on the balanced growth path equilibrium, with zero growth, then

$$w_t = r_t \frac{\gamma}{1 - \gamma} \frac{k_t}{l_t} = (\rho + \delta_k) \frac{\gamma}{1 - \gamma} \frac{k_t}{l_t};$$

$$\frac{1}{w} = \frac{\frac{1-\gamma}{\gamma} \frac{1}{\rho+\delta}}{\frac{k_t}{l_t}}. \tag{10.85}$$

Changes in parameters, such as A_G, then can be found to shift around these relations in the graphs with a new capital stock k_t identified graphically. Example 8.2 changes A_G and this will be set out graphically after first showing the baseline equilibrium of Example 8.1.

10.9.1 Baseline dynamic model

Figure 10.1 graphs the output supply and demand, and consumption supply and demand, of the baseline model of Example 8.1:

$$\frac{1}{w_t} = \frac{1}{y_t^d (1 + 0.5) - 2.3148 \left[0.03 + (1.5) 0.03\right]}, \tag{10.86}$$

$$\frac{1}{w_t} = \frac{3 \left(y_t^s\right)^2}{(0.15)^3 k_t^2}, \tag{10.87}$$

$$\frac{1}{w_t} = \frac{1}{c_t^d (1 + 0.5) - (0.03) k_t}, \tag{10.88}$$

$$c_t^s = y_t - (0.03) k_t. \tag{10.89}$$

It graphs the output equations in black and the consumption demand equation with a blue curve; the residual consumption supply equation is the dashed blue vertical line.

A normalisation that is useful for presenting all four graphs together is to divide $\frac{1}{w_t}$ by 10. This means the price of $\frac{1}{w_t} = 7.2$ will appear instead with $\frac{1}{w_t(10)}$ graphed on the

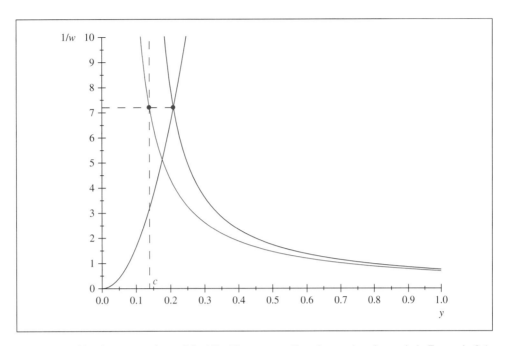

Figure 10.1 Northeast quadrant *AS–AD* with consumption demand and supply in Example 8.1

vertical axis, so that 0.72 is the equilibrium value of $\frac{1}{w_t(10)}$. The equations to be graphed are now

$$\frac{1}{w_t\left(10\right)} = \left(\frac{1}{10}\right) \frac{1}{y_t^d\left(1+0.5\right) - 2.3148\left[0.03 + \left(1.5\right)0.03\right]}, \tag{10.90}$$

$$\frac{1}{w_t\left(10\right)} = \left(\frac{1}{10}\right) \frac{3\left(y_t^s\right)^2}{\left(0.15\right)^3 k_t^2}, \tag{10.91}$$

$$\frac{1}{w_t\left(10\right)} = \left(\frac{1}{10}\right) \frac{1}{c_t^d\left(1+0.5\right) - \left(0.03\right)k_t}, \tag{10.92}$$

$$c_t^s = y_t - \left(0.03\right)k_t. \tag{10.93}$$

Figure 10.2 implements this normalisation.

The next (southeast) quadrant going down from the *AS–AD* graph is the graph of the consumer's marginal rate of substitution, in dimensions of consumption goods and labour, or $\left(c:l\right)$. The graph is of the marginal rate in terms of

$$l_t = 1 - \left(\frac{\alpha}{w_t}\right)c_t, \tag{10.94}$$

so that the slope of the line is $-\left(\frac{\alpha}{w_t}\right) = -\left(\frac{0.5}{0.13889}\right) = -3.6$, and the equation graphed is

$$l_t = 1 - \left(3.6\right)c_t. \tag{10.95}$$

With labour on the vertical axis and consumption on the horizontal, Figure 10.3 shows the dashed blue consumption line intersecting the black equation (10.95) where equilibrium labour is $l_t = 0.5$.

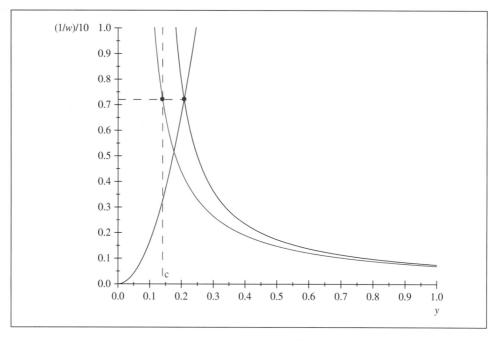

Figure 10.2 Northeast quadrant *AS–AD* normalised with $\left(\frac{1}{w_t}\right)$ /10, in Example 8.1

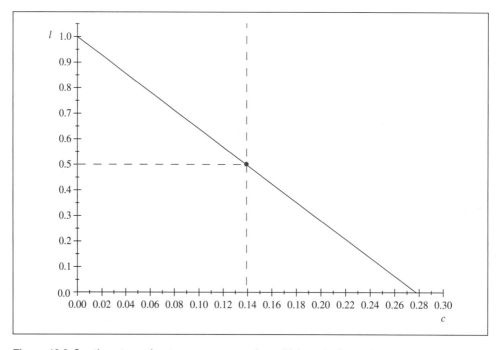

Figure 10.3 Southeast quadrant: consumer goods and labour in Example 8.1

Also note that when $l_t = 0$, this relation gives the point on the horizontal axis for c_t when $l_t = 0$:

$$0 = l_t = 1 - \left(\frac{\alpha}{w_t}\right) c_t,$$

$$c_t = \frac{w_t}{\alpha} = \frac{0.13889}{0.5} = 0.27778. \tag{10.96}$$

Therefore the intersection point on the horizontal axis is $c_t = \frac{w_t}{\alpha} = 0.278$, which is the inverse of the slope of the line, $\frac{\alpha}{w_t}$.

The third (southwest) quadrant links labour l_t to the capital to labour ratio $\frac{k_t}{l_t}$, with equation (10.83), $l_t = \frac{k_t}{\left(\frac{k_t}{l_t}\right)}$. This is a definitional equation, providing a link between l_t, and $\frac{k_t}{l_t}$, and then on into the next quadrant, to $\frac{1}{w_t}$. The equation has $\frac{k_t}{l_t}$ as a variable in the denominator. This makes the graph a hyperbola, with $k_t = 2.3148$:

$$l_t = \frac{2.3148}{\left(\frac{k_t}{l_t}\right)}. \tag{10.97}$$

Figure 10.4 graphs equation (10.97), in dotted blue. The dashed blue lines mark the equilibrium labour employment of 0.5, on the vertical axis, and the equilibrium capital to labour ratio,

$$\frac{k_t}{l_t} = \frac{2.3148}{0.5} = 4.6296,$$

on the horizontal axis. In addition is another important set of black dashed lines. These indicate that where $l_t = 1.0$, on the vertical axis, then

$$\frac{k_t}{l_t} = \frac{2.3148}{1.0} = 2.3148,$$

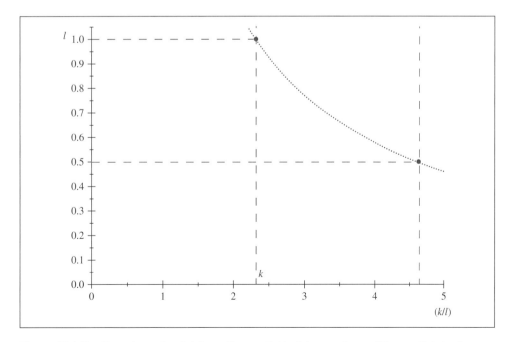

Figure 10.4 Southwest quadrant: labour, the capital to labour ratio, and the capital stock identified, in Example 8.1

as shown on the horizontal axis. This 2.3148 is the equilibrium value of k_t, shown graphically. This is the primary goal of the graphs: to identify k_t.

A further step is taken to normalise the graph in the third quadrant for this Example 8.1 economy so that it is legible. Everywhere k_t will be divided by 10. This also means that $\frac{k_t}{l_t}$ as a variable is also divided by 10. This makes the equation to be graphed in the space of $\left(l : \frac{k_t}{l_t(10)}\right)$ as

$$l_t = \frac{\left(\frac{2.3148}{10}\right)}{\left(\frac{k_t}{l_t(10)}\right)}. \tag{10.98}$$

Figure 10.5 graphs the new third (southwest) quadrant with the normalised k_t variable. The dashed blue lines mark the equilibrium labour employment of 0.5, on the vertical axis, and the equilibrium

$$\frac{k_t}{l_t(10)} = \frac{2.3148}{0.5(10)} = 0.46296,$$

on the horizontal axis. The set of black dashed lines indicates that where $l_t = 1.0$, on the vertical axis, then

$$\frac{k_t}{l_t(10)} = \frac{2.3148}{1.0(10)} = 0.23148,$$

as shown on the horizontal axis. This 0.23148 is the equilibrium value of k_t, shown graphically, when normalised by dividing by 10. This is the primary goal of these graphs: to identify k_t.

The last quadrant (northwest) links back the normalised capital to labour ratio $\frac{k_t}{l_t(10)}$ to the relative price $\frac{1}{w_t}$, through the firm's equilibrium conditions of equation (10.85). With

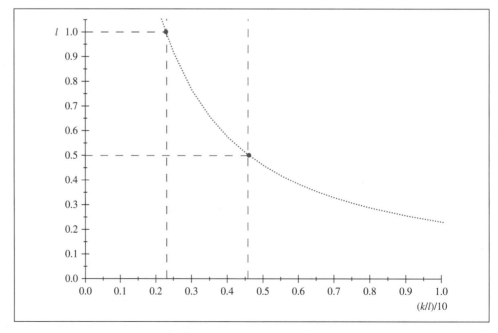

Figure 10.5 Southwest quadrant: labour and normalised capital to labour ratio $\frac{k_t}{l_t(10)}$ of Example 8.1

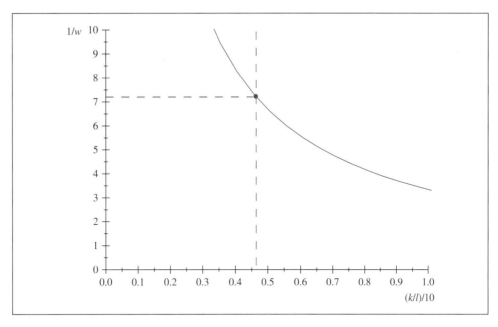

Figure 10.6 Northwest quadrant: firm's equilibrium relation between relative price and normalised capital to labour ratio in Example 8.1

the Example 8.1 assumptions, this equation is

$$\frac{1}{w} = \frac{\frac{1-\gamma}{\gamma}\frac{1}{\rho+\delta}}{\frac{k_t}{l_t}} = \frac{2}{(0.06)\frac{k_t}{l_t}}.$$

Normalising this equation so that it can be graphed in the space of $\left(\frac{1}{w_t} : \frac{k_t}{l_t(10)}\right)$, it is multiplied and divided by 10:

$$\frac{1}{w_t} = \frac{\frac{1-\gamma}{\gamma}\frac{1}{\rho+\delta}}{\frac{k_t}{l_t}} = \frac{2}{(0.06)(10)\left(\frac{k_t}{l_t(10)}\right)} = \frac{2}{(0.60)\left(\frac{k_t}{l_t(10)}\right)}. \qquad (10.99)$$

Because the variable $\frac{k_t}{l_t(10)}$ enters in the denominator of equation (10.99), the equation is again a hyperbola.

Figure 10.6 graphs equation (10.99) in blue. Also there is a blue dashed vertical line at the equilibrium normalised capital to labour ratio of $\frac{k_t}{l_t(10)} = \frac{0.23148}{0.5} = 0.46296$. And there is a horizontal black dashed line at the equilibrium price of $\frac{1}{w_t} = 7.2$, which then links back to the black dashed line in the equilibrium of the *AS–AD* output graph in the first quadrant.

Finally, the fourth quadrant also needs to be normalised by dividing $\frac{1}{w_t}$ by 10, so that the vertical axis variable is $\frac{1}{w_t(10)}$ instead of $\frac{1}{w_t}$. The graphed equation becomes

$$\frac{1}{w_t(10)} = \left(\frac{1}{10}\right)\frac{\frac{1-\gamma}{\gamma}\frac{1}{\rho+\delta}}{\frac{k_t}{l_t}} = \left(\frac{1}{10}\right)\frac{2}{(0.06)(10)\left(\frac{k_t}{l_t(10)}\right)} = \frac{2}{6\left(\frac{k_t}{l_t(10)}\right)}. \qquad (10.100)$$

Figure 10.7 shows the normalisation, with both the vertical axis variable $\frac{1}{w_t(10)}$ and the horizontal axis variable $\frac{k_t}{l_t(10)}$ now normalised by dividing by 10.

Finally all four quadrants are brought together in Figure 10.8 graphically. The blue dashed box shows the equilibrium intersection points in all four quadrants, with the

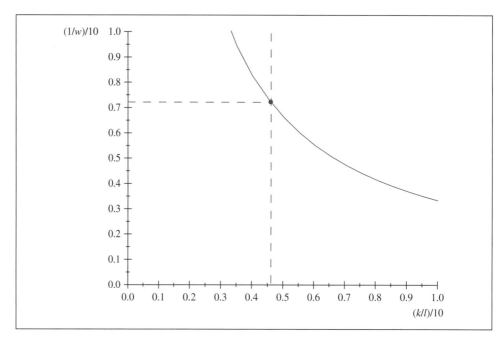

Figure 10.7 Northwest quadrant: normalised in Example 8.1

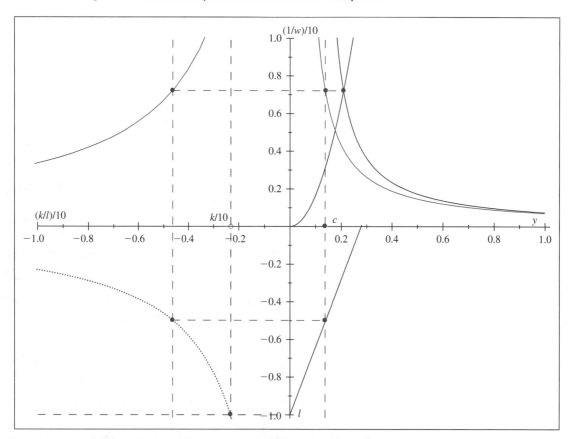

Figure 10.8 Four quadrant equilibrium in Example 8.1, with k_t determined at the black vertical dashed line

extension to the *AD* intersection point of the blue dashed line showing the equilibrium output y_t at the black line intersection point in the northeast quadrant. The capital stock is indicated by the intersection of the vertical black dashed line with the $\frac{k_t}{l_t(10)}$ horizontal axis, indicated by a circle on the axis where $\frac{k_t}{l_t(10)} = 0.23148$, at $l = 1$.

10.9.2 Example of comparative statics

In Example 8.2, the goods productivity is increased from $A_G = 0.15$ to $A_G = 0.1575$, a 5% increase. The capital stock is found to rise from 2.3148 to 2.6797, while the wage rate rises from 0.13889 to 0.16078. The increase in the capital stock can be shown graphically, as can the increase in the wage rate.

Figure 10.9 graphs the new Example 8.2 equilibrium in the new black curves, and the baseline Example 8.1 in the blue curves. In the northwest quadrant both examples share the same blue curve. The shift in the capital stock is shown by the blue dashed vertical lines. The righthand circle-dot is the baseline Example 8.1 normalised capital stock, of $\frac{k_t}{10} = 0.23148$, and the lefthand circle-dot indicates the new higher Example 8.2 normalised capital stock, of $\frac{k_t}{10} = 0.26797$, on the horizontal axis. The blue dashed line box shows the connection of the equilibrium points in the baseline Example 8.1 and the black dashed line box shows the connection of the equilibrium points with A_G increased in Example 8.2. Note that the boxes have one coinciding horizontal dashed line at -0.5, since labour remains unchanged.

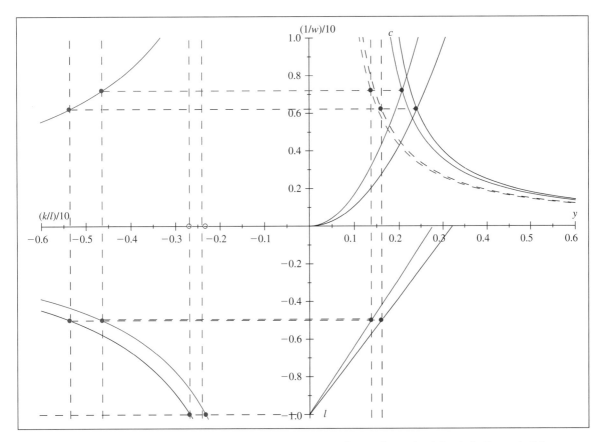

Figure 10.9 Comparative statics of an increase in goods productivity A_G in Example 8.2 compared to baseline

The higher A_G causes the *AS–AD* curves to shift out, with w_t rising and $\frac{1}{w_t}$ falling, as described in Chapter 8. The w_t increase causes the horizontal axis intercept in the southeast quadrant, of $\frac{w_t}{\alpha}$, to rise from $\frac{0.13889}{0.5} = 0.27778$ to $\frac{0.16078}{0.5} = 0.32156$. At the same time the slope of the southeast quadrant curve gets flatter, going from $\frac{\alpha}{w_t} = \frac{0.5}{0.13889} = 3.6$ to $\frac{\alpha}{w_t} = \frac{0.5}{0.16078} = 3.11$ causing the line to pivot downwards in this quadrant.

In the northwest quadrant, the black dashed line intersects with the same curve to give a higher normalised capital to labour ratio of $\frac{k_t}{l_t(10)} = \frac{2.6797}{0.5(10)} = 0.53594$. This then translates down into the southwest quadrant. In order to keep labour at 0.5, where it stays when A_G increases, and to meet a $\frac{k_t}{l_t(10)} = 0.53594$, the curve in this southwest quadrant must shift out and down. The value of $\frac{k_t}{l_t(10)}$ along this new black curve at the point where $l_t = 1$ gives the new normalised capital value of $\frac{k_t}{(10)} = 0.26797$, as indicated by the circle-dot on the horizontal axis.

10.10 Questions

1. Describe the solution methodology for determining the equilibrium capital stock in the baseline dynamic zero growth model of Part 4.

2. As a modification to Examples 8.2 and 9.2, let productivity increase by 10% instead of 5% so that now $A_G = 0.15 + 0.015 = 0.165$, with all other parameters the same as in Examples 8.1 and 9.1. Show how to find the new capital stock.

3. As a modification to Examples 8.3 and 9.3, let the time endowment increase by 10% instead of 5% so that now $T = 1.10$, with all other parameters the same as in Examples 8.1 and 9.1. Show how to find the new equilibrium capital stock.

4. In Example 9.4, both the goods productivity and time endowment rise by 5% during an economic expansion. Instead let the increase of both be 10% and find the new equilibrium capital stock.

5. In Example 9.5, both the goods productivity and time endowment fall by 5% during an economic contraction. Instead let the decrease of both be 10% and find the new equilibrium capital stock.

6. In Examples 8.1 and 9.1, with all parameters the same except that now $\delta_k = 0.05$ instead of $\delta_k = 0.03$, show how to find the new equilibrium capital stock.

7. In Examples 8.1 and 9.1, with all parameters the same except that now $\alpha = 1$ instead of $\alpha = 0.5$, show how to find the new equilibrium capital stock.

8. In Examples 8.1 and 9.1, with all parameters the same except that now $\rho = 0.05$ instead of $\rho = 0.03$, show how to find the new equilibrium capital stock.

9. In Examples 8.1 and 9.1, with all parameters the same except that now $\gamma = \frac{2}{3}$ instead of $\gamma = \frac{1}{3}$, show how to find the new equilibrium capital stock.

10. As a modification of Example 9.6, let the wage be fixed at its value as in the baseline Examples 8.1 and 9.1, and let both the goods productivity and time endowment fall by 10%, instead of by 5%. Find the new capital stock (which is the same as found in Question 5) and then find the new amount of labour employment given the fixed wage and the new equilibrium capital stock.

11. As a modification to Example 9.7,
    (a) use the *AS–AD* methodology to solve for k_t, and
    (b) prove that raising the tax rate to $\tau_l = 0.3$ gives an equilibrium capital stock of 1.9063.

12. Use the four quadrant graph to show the change in the capital stock when there is a change in the time endowment as in Examples 8.3 and 9.3 to $T = 1.05$ from a value of $T = 1$ in the baseline Examples 8.1 and 9.1.

10.11 References

Cooley, Thomas F., 1995, editor, *Frontiers in Business Cycle Research,* Princeton University Press, Princeton.

Ljungqvist, Lars and Thomas J. Sargent, 2004, *Recursive Macroeconomic Theory,* MIT Press, Cambridge.

Ohanian, Lee E., Edward C. Prescott and Nancy L. Stokey, 2009, 'Introduction to Dynamic General Equilibrium', *Journal of Economic Theory,* Elsevier, vol. 144(6): 2235–2246, November.

Ramsey, Frank, 1928, 'A Mathematical Theory of Saving', *The Economic Journal,* 38 (152, December): 543–559.

Sargent, Thomas J., 1987, *Dynamic Macroeconomic Theory,* Harvard University Press, Cambridge.

Stokey, Nancy, Robert E. Lucas, Jr. and Edward C. Prescott, 1989, *Recursive Methods in Economic Dynamics,* Harvard University Press, Cambridge.

CHAPTER (11)

Exogenous growth

11.1 Introduction

The chapter allows for exogenous technological progress in terms of a goods sector productivity factor that increases at a constant rate over time. This causes variables to grow at a constant growth rate, and given the exogeneity of the productivity increase, this model is known as the exogenous growth model. The output growth rate is a simple function of the rate of growth of the productivity factor. This growth theory is shown to also account for other basic accepted facts about the growth process.

The chapter modifies the dynamic baseline model of Part 4 by allowing the zero growth rate to be now a positive growth rate, using the exogenously growing productivity factor. The modifications to the consumption demand and the *AS–AD* analysis are developed. The interest rate is no longer equal to the simple sum of the time preference rate and the depreciation rate, but the interest rate is still determined as a function of exogenous parameters because of the exogeneity of the growth rate. A baseline growth calibration is computed with a 2% targeted growth rate. It is shown how the same interest rate can be used as in the zero growth calibration, if the rate of time preference is accordingly lowered. The wage rate then also remains the same.

The growth process is then illustrated over four periods of time in both the goods and the labour market, showing how output and the wage rate rise, while the labour employment remains unchanged. This is done simply by computing the output and wage rate at each time period, as the productivity factor rises at a steady rate over time. And it results that the variables that grow all grow at the same baseline rate of 2%.

A trend downwards in the time endowment available for goods and leisure is also introduced to capture the time used up by the trend upwards in education time. This explains how the labour time can trend downwards over time. And combined with the trend upwards in productivity, this explains the standard growth facts such as the rising wage plus the decreasing hours spent per week in work.

11.1.1 Building on the last chapters

The same analysis developed throughout Part 4 is now used in this chapter, with the extension that the growth rate is positive rather than zero. The key change comes through the intertemporal consumption margin which states how the growth rate is a function of the interest rate as discounted by the consumer's time preference. Now that this growth rate is positive, the calibration has to be changed somewhat. A calibration is shown that keeps the interest rate the same as in Part 4, with the same baseline calibration as in Part 4 except for a lower rate of time preference.

The aggregate supply and demand analysis in goods and labour markets of Part 4 is then framed within the context of the variables that grow at the same growth rate, of 2%. The same two main comparative static analyses are conducted in this chapter to explain growth facts. The goods productivity factor is increased not just once, but now steadily over time. And similarly the time endowment is not just changed once, but changed steadily over time; in particular it is decreased at a small rate over time.

These two comparative statics, of changing the goods productivity and changing the time endowment, were combined to explain business cycle expansions and contractions in Chapters 3 and 9. Here they are combined to explain long trends consistent with growth facts and labour employment. Their combination of a steady trend of each the goods productivity factor upwards and the time endowment downwards is still consistent with the fluctuations around their trends that are used to explain business cycle movements. Thus the growth theory of this chapter with trends in parameters is consistent with the business cycle theory of earlier chapters with changes both up and down in these parameters.

11.1.2 Learning objective

Seeing how the baseline exogenous growth model with zero growth can be turned into a model with positive growth is the main focus. It requires understanding how the consumer's intertemporal marginal rate of substitution determines the growth rate, and conversely how the interest rate in turn is determined once the growth rate is given. Then the necessary modification to the consumer's demand function can be understood, and the revised *AS–AD* framework developed.

Another aspect to grasp is how the growth model translates into the graphical changes of the supply and demand functions in a way that is consistent with basic growth facts. Viewing the trends of growth theory of this chapter in contrast to the fluctuations of business cycle theory of previous chapters is the challenge, as both theories use the same comparative static tools of goods and time endowment changes.

11.1.3 Who made it happen?

Robert Solow (Nobel Laureate 1987) extended the Ramsey–Harrod–Domar model of growth in his 1956 article, 'A Contribution to the Theory of Economic Growth', by recognising the stylised facts of growth and explaining them by introducing technological change. This was simultaneously developed by T.W. Swan (1956) in Australia. Subsequent articles by Solow show how to do 'growth accounting', whereby the contribution of each labour, capital and technological change can be computed over time for any country. These empirical contributions were in his articles 'Technical Change and the Aggregate Production Function', published in 1957, and 'Investment and Technological Progress' in 1960.

Ramsey's (1928) 'A Mathematical Theory of Saving' had set out the basic economic utility optimisation model in which economic growth was possible, but did not supply a theory explaining growth facts. Solow worked on the firm side of this model, using the same Ramsey neoclassical production function of aggregate output, profit maximisation and the equilibrium conditions of the real wage and real interest rate. But he assumed that consumer savings behaviour was exogenously given, rather than deriving savings endogenously through utility maximisation as did Ramsey. However Solow's breakthrough, despite using only the firm side first-order conditions, was to add into the neoclassical production function the concept of continuous technological change.

Many other theories on the firm side were competing with Solow's explanation at the time, while keeping the consumer side exogenously given. In fact, the standard theory of macroeconomics, such as set out comprehensively in R.G.D. Allen's (1968) book,

Macro-Economic Theory: A Mathematical Treatment, had no utility maximisation anywhere. Allen's book goes through the neoclassical growth model, the Harrod–Domar growth model, Keynesian growth models, Kaldorian growth models, and nowhere is there any utility maximisation, as Ramsey had first guided us.

Stimulated by Solow's ability to explain growth facts, others then folded his approach back into the Ramsey model. David Cass and T.C Koopmans independently did this in 1965 articles, so that the so-called Solow growth model became called the Ramsey–Cass–Koopmans (RCK) model of neoclassical growth; Koopmans became the 1975 Nobel Laureate for related work. This RCK model used the full consumer maximisation problem so that savings behaviour is endogenous while introducing exogenous technological change so that there is sustained growth. Allen's summary of the exogenous consumer side approach to macroeconomics marked a book-end to the dominance of the ad hoc consumer theory with growth, while Cass and Koopmans began the new age of modern macroeconomics with growth. Others continued the development of this model, such as Brock and Mirman (1972) who included uncertainty in a recursive framework, by introducing a random shock in the production function, as in the real business cycle literature.

11.2 Causes of sustained growth

Parts 2, 3, and 4 of the book allow technology progress in terms of a shift up in the output productivity parameter. If this shifted up each period would there be sustained growth? Now the task is to model formally some process by which there can be sustained growth. The most famous approach to this is indeed to let the output productivity parameter shift up each period in time, at a constant rate. And this will be the primary case considered in this chapter.

However there is a more intuitive way of thinking about growth in the baseline dynamic model that encompasses both the approach of the exogenous productivity shifting up each period and the approach of Chapter 12 to growth using human capital. This more encompassing concept presents a principle that must always be satisfied in order for there to be sustained growth in the dynamic model.

11.2.1 Principle of sustained growth

The principle of sustained growth is that all factors of the production function must somehow be enabled to grow continuously over time. Now for the physical capital factor, k_t, this is straightforward since there is a dynamic accumulation equation as given by the investment equation,

$$k_{t+1} = k_t \left(1 - \delta_k\right) + i_t.$$

As long as there is some investment of output back into capital accumulation through a positive i_t the capital stock can grow over time. In particular growth of capital will result if $i_t \geq \delta_k k_t$ since then investment exceeds that necessary to offset the depreciation of the capital stock.

11.3 Exogenous technological progress

Exogenous technological progress means exogenously augmenting the representative agent's otherwise limited raw labour time. Raw labour time cannot grow over time indefinitely, since there is a limited amount of time endowment. Therefore all of the models of growth must in essence conceive of a way in which the raw labour time is augmented continuously over time, and indefinitely into the future. The most common approach, which is now called the 'neoclassical growth model', is to allow the *total factor productivity* A_G to increase steadily over time. This A_G can be interpreted as the 'total factor productivity' when measurement is made of the production function. But here the emphasis will be how growth of A_G over time acts to augment labour so that both capital and augmented labour can grow over time.

Let A_G now depend on time and be denoted A_{Gt}, so that

$$y_t = A_{Gt} \, (l_t)^\gamma \, (k_t)^{1-\gamma}. \tag{11.1}$$

And also assume that A_{Gt} grows at the steady rate of μ:

$$A_{Gt+1} = A_{Gt} \, (1 + \mu), \tag{11.2}$$

which means that the discrete time growth rate of A_{Gt} is μ:

$$\frac{A_{Gt+1}}{A_{Gt}} - 1 = \mu.$$

To see how this can be viewed as augmenting the raw labour time, simply rewrite the production function so as to make A_{Gt} a factor of the labour time:

$$y_t = \left[l_t \, (A_{Gt})^{\frac{1}{\gamma}} \right]^\gamma \, (k_t)^{1-\gamma}. \tag{11.3}$$

This is mathematically equivalent to the original production function, except that now $A_G = A_{Gt}$ as it is a function of time. To be more transparent, define $\tilde{A}_{Gt} \equiv (A_{Gt})^{\frac{1}{\gamma}}$, then

$$y_t = \left[l_t \tilde{A}_{Gt} \right]^\gamma \, (k_t)^{1-\gamma}.$$

The result of this approach is that if both factors $l_t \tilde{A}_{Gt}$ and k_t grow at the same rate then output y_t will likewise grow at that rate.

11.3.1 Stylised facts

The primary stylised growth facts along the balanced growth path are

1. that the real wage rises,
2. while the real interest rate remains constant.

These two facts go together closely with two other facts:

3. the output to capital ratio remains constant and
4. the per capita income rises.

Start by writing the output to capital ratio as

$$\frac{y_t}{k_t} = \left[\frac{l_t \tilde{A}_{Gt}}{k_t} \right]^\gamma.$$

And in turn the real interest rate is the marginal product of capital which is just a fraction of this ratio:

$$(1 - \gamma) \frac{y_t}{k_t} = (1 - \gamma) \left[\frac{l_t \tilde{A}_{Gt}}{k_t} \right]^\gamma.$$

Both of these are viewed as being constant along the balanced growth path. Therefore it is clear that the labour to capital ratio $\frac{l_t \tilde{A}_{Gt}}{k_t}$ must also be constant in order for the theory to explain these facts. To find the common rate of growth of each, the labour in the numerator of $\frac{l_t \tilde{A}_{Gt}}{k_t}$ and the capital in the denominator of $\frac{l_t \tilde{A}_{Gt}}{k_t}$, and with the labour time l_t stationary along the BGP, consider that the growth rate of output is given by

$$1 + g = \frac{y_{t+1}}{y_t} = \frac{\left[l_{t+1} \left(A_{Gt+1} \right)^{\frac{1}{\gamma}} \right]^{\gamma} \left(k_{t+1} \right)^{1-\gamma}}{\left[l_t \left(A_{Gt} \right)^{\frac{1}{\gamma}} \right]^{\gamma} \left(k_t \right)^{1-\gamma}} = \left(1 + \mu \right) \left(\frac{k_{t+1}}{k_t} \right)^{1-\gamma}. \qquad (11.4)$$

Then the rate of growth of the capital stock is

$$\frac{k_{t+1}}{k_t} = \left(\frac{1+g}{1+\mu} \right)^{\frac{1}{1-\gamma}}.$$

The growth rate of the labour-augmenting factor $\tilde{A}_{Gt} = (A_{Gt})^{\frac{1}{\gamma}}$ is given by

$$\left(\frac{A_{Gt+1}}{A_{Gt}} \right)^{\frac{1}{\gamma}} = \left(1 + \mu \right)^{\frac{1}{\gamma}},$$

and taking the log of this

$$\ln \left(1 + \mu \right)^{\frac{1}{\gamma}} = \frac{1}{\gamma} \ln \left(1 + \mu \right) \cong \frac{\mu}{\gamma}.$$

Since the growth rate of the two factors, $l_t (A_{Gt})^{\frac{1}{\gamma}}$ and k_t, must be equal, then

$$\left(\frac{1+g}{1+\mu} \right)^{\frac{1}{1-\gamma}} = \left(1 + \mu \right)^{\frac{1}{\gamma}}$$

and so the growth rate g is found as

$$1 + g = \left(1 + \mu \right)^{\frac{1}{\gamma}}, \qquad (11.5)$$

or approximately

$$g \cong \frac{\mu}{\gamma}.$$

And indeed substituting $g = \frac{\mu}{\gamma}$ back into $\frac{k_{t+1}}{k_t} = \left(\frac{1+g}{1+\mu} \right)^{\frac{1}{1-\gamma}}$ gives that the capital stock growth rate is approximately $\frac{k_{t+1}}{k_t} = \frac{\mu}{\gamma}$. Therefore both k_t and y_t grow at the rate of $\frac{\mu}{\gamma}$.

Output per labour input also grows at this same rate of $\frac{\mu}{\gamma}$, since labour does not grow, and only the output growth rate determines the output per 'hour' growth rate. In other words, this gives that the growth rate of the wage rate is also $\frac{\mu}{\gamma}$, since the wage is a constant fraction of the output per unit of labour input, and its growth rate is the same as the growth rate of output per unit of labour input.

11.3.2 Growth accounting

Growth accounting includes a large amount of work aimed at using the standard Solow growth model and determining the contribution of each input factor to growth, and the residual contribution of the change in total factor productivity, or A_{Gt}. We have taken $\gamma = \frac{1}{3}$ in our calibration of the model. If the BGP rate of growth is say $g = 0.03$, then

$$0.03 = 3\mu,$$

and $\mu = 0.01$. This means that technological progress in the model, through a rising A_{Gt}, accounts for one-third of the total growth of output. And going back to equation (11.4), we can write the growth rate approximately as

$$g = \mu + \left(1 - \gamma \right) \frac{k_{t+1}}{k_t} = \mu + \left(1 - \gamma \right) \frac{\mu}{\gamma}.$$

Now if $\mu = 0.01$, the capital accounts for $\left(1 - \gamma\right) \frac{\mu}{\gamma} = 2\mu = 0.02$ of the growth. Or this is about two-thirds of the total of $g = 0.03$.

For capital to account for this much of the growth rate, the capital stock must be interpreted broadly so as to include both physical capital and human capital. And this is then consistent with evidence on growth accounting, for example as discussed in Aghion and Howitt (2007). But this also gives us a strong indication of how this growth process can be determined more endogenously. If we model human capital accumulation, then the growth rate no longer is a simple function of the exogenously assumed rate of technological progress μ. Rather it also depends on all of the factors that determine human capital investment.

11.4 Balanced growth path equilibrium

Such different growth alternatives are developed here, in a way consistent with our AS–AD analysis, and using the concept of a balanced growth path equilibrium that was introduced in Chapter 8. And along the balanced growth path equilibrium (BGP), all growing variables grow at the same constant rate. In particular, output, consumption, investment, and capital should all be growing at the same rate along the BGP, while the labour and leisure time allocations should be stationary, since otherwise all time ends up either in one allocation or the other rather than being balanced amongst alternative usages.

Also, along the BGP, the growth models all will need to be able to explain the stylised facts expected from any model of growth. In particular, the wage rate, income per person, and the capital to labour ratio should all be rising as consistent with experience, while the real interest rate and the output to capital ratio should be constant.

Define the balanced growth path equilibrium as the long run equilibrium in which the economy is in a steady state rate of growth, which is denoted by g; all variables that are growing do so at the common rate g. Notationally this means that y_t, c_t, k_t and i_t are growing at the rate g, or for any t,

$$\frac{y_{t+1}}{y_t} = \frac{c_{t+1}}{c_t} = \frac{k_{t+1}}{k_t} = \frac{i_{t+1}}{i_t} = 1 + g.$$

And the time allocations x_t and l_t are stationary along the BGP, meaning that they are constant.

The difference in the dynamic baseline model of Part 4 with zero growth is that now we need to assume that there is something that causes the economy to grow, so that the AD and AS curves shift out indefinitely over time. And when specified in an exogenous fashion, this is done by assuming that the productivity factor shifts up at a constant rate over time.

The exogenously specified growth is called an exogenous growth model, and the endogenously determined growth is called an endogenous growth model. The exogenous growth models are the simpler frameworks and the endogenous growth models are more complicated but can show for example how taxes affect growth. Next the AS and AD are developed with $g > 0$, within exogenous growth.

11.4.1 Consumer demand with growth

The consumer's budget constraint is that consumption equals income minus investment in capital, or

$$c_t^d = w_t l_t + r_t k_t - k_{t+1} + k_t \left(1 - \delta_k\right).$$

Now with the capital stock growth rate equal to the balanced growth path rate of $\frac{k_{t+1}}{k_t} = 1 + g$ rather than $\frac{k_{t+1}}{k_t} = 1$ as in Chapter 8, the budget constraint can be written as

$$c_t^d = w_t l_t + r_t k_t - k_t \left(1 + g\right) + k_t \left(1 - \delta_k\right).$$

Simplifying,

$$c_t^d = w_t l_t + k_t \left(r_t - \delta_k - g\right).$$

Substituting in for l_t from the marginal rate of substitution between goods and leisure, whereby

$$l_t = T - \frac{\alpha c_t}{w_t},$$

the consumer demand for goods with exogenous growth is given by

$$c_t^d = \frac{T w_t + k_t \left(r_t - \delta_k - g\right)}{1 + \alpha}. \tag{11.6}$$

The consumer's intertemporal marginal rate of substitution gives the relation between growth g and r_t:

$$1 + g = \frac{\left(c_{t+1}\right)^d}{\left(c_t\right)^d} = \frac{1 + r_t - \delta_k}{1 + \rho}. \tag{11.7}$$

Solving for

$$r_t - \delta_k = \left(1 + g\right)\left(1 + \rho\right) - 1, \tag{11.8}$$

then

$$r_t - \delta_k - g = \left(1 + g\right)\left(1 + \rho\right) - 1 - g = \rho\left(1 + g\right); \tag{11.9}$$

substituting for $r_t - \delta_k - g$ into the consumer demand function, it becomes

$$c_t^d = \frac{1}{1 + \alpha} \left[T w_t + k_t \rho \left(1 + g\right)\right]. \tag{11.10}$$

11.4.2 Consumption in terms of permanent income

Therefore consumption demand is higher by the $1 + g$ factor in the demand equation (11.10), as compared to the dynamic baseline model with zero growth. This means that the permanent income level is now higher with growth, where $T w_t + k_t \rho \left(1 + g\right)$ is the permanent income, and the flow of capital income is $k_t \rho \left(1 + g\right)$. And consumption remains a constant fraction $\left(\frac{1}{1+\alpha}\right)$ of permanent income, denoted again as y_{pt}, and defined now with positive growth as

$$y_{pt} \equiv T w_t + k_t \rho \left(1 + g\right).$$

So consumption demand remains as a set fraction of permanent income,

$$c_t^d = \frac{y_{pt}}{1 + \alpha},$$

but the permanent income is higher, the higher is the exogenous growth rate.

11.4.3 Aggregate demand with growth

To get the aggregate demand for goods, or AD, when there is positive growth in the economy, take the consumption demand of equation (11.10) and add the consumer savings to it, so that

$$y_t^d = c_t^d + s_t. \tag{11.11}$$

Consumer savings is given as $s_t = k_{t+1}^s - k_t^s (1 - \delta_k)$, and in terms of growth, this is

$$s_t = k_t^s \left[\frac{k_{t+1}^s}{k_t^s} - (1 - \delta_k) \right] = k_t^s \left[(1 + g) - (1 - \delta_k) \right] = k_t^s (g + \delta_k). \tag{11.12}$$

This compares to $s_t = \delta_k k_t^s$ in Part 4 where growth is assumed to be zero; also $s_t = i_t$.

Aggregate demand for goods, AD, is therefore, from equations (11.10), (11.11) and (11.12), and given $k_t = k_t^s$, equal to

$$y_t^d = \frac{Tw_t + k_t \rho (1 + g)}{1 + \alpha} + k_t (g + \delta_k)$$

$$y_t^d = \frac{1}{1 + \alpha} \left(Tw_t + k_t \left[\rho (1 + g) + (g + \delta_k) (1 + \alpha) \right] \right). \tag{11.13}$$

Positive growth increases the level of AD for a given k_t and wage rate w_t.

The inversion of the AD function that solves for $\frac{1}{w_t}$ is given by

$$\frac{1}{w_t} = \frac{T}{y_t^d (1 + \alpha) - k_t \left[\rho (1 + g) + (g + \delta_k) (1 + \alpha) \right]}.$$

11.4.4 Aggregate supply with growth

Aggregate supply AS of goods is the same as in Part 4, as it is not affected by growth when written in terms of k_t. From equation (8.37), the labour demand is $l_t^d = \left(\frac{\gamma A_G}{w_t} \right)^{\frac{1}{1-\gamma}} k_t$, from equation (8.11) production is $y_t^s = A_G (l_t^d)^\gamma (k_t)^{1-\gamma}$, and aggregate output supply is as before given by

$$y_t^s = A_G \left(\frac{\gamma A_G}{w_t} \right)^{\frac{\gamma}{1-\gamma}} (k_t)^\gamma (k_t)^{1-\gamma} = A_G^{\frac{1}{1-\gamma}} \left(\frac{\gamma}{w_t} \right)^{\frac{\gamma}{1-\gamma}} k_t. \tag{11.14}$$

The inversion in terms of $\frac{1}{w_t}$ as before is

$$\frac{1}{w_t} = \frac{(y_t^s)^{\frac{1-\gamma}{\gamma}}}{\gamma A_G^{\frac{1}{\gamma}} (k_t)^{\frac{1-\gamma}{\gamma}}}. \tag{11.15}$$

11.5 *AS–AD* analysis

Having now derived both AD and AS under the case with positive growth, a baseline dynamic growth case can be presented graphically. Then it can be seen that the comparative static changes in the productivity factor A_{Gt}, and other parameters, are very similar to those of Part 4. The new comparative static exercise is to allow for a change in g itself. Then the comparative statics are examined and how the growth process causes the AS and AD curves to shift out over time.

11.5.1 Example 11.1: Calibration

Consider using the same baseline calibration of the model for the parameters $\gamma = \frac{1}{3}$, $\alpha = 0.5$, $\rho = 0.03$, $T = 1$, and $\delta_k = 0.03$. In addition, consider that at time t, the goods sector productivity takes on the same baseline value of $A_{Gt} = 0.15$. In addition, the growth rate of A_{Gt}, which is denoted by μ, must be specified exogenously, as an assumed parameter.

The specification of μ in turn, according to equation (11.5), whereby $1 + g = (1 + \mu)^{\frac{1}{\gamma}}$, implies the growth rate g. If $\mu = 0$, then $g = 0$, and the zero growth case of Part 4 results. Consider targeting $g = 0.02$, a 2% growth rate, as the baseline dynamic growth model calibration. Then the value for μ follows:

$$1 + g = (1 + \mu)^{\frac{1}{\gamma}},$$
$$1.02 = (1 + \mu)^3,$$
$$\mu = (1.02)^{\frac{1}{3}} - 1,$$
$$\mu = 0.0066227.$$

Given γ, the parameterisation of μ directly implies the growth rate g, and with $\gamma = \frac{1}{3}$, a 2% growth follows from $\mu = 0.00662$. Therefore, the calibration can be said to be setting g directly, or setting μ which directly implies g. Either specifying g as 0.02 or μ as 0.0066227 is equivalent. Setting g is more intuitive and will be used in the chapter.

The *AS–AD* functions as calibrated are

$$\frac{1}{w_t} = \frac{T}{y_t^d (1 + \alpha) - k_t \left[\rho (1 + g) + (g + \delta_k)(1 + \alpha) \right]},$$
$$\frac{1}{w_t} = \frac{1}{y_t^d (1.5) - k_t \left[0.03 (1.02) + (0.02 + 0.03)(1.5) \right]}, \quad (11.16)$$

for *AD* and as before for *AS*:

$$\frac{1}{w_t} = \frac{(y_t^s)^{\frac{1-\gamma}{\gamma}}}{\gamma A_{Gt}^{\frac{1}{\gamma}} (k_t)^{\frac{1-\gamma}{\gamma}}}$$
$$\frac{1}{w_t} = \frac{3 (y_t^s)^2}{(0.15)^3 (1.0161)^2}. \quad (11.17)$$

All that remains necessary before the *AS* and *AD* can be graphed in terms of price $\left(\frac{1}{w_t} \right)$ and quantity (y_t) is the new equilibrium value of the capital stock k_t.

Building upon the solution methodology presented in Chapter 10, the new equilibrium capital stock can be solved for as a function of only the exogenous parameters. This methodology extension is presented in Appendix A11 to this chapter. It shows that $k_t = 1.0161$.

Figure 11.1 graphs in black the new *AS–AD* equilibrium with $g = 0.02$ and $k_t = 1.0161$ from equations (11.16) and (11.17), with the original zero growth baseline equilibrium of Example 8.1 in blue.

The decrease in the capital stock causes supply and demand to shift back relative to the original equilibrium with $g = 0$.

This result can be understood by thinking about how the exogenous growth works. With $r_t = (1 + g)(1 + \rho) + \delta_k - 1$, then if the growth rate increases, and no other parameters are changed, this is just like increasing the real interest rate. A higher interest rate induces the need for the firm to raise the marginal product of capital, in order to stay in equilibrium. And that can be done by reducing the capital stock.

11.5.2 Example 11.2: Alternative baseline calibration

An alternative calibration involves thinking about what might cause g to increase, relative for example to the baseline model with zero growth. Since growth is exogenously

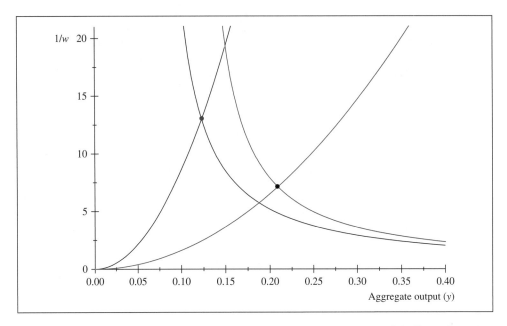

Figure 11.1 *AS–AD* equilibrium with 2% exogenous growth and zero growth in Example 11.1

determined, through the setting of μ, thinking about what causes growth to increase, other than an increase in μ, is somewhat difficult.

However, given such qualifications, one way to think of the exogenous growth analysis is to change not just the g but also for example the rate of time preference ρ. For example, if $g = 0.02$, instead of $g = 0$, with other parameters as in the baseline model of Example 8.1, then consider lowering ρ so that r continues to equal 0.06 as in the baseline model. This r could well be targeted as a variable that should remain the same in the baseline calibration with positive exogenous growth.

Consider continuing to let $r = 0.06$, as in the zero growth baseline calibration of Part 4. And also let the target growth rate be $g = 0.02$, while keeping the depreciation rate unchanged. Then using equation (11.8),

$$r_t = \left(1 + g\right)\left(1 + \rho\right) + \delta_k - 1,$$
$$r_t = \left(1 + 0.02\right)\left(1 + \rho\right) + 0.03 - 1 = 0.06;$$
$$\rho = \frac{1.03}{\left(1.02\right)} - 1 = 0.0098039.$$

This implies an alternative calibration value of $\rho = 0.0098$.

The full parameter baseline specification is therefore $\gamma = \frac{1}{3}$, $\alpha = 0.5$, $T = 1$, $\delta_k = 0.03$, and $A_{Gt} = 0.15$, with $\rho = 0.0098039$, and $g = 0.02$. Now re-evaluate the capital stock in Appendix A11, and the result is that $k_t = 2.7778$. This represents a fractional increase over the zero growth baseline capital stock of $k_t = 2.3148$ equal to $\frac{2.7778 - 2.3148}{2.3148} = 0.200$, or 20%.

Instead of equations (11.16) and (11.17), the revised calibrated *AS–AD* equations at time t are

$$\frac{1}{w_t} = \frac{1}{y_t^d\left(1.5\right) - 2.7778\left[0.0098039\left(1.02\right) + \left(0.02 + 0.03\right)\left(1.5\right)\right]}, \tag{11.18}$$

$$\frac{1}{w_t} = \frac{3\left(y_t^s\right)^2}{\left(0.15\right)^3\left(2.7778\right)^2}. \tag{11.19}$$

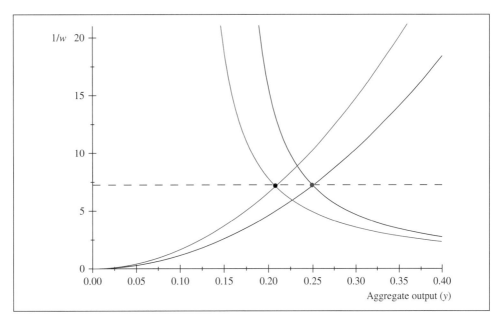

Figure 11.2 *AS–AD* equilibrium with 2% exogenous growth and a lower rate of time discount

Figure 11.2 graphs these *AS–AD* functions of equations (11.18) and (11.19) in black, with the original Example 8.1 zero growth baseline equilibrium in blue. The *AS* and *AD* shift out relative to the baseline; output rises while the real wage remains the same.

It is easy to check why the real wage is exactly the same. If r_t is held constant, while the capital stock rises by 20%, then by the marginal product of capital condition,

$$0.06 = r_t = (1 - \gamma) \left(\frac{l_t}{k_t} \right)^{\gamma};$$

this implies that the equilibrium employment l_t must also rise by 20%. This means the labour to capital ratio remains constant. And since the wage rate depends only on this ratio, the real wage remains constant at its baseline zero growth equilibrium rate:

$$0.13889 = w_t = \gamma \left(\frac{l_t}{k_t} \right)^{\gamma - 1}.$$

Therefore, the factor prices remain as in the zero growth baseline model, while output, capital and labour employment rise. The idea here is that output might be higher at any particular time t if the economy is a growing one. But this need not be the case at all. As growth is exogenous, it is difficult to be decisive about a deeper theory of what the level of stationary equilibrium output should be if the economy is growing.

Perhaps the better interpretation here is that if the idea is to increase the exogenous growth rate, there must be some reason for this growth rate to be higher. Raising the rate of time preference is a good reason for having a higher growth rate, since then the consumer tends to save more since there is less discounting of the future. Here the combination of a higher g and a lower ρ, such that the interest rate r stays the same, results in higher output and exactly the same wage rate. This is a more intuitive way to introduce exogenous growth than in Example 11.1 and so it will be used henceforth.

11.5.3 Consumption and output

The consumption demand for Example 11.2 is given from equation (11.10) as

$$c_t^d = \frac{1}{1+\alpha} \left[Tw_t + k_t \rho \left(1 + g \right) \right],$$ (11.20)

$$= \tfrac{2}{3} \left(0.13889 + \left(2.7778 \right) \left(0.0098039 \right) \left(1.02 \right) \right) = 0.1111.$$

With zero growth the baseline consumption equals the wage rate of 0.13889. So the consumption here is a fractional decrease of $\frac{0.13889 - 0.11111}{0.13889} = 0.2000$, or 20%, the same as the percentage increase in the capital stock. Therefore, with the lower ρ, this can be interpreted as the consumer consuming less goods while getting a higher capital stock and growth rate, even though consumption is still the same fraction of permanent income.

Output from equation (11.13) is

$$y_t^d = \frac{1}{1+\alpha} \left(Tw_t + k_t \left[\rho \left(1 + g \right) + \left(g + \delta_k \right) \left(1 + \alpha \right) \right] \right),$$ (11.21)

$$= \tfrac{2}{3} \left(0.13889 + \left(2.7778 \right) \left(\left(0.0098039 \right) \left(1.02 \right) + \left(0.02 + 0.03 \right) \left(1.5 \right) \right) \right),$$

$$= 0.25.$$

This represents a fractional increase relative to the zero growth baseline of $\frac{0.25 - 0.20832}{0.20832} = 0.200$, or 20%, the same as the decrease in consumption.

Investment now equals $\left(\delta_k + g \right) k_t$ and so it equals $\left(0.03 + 0.02 \right) \left(2.7778 \right) = 0.13889$, the value of the real wage. This is an increase from the zero growth baseline model of Part 4, in which investment is $\delta_k k_t = 0.03 \left(2.3148 \right) = 0.069444$. Fractionally it is an increase of $\frac{0.13889 - 0.069444}{0.069444} = 1.0$, or 100%.

Therefore consumption falls by 20%, capital and output rise by 20%, and investment rises by 100%, compared to the baseline model of Part 4. The consumption to output ratio falls from two-thirds to $\frac{c_t^d}{y_t^d} = \frac{0.1111}{0.25} = 0.4444$. This is low relative to data. This low value is the 'cost' of lowering ρ in order to get a calibration comparable to the zero growth model, but one in which the output level is higher, rather than lower as in Example 11.1.

11.5.4 Labour market

Continuing Example 11.2, the labour market can be derived and graphed. Starting with the time allocation constraint and the marginal rate of substitution between goods and leisure,

$$T - l_t^s = x_t = \frac{\alpha c_t}{w_t}.$$

Substituting in the consumer demand for goods, $c_t^d = \frac{1}{1+\alpha} \left[Tw_t + k_t \rho \left(1 + g \right) \right]$,

$$T - l_t^s = \frac{\alpha}{1+\alpha} \frac{\left[Tw_t + k_t \rho \left(1 + g \right) \right]}{w_t},$$

and the labour supply is

$$l_t^s = T - \frac{\alpha}{1+\alpha} \left[T + \frac{k_t \rho \left(1 + g \right)}{w_t} \right].$$

The demand for labour is unchanged at

$$l_t^d = \left(\frac{\gamma A_G}{w_t} \right)^{\frac{1}{1-\gamma}} k_t.$$

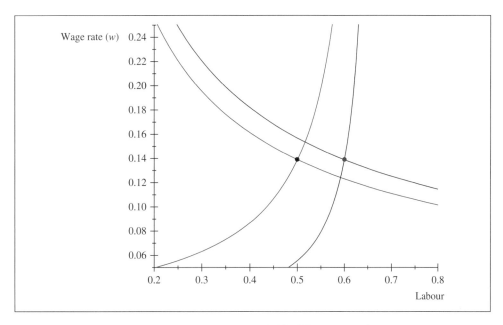

Figure 11.3 Higher employment, same wage, $g = 0.02$ of Example 11.2

The zero growth labour demand is

$$w_t = \frac{1}{3} (0.15) \left(\frac{2.3148}{l_t^d} \right)^{\frac{2}{3}}. \tag{11.22}$$

The 2% growth labour supply and demand are

$$w_t = \frac{\alpha k_t \rho (1 + g)}{T - (1 + \alpha) l_t^s}, \tag{11.23}$$

$$w_t = \frac{(0.5)(2.7778)(0.0098039)(1.02)}{1 - (1.5) l_t^s}; \tag{11.24}$$

$$w_t = \gamma A_G \left(\frac{k_t}{l_t} \right)^{1-\gamma},$$

$$w_t = \frac{1}{3} (0.15) \left(\frac{(2.7778)}{l_t^d} \right)^{\frac{2}{3}}. \tag{11.25}$$

Figure 11.3 graphs the labour market with a 2% growth rate, of equations (11.24) and (11.25), in black curves, compared to the baseline zero growth economy of Example 8.1, in blue curves. Employment rises 20% to 0.6 from 0.5, as the supply and demand for labour shift out. The real wage is unchanged at $w_t = 0.13889$.

11.6 The exogenous growth process

The growth process in the exogenous growth model is that A_{Gt} rises by $\mu\%$ each period. Consider the baseline calibration of Example 11.2 in which $g = 0.02$ and $\mu = 0.0066227$. Then each period after t, A_{Gt} is 0.66% higher than the time t value of 0.15.

11.6.1 Example 11.3: Continuous shifts in A_{Gt}

In the following example, three subsequent time periods to the initial time t are examined, with the time t equilibrium being the baseline calibration of Example 11.2. At time $t + 1$, $A_{Gt+1} = (0.15)(1.0066227) = 0.15099$, or 0.151. At time $t + 2$, $A_{Gt+2} = (0.15099)(1.0066227) = 0.15199$, or 0.152. And at time $t + 3$, $A_{Gt+3} = (0.15199)(1.0066227) = 0.153$.

As a note, the transition dynamics involved in moving from one balanced growth path equilibrium generally take more than one period. Here the periods can be interpreted as being long enough that adjustment to the new equilibrium occurs at each period. This abstraction from considering the details of transition dynamics allows a view of how the economy trends over time, from one stationary equilibrium to another.

The solution for the capital stock k_t as given in Appendix A11 does depend upon A_{Gt}, and so as the goods productivity changes, the capital stock must be recomputed. Then the aggregate supply and demand for output can be graphed accordingly.

At time $t + 1$, with $A_{Gt+1} = 0.151$, the chapter appendix shows that $k_{t+1} = 2.8331$. At time $t + 2$, $k_t = 2.8898$; and at time $t + 3$, $k_t = 2.9478$. This implies that the capital stock grows at a 2% rate.

With AS–AD functions given at time t in equations (11.18) and (11.19), the resulting calibrated supply and demand functions at time $t + 1$, $t + 2$, and $t + 3$ are

$$\frac{1}{w_{t+1}} = \frac{1}{y_{t+1}^d(1.5) - 2.8331\left[(0.0098039)(1.02) + (0.05)(1.5)\right]}, \tag{11.26}$$

$$\frac{1}{w_{t+1}} = \frac{3\left(y_{t+1}^s\right)^2}{(0.15099)^3(2.8331)^2}; \tag{11.27}$$

$$\frac{1}{w_{t+2}} = \frac{1}{y_{t+2}^d(1.5) - 2.8898\left[(0.0098039)(1.02) + (0.05)(1.5)\right]}, \tag{11.28}$$

$$\frac{1}{w_{t+2}} = \frac{3\left(y_{t+2}^s\right)^2}{(0.15199)^3(2.8898)^2}; \tag{11.29}$$

$$\frac{1}{w_{t+3}} = \frac{1}{y_{t+3}^d(1.5) - 2.9478\left[(0.0098039)(1.02) + (0.05)(1.5)\right]}, \tag{11.30}$$

$$\frac{1}{w_{t+3}} = \frac{3\left(y_{t+3}^s\right)^2}{(0.153)^3(2.9478)^2}. \tag{11.31}$$

These AS–AD equilibria can be graphed at each time period, all in the same diagram. An increasing A_{Gt} causes the real wage and output to rise. This can be seen over time as a falling relative price $\frac{1}{w}$ and a rising level of output y as the economy grows at a 2% rate. Figure 11.4 graphs equations (11.18) and (11.19) plus (11.26)–(11.31), with the AS–AD curves represented at time t by the blue dashed curves, at time $t + 1$ by the black dashed curves, at time $t + 2$ by the blue curves and at time $t + 3$ by the black curves.

11.6.2 Labour market

The labour market can be graphed similarly during the growth process. The time t calibrated labour supply and demand functions are given in equations (11.24) and (11.25).

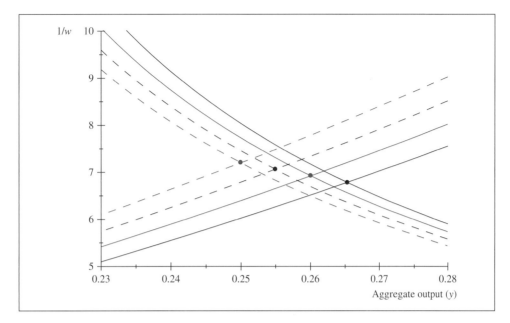

Figure 11.4 *AS–AD* equilibria over time with 2% exogenous growth in Example 11.3

At time $t+1$, $t+2$, and $t+3$, these functions are

$$w_{t+1} = \frac{(0.5)\,(2.8331)\,(0.0098039)\,(1.02)}{1 - (1.5)\,l^s_{t+1}}, \tag{11.32}$$

$$w_{t+1} = \frac{1}{3}\,(0.15099)\left(\frac{(2.8331)}{l^d_{t+1}}\right)^{\frac{2}{3}}; \tag{11.33}$$

$$w_{t+2} = \frac{(0.5)\,(2.8898)\,(0.0098039)\,(1.02)}{1 - (1.5)\,l^s_{t+2}}, \tag{11.34}$$

$$w_{t+2} = \frac{1}{3}\,(0.15199)\left(\frac{(2.8898)}{l^d_{t+2}}\right)^{\frac{2}{3}}; \tag{11.35}$$

$$w_{t+3} = \frac{(0.5)\,(2.9478)\,(0.0098039)\,(1.02)}{1 - (1.5)\,l^s_{t+3}}, \tag{11.36}$$

$$w_{t+3} = \frac{1}{3}\,(0.153)\left(\frac{(2.9478)}{l^d_{t+3}}\right)^{\frac{2}{3}}. \tag{11.37}$$

Figure 11.5 graphs equations (11.24) and (11.25), and equations (11.32) through (11.37), which present the supply and demand for labour from time t to $t+3$, with the colour coding over time the same as for the *AS–AD* Figure 11.4 above.

Labour demand shifts out while labour supply shifts back so that the equilibrium employment remains unchanged at 0.60. The wage rate rises from 0.13889 to $\frac{1}{3}\,(0.15099)\left(\frac{(2.8331)}{0.6}\right)^{\frac{2}{3}} = 0.14166$, to $\frac{1}{3}\,(0.15199)\left(\frac{(2.8898)}{0.6}\right)^{\frac{2}{3}} = 0.14449$, to

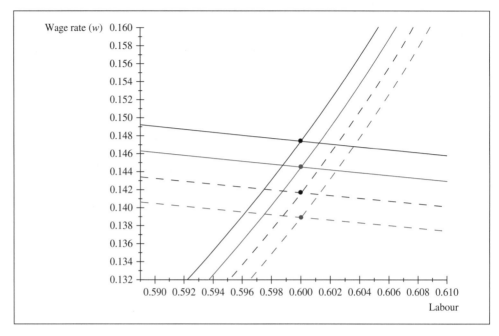

Figure 11.5 Labour market with 2% exogenous growth in Example 11.3

$\frac{1}{3}(0.153)\left(\frac{(2.9478)}{0.6}\right)^{\frac{2}{3}} = 0.14739$. These are fractional increases of $\frac{0.14166 - 0.13889}{0.13889} = 0.020$, $\frac{0.14449 - 0.14166}{0.14166} = 0.020$, and $\frac{0.14739 - 0.14449}{0.14449} = 0.020$. The wage rate rises at 2% a year.

Knowing the wage rate at each time period, the output can be determined precisely at each time period. Output at time t is 0.25 by equation (11.21). At time $t+1$, $t+2$ and $t+3$, output is given by

$$y_{t+1}^d = \frac{2}{3}\left(0.14166 + (2.8331)\left((0.0098039)(1.02) + (0.02 + 0.03)(1.5)\right)\right),$$
$$= 0.25498;$$

$$y_{t+2}^d = \frac{2}{3}\left(0.14449 + (2.8898)\left((0.0098039)(1.02) + (0.02 + 0.03)(1.5)\right)\right),$$
$$= 0.26008;$$

$$y_{t+3}^d = \frac{2}{3}\left(0.14739 + (2.9478)\left((0.0098039)(1.02) + (0.02 + 0.03)(1.5)\right)\right),$$
$$= 0.2653.$$

Therefore output rises from 0.25 to 0.25498, a $\frac{0.25498 - 0.25}{0.25} = 0.020$ fractional increase, to 0.26008, a $\frac{0.26008 - 0.25498}{0.25498} = 0.020$ fractional increase, and to 0.2653, a $\frac{0.2653 - 0.26008}{0.26008} = 0.020$ fractional increase. Again, output rises at a 2% growth rate, as do the wage rate and the capital stock.

Similarly follows the amount of consumption. Time t consumption is given in equation (11.20) at 0.1111. For time $t+1$, $t+2$, and $t+3$, consumption is

$$c_{t+1}^d = \frac{2}{3}\left(0.14166 + (2.8331)(0.0098039)(1.02)\right) = 0.11333;$$

$$c_{t+2}^d = \frac{2}{3}\left(0.14449 + (2.8898)(0.0098039)(1.02)\right) = 0.11559;$$

$$c_{t+3}^d = \frac{2}{3}\left(0.14739 + (2.9478)(0.0098039)(1.02)\right) = 0.11791.$$

The fractional increases are $\frac{0.11333 - 0.11111}{0.11111} = 0.020$, $\frac{0.11559 - 0.11333}{0.11333} = 0.020$, and $\frac{0.11791 - 0.11559}{0.11559} = 0.020$: a 2% growth rate of consumption.

11.6.3 General equilibrium

Following the Example 8.1 general equilibrium input and output market presentations, these can also be seen during the exogenous growth process. The isocost lines over time, and starting with the formation at time t as in Chapter 8, equation (8.72), are given in equations (11.38) to (11.41):

$$y_t = w_t l_t + r_t k_t,$$
$$0.25 = (0.13889) \, l_t + (0.06) \, k_t,$$
$$k_t = \frac{0.25}{0.06} - \frac{(0.13889) \, l_t}{0.06}; \tag{11.38}$$

$$k_{t+1} = \frac{0.25498}{0.06} - \frac{(0.14166)}{0.06} l_{t+1}; \tag{11.39}$$

$$k_{t+2} = \frac{0.26008}{0.06} - \frac{(0.14449)}{0.06} l_{t+2}; \tag{11.40}$$

$$k_{t+3} = \frac{0.2653}{0.06} - \frac{(0.14739)}{0.06} l_{t+3}. \tag{11.41}$$

The isoquant curves for time t to $t+3$, after developing the time t curve as in Chapter 8, equation (8.73), are given in equations (11.42) to (11.45):

$$y_t^s = A_G \left(l_t^d \right)^\gamma (k_t)^{1-\gamma},$$
$$0.25 = 0.15 \left(l_t^d \right)^{\frac{1}{3}} (k_t)^{\frac{2}{3}};$$

$$k_t = \left(\frac{(0.25)}{0.15 \left(l_t^d \right)^{\frac{1}{3}}} \right)^{\frac{3}{2}} = \frac{\left(\frac{(0.25)}{0.15} \right)^{\frac{3}{2}}}{\left(l_t^d \right)^{\frac{1}{2}}}; \tag{11.42}$$

$$k_{t+1} = \frac{\left(\frac{(0.25498)}{0.15099} \right)^{\frac{3}{2}}}{\left(l_{t+1}^d \right)^{\frac{1}{2}}}; \tag{11.43}$$

$$k_{t+2} = \frac{\left(\frac{(0.26008)}{0.15199} \right)^{\frac{3}{2}}}{\left(l_{t+2}^d \right)^{\frac{1}{2}}}; \tag{11.44}$$

$$k_{t+2} = \frac{\left(\frac{(0.2653)}{0.153} \right)^{\frac{3}{2}}}{\left(l_{t+2}^d \right)^{\frac{1}{2}}}. \tag{11.45}$$

The input ratios over time rise as capital rises and labour remains at 0.60:

$$\frac{k_t}{l_t} = \frac{2.7778}{0.60} = 4.6297; \tag{11.46}$$

$$\frac{k_{t+1}}{l_{t+1}} = \frac{2.8331}{0.60} = 4.7218; \tag{11.47}$$

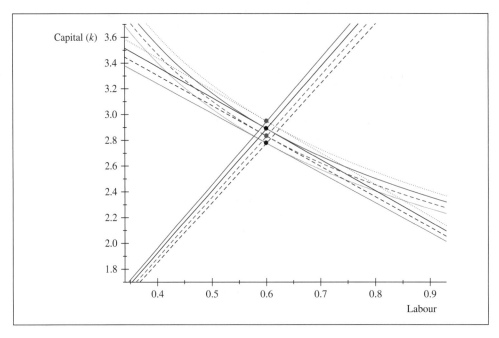

Figure 11.6 Factor market equilibrium with 2% exogenous growth in Example 11.3

$$\frac{k_{t+2}}{l_{t+2}} = \frac{2.8898}{0.60} = 4.8163; \tag{11.48}$$

$$\frac{k_{t+3}}{l_{t+3}} = \frac{2.9478}{0.60} = 4.913. \tag{11.49}$$

Figure 11.6 graphs the shifting upwards isocost lines (variants of black), the shifting up isoquants (variants of blue) and the pivoting upwards input ratios (mixed black and blue) as growth occurs through a rising A_G, in equations (11.38) through (11.49). Equilibria occur at tangencies with labour unchanged and capital rising.

Consumption can again be expressed in terms of the production function and utility level curves. Recall that investment now equals $i_t = (g + \delta_k) k_t$, which is a modification of the zero growth economy in Example 8.1. Then these functions can be set out over time following equations (8.75) and (8.76), setting out time t at length, and then more briefly for $t + 1$ to $t + 3$:

$$c_t^d = y_t^s - i_t = A_G \left(l_t^d\right)^\gamma (k_t)^{1-\gamma} - (g + \delta_k) k_t,$$

$$c_t^d = (0.15) \left(l_t^d\right)^{\frac{1}{3}} (2.7778)^{\frac{2}{3}} - (0.02 + 0.03) (2.7778); \tag{11.50}$$

$$c_{t+1}^d = (0.15099) \left(l_t^d\right)^{\frac{1}{3}} (2.8331)^{\frac{2}{3}} - (0.02 + 0.03) (2.8331); \tag{11.51}$$

$$c_{t+2}^d = (0.15199) \left(l_t^d\right)^{\frac{1}{3}} (2.8898)^{\frac{2}{3}} - (0.02 + 0.03) (2.8898); \tag{11.52}$$

$$c_{t+3}^d = (0.153) \left(l_t^d\right)^{\frac{1}{3}} (2.9478)^{\frac{2}{3}} - (0.02 + 0.03) (2.9478). \tag{11.53}$$

$$u = \ln c_t + \alpha \ln x_t = \ln c_t + \alpha \ln (1 - l_t),$$

$$-2.4527 = \ln 0.1111 + 0.5 \ln 0.4,$$

$$-2.4527 = \ln c_t + 0.5 \ln (1 - l_t),$$

$$c_t = \frac{e^{\ln 0.1111 + 0.5 \ln 0.4}}{\left(1 - l_t\right)^{0.5}}; \tag{11.54}$$

$$c_{t+1} = \frac{e^{\ln 0.11333 + 0.5 \ln 0.4}}{\left(1 - l_{t+1}\right)^{0.5}}; \tag{11.55}$$

$$c_{t+2} = \frac{e^{\ln 0.11559 + 0.5 \ln 0.4}}{\left(1 - l_{t+2}\right)^{0.5}}; \tag{11.56}$$

$$c_{t+3} = \frac{e^{\ln 0.11791 + 0.5 \ln 0.4}}{\left(1 - l_{t+3}\right)^{0.5}}. \tag{11.57}$$

The budget lines similarly are

$$c_t^d = w_t l_t^s + \rho \left(1 + g\right) k_t^s,$$

$$c_t^d = \left(0.13889\right) l_t^s + \left(0.0098039\right) \left(1 + 0.02\right) \left(2.7778\right); \tag{11.58}$$

$$c_{t+1}^d = \left(0.14166\right) l_{t+1}^s + \left(0.0098039\right) \left(1 + 0.02\right) \left(2.8331\right); \tag{11.59}$$

$$c_{t+2}^d = \left(0.14449\right) l_{t+2}^s + \left(0.0098039\right) \left(1 + 0.02\right) \left(2.8898\right); \tag{11.60}$$

$$c_{t+3}^d = \left(0.14739\right) l_{t+3}^s + \left(0.0098039\right) \left(1 + 0.02\right) \left(2.9478\right). \tag{11.61}$$

Figure 11.7 graphs equations (11.50) to (11.61), with the production functions pivoting upwards (variants of blue), the budget lines pivoting upwards (mixed black and blue), and

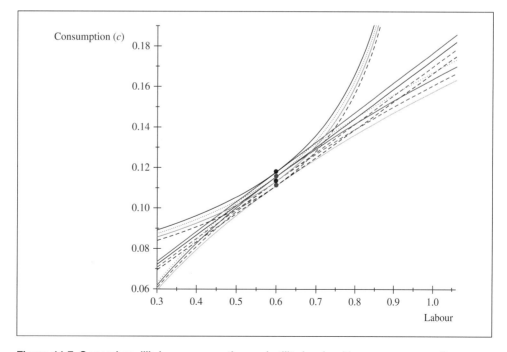

Figure 11.7 General equilibrium consumption and utility levels with exogenous growth

the utility level curves shifting upwards (variants of black) as growth takes place. Equilibria occur at the tangency points, with labour staying at 0.6 while consumption rises at the rate of $g = 0.02$.

11.7 Trend in time endowment

Part 4 with exogenous growth shows through comparative static experiments that a decrease in the time endowment T causes the employment time to fall and the wage rate to remain the same. Therefore the decrease in the long trend downwards in the time worked can potentially be explained by a long trend downwards in the time available for work and leisure, T.

Mark Aguiar and Erik Hurst (2009) report evidence of how labour time has trended down so that it has fallen by 12% over 40 years in the US from 1965 to 2005. Also they find that leisure time has trended upwards so that it has risen by 5% in the same period. With T being the sum of work and leisure time, this gives a net decrease of 7% over the 40 years. At a constant rate then T falls by 0.00182 or 0.182% over the 40 years, since $(1 - 0.00182)^{40} = 0.93$. This gives the 7% decrease down from the level of 1.

Consider the next experiment of allowing T to fall at a rate of 0.00182 per year, where T is denoted now with a time subscript as T_t. This causes the employment to fall and the output to fall, with an unchanged wage. To be consistent with facts of economic growth, such as a rising output level and wage rate, consider assuming that at the same time that T trends down, A_G trends up as before but now with $\mu = 0.0072$.

Allowing both T and A_G to change in the opposite directions simultaneously is related to the business cycle explanation of Chapters 3 and 9 in which T and A_G are both increased by the same percentage in the expansion and decreased by the same percentage in the contraction. However now, in order to explain trend behaviour, the average change over the business cycle is the interpretation for the trend changes in T and A_G. On average, over time, evidence suggests T trends down slightly while A_G trends up more significantly. A decrease in T by 0.182% per year represents this slight decreasing trend in T, and the increase in A_G by 0.72% represents the more significantly increasing trend in A_G. These long term trends still allow for fluctuations around the trend that may occur during the business cycle.

11.7.1 Example 11.4: Opposite trends in T and A_G

Let the time t equilibrium be the same as the baseline calibration of Example 11.2. At time $t + 1$, $A_{Gt} = 0.15$ rises to $A_{Gt+1} = 0.15108$ while $T_t = 1$ decreases to $T_{t+1} = 1 - 0.00182 = 0.99818$. At time $t + 2$, $A_{Gt+2} = 0.15216$, and $T_{t+2} = (0.99818)(1 - 0.00182) = 0.99636$. And at time $t + 3$, $A_{Gt+3} = 0.15327$, and $T_{t+3} = (0.99636)(1 - 0.00182) = 0.99455$.

Appendix A11 computes the capital stock at times $t + 1$, $t + 2$, and $t + 3$. The capital stock rises from $k_t = 2.7778$, to $k_{t+1} = 2.8337$, $k_{t+2} = 2.8902$, and $k_{t+3} = 2.9480$, representing a fractional increase each period of 0.02, as derived in Appendix A11. Thus the growth rate is $g = 0.02$.

The AD function is changed by the time endowment as in equation (8.57) of Chapter 8, which shows how T enters the numerator only of the AD function. Therefore, to include the change in $T_t = 1$ and the capital stock, it requires changing two terms over time, T_t and the capital stock k_t, relative to equations (11.26) to (11.31) of this chapter. The AS and

AD functions by time period are now revised to be

$$\frac{1}{w_{t+1}} = \frac{(0.99818)}{y_{t+1}^d (1.5) - (2.8337) \left[(0.0098039) (1.02) + (0.05) (1.5) \right]}, \tag{11.62}$$

$$\frac{1}{w_{t+1}} = \frac{3 \left(y_{t+1}^s \right)^2}{(0.151)^3 (2.8337)^2}; \tag{11.63}$$

$$\frac{1}{w_{t+2}} = \frac{(0.99636)}{y_{t+2}^d (1.5) - (2.8902) \left[(0.0098039) (1.02) + (0.05) (1.5) \right]}, \tag{11.64}$$

$$\frac{1}{w_{t+2}} = \frac{3 \left(y_{t+2}^s \right)^2}{(0.152)^3 (2.8902)^2}; \tag{11.65}$$

$$\frac{1}{w_{t+3}} = \frac{(0.99455)}{y_{t+3}^d (1.5) - (2.9480) \left[(0.0098039) (1.02) + (0.05) (1.5) \right]}, \tag{11.66}$$

$$\frac{1}{w_{t+3}} = \frac{3 \left(y_{t+3}^s \right)^2}{(0.153)^3 (2.9480)^2}. \tag{11.67}$$

Figure 11.8 graphs the revised growth process, of equations (11.62) to (11.67), in variants of black, plus the baseline of Example 11.2, in blue. These include the downward trend in T_t, from time t to $t + 3$, along with the goods productivity increase. The relative price of goods still falls, as the real wage rises, and output expands over time.

Output at time t is 0.25. Growing at a rate of $g = 0.02$, $y_{t+1} = (0.25) (1.02) = 0.255$, $y_{t+2} = (0.255) (1.02) = 0.26$, $y_{t+3} = (0.26) (1.02) = 0.2653$.

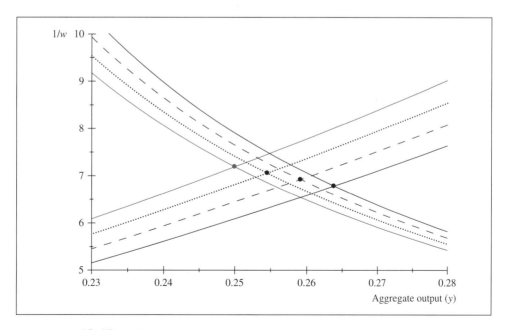

Figure 11.8 *AS–AD equilibria with A_G trending up and T trending down in Example 11.4*

11.7.2 Labour market

The labour market reveals that the time trend in T_t causes the employment to fall slightly over time. The labour supply function with T a function of time follows from the labour supply equation (11.23):

$$w_t = \frac{\alpha k_t \rho \left(1+g\right)}{T_t - \left(1+\alpha\right) l_t^s}.$$

Over time then the labour supply and demand equations are revised to

$$w_{t+1} = \frac{(0.5)\,(2.8337)\,(0.0098039)\,(1.02)}{(0.99818) - (1.5)\,l_{t+1}^s}, \tag{11.68}$$

$$w_{t+1} = \frac{1}{3}\,(0.15099)\left(\frac{(2.8337)}{l_{t+1}^d}\right)^{\frac{2}{3}}; \tag{11.69}$$

$$w_{t+2} = \frac{(0.5)\,(2.8902)\,(0.0098039)\,(1.02)}{(0.99636) - (1.5)\,l_{t+2}^s}, \tag{11.70}$$

$$w_{t+2} = \frac{1}{3}\,(0.15199)\left(\frac{(2.8902)}{l_{t+2}^d}\right)^{\frac{2}{3}}; \tag{11.71}$$

$$w_{t+3} = \frac{(0.5)\,(2.9480)\,(0.0098039)\,(1.02)}{(0.99455) - (1.5)\,l_{t+3}^s}, \tag{11.72}$$

$$w_{t+3} = \frac{1}{3}\,(0.153)\left(\frac{(2.9480)}{l_{t+3}^d}\right)^{\frac{2}{3}}. \tag{11.73}$$

Figure 11.9 graphs equations (11.68) to (11.73), for the labour supply and demand from $t+1$ to $t+3$ in variants of black, plus the baseline Example 11.2 labour supply and demand of equations (11.24) and (11.25) for time t, in blue.

As opposed to when T_t is constant over time and the employment is also stable, now the employment falls over time. The equilibrium employment slowly decreases from 0.6 down to 0.05967 over the four periods. This is true even though output and the real wage are rising.

With time T_t falling at the rate 0.00182, and labour starting at $l_t = 0.6$, then $l_{t+1} = (0.6)\,(1 - 0.00182) = 0.59891$, $l_{t+2} = (0.59891)\,(1 - 0.00182) = 0.59782$, $l_{t+3} = (0.59782)\,(1 - 0.00182) = 0.59673$.

The general equilibrium representation in input and output markets, for when T is decreasing gradually over time, is very similar to Figures 11.6 and 11.7 except that the graphs would show the labour decreasing over time as in Figure 11.9.

The trend down in T allows for an explanation of the long historical trend downwards in working hours. However at the same time the evidence suggests a trend upwards in education time, which the exogenous growth model does not address directly. The next chapter with endogenous growth can address these issues through a slight trend upwards in the productivity of human capital investment. And as in the trend down in T, this produces a slight downward trend in hours worked. And an upward trend in human capital investment time, which can be interpreted as education time, also results.

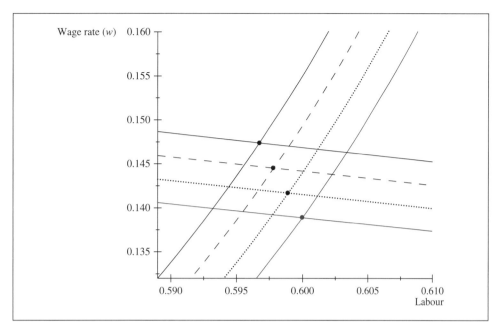

Figure 11.9 Labour market with A_G trending up and T trending down in Example 11.4

11.8 Applications

11.8.1 TFP, Japan's lost decade and the Minnesota School

The goods productivity factor A_{Gt} is known as the 'total factor productivity' or *TFP* for short. Much research has been devoted to computing the contribution of productivity increases by accounting for the change in the labour and capital inputs that enter the Cobb–Douglas production function of our baseline dynamic model. With this *TFP* approach, the growth rate of output has been explained in terms of the contribution from labour, from capital, and from exogenous technological change. This accounting process is summarised as a computation of the 'Solow residual', which is the contribution of Solow's exogenous technological change to growth within his dynamic exogenous growth model.

Such *TFP* Solow residuals have been computed for long periods of time for particular countries. Hayashi and Prescott (2002) accounted for Japan's economic stagnation in the 1990s by calling it Japan's lost decade, and by explaining the low growth in terms of a low *TFP* during this period. Therefore the *TFP* accounting is used both for growth and business cycles at the same time, given that the cycle is more of a longer term one that is more like an occasional change in the trend in the growth rate.

Others have used the *TFP* accounting strictly for explaining economic recessions and depressions around the world. One collection of studies is overviewed in the 2002 'Great Depressions of the Twentieth Century', by Timothy Kehoe and Edward Prescott, sometimes known as the Minnesota approach, for its origin from professors of the University of Minnesota. This study introduces an issue of the 2002 *Review of Economic Dynamics* of companion studies on the 1930s depression in Germany, France, Italy and the US and UK, and for the contractions in Argentina, Mexico and Chile in the 1980s and in Japan in the 1990s. This *TFP* approach to business cycles has been formalised by Chari *et al.* (2007) in their article on 'Business Cycle Accounting'.

11.9 Questions

1. Explain the stylised facts of economic growth with the dynamic baseline model of exogenous growth.

2. Define a balanced growth path equilibrium.

3. How does the determination of the growth rate, through a targeted value of g in calibration, cause the interest rate to be determined?

4. Assume that the baseline calibration of parameters in Example 11.2 is the same except that now the growth rate is targeted to be $g = 0.03$, or a 3% growth rate, and only the parameter of time preference ρ is different. What value of ρ gives a growth rate of 3% in Example 11.2?

5. The growth rate is $g = 0.02$, or 2%, in both of the Examples 11.1 and 11.2. Why is the capital stock lower than the baseline value $k_t = 2.3148$ in Example 11.1, but higher than the baseline value of $k_t = 2.3148$ in Example 11.2?

6. In Example 11.3, determine the amount invested at time t, $t+1$, $t+2$ and $t+3$ during the exogenous growth process. What is the rate of increase in investment during this growth process?

7. In Example 11.3, graph the equilibrium level curves, $c_t = \dfrac{e^{\ln 0.1111 + 0.5 \ln 0.4}}{\left(1 - l_t\right)^{0.5}}$, $c_{t+1} = \dfrac{e^{\ln 0.11333 + 0.5 \ln 0.4}}{\left(1 - l_{t+1}\right)^{0.5}}$,

    $c_{t+2} = \dfrac{e^{\ln 0.11559 + 0.5 \ln 0.4}}{\left(1 - l_{t+2}\right)^{0.5}}$ and $c_{t+3} = \dfrac{e^{\ln 0.11791 + 0.5 \ln 0.4}}{\left(1 - l_{t+3}\right)^{0.5}}$ in the space of goods and leisure, or $\left(c_t : x_t\right)$

    instead of in the space of goods and labour, or $\left(c_t : l_t\right)$ as in Figure 11.7.

8. If output is at a level of 0.25 in the year 2010, and there is constant exogenous growth of 2% a year every year, then what is the level of output in 100 years?

9. Explain what happens to labour employment over time in Example 11.3 with goods productivity steadily rising.

10. In Example 11.4, given that $\mu = 0.0072$, what rate of decrease of the time endowment T_t would cause a zero balanced path growth rate, of $g = 0$, instead of $g = 0.02$ as in Example 11.4?

11. Offer an explanation of why hours per week trend down over the long historical period in developed economies while at the same time the time spent in education trends upwards.

12. Explain what happens to labour employment over time in Example 11.4 with both goods productivity and the time endowment changing steadily over time.

13. Graph the general equilibrium goods and labour with utility, production and budget lines for Example 11.4, in $\left(c_t : l_t\right)$ dimensions. This is a modification of Figure 11.7, now with a shrinking time endowment and growing goods productivity, rather than only a growing goods productivity.

11.10 References

Aghion, Philippe and Peter Howitt, 2007, 'Capital, Innovation, and Growth Accounting', *Oxford Review of Economic Policy*, Oxford University Press, vol. 23(1), pages 79-93, Spring.

Aguiar, Mark and Erik Hurst, 2009, 'A Summary of Trends in American Time Allocation: 1965–2005', *Social Indicators Research*, 93: 57–64.

Allen, R.G.D., 1968, *Macro-Economic Theory*, Macmillan, London.

Brock, William A. and Leonard J. Mirman, 1972, 'Optimal Economic Growth and Uncertainty: The Discounted Case,' *Journal of Economic Theory*, Elsevier, vol. 4(3): 479–513, June.

Cass, David, 1965, 'Optimum Growth in an Aggregative Model of Capital Accumulation', *Review of Economic Studies*, 32: 233–240.

Chari, V. V., Patrick J. Kehoe and Ellen R. McGrattan, 2007, 'Business Cycle Accounting', *Econometrica*, Econometric Society, 75(3): 781–836.

Hayashi, Fumio and Edward C. Prescott, 2002, 'The 1990s in Japan: A Lost Decade', *Review of Economic Dynamics*, 5(1): 206–235.

Kehoe, Timothy, and Edward C. Prescott, 2002, 'Great Depressions of the Twentieth Century', *Review of Economic Dynamics*, 5(1): 1–18.

Koopmans, Tjalling C., 1965, 'On the Concept of Optimal Economic Growth', in *Econometric Approach to Development Planning,* chap. 4, pp. 225–287, North-Holland Publishing Co., Amsterdam.

Ramsey, Frank, 1928, 'A Mathematical Theory of Saving', *Economic Journal,* 38(152): 543–559.

Solow, Robert M., 1956, 'A Contribution to the Theory of Economic Growth', *The Quarterly Journal of Economics,* 70(1): 65–94.

Solow, Robert M., 1957, 'Technical Change and the Aggregate Production Function', *The Review of Economics and Statistics,* 39(3): 312–320.

Solow, Robert M., 1960, 'Investment and Technological Progress', in Kenneth Arrow, Samuel Karlin and Patrick Suppes, eds., *Mathematical Methods in the Social Sciences,* Stanford, Calif.: Stanford University Press, pp. 89–104.

Swan, Trevor W., 1956, 'Economic Growth and Capital Accumulation', *Economic Record,* 32(63): 334–361.

11.11 Appendix A11: Solution methodology for exogenous growth

The solution methodology is an extension of that of Chapter 10. Again, consider starting with the intertemporal margin condition for the consumer.

$$\frac{c_{t+1}}{c_t} = \frac{1 + r_t - \delta_k}{1 + \rho}. \tag{11.74}$$

Since output, consumption, capital and investment all grow along the balanced growth path at the rate g, then it is true that

$$1 + g = \frac{1 + r_t - \delta_k}{1 + \rho}. \tag{11.75}$$

The interest rate r_t is then solved as

$$r_t = g\left(1 + \rho\right) + \rho + \delta_k. \tag{11.76}$$

From the firm's equilibrium condition (8.38) on the marginal product of capital that

$$g\left(1 + \rho\right) + \rho + \delta_k = r_t = \left(1 - \gamma\right) A_G \left(\frac{l_t}{k_t}\right)^\gamma. \tag{11.77}$$

The solution for $\frac{l_t}{k_t}$ is

$$\frac{l_t}{k_t} = \left[\frac{g\left(1 + \rho\right) + \rho + \delta_k}{\left(1 - \gamma\right) A_G}\right]^{\frac{1}{\gamma}}. \tag{11.78}$$

This is one equation in the two variables l_t and k_t.

Taking the *AS–AD* equations of (11.13) for *AD* and (11.14) for *AS*, and setting them equal:

$$y_t^d = \frac{w_t T + k_t \left[\rho\left(1 + g\right) + \left(1 + \alpha\right)\left(g + \delta_k\right)\right]}{1 + \alpha} = A_G \left(\frac{l_t}{k_t}\right)^\gamma k_t = y_t^s. \tag{11.79}$$

Substituting into equation (11.79) the solution $\frac{l_t}{k_t} = \left[\frac{g(1+\rho)+\rho+\delta_k}{(1-\gamma)A_G}\right]^{\frac{1}{\gamma}}$ from equation (11.78), and $w_t = \gamma A_G \left(\frac{l_t}{k_t}\right)^{\gamma-1}$ from the firm's equilibrium condition (8.37),

$$\frac{\gamma A_G \left(\frac{g(1+\rho)+\rho+\delta_k}{(1-\gamma)A_G}\right)^{\frac{\gamma-1}{\gamma}} T + k_t \left[\rho\left(1 + g\right) + \left(1 + \alpha\right)\left(g + \delta_k\right)\right]}{1 + \alpha} \tag{11.80}$$

$$= A_G \left(\frac{g\left(1+\rho\right) + \rho + \delta_k}{\left(1-\gamma\right) A_G} \right) k_t. \tag{11.81}$$

Then this gives one equation in just the one unknown k_t. And this can be solved as

$$\frac{\gamma A_G \left(\frac{g(1+\rho)+\rho+\delta_k}{(1-\gamma)A_G} \right)^{\frac{\gamma-1}{\gamma}} T}{\left(1+\alpha\right) A_G \left(\frac{g(1+\rho)+\rho+\delta_k}{(1-\gamma)A_G} \right)} = k_t \left[1 - \frac{\left[\rho\left(1+g\right) + \left(1+\alpha\right)\left(g+\delta_k\right)\right]}{\left(1+\alpha\right) A_G \left(\frac{g(1+\rho)+\rho+\delta_k}{(1-\gamma)A_G} \right)} \right];$$

$$k_t = \frac{\frac{\gamma A_G \left(\frac{g(1+\rho)+\rho+\delta_k}{(1-\gamma)A_G} \right)^{\frac{\gamma-1}{\gamma}} T}{(1+\alpha)A_G \left(\frac{g(1+\rho)+\rho+\delta_k}{(1-\gamma)A_G} \right)}}{1 - \frac{[\rho(1+g)+(1+\alpha)(g+\delta_k)]}{(1+\alpha)A_G \left(\frac{g(1+\rho)+\rho+\delta_k}{(1-\gamma)A_G} \right)}},$$

$$k_t = \frac{T\gamma \left(A_G\right)^{\frac{1}{\gamma}} \left(\frac{(1-\gamma)}{g(1+\rho)+\rho+\delta_k} \right)^{\frac{1-\gamma}{\gamma}}}{\left(1+\alpha\right) \left(\frac{g(1+\rho)+\rho+\delta_k}{(1-\gamma)} \right) - \left[\rho\left(1+g\right) + \left(1+\alpha\right)\left(g+\delta_k\right)\right]}.$$

Or write this alternatively as

$$k_t = \frac{T\gamma \left(A_G\right)^{\frac{1}{\gamma}} \left(\frac{(1-\gamma)}{g(1+\rho)+\rho+\delta_k} \right)^{\frac{1-\gamma}{\gamma}}}{\left(1+\alpha\right)\delta_k \left(\frac{\gamma}{(1-\gamma)} \right) + \left(1+\alpha\right) \left(\frac{g(1+\rho)+\rho}{(1-\gamma)} \right) - \left[\rho\left(1+g\right) + \left(1+\alpha\right)g\right]}. \tag{11.82}$$

The capital stock with zero growth in Chapter 10, given by

$$k_t = \frac{T\gamma A_G^{\frac{1}{\gamma}} \left[\frac{(1-\gamma)}{\rho+\delta_k} \right]^{\frac{1-\gamma}{\gamma}}}{(\gamma + \alpha) \left(\frac{\rho+\delta_k}{(1-\gamma)} \right) - \alpha\delta_k},$$

can also be written as

$$k_t = \frac{T\gamma A_G^{\frac{1}{\gamma}} \left[\frac{(1-\gamma)}{\rho+\delta_k} \right]^{\frac{1-\gamma}{\gamma}}}{\left(1+\alpha\right)\delta_k \left(\frac{\gamma}{1-\gamma} \right) + \frac{\rho(\gamma+\alpha)}{(1-\gamma)}}.$$

Setting $g = 0$ in equation (11.82) gives the above equation, showing that the capital stock in the $g = 0$ case is the same as in Chapter 10 when there is zero growth.

11.11.1 Example 11.1: Capital stock solution

The baseline calibration of Example 11.1 assumes that $\gamma = \frac{1}{3}$, $\alpha = 0.5$, $\rho = 0.03$, $T = 1$, $\delta_k = 0.03$, $A_{Gt} = 0.15$, and $g = 0.02$. The resulting capital stock is

$$k_t = \frac{T\gamma \left(A_G\right)^{\frac{1}{\gamma}} \left(\frac{(1-\gamma)}{g(1+\rho)+\rho+\delta_k} \right)^{\frac{1-\gamma}{\gamma}}}{\left(1+\alpha\right)\delta_k \left(\frac{\gamma}{(1-\gamma)} \right) + \left(1+\alpha\right) \left(\frac{g(1+\rho)+\rho}{(1-\gamma)} \right) - \left[\rho\left(1+g\right) + \left(1+\alpha\right)g\right]},$$

$$= \frac{\left(0.15\right)^3 \left(\frac{2}{3(0.02(1.03))+0.03+0.03} \right)^2}{3\left((1.5)\left(0.03\right)\left(0.5\right) + 1.5 \left(\frac{3(0.02(1.03))+0.03}{2} \right) - \left(0.03\left(1.02\right) + \left(1.5\right)\left(0.02\right)\right)\right)},$$

$$= 1.0161.$$

With $g = 0$, this instead gives the Example 8.1 solution that $k_t = 2.3148$.

Therefore it is clear that the positive growth rate reduces the equilibrium capital stock. For example, if the growth rate doubles to $g = 0.04$ instead of $g = 0.02$, then the capital stock falls almost by half to 0.53357:

$$k_t = \frac{(0.15)^3 \left(\frac{2}{3(0.04(1.03)+0.03+0.03)}\right)^2}{3\left((1.5)(0.03)(0.5) + 1.5\left(\frac{3(0.04(1.03)+0.03)}{2}\right) - (0.03(1.04) + (1.5)(0.04))\right)},$$

$$= 0.53357.$$

11.11.2 Example 11.2

In Example 11.2, a different baseline positive growth calibration is to keep $r = 0.06$. Then with all of the other parameters the same, except that now $g = 0.02$ and $\rho = 0.0098039$ (instead of $\rho = 0.03$ in Example 11.1) the capital stock value is

$$k_t = \frac{T\gamma (A_G)^{\frac{1}{\gamma}} \left(\frac{(1-\gamma)}{g(1+\rho)+\rho+\delta_k}\right)^{\frac{1-\gamma}{\gamma}}}{(1+\alpha)\delta_k \left(\frac{\gamma}{(1-\gamma)}\right) + (1+\alpha)\left(\frac{g(1+\rho)+\rho}{(1-\gamma)}\right) - \left[\rho(1+g) + (1+\alpha)g\right]},$$

$$= \frac{(0.15)^3 \left(\frac{2}{3(0.02(1.0098)+0.0098+0.03)}\right)^2}{3\left((1.5)(0.03)(0.5) + 1.5\left(\frac{3(0.02(1.0098)+0.0098)}{2}\right) - (0.0098(1.02) + 0.03)\right)}$$

$$= 2.7778.$$

11.11.3 Example 11.3: Exogenous growth process

Using the baseline calibration of Example 11.2, with a growth rate of 0.02, A_{Gt} shifts up over time at the rate of $\mu = 0.0066227$. With $A_{Gt+1} = 0.151$, and with no other changes in the calibration, the capital stock at $t + 1$ is given as $k_t = 2.833$:

$$k_{t+1} = \frac{T\gamma (A_{Gt+1})^{\frac{1}{\gamma}} \left(\frac{(1-\gamma)}{g(1+\rho)+\rho+\delta_k}\right)^{\frac{1-\gamma}{\gamma}}}{(1+\alpha)\delta_k \left(\frac{\gamma}{(1-\gamma)}\right) + (1+\alpha)\left(\frac{g(1+\rho)+\rho}{(1-\gamma)}\right) - \left[\rho(1+g) + (1+\alpha)g\right]},$$

$$= \frac{(0.15099)^3 \left(\frac{2}{3(0.02(1.0098)+0.0098+0.03)}\right)^2}{3\left((1.5)(0.03)(0.5) + 1.5\left(\frac{3(0.02(1.0098)+0.0098)}{2}\right) - (0.0098(1.02) + 0.03)\right)},$$

$$= 2.8331.$$

At time $t + 2$, $A_{Gt+2} = 0.152$ and the capital stock is given as

$$k_{t+2} = \frac{T\gamma (A_{Gt+2})^{\frac{1}{\gamma}} \left(\frac{(1-\gamma)}{g(1+\rho)+\rho+\delta_k}\right)^{\frac{1-\gamma}{\gamma}}}{(1+\alpha)\delta_k \left(\frac{\gamma}{(1-\gamma)}\right) + (1+\alpha)\left(\frac{g(1+\rho)+\rho}{(1-\gamma)}\right) - \left[\rho(1+g) + (1+\alpha)g\right]},$$

$$= \frac{(0.15199)^3 \left(\frac{2}{3(0.02(1.0098)+0.0098+0.03)}\right)^2}{3\left((1.5)(0.03)(0.5) + 1.5\left(\frac{3(0.02(1.0098)+0.0098)}{2}\right) - (0.0098(1.02) + 0.03)\right)},$$

$$= 2.8898.$$

And at time $t+3$, $A_{Gt+3} = 0.153$, and the capital stock is

$$k_{t+3} = \frac{T\gamma \left(A_{Gt+3}\right)^{\frac{1}{\gamma}} \left(\frac{(1-\gamma)}{g(1+\rho)+\rho+\delta_k}\right)^{\frac{1-\gamma}{\gamma}}}{\left(1+\alpha\right)\delta_k \left(\frac{\gamma}{(1-\gamma)}\right) + \left(1+\alpha\right)\left(\frac{g(1+\rho)+\rho}{(1-\gamma)}\right) - \left[\rho\left(1+g\right)+\left(1+\alpha\right)g\right]},$$

$$= \frac{\left(0.153\right)^3 \left(\frac{2}{3(0.02(1.0098)+0.0098+0.03)}\right)^2}{3\left((1.5)(0.03)(0.5) + 1.5\left(\frac{3(0.02(1.0098)+0.0098)}{2}\right) - \left(0.0098(1.02)+(1.5)(0.02)\right)\right)},$$

$$= 2.9478.$$

Over time, the capital stock rises from 2.7778, to 2.833, to 2.8904, and to 2.9478. These are fractional increases of $\frac{2.8331-2.7778}{2.7778} = 0.02$, $\frac{2.8898-2.8331}{2.8331} = 0.02$, and $\frac{2.9478-2.8898}{2.8898} = 0.02$. So the capital stock grows at a 2% rate over time, as consistent with the exogenous balanced growth rate of 2%.

11.11.4 Example 11.4: Trends in both time and goods endowment

When the A_{Gt} rises to $A_{Gt+1} = 0.15108$, $A_{Gt+2} = 0.15216$, and then $A_{Gt+2} = 0.15327$, and at the same time the time T falls to $T_{t+1} = 1 - 0.00182 = 0.99818$, $T_{t+2} = (0.99818)(1-0.00182) = 0.99636$, and $T_{t+3} = (0.99636)(1-0.00182) = 0.99455$, the capital stock can be recomputed for each new equilibrium. At time $t+1$,

$$k_{t+1} = \frac{T_{t+1}\gamma \left(A_{Gt+1}\right)^{\frac{1}{\gamma}} \left(\frac{(1-\gamma)}{g(1+\rho)+\rho+\delta_k}\right)^{\frac{1-\gamma}{\gamma}}}{\left(1+\alpha\right)\delta_k \left(\frac{\gamma}{(1-\gamma)}\right) + \left(1+\alpha\right)\left(\frac{g(1+\rho)+\rho}{(1-\gamma)}\right) - \left[\rho\left(1+g\right)+\left(1+\alpha\right)g\right]},$$

$$= \frac{0.99818\left(0.15108\right)^3 \left(\frac{2}{3(0.02(1.0098)+0.0098+0.03)}\right)^2}{3\left((1.5)(0.03)(0.5) + 1.5\left(\frac{3(0.02(1.0098039)+0.0098)}{2}\right) - \left(0.0098(1.02)+0.03\right)\right)},$$

$$= 2.8337.$$

At time $t+2$,

$$k_{t+2} = \frac{T_{t+2}\gamma \left(A_{Gt+2}\right)^{\frac{1}{\gamma}} \left(\frac{(1-\gamma)}{g(1+\rho)+\rho+\delta_k}\right)^{\frac{1-\gamma}{\gamma}}}{\left(1+\alpha\right)\delta_k \left(\frac{\gamma}{(1-\gamma)}\right) + \left(1+\alpha\right)\left(\frac{g(1+\rho)+\rho}{(1-\gamma)}\right) - \left[\rho\left(1+g\right)+\left(1+\alpha\right)g\right]},$$

$$= \frac{0.99636\left(0.15216\right)^3 \left(\frac{2}{3(0.02(1.0098)+0.0098+0.03)}\right)^2}{3\left((1.5)(0.03)(0.5) + 1.5\left(\frac{3(0.02(1.0098)+0.0098)}{2}\right) - \left(0.0098(1.02)+0.03\right)\right)},$$

$$= 2.8902.$$

And at time $t+3$, $A_{Gt+3} = 0.153$, and the capital stock is

$$k_{t+3} = \frac{T_{t+3}\gamma \left(A_{Gt+3}\right)^{\frac{1}{\gamma}} \left(\frac{(1-\gamma)}{g(1+\rho)+\rho+\delta_k}\right)^{\frac{1-\gamma}{\gamma}}}{\left(1+\alpha\right)\delta_k \left(\frac{\gamma}{(1-\gamma)}\right) + \left(1+\alpha\right)\left(\frac{g(1+\rho)+\rho}{(1-\gamma)}\right) - \left[\rho\left(1+g\right)+\left(1+\alpha\right)g\right]},$$

$$= \frac{0.99455\left(0.15327\right)^3 \left(\frac{2}{3(0.02(1.0098)+0.0098+0.03)}\right)^2}{3\left((1.5)(0.03)(0.5) + 1.5\left(\frac{3(0.02(1.0098)+0.0098)}{2}\right) - \left(0.0098(1.02)+0.03\right)\right)},$$

$$= 2.9480.$$

These new values of k represent a fractional increase relative at time $t + 1$ of 0.02, at time $t + 2$ of 0.02, and at time $t + 3$ of 0.02. This growth rate comes from the difference between the growth rate in A_G of 2% and the growth rate of T of -0.181%. To see this consider the percentage change in the capital stock over time. Because only A_{Gt} and T_t change, all the other terms drop out in the ratio $\frac{k_{t+1}}{k_t}$:

$$\frac{k_{t+1}}{k_t} = \frac{\dfrac{T_{t+1}\gamma(A_{Gt+1})^{\frac{1}{\gamma}}\left(\frac{(1-\gamma)}{g(1+\rho)+\rho+\delta_k}\right)^{\frac{1-\gamma}{\gamma}}}{(1+\alpha)\delta_k\left(\frac{\gamma}{(1-\gamma)}\right)+(1+\alpha)\left(\frac{g(1+\rho)+\rho}{(1-\gamma)}\right)-[\rho(1+g)+(1+\alpha)g]}}{\dfrac{T_t\gamma(A_{Gt})^{\frac{1}{\gamma}}\left(\frac{(1-\gamma)}{g(1+\rho)+\rho+\delta_k}\right)^{\frac{1-\gamma}{\gamma}}}{(1+\alpha)\delta_k\left(\frac{\gamma}{(1-\gamma)}\right)+(1+\alpha)\left(\frac{g(1+\rho)+\rho}{(1-\gamma)}\right)-[\rho(1+g)+(1+\alpha)g]}},$$

$$\frac{k_{t+1}}{k_t} = \frac{T_{t+1}\left(A_{Gt+1}\right)^{\frac{1}{\gamma}}}{T_t\left(A_{Gt}\right)^{\frac{1}{\gamma}}} = \frac{T_t\left(1-0.00182\right)\left[A_{Gt}\left(1.0072\right)\right]^{\frac{1}{\gamma}}}{T_t\left(A_{Gt}\right)^{\frac{1}{\gamma}}}$$

$$= \left(1-0.00182\right)\left(1.0072\right)^3$$

$$= 1.02.$$

CHAPTER ⑫

Human capital and endogenous growth

12.1 Introduction

The chapter extends the standard dynamic exogenous growth model by introducing investment in human capital with the result of endogenising the growth rate. Human capital is introduced into the goods production function in a way directly comparable to the productivity factor. Now the human capital level of the agent rises over time at the constant balanced path growth rate, instead of the goods productivity factor rising exogenously over time at a constant rate.

The human capital investment is determined in a separate new sector of the economy, using part of the consumer's time allocation as the input into the human capital production. This adds a second consumer intertemporal margin, and through this second margin the growth rate is determined endogenously. It means that the return on physical capital must also equal the return on human capital in the balanced growth path equilibrium. And it also means that the state variable of the economy is no longer just the capital stock, but rather the ratio of the physical capital stock to the human capital stock.

The standard aggregate supply and demand for goods and labour are developed in a way analogous to the exogenous growth model, except with the modification of the state variable and except for the need to account for the time spent in human capital production. With these two main modifications, the AS–AD analysis is presented, and a baseline equilibrium example is set out in full. The growth rate is again targeted at 2% as in the exogenous growth model. The main new parameter in the calibration is the productivity of the human capital production sector. This helps determine the endogenous growth rate of the economy.

An alternative calibration is presented for contrast, and several simplified models of endogenous growth are also presented for comparison to the baseline endogenous growth model. These are special cases that enable explicit solutions for the amount of leisure use and the growth rate. In one case there is only human capital and no physical capital, and in the other case, no human capital but only physical capital.

The growth process over four periods of time is again set out. But now no parameters of the model change over time. All parameters are stationary and yet the model still shows the growth facts established in the exogenous growth model.

The solution for the endogenous growth economy with human and physical capital becomes more complicated because of the addition of the human capital investment sector. Now the AS–AD analysis can be used to again get a single equation in just one unknown. But the complication is that the unknown enters in an implicit quadratic equation. Since solutions to a quadratic equation are well known, this solution methodology is presented in Appendix A12 at the end of the chapter. Here, instead of solving first for the capital stock, the quadratic solution equation is presented in terms of the growth rate g. Given the calibration this solution equation implies the equilibrium growth rate, and then all of the other variables can be determined subsequently, including the state variable.

12.1.1 Building on the last chapter

The human capital analysis of this chapter extends directly the exogenous growth dynamic model of Part 4. The introduction of human capital is made so as to be seen as an alternative way of specifying the growth process developed in the last chapter. It has the advantage that the fixity of the interest rate in Part 4 now gives way to an endogenous determination of the interest rate since the growth rate is now endogenous.

The chapter shows that the *AS–AD* analysis of Part 4 can be modified with endogenous growth so as to leave the main structure of the *AS–AD* framework in place. Rather than discarding the *AS–AD* analysis, it is invigorated with its ability to show the growth process over time without requiring the assumption that parameters are exogenously changing over time. And again as in Part 4, the modified *AS–AD* analysis is used to solve for the full solution of the economy. Rather than a separate chapter devoted to this for the exogenous growth model, as in Chapter 10 of Part 4, here the solution methodology is presented in the chapter's appendix.

12.1.2 Learning objectives

Including human capital investment and so endogenising the growth rate presents a seemingly difficult extension of the baseline dynamic model. The challenge is to see the few modifications that need to be made to the *AS–AD* framework to accommodate this extension. Details of the solution methodology require the complication of solving a quadratic equation, as the appendix sets out. Understanding that endogenising the growth rate makes the interest rate endogenous is an important concept, one that is left out of the exogenous growth baseline model. Visualising the growth process over time, without changing any parameters, also is a primary objective of the chapter.

12.1.3 Who made it happen?

The importance of human capital as part of labour theory has been stressed going back to Adam Smith and Alfred Marshall, who writes 'The most valuable of all capital is that invested in human beings' (quote from Kaufman, 2008). Gary Becker (Nobel Laureate 1992) followed a long line of labour theory that emphasised 'human capital', which is the investment in skills today in order to enable labour to be more productive tomorrow. Becker helped formalise human capital theory, as did Theodore W. Schultz (Nobel Laureate 1979), along with Jacob Mincer in his 1974 book *Schooling, Experience, and Earnings*.

Within the wave of new growth theory in the 1960s, Hirofumi Uzawa in 1962 and 1963 created two-sector models of the growth process while still using the Solow assumption that consumption is just a fixed fraction of output. In these Uzawa articles, the investment good is produced by a separate technology from the consumption good. In his 1965 article, using this same approach to producing the investment good, he managed to fundamentally alter the Solow exogenous technological change approach. He made this advance by making the technological change an endogenous function of the amount of time devoted to education.

The Uzawa approach is in effect a production function for an investment good. But rather than being a production function for the investment into physical capital as in his 1963 papers, the 1965 production function is for the investment into human capital. And as a result of this investment in human capital, labour time is effectively augmented by the level of human capital, and this effective labour time could expand continuously over time along with the physical capital stock. This meant that Solow's exogenous technological change became an endogenous function of how much time was invested in accumulating human capital.

Robert E. Lucas, Jr. (1967) (Nobel Laureate 1995) showed how to have costs of adjusting the physical capital stock, similar to Uzawa (1962,1963), but in a dynamic utility maximising framework. He extended this with Ed Prescott in a 1971 paper so that there could be Solow type continuous growth, with a cost of adjusting the capital stock. The growth was still driven by exogenous technological change. Lucas in 1988 departed from exogenous growth by returning to the cost of adjusting capital with growth, but this time following Uzawa's model of costly human capital adjustment. Lucas (1988) combines the Uzawa 1965 approach with the Ramsey framework of dynamic consumer utility maximisation so as to formalise the use of human capital to explain growth in the modern framework.

12.2 Human capital investment

Human capital, denoted by h_t, is defined as that which turns raw labour time into time that yields a higher marginal product. The simplest way to think of it is an index that starts at one, $h_t = 1$, and that rises through investment in human capital. Then the wage rate now is not just w_t per unit of raw labour time, but rather $w_t h_t$ per unit of raw labour. In other words, the human capital increases the 'effective wage rate' of $w_t h_t$. As the human capital rises, the effective wage rate rises along the balanced growth path. And the time that now enters the production function, which in raw terms is l_t amount of labour time, now becomes $l_t h_t$ which is the 'effective labour time'. The time is in effect augmented by the degree of human capital. Meanwhile w_t reverts back to the wage rate of raw labour and this is now stable along the balanced growth path (instead of rising as when there is exogenous growth), so that per capita income rises only because human capital and the effective wage rate rise.

The production function for goods output then has the simple extension from the baseline dynamic model of Chapter 8 with capital and effective labour as inputs and the productivity factor not rising over time:

$$y_t^s = A_G \left(l_t^d h_t \right)^\gamma (k_t)^{1-\gamma}. \tag{12.1}$$

If human capital rises over time, so that h_t is growing, then the effective labour $l_t^d h_t$ is growing also. This allows for continuous growth. The question then becomes how does the human capital increase over time. Is it set exogenously, outside of the model, or is it part of the decision process of the consumer on how to allocate resources?

12.2.1 Relation to exogenous growth

The growth in human capital can be specified exogenously, and then this is exactly the same theory of growth as the exogenous growth model above. To see this, consider that if instead the production function were specified as $y_t^s = \left(l_t^d h_t \right)^\gamma (k_t)^{1-\gamma}$, then by also setting h_t equal to $(A_{Gt})^{\frac{1}{\gamma}}$ and substituting back into the production function would give the same production function as in the exogenous growth model:

$$y_t^s = \left(l_t^d h_t \right)^\gamma (k_t)^{1-\gamma},$$
$$h_t = (A_{Gt})^{\frac{1}{\gamma}},$$
$$y_t^s = A_{Gt} \left(l_t^d \right)^\gamma (k_t)^{1-\gamma}.$$

The resulting exogenous growth form of the output equation appears with A_{Gt} indexed by time instead of having human capital. It is clear that exogenous human capital growth would just be a renaming of the exogenous increase in the productivity factor A_{Gt}.

12.2.2 Second sector and endogenous growth

Suppose instead that the consumer must invest time in human capital accumulation in order for the human capital stock to grow. Education in schools is the most important example of such time. On the job training can also lead to an increase in human capital. And many forms of work experience increase the human capital level. There is a vast literature on this and even a new economics journal called the *Journal of Human Capital* (University of Chicago Press) that focuses exclusively on these issues.

Formally we can model this by saying that, just as with physical capital k_t, there is accumulation of human capital over time given by

$$h_{t+1} = h_t \left(1 - \delta_h\right) + i_{Ht}, \tag{12.2}$$

where $\delta_h \in [0, 1]$ is the depreciation rate of human capital, and i_{Ht} denotes the amount invested in human capital.

The investment in human capital is 'produced' either through the education sector, research and development sector, or from training on the job, and can be stated in terms of a production function itself. This is different from how physical capital accumulation is modelled in that initially we assume that output can be divided into consumption or investment, without any further cost. But for human capital, the assumption is that it requires time to invest in human capital, and it may also involve physical capital as well. Then the production function can take a standard Cobb–Douglas form. This second production function, in addition to the goods production function, makes the economy into a two-sector economy instead of the standard one-sector economy that so far has been the basis of the economy under study.

One simplification that can be made for computational purposes, as was done in Lucas's (1988) article, is to assume that the human capital investment function uses only effective labour and no physical capital. Denoting the raw time in human capital investment as l_{Ht}, and with A_H the productivity parameter of the human capital production sector, the production function for human capital investment can be written as a linear function of the effective labour $l_{Ht} h_t$:

$$i_{Ht} = A_H l_{Ht} h_t. \tag{12.3}$$

The allocation of time constraint, including time for leisure, is that one equals the fraction of time spent producing goods, l_t^s, producing human capital, l_{Ht}, and leisure x_t:

$$1 = l_{Ht} + l_t^s + x_t. \tag{12.4}$$

In comparison to exogenous growth, the time allocation of endogenous growth can be thought of as

$$T_t + l_{Ht} = 1,$$

where T_t is defined as the sum of labour and leisure time:

$$T_t \equiv l_t^s + x_t.$$

Then the time in human capital l_{Ht} can be thought of as causing a decrease in the time left for goods and leisure, in that

$$l_t^s + x_t = T_t = 1 - l_{Ht}.$$

The change in time left for goods and leisure was exogenous in the exogenous growth model, manufactured by assuming a change in T_t itself. But now T_t changes endogenously according to changes in the time used to produce human capital investment.

The consumer chooses not just labour and leisure, but also the amount of time spent in human capital accumulation. The cost of the extra time in human capital is that there is less time for current work and leisure. The benefit of the extra time is that it raises all of the future earnings of the agent by increasing the effective wage rate. This is the central trade-off.

12.3 Growth with human and physical capital

The general equilibrium decentralised representative agent problem with both human capital and physical capital accumulation can be set out as an extension of the baseline dynamic model of Chapter 8. For physical capital, as before the accumulation equation is given by

$$k_{t+1} = k_t \left(1 - \delta_k\right) + i_t. \tag{12.5}$$

Goods consumption is equal to the wages from working, now indexed by the human capital $w_t l_t h_t$, plus the rent from physical capital, $r_t k_t$, minus the investment in physical capital:

$$
\begin{aligned}
c_t^d &= w_t l_t^s h_t + r_t k_t - i_t, \\
&= w_t l_t^s h_t + r_t k_t - k_{t+1} + k_t - \delta_k k_t.
\end{aligned}
\tag{12.6}
$$

The recursive optimisation problem now has two state variables, k_t and h_t:

$$
\begin{aligned}
V\left(k_t, h_t\right) = \operatorname*{Max}_{k_{t+1}, h_{t+1}, l_t^s, l_{Ht}, x_t} \quad &: \ln\left[w_t l_t^s h_t + r_t k_t - k_{t+1} + k_t - \delta_k k_t\right] + \alpha \ln\left(x_t\right) \\
&+ \beta V\left(k_{t+1}, h_{t+1}\right),
\end{aligned}
\tag{12.7}
$$

subject to equations (12.2) to (12.4). The human capital investment function can be substituted into the optimisation problem by substituting in for h_{t+1}:

$$h_{t+1} = h_t \left(1 - \delta_h\right) + A_H l_{Ht} h_t, \tag{12.8}$$

and the time allocation can also be substituted in by solving for x_t:

$$x_t = 1 - l_{Ht} - l_t^s, \tag{12.9}$$

making the optimisation problem with respect to the three variables k_{t+1}, l_t^s, and l_{Ht}:

$$
\begin{aligned}
V\left(k_t, h_t\right) = \operatorname*{Max}_{k_{t+1}, l_t^s, l_{Ht},} \quad &: \ln\left[w_t l_t^s h_t + r_t k_t - k_{t+1} + k_t - \delta_k k_t\right] + \alpha \ln\left(1 - l_{Ht} - l_t^s\right) \\
&+ \beta V\left[k_{t+1}, h_t \left(1 - \delta_h\right) + A_H l_{Ht} h_t\right].
\end{aligned}
\tag{12.10}
$$

Plus there are now two envelope conditions, one with respect to k_t and one to h_t.

The equilibrium conditions are

$$k_{t+1} : \frac{1}{c_t^d}\left(-1\right) + \beta \frac{\partial V\left(k_{t+1}, h_{t+1}\right)}{\partial k_{t+1}} = 0, \tag{12.11}$$

$$l_t^s : \frac{1}{c_t^d}\left(w_t h_t\right) + \frac{\alpha}{x_t}\left(-1\right) = 0, \tag{12.12}$$

$$l_{Ht} : \frac{\alpha}{x_t}\left(-1\right) + \beta \frac{\partial V\left(k_{t+1}, h_{t+1}\right)}{\partial h_{t+1}}\left(A_H h_t\right) = 0; \tag{12.13}$$

plus the envelope conditions

$$k_t : \frac{\partial V(k_t, h_t)}{\partial k_t} = \frac{1}{c_t^d}\left(1 + r_t - \delta_k\right), \tag{12.14}$$

$$h_t : \frac{\partial V(k_t, h_t)}{\partial h_t} = \frac{1}{c_t^d}(w_t l_t) + \beta\frac{\partial V(k_{t+1}, h_{t+1})}{\partial h_{t+1}}\left(1 + A_H l_{Ht} - \delta_H\right). \tag{12.15}$$

Bring $\frac{\partial V(k_{t+1}, h_{t+1})}{\partial k_{t+1}}$ in equation (12.11) down one period to t, and substitute this into equation (12.14); with all growing variables growing at the rate of g along the balanced growth path equilibrium, then g is also the consumption growth rate and this implies the familiar intertemporal margin

$$1 + g_t = \frac{1 + r_t - \delta_k}{1 + \rho}. \tag{12.16}$$

Equation (12.12) gives the intratemporal margin

$$MRS_{c,x} : \frac{\alpha c_t^d}{x_t} = w_t h_t.$$

12.3.1 Second intertemporal capital margin

Equation (12.13) gives an expression for $\frac{\partial V(k_{t+1}, h_{t+1})}{\partial h_{t+1}}$:

$$\frac{\partial V(k_{t+1}, h_{t+1})}{\partial h_{t+1}} = \frac{\alpha}{\beta(A_H h_t)x_t},$$

which can be substituted in at time t and at $t+1$ into equation (12.15) to yield that

$$\frac{(h_t)x_t}{(h_{t-1})x_{t-1}} = \beta(A_H)l_t^s + \beta\left(1 + A_H l_{Ht} - \delta_H\right). \tag{12.17}$$

Along the balanced growth path equilibrium, x_t is stationary, and so $\frac{x_t}{x_{t-1}} = 1$. And with h_t growing at the rate g, with $l_t^s + l_{Ht} = 1 - x_t$ by the time allocation constraint (12.9), and with $\beta = \frac{1}{1+\rho}$, then the second intertemporal capital margin results as

$$1 + g_t = \frac{1 + A_H\left(1 - x_t\right) - \delta_h}{1 + \rho}. \tag{12.18}$$

Adding human capital means that now there is a second intertemporal condition. Comparing equations (12.16) and (12.18), it is clear that the return to capital is equal across the different forms of capital:

$$r_t - \delta_k = A_H\left(1 - x_t\right) - \delta_h. \tag{12.19}$$

This means that the economy's growth rate is determined by 1) how productive is time in human capital investment, A_H, and 2) how much time is productively employed, $1 - x$, along with 3) the marginal product of physical capital r_t.

Productive time is that time which is used in either goods or human capital production. This is the overall employment rate of the economy, when such rate is defined using all productive time across both sectors of the economy. Any factors that cause this employment rate to rise will also cause the growth rate to rise. For example, good unemployment insurance systems can make $1 - x$ higher and so the growth rate higher, while taxes can make $1 - x$ lower and so the growth rate lower.

12.4 *AS–AD* with human capital

The solution of the full equilibrium requires an extension of the methodology of Chapter 10. All of the equilibrium conditions must be used to solve for the variables. The other equilibrium conditions are the budget constraint, the time constraint, and the human capital investment technology, of equations (12.6), (12.8) and (12.9). The solution methodology is similar to that of Chapter 10, but somewhat more complex because of the human capital. Now the state variable is not k_t but rather the ratio of $\frac{k_t}{h_t}$. However h_t can be normalised to 1 so that the normalised state variable can be thought of as k_t. This methodology is supplied as Appendix A12 at the end of this chapter. The solution methodology starts with the *AS–AD* functions.

The consumption demand can be formulated in a way analogous to Chapter 8 and the baseline dynamic model. There are three changes. The physical capital to human capital ratio $\frac{k_t}{h_t}$ enters instead of just the capital k_t as the state variable. The time spent in human capital accumulation, l_{Ht}, subtracts from the time used in working. And the consumption is in terms of a ratio relative to the human capital stock h_t. To see this, the budget constraint (12.6) implies that consumption equals labour income $w_t l_t^s h_t$ plus capital income $r_t k_t$, minus investment $k_{t+1} - k_t (1 - \delta_k)$. Along the balanced growth path, $k_{t+1} = k_t (1 + g)$, and consumption is

$$c_t^d = w_t l_t^s h_t + r_t k_t - \left[k_t (1 + g) - k_t (1 - \delta_k) \right]$$
$$= w_t l_t^s h_t + k_t (r_t - \delta_k - g).$$

To solve for consumption in terms of the real wage and the state variables requires as in Chapter 8 substituting for l_t^s using the marginal rate of substitution between goods and leisure, $\frac{c_t \alpha}{w_t h_t} = x_t$, along with the allocation of time constraint, $x_t = 1 - l_t^s - l_{Ht}$:

$$\frac{c_t^d \alpha}{w_t h_t} = 1 - l_t^s - l_{Ht};$$

$$l_t^s = 1 - \frac{c_t^d \alpha}{w_t h_t} - l_{Ht}.$$

With l_t^s eliminated, the consumption function is

$$c_t^d = w_t h_t \left(1 - \frac{c_t^d \alpha}{w_t h_t} - l_{Ht} \right) + k_t (r_t - \delta_k - g).$$

Solving for c_t^d

$$c_t^d = \frac{1}{1 + \alpha} \left[w_t h_t (1 - l_{Ht}) + k_t (r_t - \delta_k - g) \right].$$

This puts the consumption demand in a form comparable to the original formulation in Chapter 8, except that now the effective wage of $w_t h_t$ enters along with the subtraction of time spent in human capital accumulation l_{Ht}. This means the raw wage w_t is factored by the amount of human capital h_t that the consumer has. And the time l_{Ht} is invested in increasing human capital, which increases growth, but at the cost of less current wages since the time is used up in the investment process.

Solving for $r_t - \delta_k - g$ from the intertemporal marginal rate of substitution, in terms of g,

$$1 + g = \frac{1 + r - \delta_k}{1 + \rho};$$

$$r_t - \delta_k - g = \rho (1 + g).$$

The consumption function becomes

$$c_t^d = \frac{1}{1+\alpha} \left[w_t h_t \left(1 - l_{Ht} \right) + k_t \rho \left(1 + g \right) \right].$$

In the BGP equilibrium, the human capital investment function implies that l_{Ht} can be written as a function of g:

$$h_{t+1} = h_t \left(1 + A_H l_{Ht} - \delta_H \right),$$

$$1 + g = \frac{h_{t+1}}{h_t} = 1 + A_H l_{Ht} - \delta_H,$$

$$l_{Ht} = \frac{g + \delta_H}{A_H}. \tag{12.20}$$

The higher is l_{Ht} the higher is the growth rate for given δ_H and A_H parameters. Substituting in for l_{Ht}, the consumption function with endogenous growth is now

$$c_t^d = \frac{1}{1+\alpha} \left[w_t h_t \left(1 - \frac{g + \delta_H}{A_H} \right) + k_t \rho \left(1 + g \right) \right], \tag{12.21}$$

or as normalised by h_t:

$$\frac{c_t^d}{h_t} = \frac{1}{1+\alpha} \left[w_t \left(1 - \frac{g + \delta_H}{A_H} \right) + \frac{k_t}{h_t} \rho \left(1 + g \right) \right].$$

Once the equilibrium g is known along with the state variable $\frac{k_t}{h_t}$, then the consumption demand can be graphed as a function of w_t, as before. Thus the difference from the exogenous growth model is that the time invested l_{Ht} determines the growth rate endogenously, and l_{Ht} itself is an endogenous variable of the model.

12.4.1 Permanent income and wealth

Consumption is a function of permanent income in equation (12.21):

$$c_t^d = \left(\frac{1}{1+\alpha} \right) y_{Pt}; \tag{12.22}$$

$$y_{Pt} = w_t h_t \left(1 - \frac{g + \delta_H}{A_H} \right) + k_t \rho \left(1 + g \right). \tag{12.23}$$

Letting T_t denote the time endowed for work and leisure,

$$T_t = 1 - \frac{g + \delta_H}{A_H}.$$

And the permanent income is

$$y_{Pt} = w_t h_t T_t + k_t \rho \left(1 + g \right).$$

With the normalisation of $h_t = 1$, then permanent income is the same as in Part 4 except that now T_t is endogenously determined.

Consider that wealth, denoted by W_t, can be defined as the discounted stream of permanent income. With R_t^W denoting the wealth discount factor, then

$$W_t = \frac{y_{Pt}}{R_t^W} = \frac{w_t h_t T_t + k_t \rho \left(1 + g \right)}{R_t^W}.$$

And if $R_t^W = \rho \left(1 + g \right)$, then the wealth constraint is

$$W_t = \frac{w_t h_t T_t}{\rho \left(1 + g \right)} + k_t. \tag{12.24}$$

Wealth equals the discounted stream of human capital earnings plus physical capital. Human capital is capitalised into the wealth stock of $\frac{w_t h_t T_t}{\rho(1+g)}$.

12.4.2 Aggregate demand *AD*

Total output demand then requires adding the investment to the consumption:

$$y_t^d = c_t^d + \left[k_{t+1} - k_t\left(1-\delta_k\right)\right];$$

$$y_t^d = c_t^d + k_t\left(g+\delta_k\right);$$

$$y_t^d = \frac{1}{1+\alpha}\left[w_t h_t\left(1 - \frac{g+\delta_H}{A_H}\right) + k_t\rho\left(1+g\right) + k_t\left(g+\delta_k\right)\left(1+\alpha\right)\right];$$

$$y_t^d = \frac{1}{1+\alpha}\left[w_t h_t\left(1 - \frac{g+\delta_H}{A_H}\right) + k_t\left[\rho\left(1+g\right) + \left(g+\delta_k\right)\left(1+\alpha\right)\right]\right].$$

$$(12.25)$$

Dividing through by h_t,

$$\frac{y_t^d}{h_t} = \frac{1}{1+\alpha}\left[w_t\left(1 - \frac{g+\delta_H}{A_H}\right) + \frac{k_t}{h_t}\left[\rho\left(1+g\right) + \left(g+\delta_k\right)\left(1+\alpha\right)\right]\right].$$

Inversely, the *AD* function can be solved in terms of the relative price $\frac{1}{w_t}$:

$$\frac{1}{w_t} = \frac{1 - \frac{g+\delta_H}{A_H}}{\frac{y_t^d}{h_t}\left(1+\alpha\right) - \frac{k_t}{h_t}\left[\rho\left(1+g\right) + \left(g+\delta_k\right)\left(1+\alpha\right)\right]}.$$

$$(12.26)$$

In these equations, h_t can be normalised to $h_t = 1$.

12.4.3 Aggregate supply *AS*

The supply comes from the firm problem. The firm maximises profit, which now includes as labour cost the wage rate w_t factored by the effective labour demanded $l_t^d h_t$:

$$\underset{l_t^d, k_t}{\text{Max}} \ \Pi_t = y_t^s - w_t l_t^d h_t - r_t k_t.$$

This maximisation problem is subject to the production function, with the equilibrium condition with respect to labour that

$$w_t = \gamma A_G\left(l_t^d h_t\right)^{\gamma-1}\left(k_t\right)^{1-\gamma},$$

and with respect to capital,

$$r_t = \left(1-\gamma\right)A_G\left(l_t^d h_t\right)^{\gamma}\left(k_t\right)^{-\gamma}.$$

From the labour equilibrium condition, the demand for labour is

$$l_t^d = \left(\frac{\gamma A_G}{w_t}\right)^{\frac{1}{1-\gamma}}\frac{k_t}{h_t}.$$

With the production function,

$$y_t^s = A_G\left(l_t^d h_t\right)^{\gamma}\left(k_t\right)^{1-\gamma},$$

and substituting in for l_t^d,

$$y_t^s = A_G\left(\frac{\gamma A_G}{w_t}\right)^{\frac{\gamma}{1-\gamma}}k_t,$$

$$(12.27)$$

or in terms of per unit of human capital, the supply function is

$$\frac{y_t^s}{h_t} = A_G \left(\frac{\gamma A_G}{w_t}\right)^{\frac{\gamma}{1-\gamma}} \frac{k_t}{h_t}. \tag{12.28}$$

Inversely, in terms of $\frac{1}{w_t}$ aggregate supply can be written as

$$\frac{1}{w_t} = \frac{1}{\gamma A_G} \left(\frac{y_t^s}{A_G k_t}\right)^{\frac{1-\gamma}{\gamma}}. \tag{12.29}$$

It is exactly the same *AS* function as in Chapter 8 when there is exogenous growth.

12.4.4 Example 12.1: Baseline calibration

One way to calibrate the model, for a baseline from which to conduct comparative statics, is to target the growth rate which is now an endogenous variable. In particular the target will be $g = 0.02$, as in the exogenous growth model of Chapter 11. Appendix A12 provides the solution methodology for the equilibrium. It derives the equilibrium of all variables as a function of g, and uses the *AS–AD* to get an excess demand equation in terms of only g. This gives an implicit solution for g, given the calibration of the parameters.

Assume again that $\gamma = \frac{1}{3}$ as in Chapter 8. This will give an aggregate supply curve that slopes up at an increasing rate, and it will be the baseline calibration for the human capital model. In addition, let $\alpha = 1$, $A_h = 0.189$, $\delta_k = 0.05$, $\delta_h = 0.015$, $\beta = \frac{1}{1+\rho} = 0.95$, $\rho = \frac{1}{0.95} - 1 = 0.0526$, $A_G = 0.28224$.

For this baseline calibration, the target of $g = 0.020$ is achieved. The state variable $\frac{k_t}{h_t} = 1.00$. With human capital stock normalised to 1, so that $h_t = 1$, then also $k_t = 1$ in this equilibrium.

Other variables in equilibrium here are $l_H = 0.18526$, $l = 0.28405$, $1 - x = 0.18526 + 0.28405 = 0.46931$. Leisure is 0.531, which is close to some calculations in related models, such as Gomme and Rupert (2007). The interest rate is $r = 0.1237$, or 12.37%, and the wage rate is $w = 0.21772$, or $\frac{1}{w_t} = 4.59$.

Another point of the calibration that compares to evidence is the return on human capital, which Zhang (2006) reports in the range of 9.6% to 10.6%. In the model, equations (12.16) and (12.18) imply that $A_H (1 - x_t) - \delta_h = r_t - \delta_k$. Thus one way to define the return on human capital is the marginal product of labour in the human capital investment, which equals $A_H (1 - x_t) = r_t - \delta_k + \delta_h = 0.1237 - 0.05 + 0.015 = 0.0887$. This 8.87% return is close to the range reported by Zhang.

Figure 12.1 graphs the *AS–AD* equilibrium of equations (12.26) and (12.29) with the calibrated values of the parameters and the equilibrium growth rate $g = 0.02$ substituted in, as in the following equations:

$$\frac{1}{w_t} = \frac{\left(1 - \frac{0.02 + 0.015}{0.189}\right)}{\gamma (1 + 1) - 1 \left[(0.0526)(1 + 0.02) + (0.02 + 0.05)(1 + 1)\right]};$$

$$\frac{1}{w_t} = \frac{3}{0.28224} \left(\frac{1}{(0.28224) \, 1}\right)^2 y_t^2.$$

12.4.5 Equilibrium wage rate

A way to see the solution for the equilibrium wage is to use the market clearing condition for aggregate output. Defining the excess demand by $Y(w_t) = y_t^d - y_t^s$, as in Chapter 8, market clearing implies that the equilibrium wage rate is that at which $Y(w_t) = 0$. Using

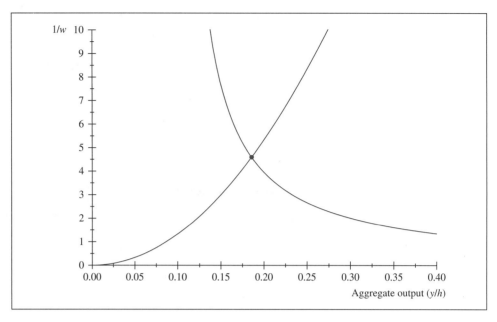

Figure 12.1 *AS–AD* with human capital and endogenous growth in Example 12.1

the aggregate output demand and supply equations (12.25) and (12.27),

$$
\begin{aligned}
0 &= Y\left(w_t\right) \\
&= \frac{\left[w_t h_t \left(1 - \frac{g + \delta_H}{A_H}\right) + k_t \left[\rho\left(1 + g\right) + \left(g + \delta_k\right)\left(1 + \alpha\right)\right]\right]}{1 + \alpha} - A_G \left(\frac{\gamma A_G}{w_t}\right)^{\frac{\gamma}{1-\gamma}} k_t. \quad (12.30)
\end{aligned}
$$

With the baseline human capital model calibration, with $h_t = 1$, the calibrated $Y\left(w_t\right) = 0$ function is

$$
0 = Y\left(w_t\right) = \frac{\left(w_t \left(1 - \frac{0.02 + 0.015}{0.189}\right) + 1\left(0.0526\left(1 + 0.02\right) + \left(0.02 + 0.05\right)\left(1 + 1\right)\right)\right)}{1 + 1}
$$

$$
- 0.28224 \left(\frac{0.28224}{3\left(w_t\right)}\right)^{0.5} (1).
$$

Figure 12.2 graphs the excess output demand function.

This excess demand is zero at the equilibrium wage rate of 0.2177. At a lower wage rate than this, the relative price of output $\frac{1}{w_t}$ is higher, demand is lower, supply is higher, and so there is an excess supply of goods, or equally, a negative excess demand for goods. At at higher wage rate than the equilibrium, the relative price $\frac{1}{w_t}$ is lower, demand is higher, supply is lower and there is an excess demand for output.

12.4.6 Consumption and output

Consumption is given as $c_t^d = \frac{1}{1+\alpha}\left[w_t h_t \left(1 - \frac{g + \delta_H}{A_H}\right) + k_t \rho\left(1 + g\right)\right]$, which can be solved at $g = 0.20$, $w_t = 0.2177$ and $k_t = 1$ as

$$
c_t^d = \frac{1}{1+1}\left(0.21772\left(1 - \frac{0.020 + 0.015}{0.189}\right) + 0.0526\left(1 + 0.020\right)\right) = 0.11553.
$$

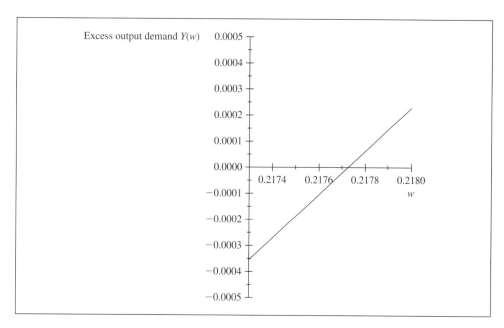

Figure 12.2 Excess output demand with baseline endogenous growth in Example 12.1

Output similarly is given in equilibrium as $y_t^d = \dfrac{\left[w_t h_t \left(1 - \frac{g+\delta_H}{A_H}\right) + k_t [\rho(1+g)+(g+\delta_k)(1+\alpha)]\right]}{1+\alpha}$, which is equal to

$$y_t^d = \frac{\left(0.21772 \left(1 - \frac{0.02+0.015}{0.189}\right) + 1\left(0.0526\left(1+0.02\right) + \left(0.02+0.05\right)\left(1+1\right)\right)\right)}{1+1}$$

$$= 0.18553.$$

This makes the consumption to output ratio $\frac{c_t^d}{y_t^d} = \frac{0.11553}{0.18553} = 0.6227$; consumption is 62% of output. Investment is the remaining 38%.

12.4.7 General equilibrium

The general equilibrium Example 12.1 comparison in input and output markets is modified somewhat in the model with human capital and endogenous growth. Following the framework of Chapter 8, in formulating the isocost, isoquant and input ratio at the equilibrium, the isocost line is

$$y_t^s = w_t l_t^d h_t + r_t k_t,$$

$$\frac{0.18553}{h_t} = \left(0.2177\right) l_t^d + \left(0.1237\right)\frac{k_t}{h_t},$$

$$\frac{k_t}{h_t} = \frac{0.18553}{0.1237 h_t} - \frac{\left(0.2177\right) l_t^d}{0.1237}. \tag{12.31}$$

The isoquant curve is

$$y_t^s = A_G \left(l_t^d h_t\right)^\gamma (k_t)^{1-\gamma},$$

$$0.18553 = \left(0.28224\right)\left(l_t^d h_t\right)^{\frac{1}{3}}(k_t)^{\frac{2}{3}};$$

$$\frac{k_t}{h_t} = \left(\frac{\left(0.18553\right)}{\left(0.28224\right) h_t \left(l_t^d\right)^{\frac{1}{3}}}\right)^{\frac{3}{2}} = \frac{\left(\frac{0.18553}{\left(0.28224\right)h_t}\right)^{\frac{3}{2}}}{\left(l_t^d\right)^{\frac{1}{2}}}. \tag{12.32}$$

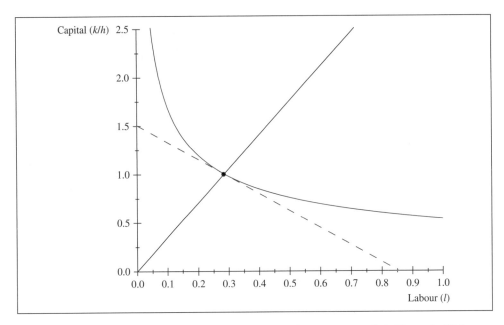

Figure 12.3 Factor market equilibrium with baseline endogenous growth in Example 12.1

The factor input ratio can be formulated as

$$\frac{k_t}{h_t} = \frac{1}{0.28405} l_t^d = (3.5205) \, l_t^d. \tag{12.33}$$

Figure 12.3 graphs in $\left(\frac{k_t}{h_t} : l_t\right)$ space the equations (12.31), (12.32) and (12.33), with $h_t = 1$, in dashed blue, solid blue and black respectively.

The blue isoquant is tangent to the dashed blue isocost at the point where the black input ratio intersects the tangency along a ray from the origin.

For goods and leisure in general equilibrium, consumption in terms of output production minus investment is

$$c_t^d = y_t^s - i_t = A_G \left(l_t^d h_t\right)^\gamma (k_t)^{1-\gamma} - (g + \delta_k) k_t,$$

$$\frac{c_t^d}{h_t} = (0.28224) \left(l_t^d\right)^{\frac{1}{3}} (1)^{\frac{2}{3}} - (0.02 + 0.05) \, (1). \tag{12.34}$$

Time t utility at the equilibrium, with $h_t = 1$, when graphing the utility level curve in dimensions of goods c_t and labour l_t, needs to account for the time in human capital, $l_{Ht} = 0.18526$. Using the notation that the time endowment for leisure and work is $T_t = 1 - l_{Ht}$, then utility can be expressed this way. First, getting the equilibrium utility level by substituting in for equilibrium goods and leisure, and then writing utility in terms of c_t^d and l_t^s alone, the level curve can be graphed.

$$u = \ln c_t^d + \alpha \ln x_t = \ln c_t^d + \alpha \ln \left(1 - l_{Ht} - l_t^s\right),$$

$$-2.7912 = \ln 0.11553 + 1 \ln \left(0.531\right),$$

$$-2.7912 = \ln c_t^d + \ln \left(T_t - l_t^s\right),$$

$$c_t^d = \frac{e^{-2.7912}}{\left(1 - 0.18526 - l_t^s\right)}. \tag{12.35}$$

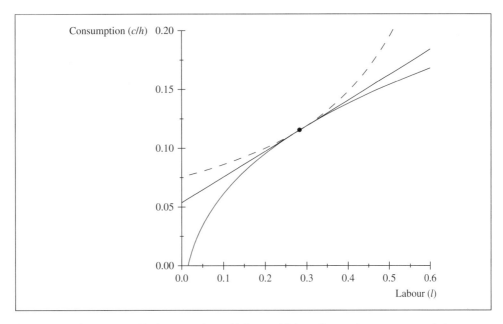

Figure 12.4 General equilibrium goods and labour with baseline endogenous growth in Example 12.1

The equilibrium budget line is

$$c_t^d = w_t l_t^s h_t + \rho \left(1 + g \right) k_t^s$$

$$\frac{c_t^d}{h_t} = \left(0.2177 \right) l_t^s + 0.052632 \left(1 + 0.02 \right) \left(1 \right). \tag{12.36}$$

With $h_t = 1$, Figure 12.4 graphs the production function based consumption (blue), the budget line (black), and the utility level curve (dashed blue), of equations (12.34), (12.35) and (12.36). The three are all tangent to each other at the equilibrium $l_t = 0.28405$.

12.5 Labour market

The labour supply reduces down to the same function as in Chapter 9 except for the subtraction of a fraction $\frac{1}{1+\alpha}$ of the time allocated to human capital activity. To see this, start from the intratemporal marginal rate of substitution between goods and leisure, solved in terms of leisure.

$$\frac{c_t^d \alpha}{w_t h_t} = x_t.$$

Then substitute in for leisure x_t using the allocation of time constraint,

$$\frac{c_t^d \alpha}{w_t h_t} = 1 - l_t^s - l_{Ht};$$

and solve for the labour supply:

$$l_t^s = 1 - \frac{c_t^d \alpha}{w_t h_t} - l_{Ht}. \tag{12.37}$$

The next step is to substitute in for $\frac{c_t^d}{h_t}$ in the above labour supply equation using the goods demand function,

$$\frac{c_t^d}{h_t} = \frac{1}{1+\alpha}\left[w_t\left(1 - l_{Ht}\right) + \frac{k_t}{h_t}\rho\left(1+g\right)\right]. \tag{12.38}$$

Substituting equation (12.38) into equation (12.37) we get that

$$l_t^s = 1 - \frac{\alpha}{w_t}\frac{1}{1+\alpha}\left[w_t\left(1 - l_{Ht}\right) + \frac{k_t}{h_t}\rho\left(1+g\right)\right] - l_{Ht}.$$

Simplifying the labour supply function,

$$l_t^s = 1 - \frac{\alpha}{1+\alpha}\left[1 - l_{Ht} + \frac{k_t}{w_t h_t}\rho\left(1+g\right)\right] - l_{Ht}$$

$$= 1 - \frac{\alpha}{1+\alpha}\left[1 + \frac{k_t}{w_t h_t}\rho\left(1+g\right)\right] - l_{Ht}\left(1 - \frac{\alpha}{1+\alpha}\right)$$

$$= 1 - \frac{\alpha}{1+\alpha}\left[1 + \frac{k_t}{w_t h_t}\rho\left(1+g\right)\right] - l_{Ht}\left(\frac{1}{1+\alpha}\right).$$

The final form of the labour supply is found by substituting in for l_{Ht} in terms of the growth rate. From equation (12.20), $l_{Ht} = \frac{g+\delta_H}{A_H}$

$$l_t^s = 1 - \frac{\alpha}{1+\alpha}\left[1 + \frac{k_t}{w_t h_t}\rho\left(1+g\right)\right] - \frac{g+\delta_H}{A_H\left(1+\alpha\right)}. \tag{12.39}$$

With the normalisation that $h_t = 1$, this function is the same as in Chapter 10 except for the subtraction of time due to time in the human capital sector. And the other more subtle difference is that now the growth rate g is endogenously determined rather than being an assumed exogenous value.

Labour demand is as in Chapters 9 and 10 except that now h_t enters into $\frac{k_t}{h_t}$ rather than just having k_t. But again with $h_t = 1$ as a normalisation, the functional form is identical to Chapters 8 and 10. From the firm's equilibrium condition with respect to labour,

$$w_t = \gamma A_G \left(l_t^d h_t\right)^{\gamma-1}\left(k_t\right)^{1-\gamma}.$$

Solving for labour demand,

$$l_t^d = \left(\frac{\gamma A_G}{w_t}\right)^{\frac{1}{1-\gamma}}\frac{k_t}{h_t},$$

and with $h_t = 1$,

$$l_t^d = \left(\frac{\gamma A_G}{w_t}\right)^{\frac{1}{1-\gamma}} k_t, \tag{12.40}$$

it is the same as equation (9.6)

To graph the labour market, rewrite the labour supply equation (12.39) and labour demand equation (12.40) by solving for the real wage w_t:

$$w_t = \frac{\alpha\rho\left(1+g\right)\left(\frac{k_t}{h_t}\right)}{1 - \left(1+\alpha\right)l_t^s - \frac{(g+\delta_H)}{A_H}}; \tag{12.41}$$

$$w_t = \gamma A_G\left(\frac{k_t}{h_t l_t^d}\right)^{1-\gamma}. \tag{12.42}$$

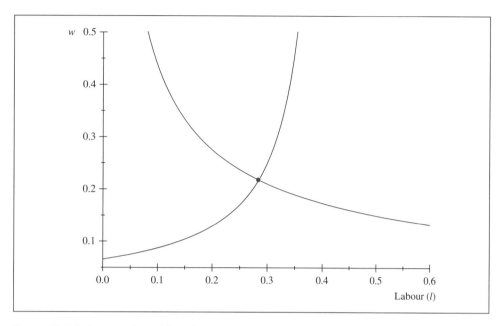

Figure 12.5 Labour market with endogenous growth baseline model in Example 12.1

Using the baseline calibration, with $\gamma = 0.3333$, $\alpha = 1$, $A_h = 0.189$, $\delta_k = 0.05$, $\delta_h = 0.015$, $\beta = \frac{1}{1+\rho} = 0.95$, $\rho = \frac{1}{0.95} - 1 = 0.0526$, $A_G = 0.28224$, and with the implied value of $\frac{k_t}{h_t} = 1$, and $g = 0.020$, the calibrated labour market equations become

$$w_t = \frac{1\,(0.0526)\,(1+0.02)}{1 - (1+1)\,l_t^s - \frac{(0.02+0.015)}{0.189}};$$

(12.43)

$$w_t = \frac{(0.28224)\,(1)^{\frac{2}{3}}}{3} \cdot \frac{1}{\left(l_t^d\right)^{\frac{2}{3}}}.$$

(12.44)

Figure 12.5 graphs equations (12.43) and (12.44) to illustrate the labour market with a wage of $w = 0.21772$ and employment of $l_t = 0.28405$.

The equilibrium wage rate is $w = 0.21772$ in the labour market just as it was this same value in the goods market, in which $\frac{1}{w} = \frac{1}{0.21772} = 4.59$.

The excess labour demand $L\,(w_t) = 0$ can also be formulated and graphed in a way similar to that in Chapter 9, equation (9.10). Labour demand is the same as in the baseline exogenous growth model while the endogenous growth labour supply is given by equation (12.39), allowing the formulation of $L\,(w_t) = l_t^d - l_t^s = 0$ as

$$L\,(w) = \left(\frac{\gamma A_G}{w_t}\right)^{\frac{1}{1-\gamma}} \frac{k_t}{h_t} - \left(1 - \frac{\alpha}{1+\alpha}\left[1 + \frac{k_t}{w_t h_t}\rho\,(1+g)\right] - \frac{g + \delta_H}{A_H\,(1+\alpha)}\right) = 0.\ (12.45)$$

And in calibrated form this becomes

$$L\,(w) = \left(\frac{0.28224}{3w_t}\right)^{1.5} 1 - \left(1 - \frac{1}{1+1}\left(1 + \frac{0.0526\,(1+0.02)}{w_t}\right) - \frac{0.02+0.015}{0.189\,(1+1)}\right) = 0.$$

(12.46)

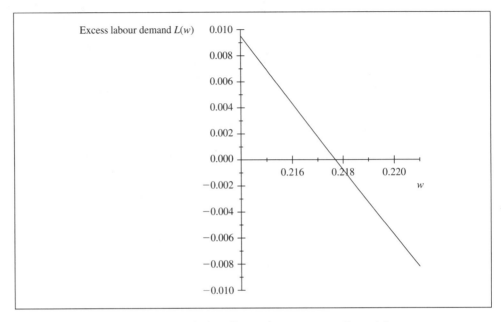

Figure 12.6 Excess labour demand in baseline endogenous growth model

Figure 12.6 graphs equation (12.46) and shows that the labour demand is in excess when the wage is less than 0.2177, while the labour supply is in excess when the wage exceeds 0.2177.

12.6 Endogenous growth process

The growth in variables c_t, y_t, k_t, h_t, i_t, all occurs without any change in exogenous parameters. In contrast the exogenous growth model requires A_{Gt} to increase over time. But now, all growing variables grow at the balanced path growth rate of g without any change in any exogenous parameters.

The growth process with endogenous growth occurs because the interest rate $r_t - \delta_k$ exceeds the rate of time preference ρ in equilibrium. And this occurs because of the added human capital equilibrium condition (12.19) that says that $r - \delta_k = A_H(1 - x) - \delta_h$. As long as the consumer's choice of leisure x_t is such that $A_H(1 - x) - \delta_h$ exceeds ρ then the variables of the economy that grow, will grow at the rate $g > 0$. Stationary variables such as time allocations remain constant.

This makes it straightforward to show output growing over time in a graph that compares to Figure 11.4. To do this, consider the same baseline endogenous growth calibration of Example 12.1 and use this to show how the *AS–AD* curves change over time. The *AS* and *AD* functions are

$$y_t^d = \frac{1}{1+\alpha}\left[w_t h_t\left(1 - \frac{g + \delta_H}{A_H}\right) + k_t\left[\rho(1+g) + (g+\delta_k)(1+\alpha)\right]\right];$$

$$y_t^s = A_G\left(\frac{\gamma A_G}{w_t}\right)^{\frac{\gamma}{1-\gamma}} k_t.$$

It is clear that with h_t and k_t each growing at a rate of 2% per period, then output demanded and supplied will also grow by 2% each period.

Inversely the AD function can be written as

$$\frac{1}{w_t} = \frac{h_t\left(1 - \frac{g+\delta_H}{A_H}\right)}{y_t^d\left(1+\alpha\right) - k_t\left[\rho\left(1+g\right) + (g+\delta_k)\left(1+\alpha\right)\right]}.$$

With h_t, k_t and y_t^d all growing by 2%, then it is clear that the wage rate w_t will be constant. And this function will not shift out over time. However, dividing by h_t gives that

$$\frac{1}{w_t h_t} = \frac{1 - \frac{g+\delta_H}{A_H}}{y_t^d\left(1+\alpha\right) - k_t\left[\rho\left(1+g\right) + (g+\delta_k)\left(1+\alpha\right)\right]}.$$

This function will shift out over time. This makes sense. The effective wage rate is w_t factored by h_t. Therefore a rising wage rate in this model is captured by the effective wage $w_t h_t$ rising over time by 2%, as in the Solow growth facts of Chapter 11. Then the relative price of output $\frac{1}{w_t h_t}$ falls over time, as h_t, k_t and y_t^d all grow by 2%.

The inverse supply equation (12.29) can be divided by h_t, and multiplied by $\frac{k_t}{k_t}$ and written as

$$\frac{1}{w_t h_t} = \left(\frac{y_t^s}{k_t A_G}\right)^{\frac{1-\gamma}{\gamma}} \frac{1}{\gamma A_G h_t} \frac{k_t}{k_t}$$

$$\frac{1}{w_t h_t} = \left(\frac{y_t^s}{k_t A_G}\right)^{\frac{1-\gamma}{\gamma}} \frac{k_t}{h_t} \frac{1}{\gamma A_G k_t}.$$

Again it is clear that w_t and $\frac{k_t}{h_t}$ are stationary, but $w_t h_t$ rises at the rate of 2%, since also $\frac{y_t^s}{k_t}$ is stationary, while k_t rises at 2%. It follows that $\frac{1}{w_t h_t}$ falls at a 2% rate along the balanced growth path.

12.6.1 Example 12.2: BGP growth

The balanced growth path growth of output can be seen by graphing the AS–AD functions at time t, $t+1$, $t+2$, and $t+3$. The calibration is assumed to be that $\alpha = 1$, $A_h = 0.189$, $\delta_k = 0.05$, $\delta_h = 0.015$, $\beta = \frac{1}{1+\rho} = 0.95$, $\rho = \frac{1}{0.95} - 1 = 0.0526$, $A_G = 0.28224$; and this implies that $g = 0.020$ and $\frac{k_t}{h_t} = 1.00$. At time $t+1$, the 2% growth causes the capital stock to rise from $k_t = 1$ to $k_{t+1} = 1.02$. With h_t normalised to 1, then at time $t+1$, $h_{t+1} = 1.02$.

If we graph the AS–AD functions in terms of $\frac{1}{w_t}$ as the vertical axis and $\frac{y_t}{h_t}$ as the horizontal axis, then there is no change over time in the AS–AD functions; it is a stationary equilibrium of w_t and the output per unit of human capital $\frac{y_t}{h_t}$. But written in terms of the inverse of the effective wage $\frac{1}{w_t h_t}$ on the vertical axis and y_t on the horizontal axis gives the comparison to the growth process seen for the exogenous growth model. And this is true even though all parameters are constant.

Consider at time $t+1$, the AD and AS inverse functions are

$$\frac{1}{w_{t+1} h_{t+1}} = \frac{1 - \frac{g+\delta_H}{A_H}}{y_{t+1}^d\left(1+\alpha\right) - k_{t+1}\left[\rho\left(1+g\right) + (g+\delta_k)\left(1+\alpha\right)\right]};$$

$$\frac{1}{w_{t+1} h_{t+1}} = \left(\frac{y_{t+1}^s}{k_{t+1} A_G}\right)^{\frac{1-\gamma}{\gamma}} \frac{k_{t+1}}{h_{t+1}} \frac{1}{\gamma A_G k_{t+1}}.$$

Writing k_{t+1} and h_{t+1} in terms of time t, using the 2% stationary growth whereby $k_{t+1} = k_t (1+g)$ and $h_{t+1} = h_t (1+g)$, these functions can be written as

$$\frac{1}{w_{t+1}h_{t+1}} = \frac{1 - \frac{g+\delta_H}{A_H}}{y_{t+1}^d (1+\alpha) - k_t (1+g) \left[\rho (1+g) + (g + \delta_k)(1+\alpha)\right]}; \tag{12.47}$$

$$\frac{1}{w_{t+1}h_{t+1}} = \left(\frac{y_{t+1}^s}{k_t (1+g) A_G}\right)^{\frac{1-\gamma}{\gamma}} \frac{k_t (1+g)}{h_t (1+g)} \frac{1}{\gamma A_G k_t (1+g)}, \tag{12.48}$$

with time $t+2$ and $t+3$ functions being

$$\frac{1}{w_{t+2}h_{t+2}} = \frac{1 - \frac{g+\delta_H}{A_H}}{y_{t+2}^d (1+\alpha) - k_t (1+g)^2 \left[\rho (1+g) + (g + \delta_k)(1+\alpha)\right]}; \tag{12.49}$$

$$\frac{1}{w_{t+2}h_{t+2}} = \left(\frac{y_{t+2}^s}{k_t (1+g)^2 A_G}\right)^{\frac{1-\gamma}{\gamma}} \frac{k_t (1+g)^2}{h_t (1+g)^2} \frac{1}{\gamma A_G k_t (1+g)^2}; \tag{12.50}$$

$$\frac{1}{w_{t+3}h_{t+3}} = \frac{1 - \frac{g+\delta_H}{A_H}}{y_{t+3}^d (1+\alpha) - k_t (1+g)^3 \left[\rho (1+g) + (g + \delta_k)(1+\alpha)\right]}; \tag{12.51}$$

$$\frac{1}{w_{t+3}h_{t+3}} = \left(\frac{y_{t+3}^s}{k_t (1+g)^3 A_G}\right)^{\frac{1-\gamma}{\gamma}} \frac{k_t (1+g)^3}{h_t (1+g)^3} \frac{1}{\gamma A_G k_t (1+g)^3}. \tag{12.52}$$

Using the assumed parameters, Figure 12.7 graphs the time t, $t+1$, $t+2$ and $t+3$ relative prices $\frac{1}{wh}$ and output y of equations (12.47) to (12.52). It shows how the relative

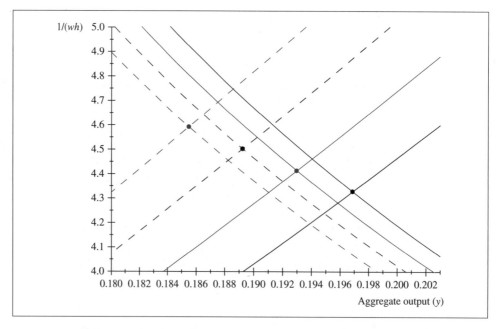

Figure 12.7 Endogenous growth shifts in *AS–AD* from time t to $t+3$ in Example 12.2

price $\frac{1}{wh}$ falls over time from the calibrated equilibrium of $\frac{1}{0.2177} = 4.5935$ at time t (dashed blue) to $\frac{1}{0.2177(1.02)} = 4.5034$ at time $t+1$ (dashed black), to $\frac{1}{0.2177(1.02)^2} = 4.4151$ at time $t+2$ (blue), to $\frac{1}{0.2177(1.02)^3} = 4.3285$ at time $t+3$ (black). Meanwhile output rises from 0.1855 at time t (dashed blue), to $(0.1855)(1.02) = 0.18921$ at time $t+1$ (dashed black), to $(0.1855)(1.02)^2 = 0.19299$ at time $t+2$ (blue), to $(0.1855)(1.02)^3 = 0.19685$ at time $t+3$ (black).

12.6.2 Labour market

The endogenous growth effect on the labour market can also be demonstrated. Again, if graphed in terms of $\frac{1}{w_t}$ and l_t, then over time there is no change in the equilibrium, as both the wage rate w_t and employment l_t are stationary. However the effective wage $w_t h_t$ and the effective labour employment $l_t h_t$ both rise over time. Writing the labour demand and supply in terms of the effective wage, equations (12.41) and (12.42) become

$$w_t h_t = \frac{\alpha \rho \left(1+g\right)(k_t)}{1 - \left(1+\alpha\right) l_t^s - \frac{(g+\delta_H)}{A_H}};$$
(12.53)

$$w_t h_t = \gamma A_G \frac{\left(\frac{h_t}{k_t}\right)^{\gamma}}{\left(l_t^d\right)^{1-\gamma}} k_t.$$
(12.54)

At time $t+1$, the supply and demand for labour are

$$w_{t+1} h_{t+1} = \frac{\alpha \rho \left(1+g\right)^2 (k_t)}{1 - \left(1+\alpha\right) l_{t+1}^s - \frac{(g+\delta_H)}{A_H}};$$
(12.55)

$$w_{t+1} h_{t+1} = \gamma A_G \frac{\left(\frac{h_t}{k_t}\right)^{\gamma}}{\left(l_{t+1}^d\right)^{1-\gamma}} k_t \left(1+g\right).$$
(12.56)

At time $t+2$ and $t+3$,

$$w_{t+2} h_{t+2} = \frac{\alpha \rho \left(1+g\right)^3 (k_t)}{1 - \left(1+\alpha\right) l_{t+2}^s - \frac{(g+\delta_H)}{A_H}};$$
(12.57)

$$w_{t+2} h_{t+2} = \gamma A_G \frac{\left(\frac{h_t}{k_t}\right)^{\gamma}}{\left(l_{t+2}^d\right)^{1-\gamma}} k_t \left(1+g\right)^2.$$
(12.58)

$$w_{t+3} h_{t+3} = \frac{\alpha \rho \left(1+g\right)^4 (k_t)}{1 - \left(1+\alpha\right) l_{t+3}^s - \frac{(g+\delta_H)}{A_H}};$$
(12.59)

$$w_{t+3} h_{t+3} = \gamma A_G \frac{\left(\frac{h_t}{k_t}\right)^{\gamma}}{\left(l_{t+3}^d\right)^{1-\gamma}} k_t \left(1+g\right)^3.$$
(12.60)

Figure 12.8 graphs equations (12.53) to (12.60) of the supply and demand for labour from time t to $t+3$ with the baseline endogenous growth calibration of Example 12.1. With the effective wage on the horizontal axis, the effective wage rises over time as the labour employment is stationary. This replicates the exogenous growth Solow facts of a rising wage rate, as seen in Figure 11.5, but now in terms of the effective wage rising as human capital rises at the rate g.

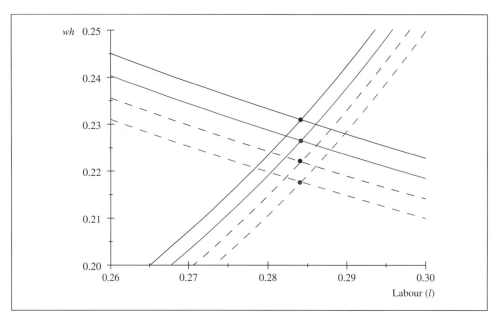

Figure 12.8 Labour market with endogenous growth baseline model in Example 12.2

12.7 Labour intensity increase

The labour share of output γ can be changed. For example some would suggest a value of $\gamma = \frac{2}{3}$. Here this example is given, but an undesired result is that it produces a marginal cost that is concave rather than convex as in a typical supply curve.

12.7.1 Example 12.3

A calibration with the effective labour share higher at $\gamma = \frac{2}{3}$ is made here with all of the other parameters the same except for now with a lower $A_h = 0.154$, and with a higher $A_G = 0.74955$. Let $\gamma = 0.667$ with $\alpha = 1$, $\delta_k = 0.05$, $\delta_h = 0.015$, $\beta = 0.95$. Again $\frac{k}{h} = 1$ and the growth rate is the same at $g = 0.0200$, or 2%, while the labour and human capital time change to $l = 0.3486$; $l_H = 0.2274$, with $1 - x = 0.2274 + 0.3486 = 0.576$. And $w = 0.71012$; $\frac{1}{w} = \frac{1}{0.71012} = 1.4082$.

By increasing γ while maintaining the same BGP growth rate of $g = 0.02$, the human capital productivity must be lower. This means that with greater labour intensity in the production of goods, a less productive human capital sector is necessary to get the same growth rate. Compared to the baseline calibration in Example 12.1, the time in the human capital sector increases from 18% to 23% while goods production labour time rises from 27% to 35%; leisure time decreases some from 47% to 42%.

The *AS–AD* equations become now:

$$\frac{1}{w_t} = \frac{\left(1 - \frac{0.02 + 0.015}{0.154}\right)}{y^d \left(1 + 1\right) - 1 \left(\left(0.0526\right) \left(1 + 0.02\right) + \left(0.07\right) \left(1 + 1\right)\right)}; \tag{12.61}$$

$$\frac{1}{w_t} = \frac{1}{\left(0.667\right) 0.74955} \left(\frac{1}{\left(0.74955\right) 1}\right)^{\frac{1 - (0.667)}{(0.667)}} \left(y_t^s\right)^{\frac{1 - (0.667)}{(0.667)}}. \tag{12.62}$$

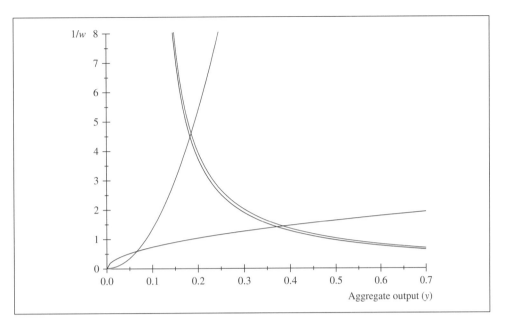

Figure 12.9 *AS–AD* with human capital and high labour intensity in Example 12.3

Figure 12.9 graphs equations (12.61) and (12.62) to show the new *AS–AD* equilibrium in the black curves, in comparison to the original calibration of Example 12.1 in the blue curves. The *AD* curve changes only slightly as A_H changes a bit. But the *AS* curve changes a lot. The primary problem here is the concave shape of the *AS* curve. With any calibration in which $\gamma > 0.5$, the aggregate marginal cost supply curve is concave to the origin. In contrast it is convex, with $\gamma < 0.5$, or it is linear, with $\gamma = 0.5$.

12.7.2 Interpretation

The calibration of γ is an important issue in growth theory. Some have argued that growth estimation results imply that empirically γ needs to be around 0.33, as in Mankiw *et al.* (1992). And Mankiw *et al.* argue that the large capital share of $1 - \gamma = 0.67$ is consistent with theory incorporating human capital. In other words, Mankiw *et al.* interpret the large share for capital as consistent with human capital models of endogenous growth. As Obstfeld and Rogoff (1996) summarise the issue,

> The crux of the problem is that with $1 - \gamma = 0.33$, there are sharply decreasing returns to capital accumulation.... If, however, one assumes that $1 - \gamma = 0.67$, diminishing returns set in more slowly and the model becomes much more plausible.

In Figure 12.9 above, the issue is put more simply: the need for $\gamma < 0.5$ in order to have a normal *AS* function. And given the need for $\gamma < 0.5$, the calibration of $\gamma = 0.33$ is also consistent with Obstfeld and Rogoff (1996).

12.8 Special cases of endogenous growth

There are two special cases in particular, where only human capital is used, or when only physical capital is used. These are worth examining in that they allow for simpler solutions that provide for sometimes easier intuition. With only human or physical capital, the production function of goods becomes a linear function using either only effective labour, when there is only human capital and no physical capital, or the production function is a linear function of only physical capital, when there is no human capital. The former is called an *Ah* economy while the latter is called an *Ak* economy, after the nature of the linear goods production functions.

12.8.1 Example 12.4: Human capital only

The goods production function can be specified as a simple linear function of the effective labour time:

$$y_t = A_G l_t h_t. \tag{12.63}$$

And the human capital investment function similarly, as in equation (12.3), is now simply

$$i_{ht} = A_H l_{Ht} h_t. \tag{12.64}$$

The human capital investment is a linear function of the effective time $l_{Ht} h_t$. Then the accumulation equation for human capital is

$$h_{t+1} = h_t \left(1 - \delta_h\right) + A_H l_{Ht} h_t. \tag{12.65}$$

This constraint needs to be added to the example economy.

The consumer problem is

$$V\left(h_t\right) = \underset{c_t, x_t, l_t, l_{Ht}, h_{t+1}}{\text{Max}} : u\left(c_t, x_t\right) + \beta V\left(h_{t+1}\right), \tag{12.66}$$

subject to the output production,

$$c_t = y_t = w_t l_t h_t, \tag{12.67}$$

time allocation,

$$x_t = 1 - l_t - l_{Ht}, \tag{12.68}$$

and human capital investment

$$h_{t+1} = h_t \left(1 - \delta_h\right) + A_H l_{Ht} h_t. \tag{12.69}$$

Substituting in the goods production and time constraints from the above gives a simpler problem.

And using log utility, $u_t = \ln c_t + \alpha \ln x_t$, the problem can be written as

$$V\left(h_t\right) = \underset{l_t, l_{Ht}}{\text{Max}} : \ln\left(w_t l_t h_t\right) + \alpha \ln\left(1 - l_t - l_{Ht}\right) + \beta V\left[h_t \left(1 - \delta_h\right) + A_H l_{Ht} h_t\right]. \tag{12.70}$$

Similar equilibrium conditions as for the full economy with physical capital result. The marginal rate of substitution between goods and leisure is again,

$$\frac{\alpha c_t}{x_t} = w_t h_t.$$

And now the only intertemporal margin implies that

$$1 + g = \frac{1 + A_H \left(1 - x\right) - \delta_h}{1 + \rho}. \tag{12.71}$$

The full solution can be found explicitly using all of the equilibrium conditions. Equilibrium leisure is

$$x = \frac{\alpha \rho}{A_H} \left[\frac{1 + A_H - \delta_h}{1 + \rho \left(1 + \alpha\right)}\right]. \tag{12.72}$$

This can be substituted into the growth equation to give the equilibrium BGP growth rate g:

$$g = \frac{A_H - \delta_h - \alpha\rho\left[\frac{1+A_H-\delta_h}{1+\rho(1+\alpha)}\right] - \rho}{1+\rho}. \tag{12.73}$$

For example, consider the case when the preference for leisure is zero, in that $\alpha = 0$. Then the growth rate is just $g = \frac{1+A_H-\delta_h}{1+\rho} - 1$, and the marginal product of human capital in producing human capital investment, $A_H - \delta_H$, is the main determinant of the growth rate along with the time discount factor ρ. This gives a trivial determination of the growth rate in that it is determined simply by the specification of parameters A_H and δ_H. This shows that positive leisure use is crucial for the non-trivial endogenisation of the growth rate.

The importance of leisure is one result here that carries through to the full economy with human and physical capital. There is another such result regarding A_G. Since the goods producer's production function is $y_t = w_t l_t h_t$, the firm's equilibrium condition for labour demand implies simply that $w_t = A_G$. Notice that A_G does not affect the growth rate in this economy, as it does not enter equation (12.73). Yet A_G is the main channel for growth in the exogenous growth model. This result of no effect of A_G on growth g also holds in the full economy with both human and physical capital.

Other results also found in the full economy are with respect to A_H. An increase in A_H, the human capital investment productivity, does increase the growth rate; $\frac{\partial g}{\partial A_H} > 0$. Further, an increase in A_H also causes more time to be invested in human capital investment. To see this, consider that

$$l_H = \frac{g + \delta_H}{A_H};$$

using the solution for the growth rate in equation (12.73), l_H can be written as

$$l_H = \frac{1 + \frac{\alpha\rho}{1+\rho(1+\alpha)}}{1+\rho} - \frac{\rho\left(1 - \delta_H\right) - \frac{\alpha\rho(1-\delta_h)}{1+\rho(1+\alpha)}}{A_H\left(1+\rho\right)}.$$

It is clear that an increase in A_H causes an increase in the human capital time l_H; or taking the derivative, $\frac{\partial l_H}{\partial A_H} > 0$. Therefore the time in human capital accumulation rises with A_H. This decreases the amount of time left for labour in the goods sector and for leisure, just like a decrease in the time endowment for labour and leisure, but now it is an endogenous decrease in this time endowment. The increases in g and l_H from an increase in A_H are results that also hold in the full economy with human and physical capital. These results will be exploited more in Chapter 13.

12.8.2 Example 12.5: Physical capital only

An alternative model of simple growth is given by the Ak model, in which there is only physical capital and no human capital. Like the Ah model, this is nested within the full economy with both human and physical capital. Let there be only one sector, the one producing goods, given by a linear technology in terms of only physical capital rather than human capital:

$$y_t = A_G k_t. \tag{12.74}$$

Physical capital investment is as usual $i_t = k_{t+1} + k_t\left(1 - \delta_k\right)$. And consumption is then output minus investment or

$$c_t = r_t k_t - k_{t+1} + k_t\left(1 - \delta_k\right). \tag{12.75}$$

With no time endowment at all, there is no leisure in the utility function and so utility is simply given by $u_t = \ln c_t$. The consumer problem is

$$V(k_t) = \underset{k_{t+1}}{\text{Max}} : \ln\left(r_t k_t - k_{t+1} + k_t\left(1 - \delta_k\right)\right) + \beta V\left(k_{t+1}\right). \tag{12.76}$$

The equilibrium conditions are, first for k_{t+1},

$$\frac{1}{c_t}(-1) + \beta\frac{\partial V\left(k_{t+1}\right)}{\partial k_{t+1}} = 0. \tag{12.77}$$

The envelope condition from partially differentiating with respect to k_t is that

$$\frac{\partial V(k_t)}{\partial k_t} = \frac{1}{c_t}\left[r_t + \left(1 - \delta_k\right)\right]. \tag{12.78}$$

Taking the first equilibrium condition back one time period to $t-1$,

$$\frac{1}{c_{t-1}} = \beta\frac{\partial V(k_t)}{\partial k_t}, \tag{12.79}$$

so that the second first-order condition implies that

$$\frac{c_t}{\beta c_{t-1}} = 1 + r_t - \delta_k. \tag{12.80}$$

The growth rate along the BGP is g such that

$$1 + g_t = \frac{c_t}{c_{t-1}} = \beta\left(1 + r_t - \delta_k\right). \tag{12.81}$$

From the firm problem, $r_t = A_G$ and so the growth rate is solved in terms of A_G, δ_k and $\beta = \frac{1}{1+\rho}$:

$$g_t = \frac{A_G - \delta_k - \rho}{1 + \rho}. \tag{12.82}$$

Growth is 'endogenous' but totally given by the exogenous constant marginal product of capital, A_G, plus the depreciation rate δ_k and time preference ρ.

The 'Ak' economy is called endogenous growth by many, but it is a trivial special case since growth is determined simply by the assumed values of A_G and δ_k. This economy is equivalent to the human only economy in the case when leisure preference α is zero, and when $A_H = A_G$ and $\delta_h = \delta_k$.

12.9 Applications: income distribution, Marx and human capital

Thorstein Veblen wrote the *Theory of the Leisure Class* in 1899, putting forth the idea that lower income class people sought to emulate higher income class people, through 'conspicuous consumption'; see Heilbroner (1961). Alternatively, one interpretation/ extension of Veblen is that such emulation could take place by low income workers getting the skills and education so as to advance to higher income levels.

Attaining education and skills provides a theory of social stability with transitionally different income classes rather than that of social instability with rigid class segregation, as was found in Karl Marx's 1867 earlier application of the classical labour theory. Marx divided the classes into worker and capitalist, and proposed redistributing the capitalist income to the workers within a setting where there was a constant dividing tension between the classes. The alternative theory of marginal productivity arose in which a socially stable framework could include lower income classes choosing to get the education necessary for an upward class movement, within a decentralised competitive society. Marx's theory of class rigidity required a centralised government to intervene and create a levelling of income amongst classes. The marginal productivity theory of income distribution instead allows anyone to own small shares of capital, and so become in a small or big way a capitalist along with a worker. Such marginal productivity theory evolved gradually, as for example J. M. Clark (1931) describes.

Some generations after Veblen, a tradition of human capital theory evolved whereby people could invest in education and so cause their productivity to jump up, along with their income class. Theodore W. Schultz for example continued the development of human capital theory, such as in his 1960 'Capital Formation by Education' article in the *Journal of Political Economy*. He further emphasised education and human capital investment in other well-known articles (1961a, 1961b) and wrote about how agrarian classes could be transformed to higher income classes through human capital investment, such as in his 1964 book *Transforming Traditional Agriculture*. His human capital work was cited in his Nobel Prize award in 1979. Class mobility through education provides an enduring alternative to class struggle that has become part of mainstream economics through endogenous growth theory.

12.10 Questions

1. Express the goods output production function of equation (12.1) in a form similar to the exogenous growth model of Part 4 by redefining the human capital stock.

2. Derive the second intertemporal margin of the consumer with respect to human capital found in equation (12.18).

3. How does the aggregate demand AD equation (12.26) compare to the AD equation
   (a) when growth is exogenous and $g > 0$, and
   (b) when growth is exogenous and $g = 0$?

4. As a modification to Example 12.1, find the full equilibrium of the economy when the only difference in the given parameters is that $A_H = 0.20$ instead of $A_H = 0.189$.

5. In Example 12.2, the growth process over time in Figures 12.7 and 12.8 are shown by graphing $w_t h_t$, the effective wage, on the vertical axis, either as $\frac{1}{w_t h_t}$ in Figure 12.7 for the goods market, or just as $w_t h_t$ in Figure 12.8 for the labour market. The figures show that the effective wage rises over time, as does output, while labour is constant. What would Figures 12.7 and 12.8 look like if instead the vertical axis variable was $\frac{1}{w_t}$ for 12.7, and w_t for 12.8, and the horizontal axes were $\frac{y_t}{h_t}$ and l_t respectively?

6. In Example 12.3, the AS curve with $\gamma = \frac{2}{3}$ has a concave shape relative to the origin, while in the baseline Example 12.2 the AS curve is convex relative to the origin. What value of γ would make the AS curve perfectly linear?

7. In Example 12.4, derive the solution for leisure given in equation (12.72), the solution for growth in equation (12.73), and prove that an increase in human capital investment productivity, A_H, will increase the growth rate.

8. In Example 12.5, derive the solution for the growth rate in equation (12.82) and explain in what sense this 'endogenous' growth rate model is similar to an 'exogenous' growth rate model.

9. In the chapter appendix, how is the excess demand for output used to find the solution for the growth rate g?

10. In the chapter appendix, explain whether the quadratic solution methodology to finding a solution for g is equivalent to graphing the normalised excess demand for output of equations (12.98).

12.11 References

Cass, David, 1965, 'Optimum Growth in an Aggregative Model of Capital Accumulation', *Review of Economic Studies*, 32: 233–240.

Clark, John Maurice, 1931, 'Distribution', *Encyclopedia of the Social Sciences*, 5: 167–173; reprinted in William Fellner and Bernard F. Haley, editors, *Readings in the Theory of Income Distribution*, The Blakiston Company, Philadelphia, 1946.

Gaume, Paul and Peter Rupert, 2007, 'Theory, Measurement and Calibration of Macroeconomic Models', *Journal of Monetary Economics*, Elsevier, 54(2) (March): 460–497.

Heilbroner, Robert L., 1961, *The Worldly Philosophers*, Revised Edition, Chapter VIII, 'The Savage World of Thorstein Veblen', Simon and Schuster, New York.

Kaufman, Bruce E., 2008, 'Jacob Mincer's Contribution to Modern Labor Economics: A Review Essay', Working Paper 2008-8-1, Andrew Young School of Policy Studies, July.

Lucas, Robert Jr., 1967, 'Adjustment Costs and Theory of Supply', *Journal of Political Economy*, 75: 321.

Lucas, Robert Jr., 1988, 'On the Mechanics of Economic Development', *Journal of Monetary Economics*, Elsevier, 22(1): 3–42, July.

Lucas, Robert Jr. and Edward, C. Prescott, 1971, 'Investment under Uncertainty', *Econometrica*, 39(5) (September): 659–681.

Mankiw, N. Gregory, David Romer and David N. Weil, 1992, 'A Contribution to the Empirics of Economic Growth', *The Quarterly Journal of Economics*, MIT Press, 107(2)(May): 407–437.

Marx, Karl, 1867, *Capital*, Volume I. Translated by Ben Fowkes. London: Penguin, 1990.

Mincer, Jacob, 1974, *Schooling, Experience, and Earnings*, New York: Columbia University Press.

Obstfeld, Maurice and Kenneth Rogoff, 1996, *Foundations in International Macroeconomics*, The MIT Press, Cambridge.

Schultz, Theodore W., 1960, 'Capital Formation by Education', *Journal of Political Economy*, 6 December.

Schultz, Theodore W., 1961a, 'Education and Economic Growth', in *Social Forces Influencing American Education*, N.B. Henry, ed., Chicago: University of Chicago Press.

Schultz, Theodore W., 1961b, 'Investment in Human Capital', *American Economic Review LI*, March, 1–17; American Economic Association Presidential Address.

Schultz, Theodore W., 1964, *Transforming Traditional Agriculture*, The University of Chicago Press, Chicago.

Uzawa, H., 1962, 'On a Two-Sector Model of Economic Growth', *Review of Economic Studies*, 29: 40–47.

Uzawa, H., 1963, 'On a Two-Sector Model of Economic Growth II', *Review of Economic Studies*, 30(2): 105–118.

Uzawa, H., 1965, 'Optimal Growth in a Two-Sector Model of Capital Accumulation', *Review of Economic Studies*, 31: 1–25.

Veblen, Thorstein, 1899, *The Theory of the Leisure Class: an Economic Study of Institutions*, Macmillan, New York.

Zhang, Qiang, 2006, 'Human Capital, Weak Identification, and Asset Pricing', *Journal of Money, Credit, and Banking*, 38(4): 873–899.

12.12 Appendix A12: Solution methodology

The solution approach will begin with the equilibrium of aggregate demand for output being equal to aggregate supply of output. Subtracting aggregate output supply from both sides gives an excess demand function which equals zero in equilibrium. This excess demand is then reformulated in terms of only one variable, the growth rate g, so that it is one equation in one unknown, g. It could be solved in terms of any particular variable. The growth rate is chosen since $g = 0.02$ is the primary target of the calibration. By solving for g, and then specifying a calibration, the target of $g = 0.02$ can be achieved exactly. The excess demand equation as a function of g is then equal to zero when $g = 0.02$.

Note that the solution methodology is simpler in Chapter 10 with exogenous growth since the intertemporal consumption margin implies that the interest rate is a constant, given the exogenous growth rate. But with endogenous growth, the growth rate is determined within the model. This is the additional complication which is a significant one. Now there are three intertemporal margins and these are key to solving the model.

12.12.1 Solving for *g* with *AS–AD*

Starting with the *AS* and *AD* functions of equations (12.25) and (12.27), and setting them equal, the result is that

$$\frac{1}{1+\alpha}\left[w_t h_t \left(1 - \frac{g + \delta_H}{A_H}\right) + k_t \left[\rho\left(1+g\right) + \left(g + \delta_k\right)\left(1+\alpha\right)\right]\right] = A_G \left(\frac{\gamma A_G}{w_t}\right)^{\frac{\gamma}{1-\gamma}} k_t.$$

Define the excess demand for output as $Y(w_t, h_t, k_t, g)$ as demand for output minus supply of output, which can be seen to depend on the four variables of w_t, h_t, k_t and g, and set it equal to zero:

$$Y(w_t, h_t, k_t, g) = \frac{1}{1+\alpha}\left[w_t h_t \left(1 - \frac{g + \delta_H}{A_H}\right) + k_t \left[\rho\left(1+g\right) + \left(g + \delta_k\right)\left(1+\alpha\right)\right]\right]$$

$$- A_G \left(\frac{\gamma A_G}{w_t}\right)^{\frac{\gamma}{1-\gamma}} k_t = 0. \tag{12.83}$$

The next steps are to find solutions for the wage w_t and the physical capital to human capital ratio, $\frac{k_t}{h_t}$, in terms of only the growth rate g. This will give one equation in one unknown g, that can be solved for g given a particular calibration. All of the equilibrium conditions must be used to find $w_t(g)$ and $\frac{k_t}{h_t}(g)$, so there are no real shortcuts.

However, the endogenous growth model does offer three different equations for the growth rate. These can be used to solve the rest of the model, in the approach described above. Consider the three growth equations that result along the balanced growth path:

$$1 + g = \beta\left(1 + r_t - \delta_k\right); \tag{12.84}$$
$$1 + g = \beta\left[1 + A_H\left(1 - x_t\right) - \delta_H\right]; \tag{12.85}$$
$$1 + g = 1 + A_H l_{Ht} - \delta_H. \tag{12.86}$$

The first of these growth equations is the standard growth condition from the intertemporal marginal rate of substitution when there is capital in the model. The second growth equation results when there is human capital, another intertemporal margin. Therefore it is clear that this is setting the return on physical capital $r_t - \delta_k$ to the return on human capital, which is $A_H\left(1 - x_t\right) - \delta_h$. The third growth equation follows directly from the human capital investment function, given that human capital also grows at the rate of g:

$$h_{t+1} = h_t\left(1 - \delta_H\right) + A_H l_{Ht} h_t;$$
$$1 + g = \frac{h_{t+1}}{h_t} = 1 + A_H l_{Ht} - \delta_H.$$

The first growth equation (12.84) implies a function for how r_t depends on g and exogenous parameters:

$$r_t = \frac{1+g}{\beta} + \delta_k - 1.$$

Now consider using the second and third growth equations to solve the three time allocations, of l_{Ht}, x_t and l_t in terms of functions of g. The third growth equation, equation

(12.86), directly implies that

$$l_{Ht} = \frac{g + \delta_H}{A_H}.$$

Next, the second and third growth equations, equations (12.85) and (12.86), can be combined to imply a function for $1 - x_t$ in terms of g:

$$\beta \left[1 + A_H \left(1 - x_t \right) - \delta_H \right] = 1 + A_H l_{Ht} - \delta_H; \tag{12.87}$$

$$A_H \left(1 - x_t \right) = \frac{1 + A_H l_{Ht} - \delta_H}{\beta} + \delta_H - 1; \tag{12.88}$$

$$1 - x_t = \frac{1 + A_H l_{Ht} - \delta_H}{A_H \beta} + \frac{\delta_H - 1}{A_H}; \tag{12.89}$$

$$1 - x_t = \frac{1 + A_H \left(\frac{g + \delta_H}{A_H} \right) - \delta_H}{A_H \beta} + \frac{\beta \left(\delta_H - 1 \right)}{A_H \beta}; \tag{12.90}$$

$$1 - x_t = \frac{\left(1 - \delta_H \right) \left(1 - \beta \right) + g + \delta_H}{A_H \beta}. \tag{12.91}$$

Using the allocation of time constraint that

$$l_t = 1 - x_t - l_{Ht},$$

and the just derived expressions for each l_{Ht} and $1 - x_t$, then l_t can be expressed as a function of g:

$$l_t = \frac{\left(1 - \delta_H \right) \left(1 - \beta \right) + g + \delta_H}{A_H \beta} - \frac{g + \delta_H}{A_H};$$

$$l_t = \frac{\left(1 - \delta_H \right) \left(1 - \beta \right) + (g + \delta_H) \left(1 - \beta \right)}{A_H \beta};$$

$$l_t = \frac{\left(1 + g \right) \left(1 - \beta \right)}{A_H \beta}. \tag{12.92}$$

Given $r\,(g)$, $l_{Ht}\,(g)$, $x_t\,(g)$, and $l_t\,(g)$, now the other variables can be solved in terms of g, and then these can be substituted back into the excess demand for output equation (12.83) to get one equation in one unknown g. Using the marginal product of capital condition and the function $l_t\,(g)$, the ratio $\frac{k_t}{h_t}$ can be solved as a function of g:

$$r_t = \left(1 - \gamma \right) A_G \left(\frac{k_t}{h_t} \right)^{-\gamma} (l_t)^{\gamma},$$

$$\frac{k_t}{h_t} = \left(\frac{\left(1 - \gamma \right) A_G}{r_t} \right)^{\frac{1}{\gamma}} l_t, \tag{12.93}$$

$$\frac{k_t}{h_t} = \left(\frac{\beta \left(1 - \gamma \right) A_G}{1 + g + \beta \left(\delta_k - 1 \right)} \right)^{\frac{1}{\gamma}} \frac{\left(1 + g \right) \left(1 - \beta \right)}{A_H \beta}. \tag{12.94}$$

The wage rate as a function of g is found from the marginal product of labour,

$$w_t = \gamma A_G \left(\frac{k_t}{h_t} \right)^{1-\gamma} (l_t)^{\gamma - 1},$$

$$w_t = \gamma A_G \left(\frac{\beta \left(1 - \gamma \right) A_G}{1 + g + \beta \left(\delta_k - 1 \right)} \right)^{\frac{1-\gamma}{\gamma}}. \tag{12.95}$$

Divide the excess demand equation through by h_t and w_t, so that

$$\frac{1}{1+\alpha}\left[\left(1-\frac{g+\delta_H}{A_H}\right)+\frac{k_t}{w_t h_t}\left[\rho\left(1+g\right)+\left(g+\delta_k\right)\left(1+\alpha\right)\right]\right]-A_G\left(\frac{\gamma A_G}{w_t}\right)^{\frac{\gamma}{1-\gamma}}\frac{k_t}{w_t h_t}=0.$$

(12.96)

And now substituting in for $\frac{k_t}{h_t}$ and w_t using equations (12.94) and (12.95), an equation with only one unknown g results:

$$0=\frac{1}{1+\alpha}\left[\left(1-\frac{g+\delta_H}{A_H}\right)+\frac{\left(1+g\right)\left(1-\beta\right)\left(1-\gamma\right)}{\left(1+g+\beta\left(\delta_k-1\right)\right)A_H\gamma}\left[\rho\left(1+g\right)+\left(g+\delta_k\right)\left(1+\alpha\right)\right]\right]$$
$$-\frac{\left[1+g+\beta\left(\delta_k-1\right)\right]}{\beta\left(1-\gamma\right)}\frac{\left(1+g\right)\left(1-\beta\right)\left(1-\gamma\right)}{\left(1+g+\beta\left(\delta_k-1\right)\right)A_H\gamma}.$$

(12.97)

Further simplifying, this gives the same excess demand of equation (12.83) except that it has been divided through by various terms. This gives what can be called a 'normalised' excess demand function:

$$Y(g)=\beta\left(A_H-g-\delta_H\right)\left(1+g+\beta\left(\delta_k-1\right)\right)\gamma$$
$$+\beta\left(1+g\right)\left(1-\beta\right)\left(1-\gamma\right)\left[\rho\left(1+g\right)+\left(g+\delta_k\right)\left(1+\alpha\right)\right]$$
$$-\left(1+\alpha\right)\left(1+g\right)\left(1-\beta\right)\left[1+g+\beta\left(\delta_k-1\right)\right]=0.$$

(12.98)

This gives one equation in g and by substituting in the assumed parameter values, g can be solved. The normalised excess demand of equation (12.98) can be graphed with the equilibrium g occurring where the graph crosses zero. Alternatively, the analytic solution is a quadratic equation in g; it can be solved that way explicitly for an exact functional form.

Example 12.1

The parameters are $\alpha=1$, $A_h=0.189$, $\delta_k=0.05$, $\delta_h=0.015$, $\beta=\frac{1}{1+\rho}=0.95$, $\rho=\frac{1}{0.95}-1=0.0526$, $A_G=0.28224$, $\gamma=\frac{1}{3}$. Substituting into equation (12.98),

$$Y(g)=\left(0.95\right)\left(\left(0.189\right)-\left(g+0.015\right)\right)\left(1+g+\left(0.95\right)\left(0.05-1\right)\right)\frac{1}{3}$$
$$+\left(0.95\right)\left(1+g\right)\left(1-\left(0.95\right)\right)\frac{2}{3}\left[\left(0.0526\right)\left(1+g\right)+\left(g+0.05\right)\left(2\right)\right]$$
$$-2\left(1+g\right)\left(1-\left(0.95\right)\right)\left[1+g+\left(0.95\right)\left(0.05-1\right)\right]=0.$$

(12.99)

Figure 12.10 graphs the normalised excess demand of equation (12.99), showing that it equals zero at a growth rate of $g=0.020$. This means the equilibrium endogenous growth rate for this calibration is in fact the target value of $g=0.020$.

The other variables of the equilibrium can all be expressed as a function of g, which in equilibrium is $g=0.02$, and so all of the other variables can be solved. For example, in the baseline endogenous growth calibration, equilibrium employment equals

$$l_t=\frac{\left(1+g\right)\left(1-\beta\right)}{A_H\beta}=\frac{\left(1.02\right)\left(1-0.95\right)}{\left(0.189\right)0.95}=0.28404.$$

The physical capital to human capital ratio by equation (12.94) is

$$\frac{k_t}{h_t}=\left(\frac{\beta\left(1-\gamma\right)A_G}{1+g+\beta\left(\delta_k-1\right)}\right)^{\frac{1}{\gamma}}l_t=\left(\frac{\left(0.95\right)\frac{2}{3}\left(0.28224\right)}{1.02+\left(0.95\right)\left(0.05-1\right)}\right)^{3}\left(0.28404\right)=1.0.$$

Thus the baseline equilibrium has that $\frac{k_t}{h_t}=1.0$. And with h_t normalised to 1, then $k_t=1$.

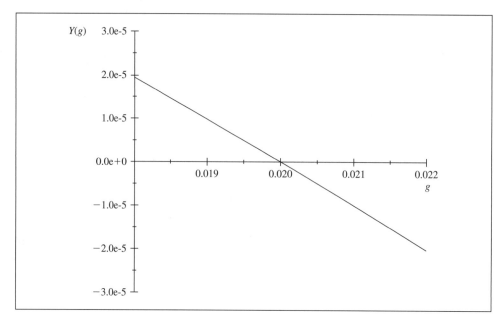

Figure 12.10 Normalised baseline excess demand $Y(g)$ as a function of g in Example 12.1

Example 12.3

Consider the calibration with $\gamma = \frac{2}{3}$ instead of $\frac{1}{3}$. And let $\alpha = 1$, $A_h = 0.154$, $\delta_h = 0.015$, $\beta = 0.95$, $A_G = 0.74955$. Again the growth rate is targeted at $g = 0.020$. The normalised excess demand equation, calibrated for this example, is

$$Y(g) = \frac{(0.95)^{\frac{1}{3}}}{2} \left(1 - \frac{g + 0.015}{0.154}\right)(1 + g + (0.95)(0.05 - 1))(0.154)^{\frac{2}{3}}$$

$$+ \frac{(0.95)^{\frac{1}{3}}}{2}(1 + g)(1 - (0.95))\frac{1}{3}[(0.0526)(1 + g) + (g + 0.05)(2)]$$

$$- [1 + g + (0.95)(0.05 - 1)](1 + g)(1 - (0.95))\frac{1}{3} = 0. \qquad (12.100)$$

Figure 12.11 graphs equation (12.100) and shows that the equilibrium is the target value of $g = 0.020$.

Other equilibrium values are $r = 0.1237$; $w = 0.710$; $\frac{k}{h} = 1.00$; $l = 0.3486$; $l_H = 0.2274$; $1 - x = 0.2274 + 0.3486 = 0.576$.

12.12.2 Quadratic equation solution of growth rate

Consider the implicit solution equation for g, in equation (12.98):

$$0 = \beta\gamma (A_h - \delta_h - g)\left[1 + \beta (\delta_k - 1) + g\right]$$
$$+ \beta (1 - \beta)(1 - \gamma)\left[\rho + \delta_k (1 + \alpha) + (1 + \alpha + \rho) g\right](1 + g)$$
$$- (1 + \alpha)(1 - \beta)\left[1 + \beta (\delta_k - 1) + g\right](1 + g).$$

This is a quadratic equation in g that can be written as $Ag^2 + Bg + C = 0$, where A, B, and C are constant terms that are functions of the given parameters of the economy. Rewriting equation (12.98) in this quadratic form, the so-called 'quadratic' term A, 'linear' term B,

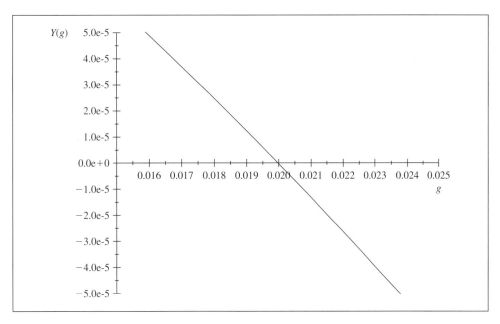

Figure 12.11 Normalised excess demand, with $\gamma = \frac{2}{3}$, as a function of g in Example 12.3

and 'constant' term C are given as

$$A \equiv -\beta\gamma + \beta \left(1 - \beta\right) \left(1 - \gamma\right) \left(1 + \alpha + \rho\right) - \left(1 + \alpha\right) \left(1 - \beta\right),$$
(12.101)

$$B \equiv -\beta\gamma \left[1 + \beta \left(\delta_k - 1\right) - A_h + \delta_h\right]$$
(12.102)
$$+ \beta \left(1 - \beta\right) \left(1 - \gamma\right) \left[\rho + \delta_k \left(1 + \alpha\right) + 1 + \alpha + \rho\right]$$
$$- \left(1 + \alpha\right) \left(1 - \beta\right) \left[2 + \beta \left(\delta_k - 1\right)\right],$$

$$C \equiv \beta\gamma \left(A_h - \delta_h\right) \left[1 + \beta \left(\delta_k - 1\right)\right]$$
(12.103)
$$+ \beta \left(1 - \beta\right) \left(1 - \gamma\right) \left[\rho + \delta_k \left(1 + \alpha\right)\right]$$
$$- \left(1 + \alpha\right) \left(1 - \beta\right) \left[1 + \beta \left(\delta_k - 1\right)\right].$$

The solution for this quadratic equation in the general form has the two real roots:

$$g = \frac{-B \pm \sqrt{B^2 - 4AC}}{2A}$$
(12.104)

One solution is positive and one negative. Only the positive solution is economically relevant, so the negative solution for g, $\frac{-B-\sqrt{B^2-4AC}}{2A}$, is discarded and only the positive solution $\frac{-B+\sqrt{B^2-4AC}}{2A}$ is used. Different calibrations will result in different values of A, B, and C, and so different values of g.

Example 12.1
For the calibration $\alpha = 1$, $A_h = 0.189$, $\delta_k = 0.05$, $\delta_h = 0.015$, $\beta = \frac{1}{1+\rho} = 0.95$, $\rho = \frac{1}{0.95} - 1 = 0.0526$, $A_G = 0.28224$, $\gamma = \frac{1}{3}$:

$$\text{Quadratic term:} \quad A = -0.3517,$$
$$\text{Linear term:} \quad B = -0.0157,$$
$$\text{Constant term:} \quad C = 0.00045558.$$

The corresponding solution for g is 0.020, where the negative root -0.0893 is not used.

Example 12.3

Here the calibration is $\gamma = \frac{2}{3}$ instead of $\frac{1}{3}$, and $\alpha = 1$, $A_h = 0.154$, $\delta_h = 0.015$, $\beta = 0.95$, $A_G = 0.74955$.

$$\begin{aligned}
\text{Quadratic term:} \quad & A = -0.7008, \\
\text{Linear term:} \quad & B = -0.0486, \\
\text{Constant term:} \quad & C = 0.0012.
\end{aligned}$$

Again the growth rate is $g = 0.020$.

CHAPTER 13

Explaining cycles and trends

13.1 Introduction

The chapter presents two main comparative static analyses of the endogenous growth economy and applies these to describe business cycles and long term trends. Using a baseline endogenous growth example, an increase in goods sector productivity is assumed, and the new equilibrium is studied in both goods and labour markets, as well as in general equilibrium input and output realms. The increased goods productivity shifts out aggregate output supply and demand so as to lower the relative price of goods, and increase output. In the labour market the supply shifts back, the demand shifts out, and the wage rate rises while employment remains unchanged. In both goods and labour markets, these effects are qualitatively similar to the baseline exogenous growth model. However changes in the goods productivity factor leaves the growth rate unchanged in the endogenous growth model.

The second comparative static analysis is to increase the productivity of the human capital investment sector. This causes the time spent in human capital investment to increase, thereby decreasing the time left over for labour and leisure use. This makes an increase in human capital productivity analogous to a decrease in the exogenous time endowment for labour and leisure in the exogenous growth model. In the goods market, the human capital productivity increase shifts back aggregate demand and supply with the result that the relative price of goods rises and the output decreases. In the labour market, the supply shifts out while the demand shifts back by more, with the result that both the real wage and the employment level fall. These results are similar to a decrease in the time endowment in the exogenous growth model, with the output and employment level falling. But while the wage rate is unchanged in the exogenous growth model, with the time endowment decrease, here with endogenous growth the real wage falls. In addition, changes in the goods productivity factor cause changes in the endogenous growth rate.

The comparative statics of goods sector and human capital sector productivity changes are then applied to explain business cycles and long term trends. For business cycles, the goods productivity change serves exactly the same role as in the exogenous growth dynamic model. It still has no effect on employment but moves output and wage rates as in a business cycle. The human capital productivity change now accounts for both output and wage rate changes as in a business cycle, and in addition for the changes of employment as in a business cycle. Therefore it can be used by itself to explain business cycle changes. Or it can be combined with the goods productivity shock to explain larger wage and output changes than when there is only the human capital productivity change by itself. But only the human capital productivity change can account for the employment changes, just as only the time endowment changes in the exogenous growth model could account for the employment changes. The difference is that now the time endowment change occurs endogenously as the human capital productivity is changed.

The nature of shocks rather than simple comparative statics is discussed. Then the chapter compares how output growth is accounted for when there is endogenous growth versus exogenous growth. Following this is an application of the same comparative statics to explain trends with the endogenous growth model. The goods productivity factor cannot explain growth rate trends because it does not affect the growth rate. However, the slowly rising growth rate from pre-industrial revolution times in western economies to the higher growth rates of today can be explained by a slightly rising trend in the human capital productivity factor. The same slightly rising trend in human capital productivity also can simultaneously explain rising education levels and gradually shrinking hours worked per week, which again cannot be explained by the goods productivity factor.

13.1.1 Building on the last chapters

The chapter uses the baseline Example 12.2 of the last chapter for the comparative static exercises in Examples 13.1 and 13.2. And the same methodology for solving the endogenous growth economy as is described in the last chapter's Appendix A12 is used in this chapter's examples. Therefore it directly extends the endogenous growth model that is formulated in the last chapter to apply it to describe business cycles and economic trends.

The application of the last chapter methodology to business cycles through comparative statics is similar to what is done in Chapters 3, 6, and 9. Chapter 3 takes the labour–leisure economy of Chapter 2 and then uses comparative statics to explain business cycles. Chapter 6 takes the two-period intertemporal economy introduced in Chapter 5 to explain business cycles again using comparative statics. Chapter 3 combines comparative static changes in goods productivity and the time endowment. The Chapter 6 business cycle application combines comparative static changes in goods productivity and in the current income endowment. In Chapter 9, the dynamic zero-growth model developed in Chapter 8 is applied again to explain business cycles using a combination of comparative static changes in goods productivity and the time endowment.

In this chapter the comparative static changes used to explain the business cycle are most directly similar to Chapters 3 and 9. But now rather than requiring a combination of goods productivity and time endowment changes, only the change in human capital investment productivity is essential to explain the business cycle. But it can be combined with the goods sector productivity change as well. The time endowment is now changed endogenously when the human capital productivity is changed, which contrasts to the exogenous change in the time endowment in Chapters 3 and 9. The result is that here the business cycle is explained by changing only the goods and human capital sectoral productivities.

13.1.2 Learning objective

Seeing the same type of comparative static analysis with endogenous growth allows for an understanding of how to use the dynamic model to try to improve upon a basic explanation of business cycles. This allows realisation that reliance on the exogenous time endowment change in Chapter 9 is replaced here by a change in the human capital sector productivity, which in turn causes an endogenous change in the time for labour and leisure.

Another challenge is to see the intuition of how a change in the human capital sector can be plausible. A rising productivity in that sector occurs as people shift into the sector while leaving the goods production sector, during an economic contraction. And conversely as an economic expansion occurs, people leaving the human capital, or 'education' sector, cause less productivity in the human capital sector. This intuition is important but it lies outside of the model, in that the comparative statics simply change sectoral productivities in an exogenous fashion, without explaining why they occur.

The other expansion of intuition is to apply the endogenous growth model to understanding long term trends. A slight upward trend in human capital productivity allows for several fundamental long term trends to be explained that otherwise elude explanation. The simultaneous business cycle and long term trend power of the chapter's analysis gives credence to the endogenous growth approach.

13.1.3 Who made it happen?

Nobel Laureate (1996) Robert E. Lucas Jr. in 1977 set an agenda for business cycles by stressing that this means understanding how main variables of the aggregate economy move together during economic expansions and contractions; in doing so he began the list of stylised facts that the business cycle should explain, just as Solow did for growth theory. Lucas set the standard for formulating such a model, following a 1975 paper on 'An Equilibrium Model of the Business Cycle', which suggested specifying changes in the money supply as a key for explaining cycles; this monetary approach extended the view of Friedman (1971).

However, instead of a monetary approach Kydland and Prescott (1982) and Long and Plosser (1983) used changes in the goods productivity factor as the main effect. This approach exploded open the research in business cycle theory, which to this day has not abated. Finn E. Kydland and Edward C. Prescott shared the 2004 Nobel prize specifically for this work. By modifying Lucas's approach, they at the same time built upon Slutsky's (1937) work showing that random shocks can give rise to cycles that look like business cycle fluctuations.

The real business cycle theory also led to the beginning of the new Keynesian approach of utilising this same model, but modified by adding in price rigidities and monopoly power following Calvo (1983) and Dixit and Stiglitz (1977) (see also Romer, 1993, 2006, and Blanchard and Fischer, 1989). According to Lucas (2005), wage rigidity was also in the first 1978 version of the Kydland and Prescott paper but later dropped from the published 1982 version. The result is a broad macroeconomic focus on dynamic general equilibrium models. As Lucas reflected in 2005:

> I call the conclusion that postwar US business cycles were mainly real in origin a discovery, but not because everyone working on business cycles at the time agreed with it. In fact, we all thought that there must be some other way to interpret Ed and Finn's results. Ours was a generation that learned economics in the shadow of the 1930s, and we were sure that a capitalist economy needed a lot of centralized direction in order to do a decent job of utilizing resources. But over the two decades since it appeared, every aspect of this paper has been gone over in detail, dozens of variations in the model have been explored indeed, many improvements have been found – and this central substantive finding has stood up.

Lucas developed the endogenous growth model in 1988 as an extension of the production function of the real business cycle approach. The chapter here combines the Kydland and Prescott goods productivity approach with the human capital productivity in the Lucas (1988) approach. This combination looks to explain both cycles and growth trends.

13.2 Business cycles with endogenous growth

The same factors that explain the business cycles within endogenous growth also explain long term economic trends, making the endogenous growth extension of the baseline dynamic model attractive. The central comparative static exercises used in Chapters 3 and 9 to explain the business cycle can be used similarly within endogenous growth but with one significant modification. Now the time endowment change is not an exogenous change in T_t but rather an endogenous change in the time left for work and leisure that arises from a change in the productivity parameter of the human capital sector, A_H.

A change in A_H causes time spent in human capital accumulation l_{Ht} to change thereby inducing an endogenous change in the time left over, T_t. The change in A_H is responsible for the change in employment that is crucial in explaining a business cycle. And a change in A_H causes a change in the consumption to output ratio in a direction consistent with evidence. This offers to help resolve a central puzzle concerning the change in the consumption to output ratio.

A rise in A_G still has no effect on the consumption to output ratio, the growth rate g, or the employment level. But a change in A_G causes a change in the wage rate, the capital stock and in aggregate output, in ways central to explaining business cycles.

13.3 Goods sector productivity increase

Using the endogenous growth baseline model of Chapter 12, consider how a change in goods sector productivity affects the AS–AD curves. Start from the baseline calibration of Example 12.1. If the goods sector productivity $A_G = 0.28224$ is increased, and no other parameters are changed, then there is no effect on growth at all in the stationary state. The real interest rate, and so the growth rate, is determined independently of the goods sector productivity level A_G. But the state variable, in terms of $\frac{k_t}{h_t}$, is affected.

Just as was the case with a productivity increase in the exogenous growth baseline model of Chapter 8, the AD curve is affected only from the change in the state variable $\frac{k_t}{h_t}$. And also as in the exogenous growth dynamic model, the AS curve is affected both by change in A_G directly and by the change in the state variable $\frac{k_t}{h_t}$.

13.3.1 Example 13.1

Assume the same model as in Example 12.1. The inverted AS–AD equations as derived in Chapter 12 in equations (12.26) and (12.29) are

$$\frac{1}{w_t} = \frac{1 - \frac{g+\delta_H}{A_H}}{\frac{y_t^d}{h_t}\left(1+\alpha\right) - \frac{k_t}{h_t}\left[\rho\left(1+g\right) + (g+\delta_k)\left(1+\alpha\right)\right]}, \tag{13.1}$$

$$\frac{1}{w_t} = \frac{1}{\gamma A_G}\left(\frac{h_t}{A_G k_t}\right)^{\frac{1-\gamma}{\gamma}}\left(\frac{y_t}{h_t}\right)^{\frac{1-\gamma}{\gamma}}. \tag{13.2}$$

The assumed parameters of Example 12.1 are $\alpha = 1$, $A_h = 0.189$, $\delta_k = 0.05$, $\delta_h = 0.015$, $\beta = \frac{1}{1+\rho} = 0.95$, $\rho = \frac{1}{0.95} - 1 = 0.0526$, $A_G = 0.28224$. The growth rate is $g = 0.02$ with this calibration, and $\frac{k}{h} = 1.0$. And h_t is normalised to $h_t = 1$. Suppose A_G increases by 5% from 0.28224 to $0.28224\left(1.05\right) = 0.29635$.

Appendix A12 of Chapter 12 shows that the growth rate g, the labour employment, and the real interest rate are all independent of A_G and so do not change. This means the new $\frac{k}{h}$ can be computed directly from the marginal product of capital: $r = \left(1 - \gamma\right) A_G \left(\frac{k_t}{h_t l_t}\right)^{-\gamma}$. Given that r_t and l_t do not change, the change in A_G alone causes $\frac{k}{h}$ to rise to $\frac{k}{h} = \left(\frac{(1-\gamma)A_G}{r}\right)^{\frac{1}{\gamma}} l = \left(\frac{2(0.29635)}{3(0.12368)}\right)^3 \left(0.28405\right) = 1.1578$, an increase of 15.8%.

Similarly, given the new $\frac{k}{h}$, and that employment does not change, the wage rate can be calculated to rise to $w = \gamma A_G \left(\frac{k_t}{h_t l_t}\right)^{1-\gamma} = \frac{1}{3}\left(0.29635\right)\left(0.28405\right)^{\frac{-2}{3}}\left(1.1578\right)^{\frac{2}{3}} = 0.25206$ from 0.21772 in the baseline case, which is a fractional increase of $\frac{0.25206 - 0.21772}{0.21772}$

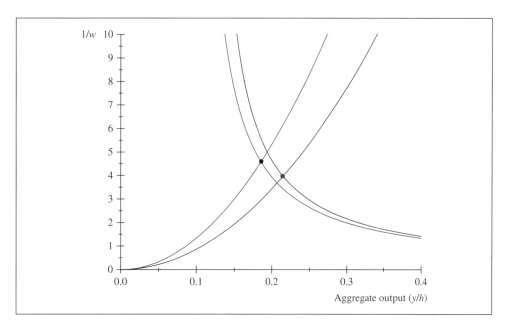

Figure 13.1 *AS–AD* with human capital and endogenous growth in Example 13.1

$= 0.15773$, or 15.8%. And $\frac{1}{w_t}$ falls from $\frac{1}{0.21772} = 4.5931$ to $\frac{1}{0.25207} = 3.9672$. These facts can be seen in the goods and labour market equilibria.

For the goods market, the *AS–AD* equations in calibrated form are

$$\frac{1}{w_t} = \frac{\left(1 - \frac{0.02+0.015}{0.189}\right)}{y_t^d \left(1+1\right) - 1.1578 \left((0.0526)\left(1+0.02\right) + \left(0.07\right)\left(2\right)\right)}; \tag{13.3}$$

$$\frac{1}{w_t} = \frac{3}{0.29635} \left(\frac{1}{(0.29635)\,1.1578}\right)^2 \left(y_t^s\right)^2. \tag{13.4}$$

The graph of equations (13.3) and (13.4) is given in Figure 13.1, with the baseline calibration of Example 12.1 given in blue, and the new equilibrium with the higher A_G given in black. Both *AS* and *AD* shift out, but *AS* shifts out by more than *AD*, causing the relative price of output, $\frac{1}{w_t}$, to fall. Output rises and the real wage rises. This is just as occurs in the standard dynamic model of Chapters 8 and 11, which makes sense in that the growth rate is not affected here while it is constant in Chapters 8 and 11.

13.3.2 Equilibrium wage

The excess demand is again given by $Y(w_t) = y_t^d - y_t^s$, as in equation (12.30), with the revised $Y(w_t)$ for the now higher A_G; with $\alpha = 1$, $A_h = 0.189$, $\delta_k = 0.05$, $\delta_h = 0.015$, $\beta = \frac{1}{1+\rho} = 0.95$, $\rho = \frac{1}{0.95} - 1 = 0.0526$, $g = 0.020$, $A_G = 0.296$ and $k_t = 1.1578$, the calibrated $Y(w_t) = 0$ function is

$$0 = Y(w_t)$$

$$= \frac{\left(w_t \left(1 - \frac{0.02+0.015}{0.189}\right) + 1.1578 \left(\left(\frac{1}{0.95} - 1\right)\left(1+0.02\right) + \left(0.02+0.05\right)\left(1+1\right)\right)\right)}{1+1}$$

$$- 0.29635 \left(\frac{0.29635}{3\,(w_t)}\right)^{0.5} (1.1578).$$

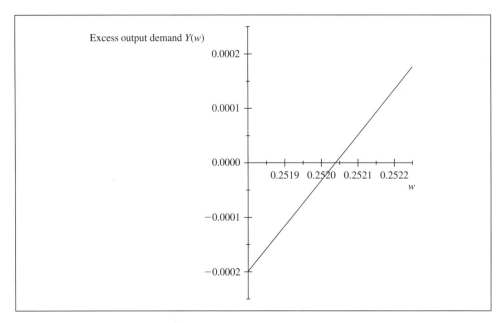

Figure 13.2 Excess output demand in endogenous growth with goods productivity increase in Example 13.1

Figure 13.2 graphs the excess output demand and illustrates how the wage rate has risen to 0.25205, from 0.21772, the same 15.8% increase as the capital stock k_t. The excess demand is positive for higher wage rates, and lower $\frac{1}{w_t}$, and excess demand is negative for lower wage rates, and higher $\frac{1}{w_t}$.

The equal increase in the wage rate and in the capital stock was also found in the baseline dynamic model with exogenous growth in Chapter 8 when A_G was increased.

13.3.3 Consumption and output

Consumption is now equal to

$$c_t^d = \frac{1}{1+1}\left(0.25206\left(1 - \frac{0.020+0.015}{0.189}\right) + (1.1578)(0.0526)(1+0.020)\right) = 0.13375,$$

and output is

$$y_t^d = \frac{\left(0.25206\left(1 - \frac{0.02+0.015}{0.189}\right) + (1.1578)(0.0526(1+0.02) + (0.02+0.05)(1+1))\right)}{1+1},$$

$$= 0.21480.$$

The consumption to output ratio is $\frac{c_t^d}{y_t^d} = \frac{0.13375}{0.21480} = 0.62267$, unchanged from the baseline value of 0.6227. Finding the same consumption to output ratio is again the same result as when A_G was increased in Chapter 8 with exogenous growth.

13.3.4 Labour market

Not surprisingly, the labour market also shows the same effects of an A_G increase as in the exogenous growth model of Chapter 8: no change in employment. The labour market

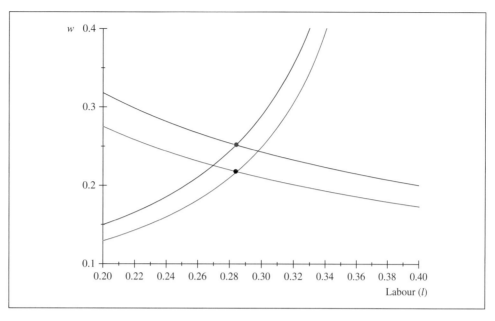

Figure 13.3 Labour market with endogenous growth and a 5% increase in A_G in Example 13.1

supply and demand equations, in calibrated form from equations (12.41) and (12.42), are now

$$w_t = \frac{(1.1578)\,(0.0526)\,(1+0.02)}{1-(1+1)\,l_t^s - \frac{(1+1)(0.02+0.015)}{0.189(1+1)}}; \tag{13.5}$$

$$w_t = \frac{0.296\,\left((1.1578)\right)^{\frac{2}{3}}}{3} \frac{}{\left(l_t^d\right)^{\frac{2}{3}}}. \tag{13.6}$$

Graphing the labour market, Figure 13.3 shows the baseline endogenous growth equilibrium supply and demand for labour in blue, and the new equilibrium in black.

The supply and demand for labour both shift up so that there is no change in employment, as in Chapters 2, 3, and 9 when A_G is increased in those simpler models.

The excess labour demand function $L(w_t) = 0$, as modified from equation (12.46) for the 5% increase in A_G, is given as

$$0 = L(w) = \left(\frac{0.29635}{3\,(0.25206)}\right)^{1.5} (1.1578)$$

$$- \left(1 - \frac{1}{1+1}\left(1+(1.1578)\frac{\left(\frac{1}{0.95}-1\right)(1+0.02)}{0.25206}\right) - \frac{0.02+0.015}{0.189\,(1+1)}\right). \tag{13.7}$$

Figure 13.4 graphs the excess demand and shows the wage rate to be 0.252, as in the goods market.

13.3.5 General equilibrium

The new general equilibrium in Example 13.1 with the goods productivity increase can be shown in input and output space. Following the baseline endogenous growth of

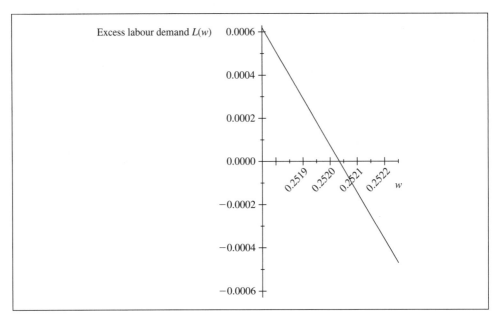

Figure 13.4 Excess demand and the real wage when A_G increases 5% in Example 13.1

Chapter 12, with $h_t = 1$, the isocost line has a higher output level and wage rate:

$$y_t = w_t l_t h_t + r_t k_t,$$

$$\frac{0.21480}{h_t} = \left(0.25206\right) l_t + \left(0.1237\right) \frac{k_t}{h_t},$$

$$\frac{k_t}{h_t} = \frac{0.21480}{0.1237\left(1\right)} - \frac{\left(0.25206\right) l_t}{0.1237}. \tag{13.8}$$

The isoquant curve has a higher output level and A_G:

$$y_t^s = A_G \left(l_t^d h_t\right)^{\gamma} \left(k_t\right)^{1-\gamma},$$

$$\frac{0.21480}{h_t} = \left(0.29635\right) \left(l_t^d\right)^{\frac{1}{3}} \left(\frac{k_t}{h_t}\right)^{\frac{2}{3}};$$

$$\frac{k_t}{h_t} = \left(\frac{0.21480}{\left(0.29635\right) \left(l_t^d\right)^{\frac{1}{3}}}\right)^{\frac{3}{2}} = \frac{\left(\frac{0.21480}{0.29635}\right)^{\frac{3}{2}}}{\left(l_t^d\right)^{\frac{1}{2}}}. \tag{13.9}$$

The factor input ratio is higher at

$$\frac{k_t}{h_t l_t} = \frac{1.1578}{0.28405} = 4.076. \tag{13.10}$$

Figure 13.5 graphs equations (13.8), (13.9) and (13.10) with the new equilibrium in the blue isoquant, the dashed blue isocost, and the dotted blue input ratio, along with the baseline Example 12.1 in black, dashed black and dotted black. The isocost and isoquant shift up and the factor input ratio pivots upwards, while the equilibrium labour employment stays the same.

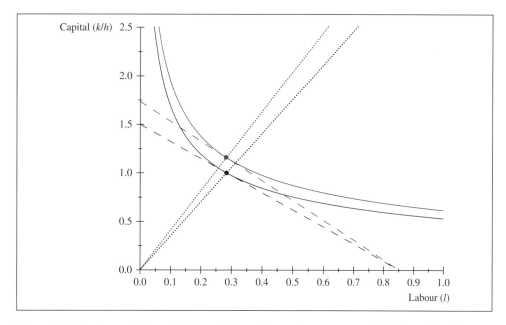

Figure 13.5 Factor market equilibrium with baseline endogenous growth in Example 13.1

For goods and leisure in general equilibrium, output production has a higher A_G and a higher capital k_t:

$$c_t^d = y_t^s - i_t = A_G \left(l_t^d h_t\right)^{\gamma} \left(k_t\right)^{1-\gamma} - (g + \delta_k) k_t,$$

$$\frac{c_t^d}{h_t} = (0.29635) \left(l_t^d\right)^{\frac{1}{3}} (1.1578)^{\frac{2}{3}} - (0.02 + 0.05)(1.1578). \tag{13.11}$$

For utility, consumption has risen, while time allocations are all the same. The level curve is

$$u = \ln c_t^d + \alpha \ln x_t = \ln c_t + \alpha \ln \left(1 - l_{Ht} - l_t^s\right),$$
$$-2.6448 = \ln 0.13375 + 1 \ln (0.531),$$
$$-2.6448 = \ln c_t^d + \ln \left(T_t - l_t^s\right),$$
$$\frac{c_t^d}{h_t} = \frac{e^{-2.6448}}{(1)\left(1 - 0.18526 - l_t^s\right)}. \tag{13.12}$$

The equilibrium budget line has a higher wage rate:

$$c_t^d = w_t l_t^s h_t + \rho \left(1 + g\right) k_t^s,$$
$$\frac{c_t^d}{h_t} = (0.25206) l_t^s + 0.052632 (1 + 0.02)(1.1578). \tag{13.13}$$

Figure 13.6 graphs the new production function, budget line, and the utility level curve, of equations (13.11), (13.12) and (13.13), in blue, dashed blue and dotted blue, while also graphing the baseline endogenous growth model of Example 13.1, in black, dashed black and dotted black. The new production function has shifted upwards, as have utility and the budget line, while labour stays the same and consumption rises.

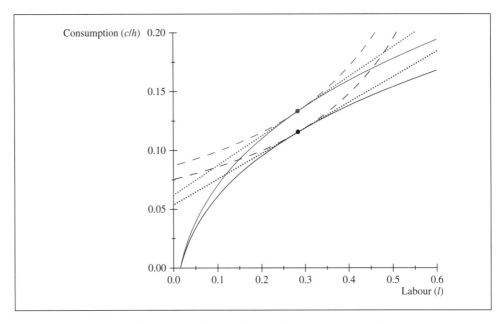

Figure 13.6 General equilibrium goods and labour with goods productivity increase in Example 13.1

13.4 Human capital sector productivity increase

An increase in A_H, the productivity in producing human capital, causes the growth rate to increase. It also causes the time spent in human capital investment to increase. This has an effect similar to a decrease in the time endowment found in Chapters 2, 3, 8 and 9. The employment goes down, as in those earlier simpler models. But now besides endogenising the decrease in the time endowed for labour and leisure, that was exogenous in earlier chapters, and besides also endogenising the growth rate, there is another marked effect. The consumption to output ratio falls. This is a new dimension that breaks the fixity of the consumption to output ratio found in the exogenous growth baseline dynamic model, when either the exogenous time endowment T or the goods productivity A_G is changed.

13.4.1 Example 13.2

Consider the baseline calibration with the only change from Examples 12.1 and 13.1 being a 5% increase in A_H from 0.189 to $(0.189)(1.05) = 0.2$. The other parameters are $\alpha = 1$, $\delta_k = 0.05$, $\delta_h = 0.015$, $\beta = \frac{1}{1+\rho} = 0.95$, $\rho = \frac{1}{0.95} - 1 = 0.0526$, $A_G = 0.28224$.

The A_H enters the general solution equation (12.98) of Appendix A12 in two places, and these two values need to be changed to find the new solution. Using the calibrated version of the solution equation for excess output demand, $L(g) = 0$ in equation (12.99) of Appendix A12, the revised equation for g is

$$L(g) = (0.95)\left((0.2) - g + 0.015\right)\left(1 + g + (0.95)(0.05 - 1)\right)^{\frac{1}{3}}$$
$$+ (0.95)(1 + g)(1 - (0.95))^{\frac{2}{3}}\left[(0.0526)(1 + g) + (g + 0.05)(2)\right]$$
$$-2(1 + g)(1 - (0.95))\left[1 + g + (0.95)(0.05 - 1)\right] = 0. \tag{13.14}$$

The solution for g is found where the function in equation (13.14) equals zero, as graphed in Figure 13.7. It shows the equilibrium occurs at $g = 0.0333$.

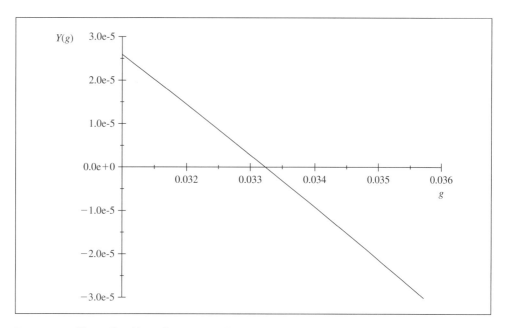

Figure 13.7 Normalised baseline excess demand as a function of *g* in Example 13.2

Alternatively, instead of graphing the solution, the quadratic solution equation for g can be used to determine g directly. Writing the solution equation as $Ag^2 + Bg + C = 0$, with the solution of equation (12.104), the terms A, B, and C are given by equations (12.101) to (12.103) and equal:

Quadratic term: $A = -0.3517$,

Linear term: $B = -0.0122$,

Constant term: $C = 0.00079521$,

with the growth rate given by $g = 0.0333$.

The change in g causes changes in all of the other variables. Other variables in equilibrium are $l_H = \frac{g + \delta_H}{A_H} = \frac{0.95(1+0.1377-0.05)-1+0.015}{0.2} = 0.242$, $l = \frac{(0.1377+(1-0.05))(1-0.95)}{0.2} = 0.27193$, $x = 0.486$, and an interest rate of $r = 0.1377$, or 13.77%. The state variable is $\frac{k}{h} = \left(\frac{(1-\gamma)A_G}{r}\right)^{\frac{1}{\gamma}} l = \left(\frac{(1-0.3333)(0.28224)}{0.1377}\right)^{\frac{1}{0.3333}} (0.27193) = 0.694$. This state variable falls since the interest rises and the labour employed in the goods sector both fall. With h_t normalised to 1, then $k_t = 0.694$. This is a substantial fall of 31% as compared to only a 16% rise in $\frac{k}{h}$ when A_G was increased by 5%.

This makes the equilibrium wage rate fall to $w = \frac{1}{3}(0.28224)(0.27193)^{\frac{-2}{3}}(0.694)^{\frac{2}{3}} = 0.1757$; and $\frac{1}{w_t} = \frac{1}{0.1757} = 5.69$. The aggregate output falls.

The *AS–AD* graphs can be seen when productivity increases. The *AS–AD* equations become

$$\frac{1}{w_t} = \frac{\left(1 - \frac{0.0333+0.015}{0.2}\right)}{y_t^d (1+1) - 0.694\left((0.0526)(1+0.0333) + (0.0833)(2)\right)}; \tag{13.15}$$

$$\frac{1}{w_t} = \frac{3}{0.28224}\left(\frac{1}{(0.28224)\,0.694}\right)^2 (y_t^s)^2. \tag{13.16}$$

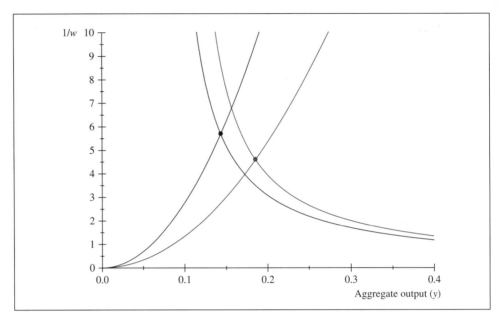

Figure 13.8 *AS–AD* with endogenous growth and a 5% increase in A_H in Example 13.2

Figure 13.8 graphs equations (13.15) and (13.16) in black along with the baseline of Example 12.1 in blue.

The *AS* and *AD* curves shift back with a higher relative price $\frac{1}{w_t}$ resulting. The increase in A_H causes an increase in the time spent in human capital accumulation. This leaves less time for the traditional activities of labour in the goods sector and of leisure. This is similar to when the time endowment for goods labour and leisure in Chapters 2 and 8 are decreased: aggregate output and the equilibrium goods sector labour both fall.

13.4.2 Equilibrium wage

The excess demand $Y(w_t) = y_t^d - y_t^s$ in the new equilibrium, with $A_h = 0.20$, $\alpha = 1$, $\delta_k = 0.05$, $\delta_h = 0.015$, $\beta = \frac{1}{1+\rho} = 0.95$, $\rho = \frac{1}{0.95} - 1 = 0.0526$, $A_G = 0.28224$, $k_t = 0.694$ and $g = 0.0333$, is

$$0 = Y(w_t)$$
$$= \frac{\left(w_t\left(1 - \frac{0.0333 + 0.015}{0.2}\right) + 0.694\left(0.0526\left(1 + 0.0333\right) + \left(0.0333 + 0.05\right)\left(1 + 1\right)\right)\right)}{1+1}$$
$$- 0.28224\left(\frac{0.28224}{3w_t}\right)^{0.5}(0.694).$$

Figure 13.9 shows that the wage rate has fallen to 0.1757 from the baseline endogenous growth wage rate of 0.2177, a fractional increase of $\frac{0.1757 - 0.21772}{0.2177} = -0.19302$, or a 19.3% decrease.

Now the wage rate has fallen, as during a recession. This is a different result from the Chapter 8 baseline dynamic exogenous growth model, in which the wage rate stays the same when the time endowment T is changed. Further, when the time endowment goes down in the Chapters 2 and 3 model, the wage rate rises somewhat as the labour supply

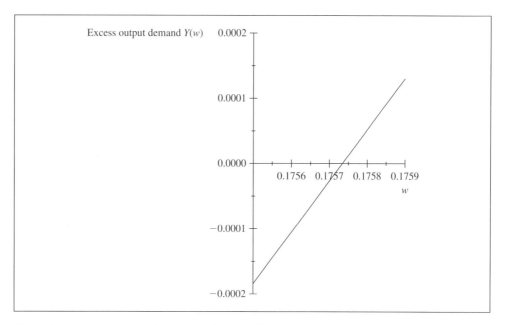

Figure 13.9 Excess output demand and the equilibrium wage when A_H rises by 5% in Example 13.2

shifts back. But here, when the A_H goes up and the remaining time endowment for work and leisure of $T - l_{Ht}$ goes down, the wage rate falls. Looking at the labour market will clarify this, in combination with the consumption to output ratio.

13.4.3 Consumption and output

Consumption is now equal to

$$c_t^d = \frac{1}{1+1}\left(0.1757\left(1 - \frac{0.0333 + 0.015}{0.2}\right) + (0.694)(0.0526)(1 + 0.0333)\right) = 0.08549,$$

and output is

$$y_t^d = \frac{\left(0.1757\left(1 - \frac{0.0333 + 0.015}{0.2}\right) + 0.694\left(0.0526(1 + 0.0333) + (0.0333 + 0.05)(1 + 1)\right)\right)}{1 + 1},$$

$$= 0.1433.$$

Both consumption and output fall and the consumption to output ratio is $\frac{c_t^d}{y_t^d} = \frac{0.08549}{0.1433} = 0.5966$, which is a fall from 0.623 in the baseline. This result differs from the baseline dynamic model in that the time endowment T change causes no change in the consumption to output ratio.

13.4.4 Labour market

For the labour market, the employment does change when A_H increases. In particular labour falls from the baseline endogenous growth value of 0.28405 to a lower value of 0.27193. This is a fractional decrease of $\frac{0.28405 - 0.27193}{0.28405} = 0.04267$, or 4.3%. In terms of

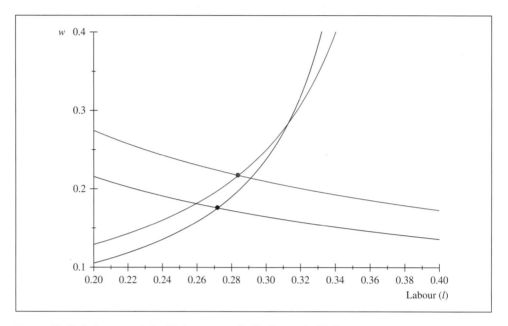

Figure 13.10 Labour market with human capital in Example 13.2

the supply and demand for labour, the new calibrated equations are

$$w_t = \frac{(0.694)(0.0526)(1+0.0333)}{1-(1+1)\,l_t^s - \frac{(0.0333+0.015)}{0.20}}; \tag{13.17}$$

$$w_t = \frac{0.28224}{3}\frac{\left((0.694)\right)^{\frac{2}{3}}}{\left(l_t^d\right)^{\frac{2}{3}}}. \tag{13.18}$$

Figure 13.10 graphs these equations in black along with the baseline supply and demand for labour of Example 12.1 in blue.

The supply and demand for labour both shift down, but do so such that the employment falls. The labour supply change is more of a pivot that makes it steeper at every level of employment. This contrasts with the experiment of decreasing the time endowment in Chapters 2, 3 and 9 in that the labour supply shifts back there while here it actually pivots outwards in the relevant range. Thus while the employment falls in Chapters 2, 3 and 9 with a time endowment decrease and also falls here with an A_H increase, which creates a $T - l_{Ht}$ decrease, the effect of the wage rate ends up being different. There is no effect in Chapters 2, 3 and 9, but here the wage rate falls because of the labour demand shifting back by more than the labour supply shifts out.

The fall in the real wage, in the consumption level, in the output level and in the employment level are all typical of what happens in an economic downturn.

13.4.5 General equilibrium

The general equilibrium with a human capital investment productivity increase finds more changes than when there is a goods productivity shift. The isocost line has a lower output level and wage rate:

$$y_t^s = w_t l_t^d h_t + r_t k_t,$$

$$\frac{0.1433}{h_t} = (0.1757) l_t^d + (0.1377) \frac{k_t}{h_t},$$

$$\frac{k_t}{h_t} = \frac{0.1433}{0.1377(1)} - \frac{(0.1757) l_t^d}{0.1377}. \tag{13.19}$$

The isoquant curve has a lower output level:

$$y_t^s = A_G \left(l_t^d h_t\right)^\gamma \left(k_t\right)^{1-\gamma},$$

$$0.1433 = (0.28224) \left(l_t^d h_t\right)^{\frac{1}{3}} \left(k_t\right)^{\frac{2}{3}};$$

$$\frac{k_t}{h_t} = \left(\frac{0.1433}{(0.28224)(1)\left(l_t^d\right)^{\frac{1}{3}}}\right)^{\frac{3}{2}} = \frac{\left(\frac{0.1433}{(0.28224)h_t}\right)^{\frac{3}{2}}}{\left(l_t^d\right)^{\frac{1}{2}}}. \tag{13.20}$$

The factor input ratio is lower at

$$\frac{k_t}{h_t l_t^d} = \frac{0.694}{0.27193} = 2.5521. \tag{13.21}$$

Figure 13.11 graphs with $h_t = 1$ the new equilibrium of equations (13.19), (13.20) and (13.21) again with the blue isoquant, the dashed blue isocost, and the dotted blue input ratio, along with the baseline of Example 12.1 in black, dashed black, and dotted black.

The isocost pivots down, the isoquant shifts down and the factor input ratio pivots downwards. Equilibrium labour employment falls 4.3%.

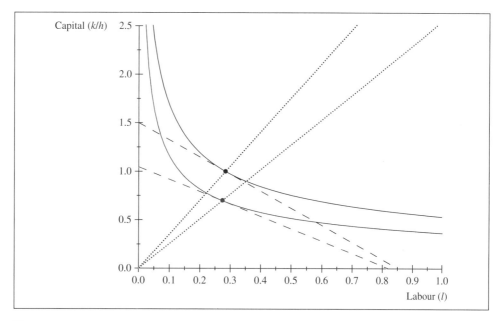

Figure 13.11 Factor market equilibrium with human capital productivity increase in Example 13.2

For goods and leisure in general equilibrium, output production has a higher A_G and a higher capital k_t:

$$c_t^d = y_t^s - i_t = A_G \left(l_t^d h_t\right)^\gamma \left(k_t\right)^{1-\gamma} - \left(g + \delta_k\right)k_t,$$

$$\frac{c_t^d}{h_t} = (0.28224)\left(l_t^d\right)^{\frac{1}{3}}(0.694)^{\frac{2}{3}} - (0.0333 + 0.05)(0.694). \qquad (13.22)$$

For utility, consumption has risen, while time allocations are all the same. The level curve is

$$u = \ln c_t^d + \alpha \ln x_t = \ln c_t + \alpha \ln \left(1 - l_{Ht} - l_t^s\right),$$
$$-3.1809 = \ln 0.08549 + 1\ln(0.486),$$
$$-3.1809 = \ln c_t^d + \ln \left(T_t - l_t^s\right),$$
$$c_t^d = \frac{e^{-3.1809}}{\left(1 - 0.242 - l_t^s\right)}. \qquad (13.23)$$

The equilibrium budget line has a higher wage rate:

$$c_t^d = w_t l_t^s h_t + \rho \left(1 + g\right) k_t^s,$$

$$\frac{c_t^d}{h_t} = (0.1757)\, l_t^s + 0.052632\,(1 + 0.0333)\,(0.694). \qquad (13.24)$$

Figure 13.12 graphs the new production function, budget line, and the utility level curve, of equations (13.22), (13.23) and (13.24), in blue, dashed blue and dotted blue, with the baseline endogenous growth model of Example 12.1 in black, dashed black and dotted black.

The new production function has shifted down, as have utility and the budget line, while labour employment falls. The budget line has a flatter slope in equilibrium as the input price ratio $\frac{w_t}{r_t} = \frac{0.1757}{0.1377} = 1.2760$ has fallen from the baseline of $\frac{w_t}{r_t} = \frac{0.21772}{0.1237} = 1.7601$ while the physical capital to human capital ratio $\frac{k_t}{h_t}$, and the physical capital to effective labour ratio $\frac{k_t}{h_t l_t}$, have also fallen.

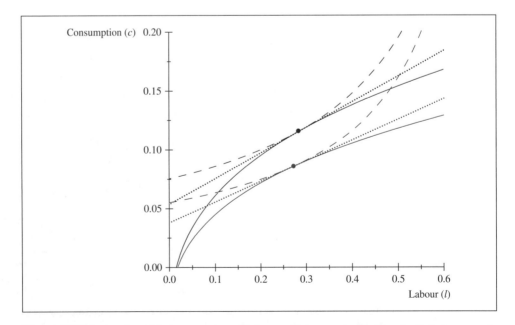

Figure 13.12 General equilibrium goods and labour with human capital productivity increase in Example 13.2

13.5 Economic expansion and contraction

Endogenous growth comparative static changes in the goods sector and human capital sector productivities, A_G and A_H, can be used to provide an explanation of business cycles that improves upon the exogenous growth dynamic model. For an expansion, in the exogenous growth dynamic model the comparative static increase in A_G causes the wage and output but not employment to rise. Therefore the change in the time endowment T was added. An increase in T causes employment to rise but the wage rate to stay unchanged. Combining these two comparative statics allows for the basic facts of the business cycle to be replicated of a rising output, employment and wage rate. However the consumption to output ratio does not change from either a change in A_G or in T. For a contraction decreases in A_G and T cause output, employment and the wage rate to fall.

In endogenous growth, the comparative statics are different. Here a change in A_H causes an endogenous change in time left for goods and leisure. If A_H goes down, then time in human capital investment, l_{Ht}, goes down as well. Then the remaining time T_t left for goods and leisure goes up. This expansion in T_t leads to an increase in $\frac{k_t}{h_t}$ and an increase in both the supply and demand for goods and labour. Because the shift out in the demand for labour is bigger than the shift out in the supply of labour, and similarly because the shift out in the supply of goods is bigger than the shift out in demand for goods, the real wage rises. And employment and output also rise. Therefore this explains the salient facts of an expansion even without any other comparative static change.

Conversely, if A_H goes up, then time in human capital investment also rises. This decreases T_t and $\frac{k_t}{h_t}$, and the supply and demand for both goods and labour shift back, with the real wage falling. Again these are the main facts we associate with a recession.

It could be that bigger changes in the wage rate and in the output level are wanted, and then a comparative static change in A_G could be combined with a comparative static change in A_H. An increase in A_G, while A_H also falls, would produce increases in output and in the real wage from each the increase in A_G and the decrease in A_H. And in a contraction, a decrease in A_G combined with an increase in A_H would make the decrease in output and the real wage even bigger than from just increasing A_H.

13.5.1 Consumption–output puzzle

Explaining business cycles with just changes in A_H, or in combination with A_G, is attractive in its simplicity. One important part of this explanation is that another fact is explained with endogenous growth that is not explained with exogenous growth. The consumption to output ratio falls empirically in an expansion and to rises in a contraction. But the problem is in the standard dynamic models, with the business cycle generated from changes in A_G, that the fall in the consumption–output ratio is larger than what appears in the data. The fact that changes in A_G cannot produce this change in the exogenous or endogenous growth model is sometimes known as the consumption–output puzzle. And it is also said that consumption is too smooth in the standard models when A_G changes, another way of looking at this puzzle.

By adding not just a comparative static change in A_G, but a random shock to A_G, our dynamic model could be used to show that the consumption–output ratio falls. But it falls by more than in the data. However, restricting ourselves here to simpler comparative static analysis, there is no change in the consumption–output ratio at all with A_G changes. And it is this lack of change in the consumption–output ratio that is behind the result of a consumption–output ratio that falls too much when there is a stochastic A_G process within the model.

In contrast, the consumption–output ratio rises when A_H falls during an expansion. The increase in the consumption–output ratio, if extended to a stochastic version of the endogenous growth model, suggests that the consumption–output ratio would fall by less, thereby being able to be closer to the data. Such solutions to the consumption–output puzzle with endogenous growth have been reported in the literature, such as in a 2000 article by Maffezzoli in the international context.

13.5.2 Two-sector business cycle models

Hansen (1985) and Rogerson (1988) are well-known for showing how the standard exogenous growth dynamic model can be modified to allow for a change in employment. Alongside the internal labour margin, of how many hours to work, they introduce the external labour margin, of whether to enter the labour force or not. As a result of adding this external margin, changes in employment occur as during a business cycle. This is the same idea behind the exogenous change in the time endowment T within the baseline dynamic exogenous growth model, used in Chapter 9 to show changes in employment as during the business cycle.

An alternative approach to modelling changes to this external margin was taken in the early 1990s, in articles by Greenwood and Hercowitz (1991) and Benhabib *et al.* (1991). They allow for a second sector besides the goods sector. The second sector is called the non-market sector, or the household sector, while the goods sector is called the market sector. With this second sector, they explain changes in employment over the business cycle as occurring as labour flows from the goods sector to the household sector during an economic contraction, and back from the household non-market sector to the market goods sector during an economic expansion. This flow of labour between sectors is like a change in the external margin of participation of labour within each sector. Such a change in the labour within each sector is a normal general equilibrium result when there are two complementary competitive sectors and the relative prices within the economy change due to some change in the exogenous parameters, such as a change in A_G.

Explaining business cycles with the comparative statics of changing A_G and also a parameter similar to A_H is thereby originally found in these two-sector models of the business cycle. The idea is that labour and capital move into the market sector from the household sector as productivity in the market rises and productivity in the household sector falls. Employment rising in the market sector is the key fact of an expansion that cannot be captured well with just a market sector and changes in goods productivity. Similarly when the productivity falls in the market sector, and rises in the household sector, labour moves from the market sector to the household sector. Falling employment results as in an economic contraction.

Making the second sector one that produces human capital investment is a particular specification of what the household sector is actually producing, which a variety of researchers have pursued, such as Jones *et al.* (2005). Raising children, getting formal schooling, and taking care of family when retired are all forms of what can be considered human capital investment. This is the broader concept than just formal education. When people leave employment in the market sector, it is plausible that they then spend their time productively in such non-market activities.

The rise in A_H during a contraction is exogenously specified here, but it also can be interpreted in terms of the flow of labour in and out of the human capital investment sector. When labour leaves the market sector and starts working instead in the human capital sector, it may well bring more productivity to the human capital sector because of experience in the market sector. This is a way to think of why A_H rises during an economic contraction.

Similarly, when labour leaves the human capital investment activity and goes into the goods sector, it is reasonable to think that the productivity in the human capital sector may suffer as a result, so that A_H falls. This means that during an economic expansion, it is plausible that A_H could fall as postulated in the comparative statics.

By the same reasoning, with labour entering the goods production, or market, sector it is plausible to think that the productivity in the goods sector might increase, so that A_G rises. This would mean that A_G rises even as A_H falls during an economic expansion. And in reverse, A_G plausibly might fall when labour leaves the goods production sector, even as A_H rises. Then A_G would be falling when A_H is rising, during an economic contraction.

13.5.3 Cyclical change in growth rate

However when A_H falls during an expansion, the balanced path growth rate g also falls. This can appear to be contradictory because we associate expansions with increases in the growth rate and not decreases. However the business cycle facts do not show in general a high correlation between the actual growth rate and the level of output. It is typically much closer to zero than to one. The reason is that the growth rate of output starts falling in the early part of expansions, at the point at which the rise in output stops accelerating. And the output growth rate starts rising just as contractions are taking hold and the output starts decelerating its decrease. Therefore the comparative static of a fall in A_H and a fall in the growth rate can still be consistent with expansions taking place.

Another qualification to the comparative static explanation of business cycles is that some would argue that the economy never reaches a steady state equilibrium during a business cycle. Yet it is a first approximation to understand the nature of the basic changes during a business cycle, the rise and fall of output and employment, through comparative statics of the model. Even with a fully stochastic dynamic model, with A_G being stochastic in the exogenous growth models and also with A_H stochastic in endogenous growth models, the economy moves towards its stationary equilibrium each time there is a change in the parameters. The comparative static approach tells us that the A_G change is insufficient to explain business cycles, and that A_H changes help rectify this, in ways not inconsistent with fully stochastic models.

Specifying shocks within the model typically is done so that A_G gradually rises and then gradually falls. This process is abstracted from in our dynamic models without uncertainty by considering shifts up and down in productivity parameters, such as A_G and A_H. Explaining a business cycle this way means that on average the economy stays at the baseline calibration. But the productivity parameters shift up and then down, around the baseline value, so as to mimic the elements of the business cycle. To see how the productivity parameters gradually rise and fall with a stochastic specification, the next section shows how the shocks are specified so that productivity gradually rises and falls.

13.6 Shocks within a business cycle model

The way in which shocks affect the model in a way related to comparative static changes can be seen also by analysing the type of shocks that are actually specified in a fully dynamic baseline exogenous growth model. Let output be given as with a shock factor Z_t so that now

$$y_t = A_{Gt} Z_t \left(l_t\right)^\gamma \left(k_t\right)^{1-\gamma}.$$

When $Z_t = 1$, then there is no effect on output. If it rises above 1 or falls below 1 then it pushes output in a positive or negative direction. Meanwhile A_{Gt} can still trend upwards.

Technically, macroeconomic variables tend to be 'log-normally distributed', rather than normally distributed. So that means that if we take the log of y_t, then statistically it would be found to be normally distributed. Therefore consider defining the shock Z_t so that it is log-normally distributed. To do this, let

$$e^{z_t} \equiv Z_t, \tag{13.25}$$

where

$$z_t = \phi z_{t-1} + \varepsilon_t, \tag{13.26}$$

and where ϕ is called the persistence factor. It is between 0 and 1, but typically specified as very close to 1. This makes z_t change only slowly over time. The high value of ϕ, typically above 0.90, means that A_{Gt} does not move very much. Rather it gradually rises up, and gradually falls down, as the shocks ε_t accumulate up or down during an expansion or a contraction. Therefore, the gradual rise and fall in $A_{Gt}Z_t$ is not so different from a comparative static shift up in A_G and down in A_G. This can be seen more fully by examining the shocks ε_t in more detail.

The shock ε_t is normally distributed with zero mean. With this definition, then taking the log of the output involves a term with the $\ln Z_t$, and this equals just z_t, which is normally distributed since ε_t is normally distributed. So the $\ln y_t$ is normally distributed, and y_t is said to be log-normally distributed, as is consistent with data.

13.6.1 Example 13.3: Zero persistence

And at time 0, let $z_0 = 0$. Then $Z_0 = e^{z_0} = e^0 = 1$. So Z starts out at 1. Then say that from time 1 to 4 the following sequence of shocks occurs:

$\varepsilon_1 = 0.1$;
$\varepsilon_2 = 0.1$;
$\varepsilon_3 = 0.0$;
$\varepsilon_4 = -0.1$.

Consider that with zero persistence, then $\phi = 0$ and $z_t = \varepsilon_t$ by equation (13.26). So for the first period at time 1,

$$z_1 = \phi z_0 + \varepsilon_1 = (0)(0) + 0.1 = 0.1.$$

And in brief, $z_1 = \varepsilon_1$, $z_2 = \varepsilon_2$, $z_3 = \varepsilon_3$ and $z_4 = \varepsilon_4$. Given the same sequence of the ε shocks, the productivity shock would be in this case $Z_1 = e^{\varepsilon_1} = e^{0.1} = 1.1$, $Z_2 = e^{\varepsilon_2} = e^{0.1} = 1.1$, $Z_3 = e^{\varepsilon_3} = e^0 = 1$, $Z_4 = e^{\varepsilon_4} = e^{-0.1} = 0.90$. In sum,

$Z_0 = 1.0$;
$Z_1 = 1.1$;
$Z_2 = 1.1$;
$Z_3 = 1.0$;
$Z_4 = 0.90$.

The productivity shock would move directly in line with the shock 'innovation' ε. This would result in aggregate variable changes that are viewed as too sudden, with insufficient persistence relative to the movements seen in the data.

13.6.2 Example 13.4: Full persistence

Assume the shock structure, the same initial value and the same sequence of ε as in Example 13.3. But now assume full persistence whereby the factor ϕ is equal to 1 in equation (13.26). To see what happens to Z_t over time in this case, write out that at time 1

$$z_1 = \phi z_0 + \varepsilon_1 = (1)(0) + 0.1 = 0.1.$$

And it follows that

$$Z_1 = e^{z_1} = e^{0.1} = 1.1.$$

Thus there is a 10% increase in Z from time 0 to time 1. This is a 10% jump in goods productivity.

At time 2, with $z_1 = 0.1$, and by assumption $\varepsilon_2 = 0.1$, then it follows that the z shock at time 2 is given by

$$z_2 = z_1 + \varepsilon_2 = 0.1 + 0.1 = 0.2.$$

Then it must be that Z_2 is now $e^{0.2}$:

$$Z_2 = e^{z_2} = e^{0.2} = 1.22.$$

With $Z_2 = 1.22$, the goods productivity has risen by 22% from its initial position of $Z_0 = 1$.

At time 3, with z_2 given at 0.2, and with $\varepsilon_2 = 0$ by assumption, then

$$z_3 = z_2 + \varepsilon_3 = 0.2 + 0 = 0.2.$$

So the Z remains the same at $Z_3 = e^{z_3} = e^{0.2} = 1.22$. Goods productivity does not change.

At time 4, with z_3 given at 0.2 again, and with a negative shock assumed at $\varepsilon_4 = -0.1$, then

$$z_4 = z_3 + \varepsilon_4 = 0.2 - 0.1 = 0.1.$$

This means that productivity drops back down to 1.1, since $Z_4 = e^{z_4} = e^{0.1} = 1.1$. Now goods productivity has fallen from the last period's level of 1.22. In sum,

$$Z_0 = 1;$$
$$Z_1 = 1.1;$$
$$Z_2 = 1.22;$$
$$Z_3 = 1.22;$$
$$Z_4 = 1.1.$$

This is a much more gradual rise and fall in Z that is viewed as more consistent with the data.

13.6.3 Example 13.5: High degree of shock persistence

Again starting with Example 13.3, allow for a more typical shock specification by setting the persistence to be high but less than 100%. Let $\phi = 0.9$. Assume the same sequence of shocks and initial values. Then the following pattern results:

$$z_0 = 0;$$
$$z_1 = \phi z_0 + \varepsilon_1 = (0.9)(0) + 0.1 = 0.1;$$
$$z_2 = (0.9) z_1 + \varepsilon_2 = 0.9(0.1) + 0.1 = 0.19;$$
$$z_3 = (0.9) z_2 + \varepsilon_3 = 0.9(0.19) + 0 = 0.17;$$
$$z_4 = (0.9) z_3 + \varepsilon_4 = 0.9(0.17) - 0.1 = 0.05.$$

These shocks give rise to the sequence of Z: $Z_1 = e^{0.1} = 1.1$, $Z_2 = e^{0.19} = 1.21$, $Z_3 = e^{0.17} = 1.19$, $Z_4 = e^{0.05} = 1.05$, or in sum

$Z_0 = 1.00$;

$Z_1 = 1.10$;

$Z_2 = 1.21$;

$Z_3 = 1.19$;

$Z_4 = 1.105$.

Thus the productivity factor still rises from 1 and then starts to fall, but now in a way that carries over a slightly lesser part of each of the shocks of the past compared to full persistence. As compared to full persistence of the shock when $\phi = 1$, the shock does not rise quite as high, it starts falling sooner, and it falls more quickly and farther, in the four time periods. This type of lesser persistence, of $\phi = 0.9$ is a typical specification of the goods productivity shock, which is usually in the range of $\phi = 0.9$ to 0.95. The actual degree of persistence is chosen in calibrations so as to best explain the stylised business cycle facts.

McCandless's (2008) *The ABCs of RBCs* provides a full development of how to make stochastic the standard dynamic general equilibrium models.

13.7 Growth accounting

The emphasis on changing A_{Gt} in typical exogenous growth dynamic models of the business cycle is fortified by what is called 'growth accounting' that is done within the exogenous growth framework. This growth accounting focuses on the calculation of A_{Gt} and in the process self-reinforces the idea that the business cycle explanations should be based on changes in A_{Gt}. However this accounting does not support such a view when framed within an endogenous growth setting.

Consider the production function of output with human capital. Equation (12.1) can also be written as

$$y_t = A_G h_t^\gamma \left(l_t\right)^\gamma \left(k_t\right)^{1-\gamma}. \tag{13.27}$$

In comparison, the exogenous growth production function of Chapter 11 is

$$y_t = A_{Gt} \left(l_t\right)^\gamma \left(k_t\right)^{1-\gamma}. \tag{13.28}$$

Clearly the two production functions are equivalent if

$$A_{Gt} = A_G h_t^\gamma. \tag{13.29}$$

This simple comparison is the basis of why the growth accounting used in an exogenous growth framework that focuses on A_{Gt} can similarly be stated within an endogenous growth context. The A_{Gt} is called the 'total factor productivity' in exogenous growth and it is assumed to grow over time. In endogenous growth, human capital grows over time at the balanced path growth rate.

Exogenous growth accounting specifically attributes some fraction of the economy's growth to an exogenous change in A_{Gt}. To do this using actual data, use the production function of equation (13.28) and write it in percentage change terms, which is a way of putting it in terms of growth rates. One way to do this is use the production function to write the ratio of output at time $t+1$ and at time t:

$$\frac{y_{t+1}}{y_t} = \frac{A_{Gt+1} \left(l_{t+1}\right)^\gamma \left(k_{t+1}\right)^{1-\gamma}}{A_{Gt} \left(l_t\right)^\gamma \left(k_t\right)^{1-\gamma}}. \tag{13.30}$$

Using g_y, g_A, g_l and g_k to write the growth rate of the variables y_t, A_{Gt}, l_t and k_t, during time t to $t + 1$, this equation can be expressed as

$$1 + g_y = (1 + g_A)(1 + g_l)^{\gamma}(1 + g_k)^{1-\gamma}. \tag{13.31}$$

Taking the natural logarithm of this growth equation, the growth rate of output is approximated by

$$g_y = g_A + \gamma g_l + (1 - \gamma) g_k. \tag{13.32}$$

And since the labour l_t is the labour of a representative agent, this is the same as the amount of labour per person, and this does not grow over time; so $g_l = 0$. Solving for the growth of the A_{Gt}, which is otherwise unobservable,

$$g_A = g_y - (1 - \gamma) g_k. \tag{13.33}$$

From equation (13.33), the 'TFP residual', which is a name for g_A, is calculated in the typical way. Data for g_y and g_k is averaged over some time period for some country, such as the US, and a value of γ is assumed, and the contribution of the shift over time in A_{Gt} to the average per capita output growth rate is computed. For example, using typical values in this literature, with $1 - \gamma$ assumed to be near to 0.4, a per capita output growth rate of 2.0, and a capital growth rate of 1%, the residual contribution of TFP is $0.02 - 0.4 (0.01) = 0.016$. This would be a 1.6% growth rate from just the change in A_{Gt} alone. This is large and therefore it suggests that such exogenous TFP increases are important to study.

However, now consider the same growth accounting within the endogenous growth economy, in which the only difference is that the TFP is interpreted as in equation (13.29). From equation (13.27), using time periods t and $t+1$, and g_h for the growth rate of human capital,

$$\frac{y_{t+1}}{y_t} = \frac{A_G (h_{t+1})^{\gamma} (l_{t+1})^{\gamma} (k_{t+1})^{1-\gamma}}{A_G (h_t)^{\gamma} (l_t)^{\gamma} (k_t)^{1-\gamma}}; \tag{13.34}$$

$$g_y = \gamma g_h + \gamma g_l + (1 - \gamma) g_k. \tag{13.35}$$

With $g_l = 0$ also in endogenous growth, the same measure of TFP in exogenous growth, which is $g_y - (1 - \gamma) g_k$, is now equal to γg_h:

$$g_y - (1 - \gamma) g_k = \gamma g_h. \tag{13.36}$$

Thus the growth rate of human capital, factored by γ, is exactly the TFP residual.

The fact that the TFP residual of exogenous growth is just a fraction of the growth rate of human capital in endogenous growth does not invalidate the whole TFP literature. But it qualifies it by showing that the measure of TFP could simply be the measure of human capital's contribution to output growth. Further consider that along the balanced growth path equilibrium, no unexplained residual is possible. In equation (13.36), when the growth rate of output, capital and human capital all equal g, which is 0.020 in the baseline endogenous growth model, then it is an identity that

$$g_y - (1 - \gamma) g_k = \gamma g_h; \tag{13.37}$$

$$0.020 - \left(\frac{2}{3}\right) 0.020 = \frac{1}{3} 0.020. \tag{13.38}$$

This suggests that the TFP issue may be more of a measurement problem than a reason for suggesting that growth and business cycles are explained by changes in A_G. Indeed, it may be that neither growth nor business cycles require an explanation based on A_G, once viewed from the endogenous growth perspective.

Because human capital is hard to measure quantitatively, and can include components such as family education that occurs naturally over time in the home, it is difficult to contradict that *TFP* residuals may be simply human capital growth. Measurements have included human capital and still argue that there is a residual from A_{Gt}. This may be true, but certainly on theoretical grounds, the *TFP* residual can be fully captured by the human capital growth within the endogenous growth framework, with no required change in A_G over time. This is an identity that can be characterised as an 'observational equivalence' between *TFP* residual measures and the human capital growth contribution, since equation (13.29) equates A_{Gt} to $A_G h_t^\gamma$.

The importance of the comparison of growth accounting between the exogenous growth and endogenous growth frameworks is the result that it is fully conceivable to conduct business cycle comparative statics emphasising A_H changes, as much as or more than A_G changes. And the importance of A_H changes is further enhanced in explaining long term trends. Human capital growth can explain long term economic growth in a growth accounting sense. But it can explain much more that is difficult to explain comprehensively otherwise.

13.8 Historical trends with endogenous growth

While any such trend that may exist in the goods productivity factor A_G cannot explain changes in the growth rate, in the endogenous growth model, there is a significant set of trends that can be explained by a small trend upwards in A_H. These trends include time allocation trends, infrastructure trends, and trends in historical evolution of industry. Industry evolution trends include the industrial revolution, development of nations, and industry realignment from agriculture to manufacturing to services.

13.8.1 Time allocation trends

In Chapter 11 on exogenous growth, trends in the work week were explained in terms of an exogenous fall in the time T available for work and leisure. However this fall in T cannot address education time. Another explanation is provided with endogenous growth through a slight trend upwards in human capital investment productivity A_H.

Comparing Example 12.1, the baseline endogenous growth model, with Example 13.2, which increases only A_H by 5%, the results of increasing A_H upwards over time can be suggested. Time in human capital investment l_{Ht} rises and work time l_t falls. If the percentage increase in A_H each year was very slight but steady, this would provide an explanation of the long trend towards greater educational attainment in formal schooling that is apparent across developed nations over the last few centuries. This also explains why the work week might fall. Working is a productive use of time, but so also is human capital investment. And when this investment takes away from work time, over time, then perhaps the most natural of all explanations for the long trend downwards in work time is the long trend upwards in education time. And the endogenous growth model does provide this explanation.

An important qualification is that the specification used in the baseline endogenous growth model is a simplistic one, with only labour and human capital used in the linear production of human capital investment. This specification simplifies the analysis from one in which the human capital investment function also uses physical capital, in a Cobb–Douglas specification similar to the one used for the goods sector in the endogenous growth setting.

For example, with i_{Ht} indicating the investment in human capital, then instead of $i_{Ht} = A_H l_{Ht} h_t$, as in the baseline model, the more general model is

$$i_{Ht} = A_H \left(l_{Ht} h_t\right)^\eta \left(s_{Ht} k_t\right)^{1-\eta}, \tag{13.39}$$

with the goods sector specified as

$$y_t = A_G \left(l_t h_t \right)^\gamma \left(s_{Gt} k_t \right)^{1-\gamma}. \tag{13.40}$$

The s_{Gt} and s_{Ht} are the shares of capital devoted to the goods sector and the human capital sector, with the sum of the shares equal to 1:

$$s_{Gt} + s_{Ht} = 1.$$

This model complicates the solution methodology significantly and is not presented here. But the implication is that when A_H increases exogenously, in a comparative static fashion, the time in human capital investment, l_{Ht}, still rises but not by as much.

In Example 13.2, the time increase in l_{Ht} from a 5% increase in A_H is very substantial; l_{Ht} rises 0.185 to 0.242, which is a fractional increase of $\frac{0.242 - 0.185}{0.185} = 0.30811$, or 31%. This 31% is the same as the fall in the physical capital to human capital ratio, which goes from 1 to 0.069. The rise in human capital investment time leads to a rise in human capital accumulation and a fall in $\frac{k_t}{h_t}$. But the qualification is that with Cobb–Douglas technologies in both goods and human capital sectors as in equations (13.39) and (13.40), this rise in l_{Ht} and fall in $\frac{k_t}{h_t}$ would likely be smaller. This makes it difficult to gauge the level of the small percentage increase in A_H that would be necessary to be able to explain quantitatively the observed average fall in working hours and rise in education time. It would be useful to solve the extended model with equations (13.39) and (13.40).

13.8.2 Economic development

The rise in the world average growth rate from the times of zero per capita income growth in Europe, known as the Malthusian (after Malthus, 1798) zero growth equilibrium, to the much higher growth rate during the industrial revolution and into modern time can be explained also by a small gradual rise in A_H. And this explanation is consistent with a large literature related to human capital.

For example, Lucas (2002) takes up explaining the transformation from low growth Malthusian times to high growth industrial revolution times by a model in which investment in human capital passes a critical level. Then demographic changes occur as there is greater investment in the quality of children, through education, than in the quantity of children. Such substitution was introduced by Becker and Lewis (1973), and advanced by Becker and Barro (1988). And this allows explanation of long run demographic trends towards lower fertility rates at the same time that the trend growth rate rises.

In particular, investment in human capital has been put forth as the reason why economies went from a zero to high growth rates. The idea of human capital theorists is that when the return on human capital is so low, which corresponds in the baseline endogenous growth model to a very low A_H, then little investment in human capital takes place. The economy remains in a low growth equilibrium. But when the return on human capital rises, investment in human capital increases and so does the economy's growth rate.

An explanation of rising growth certainly results from a slowly rising A_H. However since the rise in A_H is exogenous, this is only a formalistic explanation, but not one that explains why A_H would or could be trending slowly up. Unfortunately, there is no generally accepted explanation for why A_H might be rising. It can only be the result of a whole cultural technology of a nation or group of nations over time. And in this sense, culture would seem to determine the level of A_H.

A policy of building schools, as exemplified by a massive such increase in China under Deng, would probably be one way to cause A_H to rise. A technology becomes more productive as it is used more widely, an idea behind the human capital learning literature that says in short that productivity rises slowly in line with the level of production.

Many have suggested that low levels of human capital in a country can be alleviated by bringing large amounts of physical capital into the country, with the result that the growth rises. Lucas addresses this issue in his 1990 article 'Why Doesn't Capital Flow from Rich to Poor Countries?' The problem however can be seen within the baseline endogenous growth model. The equilibrium is determined by the level of physical capital relative to human capital. Bringing in large amounts of physical capital would simply drive the return to capital that is already very low in undeveloped countries to an even lower level. And this is why the capital does not simply flow into an undeveloped nation: the low return to capital. Schultz (1964) provided the answer related to A_H in his work on human capital theory and evidence. His works suggests that the only way to raise the growth rate is to raise the return on human capital. Then the physical capital will flow into a country, as it does now into China.

13.8.3 Industrial transformation

As economies develop they tend to focus on different industries. First, in early stages of development, it is agriculture. In more advanced stages, it is manufacturing. And finally the service sector takes on increasing importance at the expense of manufacturing. This is a curious trend that has long been researched. And it is known as the 'structural transformation' that economies go through.

Human capital endogenous growth theory provides a very simple way to explain the structural transformation. Rather than relying on a special specification of the tastes of the consumer for different goods, as has been done in the exogenous growth literature, or on the prices of different industries following certain inverted patterns over time, as has also been proposed in the exogenous growth literature, human capital theory needs only that the industries have different degrees of human capital usage.

Combining a slight trend upwards in A_H with agriculture, manufacturing and services that each has a different degree of human versus physical capital usage provides an explanation of the trend shift across industries. Consider breaking down the goods production into three sectors instead of one. Human capital investment would then be a fourth sector. Notationally represent these sectors as output in agriculture y_a, output in manufacturing y_m and output in services y_s. And let the production functions of these sectors be given as

$$y_{at} = A_a \left(l_{at} h_t \right)^{\gamma_a} \left(s_{at} k_t \right)^{1-\gamma_a};$$
$$y_{mt} = A_m \left(l_{mt} h_t \right)^{\gamma_m} \left(s_{mt} k_t \right)^{1-\gamma_m};$$
$$y_{st} = A_s \left(l_{st} h_t \right)^{\gamma_s} \left(s_{st} k_t \right)^{1-\gamma_s};$$

with human capital given as

$$i_{Ht} = A_H \left(l_{Ht} h_t \right)^{\eta} \left(s_{Ht} k_t \right)^{1-\eta}.$$

The share of time and share of capital constraint would then be

$$s_{at} + s_{mt} + s_{st} + s_{Ht} = 1.$$
$$l_{at} + l_{mt} + l_{st} + l_{Ht} + x_t = 1.$$

Also consider assuming that the agriculture sector is least intensive in human capital augmented labour, $l_{at} h_t$, while manufacturing is medium intensive in its effective labour $l_{mt} h_t$, and the services sector is most intensive in its effective labour $l_{st} h_t$. Then the Cobb–Douglas parameters would be ranked as $\gamma_a < \gamma_m < \gamma_s$.

This might appear a surprising assumption at first glance, in that we typically think of agriculture as the most labour intensive sector given how most of the labour force works in agriculture in undeveloped countries. But consider developed countries: modern agriculture is without doubt the least labour intensive industry of the economy. The way to explain this puzzle is that in undeveloped countries agriculture is often the only industry, not the most labour intensive one. So most people work in agriculture. But as the human capital level rises in a country, the amount of effective labour in modern agriculture is actually small compared to machine use, and so labour migrates from rural to urban areas. Labour gets absorbed in manufacturing within cities where the effective labour share of output is significantly higher. And then $\frac{w_t l_{at} h_t}{y_{at}} = \gamma_a$ (by the nature of the Cobb–Douglas technology) and $\frac{w_t l_{mt} h_t}{y_{mt}} = \gamma_m$, with $\gamma_a < \gamma_m$.

The same reasoning applies to the eventual migration of labour into services. Services are also thought of as a labour intensive industry. So the transformation from agriculture to manufacturing to services seems odd by exogenous growth reasoning. When there is no human capital in the model then such a transformation might be viewed as going from a labour intensive agriculture sector to a capital intensive manufacturing sector and then back to a labour intensive services sector. And this is why tortured utility functions have been devised, or special price trends, so as to fit the explanation of the transformation into the exogenous growth framework.

With endogenous growth it is much easier. Services are then considered the most effective labour, or human capital, intensive sector. Think of the major service sector industries: computer services, health services, insurance and banking. The concept of restaurants representing the growth of the service sector is probably an anachronism. Services are a huge major industry and arguably employ the highest proportion of human capital. And so this would justify the assumption that $\gamma_s > \gamma_m > \gamma_a$.

The implications of such a model are basic although not worked out fully here in the text since a model with so many sectors is beyond the scope of the text. Consider that as A_H trends up slightly over time, the sectors that are intensive in human capital will expand and the sectors that are less intensive in human capital will contract relative to the other sectors. This is the explanation of the structural transformation within the endogenous growth model. As A_H slightly trends up, the price of those sectors using human capital intensively goes down relatively and these sectors expand relatively. Agriculture shrinks relative to manufacturing which eventually shrinks relative to services.

13.8.4 Policy

The most important policy implication of the analysis of historical trends using the endogenous growth baseline model is that it is important to raise A_H. This can be done by infrastructure development generally, but especially infrastructure that develops the ability to increase human capital. This means building schools, hospitals, and health education and service.

There is a way to talk about such policy more specifically within the growth models. This is through the assumption of the initial human and physical capital stock, which can be denoted by h_0 and k_0. Governments can push up these given stocks at any time period t through good infrastructure policy. This can be thought of as raising h_t or k_t directly, but it probably is better to think of such policy in terms of raising A_H, the productivity of producing human capital. And a further extension is to model explicitly a sector that produces the investment in physical capital, similar to an i_{Ht} function, but instead an i_{Kt} function. And this would have a productivity parameter A_{Kt} that the government could raise through physical capital infrastructure development.

For example the specification of the sector investing in physical capital could be

$$i_{Kt} = A_K \left(l_{Kt} h_t\right)^\kappa \left(s_{Kt} k_t\right)^{1-\kappa},$$

with l_{Kt} and s_{Kt} being the shares of labour and capital devoted to that sector. The marginal product of capital $\kappa A_K \left(\frac{k_{Kt}}{l_{Kt}}\right)^{1-\kappa}$ would influence the endogenous growth rate in an extended endogenous growth economy. And so an infrastructure development policy that raises A_K, just as one that raises A_H, would help increase the growth rate of an economy.

Our baseline models abstract away from this complication of modelling investment i_t in terms of a separate sector, with the technology of $A_K \left(l_{Kt} h_t\right)^\kappa \left(s_{Kt} k_t\right)^{1-\kappa}$, and instead just assume that output is turned costlessly into investment, with $i_t = y_t - c_t$. This is a simplifying assumption. Realising this simplification allows for a policy focus on raising A_H and at the same time on raising this additional productivity factor A_K. This is how we explain for example the huge government investment in transportation, through highways, metro trains, and other commuter means, as well as investment in education. Such infrastructure increases the productivity of other private investment, both in human and physical capital.

13.9 Application: capital symmetry in growth theory

George Stigler, in his 1939 article on 'Production and Distribution in the Short Run', introduced the idea that having flexibility to expand output can be achieved at the cost of a higher marginal cost for a given output. Here the concept is formalised by having some of the capital lie idle, which incurs the additional rental cost of the unused capital. On the benefit side, the model assumes there is no depreciation of the capital that is not used. By adding this feature of unused physical capital, just like leisure time represents time when human capital stands unused, the model moves towards a symmetric treatment of human and physical capital. By also treating depreciation of physical and human capital symmetrically, the model gives a fully symmetric theory of growth with respect to both types of capital. And this can be useful for better explaining business cycles and trends.

In equation (12.19) of Chapter 12, the endogenous growth economy introduces the equalisation between the real interest rate net of depreciation on physical capital $r_t - \delta_k$ and the total productive time $1 - x_t$ as factored by A_H, and again net of depreciation on human capital: $r_t - \delta_k = A_H \left(1 - x_t\right) - \delta_H$. Yet this equality of returns on physical and human capital highlights what is missing on the physical capital side: a term such as $1 - x_t$ that indicates the utilisation rate of physical capital, just as $1 - x_t$ is in effect equal to the utilisation rate of human capital. Indeed, the physical capital capacity utilisation rate has been focused upon in literature on business cycles. And such capacity utilisation would also affect the long run growth rate.

The lack of symmetry in the standard endogenous growth theory stands out as a result. Human capital's return includes the capacity utilisation rate, while physical capital's return does not. A second asymmetry is also clear here. The physical capital marginal product equals r_t and depends on the ratio of effective labour to physical capital. But with the linear production function for human capital investment, the marginal product of human capital investment with respect to effective labour is just the constant A_H, rather than a marginal product that depends upon the ratio of effective labour to physical capital as with r_t.

Both of the sources of asymmetry can be rectified with extensions of the baseline model. Here these extensions are briefly set out, with the full analysis left for further work. Consider defining a percentage of the time that factories are operating, such as 80%, as u_t. Then $1 - u_t$ is the spare capacity rate of 20% in this case, and u_t is the capacity utilisation rate. This means that to produce output only some of the capital is used, the fraction u_t, just as only a fraction l_t of the human capital is used in goods production. The production of output with both physical and human capital is modified from equation (12.1) to be

$$y_t = A_G \left(l_t h_t\right)^\gamma \left(u_t k_t\right)^{1-\gamma}. \tag{13.41}$$

The benefit of not using all of the capital is assumed to be that instead of the full capital stock depreciating, only the amount of capital in use will depreciate. Thus the depreciation rate δ_k applies to a smaller amount of capital, $u_t k_t$, rather than to the whole capital stock k_t. The capital accumulation condition is now

$$i_t = k_{t+1} - k_t + \delta_k u_t k_t. \tag{13.42}$$

However without any additional benefit of unused capital, the problem gives a trivial solution for the interest rate in terms of the depreciation rate. Complicated ways of adding in the unused capital exist, including having a market in the 'scrap value' of unused capital. Here consider that there is managerial capability required to run a firm, which Friedman (1976) calls 'entrepreneurial capacity'. With full utilisation of a factory, 24 hours a day, entrepreneurial capacity is pushed to the limit. To formalise the benefit of not fully using capital in terms of the representative agent's entrepreneurial capacity, a factor is added to the utility function, $\psi \ln (1 - u_t)$ with $\psi \geq 0$, just as leisure enters the utility function. This gives another free parameter that in calibration can be used to get an empirical fit to the data on capacity utilisation, just as leisure preference is used to fit the employment share to data.

Consider the problem in a centralised form in which the consumer produces output along with investing in physical and human capital. Then consumption is output minus investment,

$$c_t = A_G \, (l_t h_t)^\gamma \, (u_t k_t)^{1-\gamma} - k_{t+1} + k_t - \delta_k u_t k_t, \tag{13.43}$$

and using the same time allocation constraint to substitute in for l_t, the maximisation problem including $\psi \ln (1 - u_t)$ in the utility function is

$$V (k_t, h_t) = \underset{l_{Ht}, x_t, u_t, k_{t+1}, h_{t+1}}{\text{Max}} \tag{13.44}$$

$$\ln \left[A_G \left[(1 - x_t - l_{Ht}) \, h_t \right]^\gamma (u_t k_t)^{1-\gamma} - k_{t+1} + k_t - \delta_k u_t k_t \right] \tag{13.45}$$

$$+ \ln x_t + \psi \ln (1 - u_t) + \beta V \left(k_{t+1}, h_{t+1} \right). \tag{13.46}$$

The new equilibrium condition with respect to capacity utilisation u_t is

$$\frac{-\psi}{(1 - u_t)} - (1 - \gamma) \, A_G \left(\frac{l_t h_t}{u_t k_t} \right)^\gamma k_t + \delta_k k_t = 0. \tag{13.47}$$

The equilibrium condition for k_{t+1} is the same as before at

$$\frac{1}{c_t} (-1) + \beta \frac{\partial V \left(k_{t+1}, h_{t+1} \right)}{\partial k_{t+1}^s} = 0. \tag{13.48}$$

The envelope condition from partially differentiating with respect to k_t is

$$\frac{\partial V \left(k_t^s \right)}{\partial k_t^s} = \frac{1 + u_t \left((1 - \gamma) \, A_G \left(\frac{l_t h_t}{u_t k_t} \right)^\gamma - \delta_k \right)}{c_t}. \tag{13.49}$$

Taking the first equilibrium condition back one time period to $t - 1$,

$$\frac{1}{c_{t-1}} = \beta \frac{\partial V (k_t, h_t)}{\partial k_t^s}, \tag{13.50}$$

so that the second first-order condition implies that

$$\frac{c_t}{\beta c_{t-1}} = 1 + u_t \left((1 - \gamma) \, A_G \left[\frac{l_t h_t}{u_t k_t} \right]^\gamma - \delta_k \right). \tag{13.51}$$

If we decentralise the economy between the consumer and the firm, the real interest rate r_t would be given by

$$r_t = (1 - \gamma) \, A_G \left[\frac{l_t h_t}{u_t k_t} \right]^\gamma. \tag{13.52}$$

Using this simplification, the balanced growth intertemporal margin gives the growth rate along the BGP such that

$$1 + g_t = \frac{c_t}{c_{t-1}} = \frac{1 + (r_t - \delta_k) u_t}{1 + \rho}. \tag{13.53}$$

To avoid a constant A_H, as the marginal product of effective labour in human capital investment, the next extension is to postulate a Cobb–Douglas production function of human capital investment, which is a standard extension. This means that part of the capital stock, denoted by s_{Ht}, is used for human capital investment and the other part, denoted by s_{Gt}, is used for goods production, with the constraint

$$s_{Gt} + s_{Ht} = 1.$$

But in the production function in the goods sector, only a fraction u_t of the total capital in the goods sector, $s_{Gt} k_t$, is used in production.

$$y_t = A_G (l_t h_t)^{\gamma} (s_{Gt} u_t k_t)^{1-\gamma}. \tag{13.54}$$

Similarly, let the new human capital investment function be specified so that u_t of the physical capital $s_{Ht} k_t$ is used in the active production of human capital:

$$i_{Ht} = A_H (l_{Ht} h_t)^{\eta} (s_{Ht} u_t k_t)^{1-\eta}.$$

The last modification to make is to the human capital accumulation equation. Instead of the standard form as in equation (12.8), now there will be a similar form to the physical capital equation (13.42), but for human capital. In particular, let human capital depreciate by less if leisure is taken, such that the amount of depreciated human capital is $\delta_h h_t (1 - x_t)$, just as it is $\delta_k u_t k_t$ for physical capital with capacity utilisation. The human capital investment function becomes

$$h_{t+1} = h_t - \delta_h (1 - x_t) h_t + i_{Ht},$$
$$h_{t+1} = h_t - \delta_h (1 - x_t) h_t + A_H (l_{Ht} h_t)^{\eta} (s_{Ht} u_t k_t)^{1-\eta}.$$

The intuition here is that when a person works night and day, non-stop, then they get sick and become non-performing. Their human capital depreciates too much as a result, as compared to a normal use of human capital, with plenty of time taken out for leisure. Leisure keeps the workload from becoming too stressful, and allows human capital to depreciate at a normal, lower, rate than when we work all the time for a while until collapsing.

Substituting in $1 - s_{Ht}$ for s_{Gt} in the goods production function, the representative agent problem now is

$$V(k_t, h_t) = \underset{l_{Ht}, x_t, u_t, k_{t+1}, h_{t+1}}{\text{Max}} \ln(x_t) + \psi \ln(1 - u_t)$$

$$+ \ln \left[A_G \left[(1 - x_t - l_{Ht}) h_t \right]^{\gamma} \left[(1 - s_{Ht}) u_t k_t \right]^{1-\gamma} - k_{t+1} + k_t - \delta_k u_t k_t \right]$$
$$+ \beta V \left(k_{t+1}, h_t - \delta_h (1 - x_t) h_t + A_H (l_{Ht} h_t)^{\eta} (s_{Ht} u_t k_t)^{1-\eta} \right). \tag{13.55}$$

After some significant work, not shown here, it results that the equilibrium BGP growth rate is given by

$$g_t = \frac{(r_t - \delta_k) u_t - \rho}{1 + \rho} = \frac{(r_{Ht} - \delta_h)(1 - x_t) - \rho}{1 + \rho}, \tag{13.56}$$

where r_{Ht} is defined as the marginal product of human capital in producing human capital investment:

$$r_{Ht} \equiv \eta A_H \left(\frac{l_{Ht} h_t}{s_{Ht} u_t k_t} \right)^{\eta-1}. \tag{13.57}$$

And it follows that

$$\left(r_t - \delta_k \right) u_t = \left(r_{Ht} - \delta_h \right) \left(1 - x_t \right). \tag{13.58}$$

This is the key result that shows a perfect type of symmetry between physical capital return of $(r_t - \delta_k) u_t$, and human capital return of $(r_{Ht} - \delta_h) (1 - x_t)$. One factor is the marginal product net of depreciation, and the other factor is the capacity utilisation rate, for each physical and human capital.

The result of creating symmetry in growth is that the employment rate of labour and the physical capital utilisation rate both help determine an economy's long term growth. More efficient manufacturing, such as the Japanese 'just-in-time' inventory systems, means a higher capital utilisation rate and higher growth. This adds the other dimension to growth theory that can be developed for its implications much further. For business cycles, having the extra dimension of the physical capital capacity utilisation rate makes it easier to have swings in the aggregate output without requiring shifts in the productivity factor A_G.

13.10 Questions

1. An increase in the goods productivity factor A_G in the baseline endogenous growth model causes
   (a) aggregate goods demand and goods supply to both shift out,
   (b) the physical capital to human capital ratio to rise,
   (c) the relative price of goods to fall,
   (d) all of the above.
2. An increase in the goods productivity factor A_G in the baseline endogenous growth model causes
   (a) labour demand to shift out,
   (b) labour supply to shift out,
   (c) employment to rise,
   (d) all of the above.
3. An increase in the goods productivity factor A_G in the baseline endogenous growth model causes
   (a) the growth rate to increase,
   (b) the wage rate to increase,
   (c) physical capital investment to decrease,
   (d) all of the above.
4. In Example 13.1, instead of letting A_G increase by 5% from 0.28224 to 0.29635, assume instead that A_G increases by 10% to 0.31.
   (a) Find the equilibrium growth rate.
   (b) Find the equilibrium physical capital to human capital ratio.
   (c) Find the equilibrium wage rate.
   (d) Graph the AS–AD output market and the labour market, in comparison to the equilibrium in Example 13.1.

5. A decrease in the human capital productivity factor A_H in the baseline endogenous growth model causes
   (a) aggregate goods demand and goods supply to both shift out,
   (b) the physical capital to human capital ratio to rise,
   (c) the relative price of goods to fall,
   (d) all of the above.

6. A decrease in the human capital productivity factor A_H in the baseline endogenous growth model causes
   (a) labour demand to shift out,
   (b) labour supply to shift back,
   (c) employment to rise,
   (d) all of the above.

7. A decrease in the human capital productivity factor A_H in the baseline endogenous growth model causes
   (a) the growth rate to increase,
   (b) the wage rate to increase,
   (c) physical capital investment to decrease,
   (d) all of the above.

8. In Example 13.2, instead of letting A_H increase by 5% from 0.189 to 0.20, let A_H increase by 10% to 0.208.
   (a) Find the equilibrium growth rate.
   (b) Find the equilibrium physical capital to human capital ratio.
   (c) Find the equilibrium wage rate.
   (d) Graph the AS–AD output market and the labour market, in comparison to the equilibrium in Example 13.1.

9. Explain business cycles within the endogenous growth model using comparative static changes in A_G and A_H.

10. As a modification to Example 13.5, consider an alternative sequence of ε shocks over time: 0.1, 0.2, 0.3, 0.2, 0.1, −0.1, −0.2, again with a persistence factor of $\phi = 0.9$.
    (a) Compute the sequence of productivity factors Z_t over time.
    (b) In what sense might stock markets anticipate recessions, through predictions of current period ε, and so experience stock price decreases even before recessions begin?

11. Compare growth accounting for the total factor productivity residual in the exogenous growth model versus the endogenous growth model.

12. Explain trends over time in working hours per week, average time spent in education, and the gradually rising growth rate of output using changes in A_G and in A_H.

13.11 References

Becker, Gary S. and Robert J. Barro, 1988, 'A Reformulation of the Economic Theory of Fertility', *The Quarterly Journal of Economics*, MIT Press, 103(1): 1–25, February.

Becker, Gary S. and H. Gregg Lewis, 1973, 'On the Interaction between the Quantity and Quality of Children', *Journal of Political Economy*, University of Chicago Press, 81(2): S279–88, Part II.

Benhabib, Jess, Richard Rogerson and Randall Wright, 1991, 'Homework in Macroeconomics: Household Production and Aggregate Fluctuations', *Journal of Political Economy*, University of Chicago Press, 99(6): 1166–1187, December.

Blanchard, Olivier Jean and Stanley Fischer, 1989, *Lectures on Macroeconomics*, The MIT Press, Cambridge.

Calvo, Guillermo, 1983, 'Staggered Prices in a Utility-Maximizing Framework', *Journal of Monetary Economics*, 12: 383–398.

Clark, John Maurice, 1931, 'Distribution', *Encyclopedia of the Social Sciences*, 5: 167–173; reprinted in William Fellner and Bernard F. Haley, editors, *Readings in the Theory of Income Distribution*, The Blakiston Company, Philadelphia, 1946.

Dixit, A. and J. Stiglitz, 1977, 'Monopolistic Competition and the Optimum Product Diversity', *American Economic Review*, 67: 297–308.

Friedman, Milton, 1971, 'A Monetary Theory of Nominal Income', *Journal of Political Economy*, 79(2): 323–337.

Friedman, Milton, 1976, *Price Theory*, Aldine Publishing Company, Chicago.

Greenwood, Jeremy and Zvi Hercowitz, 1991, 'The Allocation of Capital and Time over the Business Cycle', *Journal of Political Economy*, University of Chicago Press, 99(6): 1188–1214, December.

Hansen, Gary D. 1985, 'Indivisible Labor and the Business Cycle', *Journal of Monetary Economics*, 56: 309–327.

Jones, Larry E., Rodolfo E. Manuelli and Henry E. Siu, 2005, 'Fluctuations in Convex Models of Endogenous Growth II: Business Cycle Properties', *Review of Economic Dynamics*, Elsevier for the Society for Economic Dynamics, 8(4): 805–828, October.

Kydland, Finn E. and Edward C. Prescott, 1982, 'Time to Build and Aggregate Fluctuations', *Econometrica*, Econometric Society, 50(6): 1345–1370, November.

Long, John B., Jr., and Charles I. Plosser, 1983, 'Real Business Cycles', *Journal of Political Economy*, University of Chicago Press, 91(1): 39–69, February.

Lucas, Robert E., Jr., 1975. 'An Equilibrium Model of the Business Cycle', *Journal of Political Economy*, University of Chicago Press, 83(6): 1113–1144, December.

Lucas, Robert E., Jr., 1977, 'Understanding Business Cycles', Carnegie-Rochester Conference Series on Public Policy, Volume 5, 1977, pp. 7–29.

Lucas, Robert E., Jr., 1987, *Models of Business Cycles*, Basil Blackwell, Oxford.

Lucas, Robert E., Jr., 1988, 'On the Mechanics of Economic Development', *Journal of Monetary Economics*, Elsevier, 22(1): 3–42, July.

Lucas, Robert E, Jr., 1990, 'Why Doesn't Capital Flow from Rich to Poor Countries?', *American Economic Review*, American Economic Association, 80(2): 92–96, May.

Lucas, Robert E., Jr. 2002, *Lectures on Economic Growth*, Harvard University Press, Cambridge.

Lucas, Robert E. Jr., 2005, 'Present at the Creation: Reflections on the 2004 Nobel Prize to Finn Kydland and Edward Prescott', *Review of Economic Dynamics* 8: 777–779.

McCandless, George, 2008, *The ABCs of RBCs*, Harvard University Press, Cambridge.

Malthus, Robert Thomas, 1798, *An Essay on the Principle of Population*, Church-Yard, St.Paul's, London.

Rogerson, Richard, 1988, 'Indivisible Labor, Lotteries and Equilibrium', *Journal of Monetary Economics*, 21: 3–16.

Romer, David, 1993, 'The New Keynesian Synthesis', *The Journal of Economic Perspectives*, 7(1, Winter): 5–22.

Romer, David, 2006, *Advanced Macroeconomics*, 3rd edition, McGraw-Hill.

Schultz, Theodore W., 1964, *Transforming Traditional Agriculture*, The University of Chicago Press, Chicago.

Slutsky, Eugene, 1937, 'The Summation of Random Causes as the Source of Cyclic Processes', *Econometrica*, 5: 105–146.

Stigler, George, 1939, 'Production and Distribution in the Short Run', *Journal of Political Economy* 47(June): 305–327; reprinted in *Readings in the Theory of Income Distribution*, edited by William Fellner and Bernard F. Haley, The Blakiston Company, Philadelphia, 1946.

CHAPTER (14)

International trade

14.1 Introduction

Two agents with different productivities in the human capital sector are specified, with all other factors being the same. The two agents can be viewed as two different countries. There is just one output good that both agents produce, and both have the exact same goods sector technology. In autarky, with no world market clearing conditions specified, each agent exists in isolation from the other with different growth rates, different interest rates and different wage rates. The first agent is specified exactly as in the baseline endogenous growth economy of Example 12.2. And the second agent has a 15% higher human capital investment productivity.

To make clear each agent's independent economy, the autarky, no trade equilibria are first set out. Then with world market clearing allowed, the agents adjust their physical capital to human capital ratios so that their growth rates and interest rates converge to the same levels. This is factor price equalisation in terms of the interest rate. At the same time, the agents trade goods and labour so that the wage rate also moves to the same level. This produces factor price equalisation in terms of the wage rate, so that there is complete factor price equalisation with trade.

Trade patterns result from factor price equalisation and the given initial differences in human capital productivity between the agents. The first agent with a lower human capital productivity supplies excess labour, while demanding excess goods. The second agent with the higher human capital productivity supplies excess goods, while demanding excess labour. The first agent consumes less goods and less leisure than does the second agent, and spends more time in human capital accumulation than the second agent.

Thus it could be said that the first agent specialises in human capital investment production, given the higher allocation of time to human capital investment and the excess supply of labour, while the second agent specialises in goods production, in the sense of the excess supply of goods. Because the first agent is less productive in human capital, the agent becomes the one to supply excess labour. The second agent is more productive in human capital and becomes the one to supply excess goods. The greater human capital productivity allows for easier augmentation of the effective labour in the country 2 economy and leads to an excess supply of goods. This makes the two-country world economy similar to a developing country for agent 1 with lower human capital productivity, and a developed country for agent 2 with a higher human capital productivity.

The chapter also discusses how with an exogenous growth dynamic model, and a single output good with two agents differing only in goods productivities, factor price equalisation is not possible. The exogenous growth fixes the interest rate, determines the capital to labour ratio, and this in turn fixes the wage rate. If interest rates and wage rates start out different between two agents with exogenous growth, the factor prices can never become equal.

Changes in productivity factors are also discussed, along with showing how to compute the equilibrium with any number of the two different agents. Only the market clearing condition is modified with different numbers of each agent. This however gives a different world growth rate and other equilibrium values.

14.1.1 Building on the last chapters

The chapter extends the endogenous growth model by allowing for two agents, differing only in their human capital productivity. This makes use of the equilibrium worked out in Example 12.1, by specifying this economy for the first agent. The comparative static exercise in the last chapter, in Example 13.2, of increasing the human capital productivity is then used for the second agent. While Example 13.2 assumes a 5% increase in human capital productivity over the baseline Example 12.1 value, here the second agent is assumed to have a 15% higher human capital productivity factor. The bigger increase of 15% is useful because the trade flows are more pronounced and easier to see.

Only with endogenous growth can factor price equalisation occur in this one output good economy. This enables simultaneously both the wage equalisation of Chapter 4 and the interest rate equalisation of Chapter 7. And at the same time this means growth rate convergence to the same endogenous growth rate. Factor price equalisation cannot be shown with the Part 4 dynamic model with exogenous growth because the exogenous growth facet in effect fixes the factor prices.

A key difference from the earlier static equilibrium Chapters 4 and 7 is that now there are capital ratio state variables that vary as trade opens and factor prices are equalised. In establishing the equilibrium trade flows, the factor price equalisation demands that the capital to effective labour ratios are equalised between countries. And the growth rate equalisation is another dimension of this. This change in the capital ratios in each country also makes it not possible to provide a simple computation of the utility gains from trade, since now the transition dynamics impact on the computation of these gains; transition dynamics are left for more advanced work.

The only new part of the solution methodology is that now world aggregate demand must be set to world aggregate supply, in both goods and labour markets, while only one such condition was necessary in Chapters 4 and 7. This is an extension of the endogenous growth solution methodology presented in the Chapter 12 Appendix A12. And just as the trade Chapters 4 and 7 marked the end of Parts 2 and 3 respectively, now this trade chapter marks the end of Part 5.

14.1.2 Learning objective

It is a challenge to understand that with one output good, world trade can equalise factor prices only if human capital productivity factors are different. Once it is realised that endogenous growth is central to showing factor price equalisation, the result of how interest rates and wage rates are equalised comes more easily. It is also key to see that the movement from autarky to trade now involves adjustment of capital ratios before the trade patterns can be found. Therefore drawing in the excess supply and demand for goods on the trade graphs can only be done to the supply and demand after the capital ratios have adjusted.

14.1.3 Who made it happen?

The Heckscher–Ohlin trade theory with its Samuelson factor price equalisation remains central to the analysis of the chapter. But this is extended beyond standard analysis with its dynamic endogenous growth setting. Certain studies in modern international business cycles have used such endogenous growth specifications for each agent. In particular the 2000 article by Marco Maffezzoli on 'Human Capital and International Real Business Cycles' uses a model similar to this chapter except that it is stochastic and with human capital externalities that we avoid for simplification.

Maffezzoli (2000) shows that he can simulate the output, investment, and labour correlations between two countries well, in comparison to data, and that he reproduces a near unity correlation between savings and investment within a country. This observed correlation is well-known starting with Feldstein and Horioka's (1980) work. In the chapter here, savings equals investment in each country in equilibrium, consistent with the 0.97 simulated correlation reported in Maffezzoli.

14.2 Autarky

Let each agent, denoted by agent/country 1 and agent/country 2, have the same log utility function of goods and leisure as in the baseline dynamic Chapter 12 model. With no trade, then each agent/country will exist in isolation from the other one. Consider assuming that all parameters are the same in the two isolated economies except that country 2 has a 15% higher human capital investment productivity than country 1.

Assume the same parameters as those in the baseline dynamic model of Chapter 12, Example 12.1, for country 1. And then assume the same parameters for country 2 except that A_{2H} is 15% higher than A_{1H}. The output is the same in each country 1 and 2 and so the price of the output is the same, again normalised to one along the balanced growth path. From Chapter 12, the AD and AS functions are therefore the same as previously derived, but now with country subscripts 1 and 2 which indicate that the productivity parameters, employment, and capital ratios may differ. For AD,

$$y_{1t}^d = \frac{w_{1t}h_{1t}\left(1 - \frac{g_1+\delta_H}{A_{1H}}\right) + k_{1t}\left[\rho\left(1+g_1\right) + \left(1+\alpha\right)\left(\delta_k+g_1\right)\right]}{1+\alpha}; \tag{14.1}$$

$$y_{2t}^d = \frac{w_{2t}h_{2t}\left(1 - \frac{g_2+\delta_H}{A_{2H}}\right) + k_{2t}\left[\rho\left(1+g_2\right) + \left(1+\alpha\right)\left(\delta_k+g_2\right)\right]}{1+\alpha}. \tag{14.2}$$

Similarly, the AS functions are

$$y_{1t}^s = \left(A_{1G}\right)^{\frac{1}{1-\gamma}}\left(\frac{\gamma}{w_{1t}}\right)^{\frac{\gamma}{1-\gamma}}k_{1t}; \tag{14.3}$$

$$y_{2t}^s = \left(A_{2G}\right)^{\frac{1}{1-\gamma}}\left(\frac{\gamma}{w_{2t}}\right)^{\frac{\gamma}{1-\gamma}}k_{2t}. \tag{14.4}$$

The inverse AD and AS functions can be written, first for AD as

$$\frac{1}{w_{1t}} = \frac{h_{1t}\left(1 - \frac{g_1+\delta_H}{A_{1H}}\right)}{y_{1t}^d\left(1+\alpha\right) - k_{1t}\left[\rho\left(1+g_1\right) + \left(1+\alpha\right)\left(\delta_k+g_1\right)\right]}, \tag{14.5}$$

$$\frac{1}{w_{2t}} = \frac{h_{2t}\left(1 - \frac{g_2+\delta_H}{A_{2H}}\right)}{y_{2t}^d\left(1+\alpha\right) - k_{2t}\left[\rho\left(1+g_2\right) + \left(1+\alpha\right)\left(\delta_k+g_2\right)\right]}, \tag{14.6}$$

and for AS as

$$\frac{1}{w_{1t}} = \frac{1}{\gamma \left(A_{1G}\right)^{\frac{1}{\gamma}}} \left(\frac{y_{1t}^s}{k_{1t}}\right)^{\frac{1-\gamma}{\gamma}} ; \tag{14.7}$$

$$\frac{1}{w_{2t}} = \frac{1}{\gamma \left(A_{2G}\right)^{\frac{1}{\gamma}}} \left(\frac{y_{2t}^s}{k_{2t}}\right)^{\frac{1-\gamma}{\gamma}} . \tag{14.8}$$

14.2.1 Example 14.1: Autarky

As in Example 12.1, for country 1, let $\alpha = 1$, $\delta_k = 0.05$, $\delta_h = 0.015$, $\beta = \frac{1}{1+\rho} = 0.95$, $\rho = \left(\frac{1}{0.95} - 1\right) = 0.052632$, and $A_{1G} = 0.28224$. Also assume $A_{1H} = 0.189$, and the same goods sector and human capital investment sector technologies as in Example 12.1. For country 2, all parameters and technologies are the same except that $A_{2H} = (0.189)(1.15) = (0.21735)$. With these assumptions the growth rate in country 1 is $g = 0.02$, and $k_t = 1$, as in Example 12.1.

For country 2, the autarky equilibrium can be found as in Example 12.1. The balanced path growth rate is $g = 0.05271$; and the physical capital to human capital equilibrium value is $\frac{k_{2t}}{h_{2t}} = 0.42984$. To see this in terms of AS–AD, the excess output demand function for country 2 is

$$0 = Y\left(w_{2t}, g_2; \frac{k_{2t}}{h_{2t}}\right) = y_{2t}^d - y_{2t}^s.$$

With the functional forms substituted in,

$$\begin{aligned} Y\left(w_{2t}, g_2; k_{2t}, h_{2t}\right) \\ = \left(\frac{1}{1+\alpha}\right) \left[w_{2t}h_{2t}\left(1 - \frac{g_2 + \delta_H}{A_{2H}}\right) + k_{2t}\left[\rho\left(1+g_2\right) + \left(1+\alpha\right)\left(\delta_k + g_2\right)\right]\right] \\ - \left(A_{2G}\right)^{\frac{1}{1-\gamma}} \left(\frac{\gamma}{w_{2t}}\right)^{\frac{\gamma}{1-\gamma}} k_{2t} = 0. \end{aligned}$$

Appendix A12, equation (12.98) shows how this can be solved in terms of only the growth rate g_2, in the normalised excess output demand equation:

$$\begin{aligned} Y\left(g_2\right) &= \left(1+g_2+\beta\left(\delta_k - 1\right)\right)\gamma\left[\left(A_{2H} - \left(g_2 + \delta_H\right)\right)\right] \\ &\quad + \left(1+g_2\right)\left(1-\beta\right)\left(1-\gamma\right)\left[\rho\left(1+g_2\right) + \left(1+\alpha\right)\left(\delta_k + g_2\right)\right] \\ &\quad - \left(1+\alpha\right)\left(1+g_2\right)\rho\left(1+g_2+\beta\left(\delta_k - 1\right)\right) = 0. \end{aligned} \tag{14.9}$$

In calibrated form, this excess demand is

$$\begin{aligned} Y\left(g_2\right) &= \left(0.95\right)\left(1+g_2+0.95\left(0.05-1\right)\right)\tfrac{1}{3}\left(\left(0.21735\right) - \left(0.95\right)\left(g_2 + 0.015\right)\right) \\ &\quad + \left(1+g_2\right)\left(1-0.95\right)\left(\tfrac{2}{3}\right)\left[\left(1-\left(0.95\right)\right)\left(1+g_2\right) + 2\left(0.95\right)\left(0.05+g_2\right)\right] \\ &\quad - 2\left(1+g_2\right)\left(1-0.95\right)\left(1+g_2+0.95\left(0.05-1\right)\right) = 0. \end{aligned} \tag{14.10}$$

Figure 14.1 graphs equation (14.10) and shows that the excess demand is zero at $g_2 = 0.05271$.

Alternatively, following Appendix A12 and writing the solution equation in terms of $Ag^2 + Bg + C = 0$, the solution of equation (14.9), in terms of A, B and C, is given by

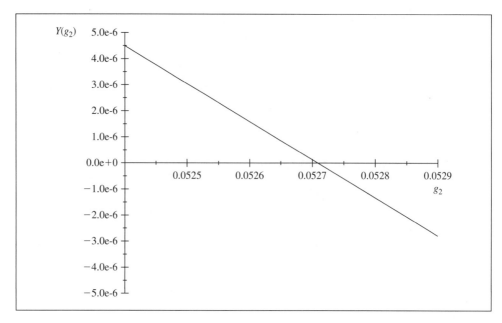

Figure 14.1 Normalised country 2 excess demand as a function of g_2 in Example 14.1

equations (12.101) to (12.103) of Appendix A12 as:

$$\text{Quadratic term: } \quad A = -0.3517,$$
$$\text{Linear term: } \quad B = -0.0067,$$
$$\text{Constant term: } \quad C = 0.0013.$$

These values imply a balanced path growth rate of $g_2 = 0.05271$.

With the equilibrium g_2 for country 2 in autarky, the labour employment follows by using the allocation of time constraint, and from equation (12.92) it is

$$l_{2t}^s = \frac{(1 + g_2)(1 - \beta)}{A_{2H}\beta} = \frac{(1.05271)(1 - 0.95)}{(0.21735)\,0.95} = 0.25492.$$

And the labour in human capital investment is

$$l_{2Ht} = \frac{g_{2t} + \delta_H}{A_{2H}} = \frac{0.05271 + 0.015}{0.21735} = 0.31153.$$

The capital to human capital ratio follows from equation (12.94), and with $l_{2t}^s = l_{2t}^d$, as

$$\frac{k_{2t}}{h_{2t}} = \left(\frac{\beta (1 - \gamma) A_{1G}}{1 + g_2 + \beta (\delta_k - 1)} \right)^{\frac{1}{\gamma}} l_{2t}^d;$$

$$\frac{k_{2t}}{h_{2t}} = \left(\frac{(0.95)\frac{2}{3}(0.28224)}{(1.05271) + (0.95)(0.05 - 1)} \right)^3 (0.25492) = 0.42960.$$

And the equilibrium wage in country 2 is

$$w_{2t} = \gamma A_{2G} \left(\frac{k_{2t}}{h_{2t} l_{2t}^d} \right)^{1-\gamma} = \frac{1}{3}(0.28224) \left(\frac{0.4296}{0.25492} \right)^{\frac{2}{3}} = 0.13323. \tag{14.11}$$

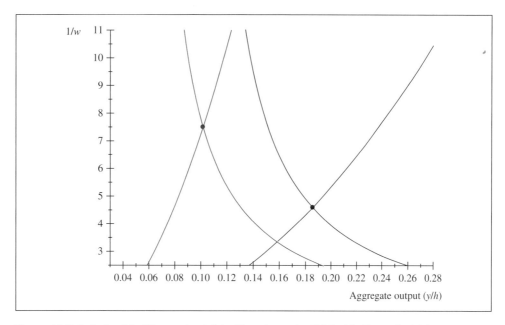

Figure 14.2 Autarky *AS–AD*; country 1 (black) and country 2 (blue) in Example 14.1

This makes the relative price of output $\frac{1}{w_{2t}} = \frac{1}{0.13323} = 7.5058$. And output with h_{2t} normalised to one, is $y_2 = (0.28224)(0.4296)^{\frac{2}{3}} 0.25492^{\frac{1}{3}} = 0.10189$.

Given $\frac{k_{2t}}{h_{2t}} = 0.4296$, the *AS–AD* can be graphed in terms of relative price $\frac{1}{w_t}$ and y_t. Figure 14.2 graphs the *AS–AD* from equations (14.5) to (14.8), using Example 12.1 for country 1 (black curves), and the just-derived equilibrium for country 2 (blue curves). The equilibrium represents the different relative output prices and wage rates in each country prior to the opening of trade, while in autarky.

The real interest rate is given by

$$r = \frac{1 + g + \beta\left(\delta_k - 1\right)}{\beta} = \frac{(1.05271) + 0.95\left(0.05 - 1\right)}{0.95} = 0.15812.$$

Consumption and output are given as

$$c_{2t}^d = \left(\frac{1}{1+\alpha}\right)\left[w_{2t}h_{2t}\left(1 - \frac{g_2 + \delta_H}{A_{2H}}\right) + k_{2t}\rho\left(1 + g_1\right)\right],$$

$$= \left(\frac{1}{1+1}\right)\left(0.13323\left(1 - \frac{0.05271 + 0.015}{(0.21735)}\right) + 0.4296\left(0.052632\right)\left(1.05271\right)\right),$$

$$= 0.057764.$$

$$y_{2t}^s = \left(A_{2G}\right)^{\frac{1}{1-\gamma}}\left(\frac{\gamma}{w_{2t}}\right)^{\frac{\gamma}{1-\gamma}} k_{2t} = \left(0.28224\right)^{1.5}\left(\frac{1}{3\left(0.13323\right)}\right)^{0.5} 0.42960,$$

$$= 0.10189.$$

14.2.2 Labour market

The equilibrium of Example 12.1 gives the country 1 autarky equilibrium. The labour supply and demand from Chapter 12, equations (12.39) and (12.40), now stated for each country 1 and 2, are

$$l_{1t}^s = 1 - \frac{\alpha}{1+\alpha}\left[1 + \frac{k_{1t}}{w_{1t}h_{1t}}\rho\left(1+g_1\right)\right] - \frac{g_1+\delta_H}{A_{1H}\left(1+\alpha\right)}, \tag{14.12}$$

$$l_{2t}^s = 1 - \frac{\alpha}{1+\alpha}\left[1 + \frac{k_{2t}}{w_{2t}h_{2t}}\rho\left(1+g_2\right)\right] - \frac{g_2+\delta_H}{A_{2H}\left(1+\alpha\right)}; \tag{14.13}$$

$$l_{1t}^d = \left(\frac{\gamma A_{1G}}{w_t}\right)^{\frac{1}{1-\gamma}} k_{1t}, \tag{14.14}$$

$$l_{2t}^d = \left(\frac{\gamma A_{2G}}{w_t}\right)^{\frac{1}{1-\gamma}} k_{2t}. \tag{14.15}$$

Inversely solved for w_t, and with calibrated values, these supply and demand equations are

$$w_{1t} = \frac{\alpha\rho\left(1+g_1\right)\left(\frac{k_{1t}}{h_{1t}}\right)}{1-\left(1+\alpha\right)l_{1t}^s - \frac{(g_1+\delta_H)}{A_{1H}}} = \frac{1\left(0.0526\right)\left(1+0.02\right)1}{1-\left(1+1\right)l_{1t}^s - \frac{(0.02+0.015)}{0.189}}, \tag{14.16}$$

$$w_{2t} = \frac{\alpha\rho\left(1+g_2\right)\left(\frac{k_t}{h_t}\right)}{1-\left(1+\alpha\right)l_{2t}^s - \frac{(g_2+\delta_H)}{A_{2H}}} = \frac{1\left(0.0526\right)\left(1.05271\right)\left(0.43\right)}{1-\left(1+1\right)l_{2t}^s - \frac{(0.053+0.015)}{0.21735}}; \tag{14.17}$$

$$w_{1t} = \gamma A_{1G}\left(\frac{k_{1t}}{h_{1t}l_{1t}^d}\right)^{1-\gamma} = \frac{(0.28224)}{3}\left(\frac{1}{l_{1t}^d}\right)^{\frac{2}{3}}, \tag{14.18}$$

$$w_{2t} = \gamma A_{2G}\left(\frac{k_{2t}}{h_{2t}l_{2t}^d}\right)^{1-\gamma} = \frac{(0.28224)}{3}\left(\frac{0.42984}{l_{2t}^d}\right)^{\frac{2}{3}}. \tag{14.19}$$

Figure 14.3 graphs equations (14.16) to (14.19).

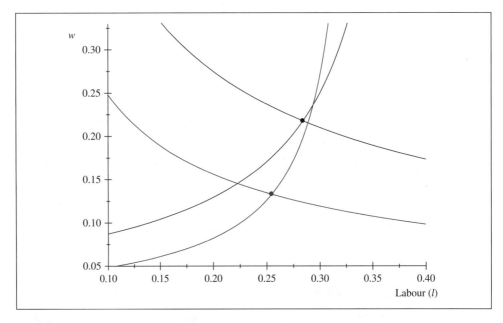

Figure 14.3 Labour market with autarky of country 1 (black) and 2 (blue) in Example 14.1

Employment under autarky for country 1 is $l_{1t} = 0.28405$ and for country 2 is $l_{2t} = 0.25492$. And the autarky wage rates are $w_{1t} = 0.21772$, and $w_{2t} = 0.13323$.

14.3 Trade

Now assume that the agent/countries can trade freely with each other. This requires an extension of the dynamic model to allow such trade. Since the equilibrium conditions are the same Chapter 12 general form for each country, the solution methodology is a modest extension of that in Chapter 12, Appendix A12. The difference is that now the market clearing condition, or excess demand function, must set the sum of demand from both countries equal to the sum of supply from both countries, as in Chapters 4 and 7.

With trade, factor prices are common to both countries. The interest rate r_t will be equal across countries, and the wage rate w_t will also be equal across countries. This is the key result of trade, often called factor price equalisation, after Paul Samuelson's 'factor price equalisation theorem'. This equalisation of factor prices occurs along the balanced growth path equilibrium.

14.3.1 World market clearing

With trade, the market clearing condition is that the sum of the output demand equals the sum of the output supply:

$$y_{1t}^d + y_{2t}^d = y_{1t}^s + y_{2t}^s. \tag{14.20}$$

From the market clearing condition (14.20) the world excess demand function can be defined as the total demand minus the total supply, or

$$0 = Y\left(w_t, g; k_{1t}, k_{2t}, h_{1t}, h_{2t}\right) = y_{1t}^d + y_{2t}^d - y_{1t}^s - y_{2t}^s.$$

Substituting in the AD and AS functions from equations (14.5) to (14.8), the excess output demand is

$$
\begin{aligned}
Y\left(w_t, g; k_{1t}, k_{2t}, h_{1t}, h_{2t}\right) \\
= \left(\frac{1}{1+\alpha}\right)\left[w_t h_{1t}\left(1 - \frac{g+\delta_H}{A_{1H}}\right) + k_{1t}\left[\rho\left(1+g\right) + \left(1+\alpha\right)\left(\delta_k + g\right)\right]\right] \\
+ \left(\frac{1}{1+\alpha}\right)\left[w_t h_{2t}\left(1 - \frac{g+\delta_H}{A_{2H}}\right) + k_{2t}\left[\rho\left(1+g\right) + \left(1+\alpha\right)\left(\delta_k + g\right)\right]\right] \\
- \left(A_{1G}\right)^{\frac{1}{1-\gamma}}\left(\frac{\gamma}{w_t}\right)^{\frac{\gamma}{1-\gamma}} k_{1t} - A_{2G}^{\frac{1}{1-\gamma}}\left(\frac{\gamma}{w_t}\right)^{\frac{\gamma}{1-\gamma}} k_{2t} = 0. \tag{14.21}
\end{aligned}
$$

14.3.2 Solution methodology

To solve the equilibrium, and so identify the trade flows, the world excess output demand function can be used as the starting point. This gives output as a function of g, w_t and $\frac{k_{1t}}{h_{1t}}$ and $\frac{k_{2t}}{k_{1t}}$. The complication relative to Chapter 12, Appendix A12 solution methodology, is that now the capital ratio $\frac{k_{2t}}{k_{1t}}$ is added into the world excess output function.

The way to solve for both $\frac{k_{1t}}{h_{1t}}$ and $\frac{k_{2t}}{k_{1t}}$ comes from using the world labour market clearing condition, in addition to the world goods market clearing condition that is used in the excess output demand equation. In particular, by using the equilibrium conditions for labour supply for each country, the total labour supplied is solved in terms of g. Then from the labour demand, a relation for $\frac{k_{1t}}{h_{1t}}$ and $\frac{k_{2t}}{k_{1t}}$ can be solved for in terms of g by also using the labour supply solution in terms of g. This same relation for $\frac{k_{1t}}{h_{1t}}$ and $\frac{k_{2t}}{k_{1t}}$ then can be substituted into the world excess output demand, and this can then be expressed as a single equation in g, and so solved as a quadratic equation again as in Chapter 12.

First the excess output demand of equation (14.21) will be rewritten by dividing through by h_{1t} and by writing $\frac{k_{2t}}{h_{1t}}$ as $\frac{k_{2t}}{k_{1t}}\frac{k_{1t}}{h_{1t}}$ by multiplying and dividing by k_{1t}:

$$
\frac{Y\left(w_t, g; k_{1t}, k_{2t}, h_{1t}, h_{2t}\right)}{h_{1t}}
$$

$$
= \left(\frac{1}{1+\alpha}\right)\left[w_t\left(1 - \frac{g+\delta_H}{A_{1H}}\right) + \frac{k_{1t}}{h_{1t}}\left[\rho\left(1+g\right) + \left(1+\alpha\right)\left(\delta_k + g\right)\right]\right]
$$

$$
+ \left(\frac{1}{1+\alpha}\right)\left[w_t\frac{h_{2t}}{h_{1t}}\left(1 - \frac{g+\delta_H}{A_{2H}}\right) + \frac{k_{2t}}{k_{1t}}\frac{k_{1t}}{h_{1t}}\left[\rho\left(1+g\right) + \left(1+\alpha\right)\left(\delta_k + g\right)\right]\right]
$$

$$
- \left(A_{1G}\right)^{\frac{1}{1-\gamma}}\left(\frac{\gamma}{w_t}\right)^{\frac{\gamma}{1-\gamma}}\frac{k_{1t}}{h_{1t}} - \left(A_{2G}\right)^{\frac{1}{1-\gamma}}\left(\frac{\gamma}{w_t}\right)^{\frac{\gamma}{1-\gamma}}\frac{k_{2t}}{k_{1t}}\frac{k_{1t}}{h_{1t}} = 0. \tag{14.22}
$$

Normalising $\frac{h_{2t}}{h_{1t}} = 1$, substituting in that $A_{1G} = A_{2G}$, and gathering terms,

$$
\frac{Y\left(w_t, g; k_{1t}, k_{2t}, h_{1t}\right)}{h_{1t}}
$$

$$
= \left(\frac{1}{1+\alpha}\right)w_t\left(2 - \frac{\left(A_{1H} + A_{2H}\right)\left(g + \delta_H\right)}{A_{1H}A_{2H}}\right)
$$

$$
+ \left(\frac{1}{1+\alpha}\right)\left[\rho\left(1+g\right) + \left(1+\alpha\right)\left(\delta_k + g\right)\right]\frac{k_{1t}}{h_{1t}}\left(1 + \frac{k_{2t}}{k_{1t}}\right)
$$

$$
- \left(A_{1G}\right)^{\frac{1}{1-\gamma}}\left(\frac{\gamma}{w_t}\right)^{\frac{\gamma}{1-\gamma}}\frac{k_{1t}}{h_{1t}}\left(1 + \frac{k_{2t}}{k_{1t}}\right) = 0. \tag{14.23}
$$

This requires a solution in terms of g only for two terms, w_t and $\frac{k_{1t}}{h_{1t}}\left(1 + \frac{k_{2t}}{k_{1t}}\right)$.

To solve for w_t in terms of g requires expressing the marginal product of labour in terms of the capital to effective labour ratio and then using the two facts about the interest rate r. It is given in terms of g from the consumer's intertemporal margin, and it also is a function only of the capital to effective labour ratio. First consider the marginal product conditions for w_t and r_t and the consumer intertemporal margin:

$$
w_t = \gamma A_{1G}\left(\frac{k_{1t}}{h_{1t}l_{1t}^d}\right)^{1-\gamma};
$$

$$
1 + g = \frac{1 + r_t - \delta_k}{1 + \rho} = \beta\left(1 + r_t - \delta_k\right),
$$

$$
r_t = \frac{1 + g + \beta\left(\delta_k - 1\right)}{\beta}; \tag{14.24}
$$

$$
r_t = \left(1 - \gamma\right)A_{1G}\left(\frac{k_{1t}}{h_{1t}l_{1t}^d}\right)^{-\gamma}.
$$

These imply the capital to effective labour ratio in terms of g:

$$
\frac{k_{1t}}{h_{1t}l_{1t}^d} = \left(\frac{\left(1 - \gamma\right)A_{1G}}{r_t}\right)^{\frac{1}{\gamma}} = \left(\frac{\beta\left(1 - \gamma\right)A_{1G}}{1 + g + \beta\left(\delta_k - 1\right)}\right)^{\frac{1}{\gamma}},
$$

and in turn the wage rate in terms of g:

$$w_t = \gamma A_{1G} \left(\frac{\beta \left(1 - \gamma\right) A_{1G}}{1 + g + \beta \left(\delta_k - 1\right)} \right)^{\frac{1-\gamma}{\gamma}}. \tag{14.25}$$

Now it remains only to solve for $\frac{k_{1t}}{h_{1t}} \left(1 + \frac{k_{2t}}{k_{1t}}\right)$ in terms of g. And this requires the world labour market clearing conditions plus the human capital intertemporal margins which constitute the other growth rate conditions.

The other growth rate equations for each country, using Appendix A12 but now with country subscripts, are

$$1 + g = \beta \left[1 + A_{1H} \left(1 - x_{1t}\right) - \delta_H\right], \tag{14.26}$$
$$1 + g = 1 + A_{1H} l_{1Ht} - \delta_H; \tag{14.27}$$

$$1 + g = \beta \left[1 + A_{2H} \left(1 - x_{2t}\right) - \delta_H\right], \tag{14.28}$$
$$1 + g = 1 + A_{2H} l_{2Ht} - \delta_H. \tag{14.29}$$

These equations allow leisure (x_{1t}, x_{2t}) and time in human capital investment (l_{1Ht}, l_{2Ht}) to be different across country, since A_{1H} and A_{2H} are allowed to be different across country by assumption.

The allocation of time constraints is

$$1 - x_{1t} - l_{1Ht} = l_{1t}^s;$$
$$1 - x_{2t} - l_{2Ht} = l_{2t}^s.$$

The growth rate equations (14.27) and (14.29) imply that

$$l_{1Ht} = \frac{g + \delta_H}{A_{1H}}, \tag{14.30}$$

$$l_{2Ht} = \frac{g + \delta_H}{A_{2H}}, \tag{14.31}$$

and equations (14.26) and (14.28) imply that

$$1 - x_{1t} = \frac{\left(1 - \delta_H\right)\left(1 - \beta\right) + g + \delta_H}{A_{1H}\beta}, \tag{14.32}$$

$$1 - x_{2t} = \frac{\left(1 - \delta_H\right)\left(1 - \beta\right) + g + \delta_H}{A_{2H}\beta}. \tag{14.33}$$

Using the time allocation constraints then

$$1 - x_{1t} - l_{1Ht} = l_{1t}^s = \frac{\left(1 + g\right)\left(1 - \beta\right)}{A_{1H}\beta}. \tag{14.34}$$

Similarly, the agent 2 labour supply is

$$1 - x_{2t} - l_{2Ht} = l_{2t}^s = \frac{\left(1 + g\right)\left(1 - \beta\right)}{A_{2H}\beta}. \tag{14.35}$$

And this makes the total labour supply l_t equal to

$$l_{1t}^d + l_{2t}^d = l_t = l_{1t}^s + l_{2t}^s = \frac{\left(1 + g\right)\left(1 - \beta\right)}{A_{1H}\beta} + \frac{\left(1 + g\right)\left(1 - \beta\right)}{A_{2H}\beta},$$

$$l_t = \frac{\left(A_{1H} + A_{2H}\right)\left(1 + g\right)\left(1 - \beta\right)}{A_{1H} A_{2H}\beta}. \tag{14.36}$$

Labour demand is as in Chapters 9 and 10 except that now h_t enters into $\frac{k_t}{h_t}$ rather than just having k_t. But again with $h_t = 1$ as a normalisation, the functional form is identical to Chapters 8 and 10. From the firm's equilibrium condition with respect to labour,

$$w_t = \gamma A_{1G} \left(l_{1t}^d h_{1t} \right)^{\gamma - 1} (k_{1t})^{1-\gamma},$$

$$w_t = \gamma A_{2G} \left(l_{2t}^d h_{2t} \right)^{\gamma - 1} (k_{2t})^{1-\gamma}.$$

Solving for labour demand in each country, adding together, using that $A_{1G} = A_{2G}$, and simplifying

$$
\begin{aligned}
l_t &= l_{1t}^d + l_{2t}^d \\
&= \left(\frac{\gamma A_{1G}}{w_t} \right)^{\frac{1}{1-\gamma}} k_{1t} + \left(\frac{\gamma A_{2G}}{w_t} \right)^{\frac{1}{1-\gamma}} k_{2t} \\
&= \left(\frac{\gamma A_{1G}}{w_t} \right)^{\frac{1}{1-\gamma}} \frac{k_{1t}}{h_{1t}} \left(1 + \left(\frac{A_{2G}}{A_{1G}} \right)^{\frac{1}{1-\gamma}} \frac{\frac{k_{2t}}{h_{2t}}}{\frac{k_{1t}}{h_{1t}}} \right) = \left(\frac{\gamma A_{1G}}{w_t} \right)^{\frac{1}{1-\gamma}} \frac{k_{1t}}{h_{1t}} \left(1 + \frac{k_{2t}}{k_{1t}} \right).
\end{aligned}
$$

Use the market clearing fact that

$$l_{1t}^s + l_{2t}^s = l_t = l_{1t}^d + l_{2t}^d, \tag{14.37}$$

plus equation (14.36) for l_t in terms of g, and substitute in for w_t in terms of g from equation (14.25)

$$\frac{(A_{1H} + A_{2H})(1+g)(1-\beta)}{A_{1H} A_{2H} \beta} = l_t = \left(\frac{1}{\left(\frac{\beta(1-\gamma)A_{1G}}{1+g+\beta(\delta_k - 1)} \right)^{\frac{1-\gamma}{\gamma}}} \right)^{\frac{1}{1-\gamma}} \frac{k_{1t}}{h_{1t}} \left(1 + \frac{k_{2t}}{k_{1t}} \right).$$

And so the solution for $\frac{k_{1t}}{h_{1t}} \left(1 + \frac{k_{2t}}{k_{1t}} \right)$ as a function of g results:

$$\frac{k_{1t}}{h_{1t}} \left(1 + \frac{k_{2t}}{k_{1t}} \right) = \left(\frac{\beta(1-\gamma)A_{1G}}{1+g+\beta(\delta_k - 1)} \right)^{\frac{1}{\gamma}} \frac{(A_{1H} + A_{2H})(1+g)(1-\beta)}{A_{1H} A_{2H} \beta}.$$

Now return to equation (14.23) and substitute in for w_t and $\frac{k_{1t}}{h_{1t}} \left(1 + \frac{k_{2t}}{k_{1t}} \right)$ both in terms of g:

$$
\begin{aligned}
Y(g) &= 0 \\
&= \left(\frac{\gamma A_{1G}}{1+\alpha} \right) \left(\frac{\beta(1-\gamma)A_{1G}}{1+g+\beta(\delta_k - 1)} \right)^{\frac{1-\gamma}{\gamma}} \left(2 - \frac{(A_{1H} + A_{2H})(g + \delta_H)}{A_{1H} A_{2H}} \right) \\
&\quad + \frac{[\rho(1+g) + (1+\alpha)(\delta_k + g)]}{1+\alpha} \left(\frac{\beta(1-\gamma)A_{1G}}{1+g+\beta(\delta_k - 1)} \right)^{\frac{1}{\gamma}} \frac{(A_{1H} + A_{2H})(1+g)(1-\beta)}{A_{1H} A_{2H} \beta} \\
&\quad - \left(\frac{(A_{1G})^{\frac{1}{1-\gamma}} \gamma^{\frac{\gamma}{1-\gamma}}}{(\gamma A_{1G})^{\frac{\gamma}{1-\gamma}} \left(\frac{\beta(1-\gamma)A_{1G}}{1+g+\beta(\delta_k-1)} \right)} \right) \left(\frac{\beta(1-\gamma)A_{1G}}{1+g+\beta(\delta_k - 1)} \right)^{\frac{1}{\gamma}} \frac{(A_{1H} + A_{2H})(1+g)(1-\beta)}{A_{1H} A_{2H} \beta}.
\end{aligned}
$$

This simplifies to

$$0 = \frac{(A_{1H} + A_{2H})\,(1+g)\,(1-\beta)}{A_{1H}A_{2H}\beta} - \frac{\gamma}{1+\alpha}\left(2 - \frac{(A_{1H} + A_{2H})\,(g+\delta_H)}{A_{1H}A_{2H}}\right)$$

$$- \left(\frac{\rho\,(1+g)}{1+\alpha} + (\delta_k+g)\right)\frac{(A_{1H}+A_{2H})\,(1+g)\,(1-\beta)}{A_{1H}A_{2H}\beta}\left(\frac{\beta\,(1-\gamma)}{1+g+\beta\,(\delta_k-1)}\right),$$

or a final simplified version for solving is

$$0 = (1+\alpha)\,\left[1+g+\beta\,(\delta_k-1)\right]\,(1+g)\,(1-\beta) \tag{14.38}$$

$$- \gamma\beta\left(\frac{2A_{1H}A_{2H}}{(A_{1H}+A_{2H})} - (g+\delta_H)\right)\left[1+g+\beta\,(\delta_k-1)\right]$$

$$- \left[(1-\beta)\,(1+g) + \beta\,(1+\alpha)\,(\delta_k+g)\right]\,(1+g)\,(1-\beta)\,(1-\gamma).$$

Solving this equation using the fact that it is a quadratic equation in g, with $Ag^2 + Bg + C = 0$, then the solution is given by

$$g = \frac{-B + \sqrt{B^2 - 4AC}}{2A}, \tag{14.39}$$

where in general form the parameters A, B, and C are given by

Quadratic term: $A \equiv -\beta\gamma + (1-\beta)\,(1-\gamma)\,(1+\alpha\beta) - (1+\alpha)\,(1-\beta)$,

Linear term: $B \equiv -\beta\gamma\left[1 + \beta\,(\delta_k-1) - \frac{2A_{1h}A_{2h}}{A_{1h}+A_{2h}} + \delta_h\right]$

$$+ (1-\beta)\,(1-\gamma)\,\left[1 - \beta + \beta\,(1+\alpha)\,\delta_k + (1+\alpha\beta)\right]$$

$$- (1+\alpha)\,(1-\beta)\,\left[2 + \beta\,(\delta_k-1)\right],$$

Constant term: $C \equiv \beta\gamma\left(\frac{2A_{1h}A_{2h}}{A_{1h}+A_{2h}} - \delta_h\right)\left[1 + \beta\,(\delta_k-1)\right]$

$$+ (1-\beta)\,(1-\gamma)\,\left[1 - \beta + \beta\,(1+\alpha)\,\delta_k\right]$$

$$- (1+\alpha)\,(1-\beta)\,\left[1 + \beta\,(\delta_k-1)\right].$$

14.3.3 Example 14.2

Assume the same calibration as in Example 14.1: $\alpha = 1$, $\delta_k = 0.05$, $\delta_h = 0.015$, $\beta = \frac{1}{1+\rho} = 0.95$, $\rho = \left(\frac{1}{0.95} - 1\right) = 0.052632$, $A_{1G} = A_{2G} = 0.28224$, $A_{1H} = 0.189$, and $A_{2H} = 0.21735$. And now allow trade.

There is a new equilibrium growth rate given by equation (14.38). To find this, consider that the calibrated form of this equation is

$$0 = 2\,(1+g+0.95\,(0.05-1))\,(1+g)\,(1-0.95) \tag{14.40}$$

$$- \tfrac{1}{3}\,(0.95)\left(\frac{2\,(0.189)\,(0.21735)}{(0.189+0.21735)} - (g+0.015)\right)(1+g+0.95\,(0.05-1))$$

$$- ((1-0.95)\,(1+g) + (0.95)\,2\,(0.05+g))\,(1+g)\,(1-0.95)\left(\tfrac{2}{3}\right).$$

The solution is that $g = 0.0358$; this can be seen by graphing the normalised excess demand function of equation (14.40) as in Figure 14.4.

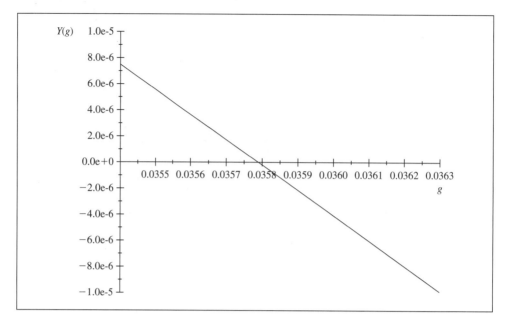

Figure 14.4 Excess world output demand $Y(g)$ and equilibrium growth g in Example 14.2

And in terms of the analytic solution in equation (14.39), for Example 14.2 the quadratic equation in g has the parameters of

Quadratic term: $A = -0.3517$,

Linear term: $B = -0.0115$,

Constant term: $C = 0.00086$.

The new capital to human capital ratios in each country can now be computed given that $g = 0.0358$. These can then be substituted into the AS–AD functions and graphed to show the trade flows within the aggregate output market. This first requires finding the new equilibrium wage rate.

From equation (14.25), substituting in the new growth rate, the equilibrium wage rate follows directly as

$$w_t = \frac{(0.28224)}{3}\left(\frac{(0.95)\frac{2}{3}(0.28224)}{(1.0358)+(0.95)(0.05-1)}\right)^2 = 0.16918.$$

And given the wage rate and the new labour supply levels, the capital ratios can be found. From equations (14.27) and (14.29) the new labour supplies are

$$l_{1t}^s = \frac{(1+g)(1-\beta)}{A_{1H}\beta} = \frac{(1.0358)(1-0.95)}{(0.189)0.95} = 0.28844; \qquad (14.41)$$

$$l_{2t}^s = \frac{(1+g)(1-\beta)}{A_{2H}\beta} = \frac{(1.0358)(1-0.95)}{(0.21735)0.95} = 0.25082. \qquad (14.42)$$

Using the labour supply functions of equations (14.12) and (14.13), and substituting in the wage w_t and the labour supply values, the capital ratios result:

$$l_{1t}^s = 1 - 0.5\left[1 + \frac{k_{1t}}{(0.16918)h_{1t}}(0.0526)(1.0358)\right] - \frac{(0.5)\,0.0508}{(0.189)}, \qquad (14.43)$$

$$= 0.28844, \qquad (14.44)$$

$$\frac{k_{1t}}{h_{1t}} = \frac{\left(2\left(1 - 0.28844 - \left(\frac{0.0508}{(0.189)(2)}\right)\right) - 1\right)(0.169)}{(0.052632)(1.0358)} = 0.47895; \tag{14.45}$$

$$l_{2t}^s = 1 - 0.5\left[1 + \frac{k_{2t}}{(0.16918)\, h_{2t}}\,(0.0526)\,(1.0358)\right] - \frac{(0.5)\,0.0508}{(0.217)} \tag{14.46}$$

$$= 0.25082, \tag{14.47}$$

$$\frac{k_{2t}}{h_{2t}} = \frac{\left(2\left(1 - 0.25082 - \left(\frac{0.0508}{(0.21735)(2)}\right)\right) - 1\right)(0.169)}{(0.052632)(1.0358)} = 0.82124. \tag{14.48}$$

Trade causes the capital ratio in country 1, $\frac{k_{1t}}{h_{1t}}$, to fall from 1 in autarky to 0.47895 under trade, and the capital ratio in country 2 to rise from 0.4296 in autarky to 0.82124 under trade.

14.3.4 Graphing AS–AD

Each individual country AS–AD can now be graphed with their respective capital ratios. And the total world AD and world AS can also be graphed similarly. The individual country AS–AD graphs show the trade flow while the total world AS–AD shows the equilibrium total output and relative price, $\frac{1}{w_t}$. And these equilibrium AS–AD functions under trade can also be compared in the same graph to the autarky equilibrium AS–AD functions.

The new individual AS–AD functions under trade with $g = 0.0358$ are for AD:

$$\frac{1}{w_t} = \frac{\left(1 - \frac{0.0358 + 0.015}{0.189}\right)}{y_{1t}^d\,(2) - 0.47895\left[\left(\frac{1}{0.95} - 1\right)(1.0358) + (2)(0.0858)\right]}, \tag{14.49}$$

$$\frac{1}{w_t} = \frac{\left(1 - \frac{0.0358 + 0.015}{(0.21735)}\right)}{y_{2t}^d\,(2) - 0.82124\left[\left(\frac{1}{0.95} - 1\right)(1.0358) + (2)(0.0858)\right]}; \tag{14.50}$$

and for AS:

$$\frac{1}{w_t} = \frac{3}{(0.28224)^3}\left(\frac{y_{1t}^s}{0.47895}\right)^2, \tag{14.51}$$

$$\frac{1}{w_t} = \frac{3}{(0.28224)^3}\left(\frac{y_{2t}^s}{0.82124}\right)^2. \tag{14.52}$$

To graph the total world AS–AD requires deriving the total aggregate demand function for output, and then stating the function inversely by solving for $\frac{1}{w_t}$. The sum of demand from countries 1 and 2, from equations (14.1) and (14.2), is equal to

$$\begin{aligned}
y_t^d &= y_{1t}^d + y_{2t}^d \\
&= \frac{w}{1+\alpha}\left(2 - (g + \delta_H)\left(\frac{1}{A_{1H}} + \frac{1}{A_{2H}}\right)\right) \\
&\quad + \frac{(k_{1t} + k_{2t})}{1+\alpha}\left[\rho\,(1+g) + (1+\alpha)\,(\delta_k + g)\right].
\end{aligned}$$

Inversely, total AD is

$$\frac{1}{w_t} = \frac{(2 - (g + \delta_H))\left(\frac{1}{A_{1H}} + \frac{1}{A_{2H}}\right)}{(y_t^d)\,(1+\alpha) - (k_{1t} + k_{2t})\left[\rho\,(1+g) + (1+\alpha)\,(\delta_k + g)\right]}.$$

In calibrated form this becomes

$$\frac{1}{w_t} = \frac{\left(2 - (0.0358 + 0.015)\left(\frac{1}{0.189} + \frac{1}{(0.21735)}\right)\right)}{\left(y_{1t}^d + y_{2t}^d\right)(2) - (0.47895 + 0.82124)\left(0.052632\left(1.0358\right) + (2)\left(0.0858\right)\right)}. \tag{14.53}$$

The total world aggregate supply of output is the sum of supply from equations (14.3) and (14.4):

$$y_t^s = y_{1t}^s + y_{2t}^s = (A_{1G})^{\frac{1}{1-\gamma}}\left(\frac{\gamma}{w_t}\right)^{\frac{\gamma}{1-\gamma}} k_{1t} + (A_{2G})^{\frac{1}{1-\gamma}}\left(\frac{\gamma}{w_t}\right)^{\frac{\gamma}{1-\gamma}} k_{2t}. \tag{14.54}$$

Inversely, this world AS is

$$\frac{1}{w_t} = \frac{\left(y_t^s\right)^{\frac{1-\gamma}{\gamma}}}{\gamma\left(A_{1G}\right)^{\frac{1}{\gamma}} k_{1t}^{\frac{1-\gamma}{\gamma}} \left(1 + \left(\frac{A_{2G}}{A_{1G}}\right)^{\frac{1}{1-\gamma}} \frac{k_{2t}}{k_{1t}}\right)^{\frac{1-\gamma}{\gamma}}}, \tag{14.55}$$

calibrated as

$$\frac{1}{w_t} = \frac{3\left(y_t^s\right)^2}{(0.28224)^3 (0.47895)^2 \left(1 + \frac{0.82124}{0.47895}\right)^2}. \tag{14.56}$$

All of the AS–AD functions can be graphed together for comparison. Figure 14.5 graphs these three sets of AS–AD functions: for autarky, equations (14.5) to (14.8) in calibrated

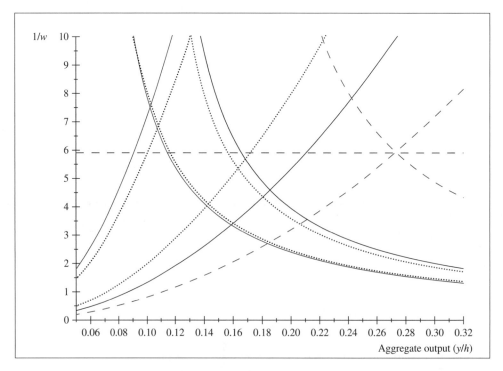

Figure 14.5 *AS–AD* under autarky (black and blue) and trade (dotted black and dotted blue), with world equilibrium (dashed blue) in Example 14.2

form, in blue and black as in Figure 14.2; for the total aggregate world supply and demand, equations (14.53) and (14.56) in dashed blue; and for the *AS–AD* of each country under trade after their capital stocks have adjusted, equations (14.49) to (14.52), in dotted black for country 1 and dotted blue for country 2.

The dashed blue equilibrium shows the equilibrium world relative price of $\frac{1}{w_t} = \frac{1}{0.16918} = 5.9109$, or $w = 0.16918$. In the autarky equilibrium, the price of 5.9109 indicates that country 1 would have a large excess supply of output, while country 2 would have a large excess demand. However this is not an equilibrium amount of excess supply and demand, as it was in Chapters 4 and 7, since here the countries have to adjust their capital ratios to the new equilibrium prices of capital and labour. After adjustment of the capital ratios, the dotted black and dotted blue equilibriums now show an excess demand by 1 and excess supply for 2.

The country more productive in human capital, country 2, becomes the one that supplies excess output, while the country less productive in human capital investment, country 1, ends up demanding more output than it produces. These trade flows can be detailed more clearly.

14.4 Trade flows

To highlight these trade flows, Figure 14.5 is zoomed in for the dotted black and dotted blue *AS–AD* under trade of each country. Figure 14.6 indicates the same dotted blue supply and demand for country 2 and the same dotted black supply and demand for country 1, of Figure 14.5. The excess demand of country 1 is met exactly by the excess supply of country 2, with output thereby exported from 2 to 1. To determine the magnitude of export requires computing the output supply and demand of each country given the price of $\frac{1}{w_t} = \frac{1}{0.16918} = 5.9109$.

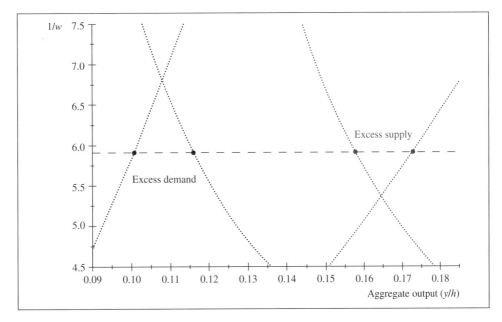

Figure 14.6 *AS–AD* output trade flow with excess demand and excess supply in Example 14.2

Going back to equations (14.5) to (14.8), and substituting in the parameters and equilibrium values of variables, the demand quantities are

$$y_{1t}^d = \left(\frac{1}{1+\alpha}\right)\left[w_t h_{1t}\left(1 - \frac{g + \delta_H}{A_{1H}}\right) + k_{1t}\left[\rho\left(1+g\right) + \left(1+\alpha\right)\left(\delta_k + g\right)\right]\right],$$

$$= 0.5\left(0.16918\right)\left(1 - \frac{0.0358 + 0.015}{0.189}\right) \tag{14.57}$$

$$+ 0.5\left(0.47895\right)\left(\left(\frac{1}{0.95} - 1\right)\left(1.0358\right) + \left(2\right)\left(0.05 + 0.0358\right)\right), \tag{14.58}$$

$$= 0.116; \tag{14.59}$$

$$y_{2t}^d = \left(\frac{1}{1+\alpha}\right)\left[w_t h_{2t}\left(1 - \frac{g + \delta_H}{A_{2H}}\right) + k_{2t}\left[\rho\left(1+g\right) + \left(1+\alpha\right)\left(\delta_k + g\right)\right]\right],$$

$$= 0.5\left(0.16918\right)\left(1 - \frac{0.0358 + 0.015}{0.21735}\right)$$

$$+ 0.5\left(0.82124\right)\left(\left(\frac{1}{0.95} - 1\right)\left(1.0358\right) + \left(2\right)\left(0.05 + 0.0358\right)\right), \tag{14.60}$$

$$= 0.15767. \tag{14.61}$$

And the supply quantities are

$$y_{1t}^s = \left(A_{1G}\right)^{\frac{1}{1-\gamma}}\left(\frac{\gamma}{w_t}\right)^{\frac{\gamma}{1-\gamma}}k_{1t},$$

$$= \left(0.28224\right)^{1.5}\left(\frac{1}{3\left(0.16918\right)}\right)^{0.5}\left(0.47895\right),$$

$$= 0.10081; \tag{14.62}$$

$$y_{2t}^s = \left(A_{2G}\right)^{\frac{1}{1-\gamma}}\left(\frac{\gamma}{w_t}\right)^{\frac{\gamma}{1-\gamma}}k_{2t},$$

$$= \left(0.28224\right)^{1.5}\left(\frac{1}{3\left(0.16918\right)}\right)^{0.5}\left(0.82124\right),$$

$$= 0.17285. \tag{14.63}$$

The excess demand of country 1 is

Excess demand (1): $y_{1t}^d - y_{1t}^s = 0.116 - 0.10081 = 0.0152.$ \qquad (14.64)

The excess supply of country 2 is

Excess supply (2): $y_{2t}^s - y_{2t}^d = 0.17285 - 0.15767 = 0.0152.$ \qquad (14.65)

Thus 0.0152 output is exported from 2 to 1. And this is the fraction of output produced by country 1 of $\frac{0.0152}{0.10081} = 0.15078$, or 15%. These trade flows in output are paid for through trade flows in labour.

14.5 Labour market

The labour market shows how trade affects the supply and demand for labour. It is the factor market dimension of the economy that is seen in the output market through AS–AD. A figure comparable to Figure 14.4 with the autarky and trade equilibrium can be constructed in the labour market in a similar fashion, again using Example 14.2.

14.5.1 Trade

The total world labour demand is the sum of the individual country labour demands, and this is equal to the sum of the individual country labour supplies. The labour market clearing condition with a single growth rate g and wage rate w_t is

$$l_{1t}^s + l_{2t}^s = l_{1t}^d + l_{2t}^d.$$

From equations (14.12) and (14.13), aggregate labour demand is

$$
\begin{aligned}
l_{1t}^d + l_{2t}^d &= 1 - \frac{\alpha}{1+\alpha}\left[1 + \frac{k_{1t}}{w_t h_{1t}}\rho\left(1+g\right)\right] - \frac{g+\delta_H}{A_{1H}\left(1+\alpha\right)} \\
&\quad + 1 - \frac{\alpha}{1+\alpha}\left[1 + \frac{k_{2t}}{w_t h_{2t}}\rho\left(1+g\right)\right] - \frac{g+\delta_H}{A_{2H}\left(1+\alpha\right)}, \\
&= \frac{2}{1+\alpha} - \frac{\alpha\rho\left(1+g\right)}{\left(1+\alpha\right)w_t}\left(\frac{k_{1t}}{h_{1t}} + \frac{k_{2t}}{h_{2t}}\right) - \frac{g+\delta_H}{\left(1+\alpha\right)}\left(\frac{1}{A_{1H}} + \frac{1}{A_{2H}}\right).
\end{aligned}
$$

Inversely, total aggregate labour demand is given as

$$w_t = \frac{\alpha\rho\left(1+g\right)\left(\frac{k_{1t}}{h_{1t}} + \frac{k_{2t}}{h_{2t}}\right)}{\left(1+\alpha\right)\left(\frac{2}{1+\alpha} - \frac{g+\delta_H}{\left(1+\alpha\right)}\left(\frac{1}{A_{1H}} + \frac{1}{A_{2H}}\right) - \left(l_{1t}^d + l_{2t}^d\right)\right)}; \tag{14.66}$$

in calibrated form this becomes

$$w_t = \frac{1\left(\frac{1}{0.95} - 1\right)\left(1+0.0358\right)\left(0.47895 + 0.82124\right)}{\left(1+1\right)\left(\frac{2}{1+1} - \frac{0.0358+0.015}{\left(1+1\right)}\left(\frac{1}{0.189} + \frac{1}{0.21735}\right) - \left(l_{1t}^d + l_{2t}^d\right)\right)}. \tag{14.67}$$

Aggregate labour supply, from equations (14.14) and (14.15), is

$$
\begin{aligned}
l_{1t}^s + l_{2t}^s &= \left(\frac{\gamma A_{1G}}{w_t}\right)^{\frac{1}{1-\gamma}} k_{1t} + \left(\frac{\gamma A_{2G}}{w_t}\right)^{\frac{1}{1-\gamma}} k_{2t} \\
&= \left(\frac{\gamma}{w_t}\right)^{\frac{1}{1-\gamma}}\left(\left(A_{1G}\right)^{\frac{1}{1-\gamma}} k_{1t} + \left(A_{21G}\right)^{\frac{1}{1-\gamma}} k_{2t}\right),
\end{aligned}
$$

which inversely and in calibrated form is

$$w_t = \left(\frac{\left(\gamma\right)^{\frac{1}{1-\gamma}}\left(\left(A_{1G}\right)^{\frac{1}{1-\gamma}} k_{1t} + \left(A_{21G}\right)^{\frac{1}{1-\gamma}} k_{2t}\right)}{\left(l_{1t}^s + l_{2t}^s\right)}\right)^{1-\gamma}, \tag{14.68}$$

$$w_t = \left(\frac{\left(0.28224\right)^{1.5}\left(0.47895\right) + \left(0.282\right)^{1.5}\left(0.82124\right)}{3^{1.5}\left(l_{1t}^s + l_{2t}^s\right)}\right)^{\frac{2}{3}}. \tag{14.69}$$

Finally the individual country labour supply and demand equations with the new trade equilibrium are given in calibrated form as

$$w_t = \frac{\alpha\rho\left(1+g\right)\left(\frac{k_{1t}}{h_{1t}}\right)}{1 - \left(1+\alpha\right)l_{1t}^s - \frac{\left(g+\delta_H\right)}{A_{1H}}} = \frac{1\left(0.0526\right)\left(1.036\right)\left(0.47895\right)}{1 - \left(1+1\right)l_{1t}^s - \frac{\left(0.036+0.015\right)}{0.189}}, \tag{14.70}$$

$$w_t = \frac{\alpha\rho\left(1+g\right)\left(\frac{k_t}{h_t}\right)}{1 - \left(1+\alpha\right)l_{2t}^s - \frac{\left(g+\delta_H\right)}{A_{2H}}} = \frac{1\left(0.0526\right)\left(1.036\right)\left(0.82124\right)}{1 - \left(1+1\right)l_{2t}^s - \frac{\left(0.036+0.015\right)}{0.21735}}; \tag{14.71}$$

$$w_t = \gamma A_{1G} \left(\frac{k_{1t}}{h_{1t} l_{1t}^d} \right)^{1-\gamma} = \frac{(0.28224)}{3} \left(\frac{0.47895}{l_{1t}^d} \right)^{\frac{2}{3}},$$ (14.72)

$$w_t = \gamma A_{2G} \left(\frac{k_{2t}}{h_{2t} l_{2t}^d} \right)^{1-\gamma} = \frac{(0.28224)}{3} \left(\frac{0.82124}{l_{2t}^d} \right)^{\frac{2}{3}}.$$ (14.73)

Figure 14.7 shows the original autarky labour market equilibria of each country 1 (black) and country 2 (blue) and the aggregate labour supply and demand (dashed blue) that establishes the equilibrium wage near 0.17. These are equations (14.16) to (14.19), for autarky, and equations (14.67) and (14.69) for the world equilibrium.

Figure 14.8 adds into Figure 14.7 the equilibria under trade, in dotted black and dotted blue, in equations (14.70) to (14.73).

Going from autarky to trade, country 1 sees its labour demand shift back and its labour supply pivot out in the area of the equilibrium wage rate (black to dotted black). Country 2 sees its labour demand shift out, and its labour supply pivoting back (blue to dotted blue). Country 1 has an excess supply of labour at the equilibrium wage and country 2 has an excess demand. This means that country 1 is providing labour to country 2 to produce output, part of which country 2 exports to country 1.

The trade flow can be better seen by zooming in on the labour markets of both countries under trade. Figure 14.9 shows only the labour equilibria of countries 1 and 2 under trade, with a zoomed-in focus.

The figure makes clear how at the equilibrium wage (dashed black) the excess labour demand of country 2 (dotted blue) equals the excess labour supply of country 1 (dotted black), these excesses being the horizontal differences between where the supply and demand cross the real wage line, for each country. And they can be determined quantitatively.

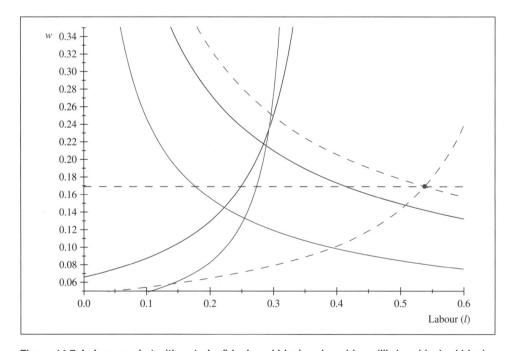

Figure 14.7 Labour market with autarky (black and blue) and world equilibrium (dashed blue)

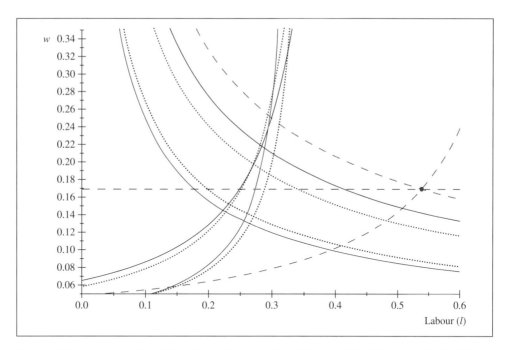

Figure 14.8 Labour market with autarky (black and blue), trade (dotted black and dotted blue), and world equilibrium (dashed blue) in Example 14.2

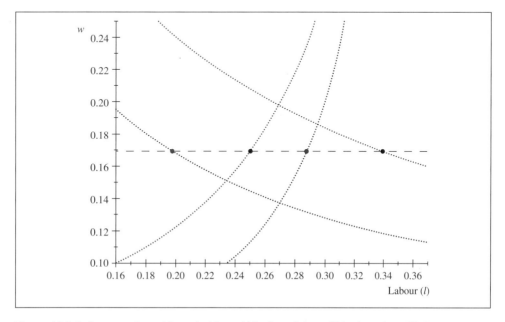

Figure 14.9 Labour market with trade (dotted black and dotted blue), and equilibrium wage (dashed black) in Example 14.2

The excess labour demand and supply can be computed from the labour demand and supply for each country:

$$l_{1t}^s = 1 - \frac{\alpha}{1+\alpha}\left[1 + \frac{k_{1t}}{w_t h_{1t}}\rho\left(1+g\right)\right] - \frac{g+\delta_H}{A_{1H}\left(1+\alpha\right)},$$

$$= 1 - 0.5\left(1 + \frac{0.47895}{(0.16918)}(0.052632)(1+0.0358)\right) - \frac{0.0358+0.015}{0.189(1+1)},$$

$$= 0.28844. \tag{14.74}$$

$$l_{2t}^s = 1 - \frac{\alpha}{1+\alpha}\left[1 + \frac{k_{2t}}{w_t h_{2t}}\rho\left(1+g\right)\right] - \frac{g+\delta_H}{A_{2H}\left(1+\alpha\right)},$$

$$= 1 - 0.5\left(1 + \frac{0.82124}{(0.16918)}(0.052632)(1+0.0358)\right) - \frac{0.0358+0.015}{0.21735(1+1)},$$

$$= 0.25082; \tag{14.75}$$

$$l_{1t}^d = \left(\frac{\gamma A_{1G}}{w_t}\right)^{\frac{1}{1-\gamma}}k_{1t} = \left(\frac{(0.28224)}{3(0.16918)}\right)^{1.5}0.47895 = 0.19862. \tag{14.76}$$

$$l_{2t}^d = \left(\frac{\gamma A_{2G}}{w_t}\right)^{\frac{1}{1-\gamma}}k_{2t} = \left(\frac{(0.28224)}{3(0.16918)}\right)^{1.5}0.82124 = 0.34056. \tag{14.77}$$

Excess labour supply by country 1 is

Excess supply (1): $l_{1t}^s - l_{1t}^d = 0.28844 - 0.19862 = 0.09,$

and excess labour demand of country 2 is

Excess demand (2): $l_{2t}^d - l_{2t}^s = 0.34056 - 0.25082 = 0.09.$

Country 1 supplies 0.09 labour to country 2 for production of output. This gives the fraction $\frac{0.09}{0.28844} = 0.312$, or 31% of country 1's total supply of labour that is exported to country 2. Note that the value of labour trade is equal to the value of output trade in equations (14.64) and (14.65); $w\left(l_{1t}^s - l_{1t}^d\right) = 0.16918\left(0.09\right) = 0.0152.$

14.6 Factor price equalisation

In autarky each country has a different growth rate, and consequently a different wage rate w_t and interest rate r_t. Trade creates a single world growth rate and this in turn implies factor price equalisation, with the same wage and interest rate in each country.

14.6.1 Interest rate

The interest rate can be expressed in terms of the growth rate by equation (14.24) for both countries:

$$r = \frac{1+g+\beta\left(\delta_k - 1\right)}{\beta} = \frac{(1.0358)+0.95\left(0.05-1\right)}{0.95} = 0.1403.$$

This global interest rate can be checked by going back to the marginal product of capital condition for each country and substituting in the parameters and variables.

$$r_t = (1 - \gamma) A_{1G} \left(\frac{h_{1t} l_{1t}^d}{k_{1t}} \right)^\gamma = \frac{2}{3} (0.28224) \left(\frac{0.47895}{0.19862} \right)^{-\frac{1}{3}} = 0.1403;$$

$$r_t = (1 - \gamma) A_{2G} \left(\frac{h_{2t} l_{2t}^d}{k_{2t}} \right)^\gamma = \frac{2}{3} (0.28224) \left(\frac{0.82124}{0.34056} \right)^{-\frac{1}{3}} = 0.1403.$$

The interest rate of 0.1403 compares to autarky of 0.1237 for country 1 and 0.15812 for country 2. The interest rate rises with trade for country 1 and falls with trade for country 2. This is comparable to the less productive country 1 in Chapter 7 and the more productive country 2 in Chapter 7. There the interest rate rises for the less productive and falls for the more productive country. The same result holds here except that now the productivity is in terms of the human capital investment sector, with country 1 less productive and country 2 more productive; $A_{1H} < A_{2H}$.

14.6.2 Wage rate

The global wage rate of $w_t = 0.16918$ results from the equilibrium balanced growth path. Computing this within each country using the marginal product of labour condition, the wage rate is confirmed at

$$w_t = \gamma A_{1G} \left(\frac{k_{1t}}{h_{1t} l_{1t}^d} \right)^{1-\gamma} = \frac{(0.28224)}{3} \left(\frac{0.47895}{0.19862} \right)^{1-\frac{1}{3}} = 0.16918,$$

$$w_t = \gamma A_{2G} \left(\frac{k_{2t}}{h_{2t} l_{2t}^d} \right)^{1-\gamma} = \frac{(0.28224)}{3} \left(\frac{0.82124}{0.34056} \right)^{1-\frac{1}{3}} = 0.16918.$$

With trade, the wage rate falls for country 1 and rises for country 2. But the drop in the capital ratio for country 1 leads to an excess supply of labour even though the wage rate falls, while the rise in the capital ratio for country 2 leads to an excess demand for labour even though the wage rate rises.

14.6.3 Capital to effective labour ratios

Notice that both the interest rate and wage rate marginal productivity conditions imply the equalisation of the capital to effective labour ratios across countries:

$$\frac{k_{1t}}{h_{1t} l_{1t}^d} = \frac{k_{2t}}{h_{2t} l_{2t}^d}, \tag{14.78}$$

$$\frac{0.47895}{0.19862} = \frac{0.82124}{0.34056} = 2.4114.$$

These input ratios can be seen diagramatically by looking at factor and output markets in general equilibrium.

14.7 General equilibrium

The autarky general equilibrium can be compared between the two countries in input and output space. Country 1 has already been set out in Example 12.1, the baseline endogenous growth model.

14.7.1 Autarky

Country 2 is presented here in terms of the isocost, isoquant, and factor input ratio in autarky. The isocost line is

$$y_{2t}^s = w_{2t}l_{2t}^d h_{2t} + r_{2t}k_{2t},$$

$$\frac{0.10189}{h_{2t}} = (0.13323) \, l_{2t}^d + (0.15812) \frac{k_{2t}}{h_{2t}},$$

$$\frac{k_{2t}}{h_{2t}} = \frac{0.10189}{(0.15812) \, h_{2t}} - \frac{(0.13323) \, l_{2t}^d}{0.15812}. \tag{14.79}$$

The isoquant curve has a lower output level:

$$y_{2t}^s = A_{2G} \left(l_{2t}^d h_{2t} \right)^\gamma \left(k_{2t} \right)^{1-\gamma}, \tag{14.80}$$

$$0.10189 = (0.28224) \left(l_{2t}^d h_{2t} \right)^{\frac{1}{3}} \left(k_{2t} \right)^{\frac{2}{3}},$$

$$\frac{k_{2t}}{h_{2t}} = \left(\frac{0.10189}{(0.28224) \, h_{2t} \left(l_{2t}^d \right)^{\frac{1}{3}}} \right)^{\frac{3}{2}} = \frac{\left(\frac{0.10189}{(0.28224)h_{2t}} \right)^{\frac{3}{2}}}{\left(l_{2t}^d \right)^{\frac{1}{2}}}.$$

The factor input ratio is lower at

$$\frac{k_{2t}}{h_{2t}l_{2t}^d} = \frac{0.42960}{0.25492} = 1.6852. \tag{14.81}$$

Figure 14.10 graphs the country 2 factor market equilibrium, of equations (14.79), (14.80) and (14.81) in variants of blue, with country 1 in variants of black. Country 2 with higher

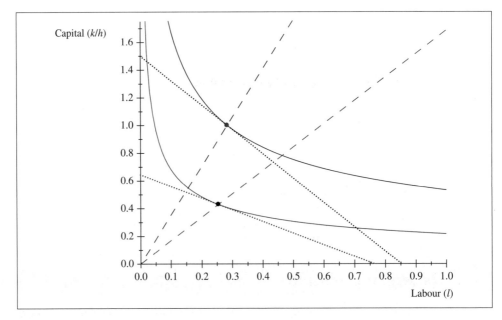

Figure 14.10 Factor market equilibrium with autarky, country 1 (variants of blue) and country 2 (variants of black) in Example 14.1

growth has a lower level of output, a lower capital to effective labour ratio, and a lower real wage to interest rate ratio.

For goods and leisure in general equilibrium, country 2 output production has a higher A_H and a lower capital $\frac{k_t}{h_t}$:

$$c_{2t}^S = y_{2t}^S - i_{2t} = A_{2G} \left(l_{2t}^d h_{2t} \right)^\gamma \left(k_{2t} \right)^{1-\gamma} - (g + \delta_k) k_{2t},$$

$$\frac{c_{2t}^S}{h_{2t}} = (0.28224) \left(l_{2t}^d \right)^{\frac{1}{3}} (0.4296)^{\frac{2}{3}} - (0.0527 + 0.05) (0.4296). \tag{14.82}$$

For utility u_{2t}, with $T_{2t} \equiv 1 - l_{2Ht}$, the country 2 level curve is

$$u_2 = \ln c_{2t}^d + \alpha \ln x_{2t} = \ln c_{2t}^d + \alpha \ln \left(1 - l_{2Ht} - l_{2t}^s \right),$$

$$-3.6871 = \ln 0.057764 + 1 \ln \left(1 - 0.31153 - 0.25492 \right),$$

$$-3.6871 = \ln c_{2t}^d + \ln \left(T_{2t} - l_{2t}^s \right),$$

$$c_{2t}^d = \frac{e^{-3.6871}}{\left(1 - 0.31153 - l_{2t}^s \right)}. \tag{14.83}$$

The country 2 equilibrium budget line has a lower wage rate:

$$c_{2t}^d = w_{2t} l_{2t}^s h_{2t} + \rho \left(1 + g \right) k_{2t}^s,$$

$$\frac{c_{2t}^d}{h_{2t}} = (0.13323) l_{2t}^s + 0.052632 \left(1 + 0.05271 \right) \left(0.42960 \right). \tag{14.84}$$

Figure 14.11 graphs the autarky equilibrium of each country in output space. Country 2 is given by the lower blue, dotted blue and dashed blue curves, the latter from equations (14.82), (14.83) and (14.84), while country 1 is the upper variants of black curves of Example 12.1.

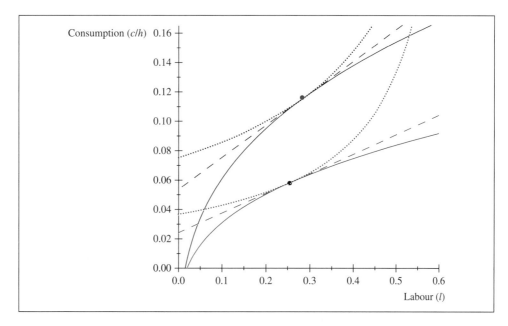

Figure 14.11 General equilibrium goods and labour with autarky of country 1 (variants of black) and country 2 (variants of blue)

14.7.2 Trade

Countries 1 and 2 are presented here in terms of the isocost, isoquant, and factor input ratio under trade. Following the same methodology, the isocost line for each country is

$$y_{1t}^s = w_t l_{1t}^d h_{1t} + r_t k_{1t},$$

$$\frac{0.10081}{h_{1t}} = (0.16918)\, l_{1t}^d + (0.14032)\, \frac{k_{1t}}{h_{1t}},$$

$$\frac{k_{1t}}{h_{1t}} = \frac{0.10081}{(0.14032)\, h_{1t}} - \frac{(0.16918)\, l_{1t}}{0.14032}. \tag{14.85}$$

$$y_{2t}^s = w_t l_{2t}^d h_{2t} + r_t k_{2t},$$

$$\frac{0.17285}{h_{2t}} = (0.16918)\, l_{2t}^d + (0.14032)\, \frac{k_{2t}}{h_{2t}},$$

$$\frac{k_{2t}}{h_{2t}} = \frac{0.17285}{(0.14032)\, h_{2t}} - \frac{(0.16918)\, l_{2t}^d}{0.14032}. \tag{14.86}$$

The isoquant curves are

$$y_{1t}^s = A_{1G} \left(l_{1t}^d h_{1t} \right)^\gamma (k_{1t})^{1-\gamma},$$

$$0.10081 = (0.28224) \left(l_{1t}^d h_{1t} \right)^{\frac{1}{3}} (k_{1t})^{\frac{2}{3}};$$

$$\frac{k_{1t}}{h_{1t}} = \left(\frac{0.10081}{(0.28224)\, h_{1t} \left(l_{1t}^d \right)^{\frac{1}{3}}} \right)^{\frac{3}{2}} = \frac{\left(\frac{0.10081}{(0.28224)h_{1t}} \right)^{\frac{3}{2}}}{\left(l_{1t}^d \right)^{\frac{1}{2}}}. \tag{14.87}$$

$$y_{2t}^s = A_{2G} \left(l_{2t}^d h_{2t} \right)^\gamma (k_{2t})^{1-\gamma},$$

$$0.17285 = (0.28224) \left(l_{2t}^d h_{2t} \right)^{\frac{1}{3}} (k_{2t})^{\frac{2}{3}};$$

$$\frac{k_{2t}}{h_{2t}} = \left(\frac{0.17285}{(0.28224)\, h_{2t} \left(l_{2t}^d \right)^{\frac{1}{3}}} \right)^{\frac{3}{2}} = \frac{\left(\frac{0.17285}{(0.28224)h_{2t}} \right)^{\frac{3}{2}}}{\left(l_{2t}^d \right)^{\frac{1}{2}}}. \tag{14.88}$$

And the factor input ratios can be written as

$$\frac{k_{1t}}{h_{1t}} = \frac{0.47895}{0.19862} l_{1t}^d = (2.411)\, l_{1t}^d. \tag{14.89}$$

$$\frac{k_{2t}}{h_{2t}} = \frac{0.82124}{0.34056} l_{2t}^d = (2.411)\, l_{2t}^d. \tag{14.90}$$

These are the same line.

Figure 14.12 again graphs the country 2 autarky factor market equilibrium in variants of blue, with country 1 autarky equilibrium in variants of black, which are found in Figure 14.11. Now the trade equilibrium is also added. Under trade the input price ratios of equations (14.89) and (14.90) are the same thick black ray from the origin. The country 1 trade isocost and isoquant, of equations (14.85) and (14.87), are in solid light black, while the country 2 trade isocost and isoquant, of equations (14.86) and (14.88), are in solid light blue.

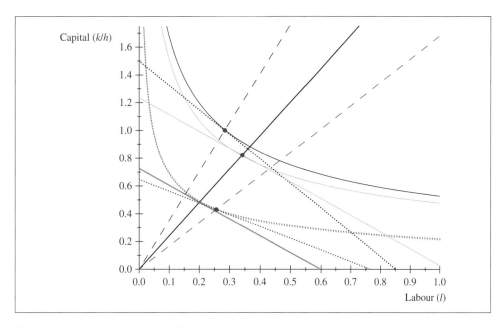

Figure 14.12 Factor market equilibrium with autarky and trade in Example 14.2

Figure 14.12 shows that the trade isoquant level falls for 1 to near the autarky level of 2, while the trade isoquant level rises for 2 to just below the autarky isoquant level of 1. In the process, the effective capital to labour becomes the same under trade, while the amount of labour demand is higher in country 2 than in country 1. The isocost curves under trade now have the same slope for each country, reflecting the equal input price

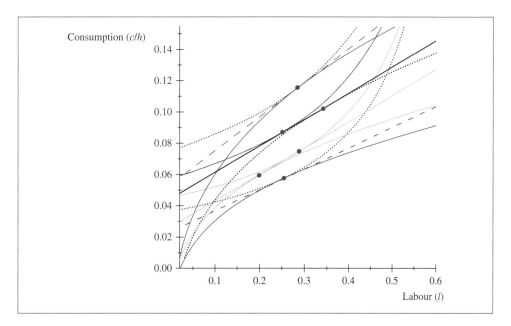

Figure 14.13 General equilibrium with autarky and trade of country 1 (upper upper-middle curves), country 2 (lower and lower-middle curves) in Example 14.2

ratios. In comparison, in autarky, the country 1 isocost line is more steeply sloped than the country 2 isocost line.

For goods and leisure in general equilibrium, again with the same methodology, consumption in terms of the output production net of investment for each country is

$$c_{1t}^s = y_{1t}^s - i_{1t} = A_{1G} \left(l_{1t}^d h_{1t} \right)^\gamma (k_{1t})^{1-\gamma} - (g + \delta_k) k_{1t},$$

$$\frac{c_{1t}^s}{h_{1t}} = (0.28224) \left(l_{1t}^d \right)^{\frac{1}{3}} (0.47895)^{\frac{2}{3}} - (0.0858) (0.47895). \tag{14.91}$$

$$c_{2t}^s = y_{2t}^s - i_{2t} = A_{2G} \left(l_{2t}^d h_{2t} \right)^\gamma (k_{2t})^{1-\gamma} - (g + \delta_k) k_{2t},$$

$$\frac{c_{2t}^s}{h_{2t}} = (0.28224) \left(l_{2t}^d \right)^{\frac{1}{3}} (0.82124)^{\frac{2}{3}} - (0.0858) (0.82124). \tag{14.92}$$

Utility levels at equilibrium are

$$u_1 = \ln c_{1t}^d + \alpha \ln x_{1t} = \ln c_{1t} + \alpha \ln \left(1 - l_{1Ht} - l_{1t}^s \right),$$

$$-3.4062 = \ln 0.074909 + 1 \ln \left(1 - 0.26878 - 0.28844 \right),$$

$$-3.4062 = \ln c_{1t}^d + \ln \left(T_{1t} - l_{1t} \right),$$

$$c_{1t}^d = \frac{e^{-3.4062}}{\left(1 - 0.26878 - l_{1t} \right)}. \tag{14.93}$$

$$u_2 = \ln c_{2t}^d + \alpha \ln x_{2t} = \ln c_{2t} + \alpha \ln \left(1 - l_{2Ht} - l_{2t}^s \right),$$

$$-3.1022 = \ln 0.087205 + 1 \ln \left(1 - 0.23372 - 0.25082 \right),$$

$$-3.1022 = \ln c_{2t}^d + \ln \left(T_{2t} - l_{2t} \right),$$

$$c_{2t}^d = \frac{e^{-3.1022}}{\left(1 - 0.23372 - l_{2t} \right)}. \tag{14.94}$$

And the equilibrium budget lines are

$$c_{1t}^d = w_t l_{1t}^s h_{1t} + \rho \left(1 + g \right) k_{1t}^s,$$

$$\frac{c_{1t}^d}{h_{1t}} = (0.16918) l_{1t}^s + 0.052632 \left(1 + 0.0358 \right) (0.47895). \tag{14.95}$$

$$c_{2t}^d = w_t l_{2t}^s h_{2t} + \rho \left(1 + g \right) k_{2t}^s,$$

$$\frac{c_{2t}^d}{h_{2t}} = (0.16918) l_{2t}^s + 0.052632 \left(1 + 0.0358 \right) (0.82124). \tag{14.96}$$

Figure 14.13 adds to the autarky equilibrium of Figure 14.11, seen in the uppermost set of curves for country 1, and the lowermost set of curves for country 2. It adds the middle two sets of curves that are the trade equilibria for country 1 (lower middle) and country 2 (upper middle), from equations (14.91) to (14.96). Each set of curves is the utility level curve, the production function, and the budget line. In the uppermost and lowermost sets, these three curves are all tangent at the same point since it is autarky.

In the middle two sets of curves there is a separate tangency between utility and the budget line, and between the production function and the budget line, for each country. However it is hard to see this in Figure 14.13. It requires zooming in on the middle two sets of curves to see the trade patterns.

Figure 14.14 focuses in on these middle curves to show the exact trade equilibria and in order to identify the trade flows. Here the lower middle curves for country 1 have a

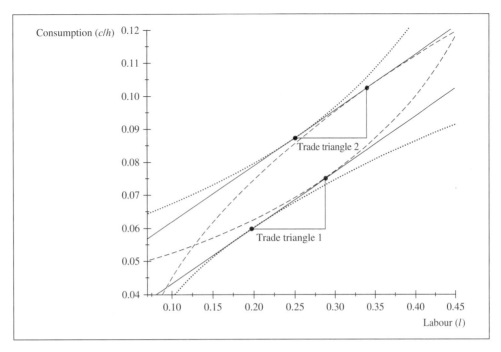

Figure 14.14 General equilibrium trade triangles of country 1 (lower middle curves) and country 2 (upper middle curves) in Example 14.2

tangency between the solid black budget line and the dotted black production function at a lower level of labour demand, and they have a tangency between the dashed black utility level curve and the solid black budget line at a higher labour supply. This country 1 utility tangency point also gives the consumption demand of country 1, which is lower than that of country 2. The upper curves, for country 2, have a tangency between production and the budget line at a higher labour demand than for 1 and a tangency between utility and the budget line at a lower labour supply than for 1. Country 2 is demanding more labour than it is supplying, with the excess demand supplied by the country 1 excess supply. Country 1 supplies more labour than it demands.

The quantitative amount of consumption goods being traded can be defined as consumption demand minus consumption supply. Consumption demand is already derived in equations (14.95) and (14.96). With the equilibrium labour supply for each country substituted in, it results that $c_{1t}^d = 0.074909$, and that $c_{2t}^d = 0.087205$. Consumption supply can be found by substituting in the labour demanded into the budget line. Using equations (14.95) and (14.96), but writing this budget line in terms of consumption supply and labour demand, instead of consumption demand and labour supply, the consumption supply is found to be

$$c_{1t}^s = w_t l_{1t}^d h_{1t} + \rho \left(1 + g\right) k_{1t},$$

$$\frac{c_{1t}^s}{h_{1t}} = \left(0.16918\right) l_{1t}^d + 0.0526 \left(1 + 0.0358\right) \left(0.47895\right), \tag{14.97}$$

$$\frac{c_{1t}^s}{h_{1t}} = \left(0.16918\right) \left(0.19862\right) + 0.052632 \left(1.0358\right) \left(0.47895\right), \tag{14.98}$$

$$= 0.059713; \tag{14.99}$$

$$c_{2t}^s = w_t l_{2t}^d h_{2t} + \rho \left(1+g\right) k_{2t},$$

$$\frac{c_{2t}^s}{h_{2t}} = (0.16918)\, l_{2t}^d + 0.0526 \left(1+0.0358\right) \left(0.82124\right), \tag{14.100}$$

$$\frac{c_{2t}^s}{h_{2t}} = (0.16918)\, (0.34056) + 0.052632 \left(1.0358\right) \left(0.82124\right), \tag{14.101}$$

$$= 0.10239. \tag{14.102}$$

And the excess consumption supply and demand are

$$\text{Excess demand } (1)\colon c_{1t}^d - c_{1t}^s = 0.074909 - 0.059713 = 0.0152. \tag{14.103}$$

$$\text{Excess supply } (2)\colon c_{2t}^s - c_{2t}^d = 0.10239 - 0.087205 = 0.0152. \tag{14.104}$$

This excess supply and demand for consumption goods is the exact same as the excess supply and demand for output in equations (14.64) and (14.65). Country 2 has an excess supply of goods that it is trading to country 1 in return for excess labour that country 1 is supplying to country 2.

14.7.3 Savings and investment

The fact that the excess demand of consumption goods by agent 1 in equation (14.103) is equal to the agent 1 excess demand of output in equation (14.64), both equal to 0.0152, implies that there is no excess demand or supply of investment by agent 1. Therefore the savings of agent 1 equals the investment of agent 1. The same can be seen for agent 2. Equations (14.65) and (14.104) show that the excess demand for output is the same as the excess demand for consumption goods, again equal to 0.0152. Therefore the savings of agent 1 equals the investment of agent 1. These are consistent with the high savings–investment correlations seen internationally even under free trade. And indeed this is a necessary result of the stationary equilibrium balanced growth path solution.

14.8 Changes in productivities

Several comparative static exercises can be conceived. Consider first allowing the goods productivities A_{1G} and A_{2G} to be different. The problem is that if $A_{1G} \neq A_{2G}$, then the wage rate cannot be equalised across countries. To see this, consider that the capital to effective labour ratios must be equal under factor price equalisation. Using the marginal input products,

$$\frac{r_t}{w_t} = \frac{(1-\gamma)\, A_{1G} \left(\frac{h_{1t} l_{1t}^d}{k_{1t}}\right)^\gamma}{\gamma A_{1G} \left(\frac{h_{1t} l_{1t}^d}{k_{1t}}\right)^{\gamma-1}} = \frac{(1-\gamma)\, A_{2G} \left(\frac{h_{2t} l_{2t}^d}{k_{2t}}\right)^\gamma}{\gamma A_{2G} \left(\frac{h_{2t} l_{2t}^d}{k_{2t}}\right)^{\gamma-1}} = \frac{r_t}{w_t}. \tag{14.105}$$

All of the parameters cancel out to give that the capital to effective labour ratios are equal in the two countries:

$$\frac{\left(\frac{h_{1t} l_{1t}^d}{k_{1t}}\right)^\gamma}{\left(\frac{h_{1t} l_{1t}^d}{k_{1t}}\right)^{\gamma-1}} = \frac{\left(\frac{h_{2t} l_{2t}^d}{k_{2t}}\right)^\gamma}{\left(\frac{h_{2t} l_{2t}^d}{k_{2t}}\right)^{\gamma-1}},$$

$$\frac{k_{1t}}{h_{1t} l_{1t}^d} = \frac{k_{2t}}{h_{2t} l_{2t}^d}.$$

And for the wage rates to be equal, it must be true that $A_{1G} = A_{2G}$:

$$\frac{w_t}{w_t} = 1 = \frac{\gamma A_{1G} \left(\frac{h_{1t}l_{1t}}{k_{1t}}\right)^{\gamma-1}}{\gamma A_{2G} \left(\frac{h_{2t}l_{2t}}{k_{2t}}\right)^{\gamma-1}};$$

$$\left(\frac{A_{1G}}{A_{2G}}\right)^{\frac{1}{1-\gamma}} = \frac{\frac{h_{1t}l_{1t}}{k_{1t}}}{\frac{h_{2t}l_{2t}}{k_{2t}}} = 1;$$

$$A_{1G} = A_{2G}.$$

Equal goods productivities make sense in that if in contrast $A_{1G} \neq A_{2G}$, then the goods are different goods, produced with a different technology. The only way to consider such a difference in productivity is to have two goods produced. Both goods can enter the utility function of each country. The differences in A_{1G} and A_{2G} are then like differences in the quality of the good. And the consumer may choose some of each quality in the consumption basket. This presents a more complex two-good economy with an exchange rate having to be specified between the consumption baskets of each country.

14.8.1 Change in human capital investment productivity

The human capital productivities of course can be changed, and the comparative statics examined. But it is clear that if A_{1H} and A_{2H} are moved closer together, then the trade amounts are reduced. If these productivity parameters are farther apart in value, then the trade flows are accordingly higher. And if the lower valued A_{1H} is decreased, the equilibrium growth rate will be lower, while the trade flows will be increased, while if the higher valued A_{2H} is increased, the equilibrium growth rate will be higher and the trade flows will be increased.

14.8.2 Exogenous growth

It is not possible to have factor price equalisation under exogenous growth. The reason is that with the growth rate exogenous, so also is the interest rate fixed. This also fixes the capital to effective labour ratio, by the marginal product of capital equation. For country 1, $r_t = (1 - \gamma) A_{1G} \left(\frac{h_{1t}l_{1t}}{k_{1t}}\right)^{\gamma}$, and so $\frac{h_{1t}l_{1t}}{k_{1t}}$ is fixed if the growth rate is exogenous, and so is the interest rate since $1 + g = \beta (1 + r_t - \delta_k)$. Therefore the interest rates cannot be equal if the growth rates are set at different exogenous values.

Consider if the growth rates are set at the same exogenous values for country 1 and 2. Then could it be possible that there is equalisation of the wage rate under trade? Again the answer is no. With the same exogenous growth rate, the ratio of the wage rates would be

$\frac{w_t}{w_t} = \frac{\gamma A_{1G} \left(\frac{h_{1t}l_{1t}}{k_{1t}}\right)^{\gamma-1}}{\gamma A_{2G} \left(\frac{h_{2t}l_{2t}}{k_{2t}}\right)^{\gamma-1}}$. But since $\frac{h_{1t}l_{1t}}{k_{1t}}$ and $\frac{h_{2t}l_{2t}}{k_{2t}}$ are fixed by the exogenous growth rate, then the wage rates are also fixed, and they cannot equalise if they start out at different levels. If they start at the same level, then both interest rates and wage rates start the same and end the same, so there is no trade. If the wage rates start at different levels, they are fixed and cannot converge. When there is only one good, only endogenous growth allows for factor price equalisation.

14.8.3 Example 14.3: Numerous agents

The equilibrium can be computed when it is assumed that there are different numbers of the agents of type/country 1 and type/country 2. This is exactly analogous to Chapters 4 and 7 when similar assumptions are made. Now the only change is to the market clearing condition.

Suppose there are 400 of agent 1 and 600 of agent 2. Then this is similar to an increase in the human capital productivity A_{2H} in that now there are more agents in country 2 than in country 1. The market clearing conditions are the same as in Chapter 4, and directly modify equations (14.20) and (14.37):

$$400y_{1t}^d + 600y_{2t}^d = 400y_{1t}^s + 600y_{2t}^s, \tag{14.106}$$

$$400l_{1t}^d + 600l_{2t}^d = 400l_{1t}^s + 600l_{2t}^s. \tag{14.107}$$

This gives a new equilibrium growth rate, interest rate and wage rate, following the same methodology already set out. And then all of the other equilibrium quantities can be found.

14.9 Applications

14.9.1 Growth convergence

The convergence of countries within a region in terms of their growth rates, and even income levels, has been a topic of great interest since Lucas's (1988) endogenous growth model appeared. Robert Barro in particular is known for his work finding empirical evidence of growth convergence in different regions, and is among the top five ranking economists in the world according to recent *RePEc* (http://repec.org) rankings. His 2001 article and his 1992 article with Sala-i-Martin find evidence of growth convergence across different regions.

The factor price equalisation of this chapter occurs only with growth convergence. Therefore the empirical findings of growth convergence support the concepts of this chapter in terms of factor price equalisation actually taking place. One element that this chapter adds to the convergence evidence is that from a theoretical point of view what defines a region of countries in which growth convergence can take place is that each of these countries has to be able to move towards the same capital to effective labour ratios.

The equalisation of the capital to effective labour ratios is also behind the Lucas (1990) question of why capital does not simply flow from rich to poor countries in order to equalise factor prices. The reason seen in the chapter here is that factor prices may only gradually equalise as the growth rates converge, through an equalisation of capital to effective labour ratios. In countries with very low human capital productivities, such as in Africa, it may take many years for the growth rates to converge towards Western levels.

14.9.2 Leontief paradox

The Leontief (Nobel Laureate 1973) paradox of 1953 is that the US was found to export labour intensive goods even though the comparative advantage of the US is thought to be capital intensive goods. The paradox could be said to still exist in that the US exports services that are again said to be labour intensive, while still the US tends to be viewed as specializing in capital intensive goods.

The paradox can be approached with the human capital endogenous growth model of trade in the same way that the structural transformation of industry over time from agriculture to manufacturing to services is discussed in Chapter 13. In particular, if the US specialises most of all in human capital intensive goods, and exports these, then with exogenous growth theory such goods look like they are labour intensive goods. This is because human capital does not enter the production function in exogenous growth theory and so is not accounted for except through the total factor productivity.

But including human capital, then the US can export service sector goods that are actually human capital intensive, rather than labour intensive goods. This would include banking services, insurance, and computer services for example that are all highly human capital intensive industries. There is no paradox since then the US is exporting what it specialises in. And it is well known that the US service sector continues to grow as a fraction of trade exports while manufacturing declines.

14.9.3 Savings–investment and Feldstein–Horioka puzzle

Small open economies are said to borrow on international markets in such a way that their demand for capital does not affect the world interest rate, since they are small. Then when small nations have investment needs during some sort of expansion, this would drive up their domestic real interest rate unless they are able to borrow internationally. This logic says that nations do such borrowing so that the investment may well exceed the amount of domestic savings.

Yet Feldstein and Horioka (1980) stimulated interest when they found that most often countries have savings that are highly correlated with investment. The sometimes close relation of national savings and investment across countries internationally, when we would expect them to diverge when international capital markets are open and well-functioning, is sometimes called the Feldstein–Horioka (1980) puzzle, for which Obstfeld and Rogoff (1996) provide a discussion.

However leaving the small open economy and using instead the world general equilibrium, here with two countries, it does not follow that the more productive countries borrow capital and have investment greater than savings. Rather the Feldstein and Horioka (1980) empirical result is found theoretically to be valid with endogenous growth. Both countries adjust their capital ratios so that their growth rates are equal, with the resulting factor price equalisation ensuing. But this means trade in goods and labour such that savings are still equal to investment within each country. See also Levy (2004) who argues that savings and investment within countries engaged in trade theoretically should be moving together empirically.

14.10 Questions

1. In Example 14.1, let the human capital investment productivity in country 1, A_{1H}, be increased. Then under autarky with no trade, in country 1
   (a) the equilibrium wage rate falls,
   (b) the growth rate rises,
   (c) the physical capital to human capital ratio falls,
   (d) all of the above.

2. In Example 14.1, country 1 is assumed to have a lower human capital productivity than country 2. Under autarky with no trade, country 1
   (a) has a lower real wage than country 2,
   (b) has a lower growth rate than country 2,
   (c) has a lower output per unit of human capital than country 2,
   (d) all of the above.

3. The solution methodology for solving for the world growth rate under trade, in Example 14.2, involves
   (a) the market clearing condition in output,
   (b) the market clearing condition in labour,

(c) the consumer's intertemporal marginal rate of substitution,

(d) all of the above.

4. What enables factor price equalisation in the endogenous growth two-country world economy?

5. In Example 14.2, let the human capital investment productivity in country 2, A_{2H}, be increased. Then under full world trade,

(a) the world equilibrium wage rate falls,

(b) the world growth rate rises,

(c) the trade flows increase in magnitude,

(d) all of the above.

6. In Example 14.2, let the human capital investment productivity in country 1, A_{1H}, be increased. Then under full world trade,

(a) the world equilibrium wage rate falls,

(b) the world growth rate rises,

(c) the trade flows decrease in magnitude,

(d) all of the above.

7. In Example 14.2, let the human capital investment productivity in country 2, A_{2H}, be decreased. Then under full world trade,

(a) the physical capital to human capital ratio in country 1 falls by more,

(b) the world growth rate falls,

(c) the world wage rate falls,

(d) all of the above.

8. In Example 14.2, the movement from autarky to full world trade implies that

(a) country 1 spends more time in human capital investment,

(b) country 2 spends more time in human capital investment,

(c) leisure time falls in both countries,

(d) all of the above.

9. In Example 14.2, let country 2 have a human capital productivity of $A_{2H} = 0.23$, instead of 0.21735. Under full free trade,

(a) find the new world growth rate,

(b) find the new world interest rate,

(c) find the new world wage rate,

(d) and find the amount of goods and labour that are traded.

10. Find the world equilibrium growth rate when Example 14.2 is modified so that there are 400 of agent type 1 and 600 of agent type 2, instead of only one agent of each type.

11. How does equalisation of the capital to effective labour ratios across countries under trade relate to the observed phenomenon of a convergence of output growth rates?

12. What is the Leontief paradox and how can endogenous growth be used to explain it?

13. The goods sector productivities A_{1G} and A_{2G} under world trade with one world output good,

(a) can be different as long as the human capital productivities A_{1H} and A_{2H} are different,

(b) must be equal because of factor price equalisation,

(c) depend on the level of the world growth rate,

(d) all of the above.

14.11 References

Barro, Robert J., 2001, 'Human Capital and Growth', *American Economic Review*, American Economic Association, 91(2): 12–17, May.

Barro, Robert J. and Xavier Sala-i-Martin, 1992, 'Convergence', *Journal of Political Economy*, University of Chicago Press, 100(2): 223–251, April.

Feldstein, M. and C. Horioka, 1980, 'Domestic Saving and International Capital Flows', *The Economic Journal,* 90: 314–329.

Leontief, Wassily, 1953, 'Domestic Production and Foreign Trade: the American Capital Position Re-examined', *Proceedings of American Philosophical Society.*

Levy, Daniel, 2004, 'Is the Feldstein–Horioka Puzzle Really a Puzzle?', in *Aspects of Globalization: Macroeconomic and Capital Market Linkages in the Integrated World Economy,* edited by C. Tsoukis, G. Agiomirgianakis and T. Biswas, London: Kluwer Academic Publishers.

Lucas, Robert Jr., 1988, 'On the Mechanics of Economic Development', *Journal of Monetary Economics,* Elsevier, 22(1): 3–42, July.

Lucas, Robert E., Jr. 1990, 'Why Doesn't Capital Flow from Rich to Poor Countries?', *American Economic Review,* American Economic Association, 80(2): 92–96, May.

Maffezzoli, Marco, 2010, 'Non-Walrasian Labor Markets and Real Business Cycles', *Review of Economic Dynamics,* Elsevier for the Society of Economic Dynamics, 4(4) (October): 860–892.

Obstfeld, Maurice and Kenneth Rogoff, 1996, *Foundations of International Macroeconomics,* The MIT Press.

RePEc (Research Papers in Economics); an online economic research service of Christian Zimmermann; at http://repec.org/.

PART 6

RISK, BANKING AND ASSETS

CHAPTER (15)

Incomplete markets and banking

15.1 Introduction

The chapter extends the Arrow and Debreu analysis of optimal consumption across states of nature to allow for incomplete markets with two 'states of nature'. The states of nature are simply a good state and a bad state. In the good state the income endowment is high. In a bad state, the income is low. With no cost of transferring income across states, markets are 'complete', and the consumer perfectly smooths consumption across states.

Costs are introduced into the process of transferring income across states. This means that perfect smoothing of consumption does not result, and so markets across states of nature are 'incomplete'. First the full equilibrium is worked out for when the costs are a simple fraction of the amount invested in transferring consumption across states. When this fraction of cost reduces to zero, as a special case, the consumer again has perfect smoothing across states.

Such costs of transferring consumption across states are then modelling using the banking sector, as modelled in the microeconomics literature on banking. This so-called financial intermediation approach to banking allows labour to be used in the banking sector to transfer income across states. The higher is the cost of banking, the less consumption smoothing that results. Instead consumption is 'tilted' towards having more in the good state than in the bad state.

As the share of labour used in the banking production goes to zero, the model reduces to a special case that is equivalent to the simple model of having the cost equal to a fraction of the amount invested. And as a further special case, this reduces back to the no cost case with perfect consumption smoothing.

The economies are set out graphically in general equilibrium with the good state consumption and bad state consumption on the axes. Equivalently these are drawn using the amount invested in transferring income across states and consumption in the bad state.

15.1.1 Building on the last chapters

Previous chapters have all involved the consumer smoothing between work and leisure, and smoothing goods consumption across time using physical and human capital investment. Now investment is focused on within another dimension. Uncertainty is introduced in the simplest way of there being only two possible states of nature, and now the consumer invests so as to smooth consumption across these states.

The same tools are used in that a log utility function is assumed and the consumer optimises subject to the constraints for consumption in each the good state and the bad state. In addition, a Cobb–Douglas utility function for output in the bad state through the banking sector is also used, just as Cobb–Douglas production was assumed for the goods sector in all previous chapters. In addition the general equilibrium graph is again constructed using the equilibrium utility level curve, the budget line, and the production function, but now these are all across states of nature, and production is of the bad state consumption through banking.

15.1.2 Learning objective

Understanding the elements of uncertainty in terms of just two states is the challenge. Why consumption is smooth across states with no cost of transferring income, and why consumption is more in the good state than in the bad state when there is a cost of transferring income are the central questions. Learning the jargon of complete versus incomplete markets is just a matter of thinking in terms of full consumption smoothing versus a lack of perfect smoothing in the equilibrium.

The banking production as a way of introducing costs allows the student to see the investment across states of nature more in terms of how it is done in the actual economy. Realising that this is the role of financial intermediation in its broadest sense requires some study. Seeing the mechanism of banking as a conduit for costly investment across states is the more immediate goal. And seeing how this reduces back down to perfect smoothing in special cases of zero cost is the other part of the broader view of the equilibrium.

15.1.3 Who made it happen?

Complete markets are an abstraction that just like perfect competition does not ever exist, but is still the baseline from which analysis of uncertainty begins. The ability to have markets for trading income perfectly across all possible states of nature is known as having 'complete markets'. This concept was pioneered by Kenneth Arrow (Nobel Laureate 1972) and Gerard Debreu (Nobel Laureate 1983) in a 1954 joint article, restated in Debreu's 1959 book, *Theory of Value*. And this is still the fundamental way to view equilibrium across states of nature.

The two-state illustration of the Arrow–Debreu equilibrium has long been a standard. For example Hirshleifer's 1970 book on *Investment, Interest and Capital* sets this out. Ehrlich and Becker (1972) wrote about 'Market Insurance, Self-Insurance, and Self-Protection', using this framework, in which the production of consumption in the bad state in the representative agent framework was called 'self-insurance'.

Instead of 'self-production', in the decentralised general equilibrium problem production becomes market production by the banking industry. The idea of the representative agent acting in part as a bank is quite old, for example, Nobel Laureate John R. Hicks in his 1935 *Economica* article on 'A Suggestion for Simplifying the Theory of Money', suggests in one paragraph on page 12 that

> So as far as banking theory is concerned ... my suggestion is that we ought to regard every individual in the community as being, on a small scale, a bank.

Clark (1984) is among the first to specify a Cobb–Douglas production function for financial intermediaries in terms of labour, capital and the deposits of financial capital, with empirical support followed up by Hancock (1985). Berger (2003) uses this approach in modern work. And now this is called the 'financial intermediation approach to banking' in textbooks such as Matthews and Thompson (2008). Here it is applied to specify the cost of transferring income across states in the Arrow–Debreu world.

15.2 Two-state analysis in general equilibrium

The complete markets economy can be simplified to a two-state world, one with a good-state good and one with a bad-state good. To have perfect smoothing, the ability to trade income across states needs to incur no costs. This means no insurance industry employment, no banking industry employment, no unemployment agencies. In this case, even though unrealistic, the basic economics underlying trading across uncertain states can be set out. And it will be seen that the amount paid during the good state, in order to buy income should the bad state occur, is equal to the expected payout in the bad state.

Incomplete markets are defined in different ways. One definition is that there is no market for trade from one particular state to another. Capturing the missing state can sometimes be done through complicated transactions using the other markets that exist across the various other states of nature. For example options pricing theory tells us how we can price the different transfers between different states of nature even if we do not have a direct market in that particular state.

The complete markets analysis results in perfect insurance and perfect consumption smoothing. The key assumption in general equilibrium concerns the production function for transforming output from one state to another state. In particular, if some consumption in the good state can be converted one-for-one into consumption in the bad state, with no loss of resources in doing this transformation, then this simple linear production function will lead to the complete markets. More generally, the transfer of resources from one state to another involves a production process. If this process involves zero costs, then this is a special case that will result in perfect consumption smoothing.

Let the probability of the good state occurring be given as $p_g \in [0, 1]$ and the probability of the bad state be given by $p_b \in [0, 1]$, where the probabilities sum to one:

$$p_g + p_b = 1. \tag{15.1}$$

The quantity of goods consumed in each the good and bad state is denoted by c_g and c_b. And the income that the consumer is endowed with in each state is y_g and y_b; the good and bad states are defined as such by the assumption that $y_g > y_b$. By having exogenously endowed income we abstract from the decisions of labour and capital in producing output, which we studied in earlier chapters. Note that endowment economies can still be general equilibrium economies within certain dimensions, and here these dimensions are good state and bad state consumption.

The social resource constraint is that the expected consumption equals the expected income:

$$p_g c_g + p_b c_b = p_g y_g + p_b y_b. \tag{15.2}$$

The expected utility, with E denoting expectations, is given by the (state-separable) utility of consumption in each state multiplied by its probability of occurring, just like with expected consumption expenditures and expected income:

$$E\left[u\left(c_g, c_b\right)\right] = p_g u\left(c_g\right) + p_b u\left(c_b\right). \tag{15.3}$$

Consider that the consumer is concerned about a low endowed income in the bad state. A way to transfer income between states is to invest funds in the good state which pay off in the bad state. Let this investment be the expected amount of funds to be deposited in the financial intermediary during the good state. Denote the amount of funds invested (or deposited) at the insurance company as d. Let the amount that the consumer receives in the bad state be denoted by y; this is similar to the amount of the insurance payout.

Consider how this investment affects the budget constraint for each state. For the good state, the expenditure is given by the sum of the consumption of goods and the investment in insurance being equal to the income endowment:

$$c_g + d = y_g. \tag{15.4}$$

For the bad state the expenditure is equal to the insurance payout plus the income endowment:

$$c_b = y + y_b. \tag{15.5}$$

Substituting the two state constraints into the social resource constraint (15.2),

$$p_g \left(y_g - d \right) + p_b \left(y + y_b \right) = p_g y_g + p_b y_b. \tag{15.6}$$

Solving for y,

$$y = \frac{p_g d}{p_b}. \tag{15.7}$$

The representative agent problem is then

$$\text{Max } Eu = p_g u \left(y_g - d \right) + p_B u \left(y + y_b \right) =$$

$$\text{Max } Eu = p_b u \left(y_g - d \right) + p_b u \left[\frac{p_g d}{p_b} + y_b \right]. \tag{15.8}$$

The equilibrium is

$$p_g \frac{\partial u \left(c_g \right)}{\partial c_g} \left(-1 \right) + p_b \frac{\partial u \left(c_b \right)}{\partial c_b} \frac{p_g}{p_b} = 0. \tag{15.9}$$

This can be simplified to equating the probability-weighted marginal rate of substitution across states to the probability-weighted marginal product of the invested funds:

$$\frac{p_b \frac{\partial u(c_b)}{\partial c_b}}{p_g \frac{\partial u(c_g)}{\partial c_g}} = \frac{p_b}{p_g}. \tag{15.10}$$

Dividing by the probabilities,

$$\frac{\partial u \left(c_b \right)}{\partial c_b} = \frac{\partial u \left(c_g \right)}{\partial c_g}, \tag{15.11}$$

and this implies that

$$c_b = c_g.$$

The equality of consumption across states creates perfect consumption smoothing across states. This happens when there are no costs in making the transfer of income across states. Markets are complete in that consumption can be smoothed perfectly across states.

15.2.1 Costly transfer of income across states

Suppose again for the good state, that consumption equals the endowed income minus the investment d:

$$c_g = y_g - d. \tag{15.12}$$

In the bad state, costs of the transformation are incurred, making consumption in the bad state:

$$c_b = y + y_b, \tag{15.13}$$

where now instead of transferring the full d, only some function of d is transferred, $f(d)$, where

$$f(d) \leq d.$$

Then the amount distributed y is given by

$$y = \frac{p_g f(d)}{p_b}. \tag{15.14}$$

First a linear production function $f(d)$ will be assumed. To construct this, consider that the deposit d is invested by the agent, but there are also costs equal to $(1 - A_F) d$. Then the total net income available after the transfer to the bad state is equal to

$$d - (1 - A_F) d = A_F d.$$

Then this is summarised by a linear production technology whereby

$$f(d) = A_F d, \tag{15.15}$$

where $A_F \leq 1$. This means that of the d that gets inputted in the good state only $A_F d$ of it is available after the transformation across states. If $A_F = 1$, then it is as if there were no costs and none of the d is lost. If $A < 1$, then some of it has been used up in the transformation. This makes the amount of insurance y paid out in the bad state equal to

$$y = \frac{p_g A_F d}{p_b}. \tag{15.16}$$

The representative agent therefore maximises the utility of equation (15.3) subject to the budget constraint for each state, equations (15.4) and (15.5), and subject to the production function of equation (15.16), with respect to consumption in each period, c_g and c_b, and the amount of funds d invested in insurance. This can be stated more simply in a one-step derivative form. Substitute in for consumption in each state using the budget constraints for each state, these being equations (15.4) and (15.5); and use the production function in equation (15.16) to substitute for y, which appears as an argument in the bad state consumption:

$$\max_d Eu = p_g u(c_g) + p_B u(c_b) = \tag{15.17}$$

$$\max_d Eu = p_b u(y_g - d) + p_b u \left[\frac{p_g f(d)}{p_b} + y_b \right]. \tag{15.18}$$

Taking the derivative with respect to d, using the chain rule of calculus again, the equilibrium condition is that:

$$p_g \frac{\partial u(c_g)}{\partial c_g} (-1) + p_b \frac{\partial u(c_b)}{\partial c_b} \frac{p_g f(d)}{p_b} = 0. \tag{15.19}$$

This can be simplified to equating the probability-weighted marginal rate of substitution across states to the probability-weighted marginal product of the invested funds:

$$\frac{p_b \frac{\partial u(c_b)}{\partial c_b}}{p_g \frac{\partial u(c_g)}{\partial c_g}} = \frac{p_b}{p_g \frac{\partial f(d)}{\partial d}} = \frac{p_b}{p_g A_F}. \tag{15.20}$$

This equilibrium looks complicated but is not. Divide through by the probability ratio $\frac{p_g}{p_b}$, and this gives that

$$\frac{\frac{\partial u(c_g)}{\partial c_g}}{\frac{\partial u(c_b)}{\partial c_b}} = \frac{\partial f(d)}{\partial d} = A_F. \tag{15.21}$$

This gives a standard condition that the ratio of marginal utilities across states of nature equals the marginal product of transforming the invested funds across the states of nature.

15.2.2 Complete consumption smoothing

Examining the equilibrium equation (15.21), a question is when would consumption be smoothed across states? This happens by definition if

$$c_g = c_b. \tag{15.22}$$

In this case then it is also true that $u\left(c_g\right) = u\left(c_b\right)$, and $\frac{\partial u(c_g)}{\partial c_g} = \frac{\partial u(c_b)}{\partial c_b}$. This leaves us with the modified equilibrium condition under perfect consumption smoothing across states of:

$$1 = \frac{\frac{\partial u(c_g)}{\partial c_g}}{\frac{\partial u(c_b)}{\partial c_b}} = \frac{\partial f\left(d\right)}{\partial d}. \tag{15.23}$$

Therefore the only way to have perfect consumption smoothing is if $\frac{\partial f(d)}{\partial d} = 1$. Consider when this would occur by going back to the production function of equation (15.16). In order to get perfect consumption smoothing, it must be the case that the marginal product of funds equals 1, or that $\frac{\partial f(d)}{\partial d} = A_F = 1$.

Implicit is that there is no cost of making this transformation. This assumption, of a simple linear production technology, is implicit in all of the complete market models with perfect consumption smoothing, even if they are in many dimensions and even if describing much more complex 'contingent claims markets' that transfer income across various states of nature.

15.2.3 Log utility and linear production

To be completely explicit, specify the general equilibrium, representative agent, problem using the linear production technology and assuming log utility. In particular substitute in log utility and substitute in for y using $f\left(d\right) = A_F d$ so that the problem now is

$$\underset{d}{\text{Max}} \, Eu = p_g \ln\left(y_g - d\right) + p_b \ln\left(\frac{p_g A_F d}{p_b} + y_b\right). \tag{15.24}$$

The equilibrium condition, from differentiating with respect to d, is

$$p_g \frac{-1}{\left(y_g - d\right)} + p_b \frac{A_F \frac{p_g}{p_b}}{\left(\frac{p_g A_F d}{p_b} + y_b\right)} = 0. \tag{15.25}$$

This simplifies to

$$c_b = \frac{p_g A_F d}{p_b} + y_b = A_F\left(y_g - d\right) = A_F c_g. \tag{15.26}$$

Therefore it is true that in this case with linear technology, the consumption is equal across states only when $A_F = 1$.

Further all of the variables of the problem can be solved in terms of exogenous parameters. From equation (15.26), the solution for the investment d is given as

$$A_F d + \frac{p_g A_F d}{p_b} = A_F d\left(1 + \frac{p_g}{p_b}\right) = A_F y_g - y_b; \tag{15.27}$$

$$d = \frac{A_F y_g - y_b}{A_F\left(1 + \frac{p_g}{p_b}\right)}. \tag{15.28}$$

Given d, and the parameters, the consumption in each state can be found from the budget constraints for each state.

$$y = \frac{p_g}{p_b} A_F d = \frac{p_g}{p_b} \left(\frac{A_F y_g - y_b}{1 + \frac{p_g}{p_b}} \right); \tag{15.29}$$

$$c_b = y + y_b = \frac{p_g}{p_b} \left(\frac{A_F y_g - y_b}{1 + \frac{p_g}{p_b}} \right) + y_b; \tag{15.30}$$

$$c_g = y_g - d = y_g - \frac{A_F y_g - y_b}{A_F \left(1 + \frac{p_g}{p_b} \right)}; \tag{15.31}$$

$$c_b = A_F c_g. \tag{15.32}$$

15.2.4 Example 15.1: Baseline

Assume that $A_F = 1$. The representative agent model is solved for general parameter values. Assume now specifically that $p_g = 0.9$, $p_b = 0.1$, $y_g = 1$, and $y_b = 0$. Think of this example as nine years in a row that have a good income, and then in the tenth year a bad income results. For example, work income flows in for 9 years and in the tenth unemployment results in no income. Then the consumer must rely on transferring income across states by investing in d.

The solution with these parameters is

$$d = \frac{A_F y_g - y_b}{A_F \left(1 + \frac{p_g}{p_b} \right)} = \frac{1}{1 + \frac{0.9}{0.1}} = 0.1; \tag{15.33}$$

$$y = \frac{p_g}{p_b} \left(\frac{A_F y_g - y_b}{1 + \frac{p_g}{p_b}} \right) = \frac{0.9}{0.1} \frac{1}{1 + \frac{0.9}{0.1}} = 0.9; \tag{15.34}$$

$$c_b = y + y_b = y + 0 = 0.9; \tag{15.35}$$

$$c_g = y_g - d = 1 - d = 1 - 0.1 = 0.9; \tag{15.36}$$

$$c_b = c_g = 0.9. \tag{15.37}$$

The amount 0.1 is invested in d deposits in the good state, and 0.9 is received as the y payout should the bad state occur. And this makes consumption the same value of 0.9 in both states. And it means that over the nine years in which a good state occurs, the consumer deposits 0.1 each year, and then in the tenth year the sum of the deposits, of $9(0.1) = 0.9$ is paid out. Of course this does not include discounting over time, such as nine years, and so the analogy is not exactly years, but rather different states occurring at the same time. This can be extended to include payouts over time, which would include explicit time discounting of the future income.

The solution can be graphed, in terms of production and utility. The equilibrium expected utility level in Example 15.1 is

$$Eu = 0.9 \ln (c_g) + 0.1 \ln (c_b),$$
$$-0.10536 = 0.9 \ln (0.9) + 0.1 \ln (0.9),$$
$$e^{-0.10536} = (c_g)^{0.9} (c_b)^{0.1},$$

$$c_b = \left(\frac{e^{-0.10536}}{(c_g)^{0.9}} \right)^{\frac{1}{0.1}}. \tag{15.38}$$

The production function is

$$f(d) = A_F d = (0.9) d.$$

Now use the two budget constraints and the production function to write the production of bad state consumption in terms of good state consumption. The bad state consumption constraint, substituting in $y = \frac{p_g f(d)}{p_b}$, and $f(d) = A_F d$, is

$$c_b = y_b + y = y_b + \frac{p_g f(d)}{p_b} = y_b + \frac{p_g A_F d}{p_b}.$$

This gives a solution for d in terms of c_b:

$$d = \frac{p_b (c_b - y_b)}{A_F p_g}.$$

Now substitute in for d in the budget constraint for good state consumption:

$$c_g = y_g - d$$
$$c_g = y_g - \frac{p_b (c_b - y_b)}{A_F p_g}.$$

Then solve for c_b in terms of c_g and put in the parameters of Example 15.1:

$$c_b = \frac{A_F p_g y_G}{p_b} + y_b - \frac{A_F p_g c_g}{p_b};$$
$$c_b = \frac{1 (0.9) 1}{(0.1)} + 0 - \frac{1 (0.9) c_g}{(0.1)}. \tag{15.39}$$

Figure 15.1 graphs the production of bad state consumption from good state consumption, of equation (15.39) in the blue line, and also graphs the utility level curve at the equilibrium, of equation (15.38) in the black curve. Here consumption in each state is 0.9, so that it is smoothed (equal) across states.

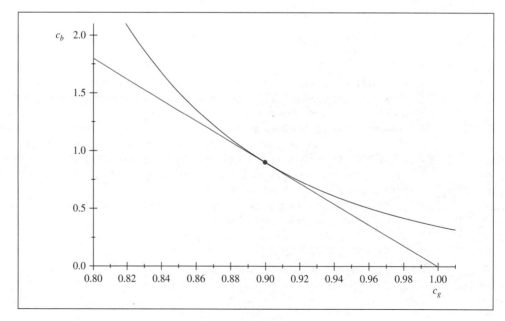

Figure 15.1 Good state and bad state consumption with consumption smoothing in Example 15.1

The equilibrium can also be graphed in terms of the bad state consumption on the vertical axis and the amount invested d in the good state as the variable on the horizontal axis; this would be $(c_b : d)$ space instead of $(c_b : c_g)$ space. It is analogous to goods and labour space versus goods and leisure space in Chapters 2 to 4.

To graph within this alternative dimension, rewrite utility in terms of c_b and d, by using the constraint that $c_g = y_g - d$:

$$c_b = \left(\frac{e^{-0.10536}}{\left(c_g\right)^{0.9}}\right)^{\frac{1}{0.1}} = \left(\frac{e^{-0.10536}}{\left(1 - d\right)^{0.9}}\right)^{\frac{1}{0.1}}. \tag{15.40}$$

Second, for the production side, in terms of $(c_b : d)$ space, write

$$c_b = \frac{A_F \, p_g \, y_G}{p_b} + y_b - \frac{A_F \, p_g c_g}{p_b},$$

$$c_b = \frac{A_F \, p_g \, y_G}{p_b} + y_b - \frac{A_F \, p_g \, (y_g - d)}{p_b},$$

$$c_b = \frac{1 \, (0.9) \, 1}{(0.1)} + 0 - \frac{1 \, (0.9) \, (1 - d)}{(0.1)},$$

$$c_b = \frac{(0.9)}{(0.1)} - \frac{(0.9)}{(0.1)} + \frac{(0.9) \, d}{(0.1)}. \tag{15.41}$$

The graph then instead becomes, in $(c_b : d)$ space, upward sloping production and utility functions rather than downward sloping ones. Figure 15.2 graphs equations (15.40) and (15.41).

The equilibrium investment in the good state is $d = 0.10$ while the consumption in the bad state is again 0.9.

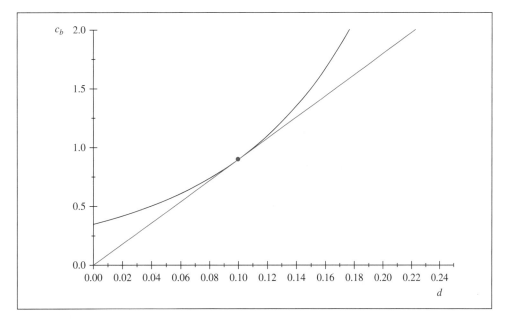

Figure 15.2 Utility and production in Example 15.1, with investment d

15.2.5 Example 15.2: Consumption tilting

Consumption tilting, with more good state consumption than bad state consumption, occurs when $A_F < 1$. Assume that $A_F = 0.8$, so that the transformation across states is costly. The representative agent model is solved for general parameter values. Assume now specifically that $p_g = 0.9$, $p_b = 0.1$, $y_g = 1$, and $y_b = 0$. Then

$$d = \frac{0.8}{0.8 \left(1 + \frac{0.9}{0.1} \right)} = 0.1 \tag{15.42}$$

$$y = 0.8 \left(\frac{0.9}{0.1} \right) \frac{0.8}{0.8 \left(1 + \frac{0.9}{0.1} \right)} = 0.72; \tag{15.43}$$

$$c_b = y = 0.72; \tag{15.44}$$

$$c_g = 1 - d = 1 - 0.1 = 0.9. \tag{15.45}$$

The solution is that 0.1 is invested in d in the good state, 0.9 consumed in the good state, but only 0.72 consumed in the bad state. Now consumption is 'tilted' towards more in the good state than in the bad state. Consumption tilting is a general result. When it is costly to transform the income across states, then perfect consumption smoothing does not result. Instead, more of the good state than bad state consumption results.

The utility level curve is now

$$Eu = 0.9 \ln \left(c_g \right) + 0.1 \ln \left(c_b \right)$$

$$-0.12767 = 0.9 \ln \left(0.9 \right) + 0.1 \ln \left(0.72 \right),$$

$$e^{-0.12767} = \left(c_g \right)^{0.9} (c_b)^{0.1},$$

$$c_b = \left(\frac{e^{-0.12767}}{\left(c_g \right)^{0.9}} \right)^{\frac{1}{0.1}}. \tag{15.46}$$

And the production line is

$$c_b = \frac{A_F \, p_g \, y_g}{p_b} + y_b - \frac{A_F \, p_g \, c_g}{p_b};$$

$$c_b = \frac{(0.8) \, (0.9) \, 1}{(0.1)} + 0 - \frac{(0.8) \, (0.9) \, c_g}{(0.1)}. \tag{15.47}$$

Figure 15.3 graphs equations (15.46) and (15.47) in dashed black and dashed blue, in comparison with the Example 15.1 equilibrium in solid black and solid blue, to show how the lower productivity A_F causes the production line to pivot down and the utility level to fall. Consumption in the good state remains the same at 0.9 but consumption in the bad state drops to 0.72.

And if written in $(c_b : d)$ space, these utility and linear production functions in Example 15.2 are

$$c_b = \left(\frac{e^{-0.12767}}{\left(1 - d \right)^{0.9}} \right)^{\frac{1}{0.1}}; \tag{15.48}$$

$$c_b = \frac{(0.8) \, (0.9) \, 1}{(0.1)} + 0 - \frac{(0.8) \, (0.9) \, (1 - d)}{(0.1)}. \tag{15.49}$$

Figure 15.4 graphs equations (15.48) and (15.49) to see the similar results. The amount invested d remains the same at $d = 0.1$, but consumption in the bad state drops.

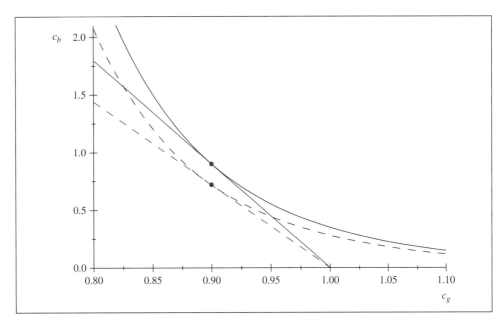

Figure 15.3 Good state and bad state consumption in Example 15.1 (black and blue) and Example 15.2 (dashed black and blue)

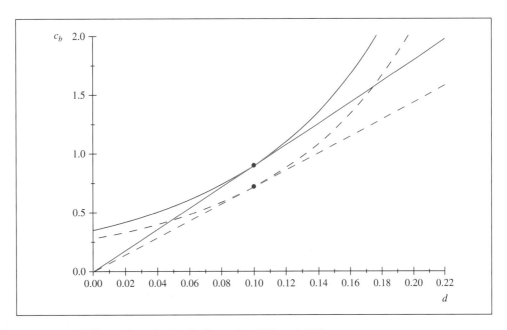

Figure 15.4 Utility and production in Examples 15.1 and 15.2

15.2.6 **Example 15.3: Change in transfer productivity**

It results that when the endowment in the bad state is zero, $y_b = 0$, then the amount invested d does not change even if productivity A_F changes. This is because the solution for d is $d = \frac{A_F y_g - y_b}{A_F \left(1 + \frac{p_g}{p_b}\right)}$, and if $y_b = 0$, then $d = \frac{y_g}{1 + \frac{p_g}{p_b}}$ and it is unaffected by A_F. This means

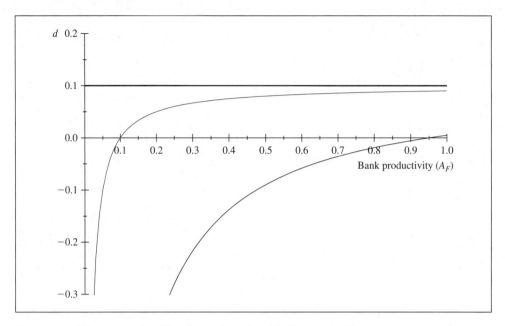

Figure 15.5 Effect of productivity A_F on deposits d in Example 15.3

that the consumer invests the same for all A_F values; the investment in d depends only on the probabilities of the states and the good state endowment.

More generally, the income in the bad state may not be zero and then the amount invested d will vary with the productivity A_F. Let $y_b = 0.1$, with all other parameters as in Example 15.2: $A_F = 0.8$, $p_g = 0.9$, $p_b = 0.1$, $y_g = 1$. Then the solution for d is

$$d = \frac{A_F y_g - y_b}{A_F \left(1 + \frac{p_g}{p_b}\right)} = \frac{0.8 - 0.1}{0.8 (1 + 9)} = 0.0875.$$

And the solution for consumption in each state then follows directly.

Given the endowments and probabilities, as A_F changes, so does d:

$$d = \frac{A_F y_g - y_b}{A_F \left(1 + \frac{p_g}{p_b}\right)} = \frac{A_F - 0.1}{A_F (1 + 9)}. \tag{15.50}$$

With $A_F = 0.6$,

$$d = \frac{A_F y_g - y_b}{A_F \left(1 + \frac{p_g}{p_b}\right)} = \frac{0.6 - 0.1}{0.6 (1 + 9)} = 0.08333. \tag{15.51}$$

Figure 15.5 graphs equation (15.50) for different values of A_F in Example 15.3. The thick black line is constant at $d = 0.1$ when $y_b = 0$ as in Example 15.2. The blue curve shows d as A_F varies given that $y_b = 0.1$; the amount invested falls as the transfer productivity A_F falls, until equalling zero at $A_F y_g = y_b = 0.1$. The thinner black line shows d as A_F varies assuming that $y_b = 0.95$; the amount of d is positive only for values of $A_F > 0.95$.

15.3 Consumer and firm decentralised problems

When we decentralise the problem between consumer and firm the price for the insurance will be seen to be the ratio of the probabilities of each state occurring, when there are no costs of income transference. The price shows the amount of goods in the bad state that is bought with each unit of goods in the good state. The consumer buys in the market a certain quantity of this insurance in the good state and gets the payout in the bad state. And the firm will receive revenues equal to the price of the insurance and the amount of insurance bought, in the good state, and pays out the insurance in the bad state.

15.3.1 Consumer problem

The amount received in the bad state is the amount of deposits d as factored by the gross rate of dividend return, denoted by $1 + R^d$, where R^d denotes the net rate of return on the amount invested in the good state. This R^d is an equilibrium price that is determined in the market.

The expected utility, with E denoting expectations, is

$$E\left[u\left(c_g, c_b\right)\right] = p_g u\left(c_g\right) + p_b u(c_b). \tag{15.52}$$

The budget constraint for each period is altered by the buying of the bad state consumption, as a means of insurance. Let the budget constraints reflect this purchase by adding d to the expenditures in the good state, and adding $\left(1 + R^d\right) d$ as income in the bad state. Then equations (15.4) and (15.5) are now

$$c_g - d = y_g. \tag{15.53}$$

For the bad state the expenditure is equal to the insurance payout plus the income endowment:

$$c_b = \left(1 + R^d\right) d + y_b. \tag{15.54}$$

The consumer maximisation problem can be simplified by substituting in for consumption in each state using these budget constraints; differentiating with respect to just the choice of d gives the equilibrium condition. The problem is

$$\underset{d}{\text{Max }} E\left[u\left(c_g, c_b\right)\right] = p_g u\left(y_g - d\right) + p_b u\left(\left(1 + R^d\right) d + y_b\right). \tag{15.55}$$

The equilibrium conditions can be arranged as

$$\frac{p_g \frac{\partial u(c_g)}{\partial c_g}}{p_b \frac{\partial u(c_b)}{\partial c_b}} = 1 + R^d. \tag{15.56}$$

If the price $\left(1 + R^d\right)$ equals the ratio of probabilities, $\frac{p_b}{p_g}$, then consumption smoothing results with $c_g = c_b$. To determine the price $\left(1 + R^d\right)$, the firm equilibrium conditions are necessary in which the price is there determined as being equal to marginal cost.

15.3.2 Firm problem

The firm takes in an amount in the good state equal to d, and pays out in the bad state the amount d plus a return $R^d d$. Assume the firm also incurs costs in the transformation of the income from the good state to bad state equal to $\left(1 - A_F\right) d$ during the good state. This makes the total net income in the good state equal to $d - \left(1 - A_F\right) d = A_F d$. In other words the net income in the good state is a function of the deposits d, given by $f(d)$. With the linear specification of this technology, whereby

$$f(d) = A_F d, \tag{15.57}$$

the net transformation $f(d)$ is the equivalent to the receipts minus the costs. The firm maximisation problem is then

$$\underset{d}{\text{Max }} E\Pi = p_g f(d) - p_b \left(1 + R^d\right) d, \tag{15.58}$$

$$= p_g \left[d - \left(1 - A_F\right) d\right] - p_b \left(1 + R^d\right) d, \tag{15.59}$$

$$= p_g A_F d - p_b \left(1 + R^d\right) d. \tag{15.60}$$

The first-order equilibrium condition is that

$$1 + R^d = \frac{p_g A_F}{p_b}. \tag{15.61}$$

15.3.3 Market clearing equilibrium

Combining the equilibrium conditions from the consumer and firm problems it results that

$$\frac{p_g \frac{\partial u(c_g)}{\partial c_g}}{p_b \frac{\partial u(c_b)}{\partial c_b}} = 1 + R^d = \frac{p_g A_F}{p_b}. \tag{15.62}$$

In the case of $A_F = 1$, this condition implies that

$$\frac{\frac{\partial u(c_b)}{\partial c_b}}{\frac{\partial u(c_g)}{\partial c_g}} = 1. \tag{15.63}$$

And this in turn means that consumption is smoothed; $c_g = c_b$.

With $A_F < 1$, and some cost in the transformation, then instead there is consumption tilting with less consumption in the bad state; assuming log utility,

$$A_F c_g = c_b. \tag{15.64}$$

Graphically the equilibrium looks the same as in Figures 15.1 to 15.4, even though now there is the additional line of the consumer's budget constraint. This is the market line that splits the production and utility sides of the problem. However here the production function is linear and so it coincides with the consumer's budget constraint, making the graphs identical to when the problem is centralised without separate consumer and firm problems. In the next section, the assumption of a linear production function is relaxed. This requires setting out the production function more generally, here using a banking approach.

15.4 The financial intermediation approach

Here the banking theory will be used for all such costly means of transferring funds from one point to another, and from one state to another, and from one time to another. This includes a general type of insurance in this chapter, and the transformation of savings into investment in Chapter 16.

The main idea of the financial intermediation approach is that the labour and the capital in the banking industry, along with the deposited funds, all need to be accounted for. In general equilibrium this means there is a production function for turning funds from one form into another. Some amount of funds are deposited in the bank. And minus the labour and capital costs, the funds are distributed in a new form, either as a loan, or as a deposit in a bank account, or as a payment of insurance when the bad state occurs. Also with the representative agent approach, the agent acts in part as a consumer, as a goods producing firm, and as a bank.

Consider that the representative agent, who acts as a bank in part therefore, becomes the owner of the bank in the decentralised problems of the consumer, the goods producer and the bank service producer. The idea is that the bank takes in funds, or deposits of money that will be denoted by d, and uses the deposits for a variety of financial services. The consumer puts funds in the bank, and gets back the funds, either at another time (for example with interest earned minus the cost of investing the funds) or at another place (minus the cost of transferring the funds) or in another state of nature (minus the cost of transferring funds across states).

With the financial intermediation approach to banking, a particular production function of the financial intermediation services is assumed. In particular, the service output in general is a Cobb–Douglas production function of labour, capital and the deposited funds. With capital in the bank sector of k_F, labour of l_F and deposits of d, the production function is

$$f(d, k_F, l_F) = A_F d^{1-\kappa_1-\kappa_2} (k_F)^{\kappa_1} (l_F)^{\kappa_2}, \tag{15.65}$$

where $\kappa_1 + \kappa_2 < 1$. With a simplifying assumption of only labour and deposited funds, this production function is

$$f(d, l_F) = A_F d^{1-\kappa} l_F^{\kappa}, \tag{15.66}$$

where $\kappa < 1$. This production function will be assumed as the function of the intermediary is specified as transferring income across states of nature.

15.5 Banking across states of nature

The production approach to transferring resources across states of nature can be stated in terms of the general financial intermediation approach. Another aspect of incomplete markets is that even if they exist between states they may require costs of transferring the income between states. The costs can be summarised in terms of the labour and capital used in the banking industry for all the different types of finance between states of nature. In the view of the financial intermediation services of the banking industry, the degree of consumption smoothing across states in turn depends on how costly it is to transfer income between states. To see how this degree of consumption smoothing depends on the production technology of the banking industry, it is also useful to set out the theory of banking. Then it is seen how it affects the price of transferring consumption across states.

Now time in banking will be used, along with labour, in producing goods. The endowment of goods in each state is instead produced with a goods sector using a linear production function with only labour time l as the input. The output in the good state, y_g, given the productivity parameter A_g, is

$$y_g = A_g l.$$

There is no leisure and the time endowment of 1 is used for goods production and banking time l_F. This means that in the good state

$$l = 1 - l_F.$$

In the bad state, all time is used for goods production, A_b is the productivity parameter, and

$$y_b = A_b l = A_b,$$

where it is assumed that

$$A_g > A_b, \tag{15.67}$$

which is what makes the good state a good state, and the bad state a bad state. The difference between the productivity parameters is therefore similar to the difference between higher goods productivity during an expansion and lower goods productivity during a recession.

15.5.1 Consumer problem

The representative agent problem can be decentralised so that there is a market for bank-provided insurance. One way to show this is to let the consumer deposit d in funds during the good state in order to receive $(1 + R^d) d$ in funds during the bad state. In this way R^d is the competitive market return on the deposited funds. And this is in the form as a dividend distribution of the bank, which the consumer owns by virtue of the deposits d.

Besides depositing the funds, the consumer produces goods output with labour time, with the output equal to $A_g l$. And the consumer works for the bank in the good state, receiving the wage value of this time as equal to $w l_F$. The allocation of time constraint is that

$$1 = l + l_F, \tag{15.68}$$

and the budget constraint for the good state is

$$
\begin{aligned}
c_g &= A_g l + w l_F - d, \\
&= A_g (1 - l_F) + w l_F - d.
\end{aligned} \tag{15.69}
$$

The consumer receives the dividend return on the deposits in the bad state of $(1 + R^d) d$ plus the income from working in the goods sector in the bad state, of A_b; the bad state budget constraint is

$$c_b = A_b + (1 + R^d) d. \tag{15.70}$$

The consumer then chooses the amount of consumption in each state and the time spent producing goods and working for the bank. Simplifying this by substituting in the time and goods budget constraints into the utility function, the decision problem is in terms of choosing d and l_F:

$$\underset{d, l_F}{\text{Max}} \ E \left[u \left(c_g, c_b \right) \right] = p_g u \left[A_g \left(1 - l_F \right) + w l_F - d \right] + p_b u \left[\left(1 + R^d \right) d + A_b \right]. \tag{15.71}$$

The equilibrium condition with respect to d implies that the marginal rate of substitution between the consumption in the good and bad state equals the gross return on deposited funds R^d:

$$\frac{p_g \frac{\partial u(c_g)}{\partial c_g}}{p_b \frac{\partial u(c_b)}{\partial c_b}} = 1 + R^d.$$

The other first-order condition with respect to l_F simply gives that the real wage equals the marginal product:

$$w = A_G. \tag{15.72}$$

15.5.2 Bank problem

The bank problem is to take in the deposit funds d during the good state and transform them so that they are available in the bad state. This is the same as saying that the output of the bank after the transformation is given by $f(d, l_F)$, where a Cobb–Douglas production function in terms of deposits d and labour l_F is specified as

$$f(d, l_F) = A_F d^{1-\kappa} l_F^\kappa. \tag{15.73}$$

The expected profit function of the bank equals expected net revenue, $p_g \left(A_F d^{1-\kappa} l_F^\kappa - w l_F \right)$, minus expect net payouts of $p_b (1 + R^d) d$:

$$\underset{d, l_F}{\text{Max}} \ E\Pi = p_g \left(A_F d^{1-\kappa} l_F^\kappa - w l_F \right) - p_b \left(1 + R^d \right) d; \tag{15.74}$$

The equilibrium condition with respect to the deposited funds d is that

$$1 + R^d = \frac{p_g \left(1 - \kappa\right) A_F \left(\frac{l_F}{d}\right)^\kappa}{p_b}. \tag{15.75}$$

The equilibrium condition with respect to the labour l_F is

$$w = \kappa A_F \left(\frac{l_F}{d}\right)^{\kappa - 1}, \tag{15.76}$$

which allows for the ratio of labour to deposits $\frac{l_F}{d}$ to be solved as

$$\frac{l_F}{d} = \left(\frac{\kappa A_F}{w}\right)^{\frac{1}{1-\kappa}}. \tag{15.77}$$

And substituting this into the first equilibrium condition gives the solution for R^d in terms of the given parameters and the real wage:

$$1 + R^d = \frac{p_g \left(1 - \kappa\right) A_F \left(\frac{\kappa A_F}{w}\right)^{\frac{\kappa}{1-\kappa}}}{p_b}. \tag{15.78}$$

15.5.3 Market clearing

Bringing together the consumer and firm equilibrium conditions, the same equilibrium results as would result in the representative agent centralised problem:

$$\frac{p_b \frac{\partial u(c_b)}{\partial c_b}}{p_g \frac{\partial u(c_g)}{\partial c_g}} = \frac{1}{1 + R^d} = \frac{p_b}{p_g \left(1 - \kappa\right) A_F \left(\frac{\kappa A_F}{w}\right)^{\frac{\kappa}{1-\kappa}}}, \tag{15.79}$$

and that

$$A_g = w, \tag{15.80}$$

$$\frac{p_b \frac{\partial u(c_b)}{\partial c_b}}{p_g \frac{\partial u(c_g)}{\partial c_g}} = \frac{1}{1 + R^d} = \frac{p_b}{p_g \left(1 - \kappa\right) A_F \left(\frac{\kappa A_F}{A_g}\right)^{\frac{\kappa}{1-\kappa}}}. \tag{15.81}$$

And with log utility, $u\left(c\right) = \ln c$, the equilibrium condition simplifies to

$$\frac{c_g}{c_b} = \frac{1}{\left(1 - \kappa\right) A_F \left(\frac{\kappa A_F}{A_g}\right)^{\frac{\kappa}{1-\kappa}}}. \tag{15.82}$$

If $\kappa > 0$, $A_F \leq 1$, and $A_g \leq 1$, then again we have that $\left(1 - \kappa\right) A_F \left(\frac{\kappa A_F}{A_g}\right)^{\frac{\kappa}{1-\kappa}} < 1$, and so

$$c_g \left(1 - \kappa\right) A_F \left(\frac{\kappa A_F}{A_g}\right)^{\frac{\kappa}{1-\kappa}} = c_b; \tag{15.83}$$

$$c_g > c_b. \tag{15.84}$$

If however $\kappa = 0$ and $A_F = 1$, then $c_g = c_b$ and there is perfect consumption smoothing. In this case but more generally,

$$\frac{c_g}{c_b} = \frac{1}{A_F}. \tag{15.85}$$

Therefore this collapses down to the same condition for the general case in equation (15.21) above. If $A_F = 1$, then there is perfect consumption smoothing across states. But if $A_F < 1$, or if $\kappa > 0$, then there are costs and imperfect consumption smoothing, with $c_g > c_b$.

To solve in general for the full equilibrium, from the budget constraints, and the solution for $1 + R^d$,

$$c_g = A_g \left(1 - l_F\right) + wl_F - d = A_g - d;$$

$$c_b = \left(1 + R^d\right) d + A_b,$$

(15.86)

$$c_b = \left(\frac{p_g \left(1 - \kappa\right) A_F \left(\frac{\kappa A_F}{A}\right)^{\frac{\kappa}{1-\kappa}}}{p_b}\right) d + A_b.$$

(15.87)

These constraints can be combined to solve for d. From equation (15.83)

$$\left(1 - \kappa\right) A_F \left(\frac{\kappa A_F}{A_g}\right)^{\frac{\kappa}{1-\kappa}} c_g = c_b.$$

(15.88)

Combining this with equations (15.86) and (15.87), then

$$\left(1 - \kappa\right) A_F \left(\frac{\kappa A_F}{A_g}\right)^{\frac{\kappa}{1-\kappa}} \left(A_g - d\right) = c_b = \frac{p_g}{p_b} \left(1 - \kappa\right) A_F \left(\frac{\kappa A_F}{A_g}\right)^{\frac{\kappa}{1-\kappa}} d + A_b,$$

$$A_g \left(1 - \kappa\right) A_F \left(\frac{\kappa A_F}{A_g}\right)^{\frac{\kappa}{1-\kappa}} - A_b = d \left(1 - \kappa\right) A_F \left(\frac{\kappa A_F}{A_g}\right)^{\frac{\kappa}{1-\kappa}} \left(1 + \frac{p_g}{p_b}\right),$$

$$d = \frac{A_g \left(1 - \kappa\right) A_F \left(\frac{\kappa A_F}{A_g}\right)^{\frac{\kappa}{1-\kappa}} - A_b}{\left(1 - \kappa\right) A_F \left(\frac{\kappa A_F}{A_g}\right)^{\frac{\kappa}{1-\kappa}} \left(1 + \frac{p_g}{p_b}\right)}.$$

And this solution for d can be substituted back into equation (15.77) to find l_F, and into the above budget constraints to find the equilibrium c_g and c_b.

In the case that $\kappa = 0$, then as with the linear production function $f(d) = A_F d$, the solution for d is

$$d = \frac{A_F A_g - A_b}{A_F \left(1 + \frac{p_g}{p_b}\right)}.$$

15.5.4 Example 15.4: Equal probabilities of states

Consider some particular probability values. One case is when the probability of the good state is equal to the probability of the bad state, so that

$$p_b = p_g.$$

(15.89)

Then the rate of return R^d is negative or equal to one, depending on the cost of transferring income to the bad state. Consider when there are no labour costs, so that $\kappa = 0$, and also assume that $A_F = 1$. Then from equation (15.78) $R^d = 0$. The deposited funds are transferred without cost from the good state to the bad state.

15.5.5 Example 15.5: Good state more probable

More typically the good state of affairs is the more likely state. Then in this case,

$$p_g > p_b.$$

(15.90)

Suppose that $p_g = 0.55$ and $p_b = 0.45$. Again assume zero cost so that $\kappa = 0$ and $A_F = 1$. Equation (15.78) implies that

$$R^d = \frac{p_g}{p_b} - 1 = \frac{0.55}{0.45} - 1 = 0.22.$$

(15.91)

And in this case consumption is perfectly smooth across states.

Now assume that there are costs. Let $\kappa = 0.05$, $A_F = 0.95$, and $w = A_g = 0.15$. Then

$$R^d = \frac{p_g \left(1 - \kappa\right) A_F \left(\frac{\kappa A_F}{w}\right)^{\frac{\kappa}{1-\kappa}}}{p_b} - 1, \tag{15.92}$$

$$= \frac{0.55 \left(1 - 0.05\right) 0.95 \left(\frac{(0.05)0.95}{0.15}\right)^{\frac{0.05}{1-0.05}}}{0.45} - 1,$$

$$= 0.038.$$

It is clear that the cost of producing the transformation of income between states can significantly lower the return on the deposited funds. In this case, the return falls from 0.22 with no costs to 0.038 with some costs. And consumption is more in the good state than the bad state.

15.5.6 Example 15.6: Rare bad state

Assume as in Example 15.2 that the bad state is much less likely, with $p_g = 0.9$ and $p_b = 0.1$. Also initially assume no costs. Then

$$R^d = \frac{p_g}{p_b} - 1 = \frac{0.9}{0.1} - 1 = 8.0.$$

The return on the deposited funds is 8.0, or 800%.

Now consider adding the same costs as in Example 15.5: $\kappa = 0.05$, $A_F = 0.95$, and $w = A_g = 1.0$ and $A_b = 0.60$. The return is then

$$R^d = \frac{p_g \left(1 - \kappa\right) A_F \left(\frac{\kappa A_F}{w}\right)^{\frac{\kappa}{1-\kappa}}}{p_b} - 1, \tag{15.93}$$

$$= \frac{0.9 \left(1 - 0.05\right) 0.95 \left(\frac{(0.05)0.95}{1}\right)^{\frac{0.05}{1-0.05}}}{0.1} - 1, \tag{15.94}$$

$$= 5.919. \tag{15.95}$$

Again the cost of the transformation is significant and it drops the return down to 592% instead of 800%. And again consumption is higher in the good than the bad state.

The full equilibrium can be found here and graphed. Given the solution for the investment d, its calibrated value is 2.2% of the income of 1 in the good state:

$$d = \frac{A_g \left(1 - \kappa\right) A_F \left(\frac{\kappa A_F}{A_G}\right)^{\frac{\kappa}{1-\kappa}} - A_b}{\left(1 - \kappa\right) A_F \left(\frac{\kappa A_F}{A_g}\right)^{\frac{\kappa}{1-\kappa}} \left(1 + \frac{p_g}{p_b}\right)}, \tag{15.96}$$

$$= \frac{1.0 \left(1 - 0.05\right) \left(0.95\right) \left(\frac{0.05(0.95)}{1.0}\right)^{\frac{0.05}{1-0.05}} - 0.6}{\left(1 - 0.05\right) \left(0.95\right) \left(\frac{0.05(0.95)}{1.0}\right)^{\frac{0.05}{1-0.05}} \left(1 + 9\right)}, \tag{15.97}$$

$$= 0.021954. \tag{15.98}$$

The consumption in each the good and bad state follows, given $d = 0.022$ and $R = 5.92$. The consumption in the good state is 97.8% of the initial income in the good state, with the consumption in the bad state only 75.2% of the initial income of the good state:

$$c_g = 1 - d = 1 - 0.021954 = 0.97805. \tag{15.99}$$

$$c_b = \left(1 + R^d\right) d + A_b = \left(6.919\right) \left(0.021954\right) + 0.60,$$

$$= 0.7519. \tag{15.100}$$

Knowing the investment d, the labour in the banking sector can also be found. It is a small amount, of $l_F = 0.000888$:

$$l_F = d \left(\frac{\kappa A_F}{A_g} \right)^{\frac{1}{1-\kappa}} = (0.021954) \left(\frac{0.05 \, (0.95)}{1.0} \right)^{\frac{1}{1-0.05}}, \tag{15.101}$$

$$= 0.00088830.$$

The solution is that 2.2% of output is invested in d in the good state, with 0.978 consumed in the good state, but only 0.75 consumed in the bad state. And 0.089% of time is used in the banking sector. Consumption is 'tilted' towards more in the good state than in the bad state. Consumption tilting is a general result. When it is costly to transform the income across states, then perfect consumption smoothing does not result. Instead, more of the good state than bad state consumption results.

The utility level curve is

$$Eu = 0.9 \ln (c_g) + 0.1 \ln (c_b),$$

$$-0.04849 = 0.9 \ln (0.97805) + 0.1 \ln (0.7519),$$

$$e^{-0.04849} = (c_g)^{0.9} (c_b)^{0.1},$$

$$c_b = \left(\frac{e^{-0.04849}}{(c_g)^{0.9}} \right)^{\frac{1}{0.1}}. \tag{15.102}$$

The production line can be found from the bank problem, where in equilibrium expenditure equals revenue and there is no profit after paying out the dividends of $(1 + R^d) d$:

$$\frac{p_g}{p_b} \left(A_F d^{1-\kappa} l_F^\kappa - w l_F \right) = (1 + R^d) d.$$

And from the consumer budget constraint for the bad state, in equation (15.70),

$$(1 + R^d) d = c_b - A_b.$$

Therefore, with l_F given, the production function in terms of d and c_b is

$$\frac{p_g}{p_b} \left(A_F d^{1-\kappa} l_F^\kappa - w l_F \right) = c_b - A_b. \tag{15.103}$$

Substituting in from the good state consumer budget constraint, equation (15.69), and using that $w = A_g$ from the consumer equilibrium condition in equation (15.72), then

$$d = A_g - c_g = 1 - c_g.$$

With d written in terms of c_g, the production function of equation (15.103) can then be also written in terms of c_g:

$$\frac{p_g}{p_b} \left(A_F (1 - c_g)^{1-\kappa} l_F^\kappa - w l_F \right) = c_b - A_b.$$

Solving for c_b,

$$c_b = \frac{p_g}{p_b} \left(A_F (1 - c_g)^{1-\kappa} l_F^\kappa - w l_F \right) + A_b.$$

Using the calibration, the production function is

$$c_b = \frac{0.9}{0.1} \left((0.95) (1 - c_g)^{1-0.05} (0.00088830)^{0.05} - 0.00088830 \right) + 0.6. \tag{15.104}$$

The consumer budget line starts with the budget constraint in the bad state, substitutes in that $d = 1 - c_g$ from the good state budget constraint, and uses the solution of

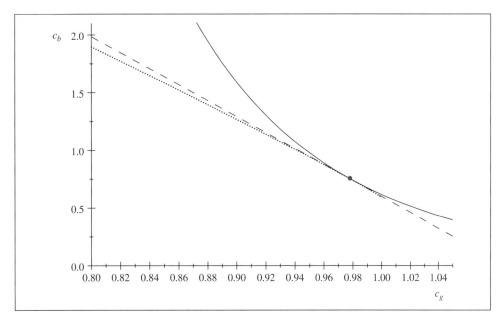

Figure 15.6 Good state and bad state consumption in Example 15.6

$1 + R = 6.919$ and the assumed parameter $A_b = 0.6$. This gives that

$$c_b = \left(1 + R^d\right) d + A_b,$$
$$c_b = \left(1 + R^d\right) \left(1 - c_g\right) + A_b,$$
$$c_b = 6.919 \left(1 - c_g\right) + 0.60. \tag{15.105}$$

Figure 15.6 graphs the utility level curve, equation (15.102), the production function, equation (15.104), and the budget line, equation (15.105). It shows the utility curve in black, the production function in dotted black and the budget line in dashed black. The equilibrium tangency point is at $c_g = 0.978$, and $c_b = 0.752$.

Note that the production line starts only at $c_g = 1$ since that is the endowment point after linear goods production. And so there is only a very slight slope difference between the dashed black budget line and the dotted black production function. But at $c_g = 1$, the dotted black production function is below the dashed black budget line, as it should be.

The equilibrium can also be seen from the perspective of the $\left(c_b : d\right)$ dimensions instead of the $\left(c_b : c_g\right)$ dimensions. Using that $c_b = 1 - d$, the utility, production and budget lines are

$$c_b = \left(\frac{e^{-0.04849}}{\left(1 - d\right)^{0.9}}\right)^{\frac{1}{0.1}};$$
$$c_b = \frac{0.9}{0.1} \left(\left(0.95\right) d^{1-0.05} \left(0.00088830\right)^{0.05} - 0.00088830\right) + 0.6;$$
$$c_b = 6.919(d) + 0.60.$$

Figure 15.7 graphs these to show how the production function starts below $c_b = 0.6$, when $d = 0$, while the budget line starts at the bad state endowment of 0.6 at $d = 0$. The production function slope is decreasing and reaches a tangency with the budget line and the utility curve at $d = 0.022$, which is the equilibrium amount of investment for the consumer. However consumption is not smoothed across states, with more in the good than in the bad state.

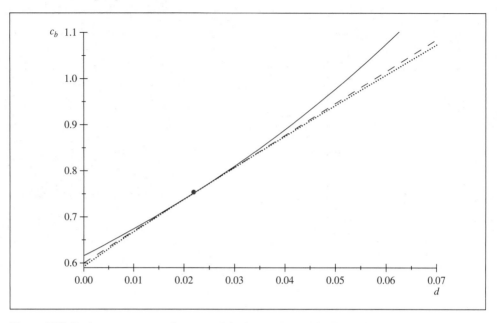

Figure 15.7 Bad state consumption c_b and the investment d, in Example 15.6

15.6 Bank production factors

There are two parameters in the bank production function, the productivity parameter A_F and the Cobb–Douglas parameter κ. Each of these determines in part the cost of banking: and each has a different effect.

15.6.1 Example 15.7: Productivity factor

Consider letting all parameters be the same as in Example 15.6 except the productivity factor. Now let $A_F = 0.80$ instead of 0.95. The other parameters are $p_g = 0.9$ and $p_b = 0.1$, $\kappa = 0.05$, $A_F = 0.95$, and $w = A_g = 1.0$, and $A_b = 0.60$. Then the solution for d and c_g is

$$d = \frac{A_g \left(1 - \kappa\right) A_F \left(\frac{\kappa A_F}{A_G}\right)^{\frac{\kappa}{1-\kappa}} - A_b}{\left(1 - \kappa\right) A_F \left(\frac{\kappa A_F}{A_g}\right)^{\frac{\kappa}{1-\kappa}} \left(1 + \frac{p_g}{p_b}\right)},$$

$$= \frac{1.0 \left(1 - 0.05\right) \left(0.80\right) \left(\frac{0.05(0.80)}{1.0}\right)^{\frac{0.05}{1-0.05}} - 0.6}{\left(1 - 0.05\right) \left(0.80\right) \left(\frac{0.05(0.80)}{1.0}\right)^{\frac{0.05}{1-0.05}} \left(1 + 9\right)},$$

$$= 0.0064781.$$

$$c_g = 1 - d = 1 - 0.0064781 = 0.99352.$$

The investment d is close to zero, and consumption in the good state close to 1.
The rate of return is

$$R^d = \frac{p_g \left(1 - \kappa\right) A_F \left(\frac{\kappa A_F}{w}\right)^{\frac{\kappa}{1-\kappa}}}{p_b} - 1$$

$$= \frac{0.9 \left(1 - 0.05\right) 0.80 \left(\frac{(0.05)0.80}{1}\right)^{\frac{0.05}{1-0.05}}}{0.1} - 1 = 4.774.$$

And the consumption in the bad state is much lower at

$$c_b = \left(1 + R^d\right) d + A_b = \left(5.774\right) \left(0.0064781\right) + 0.6,$$
$$= 0.6374.$$

The time in the bank sector is only

$$l_F = d \left(\frac{\kappa A_F}{A_g}\right)^{\frac{1}{1-\kappa}} = \left(0.0064781\right) \left(\frac{0.05 \left(0.80\right)}{1.0}\right)^{\frac{1}{1-0.05}},$$

$$= 0.00021874.$$

Graphed in $\left(c_b : d\right)$ space, the utility curve, production curve, and budget line in Example 15.7 are

$$u = 0.9 \ln\left(c_g\right) + 0.1 \ln\left(c_b\right),$$
$$-0.050887 = 0.9 \ln\left(0.99352\right) + 0.1 \ln\left(0.6374\right),$$
$$e^u = \left(c_g\right)^{0.9} \left(c_b\right)^{0.1},$$

$$c_b = \left(\frac{e^{-0.050887}}{\left(1 - d\right)^{0.9}}\right)^{\frac{1}{0.1}}; \tag{15.106}$$

$$c_b = \frac{0.9}{0.1} \left(\left(0.80\right) d^{1-0.05} \left(0.000219\right)^{0.05} - 0.000219\right) + 0.6; \tag{15.107}$$

$$c_b = 5.774 \left(d\right) + 0.60. \tag{15.108}$$

Figure 15.8 graphs this Example 15.7 equilibrium of equations (15.106), (15.107) and (15.108), in the variants of blue lines, which is pivoted down as compared to the Example 15.6 equilibrium, as shown again here in variants of black. It shows that when the

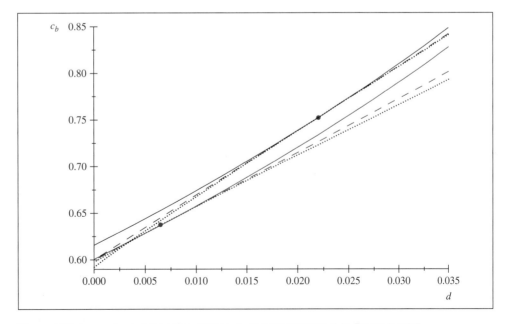

Figure 15.8 Lower bad state consumption c_b and investment d, in Example 15.7

bank sector is less productive, less is invested in transferring income across states and the consumption in the bad state is lower. The new tangency occurs at a value of d near to zero, at 0.0065.

15.6.2 Example 15.8: Larger labour costs

The other factor κ determines the share of labour cost in total bank output. Consider keeping all parameters the same as in Example 15.6 except that now $\kappa = 0.10$ instead of 0.05. Other parameters are $A_F = 0.95$, $p_g = 0.9$, $p_b = 0.1$, $w = A_g = 1.0$, and $A_b = 0.60$. The equilibrium is

$$d = \frac{A_g \left(1 - \kappa\right) A_F \left(\frac{\kappa A_F}{A_G}\right)^{\frac{\kappa}{1-\kappa}} - A_b}{\left(1 - \kappa\right) A_F \left(\frac{\kappa A_F}{A_g}\right)^{\frac{\kappa}{1-\kappa}} \left(1 + \frac{p_g}{p_b}\right)}$$

$$= \frac{1.0 \left(1 - 0.10\right) \left(0.95\right) \left(\frac{0.10(0.95)}{1.0}\right)^{\frac{0.10}{1-0.10}} - 0.6}{\left(1 - 0.10\right) \left(0.95\right) \left(\frac{0.10(0.95)}{1.0}\right)^{\frac{0.10}{1-0.10}} \left(1 + 9\right)}$$

$$= 0.0088469.$$

$$c_g = 1 - d = 1 - 0.0088469 = 0.99115.$$

Again the investment d is close to zero, and consumption in the good state close to 1. The rate of return is

$$R^d = \frac{p_g \left(1 - \kappa\right) A_F \left(\frac{\kappa A_F}{w}\right)^{\frac{\kappa}{1-\kappa}}}{p_b} - 1$$

$$= \frac{0.9 \left(1 - 0.10\right) 0.95 \left(\frac{(0.10)0.95}{1}\right)^{\frac{0.10}{1-0.10}}}{0.1} - 1$$

$$= 4.9241.$$

Consumption in the bad state is

$$c_b = \left(1 + R^d\right) d + A_b = \left(5.9241\right) \left(0.0088469\right) + 0.6$$

$$= 0.65241.$$

The time in the bank sector is

$$l_F = d \left(\frac{\kappa A_F}{A_g}\right)^{\frac{1}{1-\kappa}} = \left(0.0088469\right) \left(\frac{0.10 \left(0.95\right)}{1.0}\right)^{\frac{1}{1-0.10}}$$

$$= 0.000647.$$

And the graph would be similar to Figure 15.8.

15.6.3 Example 15.9: High labour cost

As a final example, let the bad state income be zero; $A_b = 0$. And specify a high labour cost, with $\kappa = \frac{1}{3}$, the same probabilities, with $p_g = 0.90$ and $p_b = 0.10$, and with $A_F = 0.95$, and $A_g = 1$.

The equilibrium is

$$d = \frac{A_g \left(1 - \kappa\right) A_F \left(\frac{\kappa A_F}{A_G}\right)^{\frac{\kappa}{1-\kappa}} - A_b}{\left(1 - \kappa\right) A_F \left(\frac{\kappa A_F}{A_g}\right)^{\frac{\kappa}{1-\kappa}} \left(1 + \frac{p_g}{p_b}\right)},$$

$$= \frac{1.0 \left(1 - \frac{1}{3}\right) (0.95) \left(\frac{\frac{1}{3}(0.95)}{1.0}\right)^{\frac{1}{3}}_{1-\frac{1}{3}}}{\left(1 - \frac{1}{3}\right) (0.95) \left(\frac{\frac{1}{3}(0.95)}{1.0}\right)^{\frac{1}{3}}_{1-\frac{1}{3}} \left(1 + \frac{0.90}{0.10}\right)},$$

$$= 0.1.$$

$$c_g = 1 - d = 1 - 0.1 = 0.9.$$

Again the investment d equals 0.1, and consumption in the good state close to 1.

The rate of return is

$$1 + R^d = \frac{p_g \left(1 - \kappa\right) A_F \left(\frac{\kappa A_F}{w}\right)^{\frac{\kappa}{1-\kappa}}}{p_b},$$

$$= \frac{0.90 \left(1 - \frac{1}{3}\right) 0.95 \left(\frac{\frac{1}{3} 0.95}{1}\right)^{\frac{1}{3}}_{1-\frac{1}{3}}}{0.10},$$

$$= 3.2076.$$

Consumption in the bad state is much lower than in the good state, at

$$c_b = \left(1 + R^d\right) d + A_b = (3.2076)(0.1) + 0$$
$$= 0.32076.$$

The time in the bank sector is

$$l_F = d \left(\frac{\kappa A_F}{A_g}\right)^{\frac{1}{1-\kappa}} = (0.1) \left(\frac{\frac{1}{3}(0.95)}{1.0}\right)^{\frac{1}{1-\frac{1}{3}}},$$

$$= 0.01782.$$

Utility, production and budget lines are

$$u = 0.9 \ln\left(c_g\right) + 0.1 \ln\left(c_b\right),$$
$$-0.20853 = 0.9 \ln\left(0.9\right) + 0.1 \ln\left(0.32076\right),$$
$$e^u = \left(c_g\right)^{0.9} (c_b)^{0.1},$$

$$c_b = \left(\frac{e^{-0.20853}}{(1 - d)^{0.9}}\right)^{\frac{1}{0.1}}; \tag{15.109}$$

$$c_b = \frac{0.9}{0.1} \left((0.95) d^{1-\frac{1}{3}} (0.01782)^{\frac{1}{3}} - 0.01782\right); \tag{15.110}$$

$$c_b = \left(1 + R^d\right) d + A_b,$$

$$c_b = 3.2076 d. \tag{15.111}$$

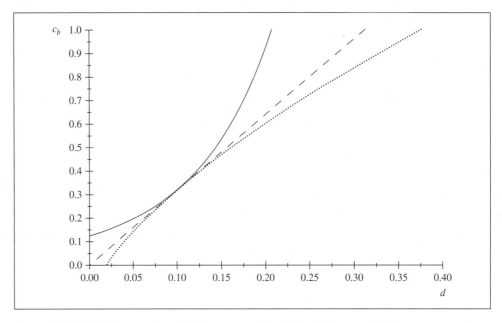

Figure 15.9 High labour costs and high consumption tilting in Example 15.9

Figure 15.9 graphs equations (15.109), (15.110) and (15.111) to show the more typical shape of the production function, with distinct curvature because the labour cost is so high a fraction of output. While this shape is more what we are used to seeing, with a big curvature for the production function, it may not be as plausible a specification, with $\kappa = \frac{1}{3}$, since this high labour cost gives a much lower consumption in the bad state. Perhaps more typical are the examples with κ being quite low. The low value of κ means that there are indeed labour costs, but these are a small fraction relative to the volume of deposits. And such a low value gives more plausible amounts of consumption smoothing across states.

15.7 Aggregate risk: falling bank productivity in the bad state

The advantage of providing the insurance explicitly through the bank sector as in actual decentralised markets is that it is easier to envision how aggregate shocks affect the ability of the market to smooth consumption across states. Consider an aggregate shock that causes the banking productivity to fall during the bad state, even though all of the contracting for the insurance takes place in the good state. So if A_F falls after the contracting has already occurred the problem is that the amount of insurance that was expected to be delivered will not be delivered. This aggregate risk by its nature cannot be insured within the market of this economy. This creates less consumption smoothing as a result.

Consider a simple way to consider this is with the above banking model. Assume a linear technology as in equation (15.57); so there are no labour costs, in that $\kappa = 0$. This implies that the return on deposits R^d is equal to

$$1 + R^d = \frac{p_g A_F}{p_b}. \tag{15.112}$$

And let $A_F = 1$. This then is an example of a costless transfer of funds across states, at their natural price of the ratio of the probabilities.

In an economy in which $\kappa = 0$ and $A_F = 1$, the consumer has perfect insurance against the bad state occurring. This happens when aggregate productivity falls from A_g to A_b with $A_g > A_b$. This fall in goods sector productivity can be typical of a business cycle contraction. Having full insurance across the business cycle is a way in which the consumer can keep consumption smooth across the business cycle and so have as high a utility level as possible.

Aggregate risk occurs in this example when A_F also falls unexpectedly, after the contract of insurance has already been made, during the bad state. Let this fall be to A'_F, with

$$A_F > A'_F. \tag{15.113}$$

As the production of insurance can be viewed as taking place during the good state, the contract for buying and selling the insurance is set with A_F as the good state level. This level of A_F is expected to remain the same when it comes time to pay out the insurance. But if for some reason it drops when the bad state occurs and the funds are meant to be paid out, then the actual less-than-contracted return on the deposited funds falls to

$$1 + R^d = \frac{p_g A'_F}{p_b}. \tag{15.114}$$

As long as this drop happens after the insurance contract has been made, the consumer is faced with this lower amount of insurance. Consumption in the bad state then falls below the expected level, and again the consumer is back to the case in which there is consumption tilting across states:

$$c_g > c_b. \tag{15.115}$$

The tilting of consumption here results because of a failure in the market to insure. Even if there was already costly insurance, with $A_F < 1$ and $\kappa > 0$, the aggregate risk factor here would make the tilting even worse. This captures the essence of the problem with aggregate risk.

What has happened in this case is something that has happened in banking crises throughout history. The transformation functions of the banks across states and time yield consumption smoothing that gets hampered by banks failing, and so unable to meet their obligations. This failure of banks within the financial intermediation market yields a market failure itself if the bank failure is widespread and if it occurs at the very time when the banks are expected to be paying out funds necessary to smooth consumption during recessions.

15.8 Application

15.8.1 Unemployment and health insurance

National unemployment and health insurance systems are effective if the amount the governments collect from each worker insured are a function of the probability of the worker's entering the bad state of being unemployed or of being sick, and of other factors such as the amount earned in both the employed and unemployed state, or in the healthy or sick states. Perfect insurance would work as in our model whereby the supply of insurance by the government can be viewed from the production function approach. And government insurance is supplemented by the private sector. Generally the productivity of the government in supplying such insurance might be thought to be lower, with a lower A_F, than in the private sector.

The problem of supplying such insurance at the aggregate level by either the government or private industry is to apply insurance policies to people with different probabilities of entering the bad state and with different endowments of income across states. Private industry does this by profiling characteristics of those it insures, while the government tends to use much less such profiling. This is one reason why the private sector is more efficient.

Profiling in the public sector for example might involve charging additional fees for emergency health care for drug and alcohol abuse health problems, since these tend to squeeze out the availability of providing normal emergency care service for the rest of the population. For unemployment, profiling by government insurance means for example allowing the insurance for a limited duration, with monitoring of efforts to find work and with pilot programmes to help train the unemployed for work. In contrast to the view that government profiling cannot be allowed on the grounds of equal treatment, careful profiling can make the unemployment and health insurance systems both more fair and more efficient. This would result in greater smoothing of consumption across states of nature in aggregate.

Unemployment, health, and in addition old age pension schemes, are huge shares of government spending in all nations. Reform that steadily introduces fair profiling at the government level enables big welfare gains.

15.9 Questions

1. In Example 15.1, modify the example by letting the probabilities be $p_g = 0.8$, and $p_b = 0.2$, instead of $p_g = 0.9$ and $p_b = 0.1$.
   (a) Find the new equilibrium consumption in each state and the investment d.
   (b) Graph the new equilibrium in both $(c_b : c_g)$ space and in $(c_b : d)$ space, in comparison with the original equilibrium of Example 15.1.
2. In Example 15.1, modify the example by letting the bad state endowment be $y_b = 0.1$ instead of $y_b = 0$.
   (a) Find the new equilibrium consumption in each state and the investment d.
   (b) Graph the new equilibrium in both $(c_b : c_g)$ space and in $(c_b : d)$ space, in comparison with the original equilibrium of Example 15.1.
3. In Example 15.1, increasing the probability of the bad state causes in equilibrium:
   (a) less consumption in the bad state,
   (b) more consumption in the good state,
   (c) less investment in deposits d to transfer income across states,
   (d) all of the above.
4. In Example 15.2, modify the example by letting $A_F = 0.7$ instead of $A_F = 0.8$.
   (a) Find the new equilibrium consumption in each state and the investment d.
   (b) Graph the new equilibrium in both $(c_b : c_g)$ space and in $(c_b : d)$ space, in comparison with the original equilibrium of Example 15.2.
5. In Example 15.2, modify the example by letting the bad state endowment be $y_b = 0.1$ instead of $y_b = 0$.
   (a) Find the new equilibrium consumption in each state and the investment d.
   (b) Graph the new equilibrium in both $(c_b : c_g)$ space and in $(c_b : d)$ space, in comparison with the original equilibrium of Example 15.2.
6. In Example 15.3, assume instead that $y_b = 0.2$, instead of $y_b = 0.1$ as in equation (15.50).
   (a) Restate equation (15.50) accordingly.
   (b) Graph the modified equation (15.50) in a figure comparable to Figure 15.5.
7. In Example 15.5, find the return on invested deposits R^d if $A_F = 0.98$ instead of $A_F = 0.95$.

8. In Example 15.6, let $A_F = 0.90$ instead of $A_F = 0.95$, and
   (a) Find the complete general equilibrium and graph it.
   (b) Determine whether consumption is more smooth or more tilted.
   (c) Explain whether investment d in the bad state increases or decreases.
9. Modify Example 15.8 by letting $\kappa = 0.07$.
   (a) Find the complete general equilibrium and graph it.
   (b) Determine whether consumption is more smooth or more tilted.
   (c) Explain whether investment d in the bad state increases or decreases.
10. Modify Example 15.9 by letting $\kappa = \frac{1}{2}$ instead of $\kappa = \frac{1}{3}$.
    (a) Find the complete general equilibrium and graph it.
    (b) Determine whether consumption is more smooth or more tilted.
    (c) Explain whether investment d in the bad state increases or decreases.

15.10 References

Arrow, K. J. and G. Debreu, 1954, 'The Existence of an Equilibrium for a Competitive Economy', *Econometrica*, vol. XXII: 265–290.

Berger, A., 2003, 'The Economic Effects of Technological Progress: Evidence from the Banking Industry', *Journal of Money, Credit, and Banking*, 35: 141–176.

Clark, J.A., 1984, 'Estimation of Economies of Scale in Banking Using a Generalized Functional Form', *Journal of Money, Credit, and Banking*, 16(1): 53–68.

Debreu, G., 1959, *Theory of Value*, New Haven and London: Yale University Press.

Ehrlich, Isaac and Gary S. Becker, 1972, 'Market Insurance, Self-Insurance, and Self-Protection', *Journal of Political Economy*, University of Chicago Press, 80(4): 623–648, July–Aug.

Hancock, D., 1985, 'The Financial Firm: Production with Monetary and Nonmonetary Goods', *Journal of Political Economy*, 93(5): 859–880.

Hicks, John R., 1935, 'A Suggestion for Simplifying the Theory of Money', *Economica*, 2(5) (February): 1–19.

Hirshleifer, J., 1970, *Investment, Interest and Capital,* Prentice-Hall, Inc., Englewood Cliffs, N.J.

Matthews, Kent, and John Thompson, 2008, *The Economics of Banking*, 2nd edition, John Wiley and Sons, Chichester, England.

CHAPTER 16

Investment and banking productivity

16.1 Introduction

The chapter shows how the consumer invests savings into capital when constrained to use financial intermediation rather than investing directly. With the costs of financial intermediation, the marginal product of capital of the goods producer is higher, and less capital is invested than with no costs of intermediation. The goods producer borrows capital from the bank, which receives the consumer's savings. Then using labour cost and a banking production function, the bank turns the savings into loans that are made to the goods producer. The cost of the loan rate to the goods producer thereby includes the cost per unit of capital of the intermediation production by the bank.

The general equilibrium is shown for the consumer who deposits in the bank, for the goods producer who borrows from the bank, and for the bank which receives the savings deposits from the consumer and lends them out to the goods producer. These are three separate problems in the decentralised economy. The resulting equilibrium is graphed in goods dimensions with the dynamic *AS–AD* framework assuming exogenous zero growth. The labour market is also graphed, as is the general equilibrium input space and the goods and leisure dimensions.

The banking depends on the productivity factor in producing the loans from the consumer deposits. The main comparative static analysis is when there is a change in the bank productivity factor. When bank productivity falls, then it is shown that output, employment, capital and the real wage all fall. This comparative static analysis is used to present the analysis of a financial crisis that results in a recession. Given a significant fall in bank productivity, the amount of the capital stock decrease, along with employment and output, is in the range of the recent bank-led recession.

An application to the issue of international bank insurance is provided. And Appendix A16 shows how the equilibrium still is solved as a closed-form solution for the capital stock, where it depends on an explicit function of the parameters of the model.

16.1.1 Building on the last chapters

The chapter applies the bank production approach developed in the last chapter to the intermediation of savings and investment. It uses the same deposits invested by the consumer, but instead of these being invested as a form of insurance as in the last chapter, now they are invested in an economy without uncertainty, but with a costly transference of income from the consumer to the goods producer. In the last chapter the costly transference was of income from one state of nature to the other; here the costly transference of income is from turning the savings into investment. Instead of a costly transference across uncertain states, this is in effect a costly transference of income across time, from consumption today to consumption in the future.

The zero exogenous growth economy is an extension of the baseline model of Part 4. The solution methodology is a modification of Chapter 10 so that now the cost of the banking is included in the calculation of the marginal product of capital for the goods producer. The solution methodology of the chapter's appendix is similar to Chapter 10 in that an explicit solution for the capital stock again results. Instead using endogenous growth as in Part 5 would be useful but is left as an extension in order to focus only on the addition of the savings–investment intermediation.

16.1.2 Learning objective

The challenge is to see that the costly intermediation process adds to the per unit cost of capital. Realising that this is reflected in the loan rate, it becomes clear that the higher the cost of intermediation, the higher must be the loan rate. Using marginal product of capital logic, whereby a higher marginal product of capital results with less capital investment, it can be seen that the intermediation cost lowers the capital stock. Then the analysis of banking crisis-led recessions can be understood intuitively from one simple comparative static exercise: a decrease in the productivity of the bank sector.

Analysing a bank crisis with a simple comparative static, in just bank productivity, in order to generate a bank-led recession allows the previous analysis of business cycles and growth trends, in terms of the productivity factor for goods and human capital production, to now be supplemented with the one additional productivity change, in banking. This eliminates the need to rely on ad hoc fixed prices as was done in Chapters 3, 6 and 9 to generate a deeper recession than with a normal business cycle. Instead now the deeper recession can be presented more fundamentally as coming from the bank sector, as in the Great Depression and in 2007–10. And the analysis of business cycles, trends over time, and deep recessions is established in the traditional way of using only sectoral productivity factors.

16.1.3 Who made it happen?

The literature on banking in general equilibrium has evolved slowly over time. Hicks (1936) suggests this approach, Pesek and Saving (1968) integrate banking further into macroeconomics, and Sealey and Lindley (1977) provide the beginnings of a rigorous financial intermediation approach to banking. The application of banking in macroeconomics most often has occurred in monetary economics, although typically the loan rate and deposit rates relation are specified exogenously.

Berk and Green (2004) investigate banking costs of intermediation albeit without a full general equilibrium production function. Goodfriend and McCallum (2007) use a production function approach for credit used in exchange. And a production function based on the Clark (1984) approach, although also for the provision of exchange credit, is found in Gillman and Kejak (2010). This approach is extended here to intertemporal credit, of savings and investment.

16.2 Savings–investment intermediation

16.2.1 Consumer problem

Financial intermediation is needed when the consumer cannot directly take savings and turn them into investment of capital. Assume this is the case, that the consumer now cannot invest directly in capital for renting to the firm or in financial markets and instead must invest through the bank. To do this the consumer deposits d_t into the bank and receives a return of $\left(1 + R_t^d\right) d_t$, where R_t^d is the dividend return. The consumer owns the bank so the dividends received are $R_t^d d_t$, which are the profit of the bank. This dividend is equivalent to interest earned on the dividends. The only difference is the ownership structure. Here the consumer is assumed to own the bank and receives the profit. Alternatively it could be assumed that the consumer rents capital to the bank in the form of deposits d_t and receives the deposits back next period plus the rental cost in the form of interest income; this interest would be equal to $R_t^d d_t$. With the ownership assumption, the way it works is that the consumer gets one share of ownership with each unit of currency deposited. The price of the share is fixed at one, but variable profits still can result. These are given back to the consumer as dividends per unit of deposited funds, with the dividend rate per unit of deposits R_t^d. By paying out all profits as these dividends the bank earns no extra profit; profit is zero after paying out dividends.

Going back to the baseline dynamic model of equations (8.27) and (8.28), the only difference is that now the investment takes the form of choosing d_{t+1}, the new deposits to make for next period, while receiving $\left(1 + R_t^d\right) d_t$ in the current period as the return of the deposited funds along with the dividends earned. Utility is the same as in equation (8.27) except that now the 'state' variable is d_t, and there is time spent working in the bank, l_{Ft}:

$$V\left(d_t\right) = \underset{c_t^d, x_t, l_t^s, l_{Ft}, d_{t+1}}{\text{Max}} \quad : \ln c_t^d + \alpha \ln x_t + \beta V\left(d_{t+1}\right). \tag{16.1}$$

And the maximisation of utility is subject to the same time constraint of equation (8.14) and a somewhat altered budget constraint as compared to equation (8.26). In particular labour income previously was just $w_t l_t^s$. But now the consumer not only owns the bank but also spends part of the time working for the bank, for the income of $w_t l_{Ft}$, where l_{Ft} denotes the time supplied to the financial intermediation sector, or in short to the bank. The other difference from the baseline model is that the dividend income $R_t^d d_t$ is added to the labour income, and the net increase invested in deposits at the bank, of $d_{t+1} - d_t$, is the investment subtracted from income. This makes consumption equal to income minus investment, in the form of the budget constraint:

$$c_t = w_t \left(l_t^s + l_{Ft}\right) + R_t^d d_t - d_{t+1} + d_t, \tag{16.2}$$

$$c_t = w_t \left(l_t^s + l_{Ft}\right) - d_{t+1} + d_t \left(1 + R_t^d\right). \tag{16.3}$$

The second constraint is the allocation of time constraint whereby time working in the goods and bank sector, plus leisure, equal the endowment of one:

$$l_t^s + l_{Ft}^s + x_t = 1. \tag{16.4}$$

This can be substituted into the goods budget constraint, so that

$$c_t = w_t \left(1 - x_t\right) - d_{t+1} + d_t \left(1 + R_t^d\right). \tag{16.5}$$

Using these two constraints, consumption and leisure can be solved for and substituted into the recursive utility problem directly:

$$V\left(d_t\right) = \underset{X_t, d_{t+1}}{\text{Max}} \ \ln \left[w_t \left(1 - x_t\right) - d_{t+1} + d_t \left(1 + R_t^d\right)\right] + \alpha \ln \left(X_t\right) + \beta V\left(d_{t+1}\right). \tag{16.6}$$

The first-order equilibrium conditions for labour X_t and deposits d_{t+1} are respectively

$$w_t = \frac{\alpha c_t}{x_t}; \tag{16.7}$$

$$\frac{1}{c_t^d} = \beta \frac{\partial V\left(d_{t+1}\right)}{\partial d_{t+1}}, \tag{16.8}$$

and the envelope condition is

$$\frac{\partial V(d_t)}{\partial d_t} = \frac{1}{c_t^d}\left(1 + R_t^d\right). \tag{16.9}$$

The first equilibrium condition is the standard marginal rate of substitution between goods and leisure with log utility. The last two equilibrium conditions imply that the intertemporal marginal rate of substitution is given by

$$\frac{c_t^d}{\beta c_{t-1}^d} = 1 + R_t^d. \tag{16.10}$$

The difference here from the baseline model is that now R_t^d is the interest rate instead of the rental rate on capital net of depreciation, $r_t - \delta_k$, when the consumer is directly investing in capital. The deposit rate R_t^d determines the amount of savings that the consumer allocates to the bank, which in turn lends it out as capital to the firm for investment.

16.2.2 Goods producer problem

The goods producer time t profit, denoted by Π_t, with q_t denoting bank loans, and R_t^q denoting the loan interest rate is given by

$$\Pi_t = A_G l_t^\gamma k_t^{1-\gamma} - w_t l_t - k_{t+1} + k_t\left(1 - \delta_k\right) + q_{t+1} - q_t\left(1 + R_t^q\right), \tag{16.11}$$

subject to the constraint that new investment in capital is paid for by new bank loans:

$$i_t = k_{t+1} - k_t = q_{t+1} - q_t. \tag{16.12}$$

This being in place from the beginning of time, say at time $t = 0$, it implies that the capital stock k_t equals the outstanding loans q_t, so that

$$k_t = q_t. \tag{16.13}$$

With this substituted into the goods producer maximisation problem, it reduces to a static problem, rather than a dynamic one, given by

$$\underset{l_t, k_t}{\text{Max}} : \Pi = A_G l_t^\gamma k_t^{1-\gamma} - w_t l_t - k_t\left(R_t^q + \delta_k\right). \tag{16.14}$$

The marginal product of capital then just equals the loan interest rate R_t^d plus the depreciation rate δ_k:

$$\left(1 - \gamma\right) A_G \left(\frac{l_t}{k_t}\right)^\gamma = R_t^q + \delta_k, \tag{16.15}$$

while the marginal product of labour equals the real wage as before:

$$w_t = \gamma A_G \left(\frac{l_t}{k_t}\right)^{\gamma - 1}. \tag{16.16}$$

16.2.3 Bank technology for producing loans

The production function for banking is that used in the banking literature, the so-called financial intermediation approach, in which the bank uses in general labour, capital and deposited funds to produce banking services. Here to simplify the equilibrium no capital except the financial capital in the form of the deposited funds will enter the production function. There remain labour costs from employing labour in the bank. Denoting this labour again by l_{Ft}, for labour in the financial intermediary, the representative agent supplies l_{Ft} when working for the bank. The total cost of the labour is the wage bill of $w_t l_{Ft}$.

The production function for the financial intermediary, or bank, service is that the loans q_t are produced using the labour l_{Ft} and the deposited funds d_t via a Cobb–Douglas production function. With the productivity parameter $A_F \geq 0$, the production function is

$$q_t = A_F \left(l_{Ft}\right)^\kappa d_t^{1-\kappa}, \tag{16.17}$$

where κ is a parameter between 0 and 1; $\kappa \in [0, 1)$.

It is very easy to see what this production function means by taking the case when κ goes towards 0. At $\kappa = 0$, the function becomes simply

$$q_t = A_F d_t. \tag{16.18}$$

This corresponds to the output of the bank in Chapter 15. In this case only deposits are used and no labour is necessary. Further if $A_F = 1$, then

$$q_t = d_t, \tag{16.19}$$

and the amount of deposits put in the bank are what get paid out as the output of the bank.

More generally, it is possible to be in an equilibrium in which deposits do equal loans, but then there is the cost of labour in producing this amount of loans. From the production function with $q_t = d_t$, in equation (16.17),

$$\frac{q_t}{d_t} = A_F \left(\frac{l_{Ft}}{d_t}\right)^\kappa = 1.$$

This equilibrium would imply a labour to deposit ratio equal to

$$\frac{l_{Ft}}{d_t} = \frac{1}{(A_F)^{\frac{1}{\kappa}}}. \tag{16.20}$$

Such labour cost requires that the return on capital ends up being lower than if there were no such cost. In the section here, the consumer will earn the return R_t^d on deposits, while the firm pays R_t^q for a loan from the bank. The difference between the two returns will be a result solely because of the labour cost of producing the loans.

16.2.4 Bank profit optimisation problem

Then the bank's time t profit, denoted by Π_{Ft}, is revenue of $q_t \left(1 + R_t^q\right) + d_{t+1}$ minus costs of $q_{t+1} + d_t \left(1 + R_t^d\right) + w_t l_{Ft}$. The dividends that are paid out, $d_t R_t^d$, are equal to the residual profit so that the profit function Π_{Ft} is zero in equilibrium:

$$0 = \Pi_{Ft} = -q_{t+1} + q_t \left(1 + R_t^q\right) + d_{t+1} - d_t \left(1 + R_t^d\right) - w_t l_{Ft}. \tag{16.21}$$

This profit Π_{Ft} is subject to the production technology in equation (16.17).

The problem is dynamic in the variables d_t and q_t and it can be stated recursively. Let $\Pi_F \left(q_t, d_t\right)$ be the value of the profit at time t and $\Pi_F \left(q_{t+1}, d_{t+1}\right)$ be the value at $t+1$. And let the firm use a discount factor that we denote by z_t. As an exception designed to simplify the understanding of the bank problem, the dynamic recursive problem will include the production technology with a Lagrangian multiplier, λ_t, rather than substituting it into the problem. The bank problem is

$$\Pi_F \left(q_t, d_t\right) = \max_{q_{t+1}, d_{t+1}, l_{Ft}} \left\{ -q_{t+1} + q_t \left(1 + R_t^q\right) + d_{t+1} - d_t \left(1 + R_t^d\right) - w_t l_{Ft} \right.$$
$$\left. -\lambda_t \left[q_t - A_F \left(l_{Ft}\right)^\kappa d_t^{1-\kappa}\right] + z_t \Pi_F \left(q_{t+1}, d_{t+1}\right) \right\}. \tag{16.22}$$

The equilibrium conditions with respect to q_{t+1} and d_{t+1} are respectively

$$-1 + z_t \frac{\partial \Pi_F \left(q_{t+1}, d_{t+1}\right)}{\partial q_{t+1}} = 0; \tag{16.23}$$

$$1 + z_t \frac{\partial \Pi_F \left(q_{t+1}, d_{t+1}\right)}{\partial d_{t+1}} = 0. \tag{16.24}$$

The derivative with respect to l_{Ft} is

$$\lambda_t = \frac{w_t}{\kappa A_F \left(\frac{l_{Ft}}{d_t}\right)^{\kappa-1}}. \tag{16.25}$$

Note that λ_t has the interpretation as the shadow cost of output of loans q_t. This makes λ_t the marginal cost of loans.

Here are the envelope conditions with respect to q_t and d_t:

$$\frac{\partial \Pi_F \left(q_t, d_t\right)}{\partial q_t} = \left(1 + R_t^q\right) - \lambda_t; \tag{16.26}$$

$$\frac{\partial \Pi_F \left(q_t, d_t\right)}{\partial d_t} = -\left(1 + R_t^d\right) + \lambda_t \left(1 - \kappa\right) A_F \left(\frac{l_{Ft}}{d_t}\right)^{\kappa}. \tag{16.27}$$

Equations (16.23) and (16.24) can be solved for z_t and then indexed in time back one period and rewritten as

$$z_t = \frac{1}{\frac{\partial \Pi_F \left(q_{t+1}, d_{t+1}\right)}{\partial q_{t+1}}} = -\frac{1}{\frac{\partial \Pi_F \left(q_{t+1}, d_{t+1}\right)}{\partial d_{t+1}}}; \tag{16.28}$$

$$\frac{\partial \Pi_F \left(q_t, d_t\right)}{\partial q_t} = -\frac{\partial \Pi_F \left(q_t, d_t\right)}{\partial d_t}. \tag{16.29}$$

The equivalence of the derivative of the value function with respect to q_t to the negative of the derivative of the value function with respect to d_t can be used to equalise the two equilibrium conditions in equations (16.26) and (16.27):

$$\left(1 + R_t^d\right) - \lambda_t \left(1 - \kappa\right) A_F \left(\frac{l_{Ft}}{d_t}\right)^{\kappa} = -\frac{\partial \Pi_F \left(q_t, d_t\right)}{\partial d_t} \tag{16.30}$$

$$= \frac{\partial \Pi_F \left(q_t, d_t\right)}{\partial q_t} \tag{16.31}$$

$$= \left(1 + R_t^q\right) - \lambda_t. \tag{16.32}$$

From these later equations, the shadow or marginal cost λ_t can be solved as

$$\left(1 + R_t^q\right) - \left(1 + R_t^d\right) = \lambda_t \left[1 - \left(1 - \kappa\right) A_F \left(\frac{l_{Ft}}{d_t}\right)^{\kappa}\right]; \tag{16.33}$$

$$\lambda_t = \frac{R_t^q - R_t^d}{1 - \left(1 - \kappa\right) A_F \left(\frac{l_{Ft}}{d_t}\right)^{\kappa}}. \tag{16.34}$$

Since the term $1 - \left(1 - \kappa\right) A_F \left(\frac{l_{Ft}}{d_t}\right)^{\kappa} \leq 1$, it is a fraction less than 1. This makes the marginal cost λ_t always equal to some multiple of the interest differential $R_t^q - R_t^d$.

It is helpful in terms of solving the equilibrium to now have the equilibrium conditions reduced to two equations, (16.25) and (16.34), that are both solved in terms of the shadow cost λ_t. Setting these two equations equal to each other implies the solution for the amount of labour per unit of deposits, $\frac{l_{Ft}}{d_t}$, to be worked in the bank sector, as a function of parameters and the real wage w_t:

$$\frac{w_t}{\kappa A_F \left(\frac{l_{Ft}}{d_t}\right)^{\kappa-1}} = \lambda_t = \frac{R_t^q - R_t^d}{1 - (1-\kappa) A_F \left(\frac{l_{Ft}}{d_t}\right)^{\kappa}}. \tag{16.35}$$

This is not a simple function in $\frac{l_{Ft}}{d_t}$. But the equilibrium solution for $\frac{l_{Ft}}{d_t}$ can be simplified further.[1]

16.2.5 Solution with deposits equal loans

It is assumed now that all of the deposits are turned into loans, so that $q_t = d_t$. This is assumed because the model has no uncertainty, and the consumer would want to invest all funds into the firm's capital. There is no less risky choice such as government bonds, which might result in some deposits going into bonds and some going into capital.

An alternative assumption is to let $d_t - q_t$ be the positive amount of capital requirements that a bank must hold, but here this direction is not taken. In a full model with uncertainty, and with a natural choice of capital invested in risk-free bonds, $d_t - q_t$, this quantity would be the capital reserves as chosen by the bank. A government constraint to hold capital reserves may or may not be binding on the bank's free market choice. Relative to the capital invested in risky equity, q_t, the bank choice of reserves $d_t - q_t$ would reflect in turn the consumer choice on risk that yields the market's diversification of assets between the risk-free bonds and the risky market portfolio.

Assuming away these interesting complications, with $q_t = d_t$, this means that the difference between the loan rate to firms and the discount rate for consumers, $R_t^q - R_t^d$, is just determined by the labour cost in producing loans that are always equal to the deposits. And the bank model is used to calculate this cost through the equilibrium production of loans. The solution shows exactly how the bank productivity affects this cost.

From equation (16.20), with $q_t = d_t$ it results simply from the production function that the required labour is $\frac{l_{Ft}}{d_t} = \frac{1}{(A_F)^{\frac{1}{\kappa}}}$. Substituting this into equation (16.35), the interest differential is solved as a simple function of the wage rate w_t and the productivity factor A_F:

$$R_t^q - R_t^d = \frac{w_t}{(A_F)^{\frac{1}{\kappa}}}. \tag{16.36}$$

Also in this case, from equation (16.34), the marginal cost is

$$\lambda_t = \frac{R_t^q - R_t^d}{\kappa}.$$

And now we can graph the supply function for the bank loan production. Solving for $\frac{l_{Ft}}{d_t}$ as

$$\frac{l_{Ft}}{d_t} = \frac{1}{(A_F)^{\frac{1}{\kappa}}} \left(\frac{q_t}{d_t}\right)^{\frac{1}{\kappa}}, \tag{16.37}$$

from the production function of equation (16.17), in which $\frac{q_t}{d_t} = A_F \left(\frac{l_{Ft}}{d_t}\right)^{\kappa}$, and substituting this $\frac{l_{Ft}}{d_t}$ into equation (16.25), gives the marginal cost of loans, denoted by MC_{qt},

[1]Only with complete markets is $\lambda_t = 0$.

and subsequent supply curve that can be graphed:

$$MC_{qt} \equiv \lambda_t = \frac{w_t}{\kappa \, (A_F)^{\frac{1}{\kappa}}} \left(\frac{q_t}{d_t}\right)^{\frac{1-\kappa}{\kappa}}. \tag{16.38}$$

16.2.6 Example 16.1: Marginal cost and bank supply

Assume that $w_t = 0.0111$, $R_t^d = \rho = 0.0525$, $\kappa = 0.333$ and $A_F = 0.95$. The wage rate w_t of 0.0111 and the value of $R_t^q = 0.0655$ are from the actual solution in the full economy in Example 16.2 below, with a full calibration that includes $\kappa = 0.333$, and $A_F = 0.95$. This makes the marginal cost curve

$$MC_{qt} = \frac{w_t}{\kappa \, (A_F)^{\frac{1}{\kappa}}} \left(\frac{q_t}{d_t}\right)^{\frac{1-\kappa}{\kappa}} = \frac{0.0111}{0.333 \, (0.95)^{\frac{1}{0.333}}} \left(\frac{q_t}{d_t}\right)^2. \tag{16.39}$$

At $\frac{q_t}{d_t} = 1$,

$$MC_{qt} = \frac{0.0111}{0.333 \, (0.95)^{\frac{1}{0.333}}} = 0.0389,$$

and in turn this marginal cost is also expressed as $\frac{R_t^q - R_t^d}{\kappa}$:

$$MC_{qt} = \frac{R_t^q - R_t^d}{\kappa} = \frac{0.06555 - 0.0526}{0.333} = 0.0389.$$

Figure 16.1 graphs equation (16.39) as the convex supply curve for an output of $\frac{q_t}{d_t}$. This means that a multiple $\frac{1}{\kappa}$ of the interest $R_t^q - R_t^d$ is the marginal cost at any point on the supply curve. The loan rate at $\frac{q_t}{d_t} = 1$ is higher than the discount rate by (0.01295), with $R_t^q - R_t^d = 0.01295$.

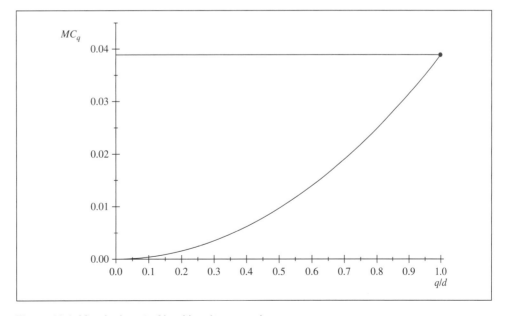

Figure 16.1 Marginal cost of banking: loan supply curve

16.2.7 *AS–AD* with banking

Consider the full economy in terms of *AS–AD* analysis in the goods market and also the labour market. Here we have assumed a zero exogenous growth rate as in Chapter 8 and not added human capital. The goods and the labour markets are exactly the same as in the market equations in Chapter 8. The only difference in the analysis is that now the level of the bank sector productivity affects the equilibrium wage rate w and the capital stock k. This means that the financial intermediation efficiency has a role in equilibrium in the goods and labour market indirectly through the determination of the levels of both w and k.

Consider that the aggregate supply and demand functions are unchanged by the introduction of banking except that the deposit interest rate R^d is now the interest rate entering these functions. However using the intertemporal consumption margin, this interest rate is substituted out of the functions so that they are in exactly the same form as in Chapter 13.

With a balanced growth path equilibrium rate of growth of g the budget constraint

$$c_t = w_t \left(1 - x_t\right) - d_{t+1} + d_t \left(1 + R_t^d\right),$$
(16.40)

becomes

$$c_t = w_t \left(1 - x_t\right) + d_t \left(R_t^d - g\right).$$

And because in equilibrium the capital stock k_t equals the amount of loans q_t which in turn equal the amount of deposits d_t, then

$$k_t = q_t = d_t$$

and the consumption demand can be written in the more familiar form of

$$c_t = w_t \left(1 - x_t\right) + k_t \left(R_t^d - g\right).$$

From the consumer's intertemporal margin, it is also true that

$$1 + g = \frac{1 + R_t^d}{1 + \rho},$$

implying that

$$R_t^d - g = \rho \left(1 + g\right),$$
(16.41)

and that consumption is

$$c_t = w_t \left(1 - x_t\right) + \rho \left(1 + g\right) k_t,$$

as in Chapter 11. As the intertemporal margin is the same also at $w_t = \frac{\alpha c_t}{x_t}$, the consumption can again be written as

$$c_t = \frac{1}{1 + \alpha} \left[w_t + \rho \left(1 + g\right) k_t\right].$$
(16.42)

This is the same consumption function as in Chapter 11.

Aggregate demand *AD* adds the investment demand to the consumption demand to get along the BGP, as before, that

$$y_t^d = c_t + i_t = \frac{1}{1 + \alpha} \left[w_t + \rho \left(1 + g\right) k_t\right] + \left(g + \delta_k\right) k_t,$$
(16.43)

or that

$$y_t^d = \frac{1}{1 + \alpha} \left\{w_t + \left[\rho \left(1 + g\right) + \left(g + \delta_k\right) \left(1 + \alpha\right)\right] k_t\right\}.$$
(16.44)

Aggregate supply AS is also the same as in Chapters 8 and 11, at

$$y_t = A_G^{\frac{1}{1-\gamma}} \left(\frac{\gamma}{w_t}\right)^{\frac{\gamma}{1-\gamma}} k_t.$$

Setting the aggregate supply and demand for goods equal implies the equilibrium wage rate w_t if the capital stock is known. The capital stock and wage rate can be determined but only by using all of other equilibrium conditions of the economy, as in Chapter 8.

Assume that the growth rate is zero, so that $g = 0$, for simplification. The task is to solve the equilibrium w_t and k_t and then see how banking productivity affects the equilibrium. With $g = 0$, equation (16.41) implies that $R_t^d = \rho$, and consumption and AD simplify to

$$c_t = \frac{1}{1+\alpha}[w_t + \rho k_t]; \tag{16.45}$$

$$y_t^d = \frac{1}{1+\alpha}\left\{w_t + \left[\rho + \delta_k\left(1+\alpha\right)\right]k_t\right\}. \tag{16.46}$$

The full solution is given in Appendix A16 at the end of the chapter. And the solution for all of the variables can be found first by letting the loan rate R_t^q that is found in the goods producer equilibrium be set equal to the loan rate R_t^q found in the bank sector. From equations (16.15) and (16.36) this gives that

$$\left(1-\gamma\right) A \left(\frac{l_t}{k_t}\right)^{\gamma} - \delta_k = R_t^q = R_t^d + \frac{w_t}{\left(A_F\right)^{\frac{1}{\kappa}}}.$$

Appendix A16 at the end of the chapter shows how to finish deriving the full solution.

16.3 Example 16.2: Baseline calibration with banking

Given the solution, the AS–AD can be graphed in the goods market, and the labour market can be graphed as well. This gives very standard diagrams as in Chapter 8. The parameter assumptions are $A_G = 0.1$, $\gamma = \kappa = 0.333$, $\delta_k = 0.05$, $\alpha = 0.5$ and $\rho = \frac{1}{\beta} - 1 = \frac{1}{0.95} - 1 = 0.052632$; also let $A_F = 0.95$.

Appendix A16 at the end of the chapter provides the solution methodology, where the variable $\frac{l_t}{k_t}$ is the first variable solved, such that the solution to all other variables follows, starting with the state variable k_t. Having the extra banking sector makes computation of this first variable $\frac{l_t}{k_t}$ somewhat more complicated than in the baseline dynamic model. Yet with $k_t = q_t = d_t$, the functional equations for the AS–AD equations remain exactly the same. The banking sector only affects the equilibrium value of k_t, which in turn affects the exact forms of the AS and AD curves graphically.

Appendix A16 shows for the given parameter values that $k_t = 0.0838$.

Then the AS–AD equations from Chapter 8 with this calibration are, for demand, from equation (8.57),

$$\frac{1}{w_t} = \frac{1}{y_t^d\left(1+\alpha\right) - k_t\left[\rho + \left(1+\alpha\right)\delta_k\right]},$$

$$\frac{1}{w_t} = \frac{1}{y_t^d\left(1.5\right) - \left(0.0838\right)\left(0.0526 + \left(1.5\right)0.05\right)}, \tag{16.47}$$

and for supply, from equation (8.62),

$$\frac{1}{w_t} = \frac{\left(y_t^s\right)^{\frac{1-\gamma}{\gamma}}}{\gamma A_G^{\frac{1}{1-\gamma}}\left(k_t\right)^{\frac{1-\gamma}{\gamma}}} = \frac{\left(y_t^s\right)^{\frac{1-0.333}{0.333}}}{0.333\left(0.1\right)^{\frac{1}{0.333}}\left(0.0838\right)^{\frac{1-0.333}{0.333}}}. \tag{16.48}$$

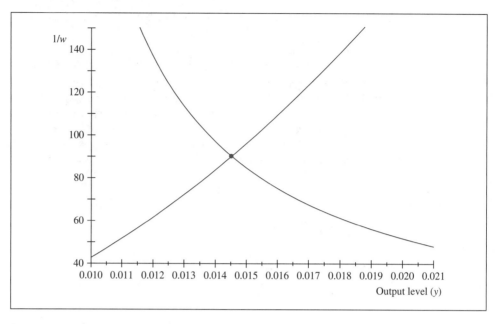

Figure 16.2 *AS–AD* baseline with intermediation of investment/savings in Example 16.2

Figure 16.2 illustrates the *AS–AD* equilibrium of equations (16.47) and (16.48).
The equilibrium relative price is $\frac{1}{w}$ = 90.24. The equilibrium output level can be computed for example from the aggregate supply function in equation (8.61):

$$y_t^s = A_G^{\frac{1}{1-\gamma}} \left(\frac{\gamma}{w_t} \right)^{\frac{\gamma}{1-\gamma}} k_t,$$

$$y_t^s = (0.1)^{\frac{1}{1-0.333}} \left(\frac{0.333}{0.011081} \right)^{\frac{0.333}{1-0.333}} (0.0838) = 0.0145.$$

The solution for the other variables is given in Appendix A16.

The loan rate on capital is 1.3% in addition to the consumer discount rate of 5.26%, for a total of a 6.56% loan rate. This 1.3% is due only to the cost of the banking. It is a plausible number. In addition the results give a share of time in the bank sector of 10%. This is a bit higher than some estimates for countries such as the US. However note that this includes all time in intermediation activity in an actual economy, implicitly including parts of the insurance industry as well as banking. The next question is how this equilibrium changes with a so-called bank crisis.

16.3.1 Bank productivity and bank crises

When there is an increase only in bank productivity, A_F, the comparative static computation of the full solution shows that the wage rate and capital stock both rise, so that the consumption, investment and output also rise. But when in contrast there is a bank crisis in which the productivity of banking falls significantly, then the wage rate and capital stock also fall significantly, as do consumption, investment and output. Such pervasive changes across the economy are consistent with the two main recessions associated with large bank crises: the 1930s depression and the 2007–09 recession.

16.3.2 Example 16.3: The bank crisis 2007–09

Consider modelling the bank crisis by letting A_F fall by more than one quarter, from the baseline value of 0.95 down to a 'crisis' level of 0.7. Appendix A16 shows that the new solution is a capital stock of $k_t = 0.0552$, a significant decrease from the baseline of $k_t = 0.0838$. In fact it is a $\frac{0.0838-0.0552}{0.0838} = 0.34129$, or 34% drop in the value of capital.

As the percentage change in the value of the capital stock is equal to the percentage change in the stock market value in a model such as this, as covered in Chapter 17 on asset prices (please see equation 17.41), a drop of 34% can be compared to what happens to the stock prices. A fall of 34.1% is exactly the same as the US Dow Jones Industrial stock average percentage drop from $13,058$ to 8599 which occurred from 2 May 2008, to 9 January 2009 during the banking crisis.

The AS–AD diagram is shifted by the change in A_F to 0.7. The decrease in the capital stock shifts back both aggregate supply and demand, as output falls, and the relative price $\frac{1}{w}$ rises. Figure 16.3 graphs the new AS–AD with the banking crisis shown by blue lines, and the baseline equilibrium shown by black lines. Output drops to

$$y_t = \frac{1}{1+\alpha}\left(w_t + \rho k_t\right) + \delta_k k_t,$$

$$y_t = \frac{1}{1.5}\left(0.008927 + \left(0.052632\right)0.0552\right) + \left(0.05\right)\left(0.0552\right) = 0.010648.$$

16.3.3 Interest rate spread

The shift back in AS and in AD occurs because the capital stock falls. The decrease in capital results because the interest rate spread that captures the cost of banking doubles. The initial interest rate spread is given by

$$R_t^q - R_t^d = \frac{w_t}{\left(A_F\right)^{\frac{1}{\kappa}}} = \frac{0.01108}{\left(0.95\right)^{\frac{1}{0.333}}} = 0.0129,$$

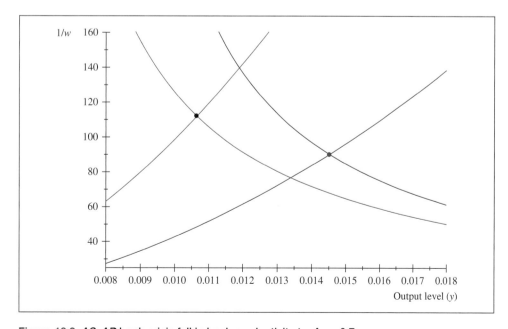

Figure 16.3 *AS–AD* bank crisis fall in bank productivity to $A_F = 0.7$

or 1.3%. When the bank productivity drops from 0.95 to 0.7, the real wage falls as well and the interest spread becomes

$$R_t^q - R_t^d = \frac{w_t}{(A_F)^{\frac{1}{\kappa}}} = \frac{0.00893}{(0.7)^{\frac{1}{0.333}}} = 0.0261.$$

This shows that the interest rate spread doubles. Although a level of only 2.61%, a doubling of the spread is significant and this is what is behind the shifts in aggregate demand and supply. These shifts can also be seen within the labour market, in which goods employment drops.

16.3.4 Labour market and bank crisis

The labour market also shows that the bank productivity fall causes lower employment in the goods sector. The labour demand comes from the firm problem and it is the same as in Chapter 9, equation (9.6),

$$l_t^d = \left(\frac{\gamma A_G}{w_t}\right)^{\frac{1}{1-\gamma}} k_t. \tag{16.49}$$

To derive the consumer's labour supply, take the marginal rate of substitution between goods and leisure, $x_t = \frac{\alpha c_t}{w_t}$, the demand for banking labour, $l_{Ft} = \frac{k_t}{(A_F)^{\frac{1}{\kappa}}}$, using that $k_t = d_t$, and the demand for goods, $c_t = \frac{1}{1+\alpha}[w_t + \rho k_t]$, and substitute these into the allocation of time constraint:

$$1 = l_t + l_{Ft} + x_t,$$

$$1 = l_t + \frac{k_t}{(A_F)^{\frac{1}{\kappa}}} + \frac{\alpha c_t}{w_t},$$

$$1 = l_t + \frac{k_t}{(A_F)^{\frac{1}{\kappa}}} + \frac{\alpha}{1+\alpha}\frac{[w_t + \rho k_t]}{w_t},$$

$$l_t^s = 1 - \frac{\alpha}{1+\alpha}\left[1 + \left(\frac{\rho}{w_t} + \frac{1+\alpha}{\alpha(A_F)^{\frac{1}{\kappa}}}\right)k_t\right]. \tag{16.50}$$

The only difference from the labour supply when there is no banking intermediation, in Chapter 9 equation (9.2) in which $l_t^s = 1 - \frac{\alpha}{1+\alpha}\left[1 + \left(\frac{\rho}{w_t}\right)k_t\right]$, is the additional term, $\frac{k_t}{(A_F)^{\frac{1}{\kappa}}}$, that comes from the time used in the bank sector.

To graph the labour market with the real wage as the vertical axis requires solving the labour demand and supply equations in terms of w_t. For labour demand, the equation is the same as in Chapter 9,

$$w_t = \gamma A_G\left(\frac{k_t}{l_t^d}\right)^{1-\gamma}. \tag{16.51}$$

For labour supply, solving for w_t gives that

$$w_t = \frac{\alpha \rho k_t}{(1+\alpha)\left(1 - l_t^s - \frac{k_t}{(A_F)^{\frac{1}{\kappa}}}\right) - \alpha}. \tag{16.52}$$

Given the Example 16.2 parameters, of $A_G = 0.1$, $\gamma = \kappa = 0.333$, $\delta_k = 0.05$, $\alpha = 0.5$, and $\rho = \frac{1}{\beta} - 1 = \frac{1}{0.95} - 1 = 0.0526$, and $A_F = 0.95$, the capital stock has the equilibrium value

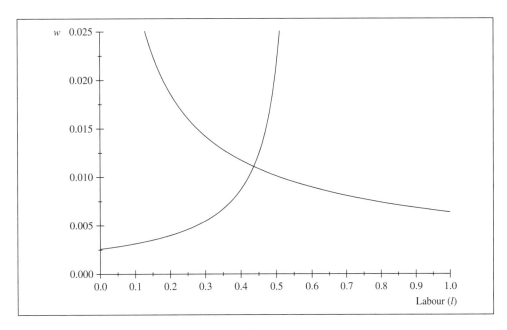

Figure 16.4 The labour market in Example 16.2

of $k_t = 0.0838$, and the labour demand and supply equations are

$$w_t = 0.333\,(0.1)\left(\frac{0.0838}{l_t^d}\right)^{1-0.333}; \tag{16.53}$$

$$w_t = \frac{(0.5)\,(0.0526)\,(0.0838)}{(1.5)\left(1 - l_t^s - \frac{(0.0838)}{(0.95)^{\frac{1}{0.333}}}\right) - 0.5}. \tag{16.54}$$

Figure 16.4 graphs equations (16.53) and (16.54) of Example 16.2. The real wage is $w_t = 0.0111$, and the labour employment is $l_t = 0.436$.

When the bank crisis is next modelled by a fall in A_F from 0.95 to 0.7, the capital stock falls to $k_t = 0.0552$. The labour demand and supply equations in calibrated form become

$$w_t = 0.333\,(0.1)\left(\frac{0.0552}{l_t^d}\right)^{1-0.333}, \tag{16.55}$$

$$w_t = \frac{(0.5)\,(0.0526)\,(0.0552)}{(1.5)\left(1 - l_t^s - \frac{(0.0552)}{(0.7)^{\frac{1}{0.333}}}\right) - 0.5}. \tag{16.56}$$

Figure 16.5 graphs equations (16.55) and (16.56) in blue, the labour market of Example 16.3, along with the labour market of Example 16.2, in black.

The drop in bank productivity causes both the labour supply and demand to shift back, with both the employment of labour and the real wage falling. The employment can be found quantitatively from setting labour supply equal to the labour demand:

$$\frac{(0.5)\,(0.0526)\,(0.0552)}{(1.5)\left(1 - l_t^s - \frac{(0.0552)}{(0.7)^{\frac{1}{0.333}}}\right) - 0.5} = 0.333\,(0.1)\left(\frac{0.0552}{l_t^d}\right)^{1-0.333},$$

$$l = 0.3973.$$

Employment falls fractionally by $\frac{0.436-0.3973}{0.436} = 0.08876$, or by 8.9%.

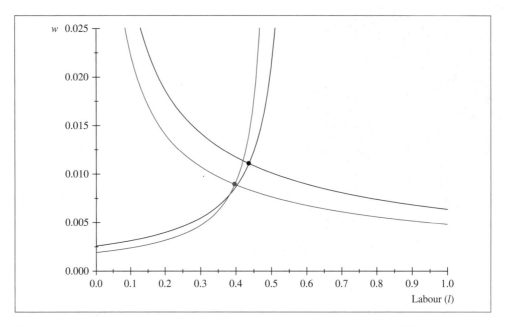

Figure 16.5 Lower employment and wage rate during bank crisis in Example 16.3 (black) compared to Example 16.2 (blue)

Therefore the labour employment drops significantly, in a way that a bank crisis can add to a drop in employment that results from a normal recession. For example with A_G and the time endowment falling by 5%, as in experiments in Chapters 3 and 9, the labour employment falls by more than 3%. Adding on top of this 3% another 9% gives a big decrease in employment, and the type of change in the employment rate that can be seen during the high unemployment of the 1930s and during 2007–10.

The banking crisis model of reduced bank productivity therefore offers a way to endogenously generate a crisis type drop in employment without the need to impose fixed prices of labour or capital. The banking extension allows the bank sector to be modelled directly, with a plausible result that the cost of investment rises, and employment, output and investment all fall significantly.

The banking time rises when A_F decreases because labour is less efficient and more is needed to produce the amount of loans needed, even though the quantity of loans and capital falls. Partly the increase in bank labour in the model is a result of the simplification of using a labour and deposit technology without physical capital. Generally physical capital also enters the bank production function and this was omitted here to make the solution more easily solvable. With capital the increase in bank labour would be less and can be reversed, depending upon the calibration.

It appears that banking labour time contracts during a bank crisis, for example with an apparently large reduction in bank employment in London during the 2007–10 crisis. However that is more exceptional since banking is one of the United Kingdom's main industries. The actual change in banking worldwide even during a banking crisis is not as easy to verify empirically since it is one sector of the economy rather than aggregate employment. And in less developed economies banking activity and the associated labour can be more informal. When international banks decrease employment, alternative banking facilitators may increase employment, as less efficient forms of banking are used more when the most productive banking firms suffer productivity declines.

16.4 General equilibrium comparison

The banking economy can be compared between when there is no crisis, and bank productivity is normal at $A_F = 0.95$, and when there is a bank crisis and bank productivity is much lower at $A_F = 0.70$. The input and output markets in general equilibrium are presented following the approach in the baseline Example 8.1. The bank economy is a zero exogenous growth dynamic model, as in Example 8.1, however the calibration and solution of the bank baseline Example 16.2 are different.

The bank crisis provides a second calibration, with only A_F changing, and a new solution, for the bank crisis case of Example 16.3. The equilibrium isocost, isoquant and factor input ratio equations for both Examples 16.2 and 16.3 are formulated here, along with the graphs. From the goods producer problem, for Example 16.2 (no crisis), the equilibrium isocost line is in accordance with the goods producer problem, in which output is given as

$$y_t = w_t l_t + \left(R_t^q + \delta_k \right) k_t. \tag{16.57}$$

Substituting in the solution values, and solving for k_t in terms of l_t, the isocost line is

$$0.014531 = \left(0.011081 \right) l_t + \left(0.06565 + 0.05 \right) k_t;$$

$$k_t = \frac{0.014531}{0.06565 + 0.05} - \frac{\left(0.011081 \right) l_t}{0.06565 + 0.05}. \tag{16.58}$$

The isoquant curve is

$$y_t^s = A_G \left(l_t^d \right)^\gamma \left(k_t \right)^{1-\gamma},$$

$$0.014531 = \left(0.1 \right) \left(l_t^d \right)^{\frac{1}{3}\gamma} \left(k_t \right)^{\frac{2}{3}};$$

$$k_t = \left(\frac{0.014531}{0.1 \left(l_t^d \right)^{\frac{1}{3}}} \right)^{\frac{3}{2}} = \frac{\left(\frac{0.014531}{0.1} \right)^{\frac{3}{2}}}{\left(l_t^d \right)^{\frac{1}{2}}}. \tag{16.59}$$

And the factor input ratio is

$$\frac{k_t}{l_t} = \frac{0.08382}{0.4363} = 0.19212. \tag{16.60}$$

Figure 16.6 graphs the factor input equilibrium of equations (16.58), (16.59) and (16.60), with the isocost in black, the isoquant in blue and the factor input ratio in dashed black.

Consumption in terms of output minus investment is

$$c_t^d = y_t^s - i_t = A_G \left(l_t^d \right)^\gamma \left(k_t \right)^{1-\gamma} - \delta_k k_t,$$

$$c_t^d = \left(0.10 \right) \left(l_t^d \right)^{\frac{1}{3}} \left(0.08382 \right)^{\frac{2}{3}} - \left(0.05 \right) \left(0.08382 \right). \tag{16.61}$$

The utility level curve is found by keeping in mind that time is allocated to working in banking, l_{Ft}, and this subtracts from the time endowment along with labour, to get the amount of leisure x_t:

$$u = \ln c_t + \alpha \ln x_t = \ln c_t + \alpha \ln \left(T_t - l_t \right),$$

$$-4.9538 = \ln 0.01034 + 0.5 \ln \left(1 - 0.098 - 0.4363 \right),$$

$$-4.9538 = \ln c_t + 0.5 \ln \left(1 - 0.098 - l_t \right),$$

$$c_t = \frac{e^{-4.9538}}{\left(1 - 0.098 - l_t \right)^{0.5}}. \tag{16.62}$$

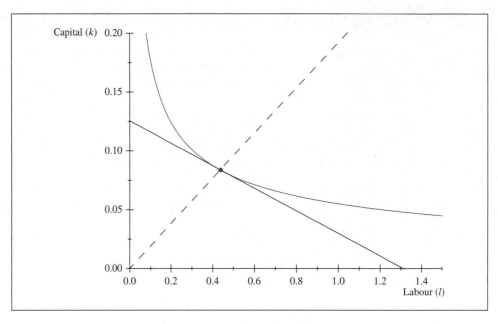

Figure 16.6 Factor market equilibrium in Example 16.2

The budget line in equilibrium has to include the wages received from working in the bank sector, $w_t l_{Ft}^s$, along with wages from the goods producer:

$$c_t^d = w_t \left(l_t^s + l_{Ft}^s \right) + \rho k_t^s = w_t l_t^s + w_t l_{Ft}^s + \rho k_t^s,$$
$$c_t^d = (0.011)\, l_t^s + (0.011)\,(0.098) + (0.0526)\,(0.084). \tag{16.63}$$

Figure 16.7 graphs the general equilibrium, of equations (16.61), (16.62) and (16.63) in blue, black, and dashed black, in the dimensions of c_t on the vertical axis and l_t on the horizontal axis.

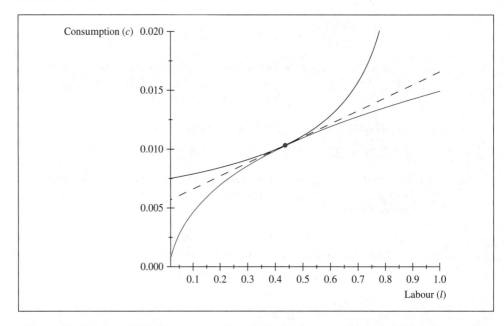

Figure 16.7 General equilibrium consumption and utility levels in Example 16.2

After the bank crisis, with a fall in bank productivity as in Example 16.3, the new iso-cost is

$$y_t = w_t l_t + \left(R_t^q + \delta_k \right) k_t;$$
$$0.01065 = (0.00893) \, l_t + (0.02606 + 0.052632 + 0.05) \, k_t;$$
$$k_t = \frac{0.01065}{(0.026 + 0.0526 + 0.05)} - \frac{(0.00893) \, l_t}{(0.026 + 0.0526 + 0.05)};$$

(16.64)

the isoquant curve is

$$y_t^s = A_G \left(l_t^d \right)^\gamma (k_t)^{1-\gamma},$$
$$0.01065 = (0.1) \left(l_t^d \right)^{\frac{1}{3}} (k_t)^{\frac{2}{3}};$$
$$k_t = \left(\frac{0.01065}{0.1 \left(l_t^d \right)^{\frac{1}{3}}} \right)^{\frac{3}{2}} = \frac{\left(\frac{0.01065}{0.1} \right)^{\frac{3}{2}}}{\left(l_t^d \right)^{\frac{1}{2}}};$$

(16.65)

and the factor input ratio is

$$\frac{k_t}{l_t} = \frac{0.0552}{0.3973} = 0.139.$$

(16.66)

Figure 16.8 graphs equations (16.64), (16.65) and (16.66), in variants of black, along with those curves for Example 16.2 in variants of blue. It shows how the bank crisis causes the isocost line to pivot down, as the wage rate to interest rate ratio falls, and the isoquant shifts down, while the capital to labour ratio pivots down and the employment level falls.

In the goods and leisure output space, consumption in terms of production minus investment is now

$$c_t^d = y_t^s - i_t = A_G \left(l_t^d \right)^\gamma (k_t)^{1-\gamma} - \delta_k k_t,$$
$$c_t^d = (0.10) \left(l_t^d \right)^{\frac{1}{3}} (0.0552)^{\frac{2}{3}} - (0.05) (0.0552).$$

(16.67)

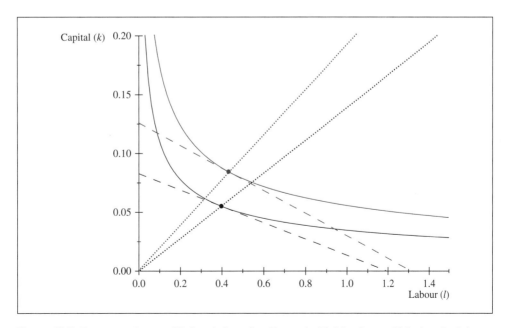

Figure 16.8 Factor market equilibrium in baseline Example 16.2 (variants of blue) and crisis Example 16.3 (variants of black)

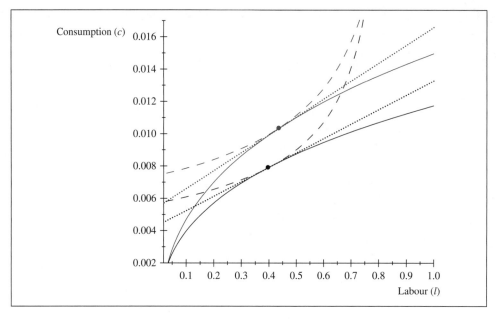

Figure 16.9 General equilibrium consumption and utility levels in baseline Example 16.2 (variants of blue) and crisis Example 16.3 (variants of black)

The utility level curve is now

$$u = \ln c_t + \alpha \ln x_t = \ln c_t + \alpha \ln (T_t - l_t),$$
$$-5.2505 = \ln 0.0078902 + 0.5 \ln \left(1 - 0.161 - 0.39713\right),$$
$$-5.2505 = \ln c_t + 0.5 \ln \left(1 - 0.161 - l_t\right),$$
$$c_t = \frac{e^{-5.2505}}{\left(1 - 0.161 - l_t\right)^{0.5}}. \tag{16.68}$$

And the budget line is

$$c_t^d = w_t \left(l_t^s + l_{Ft}^s\right) + \rho k_t^s = w_t l_t^s + w_t l_{Ft}^s + \rho k_t^s,$$
$$c_t^d = \left(0.00893\right) l_t^s + \left(0.00893\right) \left(0.161\right) + \left(0.052632\right) \left(0.0552\right). \tag{16.69}$$

Figure 16.9 graphs equations (16.67), (16.68) and (16.69) in variants of black, along with the Example 16.2 functions in variants of blue. It shows that the bank crisis causes the production function to pivot down, and utility, consumption, and employment all to fall.

16.5 Crashes of 1929 and 2008

Bank crises can arise for a variety of reasons, including industry specific risk but more likely from aggregate risk components. For example the bank crisis of 2007–09 came about after huge debt was undertaken in the US during wartime activity on two fronts in Iraq and Afghanistan. Astronomical debt increases pose the threat of future taxes which generally cause lower growth and so lower asset prices. This causes asset prices to fall. An unexpected asset price fall can lead to a bank crisis, if it includes the prices of assets that serve as collateral for loans. In 2007–09, housing prices fell after rising continuously for a long period of time. When interest rates rose as well, and so loan fees increased, consumers who found the new loan repayments too high could not sell their houses and pay back their debts since house prices had fallen. This caused bankruptcy and bank failure since many such loans were spread across banks all across the US and Europe.

Both the 1930s and the 2007–09 crises were characterised by a lack of insurance against so-called aggregate risk arising from the banking sector. The lack of effective insurance in the banking industry in effect can be interpreted as causing a large drop in bank productivity, using the outlines of the baseline model extended to include banking. The difference in the response to the crises was that the governments acted to supply insurance in banking only in 1933 for the US, through the establishment of the Federal Deposit Insurance Corporation, while international governments acted much more quickly in the 2007–09 crisis, through a variety of measures designed to insure the liabilities of banks, *ex post* after the crisis occurred. The ad hoc insurance supplied during the modern crisis enabled the recession to be much less pronounced than the 1930s depression.

However the need to use ad hoc bank insurance after the fact results in a very inefficient banking insurance system. Such insurance covered all types of financial intermediation, from commercial banking to investment banking, to insurance (the company AIG was rescued by US government action) to car financing in the form of automobile company aid from governments, especially in the US, and the government financing of new car purchases through a subsidisation of old car 'scrappage' schemes internationally. But because the shock to the banking system was not insured by the normal insurance elements already in place, the shock ended up acting as aggregate risk that was uninsured.

16.6 Application: bank insurance policy

De facto aggregate risk to the entire financial intermediation sector that is ultimately insured by governments suggests that the risk could have been insured in the first place, in a more efficient, systematic and non-discriminatory fashion. In other words aggregate risk only exists because of incomplete insurance systems. And more complete insurance systems could potentially be devised so that the amount of residual aggregate risk is minimised.

The main policy option for governments to offset the aggregate risk is to ensure the existence of a financial intermediation insurance in a systematic efficient fashion. The cleaning up of bank failures and the minimisation of the after-effects of aggregate risk occurring has been a key government policy within countries and at international levels. But with a more complete financial intermediation insurance system, such unexpected decreases in effective bank productivity might be greatly ameliorated and so the need to *ex post* supply residual insurance could be largely reduced.

16.6.1 Deposit insurance with risk-based premiums

The US enacted deposit insurance only in 1933, at the height of the depression. Previously, banks had industry-formed 'clearinghouses' which acted as a means of insuring depositors at a failing bank. This was designed to minimise the risk that a failure would spread to other banks. Therefore it was a market-based method of providing insurance against aggregate risk.

However with the establishment of the US Federal Reserve Bank in 1913, the government took over the clearinghouse functions and these private insurance mechanisms for the banks were dissolved. Yet when the banks failed during the depression the US failed to insure depositors of failing banks, and the panic then spread to other banks.

Establishment of the Federal Deposit Insurance Corporation (FDIC) in 1933 then created an insurance fund from which to insure depositors, and so avoid the spread of a bank panic. In 2005 the FDIC system was reformed to make the banks pay insurance fees, equal to our *d* in the Chapter 15 analysis, which reflected the risk of the portfolio structure of the bank. These are called 'risk-based premiums'. And they are designed to insure the system fully by taking into account the different risk factors associated with each bank.

To this day, this system has largely worked, except that financial institutions not covered by the FDIC failed during the 2008 banking crisis. This led to a type of realisation of aggregate risk that spread so as to cause a failure of FDIC insured banks. And the US government, using its specially authorised TARP funds, added funding to the FDIC fund so that it could cover the losses of the FDIC-insured bank failures that occurred. So in a sense the FDIC coverage was only partial and did not cover the entire financial intermediation industry. And this can be interpreted as resulting in the manifestation of aggregate risk of bank failure, or a fall in A_F, during the bad state of the concurrent recession of 2007–09.

For example George Soros lectured at Central European University in 2009 that

> the Basel Accords made a mistake when they gave securities held by banks substantially lower risk ratings than regular loans: they ignored the systemic risks attached to concentrated positions in securities. This was an important factor aggravating the crisis. It has to be corrected by raising the risk ratings of securities held by banks. That will probably discourage the securitization of loans.[2]

Soros is providing an example of how assets other than commercial banking assets need to be evaluated in terms of the actual risks involved. And this is also necessary in order to provide more efficient insurance to the total set of all financial intermediation liabilities.

16.6.2 Policy for global bank failure, aggregate risk and moral hazard

At the international level the widespread failure of banks within interconnected global capital markets has long been a basis for cooperative international government action. One of the main tools has been the International Monetary Fund, or IMF. This agency has been funded by governments internationally, and has acted to intervene to try to contain financial panics within countries or regions when they occur. Latin American intervention during the 1980s and Asian intervention during the 1997 international bank crisis are key examples.

What the IMF actually does is never pre-determined or clear even after the fact. This has led to criticism of it being a very inefficient way to insure against aggregate risk. And if it allows private banks to be bailed out of their insolvencies, or even just their losses from a regional failure, then criticism has been that the IMF actually increases the probability of such a recurring bank failure. And this is called 'moral hazard' when a policy action causes an increase in the probability of the bad state. This increase in the probability of the bad state, as the result of some action or system of actions, is the definition of moral hazard.

16.6.3 International finance systemic insurance

The success of the FDIC in the US suggests that if such a risk-based premium system were applied to all financial institutions and across all countries, then the aggregate risk of bank failure would be largely eliminated. The first requirement is to consider how to bring all US financial institutions into the FDIC insurance system.

---

[2]Soros, George, 2009, Lecture 2, 'Financial Markets', The Economy, Reflexivity and Open Society, Central European University; transcript at FT.com, FT Video, Soros Lectures.

Our analysis is well-suited for this. It suggests that whatever is the form of service that the bank is supplying, its expected outlays can be computed. In our analysis, the expected payout is $\left(1 + R^d\right) d$, where R^d includes the cost of the transformation as well as the probabilities of the states occurring. For deposit insurance on commercial, or 'retail' banking, such a computation has been fairly straightforward. And so the amount that commercial banks are required to pay into the FDIC is also clear. The problem is the so-called 'wholesale' banks, or really the banks that provide services for firms rather than consumers. These investment banks provide loans to firms and help firms sell equity shares to the public markets, in what is called 'underwriting'. They also help in international risk-pooling through derivative packages and other forms of hedging and risk management.

Investment banks can be brought into a government insurance system in the same way as commercial banks. The only requirement is the assessment of what is R^d on the funds deposited with such investment banks. This assessment is more complicated than for commercial banks because of the variety of risk management vehicles that investment banks offer. And the complication is also that the investment banks themselves invest in a variety of such risk transference vehicles. However, it is clear that such vehicles are subject to evaluation and a risk premium can be assessed for all deposited funds at investment banks. Allowing these banks to be a part of the FDIC in the US would allow the entire financial sector to take part in the insurance system.

At the international level, a risk-based deposit insurance system that covered both commercial and investment banks could be implemented as a replacement for the IMF's ad hoc operation in supplying such financial insurance. Insurance firms could also be brought into such domestic and global deposit insurance schemes, again on the principle of evaluating the overall average R^d that attaches to each financial intermediary.

16.7 Questions

1. In Example 16.1, the marginal cost of banking MC_{qt} is given in terms of the loans per unit of deposits, or $\frac{q_t}{d_t}$, in a function whereby $MC_{qt} = \frac{w_t}{\kappa\left(A_F\right)^{\frac{1}{\kappa}}}\left(\frac{q_t}{d_t}\right)^{\frac{1-\kappa}{\kappa}}$, and this is graphed in Figure 16.1 with $\frac{q_t}{d_t}$ on the horizontal axis. In the graph the marginal cost is a convex function relative to the horizon.

    (a) For what range of values of the parameter κ is this marginal cost graph convex,
    (b) for what range of values of the parameter κ is this marginal cost graph concave,
    (c) and for what range of values of the parameter κ is this marginal cost graph linear?

2. In Example 16.2, the aggregate supply and demand functions for output, or AS–AD, have the exact same functional form as in the zero exogenous growth model of Part 4 of the text.

    (a) What variables change in the AS–AD equations (16.47) and (16.48) when there is an increase in productivity in banking such as a result of deregulation or the elimination of onerous, wasteful regulations?
    (b) Graph the shifts in the AS–AD functions in a figure, such as Figure 16.2, when the productivity in the banking sector increases.
    (c) Explain how this bank productivity increase would affect the supply and demand for labour functions.

3. In Example 16.3 the productivity factor A_F falls by 26% and the capital stock falls by 34%.

    (a) How does this affect the labour employment in the goods sector,
    (b) the interest differential between the loan rate and the deposit rate,
    (c) and the wage rate?

4. How does the decrease in the capital stock from a banking crisis, through a productivity decrease, compare to the stock market crash that is experienced at times during bank crises?

5. How does the decrease in bank productivity reproduce elements that we expect during an economic recession?

6. Are there any aspects of the model in Example 16.3 that do not coincide with a description of a bank-crisis led recession?

7. If a bank's problems are fully insured against, then the capital stock may be little affected. In what sense does an unexpected, uninsured fall in the economy-wide bank productivity correspond to a realisation of aggregate risk in the economy?

8. In what ways are the 1930s Great Depression and the 2007–10 bank crisis led global recession explained by the bank model of the chapter?

9. What policy in terms of international bank insurance could avoid a large decrease in bank productivity and the ensuing decrease in aggregate output?

16.8 References

Berk, Jonathan B. and Richard C. Green, 2004, 'Mutual Fund Flows and Performance in Rational Markets', *Journal of Political Economy,* 112(6): 1269–1295.

Clark, J.A., 1984, 'Estimation of Economies of Scale in Banking Using a Generalized Functional Form', *Journal of Money, Credit, and Banking* 16(1): 53–68.

Gillman, Max and Michal Kejak, 2010, 'Inflation, Investment and Growth: a Money and Banking Approach', *Economica,* forthcoming; online now at 'early view' (http://www3.interscience.wiley.com/journal/120120192/issue).

Goodfriend, Marvin and Bennett T. McCallum, 2007, 'Banking and Interest Rates in Monetary Policy Analysis: A Quantitative Exploration', *Journal of Monetary Economics,* Elsevier, 54(5) (July): 1480–1507.

Hicks, John R., 1935, 'A Suggestion for Simplifying the Theory of Money', *Economica,* 2(5) (February): 1–19.

Pesek, Boris P. and Thomas R. Saving, 1968, *The Foundations of Money and Banking,* New York: The MacMillan Co.

Sealey, C.W., Jr. and James T. Lindley, 1977, 'Inputs, Outputs and a Theory of Production and Cost at Depository Financial Institutions', *The Journal of Finance,* 32(4) (September): 1251–1266.

16.9 Appendix A16

The solution to the economy with banking that intermediates savings to investment, in Section 16.4, for all of the variables can be found first by letting the loan rate R_t^q that is found in the goods producer equilibrium be set equal to the loan rate R_t^q found in the bank sector. From equations (16.15) and (16.36) this gives that

$$(1-\gamma) A \left(\frac{l_t}{k_t}\right)^{\gamma} - \delta_k = R_t^q = R_t^d + \frac{w_t}{\left(A_F\right)^{\frac{1}{\kappa}}}.$$

Since the wage rate is given as the marginal product of labour in the goods producer problem, in equation (16.16), with $w_t = \gamma A_G \left(\frac{l_t}{k_t}\right)^{\gamma-1}$, and since $R_t^d = \rho$, the above equilibrium condition gives an implicit solution for $\frac{l_t}{k_t}$ in terms of given parameters:

$$(1-\gamma) A \left(\frac{l_t}{k_t}\right)^{\gamma} - \delta_k = \rho + \frac{\gamma A_G \left(\frac{l_t}{k_t}\right)^{\gamma-1}}{\left(A_F\right)^{\frac{1}{\kappa}}}. \tag{16.70}$$

With the solution for $\frac{l_t}{k_t}$, the other variables can be determined. Next, the solution for k_t as a function of $\frac{l_t}{k_t}$ will be determined. One way to proceed is to take the allocation of time constraint, $1 = x_t + l_t + l_{Ft}$ and substitute in for l_{Ft} from the bank problem. For l_{Ft}, at

$\frac{q_t}{d_t} = 1$, from equation (16.37),

$$\frac{l_{Ft}}{d_t} = \frac{1}{\left(A_F\right)^{\frac{1}{\kappa}}}. \tag{16.71}$$

And with $k_t = d_t$, then

$$l_{Ft} = \frac{k_t}{\left(A_F\right)^{\frac{1}{\kappa}}}.$$

Substituting this l_{Ft} solution into the time allocation constraint,

$$1 = x_t + l_t + \frac{k_t}{\left(A_F\right)^{\frac{1}{\kappa}}}.$$

For x_t, it holds from the consumer's intratemporal margin between goods and leisure that $x_t = \frac{\alpha c_t}{w_t}$. And also consumption is given as $c_t = \frac{1}{1+\alpha}\left[w_t + \rho k_t\right]$. Combining these, the solution for x_t is

$$x_t = \frac{\alpha}{1+\alpha}\left[1 + \frac{\rho k_t}{w_t}\right];$$

substituting this x_t solution into the allocation of time constraint, it becomes

$$1 = \frac{\alpha}{1+\alpha}\left[1 + \frac{\rho k_t}{w_t}\right] + l_t + \frac{k_t}{\left(A_F\right)^{\frac{1}{\kappa}}}.$$

This leads directly to a solution for k_t in terms of $\frac{l_t}{k_t}$. Divide by k_t,

$$\frac{1}{k_t} = \frac{\alpha}{1+\alpha}\left[\frac{1}{k_t} + \frac{\rho}{w_t}\right] + \frac{l_t}{k_t} + \frac{1}{\left(A_F\right)^{\frac{1}{\kappa}}};$$

substitute in for $w_t = \gamma A_G \left(\frac{l_t}{k_t}\right)^{\gamma-1}$; and solve for k_t as

$$k_t = \frac{1}{\left[\frac{\alpha\rho\left(\frac{l_t}{k_t}\right)^{1-\gamma}}{\gamma A_G} + \left(1+\alpha\right)\frac{l_t}{k_t} + \frac{(1+\alpha)}{\left(A_F\right)^{\frac{1}{\kappa}}}\right]}. \tag{16.72}$$

With the solutions for $\frac{l_t}{k_t}$ and then k_t as a function of $\frac{l_t}{k_t}$, the solutions to all of the other variables follow.

16.9.1 Example 16.2

The parameters are specified as $A_G = 0.1$, $\gamma = \kappa = 0.333$, $\delta_k = 0.05$, $\alpha = 1$, and $\rho = \frac{1}{\beta} - 1 = \frac{1}{0.95} - 1 = 0.0526$, and $A_F = 0.95$. Equation (16.70) can be written as

$$\left(1-\gamma\right) A_G \left(\frac{l_t}{k_t}\right)^{\gamma} - \frac{\gamma A_G \left(\frac{l_t}{k_t}\right)^{\gamma-1}}{\left(A_F\right)^{\frac{1}{\kappa}}} - \delta_k - \rho = 0;$$

$$\left(1 - 0.333\right)\left(0.1\right)\left(\frac{l_t}{k_t}\right)^{0.333} - \frac{0.333\left(0.1\right)\left(\frac{l_t}{k_t}\right)^{0.333-1}}{\left(0.95\right)^{\frac{1}{0.333}}} - 0.1026 = 0. \tag{16.73}$$

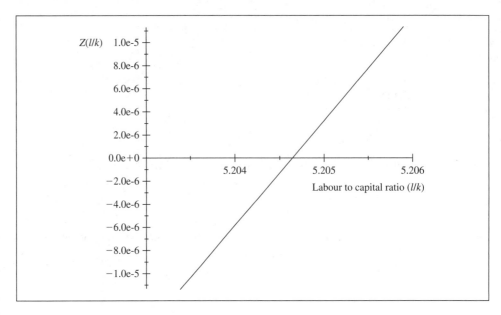

Figure 16.10 Labour to capital equilibrium solution in Example 16.2

The solution for $\frac{l_t}{k_t}$ in this equation is 5.205. The $\frac{l_t}{k_t}$ solution can be seen graphically. Equation (16.73) is a function of $\frac{l_t}{k_t}$ that is set equal to zero. In other words, this equation can be written as a function $Z\left(\frac{l_t}{k_t}\right) = 0$. Graphically, the value for $\frac{l_t}{k_t}$ at which this function equals 0 is the equilibrium value of $\frac{l_t}{k_t}$. Figure 16.10 graphs equation (16.73) to show the solution at $\frac{l_t}{k_t} = 5.205$, where $Z\left(\frac{l_t}{k_t}\right) = 0$.

Consequently the capital stock is found by substituting in $\frac{l_t}{k_t} = 5.205$ into equation (16.72):

$$k_t = \cfrac{1}{\left[\cfrac{\alpha\rho\left(\frac{l_t}{k_t}\right)^{1-\gamma}}{\gamma A_G} + \left(1+\alpha\right)\frac{l_t}{k_t} + \cfrac{(1+\alpha)}{\left(A_F\right)^{\frac{1}{\kappa}}}\right]};$$ (16.74)

$$k_t = \cfrac{1}{\cfrac{(0.5)(0.0526)(05.20525)^{1-0.333}}{(0.333)(0.10)} + \left(1.5\right)\left(05.20525\right) + \cfrac{(1.5)}{(0.95)^{\frac{1}{0.333}}}},$$ (16.75)

$$= 0.08382.$$ (16.76)

The solution for the other variables is that $w_t = 0.011081$; $\frac{l_t}{k_t} = 5.205$, $l_t = \left(\frac{l_t}{k_t}\right)k_t = \left(5.20525\right)\left(0.08382\right) = 0.4363$, $l_{Ft} = \cfrac{k_t}{\left(A_F\right)^{\frac{1}{\kappa}}} = \cfrac{(0.08382)}{(0.95)^{\frac{1}{0.333}}} = 0.098$.

Leisure is given by

$$x_t = \cfrac{\alpha}{1+\alpha}\left[1 + \cfrac{\rho k_t}{w_t}\right] = \cfrac{0.5}{1+0.5}\left(1 + \cfrac{0.0526\,(0.08382)}{0.0111}\right) = 0.4657.$$

And so the time allocation adds up exactly to 1: $0.4363 + 0.098 + 0.4657 = 1.0$. Consumption is $c_t = \frac{1}{1+\alpha}\left(w_t + \rho k_t\right) = \frac{1}{1+0.5}\left(0.0111 + 0.0526\,(0.08382)\right) = 0.01034$. Output is

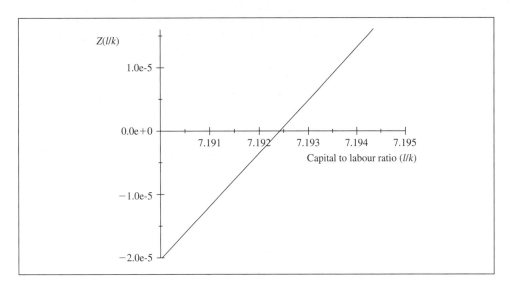

Figure 16.11 Labour to capital equilibrium solution in Example 16.3

consumption plus depreciation, or $y_t = \frac{1}{1+\alpha}(w_t + \rho k_t) + \delta_k k_t = 0.01034 + (0.05)(0.08382) = 0.014531$. The interest differential is $R_t^q - R_t^d = \frac{w_t}{(A_F)^{\frac{1}{\kappa}}} = \frac{0.0111}{(0.95)^{\frac{1}{0.333}}} = 0.012948$; with $R^q = 0.012948 + 0.052632 = 0.06558$.

16.9.2 Example 16.3

Now assume that all parameters are the same except that $A_F = 0.7$. Then it results that $\frac{l_t}{k_t} = 7.1925$. It is an increase that results as the goods producer uses less capital and more labour as the cost of capital rises because of the decreased bank productivity. This equilibrium for $\frac{l_t}{k_t}$ can be seen graphically using $Z\left(\frac{l_t}{k_t}\right) = 0$, of equation (16.73), but now with $A_F = 0.7$. This is graphed in Figure 16.11.

With this new value of $\frac{l_t}{k_t}$,

$$k_t = \frac{1}{\frac{(0.5)(0.0526)(7.193)^{1-0.333}}{(0.333)(0.10)} + (1 + (0.5))(7.193) + \frac{(1 + (0.5))}{(0.7)^{\frac{1}{0.333}}}} \tag{16.77}$$

$$= 0.05521. \tag{16.78}$$

The solution for the other variables is that $w_t = 0.333(0.10)(7.193)^{0.333-1} = 0.00893$; $l_t = \frac{l_t}{k_t} k_t = (7.193)(0.05521) = 0.397$; $l_{Ft} = \frac{k_t}{(A_F)^{\frac{1}{\kappa}}} = \frac{(0.05521)}{(0.7)^{\frac{1}{0.333}}} = 0.161$; $x_t = \frac{\alpha}{1+\alpha}\left[1 + \frac{\rho k_t}{w_t}\right] = \frac{0.5}{1+0.5}\left(1 + \frac{0.0526(0.05521)}{0.00893}\right) = 0.44173$; total time is $1 = 0.39713 + 0.16113 + 0.44173 = 1.0$; $R_t^q - R_t^d = \frac{w_t}{(A_F)^{\frac{1}{\kappa}}} = \frac{0.00893}{(0.7)^{\frac{1}{0.333}}} = 0.02606$; consumption is

$c_t = \frac{1}{1+\alpha}(w_t + \rho k_t) = \frac{1}{1+0.5}(0.00893 + 0.052632(0.0552)) = 0.0078902$; investment is $\delta_k k_t = (0.05)(0.05521) = 0.00276$; and aggregate output is $y_t = c_t + \delta_k k_t = 0.0078902 + 0.00276 = 0.01065$.

CHAPTER ⑰

Asset prices and finance

17.1 Introduction

The dynamic exogenous growth model is extended to allow the consumer not only to invest in capital directly but also to invest in government bonds. The price of government bonds is shown to be the marginal product of capital. Alternative ways of representing the bond price are presented.

The problem is then further decentralised so that the consumer can no longer directly invest in capital but instead can only buy shares in the goods producers. The goods producer in turn owns the capital and returns the profit on the capital investment to the consumer through paying dividends. The consumer can still buy government bonds and the result is that under certainty conditions the return on the share purchase, through appreciation of the stock price and the dividend payment, exactly equals the return on the bond.

The infinite horizon is considered and the idea of a limiting condition on the value of the stock price is introduced through a 'transversality condition'. And, with this condition holding, the stock price value is in direct relation to the capital stock of the firm. Constant dividends are also assumed showing the price as the discounted value of the infinite stream of dividends, which equals just the dividend divided by the interest rate. This also gives a way to think about the so-called equity premium under uncertainty.

The equity premium is the difference between the risky return on stocks and the risk free return on bonds. This is derived and then the model's failure to explain the level found empirically for the equity premium, under exogenous growth, is pointed out. Models with endogenous growth have claimed the ability to explain the empirical value of the equity premium and this concept is also presented.

17.1.1 Building on the last chapters

The chapter further develops the investment into capital found throughout the book. While in Part 4 the consumer directly accumulates capital and rents it to the firm, and while in the last chapter the consumer can only deposit savings in the bank which in turn lends it to the firm, this chapter introduces financial markets. In this chapter, the consumer can invest through financial markets. Initially, only investment in bonds is allowed. But then, instead of directly investing in capital, the consumer can invest only through financial markets.

The firm investment in capital, rather than the consumer, was also found in the last chapter. But in all previous chapters, the firm only rents capital from the consumer. The consumer in this chapter has the choice of either government bonds or shares in the firm. In previous chapters except Chapter 15 there was always full certainty. And in this situation the chapter shows how the consumer's return on bonds and on shares in the firm are the same. But then with uncertainty, which was introduced in Chapter 15, the shares in the firm are risky. The return between the firm shares and the bond prices is positive now in this chapter under uncertainty, reflecting the risk premium built into the share return to compensate for facing uncertain returns.

The model primarily uses the zero exogenous growth framework of Part 4. Positive but exogenous growth is introduced. And because the exogenous growth model does not explain well the empirical findings for the equity premium, endogenous growth of Part 5 is introduced, mainly in a discussion context of how this helps explain the empirical equity premium.

17.1.2 Learning objective

The challenge is to grasp the fundamentals of asset pricing, of bonds and shares. The extension from previous chapters is kept restricted to these dimensions so that the focus remains on how bonds and share prices reflect the marginal product of capital. Understanding that both bond and share returns are exactly the marginal product of capital under certainty, poises the student to make the leap of understanding why the share price returns exceed the bond price return under uncertainty. The focus on this difference is the key to the chapter, and one that is reflected in the macroeconomic finance literature. The other focus is how the share price reflects the discounted stream of future dividends.

17.1.3 Who made it happen?

The analysis of asset prices in the general equilibrium representative model is most widely attributed to Robert E. Lucas, Jr.'s 1978 article on asset pricing, 'Asset Prices in an Exchange Economy'. This became known as the consumption based capital asset pricing model. It built upon the work of many others to the basic finance theory analysis, albeit outside of a full general macroeconomic equilibrium, such as those recognised when the 1990 Nobel Prize was given jointly to the finance pioneers Harry M. Markowitz, Merton H. Miller, and William F. Sharpe. And it builds in Eugene F. Fama's (1970) view on how stock prices reflect the information available to the market.

Mehra and Prescott are widely known for turning the focus of the basic dynamic macroeconomic model towards explaining the difference between stock and bond returns, with their article on 'The Equity Premium: A Puzzle'. A huge amount of work has been done to offer explanations of how to make the baseline dynamic model better explain the equity premium, as Kocherlakota (1996) makes clear. This has included those using human capital, such as recent work by Zhang (2006). Cochrane (2001) links together macroeconomic theory including the equity premium with finance theory.

17.2 Modelling the return on bonds

Assume that output is Cobb–Douglas in labour and physical capital. Let utility be of the log form, including leisure. And let the consumer now invest not only in physical capital but also in government 'nominal' bonds, with the quantity of this denoted by b_t, and the interest rate return of the bonds given as R_t. By nominal bonds it is meant that the return R_t is the market price. For now the analysis does not have money included, and so the nominal return R_t will be exactly the same as the real return $r_t - \delta_k$ to capital, since in equilibrium all capital earns the same return. In Part 7, money will be introduced and the role of the inflation rate will be included in determining the nominal return R_t.

At time t, the consumer buys bonds for next period, an amount given by b_{t+1}, and receives the income and current quantity of bonds back during the current period. This means the income of the bonds is $R_t b_t$ and the redemption of the current quantity of bonds is b_t, for a total income of $b_t (1 + R_t)$. And the total new outlay is b_{t+1}. Therefore the representative agent's net investment in bonds is $b_{t+1} - b_t (1 + R_t)$. This is the only new part to be added to the dynamic equilibrium baseline model of Chapter 8, with just the one additional choice variable of b_{t+1}.

17.2.1 Extended baseline dynamic model

Consider the representative agent problem of the Chapter 8 baseline model, restated here with the production technology of the goods sector given by

$$y_t = A_G l_t^\gamma k_t^{1-\gamma}; \tag{17.1}$$

output is divided between consumption goods and investment in physical capital:

$$y_t = c_t + i_t, \tag{17.2}$$

where

$$i_t = k_{t+1} - (1 - \delta_k) k_t;$$

time is allocated between work and leisure:

$$1 = x_t + l_t. \tag{17.3}$$

With the consumer working for the goods producer and renting capital to the goods producer, the budget constraint is

$$c_t = w_t l_t + r_t k_t - k_{t+1} + k_t (1 - \delta_k). \tag{17.4}$$

The dynamic consumer maximisation problem is

$$V(k_t) = \underset{c_t, x_t, l_t, k_{t+1}}{\text{Max}} \quad : \ln c_t + \alpha \ln x_t + \beta V (k_{t+1}), \tag{17.5}$$

subject to the above constraints. It can be restated as

$$V(k_t) = \underset{l_t, k_{t+1}}{\text{Max}} : u \left(w_t l_t + r_t k_t - k_{t+1} + k_t (1 - \delta_k), 1 - l_t \right) + \beta V (k_{t+1}). \tag{17.6}$$

Now consider adding bonds as another possible investment of the consumer. Here the agent is buying the bonds from the government, and the government is selling the bonds as a way to finance government expenditure. First specify the government budget constraint. Let G_t equal government spending, and let this be financed only by selling new bonds. Denote the quantity of bonds by b_t, and the interest rate on the bonds by R_t. Then the government raises money to spend by issuing new bonds b_{t+1} at time t, while paying interest on existing bonds, of $R_t b_t$. The government budget constraint is that

$$G_t = b_{t+1} - b_t (1 + R_t).$$

The consumer receives the government spending as a lump sum transfer of income. And the consumer also buys the new bonds, and earns interest on existing bonds. The consumer budget constraint of equation (17.4) becomes

$$c_t = w_t l_t + r_t k_t - k_{t+1} + k_t (1 - \delta_k) + G_t - b_{t+1} + b_t (1 + R_t). \tag{17.7}$$

And now there is a new decision variable at time t, the quantity of bonds b_{t+1} that the consumer invests in. This also means that b_t enters the value function as a state variable along with k_t and the new maximisation problem is

$$V\left(k_t, b_t\right) = \underset{l_t, k_{t+1}, b_{t+1}}{\text{Max}} \tag{17.8}$$

$$u\left(w_t l_t + r_t k_t - k_{t+1} + k_t\left(1 - \delta_k\right) + G_t - b_{t+1} + b_t\left(1 + R_t\right), 1 - l_t\right)$$
$$+ \beta V\left(k_{t+1}, b_{t+1}\right).$$

The first-order equilibrium conditions, with respect to l_t, k_{t+1}, and the envelope condition with respect to k_t are the same:

$$\frac{1}{c_t} w_t + \frac{\alpha}{x_t}\left(-1\right) = 0; \tag{17.9}$$

$$\frac{1}{c_t}\left(-1\right) + \beta \frac{\partial V\left(k_{t+1}, b_{t+1}\right)}{\partial k_{t+1}} = 0; \tag{17.10}$$

$$\frac{\partial V\left(k_t, b_t\right)}{\partial k_t} = \frac{\partial u\left(c_t, x_t\right)}{\partial c_t}\left(1 + r_t - \delta_k\right). \tag{17.11}$$

These can be rearranged, with $\beta \equiv \frac{1}{1+\rho}$, in terms of the intertemporal marginal rate of substitution,

$$\frac{c_t}{c_{t-1}} = \frac{1 + r_t - \delta_k}{1 + \rho}, \tag{17.12}$$

and in terms of the goods to leisure marginal rate of substitution,

$$w_t = \frac{\frac{\alpha}{x_t}}{\frac{1}{c_t}}. \tag{17.13}$$

Note that from the goods producer problem, $r_t = \left(1 - \gamma\right) A_G l_t^{\gamma} k_t^{-\gamma}$ and $w_t = \gamma A_G l_t^{\gamma-1} k_t^{1-\gamma}$.

17.2.2 Equilibrium condition for bonds

The additional first-order condition with respect to bonds is the derivative with respect to b_{t+1}:

$$\frac{\partial u\left(c_t, x_t\right)}{\partial c_t}\left(-1\right) + \beta \frac{\partial V\left(k_{t+1}, b_{t+1}\right)}{\partial b_{t+1}} = 0. \tag{17.14}$$

And the second new equilibrium condition is the envelope condition with respect to b_t. Differentiating equation (17.8) with respect to b_t, this condition is

$$\frac{\partial V\left(k_t, b_t\right)}{\partial b_t} = \frac{\partial u\left(c_t, x_t\right)}{\partial c_t}\left(1 + R_t\right). \tag{17.15}$$

So now we can put together these two new conditions. To do this, bring back by one period the time t in the equation (17.14) to time $t - 1$ and the time $t + 1$ to time t:

$$\frac{\partial u\left(c_{t-1}, x_{t-1}\right)}{\partial c_{t-1}}\left(-1\right) + \beta \frac{\partial V\left(k_t, b_t\right)}{\partial b_t} = 0. \tag{17.16}$$

Then the solution for $\frac{\partial V(k_t, b_t)}{\partial b_t}$ is given from this equation as

$$\frac{\partial V\left(k_t, b_t\right)}{\partial b_t} = \frac{\partial u\left(c_{t-1}, x_{t-1}\right)}{\beta \partial c_{t-1}}. \tag{17.17}$$

Substitute this solution into equation (17.15) to get the intertemporal marginal rate of substitution as being equal to $1 + R_t$.

$$\frac{\frac{\partial u(c_{t-1}, x_{t-1})}{\partial c_{t-1}}}{\beta \frac{\partial u(c_t, x_t)}{\partial c_t}} = 1 + R_t. \tag{17.18}$$

With log utility, this condition is

$$\frac{c_t}{\beta c_{t-1}} = 1 + R_t, \tag{17.19}$$

or using that $\beta \equiv \frac{1}{1+\rho}$, it can be written in terms of the growth rate of consumption, as

$$\frac{c_t}{c_{t-1}} = \frac{1 + R_t}{1 + \rho}. \tag{17.20}$$

Comparing the equations (17.12) and (17.20), it emerges clearly that

$$R_t = r_t - \delta_k. \tag{17.21}$$

In other words, the interest rate on bonds is the same as the real return on capital, which is the marginal product of capital net of depreciation.

17.2.3 Example 17.1: Alternative bond pricing

An alternative way to look at bonds is in terms of their price, rather than yield, where the price is the inverse of the gross yield. Consider that if instead of writing the bond investment as $b_{t+1} - b_t (1 + R_t)$, we could alternatively state it as $\hat{q}_{t+1} b_{t+1} - b_t$, where $\hat{q}_{t+1}$ is the price of the new bonds b_{t+1}. Then the result would be that

$$\hat{q}_t = \frac{1}{1 + R_t}. \tag{17.22}$$

In this way the one dollar of a bond would be bought at a discount of less than one, equal to $\frac{1}{1+R_t}$. When the bond matured it would pay off b_t. And so the yield over one period of time of this so-called 'discount bond' would be R_t.

17.3 Equity capital asset market

Under certainty assumptions, if the firm issues equity shares that can be owned by the consumer, and the consumer buys these shares on the asset market, the return on holding these equity shares (also called 'stocks') of the firm is still the same marginal product of capital net of depreciation, $r_t - \delta_k$. This is also the return on holding bonds. So it would not matter to what extent the consumer holds bonds versus shares of the firm's equity.

However when there is risk associated with the firm's capital investment, then there is a significant difference in the return on risky equity versus the risk-free bonds. The return to government bonds is considered to be risk-free in that the only risk is the collapse of the government itself. It is not truly risk-free for many reasons, but this is an abstraction made here. And bonds issued by the US Treasury are typically considered the most risk-free government bonds.

17.3.1 The equity premium

The so-called 'equity premium' is the difference between the risk-free return to bonds and the average return to equity shares. It is defined so as to give the additional return from owning risky stocks. Much research has focused on the ability of the baseline dynamic model, with uncertainty assumed, to explain the observed equity premium. This asset price dimension of the model is another key facet in which the model can be put to test against the data.

A simple way to present the equity premium is to now extend the model to include the pricing of risky equity shares. The equity premium will therefore be equal to the difference in the expectation at time t, denoted by E_t, of the equity return, denoted by R_{t+1}^S, and the government bond return R_{t+1}. This is therefore given by $E_t\left[R_{t+1}^S\right] - R_{t+1}$. It remains to determine $E_t\left[R_{t+1}^S\right]$ in general equilibrium. Before taking this step, first the equity return model will be presented with perfect foresight and no uncertainty.

17.3.2 A model of asset prices under certainty

Assume that the consumer buys equity shares in the firm, as well as bonds, and no longer directly invests in physical capital accumulation. The firm instead does the investment in the capital, and sells equity shares that provide ownership of the firm to the consumer.

First with no uncertainty, assume that a share of a company's equity, denoted by s_t, can be bought on the market for the price p_t^S at time t and that it yields dividends per share each period as denoted by d_t^S. The total dividends are then $d_t^S s_t$ each period. The representative agent invests at time t in s_{t+1} shares for next period, and has the share value of $s_t p_t^S$ in the current period, plus the dividends from those shares of $d_t^S s_t$.

The consumer budget constraint accordingly is that consumption equals wages plus the government transfer G_t minus investment in bonds and equities,

$$c_t = w_t l_t + G_t - b_{t+1} + b_t \left(1 + R_t\right) - p_t^S s_{t+1} + \left(p_t^S + d_t^S\right) s_t.$$

Therefore the consumer problem is extended to

$$V\left(b_t, s_t\right) = \max_{l_t, b_{t+1}, s_{t+1}} \tag{17.23}$$
$$u\left(w_t l_t - b_{t+1} + b_t\left(1 + R_t\right) - p_t^S s_{t+1} + \left(p_t^S + d_t^S\right) s_t, 1 - l_t\right)$$
$$+ \beta V\left(b_{t+1}, s_{t+1}\right).$$

The added first-order condition with respect to s_{t+1}, which replaces the one with respect to k_{t+1}, and the new envelope condition with respect to s_t, which replaces the one with respect to k_t, are as follows:

$$\frac{\partial u\left(c_t, x_t\right)}{\partial c_t}\left(-p_t^S\right) + \beta \frac{\partial V\left(b_{t+1}, s_{t+1}\right)}{\partial s_{t+1}} = 0; \tag{17.24}$$

and the second new equilibrium condition is the envelope condition with respect to s_t. Differentiating equation (17.8) with respect to s_t, this condition is

$$\frac{\partial V\left(b_t, s_t\right)}{\partial s_t} = \frac{\partial u\left(c_t, x_t\right)}{\partial c_t}\left(p_t^S + d_t^S\right). \tag{17.25}$$

Putting these two conditions together, and denoting the equity return by R_t^S, it results that

$$\frac{\frac{\partial u\left(c_{t-1}, x_{t-1}\right)}{\partial c_{t-1}}}{\beta \frac{\partial u\left(c_t, x_t\right)}{\partial c_t}} = \frac{p_t^S + d_t^S}{p_{t-1}^S} \equiv 1 + R_t^S. \tag{17.26}$$

And adding in the previously derived equilibrium condition for bonds and for physical capital, respectively, we have that

$$\frac{\frac{\partial u(c_{t-1}, x_{t-1})}{\partial c_{t-1}}}{\beta \cdot \frac{\partial u(c_t, x_t)}{\partial c_t}} = \frac{p_t^s + d_t^s}{p_{t-1}^s} = 1 + R_t. \tag{17.27}$$

The equilibrium condition states that with no uncertainty, the stocks and bonds have the same gross return which is equal to the intertemporal marginal rate of substitution, or $1 + r_t - \delta_k$. This is an important point: all assets, physical capital k_t, financial assets of bonds b_t and stocks s_t all earn the same gross return of $1 + R_t$.

The other result here is the nature of the return to stocks. It equals the rate of increase in the stock price, or $\frac{p_t^s}{p_{t-1}^s}$, which is known commonly as the 'financial capital gain', plus the dividend yield per unit of stock of $\frac{d_t^s}{p_{t-1}^s}$. An equivalent way to write equation (17.27) is in terms of the gross capital gain, $1 + \frac{p_t^s - p_{t-1}^s}{p_{t-1}^s}$, factored by the growth dividend rate, $1 + \frac{d_t^s}{p_t^s}$:

$$\frac{p_t^s + d_t^s}{p_{t-1}^s} = \left(1 + \frac{p_t^s - p_{t-1}^s}{p_{t-1}^s}\right)\left(1 + \frac{d_t^s}{p_t^s}\right) = 1 + R_t. \tag{17.28}$$

Taking logs of the equation,

$$\ln\left(1 + \frac{p_t^s - p_{t-1}^s}{p_{t-1}^s}\right) + \ln\left(1 + \frac{d_t^s}{p_t^s}\right) = \ln\left(1 + R_t\right), \tag{17.29}$$

and given that

$$\ln\left(1 + x\right) \cong x, \tag{17.30}$$

it follows that the net return on equity is equal to the sum of the 'capital price gain' plus the dividend, which in turn equals the net return on bonds:

$$R_t^S \equiv \frac{p_t^s - p_{t-1}^s}{p_{t-1}^s} + \frac{d_t^s}{p_t^s} \simeq R_t. \tag{17.31}$$

Note that the amount of shares s_t owned by the representative agent equals exactly 1 in equilibrium since there is just one agent that owns the entire firm.

For the first time the goods producer problem is a dynamic problem since the firm chooses the amount of investment rather than the consumer. The total dividend payment to the consumer equals the quantity of shares s_t multiplied by the dividend per share, d_t^s. These dividends $s_t d_t^s$ are the residual profit of the firm, and so equal the value of the output $A_G l_t^\gamma k_t^{1-\gamma}$, minus the cost of labour $w_t l_t$ and the cost of investment $k_{t+1} - k_t \left(1 - \delta_k\right)$. The firm also receives the proceeds of the sale of equity shares to the consumer, which equal $p_t^s s_{t+1} - p_t^s s_t$. Therefore the total dividends at time t are given by

$$s_t d_t^s = A_G l_t^\gamma k_t^{1-\gamma} - w_t l_t - k_{t+1} + k_t \left(1 - \delta_k\right) + p_t^s s_{t+1} - p_t^s s_t. \tag{17.32}$$

However the dividend equation for the firm simplifies since the amount of shares owned by the representative consumer is equal to one at all time periods; $s_t = s_{t+1} = 1$. This implies that

$$p_t^s s_{t+1} - p_t^s s_t = p_t^s - p_t^s = 0.$$

Therefore the dividends can be written more simply as

$$d_t^s = A_G l_t^\gamma k_t^{1-\gamma} - w_t l_t - k_{t+1} + k_t \left(1 - \delta_k\right). \tag{17.33}$$

The goods producer dynamic maximisation problem can be written as the recursive maximisation of the value of the firm, which is the equity price p_t^S. Here the capital stock k_t is the state variable, and the price is equal to the maximised dividend value this period plus the discounted price of equity next period. The discount rate is the consumer's intertemporal marginal rate of substitution, $\dfrac{\beta \frac{\partial u\left(c_{t+1}, x_{t+1}\right)}{\partial c_{t+1}}}{\frac{\partial u(c_t, x_t)}{\partial c_t}} = \dfrac{1}{1+R_{t+1}}$. The goods producer problem is

$$p^S\left(k_t\right) = \underset{l_t, k_{t+1}}{\text{Max}}\left(d_t^S + \left(\frac{\beta \frac{\partial u(c_{t+1}, x_{t+1})}{\partial c_{t+1}}}{\frac{\partial u(c_t, x_t)}{\partial c_t}} \right) p^S\left(k_{t+1}\right) \right)$$

$$= \underset{l_t, k_{t+1}}{\text{Max}}\left(d_t^S + \frac{p^S\left(k_{t+1}\right)}{1 + R_{t+1}} \right)$$

$$= \underset{l_t, k_{t+1}}{\text{Max}}\left(A l_t^\gamma k_t^{1-\gamma} - w_t l_t - k_{t+1} + k_t\left(1 - \delta_k\right) + \frac{p^S\left(k_{t+1}\right)}{1 + R_{t+1}} \right). \tag{17.34}$$

This gives the equilibrium condition that the marginal product of capital minus depreciation equals the interest rate R_t:

$$R_t = \left(1 - \gamma\right) A_G \left(\frac{l_t}{k_t}\right)^\gamma - \delta_k. \tag{17.35}$$

And by defining the marginal product of capital as $r_t \equiv \left(1 - \gamma\right) A_G \left(\frac{l_t}{k_t}\right)^\gamma$, this gives that the bond rate is

$$R_t = r_t - \delta_k,$$

while the marginal product of labour equals the real wage as before. These are the same equilibrium conditions as when the equity prices are not made explicit as here, in this decentralisation of the asset market.

17.3.3 Value of goods producer

Another aspect of the goods producer problem is that it provides a value of the firm. In particular, the value is given by the equilibrium price $p^S\left(k_t\right)$. And this price can be evaluated in terms of k_t by substituting in for the price at time $t + 1$. Consider that in equilibrium, from equation (17.34),

$$p^S\left(k_t\right) = A_G l_t^\gamma k_t^{1-\gamma} - w_t l_t - k_{t+1} + k_t\left(1 - \delta_k\right) + \frac{p^S\left(k_{t+1}\right)}{1 + R_{t+1}}. \tag{17.36}$$

Using the Cobb–Douglas nature of the production function, it is true that output equals the income payments to factors:

$$y_t = A_G l_t^\gamma k_t^{1-\gamma} = w_t l_t + r_t k_t.$$

Substituting this in for $A_G l_t^\gamma k_t^{1-\gamma}$,

$$p^S\left(k_t\right) = w_t l_t + r_t k_t - w_t l_t - k_{t+1} + k_t\left(1 - \delta_k\right) + \frac{p^S\left(k_{t+1}\right)}{1 + R_{t+1}}, \tag{17.37}$$

$$p^S\left(k_t\right) = k_t\left(1 + r_t - \delta_k\right) - k_{t+1} + \frac{p^S\left(k_{t+1}\right)}{1 + R_{t+1}}. \tag{17.38}$$

Now consider that the price at time $t + 1$ is similarly given by

$$p^S\left(k_{t+1}\right) = k_{t+1}\left(1 + r_{t+1} - \delta_k\right) - k_{t+2} + \frac{p^S\left(k_{t+2}\right)}{1 + R_{t+2}}.$$

Substituting this into equation (17.38),

$$p^S\left(k_t\right) = k_t\left(1 + r_t - \delta_k\right) - k_{t+1}$$

$$+ \frac{k_{t+1}\left(1 + r_{t+1} - \delta_k\right) - k_{t+2} + \frac{p^S(k_{t+2})}{1 + R_{t+2}}}{1 + R_{t+1}}.$$

Now we can use equation (17.21) that shows that the bond return R_t equals the net capital marginal product $r_t - \delta_k$ to simplify the expression by cancelling out the terms involving k_{t+1}:

$$p^S\left(k_t\right) = k_t\left(1 + r_t - \delta_k\right) - k_{t+1}$$

$$+ \frac{k_{t+1}\left(1 + r_{t+1} - \delta_k\right) - k_{t+2} + \frac{p^S(k_{t+2})}{1 + R_{t+2}}}{1 + R_{t+1}},$$

$$= k_t\left(1 + r_t - \delta_k\right) - k_{t+1} + k_{t+1} - \frac{k_{t+2}}{1 + R_{t+1}} + \frac{p^S\left(k_{t+2}\right)}{\left(1 + R_{t+1}\right)\left(1 + R_{t+2}\right)}$$

$$= k_t\left(1 + r_t - \delta_k\right) - \frac{k_{t+2}}{1 + R_{t+1}} + \frac{p^S\left(k_{t+2}\right)}{\left(1 + R_{t+1}\right)\left(1 + R_{t+2}\right)}.$$

Continuing to substitute in for the one-period ahead price, all of the capital stocks drop out except in the first term. And there is a last term involving the price as t goes to infinity, so that the asset price reduces to

$$p^S\left(k_t\right) = k_t\left(1 + r_t - \delta_k\right) + \lim_{j \to \infty} \frac{p^S\left(k_j\right)}{\left(1 + R_{t+1}\right)\left(1 + R_{t+2}\right) \cdots \left(1 + R_{t+j}\right)}. \tag{17.39}$$

17.3.4 Limiting discounted price: transversality

The idea that the discounted value of the price, as t goes to infinity, must be zero is called the transversality condition. Here it is assumed that

$$\lim_{j \to \infty} \frac{p^S\left(k_j\right)}{\left(1 + R_{t+1}\right)\left(1 + R_{t+2}\right) \cdots \left(1 + R_{t+j}\right)} = 0. \tag{17.40}$$

This implies that the price does not have a 'bubble' whereby it can rise forever above its fundamental value, which is the discounted stream of dividends. Often this transversality condition is implicitly being assumed not to hold when bubbles are said to exist, or it is assumed that there are other permanent divergences from the fundamental capital income flow that is residual from the output of the firm after paying labour cost.

17.3.5 Example 17.2: Stock price and capital

In equation (17.39), and assuming that the transversality condition holds, then the price is simply equal to the value of the capital stock plus the current period net marginal product of capital:

$$p^S\left(k_t\right) = k_t\left(1 + r_t - \delta_k\right). \tag{17.41}$$

The equity price under certainty is just the value of capital owned by the firm plus the rental rate on the current period use of the capital. Note that if the timing is such that the end-of-period dividend is not yet built into the stock price, then the price reduces to just the capital stock k_t.

With zero exogenous growth assumed, and using the intertemporal consumption margin, this price reduces to

$$p^S(k_t) = k_t\left(1 + r_t - \delta_k\right) = k_t\left(1 + g\right)\left(1 + \rho\right); \qquad (17.42)$$
$$= k_t\left(1 + \rho\right). \qquad (17.43)$$

In Chapter 16, the drop in the value of the capital stock k_t due to a drop in bank productivity (A_F) was compared to the value of the stock market. This is the sense in which this is indeed true. In this model the capital stock (plus current period rents) is the value of the equity price, and a drop in k_t implies directly on an aggregate level a corresponding drop in the value of the stock market.

17.4 Under uncertainty

Suppose now that there is a shock to the productivity factor A_G, which in turn acts as a shock to the stock dividend d_t^S. This adds in uncertainty and so the consumer problem is now with respect to the expected utility. The consumer still works for the goods producer and earns certain wages, but now invests in risky equity ownership of the firm and in bonds. Therefore the representative agent problem is now extended to be

$$V(b_t, s_t) = \underset{l_t, b_{t+1}, s_{t+1}}{\text{Max}} \qquad (17.44)$$

$$E_t\left[u\left(w_t l_t - b_{t+1} + b_t\left(1 + R_t\right) - p_t^S s_{t+1} + \left(p_t^S + d_t^S\right) s_t, 1 - l_t\right)\right.$$
$$\left. + \beta V\left(b_{t+1}, s_{t+1}\right)\right].$$

The first-order conditions are as before for l_t, being that the marginal rate of substitution between goods and leisure is the real wage:

$$w_t = \frac{\frac{\partial u(c_t, x_t)}{\partial x_t}}{\frac{\partial u(c_t, x_t)}{\partial c_t}}. \qquad (17.45)$$

For b_{t+1} and s_{t+1}, expectations are necessary. Since $t+1$ is one period ahead of current period t, then the expected value at time t is used to write down the equilibrium conditions. This is needed only if the variables are at $t+1$. Variables at time t can have the expectation E_t dropped since we know the values at time t. So for b_{t+1} the derivative gives that

$$\frac{\partial u(c_t, x_t)}{\partial c_t} = \beta E_t\left[\frac{\partial V\left(b_{t+1}, s_{t+1}\right)}{\partial b_{t+1}}\right]; \qquad (17.46)$$

and for s_{t+1} the derivative implies

$$p_t^S \frac{\partial u(c_t, x_t)}{\partial c_t} = \beta E_t\left[\frac{\partial V\left(b_{t+1}, s_{t+1}\right)}{\partial s_{t+1}}\right]. \qquad (17.47)$$

For the envelope conditions, for b_t and s_t, these are

$$\frac{\partial V(b_t, s_t)}{\partial b_t} = \frac{\partial u(c_t, x_t)}{\partial c_t}\left(1 + R_t\right), \qquad (17.48)$$

and

$$\frac{\partial V(b_t, s_t)}{\partial s_t} = \frac{\partial u(c_t, x_t)}{\partial c_t}\left(p_t^S + d_t^S\right). \qquad (17.49)$$

Combining the first-order and envelope conditions, the classic pricing of equity and bonds is derived in this extended baseline dynamic model. Here the stock price condition, from equations (17.47) and (17.49), is expressed with $\frac{\partial u(c_t, x_t)}{\partial c_t}$ placed on the right-hand side so that it is under the expectations E_t, but could be factored out if desired. This equation (17.50) says that the price of equity p_t^S is the expected value of the next period price p_{t+1}^S plus the next period dividend d_{t+1}^S, as discounted back to the current period by the expected intertemporal marginal rate of substitution. $\dfrac{\beta \frac{\partial u\left(c_{t+1}, x_{t+1}\right)}{\partial c_{t+1}}}{\frac{\partial u(c_t, x_t)}{\partial c_t}}$:

$$p_t^S = E_t \left[\frac{\beta \frac{\partial u(c_{t+1}, x_{t+1})}{\partial c_{t+1}}}{\frac{\partial u(c_t, x_t)}{\partial c_t}} \left(p_{t+1}^S + d_{t+1}^S \right) \right]. \tag{17.50}$$

At the same time the equilibrium conditions for the bond imply that the expected intertemporal marginal rate of substitution is just the discount rate of 1 divided by the gross nominal interest rate $(1 + R_{t+1})$:

$$\frac{1}{1 + R_{t+1}} = E_t \left[\frac{\beta \frac{\partial u(c_{t+1}, x_{t+1})}{\partial c_{t+1}}}{\frac{\partial u(c_t, x_t)}{\partial c_t}} \right]. \tag{17.51}$$

Even though the nominal interest rate for the next period is taken to be in general unknown at present, here we are able to say that in equilibrium this interest rate for next period is in fact known today as the expected value in equation (17.51). Because the bond interest rate R_{t+1} is known, it is said to be a risk-free rate of interest.

17.4.1 Example 17.3: Asset pricing

The equity return is not risk-free. Another way to see this is to substitute in for the intertemporal marginal rate of substitution using the bond equation, to yield that

$$p_t^S = E_t \left[\frac{1}{1 + R_{t+1}} \left(p_{t+1}^S + d_{t+1}^S \right) \right]. \tag{17.52}$$

This is the basic asset pricing equation for equity (Lucas, 1978). It entails risk in that it equals the expectation of two terms that in general can have covariance.

To write the asset pricing equation in general terms, for some X_t and Y_t, the expectation of the product is the product of the two individual expected terms plus the covariance of the two:

$$E_t[X_t Y_t] = E_t[X_t] E_t[Y_t] + Cov_t[X_t Y_t]. \tag{17.53}$$

Then let

$$X_t \equiv \frac{\beta \frac{\partial u(c_{t+1}, x_{t+1})}{\partial c_{t+1}}}{\frac{\partial u(c_t, x_t)}{\partial c_t}}, \tag{17.54}$$

$$Y_t \equiv p_{t+1}^S + d_{t+1}^S. \tag{17.55}$$

This implies that

$$p_t^S = E_t[X_t Y_t]. \tag{17.56}$$

17.4.2 Example 17.4: Expectations hypothesis

And now suppose first that the covariance $Cov_t[X_tY_t] = 0$. This is a special case called the expectations hypothesis of asset pricing. It implies here that

$$p_t^S = E_t\left[\frac{1}{1+R_{t+1}}\right] E_t\left[p_{t+1}^S + d_{t+1}^S\right]. \tag{17.57}$$

Since R_{t+1} is known at time t, this can be written as

$$p_t^S = \frac{E_t\left[p_{t+1}^S + d_{t+1}^S\right]}{1+R_{t+1}}. \tag{17.58}$$

This simplification gives an intuitive way to view the asset pricing condition. It emerges more clearly as the expected discounted value of the next period price and dividend.

17.4.3 Prices and dividend streams

The asset pricing condition can be expressed also as discounted value of the infinite stream of dividends. To see this requires expanding out the asset pricing equation by substituting in for p_{t+1}^S using equation (17.58) put forward by one period of time to $t+1$:

$$p_{t+1}^S = \frac{E_{t+1}\left(p_{t+2}^S + d_{t+2}^S\right)}{1+R_{t+2}}.$$

Substitute this in for p_{t+1}^S in equation (17.58), and then substitute sequentially in for p_{t+2}^S, $p_{t+3}^S, \ldots$, to get

$$p_t^S = \frac{E_t\left[p_{t+1}^S + d_{t+1}^S\right]}{1+R_{t+1}}$$

$$= \frac{E_t\left[d_{t+1}^S + E_{t+1}\left[\frac{\left(p_{t+2}^S + d_{t+2}^S\right)}{1+R_{t+2}}\right]\right]}{1+R_{t+1}}$$

$$= \frac{E_t\left[d_{t+1}^S\right]}{1+R_{t+1}} + E_t E_{t+1}\left[\frac{p_{t+2}^S + d_{t+2}^S}{\left(1+R_{t+1}\right)\left(1+R_{t+2}\right)}\right]$$

$$= \frac{E_t\left[d_{t+1}^S\right]}{1+R_{t+1}} + E_t E_{t+1}\left[\frac{d_{t+2}^S}{\left(1+R_{t+1}\right)\left(1+R_{t+2}\right)}\right] \tag{17.59}$$

$$+ E_t E_{t+1}\left[\frac{\frac{E_{t+2}\left(p_{t+3}^S + d_{t+3}^S\right)}{1+R_{t+3}}}{\left(1+R_{t+1}\right)\left(1+R_{t+2}\right)}\right] + \cdots \tag{17.60}$$

$$p_t^S = \sum_{j=1}^{\infty} E_t\left[\frac{d_{t+j}^S}{\prod_{i=0}^{j}\left(1+R_{t+i}\right)}\right]. \tag{17.61}$$

And there is a boundary (transversality) condition that the very last discounted p_t^S, as t goes to infinity, is equal to zero. Another note here is that at time t, the expectation $E_t E_{t+1}$ simply equals E_t, and further that $E_t E_{t+1} E_{t+2} = E_t E_{t+1} E_{t+2} E_{t+3} = \cdots = E_t$.

This is because at time t, the best we can do is E_t. Finally $\prod_{i=0}^{j} (1 + R_{t+i})$ is just the product multiplier sequence, and can be understood better by looking at the case when the interest rate and dividend are constant over time.

17.4.4 Example 17.5: Constant dividend stream

Assume a constant dividend and interest rate over time. Then the price reduces simply to

$$p^S = \frac{d^S}{1+R} \left(1 + \frac{1}{1+R} + \frac{1}{(1+R)^2} + \frac{1}{(1+R)^3} + \cdots \right); \tag{17.62}$$

and this stream reduces to just $\frac{d^S}{R}$:

$$p^S = \frac{d^S}{1+R} \left(\frac{1}{1 - \frac{1}{1+R}} \right) = \frac{d^S}{R}. \tag{17.63}$$

When the economy expands because of an increase in the productivity factor A_{Gt}, then also the dividend stream of the aggregate economy shifts up. This can cause the average equity price for the whole market portfolio to increase. Market indices are such averages of the whole market portfolio of assets, and this is why these jump up when dividends are expected to rise.

Another way to view the equity return in this simple case is as the dividend rate d^S divided by the equity share price p^S, or

$$R = \frac{d^S}{p^S}.$$

Here the equity return of $\frac{d^S}{p^S}$ is just the bond return R. This is because there is no uncertainty when the dividend and the interest rate are constant over time. In general this is not the case seen in markets in which there are many sources of uncertainty.

Consider when there is uncertainty and the dividend stream is stochastically changing over time. There is a way to write the dividend stream in terms of the 'risk-adjusted' real interest rate for the risky equity capital dividend stream (Cochrane, 2001). Denoting this risk-adjusted return by R^S, and the risky dividend stream by $\hat{d}^S$, then with such uncertainty,

$$p^S = \frac{\hat{d}^S}{R^S}.$$

And the equity return R^S equals the average risky dividend divided by the equity price of the risky asset:

$$R^S = \frac{\hat{d}^S}{p^S}.$$

The risk-adjusted average equity return is higher than the risk-free bond rate, since the consumer requires some additional return in order to pay for an uncertain income stream. This difference in this return gives a simple way to think about the equity premium, in terms of the difference of $R^S - R$.

17.5 Asset prices and growth

The equity price is also affected by the balanced path growth rate. Let the production function for goods be such that the productivity factor A_{Gt} is a function of time and that it exogenously grows at a constant rate. This makes the model the exogenous growth model of Chapter 11.

17.5.1 Example 17.6: Exogenous growth

The dividend stream can be written as output minus wages and investment in physical capital:

$$d_t^S = A_{Gt} l_t^\gamma k_t^{1-\gamma} - w_t l_t - i_t. \tag{17.64}$$

Along the balanced growth path equilibrium, the output y_t, investment in capital stock i_t, and wage rate w_t all grow at the balanced growth path rate of g.

Consider how the dividend rate changes as a result over time. At time $t+1$ the dividend stream is

$$d_{t+1}^S = y_{t+1} - w_{t+1} l_{t+1} - i_{t+1}. \tag{17.65}$$

Along the balanced growth path, the ratio of dividends over time is $1 + g$:

$$\frac{d_{t+1}^S}{d_t^S} = \frac{y_{t+1} - w_{t+1} l_{t+1} - i_{t+1}}{y_t - w_t l_t - i_t} = \frac{y_t (1+g) - w_t (1+g) l_t - i_t (1+g)}{y_t - w_t l_t - i_t}$$
$$= 1 + g.$$

Now return to the determination of the equity price with no uncertainty and along the balanced growth path. The interest rate is constant along the balanced growth path but the dividends are rising over time.

As a modification to equation (17.62), the price at time t is given by the dividend at time t:

$$p_t^S = \frac{d_t^S}{1+R} + \frac{d_t^S (1+g)}{(1+R)^2} + \frac{d_t^S (1+g)(1+g)}{(1+R)^3} + \cdots;$$

$$p_t^S = \frac{d_t^S}{1+R} \left(1 + \frac{(1+g)}{(1+R)} + \frac{(1+g)^2}{(1+R)^2} + \cdots \right);$$

$$p_t^S = \frac{d_t^S}{1+R} \left(\frac{1}{1 - \frac{(1+g)}{(1+R)}} \right) = \frac{d_t^S}{1+R} \left(\frac{1+R}{(1+R) - (1+g)} \right);$$

$$p_t^S = \frac{d_t^S}{R - g}. \tag{17.66}$$

The price of equity is higher when the growth rate of the dividend stream is higher. This occurs when the economy has a higher balanced path growth rate. It predicts that when the economy is experiencing a surge in long term growth, then so also will the stock market, such as in the US in the 1990s.

17.5.2 Endogenous growth

When the asset pricing model is specified with endogenous growth, rather than exogenous growth, the dividend stream of the goods producer is almost the same, now becoming

$$d_t^S = A_G (l_t h_t)^\gamma k_t^{1-\gamma} - w_t l_t h_t - i_t. \tag{17.67}$$

The dividend still grows at the rate g along the balanced growth path equilibrium, and the asset pricing equation is again as in equations (17.66) and (17.41).

The asset pricing equation is the same. However endogenous growth shows how factors that affect the balanced path growth rate g also affect the value of equity in markets. Also the existence of human capital as well as physical capital can affect the calibration of the equity premium as some have shown.

Consider the comparative static experiments of Chapter 13, which examined the effects of changes in the productivity of the goods sector and the human capital sector, A_G and A_H. Changing the goods productivity A_G would appear to directly affect the dividend since it can be written as $d_t^S = A_G l_t^\gamma k_t^{1-\gamma} - w_t l_t - i_t$. And along the balanced growth path, with no uncertainty and h_t normalised to 1, the equity price reduces as in equation (17.41) to $p^S(k_t) = k_t (1 + r_t - \delta_k)$. An increase in A_G does not affect the growth rate g, or the interest rate r_t, but it does increase the capital stock k_t and so the equity price.

An increase in human capital productivity, A_H, causes the growth rate to increase and the price of equity under the assumption of no uncertainty to increase as g increases. But also k_t falls and r_t rises. So the effects on asset prices are ambiguous and depend on the calibration of the model.

In Example 12.1, the equilibrium balanced path interest rate is $r_t = 0.1237$ and $k_t = 1$. When A_G rises by 5% in Example 13.1, the capital stock increases to $\frac{k_t}{h_t} = 1.1578$ while the interest rate is unchanged. With $h_t = 1$ by assumption, the equity price rises by 15.78% since $p^S(k_t) = k_t (1 + r_t - \delta_k)$ and k_t rises by this amount. However in general h_t can fall as k_t rises so that $\frac{k_t}{h_t} = 1.1578$ and the rise in equity prices may not be as high.

In Example 13.2, A_H increases by 5%, the growth rate rises from $g = 0.02$ to $g = 0.0333$, the interest rate rises to $r_t = 0.1377$ from 0.1237 and $\frac{k_t}{h_t}$ falls to $\frac{k_t}{h_t} = 0.694$ from $\frac{k_t}{h_t} = 1$. The no uncertainty asset price, with $h_t = 1$, changes from

$$p^S(k) = k(1 + r - \delta_k)$$
$$= 1.0(1 + 0.1237 - 0.05)$$
$$= 1.0737,$$

to the value

$$p^S(k) = k(1 + r - \delta_k)$$
$$= 0.694(1 + 0.1377 - 0.05)$$
$$= 0.75486.$$

This is because the consumer invests more in human capital and less in physical capital, only physical capital is reflected in this model of the equity price, and h_t is restricted to stay at 1 while in general it will rise as $\frac{k_t}{h_t}$ falls. Thus $p^S(k) = 0.75486$ is a lower limit on $p^S(k)$.

The asset price focuses on k_t rather than $\frac{k_t}{h_t}$ and the endogenous growth model gives the solution to $\frac{k_t}{h_t}$. This is fine when the normalisation $h_t = 1$ is made and there are no changes in parameters. When A_G or A_H changes, then $\frac{k_t}{h_t}$ changes, and h_t in general will not stay at 1. If $\frac{k_t}{h_t}$ rises, then typically k_t will rise and h_t will fall. Therefore the equity price as given by $k(1 + r - \delta_k)$ may rise if k does not fall by much while r rises when A_H increases.

Another way to see the effect of the comparative static changes is in terms of the consumer wealth. Consider that in Chapter 12, the consumer wealth is defined in equation (12.24) as

$$W_t = \frac{w_t h_t T_t}{\rho(1 + g)} + k_t. \tag{17.68}$$

Knowing that a 5% increase in A_H causes $\frac{k_t}{h_t}$ to fall to 0.694 from 1, it can be that h_t rises significantly while k_t falls slightly. Then overall wealth W_t will increase when A_H increases. The consumer wealth with human capital plays a role in resolving the equity premium puzzle that is much discussed in modern macroeconomics.

17.6 Deriving the equity premium

The equity premium is based on the amount of covariance between the average equity price for the market portfolio and the intertemporal marginal rate of substitution. While above this covariance is assumed to be zero, as a special case, to derive the equity premium requires focusing on this covariance when it is not zero. Consider the basic Lucas (1978) asset pricing equation again:

$$p_t^S = E_t\left[\beta\frac{\frac{\partial u(c_{t+1},x_{t+1})}{\partial c_{t+1}}}{\frac{\partial u(c_t,x_t)}{\partial c_t}}\left(p_{t+1}^S + d_{t+1}^S\right)\right]. \tag{17.69}$$

This is called the 'consumption-based capital asset pricing model', or CCAPM, as opposed to the capital asset pricing model CAPM of finance theory. The difference is that the Lucas CCAPM equation is derived from the general equilibrium representative agent problem, and so it involves consumption.

Now present this equation in terms of its expected value and its covariance terms, following equation (17.53):

$$p_t^S = E_t\left[\beta\frac{\frac{\partial u(c_{t+1},x_{t+1})}{\partial c_{t+1}}}{\frac{\partial u(c_t,x_t)}{\partial c_t}}\right]E_t\left[p_{t+1}^S + d_{t+1}^S\right] + Cov_t\left[\left(\beta\frac{\frac{\partial u(c_{t+1},x_{t+1})}{\partial c_{t+1}}}{\frac{\partial u(c_t,x_t)}{\partial c_t}}\right)\left(p_{t+1}^S + d_{t+1}^S\right)\right]. \tag{17.70}$$

This can be rearranged by dividing through by p_t^S:

$$1 = \frac{1}{\left(1+R_{t+1}\right)}\frac{E_t\left[p_{t+1}^S + d_{t+1}^S\right]}{p_t^S} + Cov_t\left[\left(\beta\frac{\frac{\partial u(c_{t+1},x_{t+1})}{\partial c_{t+1}}}{\frac{\partial u(c_t,x_t)}{\partial c_t}}\right)\left(\frac{p_{t+1}^S + d_{t+1}^S}{p_t^S}\right)\right]. \tag{17.71}$$

And multiplying though by $\left(1+R_{t+1}\right)$,

$$\left(1+R_{t+1}\right) = \frac{E_t\left[p_{t+1}^S + d_{t+1}^S\right]}{p_t^S} + \left(1+R_{t+1}\right)Cov_t\left[\left(\beta\frac{\frac{\partial u(c_{t+1},x_{t+1})}{\partial c_{t+1}}}{\frac{\partial u(c_t,x_t)}{\partial c_t}}\right)\left(\frac{p_{t+1}^S + d_{t+1}^S}{p_t^S}\right)\right]. \tag{17.72}$$

Now subtract $\frac{E_t\left[p_{t+1}^S + d_{t+1}^S\right]}{p_t^S}$ and multiply by a (-1) to get that

$$\frac{E_t\left[p_{t+1}^S + d_{t+1}^S\right]}{p_t^S} - \left(1+R_{t+1}\right) \tag{17.73}$$

$$= -\left(1+R_{t+1}\right)Cov_t\left[\left(\beta\frac{\frac{\partial u(c_{t+1},x_{t+1})}{\partial c_{t+1}}}{\frac{\partial u(c_t,x_t)}{\partial c_t}}\right),\left(\frac{p_{t+1}^S + d_{t+1}^S}{p_t^S}\right)\right].$$

This is close to the equity premium. To see this more clearly, consider that the return to the stock price is the sum of the capital gain on the price and the dividend. Therefore define the gross equity return as

$$1 + E_t\left[R^S_{t+1}\right] \equiv E_t\left(\frac{p^S_{t+1} + d^S_{t+1}}{p^S_t}\right), \tag{17.74}$$

and rewrite the pricing equation as

$$E_t\left[R^S_{t+1}\right] - R_{t+1} = -\left(1 + R_{t+1}\right) Cov_t\left[\beta\frac{\frac{\partial u(c_{t+1},x_{t+1})}{\partial c_{t+1}}}{\frac{\partial u(c_t,x_t)}{\partial c_t}}, 1 + R^S_{t+1}\right]. \tag{17.75}$$

With log utility, the intertemporal marginal utility ratio reduces to the growth rate of consumption, and the asset pricing equation in which $\beta = \frac{1}{1+\rho}$ becomes

$$E_t\left[R^S_{t+1}\right] - R_{t+1} = -\left(1 + R_{t+1}\right)\beta Cov_t\left[\frac{c_t}{c_{t+1}}, 1 + R^S_{t+1}\right]. \tag{17.76}$$

$$E_t\left[R^S_{t+1}\right] - R_{t+1} = -\left(\frac{1 + R_{t+1}}{1 + \rho}\right) Cov_t\left[\frac{c_t}{c_{t+1}}, 1 + R^S_{t+1}\right]. \tag{17.77}$$

The covariance of $\frac{c_t}{c_{t+1}}$ and R^S_{t+1} is empirically found to be negative because when consumption is rising, $\frac{c_t}{c_{t+1}}$ is falling, and usually the return on the stock market is rising.

Finally consider that the calibration under uncertainty typically has the government bond interest rate R_t close in value to the rate of time preference ρ. Therefore with the simplifying assumption that $R_{t+1} = \rho$, the pricing equation reduces to a simple statement of how the equity premium, $E_t\left[R^S_{t+1}\right] - R_{t+1}$, depends upon the covariance between consumption growth and the equity return itself:

$$E_t\left[R^S_{t+1}\right] - R_{t+1} = -Cov_t\left[\frac{c_t}{c_{t+1}}, 1 + R^S_{t+1}\right]. \tag{17.78}$$

17.6.1 Example 17.7: Empirical failing of exogenous growth

One way to state the basic failing of the exogenous growth baseline model to explain evidence is in terms of the failure to explain labour movements. Another basic failing is that the covariance term $-Cov_t\left[\frac{c_t}{c_{t+1}}, 1 + R^S_{t+1}\right]$ is empirically computed, or calibrated, as being much too small to explain the actual empirical magnitude of the equity premium. In other words, the equity premium of equation (17.78) is not big enough compared to the data.

To compute the covariance, consider the statistical fact that the highest the covariance can be is the product of the variance of the two elements:

$$Cov_t\left[\frac{c_t}{c_{t+1}}, 1 + R^S_{t+1}\right] \leq Var_t\left(\frac{c_t}{c_{t+1}}\right) Var_t\left(1 + R^S_{t+1}\right). \tag{17.79}$$

Then consider some data. For example, for 90 years of US data, from 1889 to 1978, the equity premium is empirically about 6% on average per year. And the corresponding variance of consumption is 0.036, and the variance of the excess equity return is 0.167, for a product of $(0.036)(0.167) = 0.0060$. This product is off by a factor of 10, compared to 0.06 for the equity premium, even using the upper limit on the covariance as the product of the variances. Further the discount rate ρ is typically calibrated to be greater than R_t, so by assuming they are equal in equation (17.78) again overstates the ability of the model to explain the data, and still the model calibration is too small by a factor of 10. Therefore the model fails to explain the equity premium data.

17.6.2 Equity premium and human capital

One way in which the baseline dynamic model has been extended so as to account empirically for the equity premium is by introducing human capital accumulation as in Chapters 12, 13, and 14. For example this is the approach of Zhang (2006) who defines the consumer wealth as the weighted sum of human capital and non-human capital. Zhang's estimate of the share of equity in total such consumer wealth is only around 6%, which ends up being key to Zhang's ability to show that the asset pricing equity premium magnitude is consistent with data.

The idea that consumers use both human capital and physical capital in a diversified portfolio is explained nicely from one perspective by Jagannathan and Kocherlakota (1996). They argue that the workers, when young and earning wage income, own more equity stocks than bonds. This is because the wage income is a return on human capital that is of low volatility and not very risky, while the added holding of equities allows the worker to diversify and hold some more risk in the total wealth portfolio. Bonds are not needed when young because their return is a safe return comparable to the wage income on human capital.

When workers are old, wage income is no longer flowing because of retirement, inducing a substitution in the portfolio towards bonds and away from stocks in order to make up for the lost low risk human capital income. This shift to bonds from stocks allows a rebalancing of the overall risk of the wealth portfolio to make it similar to when wage income was being earned on human capital.

In our endogenous growth model with human capital, consumption demand is a fraction of permanent income, in particular, along the balanced path equilibrium,

$$c_t = \frac{1}{1+\alpha}\left[w_t h_t \left(1 - \frac{g+\delta_H}{A_H}\right) + k_t \rho \left(1+g\right)\right].$$

Permanent income, denoted by y_P, is defined as

$$y_{Pt} = w_t h_t \left(1 - \frac{g+\delta_H}{A_H}\right) + k_t \rho \left(1+g\right);$$

and consumption is a fraction of permanent income:

$$c_t = \left(\frac{1}{1+\alpha}\right) y_{Pt}.$$

Permanent income depends on the human capital income $w_t h_t \left(1 - \frac{g+\delta_H}{A_H}\right)$ and the physical capital flow $k_t \rho \left(1+g\right)$. And the permanent income can be written as a weighted average of h_t and k_t given the wage rate w_t and the parameter calibration of the model. The wealth portfolio of the consumer is therefore a combination of human and physical capital, and note that within physical capital both equity stocks and also non-financial capital such as housing (or durable goods) is included. Permanent income can be viewed as the interest return on wealth.

The question is what is the interest return on the wealth of the consumer that is a combination of both human and physical capital. For example let this wealth return be denoted by R_t^W, and let wealth be denoted by W_t. Then

$$W_t = \frac{y_{Pt}}{R_t^W} = \frac{w_t h_t \left(1 - \frac{g+\delta_H}{A_H}\right) + k_t \rho \left(1+g\right)}{R_t^W}.$$

The interest flow on wealth is then

$$R_t^W W_t = y_{Pt} = w_t h_t \left(1 - \frac{g+\delta_H}{A_H}\right) + k_t \rho \left(1+g\right).$$

In addition, consider that if R_t^W is the interest flow, then wealth next period at time $t+1$ can be given by the gross interest return minus whatever is consumed, or

$$W_{t+1} = \left(1 + R_t^W\right) W_t - c_t. \tag{17.80}$$

And since consumption is a fraction of permanent income, in terms of wealth it is given by

$$c_t = \left(\frac{1}{1+\alpha}\right) y_{Pt} = \left(\frac{1}{1+\alpha}\right) R_t^W W_t.$$

Using this expression to derive wealth net of consumption,

$$W_t - c_t = W_t - \left(\frac{1}{1+\alpha}\right) R_t^W W_t. \tag{17.81}$$

And finally equations (17.80) and (17.81) imply that the ratio of next period wealth to wealth net of consumption is

$$
\begin{aligned}
\frac{W_{t+1}}{W_t - c_t} &= \frac{\left(1 + R_t^W\right) W_t - c_t}{\left[1 - \left(\frac{1}{1+\alpha}\right) R_t^W\right] W_t} = \frac{W_t\left[\left(1 + R_t^W\right) - \left(\frac{1}{1+\alpha}\right) R_t^W\right]}{W_t\left[1 - \left(\frac{1}{1+\alpha}\right) R_t^W\right]} \\
&= \frac{\left(1 + \alpha\right)\left(1 + R_t^W\left(1 - \frac{1}{1+\alpha}\right)\right)}{1 + \alpha - R_t^W} \\
&= \frac{1 + \alpha + \alpha R_t^W}{1 + \alpha - R_t^W} \equiv R_t^m.
\end{aligned}
$$

Zhang calls this wealth ratio R_t^m, the market return on consumer wealth that is really entering the equity premium equation. And he estimates this R_t^m based on its decomposition into human and non-human capital. He finds this allows for consistency of the equity premium equation with evidence.

Deterministically, with no uncertainty, $R_t^W = R_t - g = \rho\left(1+g\right)$, and with $T_t = 1 - \frac{g+\delta_H}{A_H}$, then as in Chapter 12, equation (12.24), the wealth is $W_t = \frac{w_t h_t T_t}{\rho(1+g)} + k_t$, equal to the capitalised value of human capital plus physical capital. However under uncertainty, the discount factor R_t^W would represent a stochastic return. Second, the human capital in general is not fully capitalised.

Zhang gets his results while assuming a somewhat more general utility function that is common in finance theory. He then finds that the covariance of equity premium depends upon the covariance of consumption growth with the equity return, plus it also depends on the covariance of the consumer wealth return R_t^m with the equity return. Zhang finds that the latter covariance involving R_t^m is large and dominates the former covariance involving $\frac{c_t}{c_{t+1}}$. With this larger covariance coming from the covariance involving R_t^m, the equity premium is well explained.

Including human capital resolves the puzzle because the return on stock market equity is only one part of the return R_t^W. With equity having only a 6% share of consumer wealth, this equity return has a small weight in the total consumer return on their wealth. Human capital has the dominant share of consumer wealth. Zhang (2006) emphasises that a key to resolving the equity premium puzzle is that the return on the consumer wealth portfolio is not the same as the average return on the equity stock market. The return on human capital has different features than the return on equity. One aspect of Zhang's analysis is that the human capital return is much less volatile, which is also the basis of Jagannathan and Kocherlakota's (1996) explanation of why people switch from stocks to bonds when older.

The asset pricing equation would hold without the human capital modification of Zhang if all of the consumer's wealth was perfectly traded in asset markets. This means the human capital would need to be perfectly tradeable in equity markets. Then the return on equity markets would reflect all consumer wealth. But since human capital is only imperfectly traded in markets, through labour contracts and insurance prices, the equity premium equation appears to fail. Adjusting for the imperfect trading in human capital, Zhang finds that a comparably adjusted asset pricing equation is consistent with data on the magnitude of the equity premium.

17.7 Application: historical price–earnings ratios

Figure 17.1 shows the historical price–earnings ratio for the US Standard and Poors 500 firm index, in blue, compared to the (nominal) long term US government bond rate, in black, supplied by Professor Robert Shiller's website. One way to view the changes over the historical period is in terms of war, as well as business cycles and tax rates.

The unusual acceleration and high peak of the price–earnings ratio in the 1920s and again starting in the 1990s has one type of major event in common: war. Both were preceded by an international war that ended with peaceful prospects. And both were followed by new large-scale international wars.

The end of WWI brought about the expansion of US capital markets abroad and for US companies the prospect of higher earnings. However this future earning prospect was largely unknown in terms of what would actually be delivered through expanding markets. The bust of stock prices in 1929 could have reflected that the increase in earnings from the end of the war and international expansion of US companies was not coming to fruition as had been expected. At the same time, Germany had never been integrated into international capital markets as the WWI peace treaty demanded reparations from Germany. And this laid the foundation for the demise of the European economy that was so crucial in US post-WWI expansion expectations. As Germany's economy collapsed in the early 1930s, so did the US and much of the Western world economy.

After WWII, expectations for broad international economic expansion were dampened by the immediately ensuing Cold War between the US and Western Europe on one side

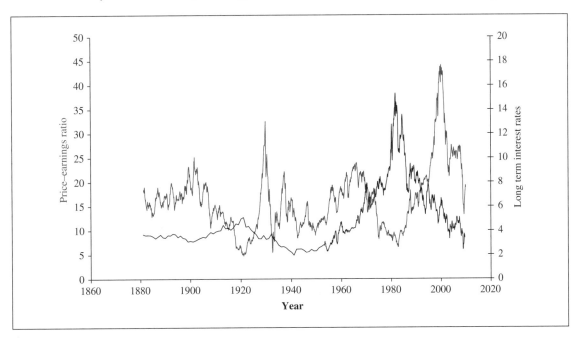

Figure 17.1 US historical price–earnings ratios (blue) and long term interest rates (black)

Source: Professor Robert Shiller, http://www.econ.yale.edu/~shiller/ Reproduced with permission

and the Soviet Union and China on the other. The Soviet Union controlled most of Eastern Europe by 1948, while the US engaged with China in the Korean War of 1950–52. Therefore the possible outbreak of higher dividends and asset prices in the US after WWII was stymied by the looming outbreak of conflict with Eastern Europe and continental Asia, with only certain 'Pacific Rim' Asian countries being newly engaged in international capital markets.

The post-WWII expansion of markets in a sense was fully delayed until post-1989, when the Cold War began its end. The huge upturn in US asset markets in the 1990s came as the Cold War dissolved in a complete fashion. Most new Eastern European countries went through financial crises of having no revenue sources and major business cycle downturns in the early 1990s, not stabilising until well after 1993. And US equity markets began accelerating upwards in the mid to late 1990s. This made sense in that huge new markets were open to the well-established US companies that could then expand internationally. For example, the information technology industry was one of the primary US industries to take advantage of such expansion.

The crash of equity markets after 2000 came about as it appeared that the incoming and likely future dividend streams could not justify such expansive valuations of equity prices. And the subsequent onset of war in central and mid-East Asia caused the possible size of new markets again to diminish. Just as the banks collapsed for several years after 1929, the banks collapsed again for years following 2007. And while all of the individual factors typically pointed to in these episodes may certainly be valid, overarching the details of the collapses are the long term episodic similarities. These similarities were the post-war prospects of new international markets and higher earnings streams, which ended up overly enthusiastic as surprising new international conflict began once again and the world's capital wealth devalued.

Besides such long term trends, cycles in the price–earnings ratio would be expected to be correlated with the business cycle. The ratio would tend to be higher during economic expansions and lower in contractions. The economy expects higher future dividends in the expansion, builds this into the market portfolio price, and so stock prices rise above the average dividend rate while the expansion is starting off. The dividends lag behind the equity price but then begin rising. Then the price–earnings ratio falls and as an economic downturn ensues, the dividend stream is expected to shift back down. This gets built into a lower price of equity: and the price–earnings ratio falls.

One particular downturn for the US in 1980 is correlated with very high interest rates. These are nominal interest rates reflecting high inflation. Inflation factors are outside the scope of this chapter but are taken up in the next, Part 7, of the text, in Chapter 20 in which inflation is shown to reduce the growth rate within endogenous growth. The drop in the price–earnings ratio during the 1970s could be caused in part by the lower dividends earned as high inflation reduces growth. This is due more to the 'inflation tax', perhaps, than to business cycle effects. So the reduction in corporate and personal income taxes, along with the inflation tax, in the 1980s, could also help explain the corresponding rise in the price–earnings ratio.

17.8 Questions

1. In Example 17.1, it is said that if the bond price, instead of being R_t in the expression for bond investment, $b_{t+1} - b_t \left(1 + R_t\right)$, were instead given as $\hat{q}_{t+1}$, with the investment in bonds being alternatively $\hat{q}_{t+1} b_{t+1} - b_t$, the equation (17.22) that relates $\hat{q}_t$ to R_t would result.

   (a) Prove that this equation (17.22) does result, with $\hat{q}_t = \frac{1}{1+R_t}$,

   (b) and explain how to interpret the alternative $\hat{q}$ price in terms of bonds that pay no interest, known as zero-coupon bonds.

2. Why must both the return on bonds and the return on shares in firms both equal the marginal product of capital under full certainty?

3. Consider the so-called transversality condition of equation (17.40).

   (a) Using this condition, explain how 'stock price bubbles' could happen for a period of time in an economy.

   (b) Explain whether such bubbles can exist indefinitely.

4. Example 17.2 explains that the share price of the firm equals the capital stock of the firm, multiplied by a factor slightly more than 1 (the gross interest rate), given that the transversality condition holds.

   (a) Use this concept to explain why stock prices can drop by large amounts during an economic recession.

   (b) Use this to explain how a banking crisis can affect stock prices such as during the Great Depression or more recently.

5. Consider the basic asset pricing condition of Example 17.3. Why is the current share price not equal simply to the discounted value of the next period's expected share price plus dividend?

6. Example 17.4 presents what is known as the expectations hypothesis of the share price. Explain this theory in terms of covariance.

7. Example 17.5 assumes a constant dividend stream and interest rate, to write the share price as the dividend divided by the interest rate, in equation (17.63).

   (a) Use this concept to derive the so-called 'price–earnings' ratio of a firm.

   (b) Explain how the share return relates to the price–earnings ratio,

   (c) and how the share return compares to the risk-free return on bonds.

8. The exogenous growth rate is allowed to be positive in Example 17.6.

   (a) How would positive growth affect the share price in equation (17.66) if the dividend did not increase when the growth rate increased?

   (b) Assuming in equation (17.66) that $R = 0.05$, $d^S = 5$, and $g = 0$, find the share price.

   (c) Now assume that with the same interest rate as (b), if the growth rate rises from $g = 0$ to $g = 0.03$, while the share price remains constant, how much does the dividend rate need to increase?

9. In Example 17.7, explain how the equity premium is calibrated numerically.

10. Explain whether equation (17.79) of Example 17.7 includes human capital in computing the equity premium.

11. How are historical trends in the price–earnings ratio explained?

12. How might business cycles affect price–earnings ratios?

17.9 References

Cochrane, John, 2001, *Asset Pricing*, Princeton University Press, Princeton.

Fama, Eugene F., 1970, 'Efficient Capital Markets: A Review of Theory and Empirical Work', *The Journal of Finance*, 25(2) (May): 383–417.

Jagannathan, Ravi and Narayana R. Kocherlakota, 1996, 'Why should Older People Invest less in Stock than Younger People?', *Quarterly Review*, Federal Reserve Bank of Minneapolis, Summer: 11–23.

Kocherlakota, Narayana R., 1996, 'The Equity Premium: It's Still a Puzzle', *Journal of Economic Literature*, American Economic Association, 34(1) (March): pp. 42–71.

Lucas, Robert E. Jr., 1978, 'Asset Prices in an Exchange Economy', *Econometrica*, 46(6) (November): 1429–1445.

Mehra, Rajnish and Edward C. Prescott, 1985, 'The Equity Premium: A Puzzle,' *Journal of Monetary Economics*, Elsevier, 15(2) (March): pp. 145–161.

Zhang, Qiang, 2006, 'Human Capital, Weak Identification, and Asset Pricing', *Journal of Money, Credit, and Banking*, 38(4): 873–899.

PART 7

FISCAL AND MONETARY POLICY

CHAPTER (18)

Public finance

18.1 Introduction

The chapter focuses on the government budget constraint. It starts with the initial period of the government operation, and builds up the budget constraints for government spending period by period. Taken to the limit, this gives the notion of the government wealth constraint. The wealth constraint includes a limiting condition on government borrowing that has import for certain policy discussion on how much a government can borrow.

The concept of Ricardian equivalence is introduced. It means that the government wealth constraint is binding and that a solvent government must repay its debt. The debt is equal to the discounted flow of revenue. The revenue is made up of explicit tax revenue and indirect inflation tax revenue. Each component of the debt and revenue stream is analysed independently to show how the components add up to give simple prescriptions that government borrowing is equal to discounted revenue, so that there is no net wealth residual.

Examples of the analysis are applied to discuss seigniorage, the revenue raised from printing money, in this case showing how it relates simply to the money to output ratio. The government debt to equity ratio is discussed with an example showing how the European Union's Maastricht Treaty link between deficits and debt makes sense mathematically. And optimal taxes are also presented in an example, with the implied deficit and debt totals presented, along with further applications being presented.

18.1.1 Building on the last chapters

The government budget constraint is introduced in the first tax example of the text in Chapter 3. Taxes and government budget constraints are found in Chapters 6 and 9 where there is further tax analysis. Borrowing by the government through bonds is introduced in the last chapter. With taxes previously introduced on goods, labour income and capital income, and bonds introduced in the last chapter, these give almost all of the main revenue sources used to finance government spending. Printing money is also added in this chapter.

The main difference from the previous chapter's treatment of the government budget constraint is that its implications over time are not fully developed. In this chapter, the budget constraints of each time period are summed up and discounted to give the wealth constraint that forms the basis of much discussion of government policy. While the government budget at any one time is not a particularly large question in policy, the sustainability of the budgets over time is pertinent. And this perspective over time is what the government wealth constraint allows.

The infinite stream of revenue and spending, and its discounting, is related to the valuation of stocks found in the last chapter. Such discounting is a key element of finance theory. Now this is applied to government finance rather than private finance.

18.1.2 Learning objective

The student is encouraged to get the main point of the wealth constraint by going through the adding up of the individual government time constraints at each period, as discounted with the interest rate. Understanding what is meant by Ricardian equivalence is the main goal. And seeing how this simple concept can be applied to a variety of financial elements, such as deficit and debt limits of the European Union, provides scope.

18.1.3 Who made it happen?

The idea that the borrowing and spending today must inevitably be paid off by taxes in the future is called 'Ricardian equivalence', after David Ricardo's treatise on *The Principles of Political Economy and Taxation*, with the last (3rd) edition of 1821. It is based on the economy's respect for the government intertemporal budget constraint: anything spent now must be paid for later by some source of government revenue, typically taxes.

One implication is that the consumer may not increase demand if given an income transfer today since this has to be paid off by future taxes that lower the consumer's permanent income by an amount equal, or even by more than, the transfer today. The uncertain impact of such policy also applies to temporary tax cuts, for which there have been numerous examples in actual economies such as the US. Non-Ricardian theories in contrast suggest that government spending can be financed by borrowing such that the 'multiplier' of government spending is large, and the net effect on the economy is positive.

Keynes (1936) prescribes increasing government spending as a way out of the 1930s Great Depression, and such policy was also proposed in the 2007–10 world recession. Keynes describes aggregate demand as being insufficient during such downturns due to an excess of savings over investment that was not being invested in the economy, a thesis he focused on in his 1930 *A Treatise on Money*. The idea that aggregate demand needs to be stimulated by the government is the most famous policy prescription that is typically associated with 'Keynesian' economics, and that can be derived in the *IS–LM* analysis that is found in traditional Keynesian macroeconomic textbooks, as Hansen (1953, 1960) discusses.

More recently, authors such as Barro (1979) revived Ricardian equivalence. And authors such as Woodford (2003) appear to formalise more of a Keynesian world. Getting out of such recessions by a Keynesian type of government borrowing and spending, without raising taxes immediately, is a possibility to help bring about a recovery. Ricardian theory reminds us that this approach can be seen as a short term solution that burdens future generations with its cost.

18.2 Government budget and wealth constraints

Consider the budget constraint of the government. As this can be expressed each period, it also can be combined into a wealth constraint covering all periods. Constructing such a wealth constraint from the sequence of budget constraints was done first in the text in Chapter 5 for a two-period model when there was just a sequence of two budget constraints; see equation (5.18). However there the wealth constraint was constructed for the consumer, using the consumer's budget constraints. Here we construct such a wealth constraint for the government, using the government budget constraints. And now it is for the infinite horizon, or an infinite sequence of current period budget constraints, rather than just for two periods.

18.2.1 Initial period revenue and spending

Initially the government has no revenue. Yet it needs to spend on setting up the infrastructure of its government. To do this, it will be allowed to borrow by issuing debt and also by issuing equity stock that gives the holder ownership over one share of government. This equity stock is nothing more than its money stock, which is not redeemable and has a fixed price of 1 so that no capital gain on it is possible.

Let time period -1 be the start-up period during which the government raises capital by issuing debt, B_0, and by issuing money, denoted by M_0. The capital they collect from the representative agent is the initial capital investment k_0. The government spends this on its initial capital infrastructure at time 0, which will be denoted by G_{-1}:

$$k_0 = B_0 + M_0 = G_{-1}. \tag{18.1}$$

During this period the government sets up the tax collection process through proportional labour income, capital income and consumption taxes, denoted by τ_l, τ_k and τ_c.

18.2.2 Subsequent periods

At time $t = 0$, the government spends G_0 as well as having to pay interest on the initial debt of $R_0 B_0$. To pay for this, it collects tax revenue $\tau_l w_0 l_0 h_0 + \tau_k r_0 k_0 + \tau_c c_0$. It also can issue new debt and money stock, $(B_1 - B_0) + (M_1 - M_0)$. This makes the period 0 budget constraint:

$$G_0 + R_0 B_0 = \left(\tau_l w_0 l_0 h_0 + \tau_k r_0 k_0 + \tau_c c_0\right) + \left(B_1 - B_0\right) + \left(M_1 - M_0\right). \tag{18.2}$$

From the point of view of the government at the initial period, the discounted stream of the spending and revenue during the two periods is

$$G_{-1} + \frac{G_0 + R_0 B_0}{1 + R_0} = B_0 + M_0 \tag{18.3}$$

$$+ \frac{\left(\tau_l w_0 l_0 h_0 + \tau_k r_0 k_0 + \tau_c c_0\right) + \left(B_1 - B_0\right) + \left(M_1 - M_0\right)}{1 + R_0}.$$

At any subsequent period t, the period budget constraint is

$$G_t + R_t B_t = (\tau_l w_t l_t h_t + \tau_k r_t k_t + \tau_c c_t) + \left(B_{t+1} - B_t\right) + \left(M_{t+1} - M_t\right). \tag{18.4}$$

18.2.3 Wealth constraint

The wealth constraint is formed by taking the two-period discounted value of expenditure and revenue and extending it to an infinite number of periods. Using the period t budget constraint (18.4) for each period after 0, this makes the infinite horizon discounted stream of spending, which is G plus debt interest RB, and revenue, which is from taxes, new bonds and new money, equal to

$$G_{-1} + \frac{G_0 + R_0 B_0}{1 + R_0} + \frac{G_1 + R_1 B_1}{\left(1 + R_0\right)\left(1 + R_1\right)} + \frac{G_2 + R_2 B_2}{\left(1 + R_0\right)\left(1 + R_1\right)\left(1 + R_2\right)} + \cdots$$

$$= B_0 + M_0 + \frac{\left(\tau_l w_0 l_0 h_0 + \tau_k r_0 k_0 + \tau_c c_0\right) + \left(B_1 - B_0\right) + \left(M_1 - M_0\right)}{1 + R_0}$$

$$+ \frac{\left(\tau_l w_1 l_1 h_1 + \tau_k r_1 k_1 + \tau_c c_1\right) + \left(B_2 - B_1\right) + \left(M_2 - M_1\right)}{\left(1 + R_0\right)\left(1 + R_1\right)}$$

$$+ \frac{\left(\tau_l w_2 l_2 h_2 + \tau_k r_2 k_2 + \tau_c c_2\right) + \left(B_3 - B_2\right) + \left(M_3 - M_2\right)}{\left(1 + R_0\right)\left(1 + R_1\right)\left(1 + R_2\right)} + \cdots \tag{18.5}$$

This is the wealth constraint of the government. It can be rearranged in various ways, and simplified under various assumptions.

The government wealth constraint says all spending is paid by taxes, money and bonds. But it says more, which can be seen in its simplification. One way to view the wealth constraint is by bringing together all of the government expenditure, the tax terms, the bond terms and the money terms. Equation (18.6) gathers these terms:

$$G_{-1} + \frac{G_0}{1 + R_0} + \frac{G_1}{(1 + R_0)(1 + R_1)} + \frac{G_2}{(1 + R_0)(1 + R_1)(1 + R_2)} + \cdots$$

$$= \frac{\tau_l w_0 l_0 h_0 + \tau_k r_0 k_0 + \tau_c c_0}{1 + R_0} + \frac{\tau_l w_1 l_1 h_1 + \tau_k r_1 k_1 + \tau_c c_1}{(1 + R_0)(1 + R_1)}$$

$$+ \frac{\tau_l w_2 l_2 h_2 + \tau_k r_2 k_2 + \tau_c c_2}{(1 + R_0)(1 + R_1)(1 + R_2)} + \cdots$$

$$B_0 - \frac{B_0}{1 + R_0} - \frac{R_0 B_0}{1 + R_0} + \frac{B_1}{1 + R_0} + \frac{B_2 - B_1 - B_1 R_1}{(1 + R_0)(1 + R_1)}$$

$$+ \frac{B_3 - B_2 - B_2 R_2}{(1 + R_0)(1 + R_1)(1 + R_2)} + \cdots$$

$$M_0 + \frac{M_1 - M_0}{1 + R_0} + \frac{M_2 - M_1}{(1 + R_0)(1 + R_1)}$$

$$+ \frac{M_3 - M_2}{(1 + R_0)(1 + R_1)(1 + R_2)} + \cdots \tag{18.6}$$

18.2.4 Bond transversality and the wealth constraint

Now consider a focus on the bond terms of the wealth constraint. In equation (18.6), the terms involving time 0 bonds, B_0, are given by

$$B_0 - \frac{B_0}{1 + R_0} - \frac{R_0 B_0}{1 + R_0} = B_0 - \frac{B_0(1 + R_0)}{1 + R_0} = B_0 - B_0 = 0.$$

In other words, they all cancel out, in that they sum to zero. The same holds for time 1 terms:

$$\frac{B_1}{1 + R_0} - \frac{B_1 + B_1 R_1}{(1 + R_0)(1 + R_1)} = \frac{B_1}{1 + R_0} - \frac{B_1(1 + R_1)}{(1 + R_0)(1 + R_1)}$$

$$= \frac{B_1}{1 + R_0} - \frac{B_1}{1 + R_0} = 0.$$

And for time 2 terms:

$$\frac{B_2}{(1 + R_0)(1 + R_1)} - \frac{B_2 + B_2 R_2}{(1 + R_0)(1 + R_1)(1 + R_2)}$$

$$= \frac{B_2}{(1 + R_0)(1 + R_1)} - \frac{B_2(1 + R_2)}{(1 + R_0)(1 + R_1)(1 + R_2)} = 0.$$

This continues forever. All bonds term cancel out until the only term left is the last term as t goes to infinity:

$$B_0 - B_0 + \frac{B_1}{1 + R_0} + \frac{B_2 - B_1\left(1 + R_1\right)}{\left(1 + R_0\right)\left(1 + R_1\right)} + \frac{B_3 - B_2\left(1 + R_2\right)}{\left(1 + R_0\right)\left(1 + R_1\right)\left(1 + R_2\right)} + \cdots$$

$$= 0 + 0 + 0 + \cdots + \lim_{j \to \infty}\left[\frac{B_{t+j}}{\left(1 + R_{t+1}\right)\left(1 + R_{t+2}\right)\cdots\left(1 + R_{t+j}\right)}\right]$$

$$= \lim_{j \to \infty}\left[\frac{B_{t+j}}{\left(1 + R_{t+1}\right)\left(1 + R_{t+2}\right)\cdots\left(1 + R_{t+j}\right)}\right].$$

And the assumption is that this last term, the present discounted value of the stock of bonds at time t, as t goes to infinity, is zero.

The limiting condition is called the transversality condition of the government problem:

$$\lim_{j \to \infty}\left[\frac{B_{t+j}}{\left(1 + R_{t+1}\right)\left(1 + R_{t+2}\right)\cdots\left(1 + R_{t+j}\right)}\right] = 0. \tag{18.7}$$

It means simply that the discounted value of the government debt in the limit converges to zero. In this way there is no permanent borrowing that is not paid back. Rather, it means all debt is paid back. Given the transversality condition, the terms involving bonds completely drop out of the government wealth constraint.

18.2.5 Ricardian equivalence

Ricardian equivalence is the recognition that all debt is eventually paid off through taxes, and that all spending must be eventually paid for by taxes. These taxes can either be explicit taxes such as on labour income, capital income and goods expenditure, or they can be from the implicit inflation tax that results from printing new money. But any spending paid for by bonds in the current period, must be paid back eventually by raising such taxes. Spending cannot be paid for only by increasing borrowing forever without raising taxes, since then debt in the limit is not zero, but positive, and the transversality condition is violated. If the transversality condition were expected to be violated, then the government could not borrow through issuing bonds since the market would view the bonds as an obligation that the government did not intend to keep.

With the transversality condition the wealth constraint becomes more simply:

$$G_{-1} + \frac{G_0}{1 + R_0} + \frac{G_1}{\left(1 + R_0\right)\left(1 + R_1\right)} + \frac{G_2}{\left(1 + R_0\right)\left(1 + R_1\right)\left(1 + R_2\right)} + \cdots$$

$$= \frac{\tau_l w_0 l_0 h_0 + \tau_k r_0 k_0 + \tau_c c_0}{1 + R_0} + \frac{\tau_l w_1 l_1 h_1 + \tau_k r_1 k_1 + \tau_c c_1}{\left(1 + R_0\right)\left(1 + R_1\right)}$$

$$+ \frac{\tau_l w_2 l_2 h_2 + \tau_k r_2 k_2 + \tau_c c_2}{\left(1 + R_0\right)\left(1 + R_1\right)\left(1 + R_2\right)} + \cdots$$

$$+ M_0 + \frac{M_1 - M_0}{1 + R_0} + \frac{M_2 - M_1}{\left(1 + R_0\right)\left(1 + R_1\right)}$$

$$+ \frac{M_3 - M_2}{\left(1 + R_0\right)\left(1 + R_1\right)\left(1 + R_2\right)} + \cdots \tag{18.8}$$

Here spending is paid for by explicit taxes and money printing. The idea is that it does not matter how you finance the spending in the current period, in that eventually it still is paid off by raising explicit or implicit taxes.

Of course with tax distortions it does matter how you finance government expenditure. And this is the focus of a big part of public finance theory. But simply using this wealth constraint reveals some simple insights into responsible government finance. One type of such a simplification is to consider the wealth constraint along the balanced growth path equilibrium. But first consider when Ricardian equivalence is assumed not to hold.

18.2.6 Impossibility theorem of non-Ricardian equivalence

If the transversality condition for bonds does not hold, so that

$$\lim_{j \to \infty} \left[\frac{B_{t+j}}{\left(1 + R_{t+1}\right)\left(1 + R_{t+2}\right)\cdots\left(1 + R_{t+j}\right)} \right] > 0,$$

then it is said that Ricardian equivalence does not hold. This is similar to assuming an asset price bubble that permanently exists. It means that the government wealth constraint is not binding in the way it has been formulated in this chapter, because somehow, in ways not specified, the debt of the government can forever stay positive and not be paid off. This is the idea of a 'non-Ricardian' world.

What a non-Ricardian world would mean is that the government does not necessarily have to raise taxes, either explicit ones or implicit ones, to pay for government expenditure. Rather the government can borrow and some of the expenditure can be paid for permanently in this way.

The problem with a non-Ricardian world is that it is impossible to prove that it could exist, or does exist. This gives rise to what can be called the 'impossibility theorem of non-Ricardian equivalence'. It means that in short it is impossible to prove that a non-Ricardian equilibrium could exist, as Kocherlakota and Phelan (1999) argue.

If the transversality condition is not binding, then there is a host of questions that are difficult to answer. Would anyone hold government debt? If they are holding debt does this not mean that the transversality condition is binding? And do not governments in fact collapse if they cannot pay off their debt?

Often non-Ricardian equivalence is taken to mean simply that taxes do not have to be increased to pay for government expenditure. This is what might be called the 'irresponsible guide to government finance' as opposed to the much less glamorous one of having to pay for expenditure with taxes, with Ricardian equivalence binding.

Some view the non-binding transversality condition to mean that government debt is an asset that the government can use to finance spending over the horizon. This bond asset acts as 'wealth' to the consumer since it finances spending that the consumer can receive. This happens in non-Ricardian models such as 'overlapping generations' models in which there are only two periods of time and government debt acts as wealth to the consumer of the current generation, but as a tax burden to future generations.

Finally, some argue that economies behave as if in a non-Ricardian world for a period of time, but not permanently. This is some type of concept in-between an infinite horizon model and one with only two periods. But it is more of a descriptive concept relating to a government issuing a lot of debt, than a mathematical description of equilibrium in a model. Unfortunately for governments, if they do not pay off debt then they lose credibility. And this is why even informally Ricardian equivalence and the transversality condition of bonds are seen as realistic parts of macroeconomics.

18.3 BGP equilibrium government spending

Assume that the balanced growth path equilibrium for an endogenous growth framework is established at time 0 and at every period after that. Also assume that inflation is zero and the nominal price of goods, denoted by P_t, is 1. Along the balanced growth path the nominal interest rate R_t is constant, as is the real interest rate r_t. With a BGP growth rate of g, variables that grow at the rate g are capitals k_t and h_t, consumption c_t, government spending G_t, and real money supply $\frac{M_t}{P_t}$. The same results derived below hold for exogenous growth.

18.3.1 Tax component

Assume the debt transversality condition holds, and now turn to deriving the present value of taxes, money revenue and spending under growth along the BGP. First the tax revenue component can be greatly simplified. The infinite stream of explicit taxes is

$$\frac{\tau_l w_0 l_0 h_0 + \tau_k r_0 k_0 + \tau_c c_0}{1 + R_0} + \frac{\tau_l w_1 l_1 h_0 + \tau_k r_1 k_1 + \tau_c c_1}{\left(1 + R_0\right)\left(1 + R_1\right)} + \frac{\tau_l w_2 l_2 h_0 + \tau_k r_2 k_2 + \tau_c c_2}{\left(1 + R_0\right)\left(1 + R_1\right)\left(1 + R_2\right)} + \cdots$$

However along the BGP constant variables are

$$r_0 = r_1 = \cdots = r_t = \cdots$$
$$w_0 = w_1 = \cdots = w_t = \cdots$$
$$R_0 = R_1 = \cdots = R_t = \cdots$$
$$l_0 = l_1 = \cdots = l_t = \cdots$$

and with w, k, h and c growing at the rate g, the discounted tax stream can be written as

$$\frac{\tau_l w_0 l_0 h_0 + \tau_k r_0 k_0 + \tau_c c_0}{1 + R_0} + \frac{\tau_l w_0 l_0 h_0 \left(1 + g\right) + \tau_k r_0 k_0 \left(1 + g\right) + \tau_c c_0 \left(1 + g\right)}{\left(1 + R_0\right)\left(1 + R_0\right)}$$
$$+ \frac{\tau_l w_0 l_0 h_0 \left(1 + g\right)^2 + \tau_k r_0 k_0 \left(1 + g\right)^2 + \tau_c c_0 \left(1 + g\right)^2}{\left(1 + R_0\right)\left(1 + R_0\right)\left(1 + R_0\right)} + \cdots$$

Now factor out $\left(\frac{1}{1 + R_0}\right)\left(\tau_l w_0 l_0 + \tau_k r_0 k_0 + \tau_c c_0\right)$, so that the tax stream is

$$\frac{\tau_l w_0 l_0 h_0 + \tau_k r_0 k_0 + \tau_c c_0}{1 + R_0} + \frac{\tau_l w_0 l_0 h_0 \left(1 + g\right) + \tau_k r_0 k_0 \left(1 + g\right) + \tau_c c_0 \left(1 + g\right)}{\left(1 + R_0\right)\left(1 + R_0\right)}$$
$$+ \frac{\tau_l w_0 l_0 h_0 \left(1 + g\right)^2 + \tau_k r_0 k_0 \left(1 + g\right)^2 + \tau_c c_0 \left(1 + g\right)^2}{\left(1 + R_0\right)\left(1 + R_0\right)\left(1 + R_0\right)} + \cdots$$
$$= \left(\frac{1}{1 + R_0}\right)\left(\tau_l w_0 l_0 h_0 + \tau_k r_0 k_0 + \tau_c c_0\right)\left(1 + \frac{1 + g}{1 + R_0} + \left(\frac{1 + g}{1 + R_0}\right)^2 + \left(\frac{1 + g}{1 + R_0}\right)^3 + \cdots\right).$$

Now using the power sequence definition that $1 + a + a^2 + \cdots = \frac{1}{1 - a}$, the tax stream reduces down to $\frac{\left(\tau_l w_0 l_0 + \tau_k r_0 k_0 + \tau_c c_0\right)}{R_0 - g}$:

$$\frac{\left(\tau_l w_0 l_0 h_0 + \tau_k r_0 k_0 + \tau_c c_0\right)}{1 + R_0}\left(\frac{1}{1 - \frac{1 + g}{1 + R_0}}\right) = \frac{\left(\tau_l w_0 l_0 h_0 + \tau_k r_0 k_0 + \tau_c c_0\right)}{1 + R_0}\left(\frac{1 + R_0}{R_0 - g}\right)$$
$$= \frac{\left(\tau_l w_0 l_0 h_0 + \tau_k r_0 k_0 + \tau_c c_0\right)}{R_0 - g}. \tag{18.9}$$

Finally take into account that the government bond rate R_t is equal to the return on capital $r_t - \delta_k$ in equilibrium, and use the intertemporal condition that

$$1 + g = \frac{1 + r_t - \delta_k}{1 + \rho}.$$

This implies that

$$R_t - g = (1+g)(1+\rho) - 1 - g = (1+g)\rho.$$

Therefore the tax stream discounts back to a value of

$$\frac{\tau_l w_0 l_0 h_0 + \tau_k r_0 k_0 + \tau_c c_0}{\rho(1+g)}. \tag{18.10}$$

18.3.2 Government spending component

Similarly the government spending component of the government wealth constraint is

$$G_{-1} + \frac{G_0}{1+R_0} + \frac{G_1}{(1+R_0)(1+R_1)} + \frac{G_2}{(1+R_0)(1+R_1)(1+R_2)} + \cdots$$

and it reduces down to $G_{-1} + \frac{G_0}{\rho(1+g)}$:

$$G_{-1} + \frac{G_0}{1+R_0} + \frac{G_1}{(1+R_0)(1+R_1)} + \cdots$$

$$= G_{-1} + \frac{G_0}{1+R_0}\left(1 + \frac{1+g}{1+R_0} + \left(\frac{1+g}{1+R_0}\right)^2 + \cdots\right)$$

$$= G_{-1} + \frac{G_0}{1+R_0}\left(\frac{1}{1 - \frac{1+g}{1+R_0}}\right)$$

$$= G_{-1} + \frac{G_0}{R_0 - g} = G_{-1} + \frac{G_0}{\rho(1+g)}.$$

18.3.3 Money printing component

When money enters the economy, this is called a 'monetary economy' rather than a 'real' economy. The difference is that in a monetary economy the price level of goods at time t, call this the 'nominal price' P_t, can rise over time simply due to inflation caused by printing money. Therefore the nominal price cannot simply be set equal to 1, as has been done implicitly in the analysis of the book up to this point. However a nominal price of $P_t = 1$ can be kept if in fact there is no inflation from printing money.

Therefore the rate of growth of the money supply needs to be explicit in the analysis of the government budget constraint. Typically this growth rate of money is set by the central bank, which is part of the government. Consider that if there is no growth in the economy, so that $g = 0$, then simply keeping the money supply constant at M will mean that money supply will equal money demand and there will be no inflation in this economy. Therefore the assumption of $P_t = 1$ is accurate when $g = 0$ and the money supply is constant over time at $M_0 = M_1 = \cdots M_t = \cdots$.

When the growth rate is positive, $g > 0$, then zero inflation again results if the money supply is assumed to grow at the same rate g. Again the result is that money supply equals money demand and the price level stays constant at $P_t = 1$. Here it will be assumed that $P_t = 1$ for all t, meaning that the underlying assumption is that M is constant when $g = 0$, and that M is growing at the rate g in general, with $g \geq 0$. Chapter 20 allows for positive inflation and examines the consequences of that.

Consider that when there is positive growth, then the money supply is growing. This means the government is collecting tax from printing money. Because there is no inflation and $P_t = 1$ for all t, this type of government revenue from printing money is sometimes called the 'natural' tax revenue of the government, or 'seigniorage'. When the government causes inflation by printing more money than at the natural seigniorage rate of g, then the government raises more implicit taxes from printing money.

Assuming that M grows at the constant growth rate g, then money supply growth equals money demand growth, which also grows at g, and the assumption that $P_t = 1$ is again valid for all t. Taking the money component of the government wealth constraint alone, this can also be reduced along the balanced growth path in a way similar to the government spending and explicit tax components. Setting $R_0 = R_1 = \cdots R_t$,

$$M_0 + \frac{M_1 - M_0}{1 + R_0} + \frac{M_2 - M_1}{(1 + R_0)(1 + R_1)} + \frac{M_3 - M_2}{(1 + R_0)(1 + R_1)(1 + R_2)} + \cdots$$

$$= M_0 + \frac{M_1 - M_0}{1 + R_0} + \frac{M_2 - M_1}{(1 + R_0)(1 + R_0)} + \frac{M_3 - M_2}{(1 + R_0)(1 + R_0)(1 + R_0)} + \cdots.$$

Substituting in the assumption that M grows at the rate g,

$$M_0 + \frac{M_1 - M_0}{1 + R_0} + \frac{M_2 - M_1}{(1 + R_0)(1 + R_0)} + \frac{M_3 - M_2}{(1 + R_0)(1 + R_0)(1 + R_0)} + \cdots$$

$$= M_0 + \frac{M_0(1 + g) - M_0}{1 + R_0} + \frac{M_0(1 + g)^2 - M_0(1 + g)}{(1 + R_0)(1 + R_0)}$$

$$+ \frac{M_0(1 + g)^3 - M_0(1 + g)^2}{(1 + R_0)(1 + R_0)(1 + R_0)} + \cdots.$$

Now factor out M_0 and rearrange in terms of infinite sequences to which can be applied the rule that $1 + a + a^2 + \cdots = \frac{1}{1-a}$:

$$M_0 \left(1 + \frac{(1 + g) - 1}{1 + R_0} + \frac{(1 + g)^2 - (1 + g)}{(1 + R_0)(1 + R_0)} + \frac{(1 + g)^3 - (1 + g)^2}{(1 + R_0)(1 + R_0)(1 + R_0)} + \cdots \right)$$

$$= M_0 \left(1 + \frac{1 + g}{1 + R_0} + \left(\frac{1 + g}{1 + R_0} \right)^2 + \cdots \right)$$

$$- \frac{M_0}{1 + R_0} \left(1 + \frac{1 + g}{1 + R_0} + \left(\frac{1 + g}{1 + R_0} \right)^2 + \cdots \right).$$

The money sequence then reduces down to

$$\left(M_0 - \frac{M_0}{1 + R_0} \right) \left(1 + \frac{1 + g}{1 + R_0} + \left(\frac{1 + g}{1 + R_0} \right)^2 + \cdots \right)$$

$$= \left(\frac{R_0 M_0}{1 + R_0} \right) \left(\frac{1}{1 - \frac{1+g}{1+R_0}} \right) = \frac{R_0 M_0}{R_0 - g}.$$

Again using that $R_0 - g = \rho(1+g)$, from Chapter 11, equation (11.9), and given that the bond price $R = r_t - \delta_k$, then

$$\frac{R_0 M_0}{R_0 - g} = M_0 \left(\frac{\rho(1+g) + g}{\rho(1+g)} \right) = M_0 \left(1 + \frac{g}{\rho(1+g)} \right). \tag{18.11}$$

18.3.4 Wealth constraint with balanced growth

Now the wealth constraint of government can bring together the components of the discounted value of spending equal to that of explicit taxes and implicit money taxes, it simplifies to

$$G_{-1} + \frac{G_0}{\rho(1+g)} = \frac{\tau_l w_0 l_0 h_0 + \tau_k r_0 k_0 + \tau_c c_0}{\rho(1+g)} + M_0 \left(1 + \frac{g}{\rho(1+g)} \right).$$

This means that the government finances the expenditure flow with the tax flow and the initial money stock plus the flow of implicit taxes from money creation at the rate of g.

Another way to view the wealth constraint here is to substitute in that $G_{-1} = M_0 + B_0$. Then the constraint is

$$M_0 + B_0 + \frac{G_0}{\rho(1+g)} = \frac{\tau_l w_0 l_0 h_0 + \tau_k r_0 k_0 + \tau_c c_0}{\rho(1+g)} + M_0 \left(1 + \frac{g}{\rho(1+g)} \right). \tag{18.12}$$

And this reduces to

$$\frac{G_0}{\rho(1+g)} = \frac{\tau_l w_0 l_0 h_0 + \tau_k r_0 k_0 + \tau_c c_0}{\rho(1+g)} + \frac{g M_0}{\rho(1+g)} - B_0. \tag{18.13}$$

This says that the flow of government expenditure, starting after the initial -1 period, is financed by revenue from the explicit tax flow, from the implicit money printing flow $g M_0$, and minus the value of the initial debt B_0.

Similarly, the government wealth constraint says that government debt equals the discounted value of revenue net of spending;

$$B_0 = \frac{(\tau_l w_0 l_0 h_0 + \tau_k r_0 k_0 + \tau_c c_0 + g M_0) - G_0}{\rho(1+g)}. \tag{18.14}$$

18.3.5 With inflation

When inflation is allowed, the economy has to be stated in 'nominal' terms, with the nominal price of goods P_t allowed to change over time. Inflation is then defined as the change in the nominal goods price. Denoting the inflation rate by π_t, it is defined as

$$1 + \pi_t \equiv \frac{P_{t+1}}{P_t}.$$

The first effect of inflation to consider is that the bond interest rate R_t now contains an inflation component. This is by the famous Fisher equation of interest rates, which is derived in Chapter 20. In short the Fisher equation is that

$$1 + R_t = (1 + \pi_t)(1 + r_t - \delta_k).$$

When $\pi_t = 0$, then R_t is just the net marginal product of capital $r_t - \delta_k$, as we have been assuming with no inflation. And in general the Fisher equation simply says that to earn a real interest rate of $r_t - \delta_k$, the nominal rate charged in bond prices must include the inflation rate plus the real rate $r_t - \delta_k$. This is because at the end of the period, nominal prices have risen by π_t.

Three effects of inflation can be found in the government wealth constraint. First the revenue from printing money rises until the inflation rate is high. If a constant money supply growth rate is denoted in general by σ, where

$$M_{t+1} = M_t \left(1 + \sigma\right),$$

then when $\sigma = g$, the same result of zero inflation occurs, and the same contribution of money printing to government revenues results as in equation (18.13) along the balanced growth path equilibrium. However in general the money revenue is

$$M_0 + \frac{M_1 - M_0}{1 + R_0} + \frac{M_2 - M_1}{\left(1 + R_0\right)\left(1 + R_0\right)} + \frac{M_3 - M_2}{\left(1 + R_0\right)\left(1 + R_0\right)\left(1 + R_0\right)} + \cdots$$

$$= M_0 + \frac{M_0\left(1+\sigma\right) - M_0}{1 + R_0} + \frac{M_0\left(1+\sigma\right)^2 - M_0\left(1+\sigma\right)}{\left(1 + R_0\right)\left(1 + R_0\right)}$$

$$+ \frac{M_0\left(1+\sigma\right)^3 - M_0\left(1+\sigma\right)^2}{\left(1 + R_0\right)\left(1 + R_0\right)\left(1 + R_0\right)} + \cdots$$

$$= \frac{R_0 M_0}{R_0 - \sigma}.$$

This sequence reduces to $\frac{R_0 M_0}{R_0-\sigma}$, instead of $\frac{R_0 M_0}{R_0-g}$ as in equation (18.11).

Accounting for initial government spending, $G_{-1} = M_0 + B_0$, the net government financing from money subtracts the initial money stock, and as revised from equation (18.12), is therefore

$$\frac{R_0 M_0}{R_0 - \sigma} - M_0 = M_0 \left(\frac{R_0 - R_0 + \sigma}{R_0 - \sigma}\right),$$

$$\frac{R_0 M_0}{R_0 - \sigma} - M_0 = \frac{\sigma M_0}{R_0 - \sigma}. \tag{18.15}$$

When the money supply growth rate rises, so does the revenue σM_0, so that the direct revenue from printing money rises. However it is true that money demand falls as σ rises, so that, forward from time t, $\sigma M_t/P_t$ can fall as the money supply growth rate, and inflation rate, is increased to a high enough level. Up until that point, the government can increase real revenue from printing money by increasing the money supply growth rate.

A second effect of printing money and causing higher inflation is that the net bond interest payments that the government owes to the consumer are decreased in present value terms by the increase in inflation. In other words, the government can reduce its interest payment liabilities on its debt by printing money, causing inflation, and seeing the nominal interest rate R_t rise because of the inflation rate increase. Since the government interest payments on debt are a particular set rate, such as R_0, then if the government later induces a higher rate of $R_t > R_0$, then the consumer is locked into receiving the lower interest rate of R_0. The new discount factor on future spending and revenue in the government wealth constraint is R_t, which since it is higher than R_0 causes the consumer to earn less than the market return on its government debt, thereby lowering the value of the debt liabilities to the government. This is how the government reduces the value of its debt liabilities through increasing the inflation rate.

A third effect is that inflation can reduce the stream of tax revenues. This is because inflation acts as a tax that can lower employment and the capital stock, and therefore the tax revenue from labour and capital income. This can thereby reduce the funds available to finance spending.

18.3.6 Example 18.1: Seigniorage wealth

How much a government actually raises from printing money depends on its rate of growth of the money supply, as well as on how much substitution occurs away from inflation-taxed goods. Consider equation (18.15) in terms of seigniorage wealth relative to output y. With the initial price of output normalised to 1, $P_0 = 1$, and real money $m \equiv \frac{M}{P}$, then

$$\frac{\frac{\sigma M_0}{R_0 - \sigma}}{P_0 y_0} = \frac{m_0}{y_0} \frac{\sigma}{R_0 - \sigma}.$$

Assume a money supply growth rate of $\sigma = 0.03$, and a nominal (market) interest rate of $R_0 = 0.06$. In general equilibrium with log utility in Chapter 20 it can be shown that $R \simeq \sigma + \rho$, with ρ the rate of time preference. So this specification of parameters is similar to assuming that $\rho = 0.03$ as in Part 4 of the text. Some estimates put ρ lower and so would increase the estimate of seigniorage wealth.

Then the seigniorage as a fraction of output is

$$\text{Seigniorage wealth:} \quad \frac{m_0}{y_0} \frac{\sigma}{R_0 - \sigma} = \frac{m_0}{y_0} \frac{0.03}{0.03} = \frac{m_0}{y_0}. \tag{18.16}$$

It equals the ratio of the money supply to output. In monetary economics, the income to money ratio $\frac{y}{m}$ is the velocity of money. And so the seigniorage ratio in this example is exactly the inverse of money velocity.

Different estimates of this ratio exist for countries such as the US, depending on the definition of money. At the high end of estimates, velocity of money can be 15–20, and at the low end, depending on the historical period, as small as 2. This implies seigniorage wealth as a ratio to output of between 5% and 50%.

Seigniorage wealth can be squandered by printing too much money, inducing consumers to use less of it relative to output, and so have a higher money velocity.

18.4 Government debt from deficits

Now some accounting will be done. The government bond held by the consumer is an asset to the consumer, but a liability, indicating negative net worth, to the government that must be paid off by future government surpluses. While currently running a government deficit, the government is running up a certain liability. The magnitude of this liability can be described using the present value framework of the wealth constraint, supposing that this deficit is run forever.

Define this debt build-up from continuous deficits as D_0, where

$$D_0 = \frac{G_0 - (\tau_l w_t l_0 h_0 + \tau_k r_0 k_0 + \tau_c c_0 + g M_0)}{\rho (1 + g)}. \tag{18.17}$$

The D_0 is the amount of liability incurred by continual deficits.

18.4.1 Debt and deficit to GDP ratios

Similarly the debt to output ratio, denoted by DY_0, can be formulated. The bonds held by the consumer are a liability to the government as

$$DY_0 = \frac{D_0}{y_0} = \frac{\frac{G_0}{\rho(1+g)} - \frac{\tau_l w_0 l_0 h_0 + \tau_k r_0 k_0 + \tau_c c_0}{\rho(1+g)} - \frac{g M_0}{\rho(1+g)}}{y_0},$$

$$= \frac{G_0 - (\tau_l w_0 l_0 h_0 + \tau_k r_0 k_0 + \tau_c c_0 + g M_0)}{y_0 \rho (1 + g)}.$$

A government with a high debt to output ratio is spending a lot relative to revenue sources. It has a high budget deficit that is financed by borrowing equal to the present value of the deficit.

Clearly when government spending each period is high relative to revenue sources, the debt to output ratio will be high. A high ratio can result in a high risk premium on government debt, under uncertainty, that increases the cost of the debt by even more.

To reduce this ratio the government must either lower government spending or raise taxes. This can lead to escalating inflation if the government cannot control spending or raises explicit taxes through tax rate increases or through economic growth. Escalating inflation can end up causing a government collapse because employment and capital fall and the debt–output ratio rises. A better route is to institute policies that raise economic growth while lowering DY_0.

18.4.2 Example 18.2: Maastricht Treaty debt and deficit limits

Now consider the relation between deficits, debt and output, or gross domestic product (GDP), as it is called statistically. The deficit to y ratio is

$$\frac{\text{Deficit}}{y_0} = \frac{G_0 - \left(\tau_l w_0 l_0 h_0 + \tau_k r_0 k_0 + \tau_c c_0 + g M_0\right)}{y_0}.$$

Now consider the European Union Maastricht Treaty limits on deficits. This limit is 0.03. At the deficit limit,

$$\frac{G_0 - \left(\tau_l w_0 l_0 h_0 + \tau_k r_0 k_0 + \tau_c c_0 + g M_0\right)}{y_0} = 0.03.$$

The question is whether this is consistent with debt limits within the Maastricht Treaty.

The Maastricht Treaty specifies a debt to GDP limit of 60%. With some EU nation at a 0.03 deficit to GDP ratio, what would be the implied debt to GDP ratio? Here we denote this debt to GDP ratio by DY_0, and it would be given as

$$DY_0 = \frac{D_0}{y_0} = \frac{G_0 - \left(\tau_l w_0 l_0 h_0 + \tau_k r_0 k_0 + \tau_c c_0 + g M_0\right)}{y_0 \rho \left(1 + g\right)} \tag{18.18}$$

$$= \frac{0.03}{\rho \left(1 + g\right)}.$$

To compute this DY_0, return to the baseline endogenous growth economy in which $\rho = 0.0526$ and $g = 0.02$. Then DY_0 equals

$$DY_0 = \frac{0.03}{\rho \left(1 + g\right)} = \frac{0.03}{0.0526 \left(1 + 0.02\right)} = 0.559. \tag{18.19}$$

This 56% ratio of debt to GDP is indeed with the limit of 60% of the Treaty guidelines. It is clear that higher deficits could lead to debt ratios above 60%.

18.5 Optimal public finance

The Ramsey solution to optimal public finance is to equalise the value of the marginal distortion from each different type of tax. This means it focuses on how to raise the taxes to pay for government expenditure. And it argues that on the margin the distortionary effects should be the same. If not, then one tax is being used too much while another is being used too little. Different marginal distortions from taxes are from the disincentive to work from labour income taxes, the disincentive to save from capital income taxes, and the disincentive to buy goods from value-added taxes on sales.

When government expenditure is modelled as exogenous occurring each period, as above in the government wealth constraint, then G_t is an exogenously determined amount every period. With this assumption, in exogenous growth theory, there is a central result: tax on intertemporally substitutable goods such as physical capital should be zero, while taxes on goods that cannot be easily substituted across time, like current period labour, should be conversely high. Therefore if only a labour income and a capital income tax were considered to be allowed, then the standard result is to collect all revenue through the labour tax and none through a capital tax.

There are many details to the zero capital tax result. For example, one is that all of the revenue is assumed to be uncollectable in the initial period through a confiscation of the agent's initial capital wealth. That is, if the government could just collect all needed capital in the initial period, it could finance all spending with the interest flow on the confiscated capital, and no taxes would be necessary after the initial confiscation of capital. This is really a technical detail that does not help explain modern government finance.

18.5.1 Spending as a constant share of output

More important however is the assumption that the government spending is exogenous. A much more realistic result follows by making two extensions to the dynamic exogenous growth baseline model that has exogenous government spending and a variety of taxes. First allow government expenditure to instead be a constant fraction of output. In our notation, this would mean that with η a constant positive fraction between 0 and 1,

$$G_t = \eta y_t. \tag{18.20}$$

This implies a constant share of government expenditure in output of $\frac{G_t}{y_t} = \eta$.

Empirical evidence on a country to country basis shows the reasonableness of such a constant share of government expenditure in output. The share of G_t in y_t does vary but it remains fairly stable over time, such as near 20% for the US.

18.5.2 Endogenous growth and a constant share

The second extension is to introduce the production of human capital investment in an endogenous growth economy. Combined with the spending as a constant share of output, a very intuitive result holds: the tax rate on physical capital equals the tax rate on human capital. Suppose again that there are only two taxes available in the economy, a labour income tax and a capital income tax. The labour income tax can be said equally to fall on human capital, or on labour, in that the income from such a tax is $\tau_l w_t h_t l_t$, or the labour income tax rate τ_l factored by the earnings on the effective time spent working, $w_t h_t l_t$.

The resulting optimal tax system can be shown to be the 'equal flat tax regime' of the labour income tax being equal to the capital income tax rate τ_k:

$$\tau_l = \tau_k.$$

Further the level of this tax rate regime is that in the best situation the tax rates should be set equal to the value of constant government share of output η:

$$\tau_l = \tau_k = \eta, \tag{18.21}$$

as shown in Azacis and Gillman (2010).

Such a regime of flat equal taxes can be seen as a way to view global trends towards less progressive tax rates, with fewer 'brackets' of tax rates, and also the tendency towards equalisation of the tax rate on capital and income. For example, these are now 35% for both the corporate income tax rate and the top personal income tax rate in the US. There are flat taxes on corporate and personal income in a host of Eastern European countries.

Azacis and Gillman (2010) extend this by allowing a goods tax as well, with endogenous growth as in Chapters 12, 13, and 14, and with equation (18.20) holding. Then it is the 'composite labour tax rate' that is set equal to the corporate income tax rate. The composite labour tax also includes the consumption tax since this tax acts just as does a tax on labour within the consumer's marginal rate of substitution between goods and leisure. With both taxes, this margin in our baseline models becomes

$$\frac{\alpha c_t}{x_t} = \frac{w_t h_t \left(1 - \tau_l\right)}{1 + \tau_c}.$$

The goods tax and labour tax both cause substitution from goods to leisure. This is why the optimal tax structure then is to set the composite tax rate on labour income equal to the corporate income tax rate, giving a somewhat more complicated version of equation (18.21). From Azacis and Gillman, the expression becomes

$$\frac{\tau_c + \tau_l}{1 + \tau_c} = \tau_k = \eta. \tag{18.22}$$

This reduces to equation (18.21) when the goods tax is zero, or $\tau_c = 0$.

A composite labour tax means that the consumption tax and labour tax both tax the return on human capital and they have to be weighed jointly against the return on physical capital. The implication is that a high labour tax should not be combined with a high value added goods tax and a low corporate income tax in that this causes too much of a distorting burden on labour income as compared to capital income. In moderation of this result, if capital can easily be invested in other countries, and if countries implicitly compete for investment through having a low corporate income tax, then these considerations would act to lower the optimal corporate tax rate relative to the composite labour tax rate.

18.5.3 Example 18.3: Optimal taxes, debt and deficit

The flat tax optimum can be applied to see what it would imply for the debt and deficit ratios to output along the balanced growth path, a focus for example of the European Union. Assume that the share of spending in output is 30%, and that there are optimal taxes on labour and capital, with no other taxes, so that

$$\tau_l = \tau_k = \eta = 0.30. \tag{18.23}$$

The government deficit ratio is

$$\frac{\text{Deficit}}{y_0} = \frac{G_0 - \left(\tau_l w_0 l_0 h_0 + \tau_k r_0 k_0 + \tau_c c_0 + g M_0\right)}{y_0}, \tag{18.24}$$

but without value-added taxes on purchases, and without money printing this reduces to

$$\frac{\text{Deficit}}{y_0} = \frac{G_0 - \left(\tau_l w_0 l_0 h_0 + \tau_k r_0 k_0\right)}{y_0}. \tag{18.25}$$

The deficit ratio can be reduced by using the Cobb–Douglas features of the production function, whereby $\gamma = \frac{wlh}{y}$ and $(1 - \gamma) = \frac{rk}{y}$. Equation (18.24) becomes

$$\frac{\text{Deficit}}{y_0} = \frac{G_0}{y_0} - \tau_l \left(\frac{w_0 l_0 h_0}{y_0}\right) - \tau_k \left(\frac{r_0 k_0}{y_0}\right),$$

$$\frac{\text{Deficit}}{y_0} = 0.30 - 0.3\gamma - 0.3\left(1 - \gamma\right) = 0. \tag{18.26}$$

There is no deficit in this equilibrium. The zero deficit carries over to a zero debt to output ratio. This is

$$DY_0 = \frac{D_0}{y_0} = \frac{G_0 - (\tau_l w_0 l_0 h_0 + \tau_k r_0 k_0)}{y_0 \rho (1+g)} = 0.$$

A zero deficit and debt could be viewed as supplying a responsible guide to government finance in the long run. Debt can be used to smooth out short run bursts in government expenditure due to wars and other crises, while it should be paid off with government current period surpluses during good periods. Considering the added revenue from money printing, research has found that inflation should not be used as a source of government revenue in the optimum.

18.6 Applications

18.6.1 Greek debt crisis and Ricardian equivalence

Greece rose far above the European deficit and debt limits during the 2007–10 world recession. In 2009, their deficit was 12.5% of output and their debt level 113% of output. At the same time there is concern within the European Union about the value of its currency, the euro.

The link between the debt, deficit, and inflation can be seen using the deficit to output ratio derived in equation (18.24). In Example 18.3 this equation is applied to show how the Maastricht deficit and debt limits can be internally consistent. A 3% deficit to output implies a 56% debt to output ratio, given the parameters.

Consider the case of Greece in 2009. The debt to output ratio, or DY_{2009}, using the wealth constraint approach that assumes these levels being maintained into the future, is

$$DY_{2009} = \frac{\frac{\text{Deficit}}{y_{2000}}}{\rho (1+g)} = \frac{0.125}{\rho (1+g)} = 1.13. \tag{18.27}$$

This directly implies a growth rate of

$$g = \frac{0.125}{\rho (1.13)} - 1 = \frac{0.125}{(0.0526) (1.13)} - 1 = 1.103,$$

or 110%. Growth rates normally trend around 0.02, or 2%. So the growth rate in Greece would have to be 50 times higher than historical averages, and on a permanent basis, in order to sustain such deficit and debt levels.

The implied growth rates are completely implausible. This suggests that Greece will need to pay for the deficit through higher taxes or less spending. And because of protests against higher taxes and less spending, the European Central Bank (ECB) is concerned about the maintenance of inflation targets in the Euro zone. Why? Because if Greece will not pay for deficits in normal ways, through direct taxes, then they might resort to trying to print money. Yet to the extent that the European Central Bank maintains monopoly control over the money supply printing, Greece will be unable to pay for the deficit by printing money.

Stark choices are the fundamentals of Ricardian equivalence in action. Greece could leave the euro and inflate its economy. The ECB could give up monopoly power on printing money and allow Greece to print money to cover its deficit, or the ECB could itself print money to buy Greek debt. This would spread the inflation tax across the whole Euro zone, raising the inflation rate everywhere the euro is used and causing its depreciation.

The first-best option is that Greece respects its government wealth constraint, and its transversality condition on debt in the limit, and so makes credible plans to pay off its debt over time. The other choice is default on government debt. In the short run, the options left are that either Greece leaves the euro and prints money and has higher inflation, or that the debt is financed in the short term by borrowing from other nations, including through the International Monetary Fund. Greece can borrow in the short term, and pay off the debt over time through higher taxes and lower spending.

There is still the danger that the Greek government may become insolvent. And therefore the real interest rate charged on Greek government debt has become high. This risk premium on Greek government borrowing has tended to spread across other high deficit and debt countries such as Portugal and Spain. This has raised the cost of capital across the whole European Union to some extent. And this can lead to lower output, as in Chapter 16 when the cost of capital is increased through higher banking costs.

Importantly, our equation (18.27) shows that a higher growth rate makes it easier for the government to satisfy its wealth constraint. Therefore it is important that during the process of reform in Greece that it also engage in tax reform that leads to higher growth rates and lower deficits, much as the US did in the 1980s and 1990s.

18.6.2 Taxes and government size

The government by nature builds public capital that adds to the wealth of a nation. This partly is in the form of all of the infrastructure that acts as a public good, or 'collective consumption good' as Nobel Laureate (1970) Paul Samuelson (1954) calls it in his famous article on public goods. Such infrastructure tends to be essential in lowering the costs by which free markets can operate. And this provision of useful public capital gives a fundamental role to government within a free market economy, a role allowed for in the law and economics tradition of Nobel Laureate (1991) Ronald H. Coase's (1960) theorem of how an exchange of property rights can decrease transaction costs of exchange.

Such useful public capital includes the legal system of laws and enforcement at all levels of government, and the physical capital and human capital infrastructure such as transportation means and public education systems. Although some of this is supplied privately, government spending that increases public capital, is a long term investment that can enhance the economy, in terms of our analysis, by shifting out the capital stock k_t with the interpretation that part of this capital stock is government supplied.

If at the same time, the provision of public capital requires a rising tax burden, then the net effect of such capital may be negative. But economists such as Milton Friedman have argued that an efficient government can provide such public capital and still allow for a shrinking share of the government expenditure as a percentage of total output. In turn, this would enable the tax burden to shrink, so that actual tax rates could fall gradually over time. This does not mean that government spending shrinks, but that it grows at a rate less than does aggregate output.

Modern society is at unprecedented levels of wealth, and a steady historical trend downwards in tax rates and government spending as a share of output is clear in developed countries such as the United States. Figure 18.1 shows this for post-1950 data for government expenditure for five developed nations. This gives room for optimism that governments may become relatively more efficient over time.

18.6.3 Flat tax policy around the world

In practice, there has been an international trend over time towards lower levels of tax rates on both capital and labour. Further, in many cases taxes have become more 'balanced' between capital and labour taxes. And they also have become more 'flat', with less different rates for different income levels.

In 1952 the US tax rate for the top-bracket of personal income was 92% and the top-bracket corporate income tax was 52%; in 2010 both of these were 35%. This shows a

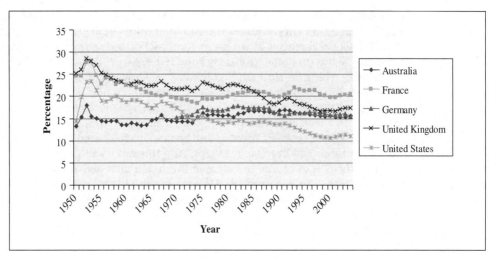

Figure 18.1 Government expenditure as a percentage of GDP

Source: Penn World Version 6.2 (188 countries, 1950–2004, 2000 as base year), government expenditure, Center for International Comparisons of Production, Income and Prices (CIC), University of Pennsylvania, http://pwt.econ.upenn.edu/php_site/pwt62/pwt62_form.php

trend down, some balancing, and there have been fewer 'brackets'. International evidence towards low flat taxes has been called 'The Global Flat Tax Revolution' (Mitchell, 2007).

A flat tax can refer to a single tax rate bracket on either personal or corporate income. There are many countries with a single tax bracket for each personal and corporate income tax rates. In some countries there are equal flat tax rates on both personal and corporate income (Romania, 16%; Serbia, 14%). And one at least even has equal rates on personal, corporate and on its value-added tax (Slovakia, 19%).

There are good reasons for these flat regimes in terms of the benefits of tax simplification for these systems, and for low tax rates in terms of decreasing the tax-induced disincentive to work, accumulate capital, and sell goods. It remains unclear however whether more balanced flat rate systems are better than more unbalanced ones. For example, the Baltic countries have low personal income tax rates but even lower corporate tax rates. The Baltic tax reforms started in 1994 in Estonia, and by 2000 the average Baltic personal tax rates had fallen to 28% and average corporate tax rates to 16%. By 2007, the average Baltic tax rates had fallen further: to 25% for personal tax rates and to 10% for corporate tax rates. And in contrast, Russia, Ukraine and Georgia have low flat corporate tax rates (24%) but even lower flat personal income tax rates (13%) (see Ivanova *et al.*, 2005).

One motivation for balanced personal and corporate rates is that tax evasion devices exist whereby the higher tax rate can be avoided in favour of the lower tax rate: for example the personal income tax rate can be evaded when company employees become self-employed consultants so that their labour income is subject to the corporate tax rate rather than the personal tax rate. But putting aside the incentive to evade taxes, an economy with balanced flat labour and capital tax rates can be more optimal, as discussed by Azacis and Gillman (2010).

18.7 Questions

1. Define Ricardian equivalence in terms of the government wealth constraint.
2. Describe the meaning of the transversality condition of equation (18.7) and discuss its role in the possible existence of non-Ricardian equilibria.

3. Compare the discounted value of government tax revenue in equation (18.9) to the value of the firm in Chapter 17, equation (17.66).

   (a) In what sense can the tax revenue stream of a government be viewed as the dividend stream to the goods producer?

   (b) How could the equity value of the government be defined in a way consistent with finance theory?

4. Assuming only taxes on labour and capital, construct the value of government debt in terms of the tax revenue using the government wealth constraint logic.

5. Consider constructing a government wealth constraint for an entire region of nations such as the European Union. What does this imply about the total debt of the EU in relation to its total tax revenue and the inflation target of the European Central Bank?

6. After the demise of the Soviet Union in 1989–90, Eastern European nations could form their own fiscal and monetary policy, but citizens never voluntarily had paid taxes, including in Russia. The International Monetary Fund initially entered the newly free region and recommended western levels of tax rates, of around 40%. Why, in contrast, did Vladimir Putin's Russian tax reform make sense, of dropping the personal income tax down to one bracket of 13% in 2001, from 12, 20 and 30% brackets previously, combined later with a lowering of the corporate income tax rate down to near 23%?

7. In Example 18.1, find the seigniorage wealth of equation (18.16) if the money velocity equals 15.

8. In Example 18.2, using equation (18.19) find the exact level of the deficit to output ratio that would yield a 60% debt to output ratio.

9. In Example 18.3, use equation (18.26) to determine the implied deficit to output ratio if as in Hungary government spending is 40% of output, the tax rate on capital is 16%, and the tax rate on labour is 40%.

10. If the growth rate rises when tax rates fall, then will the debt to output ratio of equation (18.18) be higher or lower?

18.8 References

Azacis, Helmuts and Max Gillman, 2010, 'Flat Tax Reform: The Baltics 2000–2007', *Journal of Macro-economics*, 32(2) (June): 692–708.

Barro, Robert J., 1979, 'On the Determination of the Public Debt', *Journal of Political Economy*, University of Chicago Press, 87(5) (October): 940–971.

Coase, Ronald H., 1960, 'The Problem of Social Cost', *Journal of Law and Economics*, 3(October): 1–44.

Hansen, Alvin, 1953, *A Guide to Keynes*, McGraw-Hill Book Company, Inc, New York.

Hansen, Alvin, 1960, *Economic Issues of the 1960s*, McGraw-Hill Book Company, Inc, New York.

Ivanova, Anna, Michael Keen and Alexander Klemm, 2005, 'The Russian Flat Tax Reform', International Monetary Fund Working Paper WP/05/16.

Keynes, John Maynard, 1930, *A Treatise on Money*, Macmillan and Co., London.

Keynes, John Maynard 1936, *The General Theory of Employment, Interest, and Money*, Harcourt Brace Jovanovich, first Harbinger edition, 1964.

Kocherlakota, Narayana and Christopher Phelan, 1999, 'Explaining the Fiscal Theory of the Price Level', *Quarterly Review*, Federal Reserve Bank of Minneapolis, issue Fall: pp. 14–23.

Mitchell, Daniel J., 2007, 'The Global Flat Tax Revolution', *Cato Policy Report*, 29(4) (July/August): 1 and 10–12, Cato Institute, Washington DC.

Ricardo, David, 1821, *The Principles of Political Economy and Taxation*, 3rd edition, John Murray, Albemarle Street.

Samuelson, Paul A., 1954, 'The Pure Theory of Public Expenditure', *The Review of Economics and Statistics*, 36(4) (November): 387–389.

Woodford, Michael, 2003, *Interest and Prices: Foundations of a Theory of Monetary Policy*, Princeton University Press.

CHAPTER ⑲

Taxes and growth

19.1 Introduction

The chapter shows the effect of taxes, on capital, labour and goods, on the determination of the growth rate, and the rest of the economy. This requires using the endogenous growth dynamic model. The models presented are extensions of the Part 5 baseline endogenous growth economy.

First the capital tax is added, starting with the new government budget constraint. The model solution is re-derived with this modification, using the *AS–AD* approach. An example is developed using the calibration of the baseline Example 13.2 of Chapter 13.

A 30% tax on capital income causes the growth rate to fall by 2 percentage points, and the capital ratio to fall by about half. Aggregate output supply and demand shift back while the wage rate falls. Labour demand shifts back, and labour supply shifts out, with employment falling as well as the wage rate.

The endogenous growth tax model is extended to the labour tax. An example again starts with the calibration of Example 13.2. A labour income tax rate of 14.4% yields the same decrease in the growth rate as did the 30% capital tax rate.

Differences between the capital and labour taxes include that the labour tax causes the capital to human capital ratio to rise, as the consumer substitutes from taxed human capital towards physical capital. This causes aggregate demand and supply for output to shift out, while the real wage rises. In the labour market the supply and demand for labour shift upwards while the wage rate rises, and the employment rate falls. So output growth and employment fall for both capital and labour taxes, but output and capital stocks have different effects depending on whether physical capital or human capital is being taxed. The consumption tax is also analysed and shown to be similar to the labour tax in its effect on aggregate demand for output.

19.1.1 Building on the last chapters

In Chapters 3 and 6, static models of the labour tax and the capital tax are presented, while in Chapter 9 the labour tax is shown in the baseline dynamic model with exogenous growth. However by its nature the exogenous growth economy cannot show the effect of taxes on growth since the growth rate is chosen exogenously, and cannot be affected by taxes. Therefore this chapter extends the Part 5 endogenous growth model to show how the tax rates affect growth. At the same time this produces some other results different from earlier chapters.

In Chapters 3 and 9, the labour tax decreases output and employment, while here employment falls but output rises because of substitution from human to physical capital.

But the growth rate of the economy falls here, even though the level of output rises as physical capital is used more intensively.

The solution methodology is a modest modification of that in Chapter 12, just as adding the labour tax in Chapter 9 modified the solution methodology of Chapter 10. The growth rate again can be solved either graphically or analytically through a quadratic equation in the growth rate.

19.1.2 Learning objective

That all taxes decrease the balanced path equilibrium growth rate is a startling realisation for some. The objective is to see that all of societies' major taxes, on labour, on capital, on goods, and in Chapter 20 on money use, cause the economic growth rate to decline. Rather than a detail not addressed with exogenous growth models, this is a fundamental element of macroeconomic government policy. International policy emphasis on high growth for the last quarter of a century is addressed directly by understanding how taxes affect growth.

Realising that employment falls also for all of the major taxes helps impart the importance of the results. Along the way, it is essential to grasp the difference between capital and labour taxes in terms of one taxing physical capital and the other taxing human capital. This helps the understanding of why output levels, relative to human capital, can rise with labour taxes in the equilibrium even while the growth rate and employment rates fall. The more intuitive result of a falling capital ratio and falling output per human capital level follows with the capital tax.

19.1.3 Who made it happen?

Frank Ramsey (1927) derived perhaps the original general equilibrium representative agent optimisation analysis of taxes. And his work gave rise to the specialised economics field of study called public finance. Much more modern work has found the effect of taxes on growth, following Robert E. Lucas, Jr.'s 1988 explanation of the Solow residual in terms of endogenous growth with human capital.

The effect of taxes on endogenous growth rates dates back only to 1990. It was made prominent by King and Rebelo (1990) in their article on 'Public Policy and Economic Growth: Developing Neoclassical Implications'. This was followed up for example by Rebelo's 1991 article, 'Long-Run Policy Analysis and Long-Run Growth', and Stokey and Rebelo's 1995 'Growth Effects of Flat-Rate Taxes'. These journal articles all show how tax rates reduce growth.

19.2 Capital income tax

Consider within the endogenous growth model of Chapter 12 a tax on capital income, τ_k, where income from capital now is $r_t k_t (1 - \tau_k)$ instead of $r_t k_t$. The government budget constraint is that government spending G_t is equal to the revenue from the capital tax:

$$G_t = \tau_k r_t k_t. \tag{19.1}$$

The government spending is a transfer of income back to the consumer. Consumption is now given by

$$c_t = w_t l_t h_t + r_t k_t (1 - \tau_k) - k_{t+1} + k_t - \delta_k k_t + G_t. \tag{19.2}$$

Note that after the first-order equilibrium conditions are derived, the budget constraint shows no income effect within the budget constraint of the tax, because the taxes taken out and the government transfer received cancel each other out. Therefore the tax effect is only in terms of its distortion to the consumer's margins.

Only the consumer problem is affected as the tax is on the rental income received by the consumer; the firm problem is unchanged. Modifying the consumer problem of Chapter 12 only by adding the tax τ_k and government revenue transfer G_t, the problem is

$$V(k_t, h_t) = \max_{k_{t+1}, l_t, l_{Ht},} \ln\left[w_t l_t h_t + r_t k_t (1 - \tau_k) - k_{t+1} + k_t - \delta_k k_t + G_t\right]$$

$$+ \alpha \ln\left(1 - l_{Ht} - l_t\right)$$

$$+ \beta V\left[k_{t+1}, h_t (1 - \delta_h) + A_H l_{Ht} h_t\right]. \tag{19.3}$$

Plus there are now two envelope conditions, one with respect to k_t and one to h_t. And note that after the first-order equilibrium conditions are derived, the budget constraint shows no income effect within the budget constraint, in that the taxes equal the transfer.

The equilibrium conditions are

$$k_{t+1} : \frac{1}{c_t}(-1) + \beta \frac{\partial V\left(k_{t+1}, h_{t+1}\right)}{\partial k_{t+1}} = 0, \tag{19.4}$$

$$l_t : \frac{1}{c_t}(w_t h_t) + \frac{\alpha}{x_t}(-1) = 0, \tag{19.5}$$

$$l_{Ht} : \frac{\alpha}{x_t}(-1) + \beta \frac{\partial V\left(k_{t+1}, h_{t+1}\right)}{\partial h_{t+1}}(A_H h_t) = 0; \tag{19.6}$$

plus the envelope conditions from taking the derivative with respect to k_t and h_t:

$$k_t : \frac{\partial V\left(k_t, h_t\right)}{\partial k_t} = \frac{1}{c_t}\left[1 + r_t(1 - \tau_k) - \delta_k\right], \tag{19.7}$$

$$h_t : \frac{\partial V\left(k_t, h_t\right)}{\partial h_t} = \frac{1}{c_t}(w_t l_t)$$

$$+ \beta \frac{\partial V\left(k_{t+1}, h_{t+1}\right)}{\partial h_{t+1}}\left(1 + A_H l_{Ht} - \delta_H\right). \tag{19.8}$$

Bring the time index $t+1$ in the term $\frac{\partial V(k_{t+1}, h_{t+1})}{\partial k_{t+1}}$ in equation (19.4) down one period to t, and substitute this into equation (19.7). This gives the new intertemporal consumption margin

$$\frac{c_{t+1}}{c_t} = \frac{1 + r_t(1 - \tau_k) - \delta_k}{1 + \rho}.$$

With all growing variables growing at the rate of g along the balanced growth path equilibrium, the consumption intertemporal margin shows how the growth rate is directly affected by the capital income tax:

$$1 + g = \frac{1 + r_t(1 - \tau_k) - \delta_k}{1 + \rho}. \tag{19.9}$$

Equation (19.5) gives the intratemporal margin

$$MRS_{c,x} : \frac{\alpha c_t}{x_t} = w_t h_t. \tag{19.10}$$

The second intertemporal margin coming from the human capital derivatives is unaffected directly by the tax rate. Equation (19.6) implies an expression for $\frac{\partial V(k_{t+1}, h_{t+1})}{\partial h_{t+1}}$:

$$\frac{\partial V\left(k_{t+1}, h_{t+1}\right)}{\partial h_{t+1}} = \frac{\alpha}{\beta\left(A_H h_t\right) x_t},$$

which can be substituted in at time t and at $t+1$ into equation (19.8) to yield that

$$\frac{(h_t)x_t}{(h_{t-1})x_{t-1}} = \beta(A_H)l_t + \beta(1 + A_H l_{Ht} - \delta_h). \tag{19.11}$$

Along the balanced growth path equilibrium, x_t is stationary so that $x_{t-1} = x_t$; h_t grows at the rate g; and

$$l_t + l_{Ht} = 1 - x_t. \tag{19.12}$$

With $\beta = \frac{1}{1+\rho}$, this implies

$$1 + g = \frac{1 + A_H(1 - x_t) - \delta_H}{1 + \rho}. \tag{19.13}$$

19.2.1 *AS–AD* analysis

Consumption demand can be formulated from the government budget constraint in equation (19.1), the consumer budget constraint in equation (19.2), the marginal rate of substitution between goods and leisure in equation (19.10), the allocation of time constraint in equation (19.12), the intertemporal margin of equation (19.9), and the balanced growth path assumption whereby $k_{t+1} = k_t(1+g)$. Using the government and consumer budget constraints,

$$c_t^d = w_t l_t h_t + r_t k_t (1 - \tau_k) - k_{t+1} + k_t - \delta_k k_t + G_t$$
$$= w_t l_t h_t + r_t k_t - k_{t+1} + k_t - \delta_k k_t.$$

Substituting in for l_t from the time constraint,

$$c_t^d = w_t h_t (1 - x_t - l_{Ht}) + r_t k_t - k_{t+1} + k_t - \delta_k k_t,$$

and for x_t from the intratemporal constraint between goods and leisure,

$$c_t^d = w_t h_t \left(1 - \frac{\alpha c_t}{w_t h_t} - l_{Ht}\right) + r_t k_t - k_{t+1} + k_t - \delta_k k_t,$$

so that consumption demand is the same function as in Chapter 12:

$$c_t^d = \left(\frac{1}{1+\alpha}\right)\left[w_t h_t(1 - l_{Ht}) + k_t(r_t - \delta_k - g)\right].$$

Also from the human capital investment function, as in Chapter 12, $l_{Ht} = \frac{g+\delta_H}{A_H}$:

$$c_t^d = \left(\frac{1}{1+\alpha}\right)\left[w_t h_t\left(1 - \frac{g+\delta_H}{A_H}\right) + k_t(r_t - \delta_k - g)\right].$$

One effect of the capital tax is that the term $(r_t - \delta_k - g)$, when simplified to be in terms of g by using the intertemporal margin equation (19.9), is affected by the tax rate τ_k. From that intertemporal margin, r_t is given by

$$r_t = \frac{(1+g)(1+\rho) - 1 + \delta_k}{(1 - \tau_k)}. \tag{19.14}$$

This makes the consumer demand, in terms of only $w_t h_t$, k_t and g, equal to

$$c_t^d = \frac{w_t h_t\left(1 - \frac{g+\delta_H}{A_H}\right) + k_t\left(\frac{(1+g)(1+\rho)-1+\delta_k}{(1-\tau_k)} - \delta_k - g\right)}{1+\alpha},$$

$$c_t^d = \frac{w_t h_t\left(1 - \frac{g+\delta_H}{A_H}\right) + k_t\left(\frac{\rho(1+g)+(g+\delta_k)\tau_k}{(1-\tau_k)}\right)}{1+\alpha}. \tag{19.15}$$

When the tax rate is zero, $\tau_k = 0$, then this form of the consumption function returns to its Chapter 12 form.

Aggregate demand AD is given by also adding to consumption demand the investment in capital along the balanced growth path, which is $k_t (g + \delta_k)$:

$$y_t^d = \frac{w_t h_t \left(1 - \frac{g+\delta_H}{A_H}\right) + k_t \left(\frac{\rho(1+g)+(g+\delta_k)\tau_k}{(1-\tau_k)}\right)}{1+\alpha} + k_t (g + \delta_k),$$

$$y_t^d = \frac{w_t h_t \left(1 - \frac{g+\delta_H}{A_H}\right) + k_t \left(\frac{\rho(1+g)+(g+\delta_k)[1+\alpha(1-\tau_k)]}{(1-\tau_k)}\right)}{1+\alpha}. \tag{19.16}$$

Aggregate supply AS is unchanged from Chapters 8–13, at

$$y_t^s = A_G \left(\frac{\gamma A_G}{w_t}\right)^{\frac{\gamma}{1-\gamma}} k_t. \tag{19.17}$$

19.2.2 Solution methodology

In the equilibrium, aggregate demand equals aggregate supply. Therefore consider setting up the excess aggregate output demand function $Y(w_t, h_t, k_t, g)$:

$$Y(w_t, h_t, k_t, g) = y_t^d - y_t^s = 0,$$

such that

$$0 = \frac{\left[w_t h_t \left(1 - \frac{g+\delta_H}{A_H}\right) + k_t \left(\frac{\rho(1+g)+(g+\delta_k)[1+\alpha(1-\tau_k)]}{(1-\tau_k)}\right)\right]}{1+\alpha}$$
$$- A_G \left(\frac{\gamma A_G}{w_t}\right)^{\frac{\gamma}{1-\gamma}} k_t.$$

Dividing this excess demand through by $w_t h_t$ gives that

$$0 = \frac{\left[\left(1 - \frac{g+\delta_H}{A_H}\right) + \frac{k_t}{w_t h_t} \left(\frac{\rho(1+g)+(g+\delta_k)[1+\alpha(1-\tau_k)]}{(1-\tau_k)}\right)\right]}{1+\alpha}$$
$$- A_G \left(\frac{\gamma A_G}{w_t}\right)^{\frac{\gamma}{1-\gamma}} \frac{k_t}{w_t h_t}.$$

Now we need to solve for $\frac{k_t}{w_t h_t}$ and w_t in terms of g, and then there is one equation in one unknown g and so g can be solved given the parameter calibration.

From Chapter 12's Appendix A12, equation (12.92), the employment can be expressed as a function of the growth rate g:

$$l_t = \frac{(1+g)(1-\beta)}{A_H \beta}. \tag{19.18}$$

The ratio $\frac{k_t}{h_t l_t}$ can be solved from the marginal product of capital condition of the firm equilibrium:

$$r_t = (1 - \gamma) A_G \left(\frac{k_t}{h_t l_t}\right)^{-\gamma},$$

$$\frac{k_t}{h_t l_t} = \left(\frac{(1-\gamma) A_G}{r_t}\right)^{\frac{1}{\gamma}}. \tag{19.19}$$

Using the consumer's intertemporal margin to solve for r_t, as in equation (19.14),

$$\frac{k_t}{h_t l_t} = \left(\frac{\left(1 - \gamma\right) A_G}{\frac{(1+g)(1+\rho)-1+\delta_k}{(1-\tau_k)}} \right)^{\frac{1}{\gamma}}.$$

(19.20)

With a solution in terms of g for $\frac{k_t}{h_t l_t}$, the wage rate w_t can also be expressed in terms of g. From the marginal product of labour from the firm's equilibrium condition,

$$w_t = \gamma A_G \left(\frac{k_t}{h_t l_t} \right)^{1-\gamma},$$

$$w_t = \gamma A_G \left(\frac{\left(1 - \gamma\right) A_G}{\frac{(1+g)(1+\rho)-1+\delta_k}{(1-\tau_k)}} \right)^{\frac{1-\gamma}{\gamma}}.$$

(19.21)

This gives w_t and so we still need $\frac{k_t}{w_t h_t}$ in terms of g. For this, from equations (19.18), (19.20) and (19.21),

$$\frac{k_t}{w_t h_t} = \left(\frac{k_t}{h_t l_t} \right) \frac{l_t}{w_t},$$

$$\frac{k_t}{w_t h_t} = \left(\frac{\left(1 - \gamma\right) A_G}{\frac{(1+g)(1+\rho)-1+\delta_k}{(1-\tau_k)}} \right)^{\frac{1}{\gamma}} \frac{\frac{(1+g)(1-\beta)}{A_H \beta}}{\gamma A_G \left(\frac{\left(1-\gamma\right)A_G}{\frac{(1+g)(1+\rho)-1+\delta_k}{(1-\tau_k)}} \right)^{\frac{1-\gamma}{\gamma}}},$$

$$\frac{k_t}{w_t h_t} = \left(\frac{\left(1 - \gamma\right) A_G}{\frac{(1+g)(1+\rho)-1+\delta_k}{(1-\tau_k)}} \right) \frac{\frac{(1+g)(1-\beta)}{A_H \beta}}{\gamma A_G}.$$

(19.22)

The normalised excess demand function can now have w_t and $\frac{k_t}{w_t h_t}$ substituted for in terms of g using equations (19.21) and (19.22):

$$0 = \left(\frac{1}{1+\alpha} \right) \left(1 - \frac{g + \delta_H}{A_H} \right)$$

$$+ \frac{\left(\frac{(1-\gamma)A_G}{\frac{(1+g)(1+\rho)-1+\delta_k}{(1-\tau_k)}} \right)}{1+\alpha} \frac{\frac{(1+g)(1-\beta)}{A_H \beta}}{\gamma A_G} \left(\frac{\rho\left(1+g\right)+(g+\delta_k)\left[1+\alpha\left(1-\tau_k\right)\right]}{\left(1-\tau_k\right)} \right)$$

$$- A_G \left(\frac{\gamma A_G}{\gamma A_G \left(\frac{(1-\gamma)A_G}{\frac{(1+g)(1+\rho)-1+\delta_k}{(1-\tau_k)}} \right)^{\frac{1-\gamma}{\gamma}}} \right)^{\frac{\gamma}{1-\gamma}} \left(\frac{\left(1-\gamma\right)A_G}{\frac{(1+g)(1+\rho)-1+\delta_k}{(1-\tau_k)}} \right) \frac{\frac{(1+g)(1-\beta)}{A_H \beta}}{\gamma A_G}.$$

This simplifies to

$$0 = \beta \left(A_H - g - \delta_H \right) \gamma \left[\left(1+g\right) + \beta\left(\delta_k - 1\right) \right]$$

$$+ \beta \left(1-\gamma\right)\left(1+g\right)\left(1-\beta\right)\left(\rho\left(1+g\right)+(g+\delta_k)\left[1+\alpha\left(1-\tau_k\right)\right]\right)$$

$$- \left(1+\alpha\right)\left(1+g\right)\left(1-\beta\right)\left[\left(1+g\right)+\beta\left(\delta_k - 1\right)\right].$$

(19.23)

And with zero taxes, this reduces to the same equation in Chapter 12, equation (12.98). It gives one equation in g and by substituting in the assumed parameter values, g can be solved. Analytically, the equation again is a quadratic equation in g, and can be solved that way explicitly, for an exact functional form. Or the excess demand function can be graphed and g found that way, where $Y(g) = 0$.

19.2.3 Example 19.1: Baseline calibration

Assume the same parameters as in Example 13.2: $\gamma = \frac{1}{3}$, $\alpha = 1$, $A_h = 0.20$, $\delta_k = 0.05$, $\delta_h = 0.015$, $\beta = \frac{1}{1+\rho} = 0.95$, $\rho = \frac{1}{0.95} - 1 = 0.052632$, $A_G = 0.28224$. In this Example 13.2 the growth rate is found to be $g = 0.0333$.

For government spending and taxes, the government budget constraint as divided through by y_t implies that

$$\frac{G_t}{y_t} = \frac{\tau_k r_t k_t}{y_t} = \tau_k (1 - \gamma). \tag{19.24}$$

And if government spending is assumed to be a constant share of output, and if it is assumed that $\tau_k = 0.30$, then $\frac{G_t}{y_t} = 0.30 (0.67) = 0.201$. This will be assumed for τ_k, so government spending is about 20% of output.

Consider graphically solving for g given this calibration. The normalised excess demand solution equation (19.23) with the calibration becomes

$$0 = (0.95)(0.20 - g - 0.015)\frac{1}{3}((1 + g) + 0.95(0.05 - 1)) \tag{19.25}$$

$$+ (0.95)\left(\frac{2}{3}\right)(1 + g)(0.05)(0.052632(1 + g) + (g + 0.05)[1 + 1(1 - 0.30)])$$

$$- 2(1 + g)(1 \quad 0.95)((1 + g) + 0.95(0.05 - 1)).$$

Figure 19.1 graphs equation (19.25) to show that the excess output demand function equals zero when $g = 0.0121$.

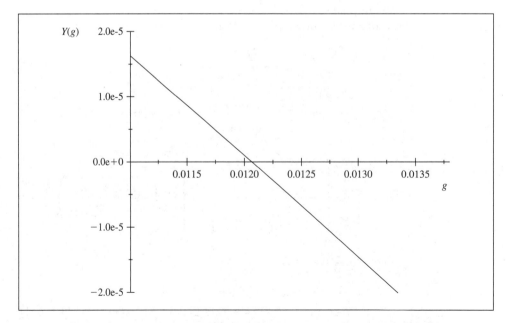

Figure 19.1 Excess output demand with capital income tax $\tau_k = 0.30$ in Example 19.1

Following Appendix A12 and writing the solution equation (19.25) in terms of $Ag^2 + Bg + C = 0$, then A, B, and C are given in general by

$$A \equiv -\beta\gamma + \beta\left(1-\beta\right)\left(1-\gamma\right)\left[1+\alpha\left(1-\tau_k\right)+\rho\right] - \left(1+\alpha\right)\left(1-\beta\right),$$

$$\begin{aligned}B \equiv &-\beta\gamma\left[1+\beta\left(\delta_k-1\right)-A_H+\delta_H\right]\\ &+\beta\left(1-\beta\right)\left(1-\gamma\right)\left\{\rho+\delta_k\left[1+\alpha\left(1-\tau_k\right)\right]+1+\alpha\left(1-\tau_k\right)+\rho\right\}\\ &-\left(1+\alpha\right)\left(1-\beta\right)\left[2+\beta\left(\delta_k-1\right)\right],\end{aligned}$$

$$\begin{aligned}C \equiv &\beta\gamma\left(A_H-\delta_H\right)\left[1+\beta\left(\delta_k-1\right)\right]\\ &+\beta\left(1-\beta\right)\left(1-\gamma\right)\left\{\rho+\delta_k\left[1+\alpha\left(1-\tau_k\right)\right]\right\}\\ &-\left(1+\alpha\right)\left(1-\beta\right)\left[1+\beta\left(\delta_k-1\right)\right],\end{aligned}$$

and given the calibration, the implied values are

$$\begin{aligned}\text{Quadratic term:}\quad &A = -0.36117,\\ \text{Linear term:}\quad &B = -0.02218,\\ \text{Constant term:}\quad &C = 0.00032021.\end{aligned}$$

This also gives a growth rate of $g = 0.0121$.

The growth rate therefore is decreased significantly by the tax on capital from 3.33% with no tax down to 1.21% with the 30% tax. This shows how taxes decrease growth, even when all proceeds are returned to the consumer through an income transfer.

With the growth rate now given, the capital ratio $\frac{k_t}{h_t}$ can be found. To do this start with the solution for employment, given as

$$l_t = \frac{\left(1+g\right)\left(1-\beta\right)}{A_H\beta} = \frac{\left(1+0.0121\right)\left(1-0.95\right)}{\left(0.20\right)0.95} = 0.26634. \tag{19.26}$$

This is a decrease in employment from the no tax case of Example 13.2, in which $l_t = 0.27192$.

The capital to effective labour ratio, by equation (19.20), is

$$\frac{k_t}{h_t l_t} = \left(\frac{\left(1-\gamma\right)A_G}{\frac{\left(1+g\right)\left(1+\rho\right)-1+\delta_k}{\left(1-\tau_k\right)}}\right)^{\frac{1}{\gamma}} = \left(\frac{\left(\frac{2}{3}\right)0.28224}{\frac{\left(1+0.0121\right)\left(1+0.052632\right)-1+0.05}{\left(1-0.30\right)}}\right)^3 = 1.488. \tag{19.27}$$

Therefore the capital ratio $\frac{k_t}{h_t}$ is $\left(\frac{k_t}{h_t l_t}\right)l_t = \left(1.488\right)\left(0.26634\right) = 0.39632$. This is lower than in Example 13.2 with no tax, in which $\frac{k_t}{h_t} = 0.694$.

The tax also shifts the AS and AD functions relative to zero tax. To graph the AS–AD with the tax, the aggregate demand and supply functions of equations (19.16) and (19.17) need to be inverted to

$$\frac{1}{w_t} = \frac{\left(1-\frac{g+\delta_H}{A_H}\right)}{\frac{y_t^d}{h_t}\left(1+\alpha\right) - \frac{k_t}{h_t}\left(\frac{\rho\left(1+g\right)+\left(g+\delta_k\right)\left[1+\alpha\left(1-\tau_k\right)\right]}{\left(1-\tau_k\right)}\right)}$$

for AD, and the same AS as previously

$$\frac{1}{w_t} = \frac{\left(y_t^s\right)^{\frac{1-\gamma}{\gamma}}}{\gamma A_G^{\frac{1}{\gamma}}\left(k_t\right)^{\frac{1-\gamma}{\gamma}}}.$$

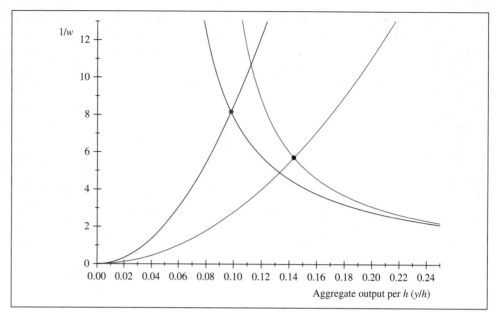

Figure 19.2 *AS–AD* with a 30% capital income tax in Example 19.1 (black) and a zero tax of Example 13.2 (blue)

Calibrated these inverse functions are

$$\frac{1}{w_t} = \frac{\left(1 - \frac{0.0121+0.015}{0.20}\right)}{2y - (0.396)\left[\frac{(0.0526)(1+0.0121)+(0.0121+0.05)(1+1(1-0.30))}{1-0.30}\right]}; \tag{19.28}$$

$$\frac{1}{w_t} = \frac{3}{0.28224}\left(\frac{1}{(0.28224)(0.39632)}\right)^2 y_t^2. \tag{19.29}$$

Figure 19.2 graphs *AS–AD* equations (19.28) and (19.29) in black, as compared to when the tax rate is zero, as in Example 13.2, in blue. It shows that the tax shifts back both supply and demand. The relative price rises from near 6 to near 8, while output falls from 0.1433 to near 0.10.

To find the exact wage, use the marginal product of labour condition, with $\frac{k_t}{h_t l_t} = 1.488$:

$$w_t = \gamma A_G \left(\frac{k_t}{h_t l_t}\right)^{1-\gamma} = \frac{1}{3}(0.28224)(1.488)^{\frac{2}{3}},$$

$$w_t = 0.12262. \tag{19.30}$$

Then the relative goods price is $\frac{1}{w_t} = \frac{1}{0.12262} = 8.1553$.

Consumption is

$$c_t^d = \left(\frac{1}{1+\alpha}\right)\left[w_t h_t \left(1 - \frac{g+\delta_H}{A_H}\right) + k_t \left(\frac{\rho(1+g)+(g+\delta_k)\tau_k}{(1-\tau_k)}\right)\right]$$

$$= \left(\frac{1}{1+1}\right)0.12262\left(1 - \frac{0.0121+0.015}{0.20}\right)$$

$$+ \left(\frac{1}{1+1}\right)(0.39632)\frac{(0.052632(1+0.0121)+(0.0121+0.05)0.30)}{1-0.30}$$

$$= 0.073356.$$

And output similarly is

$$y_t^d = \frac{w_t h_t \left(1 - \frac{g+\delta_H}{A_H}\right) + k_t \left(\frac{\rho(1+g)+(g+\delta_k)[1+\alpha(1-\tau_k)]}{(1-\tau_k)}\right)}{1+\alpha}$$

$$= \left(\frac{1}{1+1}\right) 0.12262 \left(1 - \frac{0.0121 + 0.015}{0.20}\right)$$

$$+ \left(\frac{0.39632}{2}\right) \frac{\left(0.052632 \left(1+0.0121\right) + \left(0.0121+0.05\right)\left(1+1-0.30\right)\right)}{1 - 0.30}$$

$$= 0.097968.$$

The consumption to output ratio is $\frac{c_t^d}{y_t^d} = \frac{0.073356}{0.097968} = 0.74878$. This a substantial increase from 0.5966 in Example 13.2, which is the value when the tax rate is zero. More is consumed and less is invested out of output when there is a tax on capital. The investment rate is lower.

The present value of government revenue from the labour tax, from equation (18.10) of Chapter 18, is

$$\frac{G_t}{\rho(1+g)} = \frac{\frac{G_t}{y_t} y_t}{\rho(1+g)} = \frac{\frac{\tau_k r_t k_t}{y_t} y_t}{\rho(1+g)} = \frac{\tau_k (1-\gamma) y_t}{\rho(1+g)} \tag{19.31}$$

$$= \frac{(0.30)\frac{2}{3}(0.097968)}{0.052632(1+0.0120)} = 0.36786. \tag{19.32}$$

The decrease in the investment rate can be understood also by looking at the value of the interest rate r_t. From equation (19.14),

$$r_t = \frac{(1+g)(1+\rho) - 1 + \delta_k}{(1-\tau_k)}, \tag{19.33}$$

$$r_t = \frac{(1+0.0121)(1+0.052632) - 1 + 0.05}{(1-0.30)} = 0.16481. \tag{19.34}$$

With no taxes, $r_t = 0.1377$, as in Example 13.2. Thus the real rental rate has risen. Yet the after tax rate is 11.5%:

$$r_t (1 - \tau_k) = 0.16481 (1 - 0.30) = 0.11537.$$

Therefore the after tax interest rate falls, and so the investment rate is lower since it is less worthwhile for the consumer to save and invest in capital for rent to the goods producer. Meanwhile the higher rental rate of $r_t = 0.16481$ means that the goods producer will demand less physical capital, which explains the lower capital ratio of 0.40 as compared to 0.69 with no tax.

19.2.4 Labour market

The labour supply is affected by the capital tax, while the labour demand from the goods producer remains the same function. Derive the labour supply by starting from the intratemporal marginal rate of substitution between goods and leisure, solved in terms of leisure from equation (19.10):

$$\frac{c_t^d \alpha}{w_t h_t} = x_t.$$

Substitute in for leisure x_t in the allocation of time constraint,

$$\frac{c_t^d \alpha}{w_t h_t} = 1 - l_t^s - l_{Ht};$$

and solve for the labour supply:

$$l_t^s = 1 - \frac{c_t^d \alpha}{w_t h_t} - l_{Ht}. \tag{19.35}$$

Now substitute in for $\frac{c_t^d}{h_t}$ from the consumer goods demand function of equation (19.15):

$$\frac{c_t^d}{h_t} = \left(\frac{1}{1+\alpha}\right)\left[w_t\left(1 - \frac{g+\delta_H}{A_H}\right) + \frac{k_t}{h_t}\left(\frac{\rho(1+g)+(g+\delta_k)\tau_k}{(1-\tau_k)}\right)\right], \tag{19.36}$$

and use the solution for l_{Ht} in terms of g, to get that

$$l_t^s = 1 - \frac{\left(\frac{\alpha}{1+\alpha}\right)\left[w_t\left(1 - \frac{g+\delta_H}{A_H}\right) + \frac{k_t}{h_t}\left(\frac{\rho(1+g)+(g+\delta_k)\tau_k}{(1-\tau_k)}\right)\right]}{w_t} - \frac{g+\delta_H}{A_H}.$$

Simplifying, labour supply as a function of $\frac{k_t}{h_t}$, w_t, and g is given by

$$l_t^s = 1 - \frac{\alpha}{1+\alpha}\left[1 + \frac{k_t}{w_t h_t}\left(\frac{\rho(1+g)+(g+\delta_k)\tau_k}{(1-\tau_k)}\right)\right] - \frac{g+\delta_H}{A_H(1+\alpha)}. \tag{19.37}$$

Labour demand as in Chapters 12, 13, and 14 is

$$l_t^d = \left(\frac{\gamma A_G}{w_t}\right)^{\frac{1}{1-\gamma}}\frac{k_t}{h_t}. \tag{19.38}$$

Labour supply and demand can be solved in terms of w_t so that the functions can be graphed in the traditional way. These inverse functions are

$$w_t = \frac{\alpha\left[\rho(1+g)+(g+\delta_k)\tau_k\right]\left(\frac{k_t}{h_t}\right)}{(1-\tau_k)\left[1 - (1+\alpha)l_t^s - \frac{(g+\delta_H)}{A_H}\right]}; \tag{19.39}$$

$$w_t = \gamma A_G\left(\frac{k_t}{h_t l_t^d}\right)^{1-\gamma}. \tag{19.40}$$

Using the same calibration as in Example 19.1, the calibrated labour market equations are

$$w_t = \frac{1\left[(0.0526)(1.0121)+(0.0121+0.05)0.30\right](0.396)}{(1-0.30)\left[1-(1+1)l_t^s - \frac{(0.0121+0.015)}{0.20}\right]}; \tag{19.41}$$

$$w_t = \frac{(0.28224)(0.39632)^{\frac{2}{3}}}{3}\frac{1}{\left(l_t^d\right)^{\frac{2}{3}}}. \tag{19.42}$$

Figure 19.3 graphs equations (19.41) and (19.42) in black, the labour supply and demand functions with the 30% capital income tax, along with the zero capital income tax labour market of Example 13.2 in blue. The graphs show how the labour supply is shifted out while the labour demand is shifted down, with the result that the real wage and the employment level fall.

The equilibrium employment falls to 0.26634 from 0.27192 with no tax. This is a fractional decrease of $\frac{0.27192-0.26634}{0.27192} = 0.020521$, or a 2% fall in employment.

The capital tax thereby causes output, employment, the investment rate, the wage rate, the after tax rental rate and the balanced path growth rate all to fall.

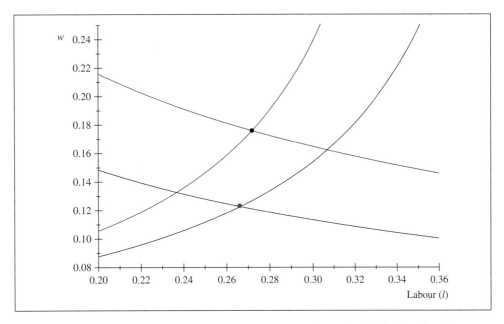

Figure 19.3 Labour market with 30% capital income tax in Example 19.1 (in black) and zero tax (in blue)

19.2.5 General equilibrium

In the general equilibrium with human capital investment there are several changes when there is a tax on capital. The isocost line has a lower output level and wage rate:

$$y_t = w_t l_t h_t + r_t k_t,$$

$$\frac{0.097968}{h_t} = (0.12262)\, l_t + (0.16481)\, \frac{k_t}{h_t},$$

$$\frac{k_t}{h_t} = \frac{0.097968}{0.16481 h_t} - \frac{(0.12262)\, l_t}{0.16481}. \qquad (19.43)$$

The isoquant curve has a lower output level. Starting with the production function, and solving for $\frac{k_t}{h_t}$ in terms of labour l_t, the isoquant at $y_t = 0.097968$ is found:

$$y_t^s = A_G \left(l_t^d h_t\right)^\gamma (k_t)^{1-\gamma},$$

$$0.097968 = (0.28224) \left(l_t^d h_t\right)^{\frac{1}{3}} (k_t)^{\frac{2}{3}};$$

$$\frac{k_t}{h_t} = \left(\frac{0.097968}{(0.28224)\, h_t \left(l_t^d\right)^{\frac{1}{3}}}\right)^{\frac{3}{2}} = \frac{\left(\frac{0.097968}{(0.28224) h_t}\right)^{\frac{3}{2}}}{\left(l_t^d\right)^{\frac{1}{2}}}. \qquad (19.44)$$

The factor input ratio is lower at

$$\frac{k_t}{h_t l_t} = \frac{0.39632}{0.26634} = 1.488. \qquad (19.45)$$

Figure 19.4 graphs equations (19.43), (19.44) and (19.45), with $h_t = 1$, in variants of black, as compared to the baseline Example 13.2 in variants of blue.

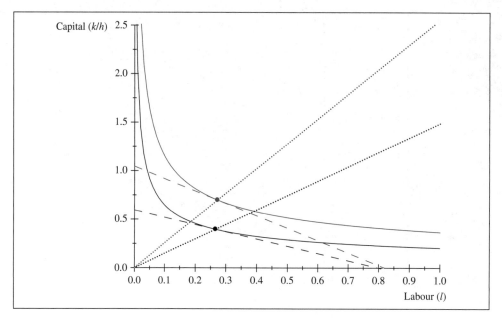

Figure 19.4 Factor market equilibrium with endogenous growth and capital income tax of $\tau_k = 0.30$

The tax causes the isocost to pivot down, with the factor input price ratio falling to $\frac{w_t}{r_t} = \frac{0.12262}{0.16481} = 0.74401$. The isoquant shifts down and the factor input ratio pivots downwards. Employment falls by 2%.

For goods and leisure in general equilibrium, consumption from output minus investment is

$$c_t^d = y_t^s - i_t = A_G \left(l_t^d h_t\right)^{\gamma} (k_t)^{1-\gamma} - (g + \delta_k) k_t,$$

$$\frac{c_t^d}{h_t} = \left(0.28224\right) \left(l_t^d\right)^{\frac{1}{3}} \left(0.39632\right)^{\frac{2}{3}} - \left(0.0121 + 0.05\right) \left(0.39632\right). \tag{19.46}$$

The level curve is

$$u = \ln c_t + \alpha \ln x_t = \ln c_t + \alpha \ln \left(1 - l_{Ht} - l_t\right),$$

$$-3.1263 = \ln 0.073356 + 1 \ln \left(1 - \left(0.26634 + 0.1355\right)\right),$$

$$-3.1263 = \ln c_t + \ln \left(T_t - l_t\right),$$

$$c_t = \frac{e^{-3.1263}}{\left(1 - 0.1355 - l_t\right)}. \tag{19.47}$$

The equilibrium budget line is

$$c_t^d = w_t l_t^s h_t + k_t \left[r_t \left(1 - \tau_k\right) - (g + \delta_k)\right] + G;$$

$$G = r_t \tau_k k_t,$$

$$c_t^d = w_t l_t^s h_t + k_t \left(r_t - \delta_k - g\right);$$

$$\frac{c_t^d}{h_t} = \left(0.12262\right) l_t^s + \left(0.39632\right) \left(\left(0.16481\right) - 0.05 - 0.0121\right). \tag{19.48}$$

Figure 19.5 graphs equations (19.46), (19.47) and (19.48), in variants of black, mostly below the baseline model of Example 13.2, in variants of blue. The production function shifts down because of the tax, as do the utility level and the budget line, while labour employment falls.

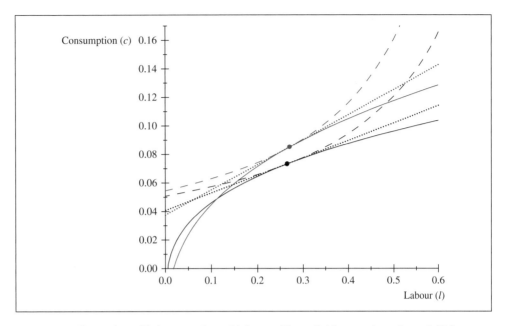

Figure 19.5 General equilibrium goods and labour with capital income tax of $\tau_k = 0.30$ in Example 19.1 compared to $\tau_k = 0$ in Example 13.2

19.3 Labour income tax

A proportional tax on labour income τ_l is introduced in Chapter 9 with exogenous growth assumed. Here it is introduced with endogenous growth whereby the tax can affect the growth rate of output. The effect of the tax is derived and then compared to its effect in the exogenous growth case, in terms of the *AS–AD* output market and the labour market.

With a tax on labour income at a rate of τ_l, only the consumer problem is affected. The goods producer has the same first-order conditions and the same supply of goods function and demand for labour function as with no tax. No other taxes exist. The consumer's wage income is $w_t \left(1 - \tau_l\right) l_t^s h_t$ and the government budget constraint is

$$G_t = \tau_l w_t l_t h_t. \tag{19.49}$$

As with the capital tax, the government transfers G_t back to the consumer so that the only result of the tax is due to its distortion on incentives, which comes through an altered marginal rate of substitution between goods and leisure.

The consumer budget constraint with the tax is modified from equation (9.46) to

$$c_t^d = w_t h_t l_t^s \left(1 - \tau_l\right) + r_t k_t + G_t - k_{t+1} + k_t \left(1 - \delta_k\right). \tag{19.50}$$

The consumer problem is

$$
\begin{aligned}
V\left(k_t, h_t\right) = \underset{k_{t+1}, l_t, l_{Ht},}{\text{Max}} \quad & \ln\left[w_t h_t l_t \left(1 - \tau_l\right) + r_t k_t - k_{t+1} + k_t - \delta_k k_t + G_t\right] \\
& + \alpha \ln\left(1 - l_{Ht} - l_t\right) \\
& + \beta V\left[k_{t+1}, h_t \left(1 - \delta_h\right) + A_H l_{Ht} h_t\right].
\end{aligned}
\tag{19.51}
$$

The equilibrium and envelope conditions are

$$k_{t+1} : \frac{1}{c_t}(-1) + \beta \frac{\partial V\left(k_{t+1}, h_{t+1}\right)}{\partial k_{t+1}} = 0, \tag{19.52}$$

$$l_t : \frac{1}{c_t}\left[w_t h_t\left(1 - \tau_l\right)\right] + \frac{\alpha}{x_t}(-1) = 0, \tag{19.53}$$

$$l_{Ht} : \frac{\alpha}{x_t}(-1) + \beta \frac{\partial V\left(k_{t+1}, h_{t+1}\right)}{\partial h_{t+1}}\left(A_H h_t\right) = 0; \tag{19.54}$$

$$k_t : \frac{\partial V\left(k_t, h_t\right)}{\partial k_t} = \frac{1}{c_t}\left(1 + r_t - \delta_k\right), \tag{19.55}$$

$$h_t : \frac{\partial V\left(k_t, h_t\right)}{\partial h_t} = \frac{1}{c_t}\left[w_t l_t\left(1 - \tau_l\right)\right]$$
$$+ \beta \frac{\partial V\left(k_{t+1}, h_{t+1}\right)}{\partial h_{t+1}}\left(1 + A_H l_{Ht} - \delta_H\right). \tag{19.56}$$

These conditions reduce down to the same balanced growth path intertemporal margins as in the baseline endogenous growth model of Chapter 12, and the same balanced growth expression for $l_{Ht} = \frac{g + \delta_H}{A_H}$. The only difference is that now the marginal rate of substitution between goods and leisure is affected by the tax. Writing this margin so as to solve for x_t, it is

$$x_t = \frac{\alpha c_t}{w_t h_t\left(1 - \tau_l\right)}. \tag{19.57}$$

The tax reduces the effective wage causing the consumer to substitute from goods towards leisure.

19.3.1 *AS–AD analysis*

The *AS* function is not affected by the tax. The aggregate demand is constructed from the consumer and government budget constraints, the marginal rate of substitution between goods and leisure, the allocation of time constraint, and the two intertemporal margins from human and physical capital. Using the government budget constraint (19.49), substituting in for $l_t = 1 - x_t - l_{Ht}$ in the consumer budget constraint (19.50), using the goods–leisure margin of equation (19.57), simplifying and substituting in that $l_{Ht} = \frac{g + \delta_H}{A_H}$, consumption demand is

$$c_t^d = w_t h_t l_t^s\left(1 - \tau_l\right) + r_t k_t + G_t - k_{t+1} + k_t\left(1 - \delta_k\right), \tag{19.58}$$

$$c_t^d = w_t h_t l_t^s + r_t k_t - k_{t+1} + k_t\left(1 - \delta_k\right), \tag{19.59}$$

$$c_t^d = w_t h_t\left(1 - x_t - l_{Ht}\right) + r_t k_t - k_{t+1} + k_t\left(1 - \delta_k\right), \tag{19.60}$$

$$c_t^d = w_t h_t\left(1 - \frac{\alpha c_t}{w_t h_t\left(1 - \tau_l\right)} - l_{Ht}\right)$$
$$+ r_t k_t - k_{t+1} + k_t\left(1 - \delta_k\right), \tag{19.61}$$

$$c_t^d\left(1 + \frac{\alpha}{\left(1 - \tau_l\right)}\right) = w_t h_t\left(1 - l_{Ht}\right) + r_t k_t - k_{t+1} + k_t\left(1 - \delta_k\right), \tag{19.62}$$

$$c_t^d = \frac{w_t h_t\left(1 - l_{Ht}\right) + r_t k_t - k_{t+1} + k_t\left(1 - \delta_k\right)}{\left(1 + \frac{\alpha}{\left(1 - \tau_l\right)}\right)}, \tag{19.63}$$

$$c_t^d = \frac{w_t h_t\left(1 - \frac{g + \delta_H}{A_H}\right) + \rho\left(1 + g\right) k_t}{\left(1 + \frac{\alpha}{\left(1 - \tau_l\right)}\right)}. \tag{19.64}$$

Adding the investment along the balanced growth path, of

$$i_t = k_{t+1} - k_t \left(1 - \delta_k\right) = k_t \left(1 + g\right) - k_t \left(1 - \delta_k\right) = k_t \left(g + \delta_k\right),$$

in order to get the aggregate demand for goods, the *AD* function is

$$y_t^d = \frac{w_t h_t \left(1 - \frac{g + \delta_H}{A_H}\right) + \rho \left(1 + g\right) k_t}{\left(1 + \frac{\alpha}{(1 - \tau_l)}\right)} + k_t \left(g + \delta_k\right),$$

$$y_t^d = \frac{w_t h_t \left(1 - \frac{g + \delta_H}{A_H}\right) + k_t \left[\rho \left(1 + g\right) + (g + \delta_k) \left(1 + \frac{\alpha}{(1 - \tau_l)}\right)\right]}{\left(1 + \frac{\alpha}{(1 - \tau_l)}\right)},$$

$$y_t^d = \frac{w_t h_t \left(1 - \tau_l\right) \left(1 - \frac{g + \delta_H}{A_H}\right) + k_t \left[\left(1 - \tau_l\right) \rho \left(1 + g\right) + (g + \delta_k) \left(1 + \alpha - \tau_l\right)\right]}{1 + \alpha - \tau_l}.$$

Inversely solving for the relative price $\frac{1}{w_t}$, the *AD* function can be graphed as

$$\frac{1}{w_t} = \frac{\left(1 - \tau_l\right) \left(1 - \frac{g + \delta_H}{A_H}\right)}{\frac{y_t^d}{h_t} \left(1 + \alpha - \tau_l\right) - \frac{k_t}{h_t} \left[\left(1 - \tau_l\right) \rho \left(1 + g\right) + (g + \delta_k) \left(1 + \alpha - \tau_l\right)\right]}.$$

The *AS* function and its inverse are again

$$y_t^s = A_G \left(\frac{\gamma A_G}{w_t}\right)^{\frac{\gamma}{1 - \gamma}} k_t; \tag{19.65}$$

$$\frac{1}{w_t} = \frac{\left(y_t^s\right)^{\frac{1 - \gamma}{\gamma}}}{\gamma A_G^{\frac{1}{\gamma}} \left(k_t\right)^{\frac{1 - \gamma}{\gamma}}}.$$

19.3.2 Solution methodology

A solution methodology very similar to the last section can be used. Let the excess aggregate output demand function $Y\left(w_t, h_t, k_t, g\right)$,

$$Y\left(w_t, h_t, k_t, g\right) = y_t^d - y_t^s = 0,$$

be

$$0 = \frac{w_t h_t \left(1 - \tau_l\right) \left(1 - \frac{g + \delta_H}{A_H}\right) + k_t \left[\left(1 - \tau_l\right) \rho \left(1 + g\right) + (g + \delta_k) \left(1 + \alpha - \tau_l\right)\right]}{1 + \alpha - \tau_l}$$

$$- A_G \left(\frac{\gamma A_G}{w_t}\right)^{\frac{\gamma}{1 - \gamma}} k_t.$$

Dividing through by $w_t h_t$ implies

$$0 = \frac{\left(1 - \tau_l\right) \left(1 - \frac{g + \delta_H}{A_H}\right) + \frac{k_t}{w_t h_t} \left[\left(1 - \tau_l\right) \rho \left(1 + g\right) + (g + \delta_k) \left(1 + \alpha - \tau_l\right)\right]}{1 + \alpha - \tau_l}$$

$$- A_G \left(\frac{\gamma A_G}{w_t}\right)^{\frac{\gamma}{1 - \gamma}} \frac{k_t}{w_t h_t}.$$

And again solve for $\frac{k_t}{w_t h_t}$ and w_t in terms of g, to have an equation in only g.

Because the intertemporal conditions are unchanged from Chapter 12, it is true that

$$l_t = \frac{(1+g)\,(1-\beta)}{A_H\beta};$$

(19.66)

$$r_t = (1-\gamma)\,A_G\left(\frac{k_t}{h_t l_t}\right)^{-\gamma},$$

$$\frac{k_t}{h_t l_t} = \left(\frac{(1-\gamma)\,A_G}{r_t}\right)^{\frac{1}{\gamma}},$$

(19.67)

$$\frac{k_t}{h_t l_t} = \left(\frac{(1-\gamma)\,A_G}{(1+g)\,(1+\rho) - 1 + \delta_k}\right)^{\frac{1}{\gamma}};$$

(19.68)

$$w_t = \gamma\,A_G\left(\frac{k_t}{h_t l_t}\right)^{1-\gamma},$$

(19.69)

$$w_t = \gamma\,A_G\left(\frac{(1-\gamma)\,A_G}{(1+g)\,(1+\rho) - 1 + \delta_k}\right)^{\frac{1-\gamma}{\gamma}}.$$

(19.70)

Therefore we now have

$$\frac{k_t}{w_t h_t} = \left(\frac{k_t}{h_t l_t}\right)\frac{l_t}{w_t},$$

$$\frac{k_t}{w_t h_t} = \left(\frac{(1-\gamma)\,A_G}{(1+g)\,(1+\rho) - 1 + \delta_k}\right)^{\frac{1}{\gamma}}\frac{\frac{(1+g)(1-\beta)}{A_H\beta}}{\gamma\,A_G\left(\frac{(1-\gamma)A_G}{(1+g)(1+\rho)-1+\delta_k}\right)^{\frac{1-\gamma}{\gamma}}},$$

$$\frac{k_t}{w_t h_t} = \left(\frac{(1-\gamma)}{(1+g)\,(1+\rho) - 1 + \delta_k}\right)\frac{(1+g)\,(1-\beta)}{\gamma\,A_H\beta}.$$

(19.71)

Returning to the normalised excess demand function, with $\frac{k_t}{w_t h_t}$ and w_t substituted in,

$$0 = \frac{(1-\tau_l)\left(1 - \frac{g+\delta_H}{A_H}\right)}{1+\alpha-\tau_l}$$

$$+ \frac{\frac{(1-\gamma)(1+g)(1-\beta)}{[(1+g)(1+\rho)-1+\delta_k]\gamma A_H\beta}\left[(1-\tau_l)\,\rho\,(1+g) + (g+\delta_k)\,(1+\alpha-\tau_l)\right]}{1+\alpha-\tau_l}$$

$$- \frac{A_G}{\left(\frac{(1-\gamma)A_G}{(1+g)(1+\rho)-1+\delta_k}\right)}\left(\frac{(1-\gamma)}{(1+g)\,(1+\rho) - 1 + \delta_k}\right)\frac{(1+g)\,(1-\beta)}{\gamma\,A_H\beta}.$$

This reduces to

$$0 = \frac{(1-\tau_l)\left(1 - \frac{g+\delta_H}{A_H}\right)}{1+\alpha-\tau_l}$$

$$+ \frac{\frac{(1-\gamma)(1+g)(1-\beta)}{[(1+g)(1+\rho)-1+\delta_k]\gamma A_H\beta}\left[(1-\tau_l)\,\rho\,(1+g) + (g+\delta_k)\,(1+\alpha-\tau_l)\right]}{1+\alpha-\tau_l}$$

$$- \frac{(1+g)\,(1-\beta)}{\gamma\,A_H\beta}.$$

This simplifies to an equation only in the variable g, thereby giving the solution to g given the parameters, similar to equation (19.25):

$$
\begin{aligned}
0 = {} & \beta\gamma\left(1-\tau_l\right)\left(A_H - g - \delta_H\right)\left[\left(1+g\right) + \beta\left(\delta_k - 1\right)\right] \\
& + \beta\left(1-\gamma\right)\left(1+g\right)\left(1-\beta\right)\left[\left(1-\tau_l\right)\rho\left(1+g\right) + \left(g+\delta_k\right)\left(1+\alpha-\tau_l\right)\right] \\
& - \left(1+g\right)\left(1-\beta\right)\left[\left(1+g\right) + \beta\left(\delta_k - 1\right)\right]\left(1+\alpha-\tau_l\right).
\end{aligned}
\tag{19.72}
$$

19.3.3 Example 19.2

With the same parameters as in Example 13.2, of $\gamma = \frac{1}{3}$, $\alpha = 1$, $A_h = 0.20$, $\delta_k = 0.05$, $\delta_h = 0.015$, $\beta = \frac{1}{1+\rho} = 0.95$, $\rho = \frac{1}{0.95} - 1 = 0.052632$, $A_G = 0.28224$, and assume that $\tau_l = 0.144$. Figure 19.6 graphs the calibrated version of equation (19.72) and shows that the equilibrium growth rate is $g = 0.0120$, similar to when there is a 30% capital income tax.

Alternatively, again following Appendix A12 and writing the solution equation in terms of $Ag^2 + Bg + C = 0$, the solution of equation (19.72), in terms of A, B, and C, is given in general by

$$
\begin{aligned}
A \equiv {} & -\beta\gamma\left(1-\tau_l\right) + \beta\left(1-\beta\right)\left(1-\gamma\right)\left[1+\alpha-\tau_l+\rho\left(1-\tau_l\right)\right] - \left(1+\alpha-\tau_l\right)\left(1-\beta\right), \\
B \equiv {} & -\beta\gamma\left(1-\tau_l\right)\left[1+\beta\left(\delta_k-1\right) - A_H + \delta_H\right] \\
& + \beta\left(1-\beta\right)\left(1-\gamma\right)\left\{\rho\left(1-\tau_l\right) + \delta_k\left(1+\alpha-\tau_l\right) + \left[1+\alpha-\tau_l+\rho\left(1-\tau_l\right)\right]\right\} \\
& - \left(1+\alpha-\tau_l\right)\left(1-\beta\right)\left[2+\beta\left(\delta_k-1\right)\right], \\
C \equiv {} & \beta\gamma\left(1-\tau_l\right)\left(A_H-\delta_H\right)\left[1+\beta\left(\delta_k-1\right)\right] \\
& + \beta\left(1-\beta\right)\left(1-\gamma\right)\left[\rho\left(1-\tau_l\right) + \delta_k\left(1+\alpha-\tau_l\right)\right] \\
& - \left(1+\alpha-\tau_l\right)\left(1-\beta\right)\left[1+\beta\left(\delta_k-1\right)\right].
\end{aligned}
$$

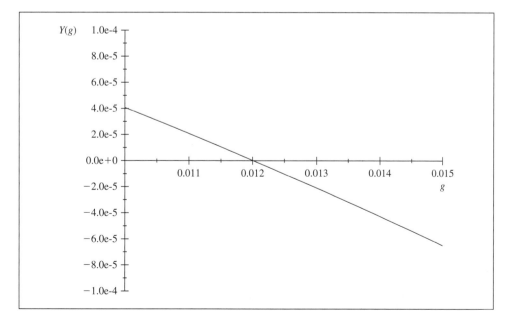

Figure 19.6 Normalised excess output demand with labour income tax of 14.4% in Example 19.2

Given the calibration, the implied values are

$$\text{Quadratic term:} \quad A = -0.3037,$$
$$\text{Linear term:} \quad B = -0.0136,$$
$$\text{Constant term:} \quad C = 0.0002067.$$

And with these inputted into the quadratic solution of Appendix A12, the growth rate is $g = 0.0120$.

The government budget constraint, divided through by y_t, implies that the 14.4% labour tax yields only about 5% of output:

$$\frac{G_t}{y_t} = \frac{\tau_l w_t l_t h_t}{y_t} = \tau_l \gamma = \frac{0.144}{3} = 0.048. \tag{19.73}$$

A 30% labour tax yields revenue of $\frac{0.30}{3} = 0.10$, or 10% of output; in comparison, for a capital tax of 30% the revenue is 20% of output. This result of relatively low tax revenue is in part due to the assumption that only effective labour enters the human capital investment production function. With physical capital as well, the increase in leisure from the labour tax would not decrease the balanced path growth rate as much; to show this would require a full analysis of the model with physical capital in both goods and human capital sectors.

The growth rate therefore is decreased significantly by the tax on capital from 3.33% with no tax down to 1.21% with the 30% tax. This shows how taxes decrease growth, even when all proceeds are returned to the consumer through an income transfer.

Other variables, with $g = 0.0120$, are

$$l_t = \frac{(1+g)\,(1-\beta)}{A_{II}\beta} = \frac{(1+0.0120)\,(1-0.95)}{(0.20)\,0.95} = 0.26632; \tag{19.74}$$

$$\frac{k_t}{h_t l_t} = \left(\frac{(1-\gamma)\,A_G}{(1+g)\,(1+\rho) - 1 + \delta_k} \right)^{\frac{1}{\gamma}},$$

$$\frac{k_t}{h_t l_t} = \left(\frac{\left(\frac{2}{3}\right) 0.28224}{(1+0.0120)\,(1+0.052632) - 1 + 0.05} \right)^{3} = 4.3502;$$

$$\frac{k_t}{h_t} = \left(\frac{k_t}{h_t l_t} \right) l_t = (4.3502)\,(0.26632) = 1.1585. \tag{19.75}$$

The calibrated AS and AD functions are

$$\frac{1}{w_t} = \frac{(1-0.144)\left(1 - \frac{0.0120+0.015}{0.20}\right)}{y\,(2-0.144) - (1.1585)\left[(1-0.144)\,(0.0526)\,(1.012) + (0.0620)\,(2-0.144)\right]}; \tag{19.76}$$

$$\frac{1}{w_t} = \frac{3}{0.28224}\left(\frac{1}{(0.28224)\,(1.1585)} \right)^{2} y_t^2. \tag{19.77}$$

Figure 19.7 graphs the inverted AS–AD equations (19.76) and (19.77) in black, as compared to when the tax rate is zero in Example 13.2 in blue.

It shows a very different result from the exogenous growth model of Chapter 9. There, the growth rate stayed the same and the aggregate demand and supply for output both shifted back with the relative price of goods $\frac{1}{w_t}$ staying the same. Here the capital stock

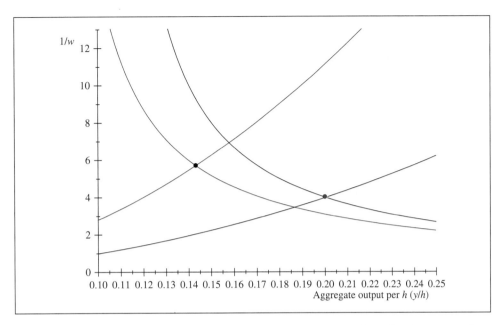

Figure 19.7 *AS–AD* with a 14.4% labour income tax in Example 19.2 (black) and a zero tax in Example 13.2 (blue)

ratio $\frac{k_t}{h_t}$ increases from 0.694 to 1.1585 and this causes the *AS* and *AD* to both shift out to give a higher level of output per unit of h_t, and a lower relative price of 4, a drop from near 6.

The rise in the output level comes however as the growth rate substantially decreases. All of this is a result in essence of taxing human capital through the labour tax and inducing more physical capital use.

The exact wage is $w_t = 0.25071$, with $\frac{1}{w_t} = \frac{1}{0.25071} = 3.9887$:

$$w_t = \gamma A_G \left(\frac{k_t}{h_t l_t}\right)^{1-\gamma} = \frac{1}{3}(0.28224)(4.3502)^{\frac{2}{3}};$$
$$w_t = 0.25071. \tag{19.78}$$

The wage rate rises from 0.1757 with no tax in Example 13.2 to 0.25071 now, and even the after tax wage rate is higher than the baseline:

$$w_t(1 - \tau_l) = 0.25071(1 - 0.144) = 0.21461.$$

Consumption is

$$\frac{c_t^d}{h_t} = \frac{(1 - \tau_l)\, w_t\left(1 - \frac{g + \delta_H}{A_H}\right) + (1 - \tau_l)\, \rho\,(1 + g)\,\frac{k_t}{h_t}}{1 + \alpha - \tau_l}$$
$$= \frac{(1 - 0.144)}{(1 + 1 - 0.144)}0.25071\left(1 - \frac{0.0120 + 0.015}{0.20}\right)$$
$$\quad + \frac{(1 - 0.144)}{1 + 1 - 0.144}(1.1585)(0.052632(1 + 0.0120))$$
$$= 0.12848.$$

Output is

$$
\frac{y_t^d}{h_t} = \frac{\left(1 - \tau_l\right) w_t \left(1 - \frac{g + \delta_H}{A_H}\right) + \frac{k_t}{h_t} \left[\left(1 - \tau_l\right) \rho \left(1 + g\right) + \left(g + \delta_k\right) \left(1 + \alpha - \tau_l\right)\right]}{1 + \alpha - \tau_l}
$$

$$
= \left(\frac{1 - 0.144}{1 + 1 - 0.144}\right) 0.25071 \left(1 - \frac{0.0120 + 0.015}{0.20}\right)
$$

$$
+ \left(\frac{(1.1585)}{2 - 0.144}\right) \left(\left(1 - 0.144\right) 0.0526 \left(1.012\right) + \left(0.0620\right) \left(1 + 1 - 0.144\right)\right)
$$

$$
= 0.20031.
$$

And $\frac{c_t^d}{y_t^d} = \frac{0.12848}{0.20031} = 0.64141$, significantly above 0.5966 in Example 13.2, the no-tax equivalent.

There is a small decrease in the investment rate, to 38% from 40%. The interest rate r_t has fallen, because of the decrease in the growth rate, to 11.5% from 13.8% with no tax:

$$
r_t = \left(1 + g\right) \left(1 + \rho\right) - 1 + \delta_k, \tag{19.79}
$$
$$
r_t = \left(1 + 0.0120\right) \left(1 + 0.052632\right) - 1 + 0.05 = 0.11526. \tag{19.80}
$$

The present value of government revenue, with h_t normalised to 1, from the labour tax is

$$
\frac{\frac{G_t}{y_t} y_t}{\rho \left(1 + g\right)} = \frac{\frac{\tau_l w_t l_t h_t}{y_t} y_t}{\rho \left(1 + g\right)} = \frac{\tau_l \gamma y_t}{\rho \left(1 + g\right)} = \frac{\left(0.144\right) \left(0.20031\right)}{0.052632 \left(1 + 0.0120\right) 3} = 0.18052. \tag{19.81}
$$

This revenue, with half the percentage tax of the 30% capital income tax, gives about half the present value of the revenue that the 30% capital income tax yields.

19.3.4 Labour market

The labour supply is affected by the labour income tax but not the labour demand. Starting with the goods–leisure margin,

$$
\frac{c_t^d \alpha}{w_t h_t \left(1 - \tau_l\right)} = x_t,
$$

substitute in for leisure x_t in the allocation of time constraint and solve for the labour supply:

$$
l_t^s = 1 - \frac{c_t^d \alpha}{w_t h_t \left(1 - \tau_l\right)} - l_{Ht}.
$$

Substitute in for c_t^d:

$$
c_t^d = \frac{\left(1 - \tau_l\right) w_t h_t \left(1 - \frac{g + \delta_H}{A_H}\right) + \left(1 - \tau_l\right) \rho \left(1 + g\right) k_t}{1 + \alpha - \tau_l}, \tag{19.82}
$$

$$
l_t^s = 1 - \left(\frac{\alpha}{1 + \alpha - \tau_l}\right) \frac{\left(1 - \tau_l\right) w_t h_t \left(1 - \frac{g + \delta_H}{A_H}\right) + \left(1 - \tau_l\right) \rho \left(1 + g\right) k_t}{w_t h_t \left(1 - \tau_l\right)} - \frac{g + \delta_H}{A_H}.
$$

Simplify to

$$
l_t^s = 1 - \left(\frac{\alpha}{1 + \alpha - \tau_l}\right) \left[1 - \frac{g + \delta_H}{A_H} + \frac{\rho \left(1 + g\right) k_t}{w_t h_t}\right] - \frac{g + \delta_H}{A_H};
$$

$$
l_t^s = \frac{\left(1 - \tau_l\right) \left(1 - \frac{g + \delta_H}{A_H}\right) - \frac{\alpha \rho \left(1 + g\right) k_t}{w_t h_t}}{1 + \alpha - \tau_l}.
$$

Labour demand is

$$l_t^d = \left(\frac{\gamma A_G}{w_t}\right)^{\frac{1}{1-\gamma}} \frac{k_t}{h_t}. \tag{19.83}$$

Inversely solved for w_t, the labour supply and demand functions are

$$w_t = \frac{\alpha\rho\left(1+g\right)\frac{k_t}{h_t}}{\left(1-\tau_l\right)\left(1-\frac{g+\delta_H}{A_H}\right) - l_t^s\left(1+\alpha-\tau_l\right)}; \tag{19.84}$$

$$w_t = \gamma A_G \left(\frac{k_t}{h_t l_t^d}\right)^{1-\gamma}. \tag{19.85}$$

Using the same calibration as in Example 19.1, the calibrated labour market equations are

$$w_t = \frac{1\left(0.052632\right)\left(1+0.0120\right)\left(1.1585\right)}{\left(1-0.144\right)\left(1-\frac{(0.0120+0.015)}{0.20}\right) - l_t^s\left(1+1-0.144\right)}; \tag{19.86}$$

$$w_t = \frac{\left(0.28224\right)\left(1.1585\right)^{\frac{2}{3}}}{3}\frac{}{\left(l_t^d\right)^{\frac{2}{3}}}. \tag{19.87}$$

Figure 19.8 graphs equations (19.86) and (19.87) in black, showing the labour market in Example 19.2, as compared to the Example 13.2 labour market in blue.

The supply of labour shifts back and the demand for labour shifts out. The wage rate rises and the employment level falls by the same 2% as it does for the 30% capital income tax in Example 19.1.

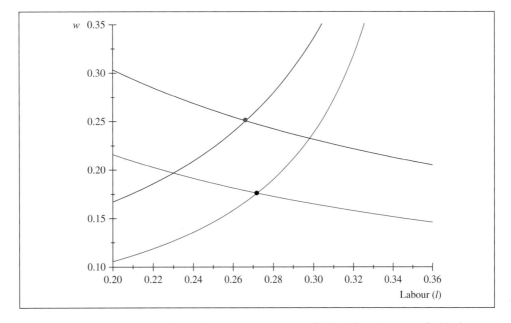

Figure 19.8 Labour market with 14.4% labour income tax (in black) and zero tax (in blue)

19.3.5 General equilibrium

The general equilibrium with a labour income tax can also be found, in terms of graphing the input and output markets. Output is 0.20031, the wage rate 0.25071 and the interest rate 0.11526 so that the isocost line with the labour tax is

$$y_t = w_t l_t h_t + r_t k_t,$$

$$\frac{0.20031}{h_t} = (0.25071) \, l_t + (0.11526) \, \frac{k_t}{h_t},$$

$$\frac{k_t}{h_t} = \frac{0.20031}{0.11526 h_t} - \frac{(0.25071) \, l_t}{0.11526}. \tag{19.88}$$

The isoquant curve is

$$y_t^s = A_G \left(l_t^d h_t \right)^\gamma (k_t)^{1-\gamma},$$

$$0.20031 = (0.28224) \left(l_t^d h_t \right)^{\frac{1}{3}} (k_t)^{\frac{2}{3}};$$

$$\frac{k_t}{h_t} = \left(\frac{0.20031}{(0.28224) \, h_t \left(l_t^d \right)^{\frac{1}{3}}} \right)^{\frac{3}{2}} = \frac{\left(\frac{0.20031}{(0.28224) h_t} \right)^{\frac{3}{2}}}{\left(l_t^d \right)^{\frac{1}{2}}}. \tag{19.89}$$

And the factor input ratio is

$$\frac{k_t}{h_t l_t} = \frac{1.1585}{0.26632} = 4.35. \tag{19.90}$$

Figure 19.9 graphs equations (19.88), (19.89) and (19.90) in variants of black, as compared to the Example 13.2 equilibrium in variants of blue.

It shows that the isoquant shifts up, the isocost pivots up and the capital to labour ratio pivots up. The rise in the physical capital to human capital ratio drives all of these results as the labour tax reduces the return on human capital and induces a shift towards physical capital that raises output while lowering the growth rate.

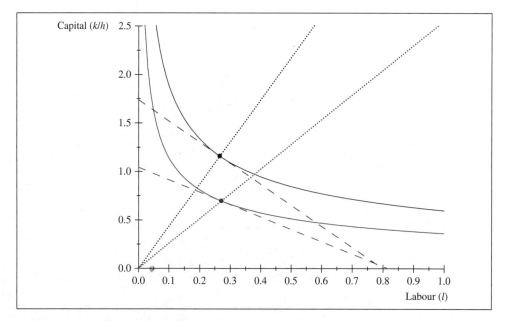

Figure 19.9 Factor market equilibrium with a labour income tax of $\tau_l = 0.144$ in Example 19.2 compared to the zero tax Example 13.2

For goods and leisure in general equilibrium, output minus investment is

$$c_t^d = y_t^s - i_t = A_G \left(l_t^d h_t\right)^\gamma (k_t)^{1-\gamma} - (g + \delta_k) k_t,$$

$$\frac{c_t^d}{h_t} = (0.28224) \left(l_t^d\right)^{\frac{1}{3}} (1.1585)^{\frac{2}{3}} - (0.0120 + 0.05)(1.1585). \tag{19.91}$$

The level curve requires the equilibrium human capital time, $l_{Ht} = \frac{g + \delta_H}{A_H} = \frac{0.0120 + 0.015}{0.20} = 0.135$. Then it is

$$u = \ln c_t + \alpha \ln x_t = \ln c_t + \alpha \ln \left(1 - l_{Ht} - l_t\right),$$

$$-2.565 = \ln 0.12848 + 1 \ln \left(1 - (0.26632 + 0.135)\right),$$

$$-2.565 = \ln c_t + \ln (T_t - l_t),$$

$$c_t = \frac{e^{-2.565}}{\left(1 - 0.135 - l_t\right)}. \tag{19.92}$$

And the budget line is

$$c_t^d = w_t l_t^s h_t \left(1 - \tau_l\right) + k_t \left[r_t - (g + \delta_k)\right] + G_t;$$

$$\frac{G_t}{h_t} = w_t \tau_l l_t h_t = (0.25071)(0.144)(0.26632) = 0.0096147;$$

$$c_t^d = w_t l_t^s h_t \left(1 - \tau_l\right) + k_t \left(r_t - \delta_k - g\right) + G_t;$$

$$\frac{c_t^d}{h_t} = (0.25071) l_t^s \left(1 - 0.144\right) + (1.1585)\left((0.115) - 0.0620\right) + 0.0096. \tag{19.93}$$

Figure 19.10 graphs equations (19.91), (19.92) and (19.93) in variants of black, and zooms in on the equilibrium to show how the budget line crosses the production function.

The labour tax equilibrium sees the budget line intersecting the production function, rather than being tangential to it, in $(c : l)$ space. This is the tax wedge graphical result. Such a wedge was not apparent for the capital tax because the graph is drawn in c and l space and the capital tax does not cause a wedge in these dimensions. But the labour tax

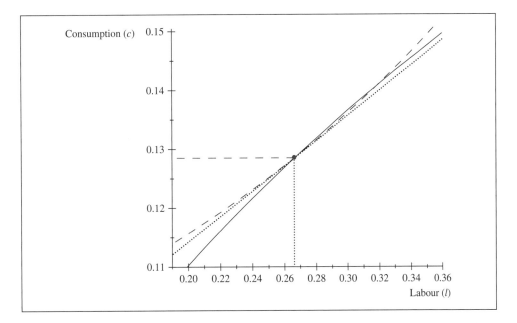

Figure 19.10 General equilibrium goods and labour with a labour income tax of $\tau_k = 0.144$ in Example 19.2

does, as in Chapter 9, with exogenous growth. Here the dashed black utility level curve is tangent to the dotted black budget line, but the level curve also intersects the black production function rather than being tangent to it. This wedge is seen graphically by noting that the black production curve is between the dotted and dashed black curves on the upper right-hand side of Figure 19.10. Normally, with no tax, the dotted black budget line is always in the middle of the production function and utility curve.

19.4 Consumption VAT

The other major tax beside inflation taxes is the tax on sales of goods. We will model this as a value-added tax denoted by τ_c as in Chapter 3. The government and consumer budget constraints are

$$G_t = \tau_c c_t;$$

$$c_t^d (1 + \tau_c) = w_t h_t l_t^s + r_t k_t + G_t - k_{t+1} + k_t (1 - \delta_k); \tag{19.94}$$

$$c_t^d = \frac{w_t h_t l_t^s + r_t k_t + G_t - k_{t+1} + k_t (1 - \delta_k)}{(1 + \tau_c)}. \tag{19.95}$$

The consumer problem is

$$V(k_t, h_t) = \underset{k_{t+1}, l_t, l_{Ht}}{\text{Max}}$$

$$\ln \left[\frac{w_t h_t l_t + r_t k_t + G_t - k_{t+1} + k_t (1 - \delta_k)}{(1 + \tau_c)} \right] + \alpha \ln (1 - l_{Ht} - l_t)$$

$$+ \beta V \left[k_{t+1}, h_t (1 - \delta_h) + A_H l_{Ht} h_t \right]. \tag{19.96}$$

The equilibrium and envelope conditions are

$$k_{t+1} : \frac{1}{c_t} \left(\frac{-1}{1 + \tau_c} \right) + \beta \frac{\partial V(k_{t+1}, h_{t+1})}{\partial k_{t+1}} = 0, \tag{19.97}$$

$$l_t : \frac{1}{c_t} \left(\frac{w_t h_t}{1 + \tau_c} \right) + \frac{\alpha}{x_t} (-1) = 0, \tag{19.98}$$

$$l_{Ht} : \frac{\alpha}{x_t} (-1) + \beta \frac{\partial V(k_{t+1}, h_{t+1})}{\partial h_{t+1}} (A_H h_t) = 0; \tag{19.99}$$

$$k_t : \frac{\partial V(k_t, h_t)}{\partial k_t} = \frac{1}{c_t} \frac{(1 + r_t - \delta_k)}{1 + \tau_c}, \tag{19.100}$$

$$h_t : \frac{\partial V(k_t, h_t)}{\partial h_t} = \frac{1}{c_t} \frac{(w_t l_t)}{1 + \tau_c}$$

$$+ \beta \frac{\partial V(k_{t+1}, h_{t+1})}{\partial h_{t+1}} (1 + A_H l_{Ht} - \delta_H). \tag{19.101}$$

Again the intertemporal margins for physical and human capital are not affected by the tax. And as with the labour tax the goods–leisure margin is affected in a similar way, just as in Chapter 3.

$$x_t = \frac{\alpha c_t (1 + \tau_c)}{w_t h_t}.$$

The equilibrium conditions imply that the goods tax enters the analysis exactly as the labour income tax enters the analysis. With a labour income tax, the leisure–goods margin is $x_t = \frac{\alpha c_t (1+\tau_c)}{w_t h_t}$. Therefore, with τ_c defined in terms of the labour tax from these margins, as

$$1 + \tau_c = \frac{1}{1 - \tau_l},$$

the analysis is exactly the same.

To see that the analysis is identical, consider the formation of the AD function; the AS is the same as with no taxes. The consumption function can be formulated again from the budget constraint and equilibrium conditions:

$$c_t^d \left(1 + \tau_c\right) = w_t h_t l_t^s + r_t k_t + G_t - k_{t+1} + k_t \left(1 - \delta_k\right),$$
$$c_t^d \left(1 + \tau_c\right) = w_t h_t l_t^s + r_t k_t + \tau_c c_t - k_{t+1} + k_t \left(1 - \delta_k\right),$$
$$c_t^d = w_t h_t l_t^s + r_t k_t - k_{t+1} + k_t \left(1 - \delta_k\right),$$
$$c_t^d = w_t h_t \left(1 - x_t - l_{Ht}\right) + r_t k_t - k_{t+1} + k_t \left(1 - \delta_k\right),$$
$$c_t^d = w_t h_t \left(1 - \frac{\alpha c_t \left(1 + \tau_c\right)}{w_t h_t} - l_{Ht}\right) + r_t k_t - k_{t+1} + k_t \left(1 - \delta_k\right),$$
$$c_t^d \left[1 + \alpha \left(1 + \tau_c\right)\right] = w_t h_t \left(1 - l_{Ht}\right) + r_t k_t - k_{t+1} + k_t \left(1 - \delta_k\right),$$
$$c_t^d = \frac{w_t h_t \left(1 - l_{Ht}\right) + r_t k_t - k_{t+1} + k_t \left(1 - \delta_k\right)}{1 + \alpha \left(1 + \tau_c\right)},$$
$$c_t^d = \frac{w_t h_t \left(1 - \frac{g + \delta_H}{A_H}\right) + \rho \left(1 + g\right) k_t}{1 + \alpha \left(1 + \tau_c\right)}.$$

This is the same consumption function for the labour income tax given that $1 + \tau_c = \frac{1}{1 - \tau_l}$. And it follows through easily to the same AD function:

$$y_t^d = \frac{w_t h_t \left(1 - \frac{g + \delta_H}{A_H}\right) + \rho \left(1 + g\right) k_t}{1 + \alpha \left(1 + \tau_c\right)} + k_t \left(g + \delta_k\right);$$
$$y_t^d = \frac{w_t h_t \left(1 - \frac{g + \delta_H}{A_H}\right) + k_t \left[\rho \left(1 + g\right) + \left(g + \delta_k\right) \left(1 + \alpha \left(1 + \tau_c\right)\right)\right]}{1 + \alpha \left(1 + \tau_c\right)}.$$

This is the same AD function with $1 + \tau_c = \frac{1}{1 - \tau_l}$.

This is why the optimal taxation analysis in Chapter 18 finds a composite labour tax in which the labour income tax and the consumption goods tax each add to this composite. There, in equation (18.22), the composite labour tax is $\frac{\tau_c + \tau_l}{1 + \tau_c}$, and it is set equal to the capital tax τ_k in the optimum. Let the labour tax in the composite be denoted by τ_l' for the moment. Then with $1 + \tau_c = \frac{1}{1 - \tau_l}$, this composite labour tax becomes

$$\frac{\tau_c + \tau_l'}{1 + \tau_c} = \frac{\frac{1}{1 - \tau_l} - 1 + \tau_l'}{\frac{1}{1 - \tau_l}} = \tau_l + \left(1 - \tau_l\right) \tau_l'.$$

If $\tau_l' = 0$, and there is no direct tax on labour income, then the composite labour tax reduces to just τ_l. Or if $\tau_c = \frac{1}{1 - \tau_l} - 1 = 0$, and there is no direct tax on goods but there is a direct tax on labour income, then the composite tax reduces to just the labour income tax τ_l'. All of this implies that the goods tax merely compounds the labour income tax. However one difference is that in this example the goods tax raises more revenue.

19.4.1 Example 19.3

Assume the calibration as in Example 19.2, including $\tau_l = 0.144$. Set $\tau_c = \frac{1}{1-\tau_l} - 1 = \frac{1}{1-0.144} - 1 = 0.16822$. The equilibrium growth rate, and goods and labour market equilibria, will be the same as derived in Example 19.2, but the present value of the revenue raised will be higher.

Consumption from Example 19.2 is 0.12438, and the present value of government revenue is

$$\frac{G_t}{\rho\left(1+g\right)} = \frac{\tau_c c_t}{\rho\left(1+g\right)} = \frac{\left(\frac{1}{1-(0.144)} - 1\right)0.12438}{0.052632\left(1+0.0120\right)} = 0.39283, \tag{19.102}$$

as compared to 0.18052 with the labour tax. This is twice the revenue from the labour income tax.

Note that the equivalence of the goods and labour taxes, and the revenue differences, holds here when only effective labour is used to produce human capital. These results would be expected to differ with physical capital also entering the human capital investment production function. Also, with heterogeneous agents and income inequality, a labour tax may possibly be more desirable than the goods tax in terms of its effect on income inequality.

19.5 Applications

19.5.1 Value-added taxes

For example, consider how value-added taxes (VAT) differ internationally in 2009. The US does not have a federal value-added tax. But nearly every state in the US has sales taxes that can be treated as if they are federal value-added taxes in other countries. Figure 19.11 shows how VAT varies substantially across nations.

The main European nations of Italy, France and Germany have the highest rates at nearly 20%. Spain and the United Kingdom follow at near the 15% level (although in the UK VAT is due to rise to 20%), with Australia and New Zealand in the 10–12.5% range, and the United States and Canada at the bottom of the range near 5%.

Figure 19.11 shows a marked segmentation by region. Europe has the highest VAT rates, Australasia the middle rates, and the US and Canada at the low end. This suggests that nations may need to keep rates comparable, because of tax evasion for example. Goods can be easily smuggled across open borders to take advantage of differences in tax treatment.

The graph also shows why European countries may lag in growth rates relative to North American countries. If a reliance on proportional goods taxes such as VAT is similar to a labour tax in its economic effects, then VAT compounds the burden of the labour tax. And labour income and capital income tax rates are already similar across all of these developed nations, at least with less variability than seen in VAT. This suggests more negative effects on growth in the high VAT regions.

19.5.2 Application: trickle down economics

When Ronald Reagan became US President one of his earliest initiatives was to reduce marginal tax rates on personal income and so aim to increase the economic growth rate. The US Economic Recovery Tax Act of 1981 reduced top marginal tax rates from 70% to 50% and the bottom tax bracket from 14% to 11%. According to Christopher Frenze, Chief Economist to the Vice-Chairman of the Joint Economic Committee, 'The Reagan tax cuts, like similar measures enacted in the 1920s and 1960s, showed that reducing excessive tax

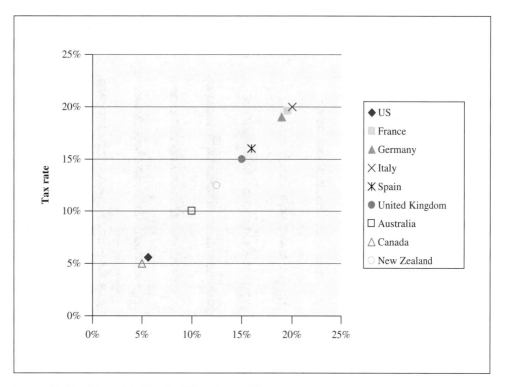

Figure 19.11 Value added tax in different countries

Sources: Value Added Taxes: TMF Group, and Worldwide-Tax.com, 'Tax Rates Around the World'; Government sources: UK HM Revenue & Customs, Australian Taxation Office, Canada Revenue Agency, New Zealand Inland Revenue.

rates stimulates growth' (April 1996, JEC Report). However this was called 'trickle down' economics that would have little effect on the common taxpayer.

This chapter's analysis shows how lower taxes increase the balanced path growth rate. And with 'trickle down', this might lead to a worse distribution of income across income classes. Figure 19.12 shows the distributional consequences of the 1980s tax cuts, which were continued in the US 1986 Tax Reform Act, as computed by The Joint Economic Committee of the US Congress (April 1996, JEC Report). It shows that the share of the total income paid in taxes increased for the income groups with the Top 1%, Top 5%, Top 10% of income, and that for the Lowest 50%, the tax share from income went down. Thus while the US growth rate experienced an increase after the 1980s tax reform, the income distribution also appeared to become more equitable.

19.5.3 Capital, market interest rates and equity value

The chapter shows how a capital tax can decrease the growth rate. The effect of taxes on stock markets and the equity premium is developed by Ellen McGrattan and Edward C. Prescott in their 2003 article 'Average Debt and Equity Returns: Puzzling?' In particular, because tax rates on corporate profit, like a capital tax, had been so high, the implied market rate of interest had been pushed high. The tax rate caused a tax wedge that pushed up the observed before-tax interest returns on equity.

The high returns created a large gap relative to the interest rates on government bonds that has proved difficult to explain without including tax analysis. But McGrattan and Prescott explain changes in this equity premium through changes in the tax rates, where

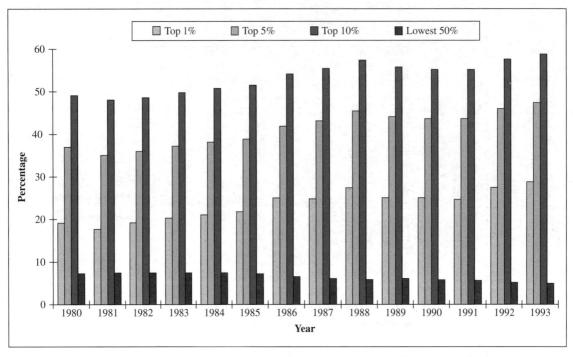

Figure 19.12 Share of total income taxes paid by income groups

Source: IRS and JEC staff calculations (The Joint Economic Committee of the US Congress, report entitled 'The Reagan Tax Cuts: Lessons for Tax Reform', April 1996, http://www.house.gov/jec/fiscal/tx-grwth/reagtxct/reagtxct.htm).

they look at over a century of data describing the US experience from 1880 to 2002. They show that the equity premium rose as the average marginal corporate tax rate in the US increased up through WWII, and this premium declined as the average corporate tax rate declined from 50% during WWII down to an average (rather than the statutory rate) below 20% in the 1990s and into 2002.

Using the same type of framework, McGrattan and Prescott explain the value of corporations in another article published in 2005 entitled 'Taxes, Regulations, and the Value of U.S. and U.K. Corporations'. There they explain changes in the market value of corporations both in the US and UK through changes in the corporate tax rate. The tax structure within their economic model is more detailed than the one in this chapter, capturing nuances of corporate tax law such as investment subsidies and differences between corporate profits and dividends. But the result is consistent with lower corporate income tax rates causing higher growth rates of output and higher dividend earning streams.

19.6 Questions

1. Derive the aggregate demand AD as a function of the wage rate, the capital ratio, and exogenous parameters including the tax rate, when there is a tax on labour income as in Example 19.1.

2. For Example 19.1, if the tax rate on capital is assumed to be $\tau_k = 0.20$ instead of $\tau_k = 0.30$, then the solution equation (19.25) is modified by only one term, and Figure 19.13 showing this modified equation shows that the normalised excess demand equals zero when $g = 0.01872$.

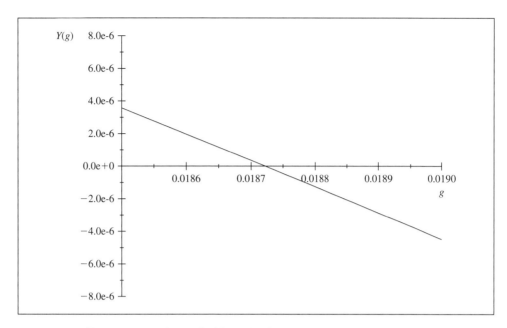

Figure 19.13 Excess output demand with capital income tax $\tau_k = 0.20$ in a modification of Example 19.1

    (a) Find the new employment level using equation (19.26) with the new tax rate and growth rate.

    (b) Find the physical capital to human capital ratio using the next equation (19.27).

3. How would a lower tax rate on capital income in Example 19.1
    (a) affect the graphed *AS* and *AD* curves of Figure 19.2?
    (b) affect the graphed labour supply and demand curves of Figure 19.3?
    (c) How would the general equilibrium input and output graphs be affected, in Figures 19.4 and 19.5?

4. In Example 19.2, the labour income tax rate is $\tau_l = 0.144$. Let the tax rate instead be $\tau_l = 0.10$. This modifies the solution equation (19.72), and this modified equation (Figure 19.14) shows that the normalised excess demand equals zero when $g = 0.01985$.
    (a) Find the new employment level using equation (19.74) with the new tax rate and growth rate.
    (b) Find the physical capital to human capital ratio using the next equation (19.75).

5. How would a lower tax rate on labour income in Example 19.2
    (a) affect the graphed *AS* and *AD* curves of Figure 19.7?
    (b) affect the graphed labour supply and demand curves of Figure 19.8?
    (c) How would the general equilibrium input and output graphs be affected, in Figures 19.9 and 19.10?

6. As in Example 19.3, if the labour tax is 10%, or $\tau_l = 0.10$,
    (a) What would be an economically equivalent level of the goods tax rate τ_c?
    (b) Would the goods tax or the labour income tax yield more revenue if they were set at equivalent levels?

7. How can relatively high value-added taxes across a region cause lower growth rates within that region, compared to other regions, given that the labour and income tax rates are comparable across the regions?

8. Suggest how capital tax rates can affect the observed equity premium.

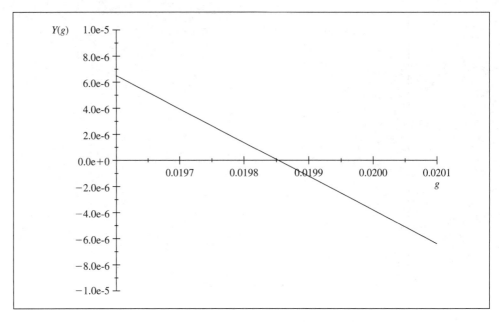

Figure 19.14 Normalised excess output demand with labour income tax of 10% in a modification of Example 19.2

19.7 References

King, Robert G. and Sergio Rebelo, 1990, 'Public Policy and Economic Growth: Developing Neoclassical Implications', *Journal of Political Economy,* University of Chicago Press, 98(5): S126-50, October.

Lucas, Robert Jr., 1988, 'On the Mechanics of Economic Development', *Journal of Monetary Economics,* Elsevier, 22(1): 3–42, July.

McGrattan, Ellen, and Edward C. Prescott, 2003, 'Average Debt and Equity Returns: Puzzling?', *American Economic Review,* American Economic Association, 93(2): 392–397, May.

McGrattan, Ellen, and Edward C. Prescott, 2005, 'Taxes, Regulations, and the Value of U.S. and U.K. Corporations', *Review of Economic Studies,* Blackwell Publishing, 72(3): 767–796.

Ramsey, Frank P., 1927, 'A Contribution to the Theory of Taxation', *Economic Journal,* 37(145): 47–61.

Rebelo, Sergio, 1991, 'Long-Run Policy Analysis and Long-Run Growth', *Journal of Political Economy,* University of Chicago Press, 99(3): 500–521, June.

Stokey, Nancy L. and Sergio Rebelo, 1995, 'Growth Effects of Flat-Rate Taxes', *Journal of Political Economy,* University of Chicago Press, 103(3): 519–550, June.

CHAPTER ⓴

Monetary theory and policy

20.1 Introduction

The chapter introduces inflation and builds fundamentals of monetary economics, including its application to central bank policy. It starts by deriving the main link between the real and the so-called 'nominal' economy in which aggregate prices are affected by inflation. This link is known as the Fisher equation of interest rates and it shows that the nominal, or market, interest rate is the sum of the real interest rate and the inflation rate. It implies, for example, that to earn any real interest on capital, the interest rate charged has to be greater than the inflation rate.

The entrance of the inflation rate into the determination of the nominal interest rate is the start of the chapter's monetary economics. Then it examines how inflation is created by financing government expenditure by printing money. It assumes that some given fraction of output is spent by the government and financed solely by printing money. And it shows how this translates into a close relation between the money supply growth rate, the inflation rate, and the fraction of output spent by the government and financed by printing money. As an application, using the relation between government spending and money supply financing, hyperinflation seen around the world is explained.

Within the formalised monetary economies that are presented, inflation as a tax falls on all purchases made with money. This is assumed to be all consumption purchases, while leisure is untaxed by inflation. This means that one main effect of the tax is to induce substitution from goods to leisure. This is why the tax causes less employment.

The full dynamic baseline exogenous growth model is extended to include money supply printing to finance government spending. This formalises the effect of the inflation tax upon the real economy. In exogenous growth, the effect is the same as a labour tax. Increasing inflation causes less equilibrium employment, output and capital. The wage rate, real interest rate and growth rate do not change because of the exogenous growth assumption.

Then the full dynamic baseline endogenous growth model is presented with the inflation tax. The results are again similar to the effect of the labour tax in endogenous growth. The employment declines, but by less than in exogenous growth, and the real interest rate and growth rate decline – the real wage increases. Also the physical capital to human capital ratio increases since the inflation tax acts as a tax on human capital. This induces an output increase, even as the growth rate decreases.

Central bank policy is discussed by deriving an equilibrium condition that describes the so-called 'Taylor rule' of interest rate determination. This is done by combining the Fisher equation of interest rates with the consumer's intertemporal marginal rate of substitution. It shows the equivalence of money supply rules and interest rate rules, and allows for interpretation of the Taylor rule as optimal consumer behaviour given the money supply rule, rather than an interest targeting rule of the central bank. The financial crisis of the last decade is then discussed in terms of monetary policy that forces deviations in the real interest rate away from its natural business cycle levels.

20.1.1 Building on the last chapters

The price level and money supply were introduced in Chapter 18 on government finance. That chapter deals only with the government budget constraint without the full representative agent optimisation. This chapter shows the implications of the increase in the price level from printing money in terms of the effect on the full equilibrium of the dynamic economies developed in Parts 4 and 5.

In the previous chapter, and in Chapter 9, taxes are introduced into the dynamic exogenous growth and endogenous growth economies. This chapter does the same. But now the tax is the inflation tax. Because this is not an explicit tax as are labour income, capital income and goods purchase taxes, it is shown how the inflation rate enters into the economy and affects it exactly like a tax. In particular, because it works on the goods to leisure margin in the same way as does the labour tax, the economic analysis in this chapter of the inflation tax is very similar to Chapters 9 and 19 on the labour tax.

20.1.2 Learning objective

The challenge is to see that the monetary economy incorporates money supply and the price level in a way that reduces down to a standard economy that has a tax imposed upon it. The tax is the inflation tax and it affects the marginal rate of substitution between goods and leisure as does a labour tax. Understanding how inflation results, from financing government expenditure that is not being financed by the regular explicit taxes, goes a long way towards seeing how inflation results and why it affects the economy as does a tax.

The examples show how much revenue is consistent with particular inflation rates and money supply growth rates, to provide intuition of what the inflation tax means when seen in the full dynamic equilibrium economies. It is key to see that the tax results in these monetary economies just as do other taxes in the non-monetary economy. Making the economy a monetary one is just the way to show the effect of the inflation tax.

20.1.3 Who made it happen?

Martin Bailey's (1956) 'The Welfare Cost of Inflationary Finance' started the modern literature in formalising the effects of the inflation tax within a monetary economy. Cagan (1956) uses the same framework to explain hyperinflation across Europe. Showing the inflation tax effects in general equilibrium exogenous growth was accomplished by Samuelson (1958) and Sidrauski (1967). Lucas (1975) introduced an inflation tax effect on capital and output within a full general equilibrium economy, albeit without specifying the explicit use for money. Lucas (1980) and Goodfriend and McCallum (1987) pioneered the economies in which money is used for exchange, as it is in this chapter. Gomme (1993) puts money used for exchange into the baseline endogenous growth model and shows how inflation reduces economic growth.

20.2 The Fisher equation: linking nominal and real

Irving Fisher, in 1896, in his theory of the interest rate (*Appreciation and Interest*) showed how the market interest rate actually contains both a real and a nominal component. This famous theory has become the cornerstone of the link in macroeconomics between the monetary and real sides of the economy. Here we show how this is derived in our dynamic baseline economy by extending it to include a second asset.

Besides physical capital, now it is also possible for the consumer to invest in financial capital, in the form of government bonds. These government bonds will be nominal bonds that are in terms of current dollar units. Dividing the nominal bonds by the aggregate price level, which is the price of goods, gives the amount of real bonds. And proceeding to account for the price level in the dynamic equation ends up introducing the inflation rate into the return on the nominal bonds. This inflation rate factor is shown to partly determine the bond return and this is how the real and the so-called nominal sides are linked together.

20.2.1 The separation of real from nominal factors

Consider introducing the nominal price level P_t into the economy and allowing it to change over time. In previous analysis it has been assumed that the nominal price of goods P_t is equal to 1 and unchanging. In this way the price level has been suppressed while focusing only on the relative price of goods $\frac{1}{w_t}$, the inverse of the real wage. Consider first what this relative price looks like when nominal factors are introduced. The price of goods relative to leisure is now the nominal price of goods P_t divided by the nominal wage rate. The nominal wage can be expressed using the real wage w_t, but this is done by factoring the real wage by the price level P_t so as to give the nominal wage of $w_t P_t$. The relative price of goods to leisure is the same as before: $\frac{P_t}{P_t w_t} = \frac{1}{w_t}$; this relative price is unaffected and the same regardless of the introduction of nominal factors. This is why putting all real variables in nominal terms in general may not have an effect on the analysis. If nominal factors have no effect on any real factors then this is called the superneutrality of money. This means there is a separation of real and nominal factors such that they do not affect each other. In particular, the inflation rate in such a case would have no effect on the real variables of the economy.

However in practice, and in our theory, the nominal factors do affect real variables in a variety of ways. This nominal to real effect is in general a way to define the topic known as monetary economics. And the nominal interest rate is a key variable that explicitly contains both nominal and real factors.

20.2.2 The nominal interest rate and the Fisher equation

To derive the 1896 Fisher equation of interest rates we need only take our economy with government bonds, while putting all variables in nominal terms. Money does not have to be added explicitly to the model. So instead of a budget constraint where all variables are expressed in real terms, we can write that constraint with all variables expressed in nominal terms. The market interest rate on government bonds is still expressed as R_t. However it will be shown to contain an inflation component, if the inflation rate is not equal to zero.

Consider the model of the consumer earning income from working for the firm, for $w_t l_t$, and renting capital to the firm, for $r_t k_t$, and also investing in capital and buying bonds, as in equation (17.8) of Section 17.1. The first difference is now to write the budget constraint in nominal terms, whereby the price level is factored to every term in the budget constraint. Second the nominal government bonds that enter the budget constraint are denoted by B_t where the relation to the 'real' government bonds in Chapter 17 is that the nominal bond divided by the price level equals the real bond:

$$\frac{B_t}{P_t} \equiv b_t. \tag{20.1}$$

Deriving the Fisher equation

The nominal budget constraint is that consumption equals income minus investment in physical capital and in nominal bonds:

$$P_t c_t = P_t w_t l_t + P_t r_t k_t - P_t k_{t+1} + P_t k_t (1 - \delta_k) - B_{t+1} + B_t (1 + R_t). \tag{20.2}$$

Solving for c_t by dividing through by P_t, this becomes

$$c_t = w_t l_t + r_t k_t - k_{t+1} + k_t (1 - \delta_k) - \frac{B_{t+1}}{P_t} + \frac{B_t}{P_t} (1 + R_t). \tag{20.3}$$

The term $\frac{B_{t+1}}{P_t}$ can be rewritten in terms of inflation. Define the gross inflation rate as the ratio of the price level over time, $\frac{P_{t+1}}{P_t}$, where π_{t+1} is used to denote the inflation rate at time $t+1$:

$$\frac{P_{t+1}}{P_t} \equiv 1 + \pi_{t+1}. \tag{20.4}$$

This makes $\frac{B_{t+1}}{P_t}$ equal to

$$\frac{B_{t+1}}{P_t} = \frac{B_{t+1} P_{t+1}}{P_{t+1} P_t} = b_{t+1} (1 + \pi_{t+1}). \tag{20.5}$$

It is clear that with a fixed price level of $P_{t+1} = P_t = P$, that $\frac{P_{t+1}}{P_t} \equiv 1$ and that the inflation rate is always zero. In this case, the model reduces down to the same model as in Chapter 17 in which it is implicitly assumed that there is zero inflation.

With a non-zero inflation rate allowed for, the budget constraint becomes

$$c_t = w_t l_t + r_t k_t - k_{t+1} + k_t (1 - \delta_k) - b_{t+1} (1 + \pi_{t+1}) + b_t (1 + R_t). \tag{20.6}$$

The consumer problem in turn is

$$V(k_t, b_t) = \max_{l_t, k_{t+1}, b_{t+1}}$$
$$\ln \left[w_t l_t + r_t k_t - k_{t+1} + k_t (1 - \delta_k) - b_{t+1} (1 + \pi_{t+1}) + b_t (1 + R_t) \right]$$
$$+ \alpha \ln (1 - l_t) + \beta V(k_{t+1}, b_{t+1}). \tag{20.7}$$

Now it was shown in Chapter 8 first that the equilibrium conditions with respect to k_{t+1} and k_t imply that the intertemporal marginal rate of substitution, and the corresponding growth rate form of the equation, with $\beta = \frac{1}{1+\rho}$ and g the growth rate, are

$$\frac{c_{t+1}}{\beta c_t} = 1 + r_t - \delta_k, \tag{20.8}$$

$$1 + g = \frac{1 + r_t - \delta_k}{1 + \rho}, \tag{20.9}$$

while the real wage equals the marginal rate of substitution between goods and leisure,

$$w_t = \frac{\frac{\alpha}{x_t}}{\frac{1}{c_t}}. \tag{20.10}$$

The two new equilibrium conditions with respect to b_{t+1} and b_t are

$$\frac{1}{\beta c_t} (1 + \pi_{t+1}) = \frac{\partial V(k_{t+1}, b_{t+1})}{\partial b_{t+1}}, \tag{20.11}$$

and that

$$\frac{\partial V(k_t, b_t)}{\partial b_t} = \frac{1}{c_t} (1 + R_t). \tag{20.12}$$

The first of these conditions differs from its previous version in Chapter 17 by the added factor of $1 + \pi_{t+1}$. Putting together these two conditions, again by bringing back by one period the time period in equation (20.11), these equations imply that

$$\frac{1}{\beta} \frac{1}{c_{t-1}} \left(1 + \pi_t\right) = \frac{1}{c_t} \left(1 + R_t\right) = 0. \tag{20.13}$$

Solving for $1 + R_t$, the equation is

$$1 + R_t = \frac{c_t}{\beta c_{t-1}} \left(1 + \pi_t\right). \tag{20.14}$$

Using equation (20.8) to substitute for $\frac{c_t}{\beta c_{t-1}}$, the Fisher equation of nominal interest rates results:

$$1 + R_t = \left(1 + r_t - \delta_k\right) \left(1 + \pi_t\right). \tag{20.15}$$

Understanding the Fisher equation

The Fisher equation of nominal interest rates shows how inflation affects the market rate of interest. If there is zero inflation, then the market rate R equals the real rate of interest $r - \delta_k$. But if there is positive inflation then the nominal interest rate is higher. Most simply, take the log of each side of the Fisher equation and use the approximation that $\ln\left(1 + x\right) \simeq x$, then

$$R_t = r_t - \delta_k + \pi_t. \tag{20.16}$$

The higher is the inflation rate, the higher is the nominal interest rate. And that makes sense. And investment today that yields 3% in one year must account for the change in the aggregate price level P_t over the year. If inflation is 2%, then the market, or nominal, interest rate must be 5% to yield a 3% real interest rate yield.

The Fisher equation of interest rates is probably the most fundamental of all equations in monetary economics. Its link between the real interest rate and the market interest rate, via addition of the inflation rate, is elegantly simple in its formulation. The return on capital, as found in everyday markets, must incorporate the inflation rate in order for a real return to be yielded as expected.

The Fisher equation also hints at how important it is to know the actual inflation rate in order to get the real return that was intended. And when the inflation that is expected ends up being for example higher than the actual inflation, then this causes a whole set of distortions. And vice versa, as distortions in the reverse direction result when inflation ends up being lower than was actually expected.

20.2.3 Unexpected inflation and the Phillips curve

Analysis of just the Fisher equation of interest rates suggests that there are both short run and long run effects, which can be very different, as a result of inflation and changes in the level of inflation. One set of analysis has to do with properly anticipated, or expected, inflation and what happens when such an inflation rate changes, also with the change being fully expected. That analysis is perhaps the most fundamental, first step, in understanding how inflation affects the economy. But more difficult, and sometimes more important when the economy has sudden shocks to government spending that it must finance, is when inflation changes in unexpected ways.

Consider equation (20.16). Suppose that the consumer lends money to banks or directly to firms at the beginning of time t at the rate of interest R_t. They expect the inflation rate to be π_t during time t. But say the government increases involvement in a war, as during the Vietnam War of the 1970s, or as in the Iraq–Afghanistan Wars of post 2001. And if this involvement is not totally anticipated, and if the means of financing such wars through money creation is not totally anticipated, then the actual inflation rate can end up significantly higher than the expected rate. In this case, the real return on the loan can end up being below the anticipated return of $r_t - \delta_k$, and can even be negative. Such negative real interest rates were found to have existed during the 1970s and during 2001–03 in the US. And during the 1970s when the world was on the Breton Woods system of fixed exchange rates anchored in the value of the US dollar, some of the US inflation was exported worldwide and resulted in negative real interest rates internationally. This is because inflation was accelerating, or continually increasing upwards from the late 1960s throughout until 1980. And such acceleration caught financial markets by surprise.

Therefore the Fisher equation shows how real interest rates can and have in fact been negative because of unanticipated inflation. The effects of this can be what is known as a Phillips curve, in the short run. Output increases because the real interest rate for borrowers, being the firms, in effect gets knocked lower than was contracted for. This creates a windfall for borrowers and they can invest more and produce more goods and so output can rise. The rise in output from unexpected acceleration of the inflation rate is the basic concept behind the Phillips curve. Statistically this relation has been found during many periods, especially when inflation is accelerating or decelerating. But it is much harder to empirically identify such a Phillips relation when inflation is changing in a mostly anticipated way, such as post 1983 in the US (Stock and Watson, 1999).

When inflation decelerates unexpectedly, the reverse happens. The real interest rate for borrowers is in effect higher than they anticipated. This causes firms to invest less and produce less, so that output falls. The decrease in output because of an unanticipated deceleration of inflation causes a Phillips curve relation also, but now in the other direction. Lower inflation causes lower output.

20.2.4 Interpreting the Phillips curve relation

The association of inflation rate levels with the economy's output level does not imply a good thing. In other words, the association comes about only because consumers and firms, borrowers and lenders, are making mistakes. This association reflects an inefficiency caused by variation, or volatility, in the inflation rate. The fact that volatility, rather than being efficient, is a bad thing for efficiency is that after a while the real interest rates end up going up because of the known risk of inflation volatility. So eventually markets respond and build the risk into rates of return so as to make borrowing more expensive, just because of the risk of fluctuating inflation rates.

The inefficiency of unanticipated inflation implies that governments are not wise to try to exploit the inflation–output association. For example, they might try to accelerate inflation so as to raise output. This often seems to happen, in practical government policy at various times. But what is more likely is the inability to finance unexpected government spending by direct taxes, leading to money printing and increased borrowing through government bond issuance.

20.3 Money supply, inflation and government expenditure

Inflation by definition occurs when the aggregate price level rises. A long historical link has been established empirically between the inflation rate and the money supply growth rate. Consider how inflation results by starting with the way in which the government can use the creation of new money for the financing of government expenditure. Assume for simplicity that the government cannot raise taxes or issue new government bonds for some additional expenditure; rather it can only use an increase in its money. Denote this new expenditure in real terms by G_t^n. And assume for simplicity that the economy starts at the BGP equilibrium, and that the stationary rate of money supply growth, as denoted by σ, along the BGP equilibrium is zero. In other words

$$\frac{M_{t+1} - M_t}{M_t} = \sigma_{t+1} = 0,$$

for all time t.

20.3.1 Money supply growth and government spending

Now with new government spending, the government budget constraint for this expenditure is

$$G_t^n = \frac{M_{t+1} - M_t}{P_t}.$$

Suppose that this additional government expenditure is prolonged, such as for a prolonged war or bank crisis or recession. And along the BGP let this be a constant fraction of output, η, so that

$$\frac{G_t^n}{y_t} = \eta.$$

Then combining the government finance equations,

$$\frac{G_t^n}{y_t} = \eta = \frac{M_{t+1} - M_t}{P_t y_t}.$$

In turn, we can ascertain the money supply rate of growth, which is no longer zero:

$$\eta = \frac{M_{t+1} - M_t}{P_t y_t} = \frac{M_{t+1} - M_t}{M_t} \frac{M_t}{P_t y_t} = \frac{\sigma_{t+1} M_t}{P_t y_t}. \tag{20.17}$$

This implies that the necessary money supply growth rate to finance the government expenditure is

$$\sigma_{t+1} = \eta \frac{P_t y_t}{M_t}. \tag{20.18}$$

Consider writing the money stock M_t in real terms. Define the real money m_t and the money supply divided by the goods price P_t:

$$m_t \equiv \frac{M_t}{P_t}.$$

Then the needed money supply growth rate σ_{t+1}, is

$$\sigma_{t+1} = \eta \frac{y_t}{m_t}. \tag{20.19}$$

The income velocity of money is defined by the ratio $\frac{y_t}{m_t}$. In the case when this velocity is 1, meaning that all output is bought with money, then the result is simply that the money supply growth rate equals the government expenditure share:

$$\sigma_{t+1} = \eta. \tag{20.20}$$

In general, for cases when velocity is greater than 1, as is typical, then the money supply growth rate exceeds the government expenditure share:

$$\sigma_{t+1} = \frac{\eta y_t}{m_t} > \eta. \tag{20.21}$$

Put differently, when less real money is held, and printing money is the way to pay for expenditure, then the money has to be printed at a faster rate in order to purchase the same expenditure. This relation is developed by showing how the money supply growth rate implies the level of the inflation rate.

20.3.2 Money supply and the inflation rate

The inflation rate can be solved along the balanced growth path equilibrium for the case when $\eta = \frac{G_t^n}{y_t}$ and this is financed by issuing more money. Then the fraction η can be written as

$$\frac{G_t^n}{y_t} = \eta = \frac{M_{t+1} - M_t}{P_t y_t} = \frac{M_{t+1} P_{t+1}}{P_{t+1} P_t y_t} - \frac{M_t}{P_t y_t} = \frac{m_{t+1}\left(1 + \pi_{t+1}\right)}{y_t} - \frac{m_t}{y_t}.$$

And consider that in general there may be positive output growth in the economy, whereby

$$\frac{y_{t+1}}{y_t} = 1 + g_{t+1}. \tag{20.22}$$

Then the fraction η, taking into account possible output growth, is

$$\eta = \frac{m_{t+1} y_{t+1}\left(1 + \pi_{t+1}\right)}{y_{t+1} y_t} - \frac{m_t}{y_t} = \frac{m_{t+1}}{y_{t+1}}\left(1 + g_{t+1}\right)\left(1 + \pi_{t+1}\right) - \frac{m_t}{y_t}. \tag{20.23}$$

20.3.3 Zero growth inflation rate determination

In the case when there is zero growth so that $g = 0$, then along the BGP $\frac{m_{t+1}}{m_t} = \frac{y_{t+1}}{y_t}$, which in turn implies that the equilibrium money per unit of output is stationary: $\frac{m_{t+1}}{y_{t+1}} = \frac{m_t}{y_t} = \frac{m}{y}$. This gives the solution for the inflation rate in terms of stationary money demand per output and η:

$$\eta = \frac{m}{y}\left(1 + \pi\right) - \frac{m}{y};$$
$$\pi = \frac{\eta y}{m}.$$

And in this case, by equation (20.19) inflation also equals the money supply growth rate:

$$\pi = \frac{\eta y}{m} = \sigma. \tag{20.24}$$

Therefore, besides its determination by the money supply growth rate σ, the inflation rate is alternatively determined by how much expenditure is financed by money, or η, and by the income velocity of money $\frac{y}{m}$. When money is used for all purchases so that $m = y$, then velocity is equal to 1. And the inflation rate in this case is just the expenditure share of output:

$$\pi = \eta. \tag{20.25}$$

And the inflation rate also equals the money supply growth rate by equation (20.19):

$$\pi = \eta = \sigma. \tag{20.26}$$

However, the higher is velocity, so that $\frac{y}{m} > 1$, the higher is the inflation rate in this example for a given η.

20.3.4 Example 20.1: Financing high spending when growth is zero

Assume that government spending equal to 10% of the output needs to be financed by printing money. Then if $g = 0$ and there is zero growth, the inflation rate equals the money supply growth rate. But to find these levels the velocity of money needs to be known. Assume that velocity is given at $\frac{y}{m} = 5$. Then the inflation rate and money supply growth rate are

$$\eta \left(\frac{y}{m} \right) = (0.10)\, 5 = 0.5. \tag{20.27}$$

And by equation (20.24),

$$\eta \left(\frac{y}{m} \right) = 0.5 = \sigma = \pi. \tag{20.28}$$

This gives a very high inflation and money supply growth rate of 50%, which is not implausible if such a large percentage of output is purchased by printing money. These rates were seen in post-Soviet economies after 1990 when new governments had few other tax sources.

20.3.5 Example 20.2: Financing low spending when growth is zero

Now assume that only 2% of spending is financed by printing money. Then again the velocity needs to be known. Assume now that velocity is smaller, since there is less incentive to avoid money use, because there is less inflation. Let $\frac{y}{m} = 2$, and then

$$\eta \left(\frac{y}{m} \right) = (0.02)\, 2 = 0.04 = \sigma = \pi. \tag{20.29}$$

This implies that a money supply growth rate and inflation rate of 4% will finance 2% of output in a zero growth economy. This is plausible, and the type of 'normal' levels of inflation tax revenue that western governments raise.

20.3.6 The inflation tax

The inflation tax results from the supply of money because the government is 'collecting' the tax when it uses new money to buy output. And then the value of the existing money supply is lower since prices rise and less real goods can be bought with the same money. Therefore there are two parts to the inflation tax: its collection as the government prints new money, and the way it imposes upon the representative agent by reducing the value of existing money. The ability to purchase less goods after the inflation tax has been imposed, and the inflation rate has risen, is the same way any tax reduces the representative agent's ability to buy goods: its real expenditure budget is decreased by the tax.

Velocity enters into the determination of the inflation tax rate, or inflation level, in that the less money that is being used by the consumer, then the higher must be the inflation tax rate in order to raise the same amount of revenue that is sufficient to pay for the constant share of government expenditure η. In other words, the broader is the 'tax base', the lower can be the tax rate and still raise a particular amount of revenue. A higher velocity means a narrower tax base for the inflation tax and so the inflation rate needs to be higher for a given government expenditure rate.

20.3.7 Inflation and growth

Having economic growth works the opposite to having a higher velocity of money with respect to the inflation rate. In particular, the same example shows that if the BGP growth rate is positive, then the inflation rate is lower. Equation (20.23) implies the solution for the inflation rate when growth is positive along the BGP:

$$\eta = \frac{m}{y}\left(1+g\right)\left(1+\pi\right) - \frac{m_t}{y_t};$$

$$\pi = \frac{\frac{\eta y}{m} - g}{\left(1+g\right)}. \tag{20.30}$$

Since the derivative of the solution for the inflation rate with respect to the growth rate is negative, the inflation rate with zero growth, as given by $\frac{\eta y}{m}$, is lower than $\frac{\eta y}{m}$ when $g > 0$. This again has straightforward intuition: if the economy is growing then there is a greater demand for money, and so there is a broader inflation tax base over time. The inflation rate from using money to finance a set fraction of output is accordingly lower.

Alternatively, for the money supply growth rate of σ, using equation (20.19) again, the same reasoning implies that the inflation rate is lower the higher is the growth rate of output:

$$\pi = \frac{\frac{\eta y}{m} - g}{(1+g)} = \frac{\sigma - g}{(1+g)}. \tag{20.31}$$

However there can be feedback between the inflation rate and the growth rate. When inflation exists it acts as a tax on the purchases of goods. And this tax can lower the growth rate of output itself. In this case, when inflation causes the BGP equilibrium growth rate g to be lower, then the inflation rate itself ends up being higher. This creates the feedback between the effect of the inflation tax on growth and between the effect of the growth rate on the level of the inflation tax as given in equation (20.30).

20.4 Inflation tax dynamics and hyperinflation

The feedback among the inflation rate π, the government share in output η, and the money supply growth rate σ can lead to extreme circumstances. In particular, if the representative agent holds less real money when inflation goes up, and so velocity $\frac{y}{m}$ increases, then the needed money supply growth rate for paying for the η share of government expenditure must rise. But as the σ rises, so does the inflation rate rise again. If $\frac{y}{m}$ increases further, then again σ must rise, and inflation again rises. This can go on and on, leading to a hyperinflation that is defined as an extremely high rate of inflation. The key cause of hyperinflation is that the government wants to pay for a certain expenditure by printing money, but the consumer does not want to hold an amount of real money that is sufficient to provide the tax base from which to raise the inflation tax. Therefore the government raises the money supply growth rate and inflation rate even higher, but the consumer continues to increase the velocity of money, by holding less real money. This can result in an ever-upward spiral of money creation and inflation until either the government collapses or the currency is re-established alongside a recapitalised government treasury that can pay for government spending without printing much money.

20.4.1 Inflation dynamics

The dynamics of inflation are well-identified in a simple way by focusing on the inflation tax equation (20.23). Let us reconsider this equation by solving for the inflation rate but without assuming that the economy is in the balanced growth path equilibrium:

$$\eta = \frac{m_{t+1}}{y_{t+1}} \left(1 + g_{t+1}\right) \left(1 + \pi_{t+1}\right) - \frac{m_t}{y_t}. \tag{20.32}$$

Solving for the inflation rate at time $t + 1$, this is given by

$$\pi_{t+1} = \frac{\eta y_{t+1}}{m_{t+1} \left(1 + g_{t+1}\right)} + \frac{m_t}{m_{t+1}} - 1. \tag{20.33}$$

Here it is apparent that an increase in money velocity $\frac{y_{t+1}}{m_{t+1}}$, a decrease in the growth rate of output g_{t+1}, and a decrease in real money demand m_{t+1} all cause the inflation rate to go up.

Along the business cycle, for example during a recession, clearly the growth rate of output falls, and this makes inflation lower. The income velocity of money also often falls in recessions and again this goes towards decreasing the inflation rate. And real money demand also may fall somewhat and result in some pressure upwards on the inflation rate.

20.4.2 Government spending and money supply

Now consider when the government expenditure share rises and this increase along with η is financed by issuing new money. Clearly the effect of η on the inflation rate in equation (20.33) is positive. And in general an increase in η leads to an even bigger increase in the inflation rate if $\frac{y_{t+1}}{m_{t+1}(1+g_{t+1})} > 1$.

During a business cycle crisis or war, the government often increases government expenditure and finances it in part by printing more money. The increase in the US inflation rate during the 1970s and 1980s can thus be attributed to the rise in spending during the Vietnam War, although there is mixed evidence about this.[1]

20.4.3 Hyperinflation in Europe and across the world

Hyperinflation typically happens when a government is trying to spend a large fraction of national output on goods purchases while financing it largely by printing new money. Dynamically, the simple equation (20.33) shows how this can happen. If η rises substantially, such as during a war, then other effects of the rising inflation feed back and make the inflation rate even higher. Consider that when η increases, and the inflation rate increases, then so does the velocity of money, while the growth rate of output typically falls. This process can accelerate in a feedback loop that causes accelerating inflation, if the amount of expenditure financed by printing money is very high. When it does accelerate it becomes completely uncontrolled: the government is wanting a stable inflation rate, and a stable inflation tax base, but instead the real money demand is falling quickly and the inflation rate can rise exponentially!

Exponentially rising inflation is the characteristic feature of what is called hyperinflation. Another definition is simply in terms of the level of inflation, with a level over 50% a month being considered hyperinflation in typical definitions. But regardless of the exact definition, what tends to happen is that both the money supply growth rate and the inflation rate rise at extreme rates. And this often ends with the government of the nation collapsing since the citizens are unwilling to hold the 'equity stock' of the nation, which is the nation's money supply.

Hyperinflation occurred in various European countries after World War I and after World War II, typically for the losing nations facing an insufficient taxable income base. These included after WWI, in the 1920s, Austria, Germany, Hungary, Poland and Russia, during WWII, Greece, and after WWII Hungary again (see Cagan, 1956). It has also happened in Latin American countries, in Argentina and Chile in the 1970s, Bolivia, Brazil,

---

[1]It is important to note that the link between the US budget deficit and the inflation rate of the 1970s is obscured in a very important way. In 1969 the US Social Security Trust Funds were running a giant surplus and in 1969 these funds were moved 'on-budget' just as the war expenditure was accelerating. This therefore masked the extent to which the general US Treasury budget reflected the Vietnam War expenditure and it thereby hid in part the link between government expenditure and the rising inflation rate during this period.

Nicaragua and Peru in the 1980s and 1990s; in Africa, in Zaire and Zimbabwe in the 1990s and presently; and in Eastern Europe after the collapse of the Soviet Union in the early 1990s, in Belarus, Bulgaria, Georgia, Romania, Russia and Ukraine.

20.5 The monetary economy

The use of money as part of the financing of government expenditure causes an inflation tax that distorts the economy. The distortion is shown within the *AS–AD* framework in the simplest case by assuming again that a certain amount of government purchases are financed with money creation or issuing new bonds.

In particular assume that

$$G_t = M_{t+1} - M_t + B_{t+1} - B_t \left(1 + R_t\right).$$

This gives the nominal money supply condition of the economy, for M_t, and it is an exogenous process. Denote the rate of growth of the money supply by σ_t at time t:

$$\frac{M_{t+1} - M_t}{M_t} \equiv \sigma_t.$$

The money demand comes out as part of the equilibrium of the economy, an endogenous choice of how much real money, or $m_t \equiv \frac{M_t}{P_t}$, to hold. The idea that money is necessary to buy goods gives a benefit from using money, this being the ability to buy goods that otherwise cannot be purchased. The cost of using money is the interest that could have been earned if money was not being held to make purchases and instead was invested in the bank at the market interest rate.

By assuming that money must be used to buy goods, an additional 'exchange constraint', or exchange technology is assumed. Suppose that only consumption goods need to be purchased by money, and that one dollar of money allows for purchase of one dollar of goods. Then the exchange technology is a simple linear one in which

$$M_t = P_t c_t. \tag{20.34}$$

In this case the consumption velocity of money is $\frac{c_t}{m_t} = 1$. While velocity in general is more than 1, this simple model shows how the inflation tax affects the allocation, in particular through raising the shadow price of goods within the marginal rate of substitution between goods and leisure.

Consider our model in equation (20.7) for the representative agent problem when government bonds are invested in by the agent along with physical capital. There the budget constraint is

$$c_t = w_t l_t + r_t k_t - k_{t+1} + k_t \left(1 - \delta_k\right) - b_{t+1} \left(1 + \pi_{t+1}\right) + b_t \left(1 + R_t\right). \tag{20.35}$$

Now also allow the consumer to invest in holding real money balances. If we take the nominal form of the budget by multiplying through by P_t, and subtract from income the investment in nominal money of $-M_{t+1} + M_t$, and add to income the real government transfer $\frac{G_t}{P_t}$, and then the budget constraint is

$$P_t c_t = P_t w_t l_t + P_t r_t k_t - P_t k_{t+1} + P_t k_t \left(1 - \delta_k\right)$$
$$- P_t b_{t+1} \left(1 + \pi_{t+1}\right) + P_t b_t \left(1 + R_t\right) - M_{t+1} + M_t + \frac{G_t}{P_t}. \tag{20.36}$$

Note that the difference with money as opposed to bonds is that bonds earn the return R_t, as evident by the term $+P_t b_t \left(1 + R_t\right)$, while money earns no interest when carried around from period to period, as evident by the term $+M_t$. The lack of interest earning is the cost of money.

Writing the budget constraint again in real terms using that $m_t \equiv \frac{M_t}{P_t}$:

$$c_t = w_t l_t + r_t k_t - k_{t+1} + k_t \left(1 - \delta_k\right) - b_{t+1} \left(1 + \pi_{t+1}\right) + b_t \left(1 + R_t\right)$$
$$- \frac{M_{t+1}}{P_t} + \frac{M_t}{P_t} + \frac{G_t}{P_t};$$
$$= w_t l_t + r_t k_t - k_{t+1} + k_t \left(1 - \delta_k\right) - b_{t+1} \left(1 + \pi_{t+1}\right) + b_t \left(1 + R_t\right)$$
$$- m_{t+1} \left(1 + \pi_{t+1}\right) + m_t + \frac{G_t}{P_t}. \tag{20.37}$$

Assuming the same log utility and Cobb–Douglas production of output, the consumer problem adds the exchange technology as a constraint. To put this in the recursive framework, consumption will be set equal to real money. At the same time, the labour supply will be solved from the budget constraint. From equation (20.37), the labour supply is

$$l_t = \frac{c_t}{w_t} - \frac{r_t k_t - k_{t+1} + k_t \left(1 - \delta_k\right) - b_{t+1} \left(1 + \pi_{t+1}\right) + b_t \left(1 + R_t\right) - m_{t+1} \left(1 + \pi_{t+1}\right) + m_t + \frac{G_t}{P_t}}{w_t}.$$

Now using equation (20.34), this labour supply is also equal to

$$l_t = \frac{m_t}{w_t} - \frac{r_t k_t - k_{t+1} + k_t \left(1 - \delta_k\right) - b_{t+1} \left(1 + \pi_{t+1}\right) + b_t \left(1 + R_t\right) - m_{t+1} \left(1 + \pi_{t+1}\right) + m_t + \frac{G_t}{P_t}}{w_t}$$
$$= \frac{-r_t k_t + k_{t+1} - k_t \left(1 - \delta_k\right) + b_{t+1} \left(1 + \pi_{t+1}\right) - b_t \left(1 + R_t\right) + m_{t+1} \left(1 + \pi_{t+1}\right) - \frac{G_t}{P_t}}{w_t} \tag{20.38}$$

Now substitute m_t in the log utility function for c_t from equation (20.34); substitute for x_t using the time allocation constraint, $x_t = 1 - l_t$, and for l_t from equation (20.38); and introduce the additional state variable m_t in the value function. This makes the recursive consumer problem

$$V\left(k_t, b_t, m_t\right) = \underset{k_{t+1}, b_{t+1}, m_{t+1}}{\text{Max}} \quad : \ln\left(m_t\right)$$
$$+ \alpha \ln \left[1 - \frac{-r_t k_t + k_{t+1} - k_t \left(1 - \delta_k\right) + b_{t+1} \left(1 + \pi_{t+1}\right) - b_t \left(1 + R_t\right) + m_{t+1} \left(1 + \pi_{t+1}\right) - \frac{G_t}{P_t}}{w_t} \right]$$
$$+ \beta V\left(k_{t+1}, b_{t+1}, m_{t+1}\right). \tag{20.39}$$

The first-order equilibrium conditions and envelope conditions imply a very similar set of conditions as before, but now they are affected by the inflation tax. The balanced growth path equilibrium marginal rate of substitution between goods and leisure is

$$\frac{\alpha c_t}{x_t} = \frac{w_t}{1 + R_t},$$

instead of the non-monetary economy standard of $\frac{\alpha c_t}{x_t} = w_t$. This means that the higher is the nominal interest rate, the more leisure that is taken and the less consumption. This distortion to the goods–leisure margin is the basic distortion of the monetary economy.

This margin shows the inflation tax in action. Only if $R_t = 0$ would there be no increase in the shadow price of goods, $1 + R_t$, as appears in the denominator of the ratio $\frac{w_t}{1 + R_t}$. Then the economy would return to the no-inflation tax case of the real economy without money. As long as $R_t > 0$, then the inflation tax is in effect positive. By this reasoning, the inflation tax is defined to be the level of R_t, rather than the level of the inflation rate π_t.

In other words the opportunity cost of using money to buy goods, R_t, is also the level of the inflation tax in an economic sense.

Other equilibrium conditions are the same. In the stationary equilibrium, the intertemporal marginal rate of substitution can be written as

$$1 + g_{t+1} = \frac{c_{t+1}}{c_t} = \frac{1 + r_{t+1} - \delta_k}{1 + \rho},$$

and the Fisher equation of interest rates is again

$$1 + R_t = \left(1 + r_t - \delta_k\right)\left(1 + \pi_t\right).$$

Assuming a zero balanced growth path exogenous rate of growth, so that $g = 0$, the result is that

$$r_t - \delta_k = \rho. \tag{20.40}$$

The Fisher equation

$$1 + R_t = \left(1 + r_t - \delta_k\right)\left(1 + \pi_t\right),$$

using equation (20.40) with zero exogenous growth can be written more simply as

$$1 + R_t = \left(1 + \rho\right)\left(1 + \pi_t\right).$$

Finally the inflation rate itself is endogenous but can be solved along the BGP. Using equation (20.34), over two time periods, t and $t + 1$,

$$1 + \sigma_{t+1} = \frac{M_{t+1}}{M_t} = \frac{P_{t+1}c_{t+1}}{P_t c_t} = \left(1 + \pi_{t+1}\right)\left(1 + g_{t+1}\right). \tag{20.41}$$

And since $g = 0$,

$$\sigma_t = \pi_t.$$

The money supply growth rate σ_t is exogenously set by the government. This implies that the solution for R_t is given by

$$1 + R_t = \left(1 + \rho\right)\left(1 + \sigma_t\right). \tag{20.42}$$

Any change in the rate of money supply growth causes a change in the nominal interest rate. Only if $R = 0$ does the economy revert back to an undistorted one in which $\frac{\alpha c_t}{x_t} = w_t$.

20.5.1 AS–AD analysis of inflation effects

Inflation lowers the capital stock and causes a shift back in both AS and AD. Inflation also causes the shadow price of goods to rise, so that demand shifts back by more than just what would result from the capital stock decreasing. A decrease in the capital stock makes output supply shift back by more than output demand. With inflation the decrease in the capital stock combined with the increase in the shadow price of goods causes AS and AD both to shift back by similar amounts. Output falls and so does employment.

The effect of inflation in lowering output and employment can be seen with the framework of the baseline dynamic model of Chapter 8 with zero exogenous growth. Aggregate supply remains exactly the same in functional form, within the monetary economy, as in Chapter 8. The aggregate demand is somewhat modified. It is derived in the same fashion by taking the consumer's budget constraint, simplifying it, and substituting in for labour l_t using the marginal rate of substitution between goods and leisure. In equilibrium, the government budget constraint is binding, and those terms drop out of the budget constraint, giving that

$$c_t = w_t l_t + r_t k_t - k_{t+1} + k_t (1 - \delta_k).$$

Along the BGP, $k_{t+1} = k_t$, so that

$$c_t = w_t l_t + (r_t - \delta_k) k_t.$$

And since $r_t - \delta_k = \rho$,

$$c_t = w_t l_t + \rho k_t.$$

This is as before in Chapter 8. Using the allocation of time constraint $l_t = 1 - x_t$, and the intratemporal marginal rate of substitution, $x_t = \frac{\alpha c_t (1 + R_t)}{w_t}$, and

$$c_t = w_t (1 - x_t) + \rho k_t$$
$$= w_t \left(1 - \frac{\alpha c_t (1 + R_t)}{w_t}\right) + \rho k_t.$$

Simplifying

$$c_t^d = w_t (1 - x_t) + \rho k_t,$$
$$c_t^d = \frac{1}{1 + \alpha (1 + R_t)} (w_t + \rho k_t). \tag{20.43}$$

Functionally, the share of permanent income that is consumed falls as the money supply growth rate, σ_t, rises, and so causes R_t to rise. The share is no longer constant as in the standard version of the permanent income hypothesis of consumption, as a result of the inflation tax distortion.

Aggregate demand AD is given by the sum of consumption demand and investment, which with zero growth is

$$y_t^d = \left(\frac{1}{1 + \alpha (1 + R_t)}\right) (w_t + \rho k_t) + \delta_k k_t,$$
$$= \left(\frac{1}{1 + \alpha (1 + R_t)}\right) \left[w_t + \left(\rho + \delta_k \left[1 + \alpha (1 + R_t)\right]\right) k_t\right]. \tag{20.44}$$

Inversely the AD can be written as

$$\frac{1}{w_t} = \frac{1}{y_t^d \left[1 + \alpha (1 + R_t)\right] - \left(\rho + \delta_k \left[1 + \alpha (1 + R_t)\right]\right) k_t}.$$

20.5.2 Example 20.3

The economy can now be calibrated with some assumed rate of growth of money supply σ. And with AS and AD analysis, the effect of an increase in σ can be found. Using the same calibration in the baseline exogenous growth economy of Example 8.1, with $\rho = 0.03$, $\gamma = \frac{1}{3}$, $\delta_k = 0.03$, $\alpha = 0.5$, $A_G = 0.15$, and assuming a money supply growth rate of $\sigma = 5\%$, then $R = \rho + \sigma + \rho\sigma = 0.03 + 0.05 + 0.03(0.05) = 0.0815$, and the value of the capital stock is $k_t = 2.2242$, as opposed to 2.3148 when $R = 0$.

Methodologically, the solution for k_t can be found from the Chapter 10 methodology. Everywhere in the solution that α appears, now this becomes instead $a\,(1+R)$:

$$k_t = \frac{T\gamma A_G^{\frac{1}{\gamma}}\left[\frac{(1-\gamma)}{\rho+\delta_k}\right]^{\frac{1-\gamma}{\gamma}}}{(\gamma+\alpha\,(1+R))\left(\frac{\rho+\delta_k}{(1-\gamma)}\right)-\alpha\,(1+R)\,\delta_k}$$

$$= \frac{\left(\frac{1}{3}\right)(0.15)^3\left(\frac{2}{3(0.06)}\right)^2}{\left(\frac{1}{3}+0.5\,(1+0.0815)\right)(0.06)\,(1.5)-0.5\,(1+0.0815)\,(0.03)}$$

$$= 2.2242.$$

The AS and AD can now be graphed, using the calibration for the supply and demand functions:

$$\frac{1}{w_t} = \frac{\left(y_t^s\right)^{\frac{1-\gamma}{\gamma}}}{\gamma A_G^{\frac{1}{\gamma}}\,(k_t)^{\frac{1-\gamma}{\gamma}}} = \frac{\left(y_t^s\right)^2}{0.333\,(0.15)^3\,(2.2242)^2}; \tag{20.45}$$

$$\frac{1}{w_t} = \frac{1}{y_t^d\left[1+\alpha\,(1+R_t)\right]-k_t\left(\rho+\delta_k\left[1+\alpha\,(1+R_t)\right]\right)},$$

$$\frac{1}{w_t} = \frac{1}{y_t^d\,(1+0.5\,(1.0815))-2.2\left[0.03+(0.03)\,(1+0.5\,(1.0815))\right]}. \tag{20.46}$$

Figure 20.1 graphs equations (20.45) and (20.46) in black, with $R=0.0815$, as compared to the Example 8.1 AS–AD economy in blue, which is the same as when $R=0$ in this Example 20.3.

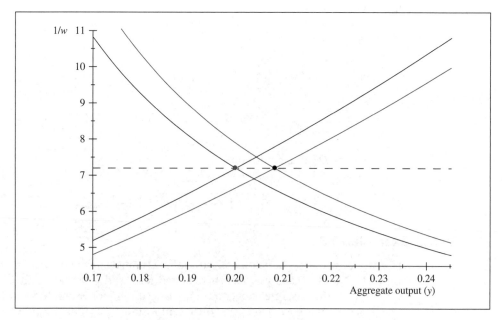

Figure 20.1 Monetary economy AS–AD with inflation tax (black) in Example 20.3 and no tax (blue) in Example 8.1

Inflation causes aggregate demand and supply to both shift back by about the same amount, in that the relative price of goods $\frac{1}{w}$ stays the same and aggregate output falls. The equilibrium output is 0.20, and the relative price $\frac{1}{w} = 7.2$, with a real wage of 0.13889. Therefore the inflation tax lowers output and the capital stock.

Consumption is

$$c_t^d = \frac{w_t + \rho k_t}{1 + \alpha\left(1 + R_t\right)} = \frac{0.1389 + 0.03\left(2.2242\right)}{1 + 0.5\left(1 + 0.0815\right)}$$
$$= 0.13346;$$

output is

$$y_t^d = \left(\frac{1}{1 + \alpha\left(1 + R_t\right)}\right)\left[w_t + \left(\rho + \delta_k\left[1 + \alpha\left(1 + R_t\right)\right]\right)k_t\right]$$
$$= \left(\frac{1}{1 + 0.5\left(1.0815\right)}\right)\left(0.139 + \left(0.03 + 0.03\left(1 + 0.5\left(1 + 0.0815\right)\right)\right)\right)\left(2.2\right)$$
$$= 0.20018.$$

And $\frac{c_t^d}{y_t^d} = \frac{0.13346}{0.20018} = 0.66670$, the same relative to 0.667 of the baseline zero exogenous growth economy of Example 8.1.

20.5.3 Labour market effects of inflation

The inflation tax lowers output and the capital stock, while keeping the wage rate the same. Using the marginal product condition, $w_t = \gamma A_G\left(\frac{k_t}{l_t}\right)^{1-\gamma}$, it is clear that the employment of labour must fall when k_t falls so as to keep w_t constant. The labour market can also be graphed, using the labour demand and supply conditions.

Labour demand is the same as in the baseline model of Chapter 8, at

$$l_t^d = \left(\frac{\gamma A_G}{w_t}\right)^{\frac{1}{1-\gamma}} k_t. \tag{20.47}$$

Labour supply can be derived from the time constraint, $l_t^s = 1 - x_t$, and the intratemporal marginal rate of substitution, $x_t = \frac{\alpha c_t(1+R_t)}{w_t}$, so that

$$l_t^s = 1 - \frac{\alpha\left(1 + R_t\right)c_t}{w_t}.$$

Substituting in the consumption demand for c_t, where $c_t = \frac{(w_t + \rho k_t)}{1 + \alpha(1+R_t)}$,

$$l_t^s = 1 - \frac{\alpha\left(1 + R_t\right)\left(1 + \frac{\rho k_t}{w_t}\right)}{\left[1 + \alpha\left(1 + R_t\right)\right]}.$$

Inversely, the function for the labour supply is

$$w_t = \frac{\alpha\left(1 + R_t\right)\rho k_t}{\left(1 - l_t^s\right)\left(1 + \alpha\left(1 + R_t\right)\right) - \alpha\left(1 + R_t\right)}, \tag{20.48}$$

and for the labour demand,

$$w_t = \gamma A_G\left(\frac{k_t}{l_t^d}\right)^{1-\gamma}. \tag{20.49}$$

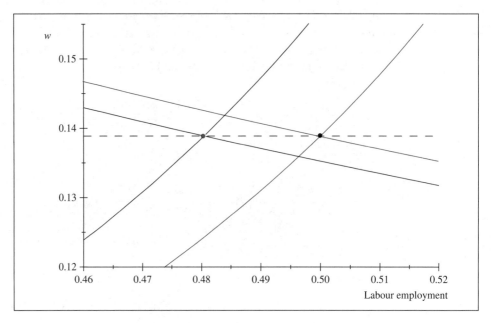

Figure 20.2 Zero growth equilibrium labour market with inflation tax of $R = 0.0815$ (black) in Example 20.3 compared to $R = 0$ (blue)

Calibrating these functions,

$$w_t = \frac{0.5 \, (1.0815) \, (0.03) \, (2.2242)}{(1 - l_t^s) \, (1 + 0.5 \, (1.0815)) - 0.5 \, (1.0815)}, \tag{20.50}$$

$$w_t = \frac{(0.15)}{3} \left(\frac{(2.2242)}{l_t^d} \right)^{\frac{2}{3}}. \tag{20.51}$$

Figure 20.2 graphs equations (20.50) and (20.51) in black, with $R = 0.0815$, as compared to the $R = 0$ equilibrium in blue.

This shows how the inflation tax shifts back labour supply and demand, decreases employment, and leaves the wage rate unchanged.

Here the equilibrium employment is

$$l_t^s = 1 - \frac{0.5 \, (1.0815) \left(1 + \frac{0.03(2.2242)}{0.13889} \right)}{(1 + 0.5 \, (1.0815))} = 0.48042.$$

20.5.4 General equilibrium

The general equilibrium with a labour income tax can also be found, in terms of graphing the input and output markets. Output is 0.20031, the wage rate 0.25071 and the interest rate 0.11526 so that the isocost line with the labour tax is

$$y_t = w_t l_t + r_t k_t,$$
$$0.20018 = (0.13889) \, l_t + (0.06) \, k_t,$$
$$k_t = \frac{0.20018}{0.06} - \frac{(0.13889) \, l_t}{0.06}. \tag{20.52}$$

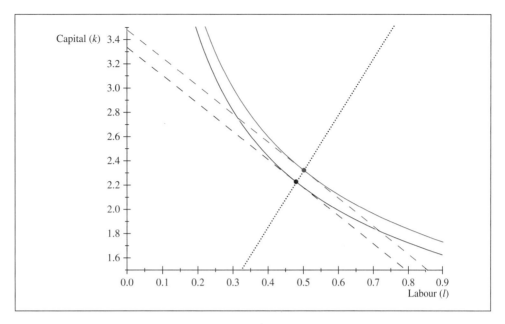

Figure 20.3 Factor market equilibrium in monetary economy with $R = 0.0815$ in Example 20.3 (black and dashed black) and $R = 0$ (blue and dashed blue)

The isoquant curve is

$$y_t^s = A_G \left(l_t^d h_t\right)^\gamma \left(k_t\right)^{1-\gamma},$$

$$0.20018 = (0.15) \left(l_t^d h_t\right)^{\frac{1}{3}} \left(k_t\right)^{\frac{2}{3}};$$

$$k_t = \left(\frac{0.20018}{(0.15) \left(l_t^d\right)^{\frac{1}{3}}}\right)^{\frac{3}{2}} = \frac{\left(\frac{0.20018}{0.15}\right)^{\frac{3}{2}}}{\left(l_t^d\right)^{\frac{1}{2}}}. \tag{20.53}$$

And the factor input ratio is

$$\frac{k_t}{l_t} = \frac{2.2242}{0.48042} = 4.6297. \tag{20.54}$$

Figure 20.3 graphs equations (20.52), (20.53) and (20.54) in black and dashed black, as compared to the baseline Example 8.1 economy, in blue and dashed blue.

It shows that the factor input ratio stays the same as in the $R = 0$, no inflation tax economy. The inflation tax however causes the isocost and isoquant levels to shift down, with a lower level of employment as a result.

Consumption can be expressed in terms of output minus investment using the goods production function. With a given capital stock k_t this consumption is a function only of labour, and can be graphed in c and l dimensions. The utility level curve can also be graphed in c and l dimensions by substituting in for $x_t = 1 - l_t$. In Example 8.1, in equilibrium $k_t = 2.3148$; now the consumption in terms of the production function and the utility level curve, comparable to equations (8.75) and (8.76), is

$$c_t^d = y_t^s - i_t = A_G \left(l_t^d\right)^\gamma \left(k_t\right)^{1-\gamma} - \delta_k k_t,$$

$$c_t^d = (0.15) \left(l_t^d\right)^{\frac{1}{3}} (2.2242)^{\frac{2}{3}} - (0.03)(2.2242) \tag{20.55}$$

$$u = \ln c_t + \alpha \ln x_t = \ln c_t + \alpha \ln \left(1 - l_t\right),$$

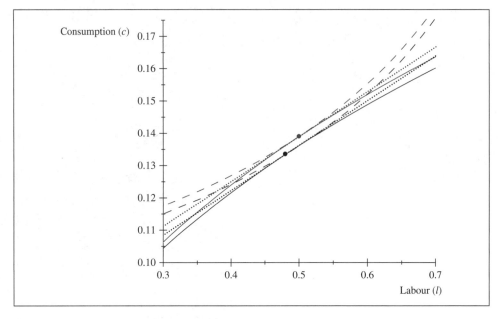

Figure 20.4 General equilibrium consumption and utility levels with inflation tax of $R = 0.0815$ in Example 20.3 (variants of black) and baseline $R = 0$ (variants of blue)

$$-2.3413 = \ln 0.13346 + 0.5 \ln \left(1 - 0.48042\right),$$
$$-2.3413 = \ln c_t + 0.5 \ln \left(1 - l_t\right),$$
$$c_t = \frac{e^{-2.3413}}{\left(1 - l_t\right)^{0.5}}. \tag{20.56}$$

The budget line in equilibrium is

$$c_t^d = w_t l_t^s + \rho k_t^s,$$
$$c_t^d = \left(0.13889\right) l_t^s + \left(0.03\right)\left(2.2242\right). \tag{20.57}$$

Figure 20.4 graphs equations (20.55), (20.56) and (20.57) in variants of black, below the baseline of Example 8.1, or $R = 0$, as seen in variants of blue.

The figure shows how the production function, utility level and budget line all shift down with an inflation tax, here of $R = 0.0815$. The employment rate and consumption level both fall with the inflation tax.

20.6 Endogenous growth and the inflation tax

The effect of inflation on growth can be analysed following the analysis of Chapter 19. The inflation tax affects only the goods–leisure margin. It does this exactly as does a consumption tax, and labour income tax, within the goods–leisure margin. Bringing together the goods tax effect, the labour income effect, and the inflation tax effect, a comparison of the taxes within this margin implies that

$$1 + \tau_c = \frac{1}{1 - \tau_l} = 1 + R.$$

The nominal interest rate R is similar analytically to the tax on goods, τ_c. Therefore, within the endogenous growth economies of Chapters 12, 13, 14 and 19, as extended with the monetary elements here, a rate of $R = 0.10$ has a similar effect on growth and goods and labour markets as a goods tax of $\tau_c = 0.10$, or a labour income tax of $\tau_l = \frac{\tau_c}{1+\tau_c} = \frac{0.10}{1.10} = 0.091$.

To see this, the endogenous growth economy of Chapter 12 is combined with the monetary economy above. The consumer problem now has human capital and an additional variable, along with the time spent in human capital investment l_{Ht}.

The consumer budget constraint is the same as equation (20.37) except that wages are factored by the human capital stock:

$$c_t = w_t l_t h_t + r_t k_t - k_{t+1} + k_t \left(1 - \delta_k\right) - b_{t+1} \left(1 + \pi_{t+1}\right) + b_t \left(1 + R_t\right)$$
$$- m_{t+1} \left(1 + \pi_{t+1}\right) + m_t + \frac{G_t}{P_t}. \tag{20.58}$$

Using the budget constraint and the allocation of time constraint to solve for labour l_t, leisure is given by

$$x_t = 1 - l_t - l_{Ht},$$
$$= 1 - l_{Ht} - \frac{-r_t k_t + k_{t+1} - k_t \left(1 - \delta_k\right) + b_{t+1} \left(1 + \pi_{t+1}\right) - b_t \left(1 + R_t\right) + m_{t+1} \left(1 + \pi_{t+1}\right) - \frac{G_t}{P_t}}{w_t h_t}.$$

The consumer problem is

$$V \left(k_t, h_t, b_t, m_t\right)$$

$$= \max_{k_{t+1}, b_{t+1}, m_{t+1}, l_{Ht}} : \ln \left(m_t\right) + \alpha \ln \left[1 - l_{Ht}\right.$$

$$\left. - \frac{-r_t k_t + k_{t+1} - k_t \left(1 - \delta_k\right) + b_{t+1} \left(1 + \pi_{t+1}\right) - b_t \left(1 + R_t\right) + m_{t+1} \left(1 + \pi_{t+1}\right) - \frac{G_t}{P_t}}{w_t h_t}\right]$$

$$+ \beta V \left(k_{t+1}, h_t \left(1 - \delta_h\right) + A_H l_{Ht} h_t, b_{t+1}, m_{t+1}\right). \tag{20.59}$$

All of the equilibrium and envelope conditions are the same as in Chapter 12 for endogenous growth, except that the marginal rate of substitution between goods and leisure is

$$x_t = \frac{\alpha \left(1 + R_t\right) c_t}{w_t h_t}. \tag{20.60}$$

The tax reduces the effective wage, or increases the goods price, depending on which perspective is preferred, causing substitution from goods to leisure.

20.6.1 *AS–AD* analysis

The *AS* function is not affected by the tax. The aggregate demand is constructed from the consumer and government budget constraints, the marginal rate of substitution between goods and leisure, the allocation of time constraint, and the two intertemporal margins from human and physical capital. Using the government budget constraint, substituting in for $l_t = 1 - x_t - l_{Ht}$ in the consumer budget constraint (20.58), using the goods–leisure margin of equation (20.60), simplifying and substituting in that $l_{Ht} = \frac{g + \delta_H}{A_H}$, consumption demand is

$$c_t^d = w_t h_t l_t^s + r_t k_t - k_{t+1} + k_t \left(1 - \delta_k\right), \tag{20.61}$$
$$c_t^d = w_t h_t \left(1 - x_t - l_{Ht}\right) + r_t k_t - k_{t+1} + k_t \left(1 - \delta_k\right), \tag{20.62}$$
$$c_t^d = w_t h_t \left(1 - \frac{\alpha \left(1 + R_t\right) c_t}{w_t h_t} - l_{Ht}\right)$$
$$+ r_t k_t - k_{t+1} + k_t \left(1 - \delta_k\right), \tag{20.63}$$

$$c_t^d \left[1 + \alpha \left(1 + R_t\right)\right] = w_t h_t \left(1 - l_{Ht}\right) + r_t k_t - k_{t+1} + k_t \left(1 - \delta_k\right), \tag{20.64}$$

$$c_t^d = \frac{w_t h_t \left(1 - l_{Ht}\right) + r_t k_t - k_{t+1} + k_t \left(1 - \delta_k\right)}{\left[1 + \alpha \left(1 + R_t\right)\right]}, \tag{20.65}$$

$$c_t^d = \frac{w_t h_t \left(1 - \frac{g + \delta_H}{A_H}\right) + \rho \left(1 + g\right) k_t}{\left[1 + \alpha \left(1 + R_t\right)\right]}. \tag{20.66}$$

Investment along the balanced growth path is

$$i_t = k_t \left(g + \delta_k\right),$$

and the *AD* function is

$$y_t^d = \frac{w_t h_t \left(1 - \frac{g + \delta_H}{A_H}\right) + \rho \left(1 + g\right) k_t}{\left[1 + \alpha \left(1 + R_t\right)\right]} + k_t \left(g + \delta_k\right);$$

$$y_t^d = \frac{w_t h_t \left(1 - \frac{g + \delta_H}{A_H}\right) + k_t \left[\rho \left(1 + g\right) + \left(g + \delta_k\right) \left[1 + \alpha \left(1 + R_t\right)\right]\right]}{\left[1 + \alpha \left(1 + R_t\right)\right]}.$$

Inversely solving for the relative price $\frac{1}{w_t}$, the *AD* function can be graphed as

$$\frac{1}{w_t} = \frac{\left(1 - \frac{g + \delta_H}{A_H}\right)}{\frac{y_t^d}{h_t} \left[1 + \alpha \left(1 + R_t\right)\right] - \frac{k_t}{h_t} \left[\rho \left(1 + g\right) + \left(g + \delta_k\right) \left[1 + \alpha \left(1 + R_t\right)\right]\right]}.$$

The *AS* function and its inverse are again

$$y_t^s = A_G \left(\frac{\gamma A_G}{w_t}\right)^{\frac{\gamma}{1 - \gamma}} k_t; \tag{20.67}$$

$$\frac{1}{w_t} = \frac{\left(y_t^s\right)^{\frac{1 - \gamma}{\gamma}}}{\gamma A_G^{\frac{1}{\gamma}} \left(k_t\right)^{\frac{1 - \gamma}{\gamma}}}.$$

20.6.2 Solution methodology

A solution methodology very similar to the last section can be used. Let the excess aggregate output demand function $Y \left(w_t, h_t, k_t, g\right)$,

$$Y \left(w_t, h_t, k_t, g\right) = y_t^d - y_t^s = 0,$$

be

$$0 = \frac{w_t h_t \left(1 - \frac{g + \delta_H}{A_H}\right) + k_t \left[\rho \left(1 + g\right) + \left(g + \delta_k\right) \left[1 + \alpha \left(1 + R_t\right)\right]\right]}{\left[1 + \alpha \left(1 + R_t\right)\right]}$$

$$- A_G \left(\frac{\gamma A_G}{w_t}\right)^{\frac{\gamma}{1 - \gamma}} k_t.$$

Dividing through by $w_t h_t$ implies

$$0 = \frac{\left(1 - \frac{g + \delta_H}{A_H}\right) + \frac{k_t}{w_t h_t} \left[\rho \left(1 + g\right) + \left(g + \delta_k\right) \left[1 + \alpha \left(1 + R_t\right)\right]\right]}{\left[1 + \alpha \left(1 + R_t\right)\right]}$$

$$- A_G \left(\frac{\gamma A_G}{w_t}\right)^{\frac{\gamma}{1 - \gamma}} \frac{k_t}{w_t h_t}.$$

And again solve for $\frac{k_t}{w_t h_t}$ and w_t in terms of g, to have an equation in only g.

Because the intertemporal conditions are unchanged from Chapter 12, it is true that

$$l_t = \frac{(1+g)(1-\beta)}{A_H \beta}; \tag{20.68}$$

$$r_t = (1-\gamma) A_G \left(\frac{k_t}{h_t l_t}\right)^{-\gamma},$$

$$\frac{k_t}{h_t l_t} = \left(\frac{(1-\gamma) A_G}{r_t}\right)^{\frac{1}{\gamma}}, \tag{20.69}$$

$$\frac{k_t}{h_t l_t} = \left(\frac{(1-\gamma) A_G}{(1+g)(1+\rho) - 1 + \delta_k}\right)^{\frac{1}{\gamma}}; \tag{20.70}$$

$$w_t = \gamma A_G \left(\frac{k_t}{h_t l_t}\right)^{1-\gamma}, \tag{20.71}$$

$$w_t = \gamma A_G \left(\frac{(1-\gamma) A_G}{(1+g)(1+\rho) - 1 + \delta_k}\right)^{\frac{1-\gamma}{\gamma}}. \tag{20.72}$$

Therefore we now have

$$\frac{k_t}{w_t h_t} = \left(\frac{k_t}{h_t l_t}\right) \frac{l_t}{w_t},$$

$$\frac{k_t}{w_t h_t} = \left(\frac{(1-\gamma) A_G}{(1+g)(1+\rho) - 1 + \delta_k}\right)^{\frac{1}{\gamma}} \frac{\frac{(1+g)(1-\beta)}{A_H \beta}}{\gamma A_G \left(\frac{(1-\gamma) A_G}{(1+g)(1+\rho) - 1 + \delta_k}\right)^{\frac{1-\gamma}{\gamma}}},$$

$$\frac{k_t}{w_t h_t} = \left(\frac{(1-\gamma)}{(1+g)(1+\rho) - 1 + \delta_k}\right) \frac{(1+g)(1-\beta)}{\gamma A_H \beta}. \tag{20.73}$$

Returning to the normalised excess demand function, with $\frac{k_t}{w_t h_t}$ and w_t substituted in,

$$0 = \frac{\left(1 - \frac{g+\delta_H}{A_H}\right) + \frac{(1-\gamma)(1+g)(1-\beta)}{[(1+g)(1+\rho) - 1 + \delta_k]\gamma A_H \beta} \left[\rho(1+g) + (g+\delta_k)\left[1 + \alpha(1 + R_t)\right]\right]}{\left[1 + \alpha(1 + R_t)\right]}$$

$$- \frac{A_G}{\left(\frac{(1-\gamma) A_G}{(1+g)(1+\rho) - 1 + \delta_k}\right)} \left(\frac{(1-\gamma)}{(1+g)(1+\rho) - 1 + \delta_k}\right) \frac{(1+g)(1-\beta)}{\gamma A_H \beta}.$$

This reduces to

$$0 = \frac{\left(1 - \frac{g+\delta_H}{A_H}\right) + \frac{(1-\gamma)(1+g)(1-\beta)}{[(1+g)(1+\rho) - 1 + \delta_k]\gamma A_H \beta} \left[\rho(1+g) + (g+\delta_k)\left[1 + \alpha(1 + R_t)\right]\right]}{\left[1 + \alpha(1 + R_t)\right]}$$

$$- \frac{(1+g)(1-\beta)}{\gamma A_H \beta}.$$

This simplifies to an equation only in the variable g, thereby giving the solution to g given the parameters, similar to equation (19.25):

$$0 = \beta\gamma (A_H - g - \delta_H)\left[(1+g) + \beta(\delta_k - 1)\right] \tag{20.74}$$
$$+ \beta(1-\gamma)(1+g)(1-\beta)\left[\rho(1+g) + (g+\delta_k)\left[1 + \alpha(1 + R_t)\right]\right]$$
$$- (1+g)(1-\beta)\left[(1+g) + \beta(\delta_k - 1)\right]\left[1 + \alpha(1 + R_t)\right].$$

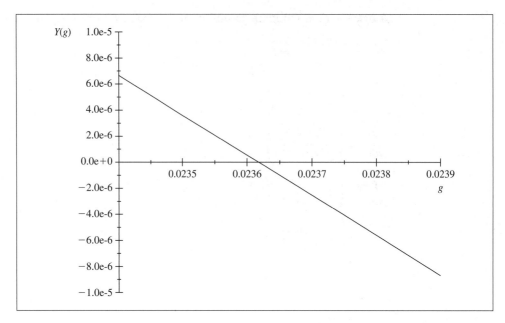

Figure 20.5 Normalised excess output demand $Y(g)$ with inflation tax of $R = 0.0815$ in Example 20.4

20.6.3 Example 20.4: Inflation tax and growth

With the same parameters as in Example 13.2, of $\gamma = \frac{1}{3}$, $\alpha = 1$, $A_h = 0.20$, $\delta_k = 0.05$, $\delta_h = 0.015$, $\beta = \frac{1}{1+\rho} = 0.95$, $\rho = \frac{1}{0.95} - 1 = 0.052632$, $A_G = 0.28224$, and a money supply growth rate of $\sigma = 2.7425\%$, then $R = \rho + \sigma + \rho\sigma = 0.0815$.

The equilibrium growth rate is given then by the quadratic equation in g, equation (20.74). Figure 20.5 graphs equation (20.74) in its calibrated form.

It implies the solution of a growth rate of $g = 0.02362$. This is a reduction from $g = 0.0333$ when there is no inflation tax, and $R = 0$, as in Example 13.2.

The alternative analytic solution is obtained, following Appendix A12, from the quadratic equation in g given by equation (20.74). Using the quadratic form, $Ag^2 + Bg + C = 0$, with

$$A \equiv -\beta\gamma + \beta\left(1-\beta\right)\left(1-\gamma\right)\left[1+\alpha\left(1+R_t\right)+\rho\right] - \left[1+\alpha\left(1+R_t\right)\right]\left(1-\beta\right),$$

$$\begin{aligned} B \equiv &-\beta\gamma\left[1+\beta\left(\delta_k-1\right)-A_H+\delta_H\right] \\ &+\beta\left(1-\beta\right)\left(1-\gamma\right)\left\{\rho+\delta_k\left[1+\alpha\left(1+R_t\right)\right]+1+\alpha\left(1+R_t\right)+\rho\right\} \\ &-\left[1+\alpha\left(1+R_t\right)\right]\left(1-\beta\right)\left[2+\beta\left(\delta_k-1\right)\right], \end{aligned}$$

$$\begin{aligned} C \equiv &\beta\gamma\left(A_H-\delta_H\right)\left[1+\beta\left(\delta_k-1\right)\right] \\ &+\beta\left(1-\beta\right)\left(1-\gamma\right)\left\{\rho+\delta_k\left[1+\alpha\left(1+R_t\right)\right]\right\} \\ &-\left[1+\alpha\left(1+R_t\right)\right]\left(1-\beta\right)\left[1+\beta\left(\delta_k-1\right)\right], \end{aligned}$$

and the given assumed parameters, then:

Quadratic term: $A = -0.3532$,

Linear term: $B = -0.0140$,

Constant term: $C = 0.0005269$.

With these terms, the quadratic solution implies a growth rate again of $g = 0.0236$.

Given this growth rate of $g = 0.02362$, the labour employment l_t, capital to effective labour ratio $\frac{k_t}{h_t l_t}$ and the capital to human capital ratio $\frac{k_t}{h_t}$ are given by

$$l_t = \frac{(1+g)(1-\beta)}{A_H \beta} = \frac{(1+0.02362)(1-0.95)}{(0.20)\,0.95} = 0.26937; \tag{20.75}$$

$$\frac{k_t}{h_t l_t} = \left(\frac{(1-\gamma)\,A_G}{(1+g)(1+\rho)-1+\delta_k} \right)^{\frac{1}{\gamma}},$$

$$\frac{k_t}{h_t l_t} = \left(\frac{\left(\frac{2}{3}\right)0.28224}{(1+0.02362)(1+0.052632)-1+0.05} \right)^{3} = 3.2144;$$

$$\frac{k_t}{h_t} = \left(\frac{k_t}{h_t l_t} \right) l_t = (3.2144)(0.26937) = 0.86586.$$

The calibrated AS and AD functions are

$$\frac{1}{w_t} = \frac{\left(1 - \frac{0.02362+0.015}{0.20}\right)}{y\,(2.0815) - (0.86586)\left[(0.0526)(1.0236)+(0.0736)(2.0815)\right]}; \tag{20.76}$$

$$\frac{1}{w_t} = \frac{3}{0.28224} \left(\frac{1}{(0.28224)(0.86586)} \right)^{2} y_t^2. \tag{20.77}$$

Figure 20.6 graphs equations (20.76) and (20.77) in black, along with the baseline Example 13.2 in blue.

The AD and AS both shift out as compared to the baseline of $R = 0$ as in Example 13.2. These shifts are because the capital ratio $\frac{k_t}{h_t}$ increases from 0.694 to 0.86586, an increase that also happened with the labour income tax. However, again, as with the labour tax, the balanced path growth rate has fallen substantially.

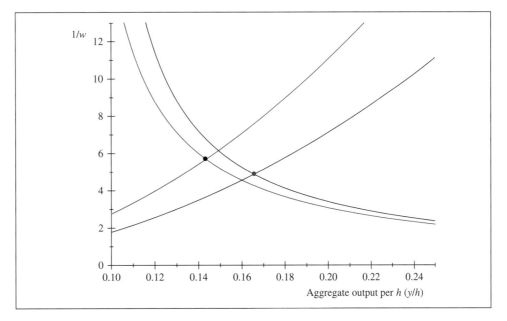

Figure 20.6 *AS–AD* with endogenous growth and an inflation tax of $R = 0.0815$ in Example 20.4 (black) versus baseline $R = 0$ in Example 13.2 (blue)

The exact wage is $w_t = 0.20491$, up from the $R = 0$ rate of 0.1757; and now $\frac{1}{w_t} = \frac{1}{0.20491} = 4.8802$:

$$w_t = \gamma A_G \left(\frac{k_t}{h_t l_t}\right)^{1-\gamma} = \frac{1}{3}(0.28224)(3.2144)^{\frac{2}{3}};$$

$$w_t = 0.20491. \tag{20.78}$$

Consumption is

$$\frac{c_t^d}{h_t} = \frac{w_t\left(1 - \frac{g+\delta_H}{A_H}\right) + \rho\left(1+g\right)\frac{k_t}{h_t}}{1 + \alpha\left(1 + R_t\right)},$$

$$= \frac{0.20491\left(1 - \frac{0.02362+0.015}{0.20}\right) + (0.052632)(1.02362)(0.86586)}{(1+1.0815)}$$

$$= 0.10184.$$

Output is

$$\frac{y_t^d}{h_t} = \frac{w_t\left(1 - \frac{g+\delta_H}{A_H}\right) + \frac{k_t}{h_t}\left[\rho\left(1+g\right) + \left(g+\delta_k\right)\left(1+\alpha\left(1+R_t\right)\right)\right]}{1 + \alpha\left(1 + R_t\right)}$$

$$= \frac{0.20491\left(1 - \frac{0.02362+0.015}{0.20}\right)}{(1+1.0815)}$$

$$+ \frac{(0.86586)\left((0.052632)(1.02362) + (0.02362+0.05)(1+1.0815)\right)}{(1+1.0815)}$$

$$= 0.16559.$$

And $\frac{c_t^d}{y_t^d} = \frac{0.10184}{0.16559} = 0.61501$, above 0.5966 in Example 13.2, the $R = 0$ equivalent.

The interest rate r_t falls because of the decrease in the growth rate to 12.75% from 13.8% with $R = 0$.

$$r_t = \left(1+g\right)\left(1+\rho\right) - 1 + \delta_k,$$
$$r_t = \left(1+0.02362\right)\left(1+0.052632\right) - 1 + 0.05 = 0.12750. \tag{20.79}$$

The inflation rate is then given by the Fisher equation

$$1 + R_t = \left(1 + r_t - \delta_k\right)\left(1 + \pi_t\right),$$

$$\left(1 + \pi_t\right) = \frac{1.0815}{\left(1.12750 - 0.05\right)} = 1.0037.$$

This is only an inflation rate of 0.37%, a rate of less than 1%. However, since the optimum in the economy is $R = 0$, it is an inflation tax rate of 8.15%.

With government bonds equal to zero, along the balanced growth path the real government expenditure is given by the inflation tax proceeds:

$$\frac{G_t}{P_t} = \frac{M_{t+1} - M_t}{P_t} = \frac{M_{t+1}\left(\frac{P_{t+1}}{P_t}\right)}{P_{t+1}} - \frac{M_t}{P_t},$$

$$= m_t\left(1+g\right)\left(1+\pi_t\right) - m_t;$$

$$\frac{G_t}{P_t y_t} = \frac{m_t\left[\left(1+g\right)\left(1+\pi_t\right) - 1\right]}{y_t}$$

$$= \frac{m_t}{c_t}\frac{c_t}{y_t}\left[\left(1+g\right)\left(1+\pi_t\right) - 1\right] = (1)\frac{0.10184}{0.16559}\left[(1.02362)(1.0037) - 1\right]$$

$$= 0.016856.$$

This inflation tax raises revenue equal to 1.7% of output. And in present value terms, this is

$$\frac{\frac{G_t}{y_t} y_t}{\rho \left(1+g\right)} = \frac{0.016856 \left(0.16559\right)}{0.052632 \left(1+0.02362\right)} = 0.051808. \tag{20.80}$$

20.6.4 Labour market

The labour supply is found from the goods–leisure margin, the allocation of time constraint and the consumption demand:

$$\frac{c_t^d \alpha \left(1+R_t\right)}{w_t h_t} = x_t,$$

$$l_t^s = 1 - \frac{c_t^d \alpha \left(1+R_t\right)}{w_t h_t} - l_{Ht}.$$

Substitute in for c_t^d in the allocation of time constraint:

$$c_t^d = \frac{w_t h_t \left(1 - \frac{g+\delta_H}{A_H}\right) + \rho \left(1+g\right) k_t}{1 + \alpha \left(1+R_t\right)}, \tag{20.81}$$

$$l_t^s = 1 - \left(\frac{\alpha \left(1+R_t\right)}{1+\alpha \left(1+R_t\right)}\right) \left[\left(1 - \frac{g+\delta_H}{A_H}\right) + \frac{\rho \left(1+g\right) k_t}{w_t h_t}\right] - \frac{g+\delta_H}{A_H};$$

$$l_t^s = 1 - \left(\frac{\alpha \left(1+R_t\right)}{1+\alpha \left(1+R_t\right)}\right) \left[1 - \frac{g+\delta_H}{A_H} + \frac{\rho \left(1+g\right) k_t}{w_t h_t}\right] - \frac{g+\delta_H}{A_H};$$

$$l_t^s = \frac{\left(1 - \frac{g+\delta_H}{A_H}\right) - \frac{\alpha(1+R_t)\rho(1+g)k_t}{w_t h_t}}{1 + \alpha \left(1+R_t\right)}.$$

Labour demand is

$$l_t^d = \left(\frac{\gamma A_G}{w_t}\right)^{\frac{1}{1-\gamma}} \frac{k_t}{h_t}. \tag{20.82}$$

Inversely,

$$w_t = \frac{\alpha \left(1+R_t\right) \rho \left(1+g\right) \frac{k_t}{h_t}}{\left(1 - \frac{g+\delta_H}{A_H}\right) - l_t^s \left(1+\alpha \left(1+R_t\right)\right)}; \tag{20.83}$$

$$w_t = \gamma A_G \left(\frac{k_t}{h_t l_t^d}\right)^{1-\gamma}. \tag{20.84}$$

Using the same calibration, these labour market equations are

$$w_t = \frac{1.0815 \left(0.052632\right) \left(1+0.02362\right) \left(0.86586\right)}{\left(1 - \frac{(0.02362+0.015)}{0.20}\right) - l_t^s \left(1+1.0815\right)}; \tag{20.85}$$

$$w_t = \frac{\left(0.28224\right) \left(0.86586\right)^{\frac{2}{3}}}{3} \frac{1}{\left(l_t^d\right)^{\frac{2}{3}}}. \tag{20.86}$$

Figure 20.7 graphs equations (20.85) and (20.86) in black, along with the baseline of Example 13.2 in blue.

As labour supply and demand shift upwards, the inflation tax causes the employment level to fall somewhat while the real wage rises because of the higher capital to human capital ratio.

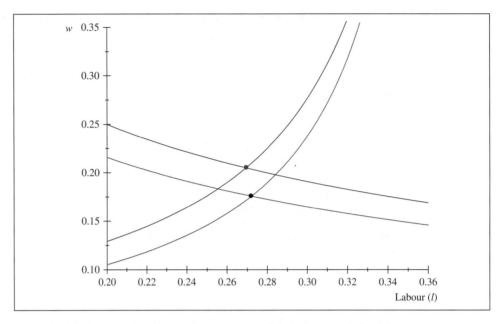

Figure 20.7 Labour market with endogenous growth inflation tax of $R = 0.0815$ in Example 20.4 (black) and $R = 0$ in Example 13.2 (blue)

20.6.5 General equilibrium

The general equilibrium with a labour income tax can also be found, in terms of graphing the input and output markets. Output is 0.20031, the wage rate 0.25071 and the interest rate 0.11526 so that the isocost line with the labour tax is

$$y_t = w_t l_t h_t + r_t k_t,$$

$$\frac{0.16559}{h_t} = (0.20491) l_t + (0.12750) \frac{k_t}{h_t},$$

$$\frac{k_t}{h_t} = \frac{0.16559}{0.12750 h_t} - \frac{(0.20491) l_t}{0.12750}. \qquad (20.87)$$

The isoquant curve is

$$y_t^s = A_G \left(l_t^d h_t \right)^{\gamma} \left(k_t \right)^{1-\gamma},$$

$$0.16559 = (0.28224) \left(l_t^d h_t \right)^{\frac{1}{3}} \left(k_t \right)^{\frac{2}{3}};$$

$$\frac{k_t}{h_t} = \left(\frac{0.16559}{(0.28224) h_t \left(l_t^d \right)^{\frac{1}{3}}} \right)^{\frac{3}{2}} = \frac{\left(\frac{0.16559}{(0.28224) h_t} \right)^{\frac{3}{2}}}{\left(l_t^d \right)^{\frac{1}{2}}}. \qquad (20.88)$$

And the factor input ratio is

$$\frac{k_t}{h_t l_t} = \frac{0.86586}{0.26937} = 3.2144. \qquad (20.89)$$

Figure 20.8 graphs equations (20.87), (20.88) and (20.89) in variants of black, as compared to the baseline with $R = 0$ as in Example 13.2, in variants of blue.

The inflation tax causes results similar to the labour tax, with employment falling and the physical capital to human capital ratio rising.

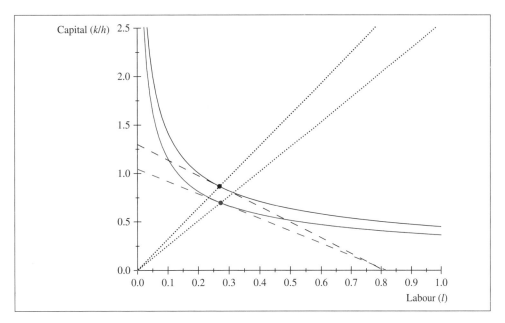

Figure 20.8 Factor market equilibrium with endogenous growth in Example 20.4 with $R = 0.0815$ (variants of black), compared to $R = 0$ (variants of blue)

For goods and leisure in general equilibrium, output minus investment is

$$c_t^d = y_t^s - i_t = A_G \left(l_t^d h_t \right)^\gamma \left(k_t \right)^{1-\gamma} - (g + \delta_k) k_t,$$

$$\frac{c_t^d}{h_t} = (0.28224) \left(l_t^d \right)^{\frac{1}{3}} (0.86586)^{\frac{2}{3}} - (0.0736) (0.866). \tag{20.90}$$

The level curve requires the equilibrium human capital time, $l_{Ht} = \frac{g + \delta_H}{A_H} = \frac{0.02362 + 0.015}{0.20} = 0.1931$. Then it is

$$u = \ln c_t + \alpha \ln x_t = \ln c_t + \alpha \ln \left(1 - l_{Ht} - l_t \right),$$
$$-2.9051 = \ln 0.10184 + 1 \ln \left(1 - (0.26937 + 0.1931) \right),$$
$$-2.9051 = \ln c_t + \ln (T_t - l_t),$$
$$c_t = \frac{e^{-2.9051}}{\left(1 - 0.1931 - l_t \right)}. \tag{20.91}$$

And the budget line is

$$c_t^d = w_t l_t^s h_t + k_t \left[r_t - (g + \delta_k) \right],$$

$$\frac{c_t^d}{h_t} = (0.20491) l_t^s + (0.86586) (0.12750 - 0.05 - 0.02362). \tag{20.92}$$

Figure 20.9 graphs equations (20.90), (20.91) and (20.92) in variants of black, as compared to the zero inflation tax equilibrium, as in Example 13.2, in variants of blue.

The inflation tax causes a shift up in the level of consumption, a decrease in labour, all while the growth rate decreases.

The equivalence of the effect of the inflation tax, through R, to other taxes implies similar growth effects. This can explain why evidence has found consistently a negative effect of inflation on the output growth rate. And this is in part why inflation targeting policy has sought to lower the inflation rate as far as is feasible.

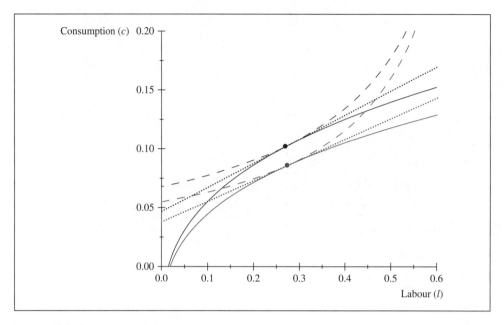

Figure 20.9 General equilibrium with endogenous growth and an inflation tax of $R = 0.0815$ in Example 20.4 (variants of black) compared to $R = 0$ (variants of blue) as in Example 13.2

In terms of optimal policy, an inflation tax simply compounds the composite labour tax, just as does the goods tax. Further this tax is avoidable by substituting away from money use towards for example credit in exchange. Producing this exchange credit uses up real resources and decreases government revenue from the inflation tax. Research has found under certain conditions that this tax should be eliminated completely, again giving impetus to the low inflation targeting policy used widely today.

20.6.6 Exogenous growth versus endogenous growth

The comparison of the effect of the inflation tax on the economy, in the exogenous growth dynamic model versus the endogenous growth one, is very similar to the same comparison for the labour tax in exogenous growth in Chapter 9 and in endogenous growth in Chapter 19.

First, the inflation tax causes a much bigger decline in employment in the exogenous growth model than in endogenous growth. This makes the endogenous growth probably closer to data, in that a moderate inflation causes only a moderate decrease in long term employment. The other part of the comparison is that in endogenous growth the wage rises instead of fixed constant exogenous growth, when inflation increases. And this makes sense in terms of the tax wedge that the inflation tax drives into the wage rate, and because the consumer substitutes from taxed human capital to untaxed physical capital. This substitution drives up the wage rate according to the marginal product of labour condition. At the same time, also absent in exogenous growth, the real interest rate falls when the substitution towards physical capital from human capital takes place. Thus factor prices move in opposite directions and the growth rate falls, all absent from exogenous growth.

The other facet is that output rises in endogenous growth even though the growth rate falls. Some would claim that this means that inflation is a good policy, since it increases output. But this would be a misguided view in that the output rises only because the consumer is forced away from the optimal use of physical capital versus human capital, and in the process, the higher physical capital to human capital ratio causes output to increase. This is a manifestation of the inefficiency of the tax, with the representative agent doing the best action given the tax. And the decline in employment is not viewed well in terms of policy.

20.6.7 Level of the inflation tax

The inflation tax enters both exogenous growth and endogenous growth economies in terms of the level of the nominal interest rate R. Therefore the level of the inflation tax is actually equal to the level of R. This can be confusing since the temptation is to think of the level of the inflation tax as the level of the inflation rate π. But a way to see why it is the whole of the nominal rate R and not just the inflation rate π is through the marginal rate of substitution between goods and leisure.

In equation (20.60), the marginal rate can be written as the ratio of marginal utilities of goods to leisure, or

$$\frac{x_t}{\alpha c_t} = \frac{1 + R_t}{w_t h_t}. \tag{20.93}$$

If $R_t = 0$, then the economy is back to the same margin here as when there is no inflation tax distortion. The margin is simply the inverse of the effective wage rate, or in exogenous growth, $\frac{x_t}{\alpha c_t} = \frac{1 + R_t}{w_t}$, and it is the inverse of the wage rate. Therefore a positive $R > 0$ is in fact the distortion that causes substitution from goods to leisure.

When in contrast $R = 0$, the economy returns to an undistorted case, and this is the 'first-best' optimum in the economy. It is like saying that the zero tax case is the best case, when the government spending is just a transfer as in this economy. So of course a zero tax case is best since it eliminates the substitution distortion. Therefore the level of the inflation tax is R. And a non-distorting economy, with money supplied at zero cost as in this economy, is to have $R = 0$. By the Fisher equation, this implies letting the inflation rate be negative, so that there is 'deflation'. In practical terms, this Friedman (1969) rule of deflation can be done by keeping the money supply constant in a growing economy. Then money earns the same real return as physical capital, a return equal to the deflation rate. However, if money cost is $r_t - \delta_k$, then $\pi = 0$ is optimal.

20.7 Application: central bank policy

With the endogenous growth economy along the balanced growth path equilibrium, the interest rate can be expressed in terms of the growth rate and the inflation rate. This gives an equilibrium derivation of what is called the 'Taylor rule' of central bank interest rate policy.

20.7.1 Deriving a Taylor rule

From the economy's Fisher equation (20.15), and substituting in for $\left(1 + r_t - \delta_k\right)$ from the consumer intertemporal margin of equation (20.9), gives that

$$1 + R_t = \left(1 + \pi_t\right)\left(1 + g_t\right)\left(1 + \rho\right). \tag{20.94}$$

Taking the logarithm and using the approximation that $\ln\left(1 + x\right) \simeq x$, for small x, gives that

$$R_t \simeq \rho + \pi_t + g_t. \tag{20.95}$$

Writing this at time t, with some 'inflation target' of π^* added and subtracted:

$$R_t \simeq \rho + \pi^* + \left(\pi_t^e - \pi^*\right) + g_t, \tag{20.96}$$

where with perfect foresight, and briefly using the expectation operator E_t, $\pi_t = E_{t-1}\pi_t \equiv \pi_t^e$.

Now this assumes log utility. With a slightly more general 'constant relative risk aversion' utility function, whereby $u_t = \frac{(c_t x_t^\alpha)^{1-\theta}}{1-\theta}$, of which log utility is a special case, this interest rate equation includes the θ parameter also:

$$R_t \simeq \rho + \pi^* + \left(\pi_t^e - \pi^*\right) + \theta g_t. \tag{20.97}$$

Consider denoting by β_π and β_g the coefficients on the inflation error term $\left(\pi_t^e - \pi^*\right)$ and the growth rate term g_t, respectively:

$$R_t \simeq \rho + \pi^* + \beta_\pi \left(\pi_t^e - \pi^*\right) + \beta_g g_t. \tag{20.98}$$

And this equation gives a form of the original Taylor (1993) rule. To see this, consider that the original rule is

$$R_t = \bar{r} + \pi_t^e + 0.5 \left(\pi_t^e - \pi^*\right) + \left(0.5\right) y_{gap,t}, \tag{20.99}$$

where $y_{gap,t}$ is a variable called the 'output gap'.

Adding and subtracting π^*, this writes as

$$R_t = \bar{r} + \pi^* + \left(\pi_t^e - \pi^*\right) + 0.5 \left(\pi_t^e - \pi^*\right) + \left(0.5\right) y_{gap,t}, \tag{20.100}$$

which simplifies as

$$R_t = \bar{r} + \pi^* + 1.5 \left(\pi_t^e - \pi^*\right) + \left(0.5\right) y_{gap,t}. \tag{20.101}$$

Finally denote by β_π and β_g the coefficients on the inflation error term $\left(\pi_t^e - \pi^*\right)$ and the output gap term $y_{gap,t}$, respectively. This gives what Taylor (1993) presents, also seen as equation (1) in Siklos and Wohar (2005).

$$R_{t+1} = \bar{r} + \pi^* + \beta_\pi \left(\pi_t^e - \pi^*\right) + \beta_g \cdot y_{gap,t}. \tag{20.102}$$

Equations (20.98) and (20.102) are identical under two conditions:

$$\bar{r} = \rho,$$
$$y_{gap,t} \equiv g_t.$$

The first condition is very much like the usual interpretation of $\bar{r}$ seen in the literature, as the historical average real interest rate. Except here the interpretation is more restricted by the general equilibrium setting to the rate of time preference. However calibration values of the rate of time preference, of 0.02 annual, are similar to values used for the historical real interest rate.

The second condition is identical to so-called 'speed limit' versions of the Taylor rule in which the output gap is defined exactly as the growth rate of output.

The coefficients of equation (20.98) are β_π and β_g. With $\beta_\pi = 1$, the general equilibrium model is replicated. This is the borderline of what is called the Taylor rule 'principle' that the change in the inflation needs to have an impact of greater than one on the interest rate. What this implies is that in the stationary equilibrium the Fisher equation (20.15) is operative and more than proportional effects are not necessary. Rather the one to one relation between inflation and the nominal interest rate keeps this coefficient at unity.

The coefficient on the growth rate in equation (20.98) is β_g, and in the model this is determined by the degree of relative risk aversion. This value typically varies in calibration between 0.5 and 2. A value of 0.5 replicates the value in Taylor (1993). But a range of values have been estimated for this term, including values above unity.

20.7.2 Taylor rule as policy in general equilibrium

The Taylor equation (20.97) is an equilibrium condition of the economy in which the government is supplying money. This implies an equivalence between money supply rules and interest rate rules. And this implies that the Taylor equation is not saying necessarily how the central bank is controlling the interest rate but rather simply says how it is printing money.

And as an equilibrium condition of the economy, this equation should not simply be added on to a general equilibrium economy, as Taylor rules typically are added on in all such different forms. In contrast it is already part of the equilibrium, and only the form that is consistent with the general equilibrium should be specified.

The Taylor equation (20.95) has a very simple prescription for keeping the inflation rate constant: let the nominal interest rate follow the economy's output growth rate. A caveat is that the employment rate may lag the output growth rate, and so can be considered as an additional factor in a dynamic version of the Taylor equation, when setting the interest rate through a certain money supply policy. Under uncertainty, a dynamic version of the general equilibrium Taylor equation has been derived, which includes the employment growth rate and the consumption growth rate. Also, when the velocity of money is changing, the central bank needs to change its degree of interest rate 'smoothing' accordingly; topics for advanced study.

More simply, an alternative approach to simply following the output growth rate is the so-called 'Taylor principle'. This is defined as conducting money supply policy so as to keep $\beta_\pi > 1$ rather than $\beta_\pi = 1$ as in the Fisher equation of interest rates. Suppose that the inflation rate is $\overline{\pi}$, and the growth rate g is unchanged. Then say that the bank decides to lower R. It follows then by the Fisher equation that the real interest rate must fall, in the short run. The way the bank lowers R is by printing money at a faster rate, and this eventually causes higher inflation. But in the meantime, before the inflation rate rises, the real interest rate is pushed down below its natural market value by the increase in the rate of money supply growth. This is a short term subsidy to borrowing in capital markets, followed by a long run increase in the inflation rate.

Conversely, if R is raised when the inflation rate is $\overline{\pi}$, and the growth rate g is unchanged, it is done by decreasing the growth rate of the money supply. The real interest rate rises in the short run until the inflation rate falls. And capital market borrowing is taxed.

This type of 'Taylor policy' amounts to subsidising borrowing by lowering the real interest rate with a subsequent increase in the inflation rate. This may be motivated by trying to stimulate the economy in a recession. And then when the inflation rate does in fact rise, and the central bank wants to lower the inflation rate, it effectively taxes borrowing by raising R and raising the real interest rate in the short run. This creates a formula for a lack of a stable inflation rate, combined with continuously either subsidising or taxing borrowing.

First the ship-of-state over-steers one way, by subsidising borrowing, and raising the inflation rate, then it over-steers the other way, by taxing borrowing and lowering the inflation rate. The economy, like a large lumbering ocean supertanker, is steered in a zigzag pattern around a targeted inflation rate, while capital markets are alternately subsidised and then taxed. All of this appears inefficient compared to a policy of letting the nominal interest rate simply follow the economy's growth rate. And such interference with capital markets can lead to financial crises.

20.7.3 Financial crises of the last decade

Policy implications of the Taylor condition can be found in terms of the financial crises over the last decade. When the nominal interest rate was kept at 1% for nearly three years from 2001–04, the inflation rate eventually increased as money was printed in order to drive down the nominal interest rate. This caused a negative real interest rate. When nominal interest rates were finally allowed to rise because of concerns over the rising inflation, the nominal rate had to jump up by almost 5 percentage points. Otherwise the real rate would have been continuously kept below its natural value by printing more money and causing more inflation.

The subsequent rise in the nominal rate was much more sudden and steeper than expected, causing consumers who borrowed to default on car and home loans. In the Chapter 16 analysis, this is equivalent to an exogenous fall in the bank sector productivity A_F. But here the explanation for why the bank productivity falls is that the monetary policy tried to subsidise lending as long as possible, before inflation became too high. And then the sudden larger-than-normal rise in market, nominal, interest rates caused bankruptcies to occur across consumers and within banks.

The lesson is that the central bank only controls the interest rate by how much money it prints. And forcing down the nominal rate below what the business cycle demands causes inflation. And in turn this further builds up pressure on allowing the nominal rate to rise.

In the very recent times, the policy of forcing down the interest rate once again for a prolonged period even after the growth rate has turned upwards, causes the roots of the financial crisis cycle to start growing all over again. The only way such mass bankruptcy can be avoided when nominal interest rates are finally allowed to rise fully again is by indirectly taxing banks through regulation so they do not lend as much as consumers want when real interest rates are negative or zero. So this becomes an even more distorted policy of subsidising borrowing by printing money in the short run, and then taxing banking to control borrowing. And of course, then the inflation rate needs to be brought down again along with government deficits.

Consider how Thomas Hoenig, Kansas City Federal Reserve Bank President, describes in May 2010, the US Federal Reserve policy of the past decade:

> So then we come to 2001–2002, and we have language that says we will have low rates for a considerable period, whatever the language was, and we kept interest rates low and real interest rates negative. The decade of the '70s and the decade of the 2000s were the periods in which we had, over 40% of the time, negative real interest rates. The consequence of that was bubbles, high leverage and financial crisis.[2]

With such low interest rate policies, Hoenig says:

> ...the saver in America is in a sense subsidising the borrower in America. We need a more normal set of circumstances so we can have an extended recovery and a more stable economy in the long run.... In other words, when we kept interest rates unusually low for a considerable period we favoured credit and the allocations related to it over savings, and we created the conditions that I think facilitated a bubble.[3]

Much better would be to allow the nominal interest rate to rise and fall with the economy's output growth rate. This is what the Taylor condition says is required for a central bank that is targeting inflation at π^*. Keeping inflation constant, the only 'policy' of a central bank is to let the nominal rate move in exact tandem with the growth rate. And then, rather than having to forecast central bank action, capital markets need only forecast the output growth rate to know how nominal interest rates will change.

---

[2]O'Grady, Mary, 2010, 'The Fed's Monetary Dissident', *Wall Street Journal*, 17 May, Opinion page.
[3]Ibid.

20.8 Questions

1. Modify Example 20.1 by assuming instead that the share of government expenditure is $\eta = 0.02$, while the velocity is the same at $\frac{y_t}{m_t} = 5$, and $g = 0$. Find the implied inflation rate and money supply growth rate.

2. Modify Example 20.2 by assuming the same share of government expenditure, $\eta = 0.02$, and that velocity is the same at $\frac{y_t}{m_t} = 2$, but now assume that there is positive growth of $g = 0.02$.

   (a) Using equation (20.31), find the implied inflation rate and money supply growth rate.

   (b) Explain why the money supply growth rate now is higher than the inflation rate.

3. Explain what causes hyperinflation, and give an example where it is currently occurring in the world, or a recent example.

4. In the exogenous growth dynamic economy,

   (a) derive the marginal rate of substitution between goods and leisure,

   (b) and explain how the inflation tax affects this margin.

5. Derive the demand for consumption in the monetary economy as given in equation (20.43).

6. In Example 20.3, the interest rate is $R = 0.0815$. Assume that the interest rate rises even higher to $R = 0.12$.

   (a) Show how the output market AS and AD functions shift graphically when R increases.

   (b) Show how the labour market supply and demand are affected when R increases.

   (c) Show how the capital to labour ratio is affected by an increase in R in terms of a graph with isocost lines and isoquant curves.

   (d) Show the effect of an increase in R on the goods and leisure in an equilibrium graph with utility level curves and production functions.

7. In Example 20.3, assume that $R = 0.12$ instead of $R = 0.0815$. It can be confirmed that this lowers the equilibrium capital stock to $k_t = 2.1838$. Given that the wage rate remains the same, unaffected by changes in R,

   (a) find the new level of employment,

   (b) find the new level of consumption and output.

8. In Example 20.4, the interest rate is $R = 0.0815$. Assume that the interest rate rises even higher to $R = 0.12$.

   (a) Show how the output market AS and AD functions shift graphically when R increases.

   (b) Show how the labour market supply and demand are affected when R increases.

   (c) Show how the capital to labour ratio is affected by an increase in R in terms of a graph with isocost lines and isoquant curves.

   (d) Show the effect of an increase in R on the goods and leisure in an equilibrium graph with utility level curves and production functions.

9. In Example 20.4, assume that $R = 0.12$ instead of $R = 0.0815$. From the excess demand solution equation (20.74), the new growth rate is $g = 0.01868$. This is illustrated by graphing the modified solution equation below in Figure 20.10.

   (a) Find the new equilibrium labour employment.

   (b) Find the new equilibrium physical capital to human capital ratio.

   (c) Find the new wage rate.

   (d) Find the new consumption and output levels, per unit of human capital.

10. Explain how a Taylor rule condition can be derived in the general equilibrium endogenous growth monetary economy.

11. Explain how central bank interest rate targeting can be equivalent to determining the rate of growth of the money supply.

12. Explain the targeting of a nominal interest rate below the inflation rate in terms of a short run subsidisation of capital investment.

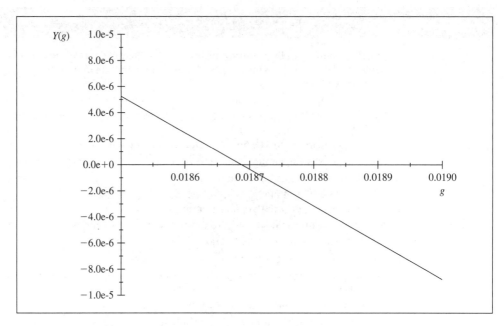

Figure 20.10 Normalised excess output demand $Y(g)$ with inflation tax of $R = 0.12$ in a modified Example 20.4

20.9 References

Bailey, Martin J., 1956, 'The Welfare Cost of Inflationary Finance', *Journal of Political Economy*, 64: 93–110.

Cagan, Phillip, 1956, 'The Monetary Dynamics of Hyperinflation', in Friedman, Milton, editor, *Studies in the Quantity Theory of Money*, Chicago: University of Chicago Press.

Friedman, Milton (editor), 1956, *Studies in the Quantitative Theory of Money*, Chicago: University of Chicago Press.

Fisher, Irving, 1896, *Appreciation and Interest*, New York: Macmillan.

Goodfriend, M.S. and B.T. McCallum, 1987, 'Demand for Money: Theoretical Studies', in Eatwell, J., Migate, M. and Newman, P. (eds), *The New Palgrave Dictionary of Economics*, Vol. 1. Macmillan: London, pp. 775–781.

Gomme, Paul, 1993, 'Money and Growth Revisited: Measuring the Costs of Inflation in an Endogenous Growth Model', *Journal of Monetary Economics*, Elsevier, 32(1) (August): 51–77.

Lucas, Robert E., Jr., 1975, 'An Equilibrium Model of the Business Cycle', *Journal of Political Economy*, University of Chicago Press, 83(6) (December): 1113–1144.

Lucas, Robert E., Jr., 1980, 'Equilibrium in a Pure Currency Economy', *Economic Inquiry*, Oxford University Press, 18(2) (April): 203–220.

Samuelson, Paul A., 1958, 'An Exact Consumption-Loan Model of Interest with or without the Social Contrivance of Money', *Journal of Political Economy*, University of Chicago Press, 66: 467.

Sidrauski, Miguel, 1967, 'Rational Choice and Patterns of Growth in a Monetary Economy', *Am. Econ. Rev. Proc.*, May 1967, 57: 534–544.

Siklos, Pierre, and Mark Wohar, 2005, 'Estimating Taylor Type Rules: An Unbalaned Regression?', in *Advances in Econometrics*, 20, Amsterdam: Elsevier.

Stock, James H. and Mark W. Watson, 1999, 'Forecasting Inflation', *Journal of Monetary Economics*, Elsevier, 44(2) (October): 293–335.

Taylor, John B., 1993, 'Discretion versus Policy Rules in Practice', *Carnegie-Rochester Conference Series on Public Policy*, 39: 195–214.

INDEX